THE UNDERGROUND RAILROAD
FROM SLAVERY TO FREEDOM

THE UNDERGROUND RAILROAD:

LEVI COFFIN RECEIVING A COMPANY OF FUGITIVES IN THE OUTSKIRTS OF CINCINNATI, OHIO.

(From a painting by C. T. Webber, Cincinnati, Ohio.)

THE UNDERGROUND RAILROAD
FROM SLAVERY TO FREEDOM
A COMPREHENSIVE HISTORY

Wilbur H. Siebert

With an Introduction by
Albert Bushnell Hart

DOVER PUBLICATIONS, INC.
Mineola, New York

Bibliographical Note

This Dover edition, first published in 2006, is an unabridged republication of *The Underground Railroad from Slavery to Freedom,* originally published by The Macmillan Company, New York and London, in 1898. The original fold-out map facing page 113 has now been set into the book on three separate pages in the same location.

International Standard Book Number

ISBN-13: 978-0-486-45039-1
ISBN-10: 0-486-45039-2

Manufactured in the United States by LSC Communications
45039205   2018
www.doverpublications.com

To My Wife

INTRODUCTION

BY ALBERT BUSHNELL HART

OF all the questions which have interested and divided the people of the United States, none since the foundation of the Federal Union has been so important, so far-reaching, and so long contested as slavery. During the first half of the nineteenth century the other great national questions were nearly all economic — taxation, currency, banks, transportation, lands, — and they had a strong material basis, a flavor of self-interest; but though slavery had also an economic side, the reasons for the onslaught upon it were chiefly moral. The first objection brought by the slave-power against the anti-slavery propaganda was the cry of the sacredness of vested and property rights against attack by sentimentalists; but what dignified the whole contest was the very fact that the sentiment for human rights was at the bottom of it, and that the abolitionists felt a moral responsibility even though property owners suffered. The slavery question, which in origin was sectional, became national as the moral issues grew clearer; and finally loomed up as the dominant question through the determination of both sides to use the power and prestige of the national government. From the moral agitation came also the personal element in the struggle, the development of strong characters, like Calhoun, Toombs, Stephens and Jefferson Davis on one side; like Lundy, Lovejoy, Garrison, Giddings, Sumner, Chase, John Brown and Lincoln on the other.

Among the many weak spots in the system of slavery none gave such opportunities to Northern abolitionists as the locomotive powers of the slaves; a "thing" which could hear its owner talking about freedom, a "thing" which could steer itself Northward and avoid the "patterollers," was a thing of impaired value as a machine, however intelligent as a human being. From earliest colonial times fugitive slaves helped to make slavery inconvenient and expensive. So long as slavery was general, every slaveholder in every colony was a member of an automatic association for stopping and returning fugitives; but, from the Revolution on, the fugitives performed the important function of keeping continually before the people of the states in which slavery had ceased, the fact that it continued in other parts of the Union. Nevertheless, though between 1777 and 1804 all the states north of Maryland threw off slavery, the free states covenanted in the Federal Constitution of 1787 to interpose no obstacle to the recapture of fugitives who might come across their borders; and thus continued to be partners in the system of slavery. From the first there was reluctance and positive opposition to this obligation; and every successful capture was an object lesson to communities out of hearing of the whipping-post and out of sight of the auction-block.

In aiding fugitive slaves the abolitionist was making the most effective protest against the continuance of slavery; but he was also doing something more tangible; he was helping the oppressed, he was eluding the oppressor; and at the same time he was enjoying the most romantic and exciting amusement open to men who had high moral standards. He was taking risks, defying the laws, and making himself liable to punishment, and yet could glow with the healthful pleasure of duty done.

To this element of the personal and romantic side of the slavery contest Professor Siebert has devoted himself in this book. The Underground Railroad was simply a form of combined defiance of national laws, on the ground that those laws were unjust and oppressive. It was the unconstitutional but logical refusal of several thousand people to acknowledge that they owed any regard to slavery or were bound to look on fleeing bondmen as the property of the slaveholders, no matter how the laws read. It was also a practical means of bringing anti-slavery principles to the attention of the lukewarm or pro-slavery people in free states; and of convincing the South that the abolitionist movement was sincere and effective. Above all, the Underground Railroad was the opportunity for the bold and adventurous; it had the excitement of piracy, the secrecy of burglary, the daring of insurrection; to the pleasure of relieving the poor negro's sufferings it added the triumph of snapping one's fingers at the slave-catcher; it developed coolness, indifference to danger, and quickness of resource.

The first task of the historian of the Underground Railroad is to gather his material, and the characteristic of this book is to consider the whole question on a basis of established facts. The effort is timely; for there are still living, or were living when the work began, many hundreds of persons who knew the intimate history of parts of the former secret system of transportation; the book is most timely, for these invaluable details are now fast disappearing with the death of the actors in the drama. Professor Siebert has rescued and put on record events which in a few years will have ceased to be in the memory of living men. He has done for the history of slavery what the students of ballad and folk-lore have done for literature; he has collected perishing materials.

Reminiscence is of course, standing alone, an insufficient basis for historical generalization. On that point Professor Siebert has been careful to explain his principle : he does not attempt to generalize from single memories not otherwise substantiated, but to use reminiscences which confirm each other, to search out telling illustrations, and to discover what the tendencies were from numerous contrasted testimonies. Actual contemporary records are scanty; a few are here preserved, such as David Putnam's memorandum, and Campbell's letter; and the crispness which they give to the narrative makes us wish for more. The few available biographies, autobiographies, and contemporary memoirs have been diligently sought out and used; and no variety of sources has been ignored which seemed likely to throw light on the subject. The ground has been carefully traversed; and it is not likely that much will ever be added to the body of information collected by Professor Siebert. His list of sources, described in the introductory chapter and enumerated in the Appendices, is really a carefully winnowed bibliography of the contemporary materials on slavery.

The book is practically divided into four parts: the Railroad itself (Chapters ii, v); the railroad hands (Chapters iii, iv, vi); the freight (Chapters vii, viii); and political relations and effects (Chapters ix, x, xi). Perhaps one of the most interesting contributions to our knowledge of the subject is the account of the beginnings of the system of secret and systematic aid to fugitives. The evidence goes to show that there was organization in Pennsylvania before 1800; and in Ohio soon after 1815. The book thus becomes a much-needed guide to information about the obscure anti-slavery movement which preceded William Lloyd Garrison, and to some degree prepared the way for him; and it will prove a source for the historian of the influence of the West in national development. As yet we know too little of the anti-slavery movement which so profoundly stirred the Western states, including Kentucky and Missouri, and which came closely into contact with the actual conditions of slavery. As Professor Siebert points out, most of the early abolitionists in the West were former slaveholders or sons of slaveholders.

Professor Siebert has applied to the whole subject a graphic form of illustration which is at the same time a test of his conclusions. How can the scattered reminiscences and records of escapes in widely separated states be shown to refer to the results of one organized method? Plainly by applying them to the actual face of the country, so as to see whether the alleged centres of activity have a geographical connection. The painstaking map of the lines of the Underground Railroad "system" is an historical contribution of a novel kind; and it is impossible to gainsay its evidence, which is expounded in detail in one of the chapters of the book. The result is a gratifying proof of the usefulness of scientific methods in historical investigation; one who lived in an anti-slavery community before the Civil War is fascinated by tracing the hitherto unknown stretches north and south from the centre which he knew. The map bears testimony not only to the wide-spread practice of aiding fugitives, but to the devotion of the conductors on the Underground Railroad. How useful a section of Mr. Siebert's map would have been to the slave-catcher in the 50's, when so many strange negroes were appearing and disappearing in the free states! The facts presented in the brief compass of the map would have been of immense value also to the leaders of the Southern Confederacy in 1861, as a confirmation of their argument that the North would not perform its constitutional duty of returning the fugitives; yet there is no record in this book of the betraying of the secrets of the U. G. R. R. by any person in the service. The moral bond of opposition to the whole slave power kept men at work forwarding fugitives by a road of which they themselves knew but a small portion. The political philosophers who think that the Civil War might have been averted by timely concessions would do well to study this picture of the wide distribution of persons who saw no peace in slavery.

Amid all the varieties of anti-slavery men, from the Garrisonian abolitionist to faint-hearted slaveholders like James G. Birney, it is interesting to see how many had a share in the Underground Railroad; and how many earned a reputation as heroes. Professor Siebert has gathered the names of about 3,200 persons known to have been engaged in this work — a roll of honor for many American families. Everybody knew that the fugitives were aided by Fred

Douglass, Thomas Wentworth Higginson, Gerrit Smith, Joshua Giddings, John Brown, Levi Coffin, Thomas Garrett and Theodore Parker; but this book gives us some account of the interest of men like Thaddeus Stevens, not commonly counted among the sons of the prophets; and performs a special service to the student of history and the lover of heroic deeds, by the brief account of the services of obscure persons who deserve a place in the hearts of their countrymen. Men like Rev. George Bourne, Rev. James Duncan and Rev. John Rankin, years before Garrison's propaganda, had begun to speak and publish against slavery, and to prepare men's minds for a righteous disregard of Fugitive Slave Acts. Joseph Sider, with his carefully subdivided peddler's wagon, deserves a place alongside the better known Henry Box Brown. The thirty-five thousand stripes of Calvin Fairbank, seventeen years a convict in the Kentucky penitentiary, range him with Lovejoy as an anti-slavery martyr. Rev. Charles Torrey had in the work of rousing slaves to escape, the same devotion to a fatal duty as that which animated John Brown. And no one who has ever heard Harriet Tubman describe her part as "Moses" of the fugitives can ever forget that African prophetess, whose intense vigor is relieved by a shrewd and kindly humanity.

The quiet recital of the facts has all the charm of romance to the passengers on the Underground Railroad: whether travelling by night in a procession of covered wagons, or boldly by day in disguises; whether boxed up as so much freight, or riding on passes unhesitatingly given by abolitionist directors of railroads; the fugitives in these pages rejoice in their prospect of liberty. The road sign near Oberlin, of a tiger chasing a negro, was a white man's joke; but it was a negro who said, apropos of his master's discouraging account of Canada: "They put some extract onto it to keep us from comin'"; and neither Whittier in his poems, nor Harriet Beecher Stowe in her novels, imagined a more picturesque incident than the crossing of the Detroit River by Fairfield's "gang" of twenty-eight rescued souls singing, "I'm on my way to Canada, where colored men are free," to the joyful accompaniment of their firearms.

To the settlements of fugitives in Canada Professor Siebert has given more labor than appears in his book; for his own visits supplement the accounts of earlier investigators; and we have here the first complete account of the reception of the negroes in Canada and their progress in civilization.

Upon the general question of the political effects of the Underground Railroad, the book adds much to our information, by its discussion of the probable numbers of fugitives, and of the alarm caused in the slave states by their departure. The census figures of 1850 and 1860 are shown to be wilfully false; and the escape of thousands of persons seems established beyond cavil. Into the constitutional question of the right to take fugitives, the book goes with less minuteness, since it is intended to be a contribution to knowledge, and not an addition to the abundant literature on the legal side of slavery.

It has been the effort of Professor Siebert to furnish the means for settling the following questions: the origin of the system of aid to the fugitives, popularly called the Underground Railroad; the degree of formal organization; methods of procedure; geographical extent and relations; the leaders and heroes of the movement; the behavior of the fugitives on their way; the effectiveness of the settlement in Canada; the numbers of fugitives; and the attitude of courts and communities. On all these questions he furnishes new light; and he appears to prove his concluding statement that "the Underground Railroad was one of the greatest forces which brought on the Civil War and thus destroyed slavery."

CONTENTS

CHAPTER I

Sources of the History of the Underground Railroad

	PAGE
The Underground Road as a subject for research	1
Obscurity of the subject	2
Books dealing with the subject	2
Magazine articles on the Underground Railroad	5
Newspaper articles on the subject	6
Scarcity of contemporaneous documents	7
Reminiscences the chief source	11
The value of reminiscences illustrated	12

CHAPTER II

Origin and Growth of the Underground Road

Conditions under which the Underground Road originated	17
The disappearance of slavery from the Northern states	17
Early provisions for the return of fugitive slaves	19
The fugitive slave clause in the Ordinance of 1787	20
The fugitive slave clause in the United States Constitution	20
The Fugitive Slave Law of 1793	21
The Fugitive Slave Law of 1850	22
Desire for freedom among the slaves	25
Knowledge of Canada among the slaves	27
Some local factors in the origin of the underground movement	30
The development of the movement in eastern Pennsylvania, in New Jersey, and in New York	33
The development of the movement in the New England states	36
The development of the movement in the West	37
The naming of the Road	44

xv

CHAPTER III

THE METHODS OF THE UNDERGROUND RAILROAD

	PAGE
Penalties for aiding fugitive slaves	47
Social contempt suffered by abolitionists	48
Espionage practised upon abolitionists	50
Rewards for the capture of fugitives and the kidnapping of abolitionists	52
Devices to secure secrecy	54
Service at night	54
Methods of communication	56
Methods of conveyance	59
Zigzag and variable routes	61
Places of concealment	62
Disguises	64
Informality of management	67
Colored and white agents	69
City vigilance committees	70
Supplies for fugitives	76
Transportation of fugitives by rail	78
Transportation of fugitives by water	81
Rescue of fugitives under arrest	83

CHAPTER IV

UNDERGROUND AGENTS, STATION-KEEPERS, OR CONDUCTORS

Underground agents, station-keepers, or conductors	87
Their hospitality	87
Their principles	89
Their nationality	90
Their church connections	93
Their party affinities	99
Their local standing	101
Prosecutions of underground operators	101
Defensive League of Freedom proposed	103
Persons of prominence among underground helpers	104

CHAPTER V

Study of the Map of the Underground Railroad System

	PAGE
Geographical extent of underground lines	113
Location and distribution of stations	114
Southern routes	116
Lines of Pennsylvania, New Jersey, and New York	120
Routes of the New England states	128
Lines within the old Northwest Territory	134
Noteworthy features of the general map	139
Complex routes	141
Broken lines and isolated place names	141
River routes	142
Routes by rail	142
Routes by sea	144
Terminal stations	145
Lines of lake travel	147
Canadian ports	148

CHAPTER VI

Abduction of Slaves from the South

Aversion among underground helpers to abduction of slaves	150
Abductions by negroes living along the northern border of the slave states	151
Abductions by Canadian refugees	152
Abductions by white persons in the South	153
Abductions by white persons of the North	154
The Missouri raid of John Brown	162
John Brown's great plan	166
Abductions attempted in response to appeals	168
Devotees of abduction	178

CHAPTER VII

Life of the Colored Refugees in Canada

Slavery question in Canada	190
Flight of slaves to Canada	192
Refugees representative of the slave class	195

	PAGE
Misinformation about Canada among slaves	197
Hardships borne by Canadian refugees	198
Efforts toward immediate relief for fugitives	199
Attitude of the Canadian government	201
Conditions favorable to their settlement in Canada	203
Sparseness of population	203
Uncleared lands	204
Encouragement of agricultural colonies among refugees	205
Dawn Settlement	205
Elgin Settlement	207
Refugees' Home Settlement	209
Alleged disadvantages of the colonies	211
Their advantages	212
Refugee settlers in Canadian towns	217
Census of Canadian refugees	220
Occupations of Canadian refugees	223
Progress made by Canadian refugees	224
Domestic life of the refugees	227
School privileges	228
Organizations for self-improvement	230
Churches	231
Rescue of friends from slavery	231
Ownership of property	232
Rights of citizenship	233
Character as citizens	233

CHAPTER VIII

Fugitive Settlers in the Northern States

Number of fugitive settlers in the North	235
The Northern states an unsafe refuge for runaway slaves	237
Reclamation of fugitives in the free states	239
Protection of fugitives in the free states	242
Object of the personal liberty laws	245
Effect of the law of 1850 on fugitive settlers	246
Underground operators among fugitives of the free states	251

CHAPTER IX

Prosecutions of Underground Railroad Men

	PAGE
Enactment of the Fugitive Slave Law of 1793	254
Grounds on which the constitutionality of the measure was questioned	254
Denial of trial by jury to the fugitive slave	255
Summary mode of arrest	257
The question of concurrent jurisdiction between the federal and state governments in fugitive slave cases	259
The law of 1793 versus the Ordinance of 1787	261
Power of Congress to legislate concerning the extradition of fugitive slaves denied	263
State officers relieved of the execution of the law by the Prigg decision, 1842	264
Amendment of the law of 1793 by the law of 1850	265
Constitutionality of the law of 1850 questioned	267
First case under the law of 1850	268
Authority of a United States commissioner	269
Penalties imposed for aiding and abetting the escape of fugitives .	273
Trial on the charge of treason in the Christiana case, 1854 . .	279
Counsel for fugitive slaves	281
Last case under the Fugitive Slave Law of 1850	285
Attempted revision of the law	285
Destructive attacks upon the measure in Congress	286
Lincoln's Proclamation of Emancipation	287
Repeal of the Fugitive Slave Acts	288

CHAPTER X

The Underground Railroad in Politics

Valuation of the Underground Railroad in its political aspect .	290
The question of the extradition of fugitive slaves in colonial times .	290
Importance of the question in the constitutional conventions . .	293
Failure of the Fugitive Slave Law of 1793	294
Agitation for a more efficient measure	295
Diplomatic negotiations for the extradition of colored refugees from Canada, 1826–1828	299
The fugitive slave a missionary in the cause of freedom . . .	300

	PAGE
Slave-hunting in the free states	302
Preparation for the abolition movement of 1830	303
The Underground Railroad and the Fugitive Slave Law of 1850	308
The law in Congress	310
The enforcement of the law of 1850	316
The Underground Road and *Uncle Tom's Cabin*	321
Political importance of the novel	323
Sumner on the influence of escaped slaves in the North	324
The spirit of nullification in the North	327
The Glover rescue, Wisconsin, 1854	327
The rendition of Burns, Boston, 1854	331
The rescue of Addison White, Mechanicsburg, Ohio, 1857	334
The Oberlin-Wellington rescue, 1858	335
Obstruction of the Fugitive Slave Law by means of the personal liberty acts	337
John Brown's attempt to free the slaves	338

CHAPTER XI

Effect of the Underground Railroad

The Underground Road the means of relieving the South of many despairing slaves	340
Loss sustained by slave-owners through underground channels	340
The United States census reports on fugitive slaves	342
Estimate of the number of slaves escaping into Ohio, 1830-1860	346
Similar estimate for Philadelphia, 1830-1860	346
Drain on the resources of the depot at Lawrence, Kansas, described in a letter of Col. J. Bowles, April 4, 1859	347
Work of the Underground Railroad as compared with that of the American Colonization Society	350
The violation of the Fugitive Slave Law a chief complaint of Southern states at the beginning of the Civil War	351
Refusal of the Canadian government to yield up the fugitive Anderson, 1860	352
Secession of the Southern states begun	353
Conclusion of the fugitive slave controversy	355
General effect and significance of the controversy	356

ILLUSTRATIONS, PORTRAITS, FACSIMILES AND MAPS

The Underground Railroad: Levi Coffin receiving a company of fugitives in the outskirts of Cincinnati, Ohio . . *Frontispiece*

	FACING PAGE
Isaac T. Hopper	17
The Runaway: a stereotype cut used on handbills advertising escaped slaves	27
Crossing-place on the Ohio River at Steubenville, Ohio . . .	47
The Rankin House, Ripley, Ohio	47
Facsimile of an Underground Message . . . . *On page*	57
Barn of Seymour Finney, Detroit, Michigan	65
The Old First Church, Galesburg, Illinois	65
William Still	75
Levi Coffin	87
Frederick Douglass	104
Caves in Salem Township, Washington County, Ohio . . .	130
House of Mrs. Elizabeth Buffum Chace, Valley Falls, Rhode Island	130
The Detroit River at Detroit, Michigan	147
Ashtabula Harbor, Ohio	147
Ellen Craft as she escaped from Slavery	163
Samuel Harper and Wife	163
Dr. Alexander M. Ross	180
Harriet Tubman	180
Group of Refugee Settlers at Windsor, Ontario, C.W. . . .	190
Theodore Parker	205
Thomas Wentworth Higginson	205
Dr. Samuel G. Howe	205
Benjamin Drew	205
Church of the Fugitive Slaves, Boston, Massachusetts . . .	235
Salmon P. Chase	254

xxi

	FACING PAGE
Thomas Garrett	254
Rush R. Sloane	282
Thaddeus Stevens	282
J. R. Ware	282
Rutherford B. Hayes	282
Gerrit Smith	290
Joshua R. Giddings	290
Charles Sumner	290
Richard H. Dana	290
Bust of Rev. John Rankin	307
Harriet Beecher Stowe	321
Captain John Brown	338
Facsimile of a Leaf from the Diary of Daniel Osborn	On pages 344, 345

MAPS

Map of the Underground Railroad System	*Facing page*	113
Map of Underground Lines in Southeastern Pennsylvania	"	113
Map of Underground Lines in Morgan County, Ohio	*On page*	136
Lewis Falley's Map of the Underground Routes of Indiana and Michigan	*On page*	138
Map of an Underground Line through Livingston and La Salle Counties, Illinois	*On page*	139
Map of Underground Lines through Greene, Warren and Clinton Counties, Ohio	*On page*	140

APPENDICES

PAGES

APPENDIX A: Constitutional Provisions and National Acts relative to Fugitive Slaves, 1787–1850 359–366

APPENDIX B: List of Important Fugitive Slave Cases . . 367–377

APPENDIX C: Figures from the United States Census Reports relating to Fugitive Slaves 378, 379

APPENDIX D: Bibliography 380–402

APPENDIX E: Directory of the names of Underground Railroad Operators and Members of Vigilance Committees . . 403–439

PREFACE

THIS volume is the outgrowth of an investigation begun in 1892–1893, when the writer was giving a portion of his time to the teaching of United States history in the Ohio State University. The search for materials was carried on at intervals during several years until the mass of information, written and printed, was deemed sufficient to be subjected to the processes of analysis and generalization.

Patience and care have been required to overcome the difficulties attaching to a subject that was in an extraordinary sense a hidden one; and the author has constantly tried to observe those well-known dicta of the historian; namely, to be content with the materials discovered without making additions of his own, and to let his conclusions be defined by the facts, rather than seek to cast these "in the mould of his hypothesis."

Starting without preconceptions, the writer has been constrained to the views set forth in Chapters X and XI in regard to the real meaning and importance of the underground movement. And if it be found by the reader that these views are in any measure novel, it is hoped that the pages of this book contain evidence sufficient for their justification. There is something mysterious and inexplicable about the whole anti-slavery movement in the United States, as its history is generally recounted. According to the accepted view the anti-slavery movement of the thirties and the later decades has been considered as altogether distinct from the earlier abolition period in our history, both in principle and external features, and as separated from it by a considerable interval of time. The earlier movement is supposed to have died a natural death, and the later to have sprung into full life and vigor with the appearance of Garrison and the *Liberator*. Issue is made with this view in the following pages, where Macaulay's rational account of revolutions in general may, perhaps, be thought to find illustration. Macaulay says in one of his essays: "As the history of states is generally written, the greatest and most momentous revolutions seem to come upon them like supernatural inflictions, without warning or cause. But the fact is, that such revolutions are almost always the consequences of moral changes, which have gradually passed on the mass of the community, and which ordinarily proceed far before their progress is indicated by any public measure. An intimate knowledge of the domestic history of nations is therefore absolutely necessary to the prognosis of political events." Or, the essayist might have added, to a subsequent understanding of them.

It is impossible for the author to make acknowledgments to all who have contributed, directly and indirectly, to the promotion of his research. A liberal use of foot-notes suffices to reduce his obligations in part only. But, although the great balance of his indebtedness must stand against him, his special acknowledgments are due in certain quarters. The writer has to thank Professor J. Franklin Jameson of Brown University for calling his attention to a rare and important little book, which otherwise would almost certainly have escaped his notice. To Professor Eugene Wambaugh of the Harvard Law School he is indebted for the critical perusal of Chapter IX, on the Prosecutions of Underground Railroad Men, — a chapter based largely on reports of cases, and involving legal points about which the layman may easily go astray. The frequent citations of the monograph on *Fugitive Slaves* by Mrs. Marion G. McDougall attest the general usefulness of that book in the preparation of the present work. For personal encouragement in the under-

PREFACE

taking after the collection of materials had begun, and for assistance while the study was being put in manuscript, the author is most deeply indebted to Professor Albert Bushnell Hart, and the Seminary of American History in Harvard University, over which he and his colleague, Professor Edward Channing, preside. The proof-sheets of this book have been read by Mr. F. B. Sanborn, of Concord, Massachusetts, and, it is hardly necessary to add, have profited thereby in a way that would have been impossible had they passed under the eye of one less widely acquainted with anti-slavery times and anti-slavery people. More than to all others the author's gratitude is due to the members of his own household, without whose abiding interest and ready assistance in many ways this work could not have been carried to completion. It should be said that no responsibility for the use made of data or the conclusions drawn from them can justly be imposed upon those whose generous offices have kept these pages freer from discrepancies than they could have been otherwise.

It is a fortunate circumstance that, by the kindness of the artist, Mr. C. T. Webber, the reproduction of his painting entitled "The Underground Railroad" can appear as the frontispiece of this book. Mr. Webber was fitted by his intimate acquaintance with the Coffin family of Cincinnati, Ohio, and their remarkable record in the work of secret emancipation, to give a sympathetic delineation of the Underground Railroad in operation.

OHIO STATE UNIVERSITY,
October, 1898.

THE UNDERGROUND RAILROAD
FROM
SLAVERY TO FREEDOM

CHAPTER I

SOURCES OF THE HISTORY OF THE UNDERGROUND RAILROAD

HISTORIANS who deal with the rise and culmination of the anti-slavery movement in the United States have comparatively little to say of one phase of it that cannot be neglected if the movement is to be fully understood. This is the so-called Underground Railroad, which, during fifty years or more, was secretly engaged in helping fugitive slaves to reach places of security in the free states and in Canada. Henry Wilson speaks of the romantic interest attaching to the subject, and illustrates the coöperative efforts made by abolitionists in behalf of colored refugees in two short chapters of the second volume of his *Rise and Fall of the Slave Power in America*.[1] Von Holst makes several references to the work of the Road in his well-known *History of the United States*, and predicts that "The time will yet come, even in the South, when due recognition will be given to the touching unselfishness, simple magnanimity and glowing love of freedom of these law-breakers on principle, who were for the most part people without name, money, or higher education."[2] Rhodes in his great work, the *History of the United*

[1] Chapters VI and VII, pp. 61-86. [2] Vol. III, p. 552, foot-note.

States from the Compromise of 1850, mentions the system, but considers it only as a manifestation of popular sentiment.[1] Other writers give less space to an account of this enterprise, although it was one that extended throughout many Northern states, and in itself supplied the reason for the enactment of the Fugitive Slave Law of 1850, one of the most remarkable measures issuing from Congress during the whole anti-slavery struggle.

The explanation of the failure to give to this "institution" the prominence which it deserves, is to be found in the secrecy in which it was enshrouded. Continuous through a period of two generations, the Road spread to be a great system by being kept in an oblivion that its operators aptly designated by the figurative use of the word "underground." Then, too, it was a movement in which but few of those persons were involved whose names have been most closely associated in history with the public agitation of the question of slavery, or with those political developments that resulted in the destruction of slavery. In general the participants in underground operations were quiet persons, little known outside of the localities where they lived, and were therefore members of a class that historians find it exceedingly difficult to bring within their field of view.

Before attempting to prepare a new account of the Underground Railroad, from new materials, something should be said of previous works upon it, and especially of the seven books which deal specifically with the subject: *The Underground Railroad*, by the Rev. W. M. Mitchell; *Underground Railroad Records*, by William Still; *The Underground Railroad in Chester and the Neighboring Counties of Pennsylvania*, by R. C. Smedley; *The Reminiscences of Levi Coffin; Sketches in the History of the Underground Railroad*, by Eber M. Pettit; *From Dixie to Canada*, by H. U. Johnson; and *Heroes in Homespun*, by Ascott R. Hope (a *nom de plume* for Robert Hope Moncrieff).

While several of these volumes are sources of original material, their value is chiefly that of collections of incidents, affording one an insight into the workings of the Under-

---

[1] *History of the United States*, Vol. II, pp. 74-77, 361, 362.

ground Railroad in certain localities, and presenting types of character among the helpers and the helped. In composition they are what one would expect of persons who lived simple, strenuous lives, who with sincerity record what they knew and experienced. They have not only the characteristics of a deep-seated, moral movement, they have also an undeniable value for historical purposes.

Mitchell's small volume of 172 pages was published in England in 1860. Its author was a free negro, who served as a slave-driver in the South for several years, then became a preacher in Ohio, and for twelve years engaged in underground work; finally, about 1855, he went to Toronto, Canada, to minister to colored refugees as a missionary in the service of the American Free Baptist Mission Society.[1] It was while soliciting money in England for the purpose of building a chapel and schoolhouse for his people in Toronto that he was induced to write his book. The range of experience of the author enabled him to relate at first hand many incidents illustrative of the various phases of underground procedure, and to give an account of the condition of the fugitive slaves in Canada.[2]

Still's *Underground Railroad Records*, a large volume of 780 pages, appeared in 1872, and a second edition in 1883. For some years before the War Mr. Still was a clerk in the office of the Pennsylvania Anti-Slavery Society in Philadelphia; and from 1852 to 1860 he served as chairman of the Acting Vigilance Committee of Philadelphia, a body whose special business it was to harbor fugitives and help them towards Canada. About 1850 Mr. Still began to keep records of the stories he heard from runaways, and his book is mainly a compilation of these stories, together with some Underground Railroad correspondence. At the end there are some biographical sketches of persons more or less prominent in the anti-slavery cause. The book is a mine of material relating to the work of the Vigilance Committee of Philadelphia.

---

[1] Mitchell, *Underground Railroad*, Preface, p. vi; p. 17.

[2] Mr. Mitchell divides his little book into two chapters, one on the "Underground Railroad," occupying 124 pages, the other on the "Condition of Fugitive Slaves in Canada," occupying 48 pages.

Operations carried on in an extended field of six or seven counties in southeastern Pennsylvania, over routes many of which led to the Quaker City, are recounted in Smedley's volume of 395 pages, published in 1883. The abundant reminiscences and short biographies were patiently gathered by the author from many aged participants in underground enterprises.

In his *Reminiscences*, a book of 732 pages, Levi Coffin, the reputed president of the Underground Railroad, relates his experiences from the time when he began, as a youth in North Carolina, to direct slaves northward on the path to liberty, till the time when, after twenty years of service in eastern Indiana and fifteen in Cincinnati, Ohio, he and his coworkers were relieved by the admission of slaves within the lines of the Union forces in the South. Mr. Coffin was a Quaker of the gentle but firm type depicted by Harriet Beecher Stowe in the character Simeon Halliday, of which he may have been the original. It need scarcely be said, therefore, that his autobiography is characterized by simplicity and candor, and supplies a fund of information in regard to those branches of the Road with which its author was connected.

Pettit's *Sketches* comprise a series of articles printed in the Fredonia (New York) *Censor*, during the fall of 1868, and collected in 1879 into a book of 174 pages. The author was for many years a "conductor" in southwestern New York, and most of the adventures narrated occurred within his personal knowledge.

Johnson's *From Dixie to Canada* is a little volume of 194 pages, in which are reprinted some of the many stories first published by him in the *Lake Shore Home Magazine* during the years 1883 to 1889 under the heading, "Romances and Realities of the Underground Railroad." The data that most of these tales embody were accumulated by research, and while the names of operators, towns and so forth are authentic, the writer allows himself the license of the story-teller instead of restricting himself to the simple recording of the information secured. His investigations have given him an acquaintance with the routes of northeastern Ohio and the adjacent portions of Pennsylvania and New York.

Hope's volume, published in 1894, does not increase the number of our sources of information, inasmuch as its materials are derived from Still's *Underground Railroad Records* and Coffin's *Reminiscences*. It was written by an Englishman apparently as a popular exposition of the hidden methods of the abolitionists.

To these books should be added a pamphlet of thirty pages, entitled *The Underground Railroad*, by James H. Fairchild, D.D., ex-President of Oberlin College, published in 1895 by the Western Reserve Historical Society.[1] The author had personal knowledge of many of the events he narrates and recounts several underground cases of notoriety; he thus affords a clear insight into the conditions under which secret aid came to be rendered to runaways.

It is surprising that a subject, the mysterious and romantic character of which might be supposed to appeal to a wide circle of readers, has not been duly treated in any of the modern popular magazines. During the last ten years a few articles about the Underground Railroad have appeared in *The Magazine of Western History*,[2] *The Firelands Pioneer*,[3] *The Midland Monthly*,[4] *The Canadian Magazine of Politics, Science, Art and Literature*[5] and *The American Historical Review*.[6] Three of these publications, the first two and the last, are of a special character; the other two, although they appeal to the general reader, cannot be said to have attempted more than the presentation of a few incidents out of the experience of certain underground helpers. From time to time the *New England Magazine* has given its readers glimpses of the Underground Road by its articles dealing with several well-known fugitive slave cases, and a bio-

---

[1] *Tract No. 87*, in Vol. IV, pp. 91-121, of the publications of the Society.
[2] March, 1887, pp. 672-682.
[3] July, 1888, pp. 19-88. This periodical is issued by the Firelands Historical Society of Ohio. The bulk of the number mentioned is made up of contributions in regard to the Underground Road in northwestern Ohio.
[4] February, 1895, pp. 173-180.
[5] May, 1895, pp. 9-16.
[6] April, 1896, pp. 455-463. This article is a preliminary study prepared by the author.

graphical sketch of the abductor Harriet Tubman.[1] But it would be quite impossible for any one to gain an adequate idea of the movement from the meagre accounts that have appeared in any of these magazines.

In contrast with the magazines, the newspapers have frequently published some of the stirring recollections of surviving abolitionists, but the result for the reader is usually that he learns only some anecdotes concerning a small section of the Road, without securing an insight into the real significance of the underground movement. Without undertaking here to print a full list of articles on the subject, it is worth while to notice a few newspapers in which series of sketches have appeared of more or less value in extending our geographical knowledge of the system, or in illustrating some important phase of its working. The New Lexington (Ohio) *Tribune*, from October, 1885, to February, 1886, contains a series of reminiscences, written by Mr. Thomas L. Gray, that supply interesting information about the work in southeastern Ohio. The Pontiac (Illinois) *Sentinel*, in 1890 and 1891, published fifteen chapters of "A History of Anti-Slavery Days" contributed by Mr. W. B. Fyffe, recording some episodes in the development of this Road in northeastern Illinois. The *Sentinel*, of Mt. Gilead, Ohio, in a series of articles, one of which appeared every week from July 13 to August 17, 1893, under the name of Aaron Benedict, affords a knowledge of the way in which the secret work was carried on in a typical Quaker community. In *The Republican Leader*, of Salem, Indiana, at various dates from Nov. 17, 1893, to April, 1894, E. Hicks Trueblood printed the results of some investigations begun at the instance of the author, which disclose the principal routes of south central Indiana. An account of the peculiar methods of the pedler Joseph Sider, an abductor of slaves, is also given by Mr. Trueblood. The Rev.

[1] Lillie B. C. Wyman: "Black and White," in *New England Magazine*, N.S., Vol. V, pp. 476–481; "Harriet Tubman," *ibid.*, March, 1896, pp. 110–118. Nina M. Tiffany: "The Escape of William and Ellen Craft," *ibid.*, January, 1890, p. 524 *et seq.*; "Shadrach," *ibid.*, May, 1890, pp. 280–283; "Sims," *ibid.*, June, 1890, pp. 385–388; "Anthony Burns," *ibid.*, July, 1890, pp. 569–576. A. H. Grimké: "Anti-Slavery Boston," *ibid.*, December, 1890, pp. 441–459.

John Todd has preserved in the columns of the Tabor (Iowa) *Beacon*, in 1890 and 1891, some valuable reminiscences, running through more than twenty numbers of the paper, under the title, "The Early Settlement and Growth of Western Iowa"; several of these are devoted to fugitive slave cases.[1]

It is not surprising, in view of the unlawful nature of Underground Railroad service, that extremely little in the way of contemporaneous documents has descended to us even across the short span of a generation or two, and that there are few written data for the history of a movement that gave liberty to thousands of slaves. The legal restraints upon the rendering of aid to slaves bent on flight to Canada were, of course, ever present in the minds of those that pitied the bondman, whether a well-informed lawyer, like Joshua R. Giddings, or an illiterate negro, who, notwithstanding his fellow-feeling, was yet sufficiently sagacious to avoid the open violation of what others might call the law of the land. Therefore, written evidence of complicity was for the most part carefully avoided; and little information concerning any part of the work of the Underground Road was allowed to get into print. It is known that records and diaries were kept by certain helpers; and a few of the letters and messages that passed between station-keepers have been preserved. These sources of information are as valuable as they are rare: they would doubtless be more plentiful if the Fugitive Slave Law of 1850 had not created such consternation as to lead to the destruction of most of the telltale documents.

The great collection of contemporaneous material is that of William Still, relating mainly to the work of the Vigilance Committee of Philadelphia. The motives and the methods of Mr. Still in keeping his register are given in the following words: "Thousands of escapes, harrowing separations, dreadful longings, dark gropings after lost parents, brothers, sisters, and identities, seemed ever to be pressing on my mind. While I knew the danger of keeping strict records, and while I did not then dream that in my day slavery would be blotted out,

[1] Other newspapers in which materials have been found are mentioned in the Appendix, pp. 395-398.

or that the time would come when I could publish these records, it used to afford me great satisfaction to take them down fresh from the lips of fugitives on the way to freedom, and to preserve them as they had given them. . . ."[1] When in 1852 Mr. Still became the chairman of the Acting Committee of Vigilance his opportunities were doubtless increased for obtaining histories of cases; and he was then directed as head of the committee "to keep a record of all their doings, . . . especially of the money received and expended on behalf of every case claiming their interposition."[2] During the period of the War, Chairman Still concealed the records and documents he had collected in the loft of Lebanon Cemetery building, and although their publication became practicable when the Proclamation of Emancipation was issued, the *Underground Railroad Records* did not appear until 1872.[3]

Theodore Parker, the distinguished Unitarian clergyman of Boston, and one of the most active members of the Vigilance Committee of that city, kept memoranda of occurrences growing out of the attempted enforcement of the Fugitive Slave Law in his neighborhood. He was outspoken in his opposition to the law, and was not less bold in gathering into a journal, along with newspaper clippings and handbills referring to the troubles of the time, manuscripts of his own bearing on the unlawful procedure of the Committee. This journal or scrapbook, given to the Boston Public Library in 1874 by Mrs. Parker,[4] was compiled day by day from March 15, 1851, to February 19, 1856, and throws much light on the rendition of the fugitives Burns and Sims.

John Brown, of Osawattomie, left a few notes of his memorable journey through Kansas and Iowa, on his way to Canada in the winter of 1858 and 1859, with a company of slaves rescued by him from bondage in western Missouri. On the back of the original draft of a letter written by Brown for the *New York Tribune* soon after the slaves had been taken from their

[1] *Underground Railroad Records*, pp. xxxiii, xxxiv.
[2] *Ibid.*, p. 611, where is printed an article from the *Pennsylvania Freeman*, December 9, 1852, giving an account of the formation of the Committee.
[3] See pp. xxxiv, xxxv, xxxvi.
[4] The title Mr. Parker gave to this scrap-book is as follows: "Memoranda of the Troubles in Boston occasioned by the infamous Fugitive Slave Law."

masters, appear the names of station-keepers of the Underground Railroad in eastern Kansas, and a record of certain expenditures forming, doubtless, a part of the cost of his trip.[1] When the fearless abductor arrived at Springdale, Iowa, late in February, he wrote to a friend in Tabor a statement concerning the " Reception of Brown and Party at Grinnell, Iowa, compared with Proceedings at Tabor," in which he set down in the form of items the substantial attentions he had received at the hands of citizens of Grinnell.[2] These meagre records, together with the letter written to the *Tribune* mentioned above, are all that Brown wrote, so far as known, giving explicit information in regard to an exploit that created a stir throughout the country.

Mr. Jirch Platt, of the vicinity of Mendon, Illinois, recorded his experiences as a station-keeper in a "sort of diary and farm record," and in a "blue-book," and appears to have been the only one of the underground helpers of Illinois that ventured to chronicle matters of this kind. The diary is still extant, and shows entries covering a period of more than ten years, closing with October, 1859; the following items will illustrate sufficiently the character of the record:—

"*May* 19, 1848. Hannah Coger arrived on the U. G. Railroad, the last $100.00 for freedom she was to pay to Thomas Anderson, Palmyra, Mo. The track is kept bright, it being the 3rd time occupied since the first of April." . . .

"*Nov.* 9, '54. Negro hoax stories have been very high in the market for a week past."

* * * * * * * *

" *Oct.* 1859. U. G. R. R. Conductor reported the passage of five, who were considered very valuable pieces of Ebony, all designated by names, such as *John Brooks, Daniel Brooks, Mason Bushrod, Sylvester Lucket* and *Hanson Gause*. Have understood also that three others were ticketed about midsummer."

In Ohio, Daniel Osborn, of the Alum Creek Quaker Settlement, in the central part of the state, kept a diary, of

---

[1] Sanborn, *Life and Letters of John Brown*, p. 482.
[2] *Ibid.*, pp. 488, 489.

which to-day only a leaf remains. This bit of paper gives a record of the number of negroes passing through the Alum Creek neighborhood during an interval of five months, from April 14 to September 10, 1844, and is of considerable importance, because it supplies data that furnish, when taken in connection with other terms, the elements for an interesting computation of the number of slaves that escaped into Ohio.[1] In the correspondence of Mr. David Putnam, of Point Hamar, near Marietta, Ohio, there were found a few letters relating to the journeys of fugitives. That even these few letters remain is doubtless due to neglect or oversight on the part of the recipient. It is noticeable that some of them bear unmistakable signs of intended secrecy, the proper names having been blotted out, or covered with bits of paper.

Underground managers who were so indiscreet as to keep a diary or letters for a season, were induced to part with such condemning evidence under the stress of a special danger. Mr. Robert Purvis, of Philadelphia, states that he kept a record of the fugitives that passed through his hands and those of his coworkers in the Quaker City for a long period, till the trepidation of his family after the passage of the Fugitive Slave Bill in 1850 caused him to destroy it.[2] Daniel Gibbons, a Friend, who lived near Columbia in southeastern Pennsylvania, began in 1824 to keep a record of the number of fugitives he aided. He was in the habit of entering in his book the name of the master of each fugitive, the fugitive's own name and his age, and the new name given him. The data thus gathered came in time to form a large volume, but after the passage of the Fugitive Slave Law Mr. Gibbons burned this book.[3] William Parker, the colored leader in the famous Christiana case, was found by a friend to have a large number of letters from escaped slaves hidden about his house at the time of the Christiana affair, September 11, 1851, and these fateful documents were quickly destroyed. Had they been discovered by the officers that visited Parker's

---

[1] See Chap. XI, p. 346.
[2] Conversation with Robert Purvis, Philadelphia, Pa., December 24, 1895.
[3] Smedley, *Underground Railroad*, pp. 56, 57.

house, they might have brought disaster upon many persons.[1] Thus, the need of secrecy constantly served to prevent the making of records, or to bring about their early destruction. The written and printed records do give a multitude of unquestioned facts about the Underground Railroad; but when wishing to find out the details of rational management, the methods of business, and the total amount of traffic, we are thrown back on the recollections of living abolitionists as the main source of information; from them the gaps in the real history of the Underground Railroad must be filled, if filled at all.

It is with the aid of such memorials that the present volume has been written. Reminiscences have been gathered by correspondence and by travel from many surviving abolitionists or their families; and recollections of fugitive slave days have been culled from books, newspapers, letters and diaries. During three years of the five years of preparation the author's residence in Ohio afforded him opportunity to visit many places in that state where former employees of the Underground Railroad could be found, and to extend these explorations to southern Michigan, and among the surviving fugitives along the Detroit River in the Province of Ontario. Residence in Massachusetts during the years 1895–1897 has enabled him to secure some interesting information in regard to underground lines in New England. The materials thus collected relate to the following states: Iowa, Wisconsin, Illinois, Indiana, Ohio, Michigan, Pennsylvania, New Jersey, New York, Connecticut, New Hampshire, Rhode Island, Massachusetts and Vermont, besides a few items concerning North Carolina, Maryland and Delaware.

Underground operations practically ceased with the beginning of the Civil War. In view of the lapse of time, the reasons for trusting the credibility of the evidence upon which our knowledge of the Underground Road rests should be stated. Some of the testimony dealt with in this chapter was put in writing during the period of the Road's operation, or at the close of its activity, and, therefore, cannot be easily questioned. But it may be said that a large part of the

[1] Smedley, *Underground Railroad*, pp. 120, 121.

materials for this history were drawn from written and oral accounts obtained at a much later date; and that these materials, even though the honesty and fidelity of the narrators be granted, are worthy of little credit for historical purposes. Such a criticism would doubtless be just as applied to reminiscences purporting to represent particular events with great detail of narration, but clearly it would lose much of its force when directed against recollections of occurrences that came within the range of the narrator's experience, not once nor twice, but many times with little variation in their main features. It would be difficult to imagine an "old-time" abolitionist, whose faculties are in a fair state of preservation, forgetting that he received fugitives from a certain neighbor or community a few miles away, that he usually stowed them in his garret or his haymow, and that he was in the habit of taking them at night in all kinds of weather to one of several different stations, the managers of which he knew intimately and trusted implicitly. Not only did repetition serve to deepen the general recollections of the average operator, but the strange and romantic character of his unlawful business helped to fix them in his mind. Some special occurrences he is apt to remember with vividness, because they were in some way extraordinary. If it be argued that the surviving abolitionists are now old persons, it should not be forgotten that it is a fact of common observation that old persons ordinarily remember the occurrences of their youth and prime better than events of recent date. The abolitionists, as a class, were people whose remembrances of the ante-bellum days were deepened by the clear definition of their governing principles, the abiding sense of their religious convictions, and the extraordinary conditions, legal and social, under which their acts were performed. The risks these persons ran, the few and scattered friends they had, the concentration of their interests into small compass, because of the disdain of the communities where they lived, have secured to us a source of knowledge, the value of which cannot be lightly questioned. If there be doubt on this point, it must give way before the manner in which statements gathered from different localities during the last five years articulate together, the testimony of different and sometimes widely separated witnesses combining to support one another.[1]

The elucidation by new light of some obscure matter already reported, the verification by a fresh witness of some fact already discovered, gives at once the rule and test of an investigation such as this. Out of many illustrations that might be given, the following are offered. Mr. J. M. Forsyth, of Northwood, Logan County, Ohio, writes under date September 22, 1894: "In Northwood there is a denomination known as Covenanters; among them the runaways were safe. Isaac Patterson has a cave on his place where the fugitives were secreted and fed two or three weeks at a time until the hunt for them was over. Then friends, as hunters, in covered wagons would take them to Sandusky. The highest number taken at one time was seven. The conductors were mostly students from Northwood. All I did was to help get up the team. . . ."

The Rev. J. S. T. Milligan, of Esther, Pennsylvania, December 5, 1896, writes entirely independently: "In 1849 my brother . . . and I went . . . to Logan Co., Ohio, to conduct a grammar school . . . at a place called Northwood. The school developed into a college under the title of Geneva Hall. J. R. W. Sloane[2] . . . was elected President and moved to Northwood in 1851. . . . The region was settled by Covenanters and Seceders, and every house was a home for the wanderers. But there was a cave on the farm of a man by the name of Patterson, absolutely safe and fairly

---

[1] The value of reminiscences and memoirs is considered in an article on "Recollections as a Source of History," by the Hon. Edward L. Pierce, in the *Proceedings of the Massachusetts Historical Society*, March and April, 1896, pp. 473-490. This, with the remarks of Professor H. Morse Stephens in his article entitled "Recent Memoirs of the French Directory," *American Historical Review*, April, 1896, pp. 475, 476, 489, should be read as a corrective by the student that finds himself constrained to have recourse to recollections for information.

[2] The Rev. J. R. W. Sloane, D.D., was the father of Professor William M. Sloane, of Columbia University, New York City. Professor Sloane, in a letter recently received, says: "The first clear, conscious memory I have is of seeing slaves taken from our garret near midnight, and forwarded towards Sandusky. I also remember the formal, but rather friendly, visitation of the house by the sheriff's posse." Date of letter, Paris, November 19, 1896.

comfortable for fugitives. In one instance thirteen fugitives, after resting in the cave for some days, were taken by the students in two covered wagons to Sandusky, some 90 miles, where I had gone to engage passage for them on the Bay City steamboat across the lake to Malden — where I saw them safely landed on free soil, to their unspeakable joy. Indeed, I thought one old man would have died from the gladness of his heart in being safe in freedom. I went from Belle Centre [near Northwood] by rail, and did not go with the land escort — but from what they told me of their experience, it was often amusing and sometimes thrilling. They were ostensibly a hunting party of 10 or 12 armed men. . . . The two covered wagons were a 'sanctum sanctorum' into which no mortal was allowed to peep. . . . The word of command, 'Stand back,' was always respected by those who were unduly intent upon seeing the thirteen deer . . . brought from the woods of Logan and Hardin counties and being taken to Sandusky."

In the same letter Mr. Milligan corroborates some information secured from the Rev. R. G. Ramsey, of Cadiz, Ohio, August 18, 1892, in regard to an underground route in southern Illinois. Mr. Ramsey related that his father, Robert Ramsey, first engaged in Underground Railroad work at Eden, Randolph County, Illinois, in 1844, and that he carried it on at intervals until the War. "The fugitives," he said, "came up the river to Chester, Illinois, and there they started northeast on the state road, which followed an old Indian trail. The stations were each in a community of Covenanters, . . ." and existed, according to his account, at Chester, Eden, Oakdale, Nashville and Centralia. "Besides my father," said Mr. Ramsey, "John Hood and two brothers, James B. and Thomas McClurkin, lived in Oakdale, where my father lived during the last thirty-five years of his life. He lived in Eden before this time. . . ."[1] The Rev. Mr. Milligan writes as follows: "My father removed to Randolph Co., Ill., in 1847, and with Rev. Wm. Sloane . . . and the Covenanter congregations under their ministry kept a very large depot wide open for slaves escaping from Mis-

[1] Conversation with the Rev. R. G. Ramsey, Cadiz, Ohio, August 18, 1892.

souri. Scores at a time came to Sparta [the post-office of the Eden settlement mentioned above] — my father's region, were harbored there, . . . and finally escorted to Elkhorn [about two miles from Oakdale], the region of Father Sloane, where they were sheltered and escorted . . . to some friends in the region of Nashville, Ill., and thence north on the regular trail which I am not able further to locate. At Sparta, Coultersville and Elkhorn there was an almost constant supply of fugitives. . . . But . . . few were ever gotten from the ægis of the Hayes and Moores and Todds and McLurkins and Hoods and Sloanes and Milligans of that region."

The evidence above quoted has the well-known value of two witnesses, examined apart, who corroborate each other; and it also illustrates the way in which the pieces of underground routes may be joined together. These letters, together with some additional testimony, enable us to trace on the map a section of a secret line of travel in southern Illinois.

Another example throws light on a channel of escape in northeastern Indiana. While Levi Coffin lived at Newport (now Fountain City), Indiana, he sometimes sent slaves northward by way of what he called "the Mississinewa route,"[1] from the Mississinewa River, near which undoubtedly it ran for a considerable distance. This road seems to have been called also the Grant County route. In the most general way only do these descriptions tell anything about the route. However, correspondence with several people of Indiana has brought it to light. One letter[2] informs us in regard to fugitives departing from Newport: "If they came to Economy they were sent to Grant Co. . . ." Now, so far as known, Jonesboro' was the next locality to which they were usually forwarded, and the line from this point northward is given us by the Hon. John Ratliff, of Marion, Indiana, who had been over it with passengers. He says that the first station north of Jonesboro' was North Manchester, where "Morris" Place

[1] *Reminiscences*, p. 184.
[2] Letter of John Charles, Economy, Wayne County, Indiana, January 9, 1896. Mr. Charles is a Quaker, and took part in the underground work at Economy.

was agent; the next station, Goshen, where Dr. Matchett harbored fugitives; and thence the line ran to Young's Prairie,[1] which is in Cass County, Michigan. The same section of Road, but with a few additional stations, is marked out by William Hayward. The additional stations may not have existed at the time when Mr. Ratliff served as a guide, or he may have forgotten to mention them. Mr. Hayward writes: "My cousin, Maurice Place, often brought carriage loads of colored people from North Manchester, Wabash Co., to my father's house, six miles west of Manchester on the Rochester road. . . . We would keep them . . . until sometime in the night; then my father would go with them to Avery Brace's . . . three miles . . . north, through the woods. He took them . . . seven miles farther . . . to Chauncey Hurlburt's in Kosciusko Co. . . . They (the Hurlburts) took them twelve miles farther . . . to Warsaw, to a man by the name of Gordon, and he took them to Dr. Matchett's in Elkhart Co., not far from Goshen. There were friends there to help them to Michigan."[2]

In weighing the testimony amassed, the author has had the advantage of personal acquaintance with many of those furnishing information; and the internal evidence of letters has been considered in estimating the worth of written testimony. Doubtless the work could have been more thoroughly executed, if the collection of materials had been systematically undertaken by some one a decade or two earlier. It is certain that it could not have been postponed to a later period. Since the inception of this research the ravages of time have greatly thinned the company of witnesses, who count it among their chiefest joys that they were permitted to live to see their country rid of slavery, and the negro race a free people.

[1] Letter from Charles W. Osborn, Economy, Indiana, March 4, 1896. Mr. Osborn obtained the names of stations in conversation with Mr. Ratliff.
[2] Letter of William Hayward.

ONE OF THE PIONEERS IN THE UNDERGROUND MOVEMENT IN
PHILADELPHIA AND NEW YORK.

Mr. Hopper is supposed to have resorted to underground methods as early as 1787.

CHAPTER II

ORIGIN AND GROWTH OF THE UNDERGROUND ROAD

THE Underground Road developed in a section of country rid of slavery, and situated between two regions, from one of which slaves were continually escaping with the prospect of becoming indisputably free on crossing the borders of the other. Not a few persons living within the intervening territory were deeply opposed to slavery, and although they were bound by law to discountenance slaves seeking freedom, they felt themselves to be more strongly bound by conscience to give them help. Thus it happened that in the course of the sixty years before the outbreak of the War of the Rebellion the Northern states became traversed by numerous secret pathways leading from Southern bondage to Canadian liberty.

Slavery was put in process of extinction at an early period in Pennsylvania, New Jersey, New York and the New England states. From the five and a fraction states created out of the Northwestern Territory slavery was excluded by the Ordinance of 1787. It is interesting to note how rapid was the progress of emancipation in the Northeastern states, where the conditions of climate, industry and public opinion were unfavorable to the continuance of slavery. In 1777 emancipation was begun by the action of Vermont, which upon its separation from New York adopted a constitution in which slavery was prohibited. Pennsylvania and Massachusetts took action three years later. Pennsylvania provided by statute for gradual abolition, and its example was followed by Rhode Island and Connecticut in 1784, by New York in 1799, and by New Jersey in 1804. Massachusetts was less direct, but not less effective, in securing the extinction of slavery; happily it had inserted in the declaration of rights prefixed to its constitution: "All men are born free and equal, and have certain natural, essential and inalienable rights."[1] This clause received at a later time strict interpretation at the bar of the state supreme court, and slavery was held to have ceased with the year 1780.

There is little to be said about the remaining group of states with which we are here concerned. Their territorial organizations were effected under the provisions of the Ordinance of 1787. One of the most important of these provisions is as follows: "There shall be neither slavery nor involuntary servitude in the said Territory, otherwise than in the punishment of crimes whereof the party shall have been duly convicted."[2] It was this feature, introduced into the great Ordinance by New England men, that rendered futile the many attempts subsequently made by Indiana Territory to have slavery admitted within its own boundaries by congressional enactment. "It is probable," says Rhodes, "that had it not been for the prohibitory clause, slavery would have gained such a foothold in Indiana and Illinois that the two would have been organized as slaveholding states."[3] The five states, Ohio, Indiana, Illinois, Michigan and Wisconsin were therefore admitted to the Union as free states. West of the Mississippi River there is one state, at least, that must be added to the group just indicated, namely, Iowa. Slaveholding was prevented within its domain by the Act of Congress of 1820, prohibiting slavery in the territory acquired under the Louisiana purchase north of latitude 36° 30', and several years before this law was abrogated Iowa had entered statehood with a constitution that fixed her place among the free commonwealths. The enfranchisement of this extended region was thus accomplished by state and national action. The ominous result was the establishment of a sweeping line of frontier between the slaveholding South and the non-slaveholding North, and thereby the propounding to the nation of a new question,

---

[1] Constitution of Massachusetts, Part I, Art. 1; quoted by Du Bois, *Suppression of the Slave Trade*, p. 225.
[2] See Appendix A, p. 359.
[3] *History of the United States*, Vol. I, p. 16.

that of the status of fugitives in free regions. The elements were in the proper condition for the crystallization of this question.

The colonies generally had found it necessary to provide regulations in regard to fugitives and the restoration of them to their masters. Such provisions, it is probable, were reasonably well observed as long as runaways did not escape beyond the borders of the colonies to which their owners belonged; but escapes from the territory of one colony into that of another were at first left to be settled as the state of feeling existing between the two peoples concerned should dictate. In 1643 the New England Confederation of Plymouth, Massachusetts, Connecticut and New Haven, unwilling to leave the subject of the delivery of fugitives longer to intercolonial comity, incorporated a clause in their Articles of Confederation providing: "If any servant runn away from his master into any other of these confederated Jurisdiccons, That in such case vpon the Certyficate of one Majistrate in the Jurisdiccon out of which the said servant fled, or upon other due proofs, the said servant shall be deliuered either to his Master or any other that pursues and brings such Certificate or proofe." About the same time an agreement was entered into between the Dutch at New Netherlands and the English at New Haven for the mutual surrender of fugitives, a step that was preceded by a complaint from the commissioners of the United Colonies to Governor Stuyvesant of New Netherlands, to the effect that the Dutch agent at Hartford was harboring one of their Indian slaves, and by the refusal to return some of Stuyvesant's runaway servants from New Haven until the redress of the grievance. It was only when some of the fugitives had been restored to New Netherlands, and a proclamation, issued in a spirit of retaliation by the Lords of the West India Company, forbidding the rendition of fugitive slaves to New Haven, had been annulled, that the agreement for the mutual surrender of runaways was made by the two parties. Negotiations in regard to fugitives early took place between Maryland and New Netherlands; at one time on account of the flight of some slaves from the Southern colony into the Northern colony, and later on account of the reversal of the conditions. The temper of the Dutch when calling for their servants in 1659 was not conciliatory, for they threatened, if their demand should be refused, " to publish free liberty, access and recess to all planters, servants, negroes, fugitives, and runaways which may go into New Netherland." The escape of fugitives from the Eastern colonies northward to Canada was also a constant source of trouble between the French and the Dutch, and between the French and English.[1]

When, therefore, emancipation acts were passed by Vermont and four other states the new question came into existence. It presented itself also in the Western territories. The framers of the Northwest Ordinance found themselves confronted by the question, and they dealt with it in the spirit of compromise. They enacted a stipulation for the territory, " that any person escaping into the same, from whom labor or service is lawfully claimed in any one of the original states, such fugitive may be lawfully reclaimed and conveyed to the person claiming his or her labor or service aforesaid."[2]

Meanwhile the Federal Convention in Philadelphia had the same question to consider. The result of its deliberations on the point was not different from that of Congress expressed in the Ordinance. Among the concessions to slavery that the Federal Convention felt constrained to make, this provision found place in the Constitution: " No person held to service or labor in one state under the laws thereof, escaping into another, shall, in consequence of any law or regulation therein, be discharged from such service or labor, but shall be delivered up on claim of the party to whom such service or labor may be due."[3] Neither of these clauses appears to have been subjected to much debate, and they were adopted by votes that testify to their acceptableness; the former received the support of all members present but one, the latter passed unanimously.

In the sentiment of the time there seems to have been no

[1] M. G. McDougall, *Fugitive Slaves*, pp. 2–11.
[2] *Journals of Congress*, XII, 84, 92.
[3] Constitution of the United States, Art. IV, § 2. See *Revised Statutes of the United States*, I, 18. See also Appendix A, p. 359.

sense of humiliation on the part of the North over the conclusions reached concerning the rendition of escaped slaves. It had been seen by Northern men that the subject was one requiring conciliatory treatment, if it were not to become a block in the way of certain Southern states entering the Union; and, besides, the opinion generally prevailed that slavery would gradually disappear from all the states, and the riddle would thus solve itself.[1] The South was pleased, but apparently not exultant, over the supposed security gained for its slave property. General C. C. Pinckney, of South Carolina, probably expressed the view of most Southerners when he said that the terms for the security of slave property gained by his section were not bad, although they were not the best from the slaveholders' standpoint, and that they permitted the recapture of runaways in any part of America — a right the South had never before enjoyed.[2] In abstract law the rights of the slave-owner had in truth been well provided for. Especially deserving of note is the fact that a constitutional basis had been furnished for claims which, in case slavery did not disappear from the country — a contingency not anticipated by the fathers — might be insisted upon as having the fundamental and positive sanction of the government. But what would be the fate of the running slave was a matter with which, after all, private principles and sympathies, and not merely constitutional provisions, would have a good deal to do in each case.

For several years the stipulations for the rendition of fugitive slaves remained inoperative. At length, in 1791, a case of kidnapping occurred at Washington, Pennsylvania, and this served to bring the subject once more to the public mind. Early in 1793 Congress passed the first Fugitive Slave Law.[3] This law provided for the reclamation of fugitives from justice and fugitives from labor. We are concerned, of course, with the latter class only. The sections of the act dealing with this division are too long to be here quoted:

[1] Elliot's *Debates*. See also George Livermore's *Historical Research Respecting the Opinions of the Founders of the Republic on Negroes, as Citizens and as Soldiers*, 1862, p. 51 *et seq*.
[2] Elliot's *Debates*, III, 277.   [3] Appendix A, pp. 359–361.

they empowered the owner, his agent or attorney, to seize the fugitive and take him before a United States circuit or district judge within the state where the arrest was made, or before any local magistrate within the county in which the seizure occurred. The oral testimony of the claimant, or an affidavit from a magistrate in the state from which he came, must certify that the fugitive owed service as claimed. Upon such showing the claimant secured his warrant for removing the runaway to the state or territory from which he had fled. Five hundred dollars fine constituted the penalty for hindering arrest, or for rescuing or harboring the fugitive after notice that he or she was a fugitive from labor.

All the evidence goes to show that this law was ineffectual; Mrs. McDougall points out that two cases of resistance to the principle of the act occurred before the close of 1793.[1] Attempts at amendment were made in Congress as early as the winter of 1796, and were repeated at irregular intervals down to 1850. Secret or "underground" methods of rescue were already well understood in and around Philadelphia by 1804. Ohio and Pennsylvania, and perhaps other states, heeded the complaints of neighboring slave states, and gave what force they might to the law of 1793 by enacting laws for the recovery of fugitives within their borders. The law of Pennsylvania for this purpose was passed the same year in which Mr. Clay, then Secretary of State, began negotiations with England looking toward the extradition of slaves from Canada (1826); but it was quashed by the decision of the United States Supreme Court in the Prigg case in 1842.[2] By 1850 the Northern states were traversed by numerous lines of Underground Railroad, and the South was declaring its losses of slave property to be enormous.

The result of the frequent transgressions of the Fugitive Slave Law on the one hand and of the clamorous demand for a measure adequate to the needs of the South on the other, was the passage of a new Fugitive Recovery Bill in 1850.[3] The

---

[1] *Fugitive Slaves*, p. 19.
[2] See Chap. IX, pp. 259–267; also Stroud, *Sketch of the Laws Relating to Slavery in the Several States*, 2d ed., pp. 220–222.
[3] Appendix A, pp. 361–366.

increased rigor of the provisions of this act was ill adapted to generate the respect that a good law secures, and, indeed, must have in order to be enforced. The law contained features sufficiently objectionable to make many converts to the cause of the abolitionists; and a systematic evasion of the law was regarded as an imperative duty by thousands. The Fugitive Slave Act of 1850 was based on the earlier law, but was fitted out with a number of clauses, dictated by a self-interest on the part of the South that ignored the rights of every party save those of the master. Under the regulations of the act the certificate authorizing the arrest and removal of a fugitive slave was to be granted to the claimant by the United States commissioner, the courts, or the judge of the proper circuit, district, or county. If the arrest were made without process, the claimant was to take the fugitive forthwith before the commissioner or other official, and there the case was to be determined in a summary manner. The refusal of a United States marshal or his deputies to execute a commissioner's certificate, properly directed, involved a fine of one thousand dollars; and failure to prevent the escape of the negro after arrest, made the marshal liable, on his official bond, for the value of the slave. When necessary to insure a faithful observance of the fugitive slave clause in the Constitution, the commissioners, or persons appointed by them, had the authority to summon the posse comitatus of the county, and "all good citizens" were "commanded to aid and assist in the prompt and efficient execution" of the law. The testimony of the alleged fugitive could not be received in evidence. Ownership was determined by the simple affidavit of the person claiming the slave; and when determined it was shielded by the certificate of the commissioner from "all molestation . . . by any process issued by any court, judge, magistrate, or other person whomsoever." Any act meant to obstruct the claimant in his arrest of the fugitive, or any attempt to rescue, harbor, or conceal the fugitive, laid the person interfering liable "to a fine not exceeding one thousand dollars, and imprisonment not exceeding six months," also liable for "civil damages to the party injured in the sum of one thousand dollars for each fugitive so lost." In all cases where the proceedings took place before a commissioner he was "entitled to a fee of ten dollars in full for his services," provided that a warrant for the fugitive's arrest was issued; if, however, the fugitive was discharged, the commissioner was entitled to five dollars only.[1]

By the abolitionists, at whom it was directed, this law was detested. A government, whose first national manifesto contained the exalted principles enshrined in the Declaration of Independence, stooping to the task of slave-catching, violated all their ideas of national dignity, decency and consistency. Many persons, indeed, justified their opposition to the law in the familiar words: "We hold these truths to be self-evident, that all men are created equal, that they are endowed by their Creator with certain inalienable rights, that among these are life, liberty, and the pursuit of happiness." The scriptural injunction "not to deliver unto his master the servant that hath escaped,"[2] was also frequently quoted by men whose religious convictions admitted of no compromise. They pointed out that the law virtually made all Northern citizens accomplices in what they denominated the crime of slave-catching; that it denied the right of trial by jury, resting the question of lifelong liberty on ex-parte evidence; made ineffective the writ of habeas corpus; and offered a bribe to the commissioner for a decision against the negro.[3] The penalties of fine and imprisonment for offenders against the law were severe, but they had no deterrent effect upon those engaged in helping slaves to Canada. On the contrary, the Fugitive Slave Law of 1850 stimulated the work of secret emancipation. "The passage of the new law," says a recent investigator, "probably increased the number of anti-slavery people more than anything else that had occurred during the whole agitation. Many of those formerly indifferent were roused to active opposition by a sense of the injustice of the Fugitive Slave Act as they saw it executed in Boston and

[1] *Statutes at Large*, IX, 462–465.
[2] *Deut.* xxiii, 15, 16.
[3] See *Some Recollections of the Anti-Slavery Conflict*, by S. J. May, p. 345 et seq.; Stroud's *Sketch of the Laws Relating to Slavery in the Several States*, 2d ed., 1856, pp. 271–280; Wilson, *History of the Rise and Fall of the Slave Power*, Vol. II, pp. 304–322.

elsewhere. . . . As Mr. James Freeman Clarke has said, 'It was impossible to convince the people that it was right to send back to slavery men who were so desirous of freedom as to run such risks. All education from boyhood up to manhood had taught us to believe that it was the duty of all men to struggle for freedom.'"[1]

The desire for freedom was in the mind of nearly every enslaved negro. Liberty was the subject of the dreams and visions of slave preachers and sibyls; it was the object of their prayers. The plaintive songs of the enslaved race were full of the thought of freedom. It has been well said that "one of the finest touches in *Uncle Tom's Cabin* is the joyful expression of Uncle Tom when told by his good and indulgent master that he should be set free and sent back to his old home in Kentucky. In attributing the common desire of humanity to the negro the author was as true as she was effective."[2] To slaves living in the vicinity, Mexico and Florida early afforded a welcome refuge. Forests, islands and swamps within the Southern states were favorite places of resort for runaways. The Great Dismal Swamp became the abode of a large colony of these refugees, whose lives were spent in its dark recesses, and whose families were reared and buried there. Even in this retreat, however, the negroes were not beyond molestation, for they were systematically hunted by men with dogs and guns.[3] Scraps of information about Canada and the Northern states were gleaned and treasured by minds recognizing their own degradation, but scarcely knowing how to take the first step towards the betterment of their condition.

There can be no doubt that the form in which slavery existed in the South during the opening decade of the present century was comparatively mild; but it is quite clear that it soon exchanged this character for one from which the amen-

---

[1] M. G. McDougall, *Fugitive Slaves*, p. 43; J. F. Clarke, *Anti-Slavery Days*, p. 92.
[2] Rhodes, *History of the United States*, Vol. I, p. 377.
[3] F. L. Olmsted, *Journey in the Back Country*, p. 155; Rev. W. M. Mitchell, *The Underground Railroad*, pp. 72, 73; M. G. McDougall, *Fugitive Slaves*, p. 57.

ities of the patriarchal type had practically disappeared. With the rapid expansion of the industries peculiar to the South after the opening up of the Louisiana purchase, the invention of the cotton gin, and the removal of the Indians from the Gulf states, came the era of the slave's dismay. The auction block and the brutal overseer became his dread while awake, his nightmare when asleep. That his fears were not ill founded is proved by the activity of the slave-marts of Baltimore, Richmond, New Orleans and Washington from the time of the migrations to the Mississippi territory until the War. Alabama is said to have bought millions of dollars worth of slaves from the border states up to 1849. Dew estimated that six thousand slaves were carried from Virginia, though not all of these were sold to other states.[1]

The fear of sale to the far South must have stimulated slaves to flight. That the number of escapes did increase is deduced from the consensus of abolitionist testimony. Our sole reliance is upon this testimony until the appearance of the United States census reports for 1850 and 1860;[2] and the exhibits on fugitive slaves in these compendiums we are constrained by various considerations to regard as inadequate. However, the flight of slaves from the South was not what the new conditions would readily account for. We must conclude, therefore, that the deterring effect of ignorance and the sense of the difficulties in the way were reënforced after 1840 by increased vigilance on the part of the slave-owning class, owing to the rise in value of slave property. "Since 1840," says a careful observer, "the high price of slaves may be supposed . . . to have increased the vigilance and energy with which the recapture of fugitives is followed up, and to have augmented the number of free negroes reduced to slavery by kidnappers. Indeed it has led to a proposition being quite seriously entertained in Virginia, of enslaving the whole body of the free negroes in that state by legislative enactment."[3] Then, too, the negro's attachment

---

[1] Edward Ingle, *Southern Side-Lights*, p. 293.

[2] These reports will be dealt with in another connection. See Chap. XI, pp. 342, 343.

[3] G. M. Weston, *Progress of Slavery in the United States*, Washington, D.C., 1858, pp. 22, 23.

(Slightly enlarged from *The Anti-Slavery Record*, published in New York City by the American Anti-Slavery Society.)

to the land of his birth, and to his kindred, when these were not torn from him, must be allowed to have hindered flight in many instances; when, however, the appearance of the dreaded slave-dealer, or the brutality of the overseer or the master, spread dismay among the hands of a plantation, flights were likely to follow. This was sometimes the case, too, when by the death of a planter the division of his property among his heirs was made necessary. William Johnson, of Windsor, Ontario, ran away from his Kentucky master because he was threatened with being sent South to the cotton and rice fields.[1] Horace Washington, of Windsor, after working nearly two years for a man that had a claim on him for one hundred and twenty-five dollars, reminded his employer that the original agreement required but one year's labor, and asked for release. Getting no satisfaction, and fearing sale, he fled to Canada.[2] Lewis Richardson, one of the slaves of Henry Clay, sought relief in flight after receiving a hundred and fifty stripes from Mr. Clay's overseer.[3] William Edwards, of Amherstburg, Ontario, left his master on account of a severe flogging.[4] One of the station-keepers of an underground line in Morgan County, Ohio, recalls an instance of a family of seven fugitives giving as the cause of their flight the death of their master, and the expected scattering of their number when the division of the estate should occur.[5]

It has already been remarked that slaves began to find their way to Canada before the opening of the present century, but information in regard to that country as a place of refuge can scarcely be said to have come into circulation before the War of 1812. The hostile relations existing between the two nations at that time caused negroes of sagacious minds to seek their liberty among the enemies of the United States.[6] Then, too, soldiers returning from the War to their homes in Kentucky

[1] Conversation with William Johnson, Windsor, Ontario, July, 1895.
[2] Conversation with Horace Washington, Windsor, Ontario, Aug. 2, 1895.
[3] *The Liberator*, April 10, 1846.
[4] Conversation with William Edwards, Amherstburg, Ontario, Aug. 3, 1895.
[5] Letter of H. C. Harvey, Manchester, Kan., Jan. 16, 1893.
[6] S. G. Howe, *The Refugees from Slavery in Canada West*, pp. 11, 12.

and Virginia brought the news of the disposition of the Canadian government to defend the rights of the self-emancipated slaves under its jurisdiction. Rumors of this sort gave hope and courage to the blacks that heard it, and, doubtless, the welcome reports were spread by these among trusted companions and friends. By 1815 fugitives were crossing the Western Reserve in Ohio, and regular stations of the Underground Railroad were lending them assistance in that and other portions of the state.[1]

After the discovery of Canada by colored refugees from the Southern states, it was, presumably, not long before some of them, returning for their families and friends, gave circulation in a limited way to reports more substantial than the vague rumors hitherto afloat. Among the escaped slaves that carried the promise of Canadian liberty across Mason and Dixon's line were such successful abductors as Josiah Henson and Harriet Tubman. In 1860 it was estimated that the number of negroes that journeyed annually from Canada to the slave states to rescue their fellows was about five hundred. It was said that these persons "carried the Underground Railroad and the Underground Telegraph into nearly every Southern state."[2] The work done by these fugitives was supplemented by the cautious dissemination of news by white persons that went into the South to abduct slaves or encourage them to escape, or while engaged there in legitimate occupations used their opportunities to pass the helpful word or to afford more substantial aid. The Rev. Calvin Fairbank, the Rev. Charles T. Torrey and Dr. Alexander M. Ross may be cited as notable examples of this class. The latter, a citizen of Canada, made extensive tours through various slave states for the express purpose of spreading information about Canada and the routes by which that country could be reached. He made trips into Maryland, Kentucky, Virginia and Tennessee, and did not think it too great a risk to make excursions into the more southern states. He went to New Orleans, and from that point set out on a journey, in the course of which he visited

[1] Wilson, *History of the Rise and Fall of the Slave Power*, Vol. II, p. 63.
[2] Redpath, *The Public Life of Captain John Brown*, p. 229.

Vicksburg, Selma and Columbus, Mississippi, Augusta, Georgia, and Charleston, South Carolina.[1] Considering the comparative freedom of movement between the slave and the free states along the border, it is easy to understand how slaves in Maryland, Virginia, Kentucky and Missouri might pick up information about the "Land of Promise" to the northward. Isaac White, a slave of Kanawha County, Virginia, was shown a map and instructed how to get to Canada by a man from Cleveland, Ohio. Allen Sidney, a negro who ran a steamboat on the Tennessee River for his master, first learned of Canada from an abolitionist at Florence, Alabama.[2] Until the contest over the peculiar institution had become heated, it was not an uncommon thing for slaves to be sent on errands, or even hired out to residents of the border counties of the free states. Notwithstanding Ohio's political antagonism to slavery from the beginning, there was a "tacit tolerance" of slavery by the people of the state down to about 1835; and "numbers of slaves, as many as two thousand it was sometimes supposed, were hired . . . from Virginia and Kentucky, chiefly by farmers." Doubtless such persons heard more or less about Canada, and when the agitation against slavery became vehement, they were approached by friends, and many were induced to accept transportation to the Queen's dominions.[3]

Depredations of this sort caused alarm among slaveholders. They sought to deter their chattels from flight by talking freely before them about the rigors of the climate and the poverty of the soil of Canada. Such talk was wasted on the slaves, who were shrewd enough to discern the real meaning of their masters. They were alert to gather all that was said, and interpret it in the light of rumors from other sources. Thus, masters themselves became disseminators of information

[1] Dr. A. M. Ross, *Recollections and Experiences of an Abolitionist*, 2d ed., 1876, pp. 10, 11, 15, 39.
[2] Conversation with White and Sidney in Canada West, August, 1895.
[3] Rufus King, *Ohio*, in *American Commonwealths*, pp. 364, 365, relates that some of these slaves were discharged from servitude "by writs of habeas corpus procured in their names," and that "numbers were abducted from the slave states and concealed, or smuggled by the 'Underground Railroad' into Canada."

they meant to withhold. In this and other ways the slaves of the border states heard of Canada. The sale of some of these slaves to the South helps to explain the knowledge of Canada possessed by many blacks in those distant parts. When Mr. Ross visited Vicksburg, Mississippi, he found that "many of these negroes had heard of Canada from the negroes brought from Virginia and the border slave states; but the impression they had was that, Canada being so far away, it would be useless to try to reach it."[1] Notwithstanding the distance, the number of successful escapes from the interior as well as from the border slave states seems to have been sufficient to arouse the suspicion in the minds of Southerners that a secret organization of abolitionists had agents at work in the South running off slaves. This suspicion was brought to light during the trial of Richard Dillingham in Tennessee in 1849.[2] The labors of Mr. Ross several years later gave color to the same notion. These facts help to explain the insistence of the lower Southern states on the passage and strict enforcement of the Fugitive Slave Law in 1850.

With the growth of a thing so unfavored as was the Underground Road, local conditions must have a great deal to do. The characteristics of small and scattered localities, and even of isolated families, are of the first importance in the consideration of a movement such as this. These little communities were in general the elements out of which the underground system built itself up. The sources of the convictions and confidences that knitted these communities together in defiance of what they considered unjust law can only be learned by the study of local conditions. The incorporation in the Constitution of the compromises concerning slavery doubtless quieted the consciences of many of the early friends of universal liberty. It was only natural, however, that there should be some that would hold such concessions to be sinful, and in violation of the principles asserted in the Declaration of Independence and in the very Preamble of the Constitution itself. These persons would cling tena-

---

[1] Dr. A. M. Ross, *The Recollections and Experiences of an Abolitionist*, p. 38.
[2] A. L. Benedict, *Memoir of Richard Dillingham*, p. 17.

ciously to their views, and would aid a fugitive slave whenever one would ask protection and help. It is not strange that representatives of this class should be found more frequently among the Quakers than any other sect. In southeastern Pennsylvania and in New Jersey the work of helping slaves to escape was, for the most part, in the hands of Quakers from the beginning. This was true also of Wilmington, Delaware, New Bedford, Massachusetts, and Valley Falls, Rhode Island, as of a number of important centres in western Pennsylvania, and eastern, central and southwestern Ohio, in eastern Indiana, in southern Michigan and in eastern Iowa.

Anti-slavery views prevailed against the first attempts at enforcement of the Fugitive Slave Law of 1793 in Massachusetts, and spread to other localities in the New England states. When the tide of emigration to the Western states set in, settlers from New England were given more frequent occasions to put their principles into practice in their new homes than they had known in the seaboard region. The western portions of New York and Pennsylvania, as well as the neighboring section of Ohio, called the Western Reserve, are dotted over with communities where negroes learned the meaning of Yankee hospitality. Like Joshua R. Giddings, the people of these communities claimed to have borrowed their abolition sentiments from the writings of Jefferson, whose "abolition tract," Giddings said, "was called the Declaration of Independence."[1] In northern Illinois there were many centres of the New England type, though, of course, not all the underground stations in that region were kept by New Englanders.

In a few neighborhoods settlers from the Southern states were helpers. These persons had left the South on account of slavery; they preferred to raise their families away from influences they felt to be harmful; and they pitied the slave. It was easy for them to give shelter to the self-freed negro. In south central Ohio, in a district of four or five counties locally known as the old Chillicothe Presbytery, a number of the early preachers were anti-slavery men from the Southern

[1] George W. Julian, *Life of Joshua R. Giddings*, p. 157.

states. Among the number were John Rankin, of Ripley, James Gilliland, of Red Oak, Jesse Lockhart, of Russellville, Robert B. Dobbins, of Sardinia, Samuel Crothers, of Greenfield, Hugh S. Fullerton, of Chillicothe, and William Dickey, of Ross or Fayette County. The Presbyterian churches over which these men presided became centres of opposition to slavery, and fugitives finding their way into the vicinity of any one of them were likely to receive the needed help.[1] The stations in Bond, Putnam and Bureau counties, Illinois, were kept in part by anti-slavery settlers from the South.

It is a fact worthy of record in this connection that the teachings of the two sects, the Scotch Covenanters and the Wesleyan Methodists, did not exclude the negro from the bonds of Christian brotherhood, and where churches of either denomination existed the Road was likely to be found in active operation. Within the borders of Logan County, Ohio, there were a number of Covenanter homes that received fugitives; and in southern Illinois, between the towns of Chester and Centralia, there was a series of such hospitable places. There were several Wesleyan Methodist stations in Harrison County, Ohio, and with these were intermixed a few of the Covenanter denomination.

It was natural that negro settlements in the free states should be resorted to by fugitive slaves. The colored people of Greenwich, New Jersey, the Stewart Settlement of Jackson County, Ohio, the Upper and Lower Camps, Brown County, Ohio, and the Colored Settlement, Hamilton County, Indiana, were active. The list of towns and cities in which negroes became coworkers with white persons in harboring and concealing runaways is a long one. Oberlin, Portsmouth and Cincinnati, Ohio, Detroit, Michigan, Philadelphia, Pennsylvania, and Boston, Massachusetts, will suffice as examples.

The principles and experience gained by a number of stu-

[1] *History of Brown County, Ohio*, p. 313 *et seq.* Also letter of Dr. Isaac M. Beck, Sardinia, O., Dec. 26, 1892. Mr. Beck was born in 1807, and knew personally the clergymen named. He joined the abolition movement in 1835. His excellent letter is verified in various points by other correspondents.

dents while attending college in Oberlin did not come amiss later when these young men established themselves in Iowa. Professor L. F. Parker, after describing what was probably the longest line of travel through Iowa for escaped slaves, says: " Along this line Quakers and Oberlin students were the chief namable groups whose houses were open to such travellers more certainly than to white men,"[1] and the Rev. William M. Brooks, a graduate of Oberlin, until recently President of Tabor College, writes: " The stations . . . in southwestern Iowa were in the region of Civil Bend, where the colony from Oberlin, Ohio, settled which afterwards settled Tabor."[2]

The origin of the Underground Road dates farther back than is generally known; though, to be sure, the different divisions of the Road were not contemporary in development. Two letters of George Washington, written in 1786, give the first reports, as yet known, of systematic efforts for the aid and protection of fugitive slaves. One of these letters bears the date May 12, and the other, November 20. In the former, Washington speaks of the slave of a certain Mr. Dalby residing at Alexandria, who has escaped to Philadelphia, and " whom a society of Quakers in the city, formed for such purposes, have attempted to liberate."[3] In the latter he writes of a slave whom he sent " under the care of a trusty overseer" to the Hon. William Drayton, but who afterwards escaped. He says: " The gentleman to whose care I sent him has promised every endeavor to apprehend him, but it is not easy to do this, when there are numbers who would rather facilitate the escape of slaves than apprehend them when runaways."[4] The difficulties attending the pursuit of the Drayton slave, like those in the other case mentioned, seem to have been associated in Washington's mind with the procedure of certain citizens of Pennsylvania; it is quite possible that he was again referring to the Quaker

---

[1] Letter from Professor L. F. Parker, Grinnell, Iowa, Aug. 30, 1894.
[2] Letter from President W. M. Brooks, Tabor, Iowa, Oct. 11, 1894.
[3] Sparks's *Washington*, IX, 158, quoted in *Quakers of Pennsylvania*, by Dr. A. C. Applegarth, Johns Hopkins Studies, X, p. 463.
[4] Lunt, *Origin of the Late War*, Vol. I, p. 20.

society in Philadelphia. However that may be, it appears probable that the record of Philadelphia as a centre of active sympathy with the fugitive slave was continuous from the time of Washington's letters. In 1787 Isaac T. Hopper, who soon became known as a friend of slaves, settled in Philadelphia, and, although only sixteen or seventeen years old, had already taken a resolution to befriend the oppressed Africans.[1] Some cases of kidnapping that occurred in Columbia, Pennsylvania, in 1804, stirred the citizens of that town to intervention in the runaways' behalf; and the movement seems to have spread rapidly among the Quakers of Chester, Lancaster, York, Montgomery, Berks and Bucks counties.[2] New Jersey was probably not behind southeastern Pennsylvania in point of time in Underground Railroad work. This is to be inferred from the fact that the adjacent parts of the two states were largely settled by people of a sect distinctly opposed to slavery, and were knitted together by those ties of blood that are known to have been favorable in other quarters to the development of underground routes. That protection was given to fugitives early in the present century by the Quakers of southwestern New Jersey can scarcely be doubted; and we are told that negroes were being transported through New Jersey before 1818.[3] New York was closely allied with the New Jersey and Philadelphia centres as far back as our meagre records will permit us to go. Isaac T. Hopper, who had grown familiar with underground methods of procedure in Philadelphia, moved to New York in 1829. No doubt his philanthropic arts were soon made use of there, for in 1835 we find him accused,

[1] L. Maria Child, *Life of Isaac T. Hopper*, 1854, p. 35.
[2] *History of Chester County, Pennsylvania*, R. C. Smedley's article on the "Underground Railroad," p. 426; also Smedley, *Underground Railroad*, p. 26.
[3] The Rev. Thomas C. Oliver, born and raised in Salem, N.J., says that the work of the Underground Railroad was going on before he was born, (1818) and continued until the time of the War. Mr. Oliver was raised in the family of Thomas Clement, a member of the Society of Friends. He graduated from the Princeton Theological Seminary in 1856. As a youth he began to take part in rescues. Although seventy-five years old when visited by the author, he was vigorous in body and mind, and seemed to have a remarkably clear memory.

though falsely this time, of harboring a runaway at his store in Pearl Street.[1] Frederick Douglass mentions the assistance rendered by Mr. Hopper to fugitives in New York; and says that he himself received aid from David Ruggles, a colored man and coworker with the venerable Quaker.[2] After the passage of the Fugitive Slave Law in 1850, New York City became more active than ever in receiving and forwarding refugees.[3] This city at the mouth of the Hudson was the entrepôt for a line of travel by way of Albany, Syracuse and Rochester to Canada, and for another line diverging at Albany, and extending by the way of Troy to the New England states and Canada; and these routes appear to have been used at an early date. The Elmira route, which connected Philadelphia with Niagara Falls by way of Harrisburg, Pennsylvania, was made use of from about 1850 to 1860. Its comparatively late development is explained by the fact that one of its principal agents was a fugitive slave, John W. Jones, who did not settle in Elmira until 1844, and that the line of the Northern Central Railroad was not completed until about 1850.[4] In western New York fugitives began to arrive from the neighboring parts of Pennsylvania and Ohio between 1835 and 1840, if not earlier. Professor Edward Orton recalls that in 1838, soon after his father moved to Buffalo, two sleigh-loads of negroes from the Western Reserve were brought to the house in the night-time;[5] and Mr. Frederick Nicholson, of Warsaw, New York, states that the underground work in his vicinity began in 1840. From this time on there was apparently no cessa-

---

[1] L. Maria Child, *Life of Isaac T. Hopper*, p. 316.
[2] *History of Florence, Mass.*, p. 131, Charles A. Sheffeld, Editor.
[3] The Underground Road was active in New York City at a much earlier date certainly than Lossing gives. He says, "After the Fugitive Slave Law, the Underground Railroad was established, and the city of New York became one of the most important stations on the road." *History of New York*, Vol. II, p. 655.
[4] Letter of Mrs. Susan L. Crane, Elmira, Sept. 14, 1896. Mrs. Crane's father, Mr. Jervis Langdon, was active in underground work at Elmira, and had a trusted co-laborer in John W. Jones, who still lives in Elmira.
[5] Conversation with Professor Orton, Ohio State University, Columbus, O., 1893.

tion of migrations of fugitives into Canada at Black Rock, Buffalo and other points.[1]

The remoteness of New England from the slave states did not prevent its sharing in the business of helping blacks to Canada. In Vermont, which seems to have received fugitives from the Troy line of eastern New York, the period of activity began "in the latter part of the twenties of this century, and lasted till the time of the Rebellion."[2] In New Hampshire there was a station at Canaan after 1830, and probably before that time.[3] The Hon. Mellen Chamberlain, of Chelsea, Massachusetts, personally conducted a fugitive on two occasions from Concord, New Hampshire, to his uncle's at Canterbury, in the same state "most probably in 1838 or 1839."[4] This thing once begun in New Hampshire seems to have continued steadily during the decades until the War of the Rebellion.[5] As regards Connecticut the Rev. Samuel J. May states that as long ago as 1834 slaves were addressed to his care while he was living in the eastern part of the state.[6] In Massachusetts the town of Fall River became an important station in 1839.[7] New Bedford, Boston, Marblehead, Concord, Springfield, Florence and other places in Massachusetts are known to have given shelter to fugitives as they travelled northward. Mr. Simeon Dodge, of Marblehead, who had per-

[1] For cases of arrivals of escaped slaves over some of the western New York branches, see *Sketches in the History of the Underground Railroad*, by Eber M. Pettit, 1879. These sketches were first published in the *Fredonia Censor*, the series closing Nov. 18, 1868.

[2] Letter of Mr. Aldis O. Brainerd, St. Albans, Vt., Oct. 21, 1895.

[3] Letter of Mr. Charles E. Lord, Franklin, Pa., July 6, 1896: "My maternal grandfather, James Furber, lived for several years in Canaan, N. H., where his house was one of the stations of the Underground Railway. His father-in-law, James Harris, who lived in the same house, had been engaged in helping fugitive negroes on toward Canada ever since 1830, and probably before that time."

[4] Letter of Judge Mellen Chamberlain, Chelsea, Mass., Feb. 1, 1896.

[5] Letter of Mr. Thomas P. Cheney, Ashland, N.H., March 30, 1896.

[6] *Recollections of the Anti-Slavery Conflict*, p. 297.

[7] Elizabeth Buffum Chace, *Anti-Slavery Reminiscences*, p. 27. Mrs. Chace says: "From the time of the arrival of James Curry at Fall River, and his departure for Canada, in 1839, that town became an important station on the so-called Underground Railroad." The residence of Mrs. Chace was a place of refuge from the year named.

sonal knowledge of what was going on, recollects that the Underground Road was active between 1840 and 1860, and his testimony is substantiated by that of a number of other persons.[1] Doubtless there was underground work going on in Massachusetts before this period, but it was probably of a less systematic character. In Maine fugitives frequently obtained help in the early forties. The Rev. O. B. Cheney, later President of Bates College, was concerned in a branch of the Road running from Portland to Effingham, New Hampshire, and northward, during the years 1843 to 1845.[2] That later conditions probably increased the labors of the Maine abolitionists appears from the statement of Mr. Brown Thurston, of Portland, that he had at one time after the passage of the second Fugitive Slave Law the care of thirty fugitives.[3]

Considering the geographical situation of Ohio and western Pennsylvania, the period of their settlement, and the character of many of their pioneers, it is not strange that this work should have become established in this region earlier than in the other free states along the Ohio River. The years 1815 to 1817 witnessed, so far as we now know, the origin of underground lines in both the eastern and western parts of this section. Henry Wilson explains this by saying that soldiers from Virginia and Kentucky, returning home after the War of 1812, carried back the news that there was a land of freedom beyond the lakes. John Sloane, of Ravenna, David Hudson, the founder of the town of Hudson, and Owen Brown, the father of John Brown of Osawattomie, were among the first of those known to have harbored slaves in the eastern part.[4] Edward Howard, the father of Colonel D. W. H. Howard, of Wauseon, and the Ottawa Indians of the village of Chief Kinjeino were among the earliest friends of fugitives

---

[1] Concerning Springfield, Mass. see Mason A. Green's *History of Springfield*, pp. 470, 471. For the sentiment of New Bedford, see Ellis's *History of New Bedford*, pp. 306, 307.

[2] Letter of the Rev. O. B. Cheney, Pawtuxet, R.I., Apr. 8, 1896.

[3] Letter of Mr. Brown Thurston, Portland, Me., Oct. 21, 1895.

[4] Wilson, *Rise and Fall of the Slave Power*, Vol. II, p. 63; Alexander Black, *The Story of Ohio*, see account of the Underground Railroad.

in the western part.¹ At least one case of underground procedure is reported to have occurred in central Ohio as early as 1812. The report is but one remove from its original source, and was given to Mr. Robert McCrory, of Marysville, Ohio, by Richard Dixon, an eye-witness. The alleged runaway, seized at Delaware, was unceremoniously taken from the custody of his mounted captor when the two reached Worthington, and was brought before Colonel James Kilbourne, who served as an official of all work in the village he had founded but a few years before. By Mr. Kilbourne's decision, the negro was released, and was then sent north aboard one of the government wagons engaged at the time in carrying military supplies to Sandusky.² That such action was not inconsistent with the character of Colonel Kilbourne and his New England associates is evidenced by the fact that as an agent for "The Scioto Company," formed in Granby, Connecticut, in the winter of 1801–1802, he had delayed the purchase of a township in Ohio for settlement until a state constitution forbidding slavery should be adopted.³ If now the testimony of the oldest surviving abolitionists from the different regions of the state be compared, some interesting results may be found. Job Mullin, a Quaker of Warren County, in his eighty-ninth year when his statement was given, says: "The most active time to my knowledge was from 1816 to 1830. . . ." In 1829 Mr. Mullin moved off the line with which he had been connected and took no further part in the work.⁴ Mr. Eliakim H. Moore, for a number of years the treasurer of Ohio University at Athens, says that the work began near Athens during 1823 and 1824. "In those years not so many attempted to escape as later, from 1845 to 1860."⁵ Dr. Thomas Cowgill, an aged Quaker of Kennard, Champaign County, recollects that the work of the Underground Railroad began in his

---

[1] Letter of Col. D. W. H. Howard, Wauseon, O., Aug. 22, 1894.
[2] Conversation with Robert McCrory, Marysville, O., Sept. 30, 1898. Mr. McCrory was educated at Oberlin College, and has an excellent memory.
[3] Howe's *Historical Collections of Ohio*, Vol. I, p. 614.
[4] Letter from Job Mullin, dictated to his son-in-law, W. H. Newport, at Springboro, O., Sept. 9, 1895.
[5] Conversation with Mr. Eliakim H. Moore, Athens, O.

neighborhood about 1824. The time between 1840 and the passage of the Fugitive Slave Law he regards as the period of greatest activity within his experience. Joseph Skillgess, a colored citizen of Urbana, now seventy-six years old, says that it is among his earliest recollections that runaways were entertained at Dry Run Church, in Ross County.[1] William A. Johnston, an old resident of Coshocton, testifies: "We had such a road here as early as the twenties, I know from tradition and personal observation."[2] Mahlon Pickrell, a prominent Quaker of Logan County, writes: "There was some travel on the Underground Railroad as early as 1820, but the period of greatest activity in this vicinity was between 1840 and 1850."[3] Finally, Mr. R. C. Corwin, of Lebanon, writes: "My first recollection of the business dates back to about 1820, when I remember seeing fugitives at my father's house, though I dare say it had been going on long before that time. From that time until 1840 there was a gradual increase of business. From 1840 to 1860 might be called the period of greatest activity."[4] Among these aged witnesses, those have been quoted whose experience, character and clearness of mind gave weight to their words. Mr. Rush R. Sloane, of Sandusky, who made some local investigations in northwestern Ohio and published the results in 1888, produces some evidence that agrees with the testimony just given. He found that, "The first runaway slave known as such at Sandusky was there in the fall of the year 1820. . . . Judge Jabez Wright, one of the three associate judges who held the first term of court in Huron County in 1815, was among the first white men upon the Firelands to aid fugitive slaves; he never failed when opportunity offered to lend a helping hand to the fugitives, secreting them when necessary, feeding them when they were hungry, clothing and employing them."[5] After reciting a number of instances of rescues occurring between 1820 and 1850, Mr. Sloane remarks

[1] Conversation with Joseph Skillgess, Urbana, O., Aug. 14, 1894.
[2] Letter of Wm. A. Johnston, Coshocton, O., Aug. 23, 1894.
[3] Letter of Hannah W. Blackburn, for her father, Mahlon Pickrell, Zanesfield, O., March 25, 1893.
[4] Letter of R. C. Corwin, Lebanon, O., Sept. 11, 1895.
[5] The *Firelands Pioneer*, July, 1888, p. 34.

that one of the immediate results of the passage of the second Fugitive Slave Law was the increased travel of fugitives through the State of Ohio.[1] The foregoing items have been brought together to show that there was no break in the business of the Road from the beginning to the end. The death or the change of residence of abolitionists may have interrupted travel on one or another route, and may even have broken a line permanently, but the history of the Underground Railroad system in Ohio is continuous.

In North Carolina underground methods are known to have been employed by white persons of respectability as early as 1819. We are informed that "Vestal Coffin organized the Underground Railroad near the present Guilford College in 1819. Addison Coffin, his son, entered its service as a conductor in early youth and still survives in hale old age.... Vestal's cousin, Levi Coffin, became an antislavery apostle in early youth and continued unflinching to the end. His early years were spent in North Carolina, whence he helped many slaves to reach the West."[2] Levi Coffin removed to Indiana in 1826. Of his own and his cousin's activities in behalf of slaves while still a resident of North Carolina, Mr. Coffin writes: "Runaway slaves used frequently to conceal themselves in the woods and thickets of New Garden, waiting opportunities to make their escape to the North, and I generally learned their places of concealment and rendered them all the service in my power.... These outlying slaves knew where I lived, and, when reduced to extremity of want or danger, often came to my room, in the silence and darkness of the night, to obtain food or assistance. In my efforts to aid these fugitives I had a zealous coworker in my friend and cousin Vestal Coffin, who was then, and continued to the time of his death — a few years later — a staunch friend to the slave."[3] When Levi Coffin emigrated in 1826 to southeastern Indiana, he did not give up his active interest in the fleeing slave, and his house at Newport (now Fountain City) became a centre

---

[1] The *Firelands Pioneer*, July, 1888, p. 34 *et seq.*
[2] Stephen B. Weeks, *Southern Quakers and Slavery*, p. 242.
[3] *Reminiscences of Levi Coffin*, 2d ed., pp. 20, 21.

at which three distinct lines of Underground Road converged. It is probable, however, that wayfarers from bondage found aid from pioneer settlers in Indiana before Friend Coffin's arrival. John F. Williams, of Economy, Indiana, says that fugitives "commenced coming in 1820," and he denominated himself "an agent since 1820," although he "never kept a depot till 1852."[1] It is scarcely necessary to make a showing of testimony to prove that an expansion of routes like that taking place in Ohio and states farther east occurred also in Indiana.

It is doubtful at what time stations first came to exist in Illinois. Mr. H. B. Leeper, an old resident of that state, assigns their origin to the years 1819 and 1820, at which time a small colony of anti-slavery people from Brown County, Ohio, settled in Bond County, southern Illinois. Emigrations from this locality to Putnam County, about 1830, led, he thinks, to the establishment there of a new centre for this work. These settlers were persons that had left South Carolina on account of slavery, and during their residence in Brown County, Ohio, had accepted the abolitionist views of the Rev. James Gilliland, a Presbyterian preacher of Red Oak; and in Illinois they did not shrink from putting their principles into practice. This account is plausible, and as it is substantiated in certain parts by facts from the history of Brown County, Ohio, it may be considered probable in those parts that are and must remain without corroboration. Concerning his father Mr. Leeper writes: " John Leeper moved from Marshall County, Tennessee, to Bond County, Illinois, in 1816. Was a hater of slavery. . . . Remained in Bond County until 1823, then moved to Jacksonville, Morgan County, and in 1831 to Putnam County, and in 1833 to Bureau County, Illinois. . . . My father's house was always a hiding-place for the fugitive

---

[1] Letter from John F. Williams, Economy, Ind., March 21, 1893. When this letter was written, Mr. Williams was eighty-one years old. He was, he says, born in 1812. In 1820 he would have been eight years old. Children were sometimes sent to carry food to refugees in hiding, or to do other little services with which they could be safely trusted. Such experiences were apt to make deep impressions on their young memories.

from slavery."[1] On the basis of this testimony, and the probability in the case, we may believe that the underground movement in Illinois dates back, at least, to the time of the admission of Illinois into the Union, that is, to 1818. Soon after 1835, the movement seems to have become well established, and to have increased in importance with considerable rapidity till the War.

It is a fact worthy of note that the years that witnessed the beginnings in Ohio, Indiana, North Carolina and Illinois of this curious method of assailing the slave power, precede but slightly those that witnessed the formulation of three several bills in Congress designed to strengthen the first Fugitive Slave Law. The three measures were drafted during the interval from 1818 to 1822.

The abolitionist enterprises of the more western states, Iowa and Kansas, came too late to be in any way connected with the proposal of these bills. The settlement of these territories was, of course, considerably behind that of Ohio, Indiana and Illinois, but the nearness of the new regions to a slaveholding section insured the opportunity for Underground Railroad work as soon as settlement should begin. Professor L. F. Parker, of Tabor College, Iowa, has sketched briefly the successive steps in the opening of his state to occupancy. "The Black-Hawk Purchase opened the eastern edge of Iowa to the depth of 40 or 50 miles to the whites in 1833. The strip . . . west of that which included what is now Grinnell was not opened to white occupancy till 1843, and it was ten years later before the white residents in this county numbered 500. Grinnell was settled in 1854, when central and western Iowa was merely dotted by a few hamlets of white men, and seamed by winding paths along prairie ridges and through bridgeless streams."[2] One of the early settlers in southeastern Iowa was J. H. B. Armstrong, who had been familiar with the midnight appeals of escaping

---

[1] Letter from H. B. Leeper, Princeton, Ill., received Dec. 19, 1895. Mr. Leeper is seventy-five years of age. His letter shows a knowledge of the localities of which he writes, Bond County in southwestern Illinois, and Bureau and Putnam Counties in the central part of the state.

[2] Letter from Professor L. F. Parker, Grinnell, Iowa, Aug. 30, 1894.

slaves in Fayette County, Ohio. Mr. Armstrong removed to the West in 1839, and settled in Lee County, Iowa. His proximity to the northeastern boundary of Missouri seems to have involved him in Underground Railroad work from the start, on the route running to Salem and Denmark. When in 1852 Mr. Armstrong moved to Appanoose County, and located within four miles of the Missouri line, among a number of abolitionists, he found himself even more concerned with secret projects to help slaves to Canada. The lines of travel of fugitive slaves that extended east throughout the entire length of Iowa were more or less associated with Kansas men and Kansas movements, and their development is, therefore, to be assigned to the time of the outbreak of the struggle over Kansas (1854). Residents of Tabor in southwestern Iowa, and of Grinnell in central Iowa, agree in designating 1854 as the year in which their Underground Railroad labors began. The Rev. John Todd, one of the founders of the college colony of Tabor, is authority for the statement that the first fugitives arrived in the summer of 1854.[1] Professor Parker states that Grinnell was a stopping-place for the hunted slave from the time of its founding in 1854.

We may summarize our findings in regard to the expansion of the Underground Railroad, then, by saying that it had grown into a wide-spread "institution" before the year 1840, and in several states it had existed in previous decades. This statement coincides with the findings of Dr. Samuel G. Howe in Canada, while on a tour of investigation in 1863. He reports that the arrivals of runaway slaves in the provinces, at first rare, increased early in the century; that some of the fugitives, rejoicing in the personal freedom they had gained and banishing all fear of the perils they must endure, went stealthily back to their former homes and brought away their wives and children. The Underground Road was of great assistance to these and other escaping slaves, and "hundreds,"

[1] Letter from Professor James E. Todd, Vermillion, South Dakota, Nov. 6, 1894. Professor Todd is the son of the Rev. John Todd.
The *Tabor Beacon*, 1890, 1891, contains a series of reminiscences from the pen of the Rev. John Todd. The first of these recounts the first arrival of fugitives in July, 1854.

says Dr. Howe, "trod this path every year, but they did not attract much public attention."[1] It does not escape Dr. Howe's consideration, however, that the fugitive slaves in Canada were soon brought to public notice by the diplomatic negotiations between England and the United States during the years 1826–1828, the object being, as Mr. Clay, the Secretary of State, himself declared, "to provide for a growing evil." The evidence gathered from surviving abolitionists in the states adjacent to the lakes shows an increased activity of the Underground Road during the period 1830–1840. The reason for flight given by the slave was, in the great majority of cases, the same, namely, fear of being sold to the far South. It is certainly significant in this connection that the decade above mentioned witnessed the removal of the Indians from the Gulf states, and, in the words of another contemporary observer and reporter, "the consequent opening of new and vast cotton fields."[2] The swelling emphasis laid upon the value of their escaped slaves by the Southern representatives in Congress, and by the South generally, resounded with terrific force at length in the Fugitive Slave Law of 1850. That act did not, as it appears, check or diminish in any way the number of underground rescues. In spite of the exhibit on fugitive slaves made in the United States census report of 1860, which purports to show that the number of escapes was about a thousand a year, it is difficult to doubt the consensus of testimony of many underground agents, to the effect that the decade from 1850 to 1860 was the period of the Road's greatest activity in all sections of the North.[3]

It is not known when the name "Underground Railroad" came to be applied to these secret trails, nor where it was first applied to them. According to Mr. Smedley the designation came into use among slave-hunters in the neighborhood of Columbia soon after the Quakers in southeastern Penn-

[1] S. G. Howe, *The Refugees from Slavery in Canada West*, 1864, pages 11, 12.
[2] G. M. Weston, *Progress of Slavery in the United States*, Washington, D.C., 1858, p. 22.
[3] Some conclusions presented in the *American Historical Review*, April, 1896, pp. 460–462, are here repeated.

sylvania began their concerted action in harboring and forwarding fugitives. The pursuers seem to have had little difficulty in tracking slaves as far as Columbia, but beyond that point all trace of them was generally lost. All the various methods of detection customary in such cases were resorted to, but failed to bring the runaways to view. The mystery enshrouding these disappearances completely bewildered and baffled the slave-owners and their agents, who are said to have declared, "there must be an Underground Railroad somewhere."[1] As this work reached considerable development in the district indicated during the first decade of this century the account quoted is seen to contain an anachronism. Railroads were not known either in England or the United States until about 1830, so that the word "railroad" could scarcely have received its figurative application as early as Mr. Smedley implies.

The Hon. Rush R. Sloane, of Sandusky, Ohio, gives the following account of the naming of the Road: "In the year 1831, a fugitive named Tice Davids came over the line and lived just back of Sandusky. He had come direct from Ripley, Ohio, where he crossed the Ohio River. . . .

"When he was running away, his master, a Kentuckian, was in close pursuit and pressing him so hard that when the Ohio River was reached he had no alternative but to jump in and swim across. It took his master some time to secure a skiff, in which he and his aid followed the swimming fugitive, keeping him in sight until he had landed. Once on shore, however, the master could not find him. No one had seen him; and after a long . . . search the disappointed slave-master went into Ripley, and when inquired of as to what had become of his slave, said . . . he thought 'the nigger must have gone off on an underground road.' The story was repeated with a good deal of amusement, and this incident gave the name to the line. First the 'Underground Road,' afterwards 'Underground Railroad.'"[2] A colored man, the Rev. W. M. Mitchell, who was for several years a resident of

---

[1] R. C. Smedley, *Underground Railroad*, pp. 34, 35.
[2] The *Firelands Pioneer*, July, 1888, p. 35.

southern Ohio, and a friend of fugitives, gives what appears to be a version of Mr. Sloane's story.[1] These anecdotes are hardly more than traditions, affording a fair general explanation of the way in which the Underground Railroad got its name; but they cannot be trusted in the details of time, place and occasion. Whatever the manner and date of its suggestion, the designation was generally accepted as an apt title for a mysterious means of transporting fugitive slaves to Canada.

[1] The *Underground Railroad*, pp. 4, 5.

A CROSSING PLACE FOR FUGITIVE SLAVES ON THE OHIO RIVER, AT STEUBENVILLE, OHIO.

(From a recent photograph.)

HOUSE OF THE REV. JOHN RANKIN, RIPLEY, OHIO.

Situated on the top of a high hill, this initial station was readily found by runaways from the Kentucky shore opposite.

(From a recent photograph.)

CHAPTER III

THE METHODS OF THE UNDERGROUND RAILROAD

By the enactment of the first Fugitive Slave Law, February 12, 1793, the aiding of fugitive slaves became a penal offence. This measure laid a fine of five hundred dollars upon any one harboring escaped slaves, or preventing their arrest. The provisions of the law were of a character to stimulate resistance to its enforcement. The master or his agent was authorized to arrest the runaway, wherever found; to bring him before a judge of the circuit or the district court of the United States, or before a local magistrate where the capture was made; and to receive, on the display of satisfactory proof, a certificate operating as a full warrant for taking the prisoner back to the state from which he had fled. This summary method of disposing of cases involving the high question of human liberty was regarded by many persons as unjust; they freely denounced it, and, despite the penalty attached, many violated the law. Secrecy was the only safeguard of these persons, as it was of those they were attempting to succor; hence arose the numerous artifices employed.

The uniform success of the attempts to evade this first Fugitive Slave Law, and doubtless, also, the general indisposition of Northern people to take part in the return of refugees to their Southern owners, led, as early as in 1823, to negotiations between Kentucky and the three adjoining states across the Ohio. It is unnecessary to trace the history of these negotiations, or to point out the statutes in which the legislative results are recorded. It is notable that sixteen years elapsed before the legislature of Ohio passed a law to secure the recovery of slave property, and that the new enactment remained on the statute books only four years. The penalties imposed by this law for advising or for enticing a slave to leave his master, or for harboring a fugitive, were a fine, not to exceed five hundred dollars, and, at the discretion of the court, imprisonment not to exceed sixty days. In addition, the offender was to be liable in an action at the suit of the party injured.[1] It can scarcely be supposed that a state Fugitive Slave Law like this would otherwise affect persons that were already engaged in aiding runaways than to make them more certain than ever that their cause was just.

The loss of slave property sustained by Southern planters was not diminished, and the outcry of the South for a more rigorous national law on the subject was by no means hushed. In 1850 Congress met the case by substituting for the Fugitive Slave Act of 1793 the measure called the second Fugitive Slave Law. The penalties provided by this law were, of course, more severe than those of the act of 1793. Any person hindering the claimant from arresting the fugitive, or attempting the rescue or concealment of the fugitive, became "subject to a fine not exceeding one thousand dollars, or imprisonment not exceeding six months," and was liable for "civil damages to the party injured by such illegal conduct in the sum of one thousand dollars for each fugitive so lost." These provisions of the new law only added fresh fuel to the fire. The determination to prevent the recovery of escaped slaves by their owners spread rapidly among the inhabitants of the free states. Many of these persons, who had hitherto refrained from acting for or against the fugitive, were provoked into helping defeat the action of a law commanding them "to aid and assist in the prompt and efficient execution" of a measure that would have set them at the miserable business of slave-catching. Clay only expressed a wish instead of a fact, when he maintained in 1851 that the law was being executed in Indiana, Ohio and other states. Another Southern senator was much nearer the truth when he complained of the small number of recaptures under the recent act.

The risk of suffering severe penalties by violating the Fugitive Slave laws was less wearing, probably, on abolitionists than was the social disdain they brought upon themselves by acknowledging their principles. During a generation or more

[1] The date of the act is February 26, 1839.

they were in a minority in many communities, and were forced to submit to the taunts and insults of persons that did not distinguish between abolition of slavery and fusion of the white and the black races. " Black abolitionist," " niggerite," " amalgamationist " and " nigger thief " were convenient epithets in the mouths of pro-slavery champions in many Northern neighborhoods. The statement was not uncommonly made about those suspected of harboring slaves, that they did so from motives of thrift and gain. It was said that some underground helpers made use of the labor of runaways, especially in harvest-time, as long as it suited their convenience, then on the pretext of danger hurried the negroes off without pay. Unreasoning malice alone could concoct so absurd an explanation of a philanthropy involving so much cost and risk.[1] Abolitionists were often made uncomfortable in their church relations by the uncomplimentary attentions they received, or by the discovery that they were regarded as unwelcome disturbers of the household of faith.[2] Even the Society of Friends is not above the charge of having lost sight, in some quarters, of the precepts of Anthony Benezet and John Woolman. Uxbridge monthly meeting is known to have disowned Abby Kelly because she gave anti-slavery lectures.[3] The church certificate given to Mrs. Elizabeth Buffum Chace when she transferred her membership from Swanzey monthly meeting to Providence (Rhode Island) monthly meeting was without the acknowledgment usually contained in such certificates that the bearer " was of orderly life and conversation."[4] A popular Hicksite minister of New York City, in commending the fugitive Thomas Hughes for consenting to return South with his master, said, " I had a thousand times rather be a slave, and spend my days with slaveholders, than to dwell in companionship with abolitionists."[5] In the Methodist Church

[1] See an article entitled "An Underground Railway," by Robert W. Carroll, of Cincinnati, O., in the *Cincinnati Times-Star*, Aug. 19, 1890; also Smedley, *Underground Railroad*, p. 182; and J. B. Robinson, *Pictures of Slavery and Anti-Slavery*, pp. 293, 294.
[2] *History of Henry County, Indiana*, p. 126 et seq.
[3] Elizabeth Buffum Chace, *Anti-Slavery Reminiscences*, p. 19.
[4] *Ibid.*, p. 18.
[5] Lydia Maria Child, *Life of Isaac T. Hopper*, pp. 388, 389.

there came to be such stress of feeling between the abolitionists and the other members, that in many places the former withdrew and organized little congregations apart, under the denominational name, Wesleyan Methodist. The truth is, the mass of the people of the free states were by no means abolitionists; they cherished an intense prejudice against the negro, and permitted it to extend to all anti-slavery advocates. They were willing to let slavery alone, and desired that others should let it alone. In the Western states the character of public sentiment is evidenced by the fact that generally the political party considered to be most favorable to slavery could command a majority, and "black laws" were framed at the behest of Southern politicians for the purpose of making residence in the Northern states a disagreeable thing for the negro.[1]

Abolitionists were frequently subjected to espionage; the arrival of a party of colored people at a house after daybreak would arouse suspicion and cause the place to be closely watched; a chance meeting with a neighbor in the highway would perhaps be the means by which some abolitionists' secrets would become known. In such cases it did not always follow that the discovery brought ruin upon the head of the offender, even when the discoverer was a person of pro-slavery views. Nevertheless, accidents of the kind described served to fasten the suspicions of a locality upon the offender. Gravner and Hannah Marsh, Quakers, living near Downington, in Chester County, Pennsylvania, became known to their pro-slavery neighbors as agents on the Underground Road. These neighbors were not disposed to inform against them, although one woman, intent on finding out how many slaves they aided in a year, with much watching counted sixty.[2] The Rev. John Cross, a Presbyterian minister living in Elba Township, Knox County, Illinois, about the year 1840, had neighbors that insisted on his answering to the law for the help he gave to some fugitives. Mr. Cross made no secret of his principles and accordingly became game for his enemies. One of these was Jacob Kightlinger, who observed a wagon-load of

[1] See President Fairchild's pamphlet, *The Underground Railroad.*
[2] Smedley, *Underground Railroad*, p. 139.

ABOLITIONISTS UNDER SURVEILLANCE 51

negroes being taken in the direction of Mr. Cross's house. Investigation by Mr. Kightlinger and several of his friends proved their suspicions to be true, and by their action Mr. Cross was indicted for harboring fugitive slaves.[1]

Parties in pursuit of fugitives were compelled to make careful and often long-continued search to find traces of their wayfaring chattels. During such missions they were, of course, inquisitive and vigilant, and when circumstances seemed to warrant it, they set men to watch the premises of the persons most suspicioned, and to report any mysterious actions occurring within the district patrolled. The houses of many noted abolitionists along the Ohio River were frequently under the surveillance of slave-hunters. It was not a rare thing that towns and villages in regions adjacent to the Southern states were terrorized by crowds of roughs eager to find the hiding-places of slaves, recently missed by masters bent on their recovery. The following extracts from a letter written by Mr. William Steel to Mr. David Putnam, Jr., of Point Harmar, Ohio, will show the methods practised by slave-hunters when in eager pursuit of fugitives: —

WOODSFIELD, MONROE CO., O.
Sept. 5, 1843.

MR. DAVID PUTNAM, JR.:

Dear Sir,— I received yours of the 26th ult. and was very glad to hear from it that Stephen Quixot had such good luck in getting his family from Virginia, but we began to be very uneasy about them as we did not hear from them again until last Saturday, . . . we then heard they were on the route leading through Summerfield, but that the route from there to Somerton was so closely watched both day and night for some time past on account of the human cattle that have lately escaped from Virginia, that they could not proceed farther on that route. So we made an arrangement with the Summerfield friends to meet them on Sunday evening about ten miles west of this and bring them on to this route . . . the abolitionists of the west part of this county have had very difficult work in getting them all off without being caught, as the whole of that part of the country has been filled with Southern blood hounds upon their track, and some of the aboli-

---

[1] *History of Knox County, Ill.*, pp. 213, 214. Mr. Kightlinger's account of this affair is published under his own name.

tionists' houses have been watched day and night for several days in succession. This evening a company of eight Virginia hounds passed through this place north on the hunt of some of their two-legged chattels. . . . Since writing the above I have understood that something near twenty Virginians including the eight above mentioned have just passed through town on their way to the Somerton neighborhood, but I do not think they will get much information about their lost chattels there. . . .

Yours for the Slave,
WILLIAM STEEL.[1]

A case that well illustrates the method of search employed by pursuing parties is that of the escape of the Nuckolls slaves through Iowa, the incidents of which are still vivid in the memories of some that witnessed them. Mr. Nuckolls, of Nebraska City, Nebraska, lost two slave-girls in December, 1858. He instituted search for them in Tabor, an abolitionist centre, and did not neglect to guard the crossings of two streams in the vicinity, Silver Creek and the Nishnabotna River. As the slaves had been promptly despatched to Chicago, this search availed him nothing. A second and more thorough hunt was decided on, and the aid of a score or more fellows was secured. These men made entrance into houses by force and violence, when bravado failed to gain them admission.[2] At one house where the remonstrance against intrusion was unusually strong the person remonstrating was struck over the head and injured for life. The outcome of the whole affair was that Mr. Nuckolls had some ten thousand dollars to pay in damages and costs, and, after all, failed to recover his slaves.[3]

Many were the inducements to practise espionage on abolitionists. Large sums were offered for the capture of fugitives, and rewards were offered also for the arrest and delivery

[1] The original letter is in the possession of the author of this book.
[2] The *Tabor Beacon*, 1890, 1891, Chapter XXI of a series of articles by the Rev. John Todd, on "The Early Settlement and Growth of Western Iowa." Mr. Todd was one of the early settlers of western Iowa. The letters were received from his son, Professor James E. Todd, of the University of South Dakota, Vermillion, S. Dak.
[3] Letter of Mr. Sturgis Williams, Percival, Ia., 1894. Mr. Williams was also one of the pioneers of western Iowa.

south of Mason and Dixon's line of certain abolitionists, who were well-enough known to have the hatred of many Southerners. "At an anti-slavery meeting of the citizens of Sardinia and vicinity, held on November 21, 1838, a committee of respectable citizens presented a report, accompanied with affidavits in support of its declarations, stating that for more than a year past there had been an unusual degree of hatred manifested by the slave-hunters and slaveholders towards the abolitionists of Brown County, and that rewards varying from $500 to $2,500 had been repeatedly offered by different persons for the abduction or assassination of the Rev. John B. Mahan; and rewards had also been offered for Amos Pettijohn, William A. Frazier and Dr. Isaac M. Beck, of Sardinia, the Rev. John Rankin and Dr. Alexander Campbell, of Ripley, William McCoy, of Russellville, and citizens of Adams County."[1] A resolution was offered in the Maryland Legislature, in January, 1860, proposing a reward for the arrest of Thomas Garrett, of Wilmington, for "stealing" slaves.[2] It is perhaps an evidence of the extraordinary caution and shrewdness employed by managers of the Road generally that so many of them escaped without suffering the penalties of the law or the inflictions of private vengeance.

Slave-owners occasionally tried to find out the secrets of an underground station or of a route by visiting various localities in disguise. A Kentucky slaveholder clad in the Friends' peculiar garb went to the house of John Charles, a Quaker of Richmond, Indiana, and meeting a son of Mr. Charles, accosted him with the words, "Well, sir, my little mannie, hasn't thee father gone to Canada with some niggers?" Young Charles quickly perceived the disguise, and pointing his finger at the man declared him to be a "wolf in sheep's clothing."[3] About the year 1840 there came into Cass County, Indiana, a man from Kentucky by the name of Carpenter, who professed to be an anti-slavery lecturer and an agent for

[1] *History of Brown County, Ohio*, p. 314.
[2] *The New Reign of Terror in the Slaveholding States*, for 1859-1860 (*Anti-Slavery Tracts*, No. 4, New Series), pp. 49, 50.
[3] Letter of Mrs. Mary C. Thorne, Selma, Clark Co., O., March 3, 1892. John Charles was an uncle of Mrs. Thorne.

certain anti-slavery papers. He visited the abolitionists and seemed zealous in the cause. In this way he learned the whereabouts of seven fugitives that had arrived in the neighborhood from Kentucky a few weeks before. He sent word to their masters, and in due time they were all seized, but had not been taken far before the neighborhood was aroused, masters and victims were overtaken and carried to the county-seat, a trial was procured, and the slaves were again set free.

Thus the penalties of the law, the contempt of neighbors, and the espionage of persons interested in returning fugitives to bondage made secrecy necessary in the service of the Underground Railroad.

Night was the only time, of course, in which the fugitive and his helpers could feel themselves even partially secure. Probably most slaves that started for Canada had learned to know the north star, and to many of these superstitious persons its light seemed the enduring witness of the divine interest in their deliverance. When clouds obscured the stars they had recourse, perhaps, to such bits of homely knowledge as, that in forests the trunks of trees are commonly moss-grown on their north sides. In Kentucky and western Virginia many fugitives were guided to free soil by the tributaries of the Ohio; while in central and eastern Virginia the ranges of the Appalachian chain marked the direction to be taken. After reaching the initial station of some line of Underground Road the fugitive found himself provided with such accommodations for rest and refreshment as circumstances would allow; and after an interval of a day or more he was conveyed, usually in the night, to the house of the next friend. Sometimes, however, when a guide was thought to be unnecessary the fugitive was sent on foot to the next station, full and minute instructions for finding it having been given him. The faltering step, and the light, uncertain rapping of the fugitive at the door, was quickly recognized by the family within, and the stranger was admitted with a welcome at once sincere and subdued. There was a suppressed stir in the house while the fire was building and food preparing; and after the hunger and chill of the wayfarer had been dispelled, he was provided with a bed in some out-of-the-way part of the house, or under the hay in the barn loft, according to the degree of danger. Often a household was awakened to find a company of five or more negroes at the door. The arrival of such a company was sometimes announced beforehand by special messenger.

That the amount of time taken from the hours of sleep by underground service was no small item may be seen from the following record covering the last half of August, 1843. The record or memorandum is that of Mr. David Putnam, Jr., of Point Harmar, Ohio, and is given with all the abbreviations:

Aug.		13/43	Sunday Morn.	2 o'clock	arrived
			Sunday Eve.	8½ "	departed for B.
		16	Wednesday Morn.	2 "	arrived
		20	Sunday eve.	10 "	departed for N.
Wife & children		21	Monday morn.	2 "	arrived from B.
			" eve.	10 "	left for Mr. H.
		22	Tuesday "	11 "	left for W.
A. L. & S. J.		28	Monday morn.	1 "	arrived left 2 o'clock.[1]

This is plainly a schedule of arriving and departing "trains" on the Underground Road. It is noticeable that the schedule contains no description, numerical or otherwise, of the parties coming and going; nor does it indicate, except by initial, to what places or persons the parties were despatched; further, it does not indicate whether Mr. Putnam accompanied them or not. It does, however, give us a clue to the amount of night service that was done at a station of average activity on the Ohio River as early as the year 1843. The demands upon operators increased, we know, from this time on till 1860. The memorandum also shows the variation in the length of time during which different companies of fugitives were detained at a station; thus, the first fugitive, or company of fugitives, as the case may have been, departed on the evening of the day of arrival; the second party was kept in concealment from Wednesday morning until the Sunday night next following before it was sent on its way; the third

---

[1] The original memorandum is written in pencil on a letter received by Mr. Putnam from Mr. John Stone, of Belpre, O., in Aug., 1843. The contents of this letter, or message, is given on page 57. The original is in possession of the author.

party seems to have been divided, one section being forwarded the night of the day of arrival, the other the next night following; in the case of the last company there seems to have existed some especial reason for haste, and we find it hurried away at two o'clock in the morning, after only an hour's intermission for rest and refreshment. The memorandum of night service at the Putnam station may be regarded as fairly representative of the night service at many other posts or stations throughout Ohio and the adjoining states.

Much of the communication relating to fugitive slaves was had in guarded language. Special signals, whispered conversations, passwords, messages couched in figurative phrases, were the common modes of conveying information about underground passengers, or about parties in pursuit of fugitives. These modes of communication constituted what abolitionists knew as the "grape-vine telegraph."[1] The signals employed were of various kinds, and were local in usage. Fugitives crossing the Ohio River in the vicinity of Parkersburg, in western Virginia, were sometimes announced at stations near the river by their guides by a shrill tremolo-call like that of the owl. Colonel John Stone and Mr. David Putnam, Jr., of Marietta, Ohio, made frequent use of this signal.[2] Different neighborhoods had their peculiar combinations of knocks or raps to be made upon the door or window of a station when fugitives were awaiting admission. In Harrison County, Ohio, around Cadiz, one of the recognized signals was three distinct but subdued knocks. To the in-

[1] The *Firelands Pioneer*, July, 1888, p. 20; also letter of S. J. Wright, Rushville, O., Aug. 29, 1894, and letter of Ira Thomas, Springboro, O., Oct. 29, 1895.

[2] This owl signal was mentioned in conversation with several residents of Marietta. Miss Martha Putnam says she has heard her father make the "hoot-owl" call hundreds of times. General R. R. Dawes designates this call the "river signal." "When I was a boy of eight," he says, "I was visiting my grandfather, Judge Ephraim Cutler. The place was called Constitution. Somehow, in the night I was wakened up, and a wagon came down over the hill to the river. Then a call was given, a hoot-owl call, and this was answered by a similar one from the other side; then a boat went out and brought over the crowd. My mother got out of bed and knelt down and prayed for them, and had me kneel with her." Conversation with General Dawes, Marietta, O., Aug. 21, 1892.

quiry, "Who's there?" the reply was, "A friend with friends."[1] Passwords were used on some sections of the Road. The agents at York in southeastern Pennsylvania made use of them, and William Yokum, a constable of the town, who was kindly disposed towards runaways, was able to be most helpful in times of emergency by his knowledge of the watchwords, one of which was "William Penn."[2] Messages couched in figurative language were often sent. The following note, written by Mr. John Stone, of Belpre, Ohio, in August, 1843, is a good example: —

BELPRE Friday Morning

DAVID PUTNAM

Business is aranged for Saturday night be on the lookout and if practicable let a cariage come & meet the carawan
J S[3]

Mr. I. Newton Peirce forwarded a number of fugitives from Alliance, Ohio, to Cleveland, over the Cleveland and Western Railroad. He sent with each company a note to a Cleveland merchant, Mr. Joseph Garretson, saying: "Please forward immediately the U. G. baggage this day sent to you. Yours truly, I. N. P."[4] Mr.

[1] Letter of the Rev. J. B. Lee, Franklinville, N.Y., Oct. 21, 1895.
[2] Smedley, *Underground Railroad*, p. 46.
[3] See the facsimile.
[4] Letter of I. Newton Peirce, Folcroft, Sharon Hill P.O., Delaware Co., Pa., Feb. 1, 1893.

G. W. Weston, of Low Moor, Iowa, was the author of similar communications addressed to a friend, Mr. C. B. Campbell, of Clinton.

Low Moor, May 6, 1859.

Mr. C. B. C.,

Dear Sir: — By to-morrow evening's mail, you will receive two volumes of the "Irrepressible Conflict" bound in black. After perusal, please forward, and oblige,

Yours truly,

G. W. W.[1]

The Hon. Thomas Mitchell, founder of Mitchellville, near Des Moines, Iowa, forwarded fugitives to Mr. J. B. Grinnell, after whom the town of Grinnell was named. The latter gives the following note as a sample of the messages that passed between them: —

Dear Grinnell: — Uncle Tom says if the roads are not too bad you can look for those fleeces of wool by to-morrow. Send them on to test the market and price, no back charges.

Yours,

Hub.[2]

There were many persons engaged in underground work that did not always take the precaution to veil their communications. Judge Thomas Lee, of the Western Reserve, was one of this class, as the following letter to Mr. Putnam, of Point Harmar, will show: —

Cadiz, Ohio, March 17th, 1847.

Mr. David Putnam,

Dear Sir: — I understand you are a friend to the poor and are willing to obey the heavenly mandate, "Hide the outcasts, betray not him that wandereth." Believing this, and at the request of Stephen Fairfax (who has been permitted in divine providence to enjoy for a few days the kind of liberty which Ohio gives to the man of colour), I would be glad if you could find out and let me know by letter what are the prospects if any

---

[1] *History of Clinton County, Iowa*, article on the "Underground Railroad," pp. 413–416.
[2] J. B. Grinnell, *Men and Events of Forty Years*, p. 217.

and the probable time when, the balance of the family will make the same effort to obtain their inalienable right to life, liberty, and the pursuit of happiness. Their friends who have gone north are very anxious to have them follow, as they think it much better to work for eight or ten dollars per month than to work for nothing.

Yours in behalf of the millions of poor, opprest and downtrodden in our land.

THOMAS LEE.

In the conveyance of fugitives from station to station there existed all the variety of method one would expect to find. In the early days of the Underground Road the fugitives were generally men. It was scarcely thought necessary to send a guide with them unless some special reason for so doing existed. They were, therefore, commonly given such directions as they needed and left to their own devices. As the number of refugees increased, and women and children were more frequently seen upon the Road, and pursuit was more common, the practice of transporting fugitives on horseback, or by vehicle, was introduced. The steam railroad was a new means furnished to abolitionists by the progress of the times, and used by them with greater or less frequency as circumstances required, and when the safety of passengers would not be sacrificed.

When fugitive travellers afoot or on horseback found themselves pursued, safety lay in flight, unless indeed the company was large enough, courageous enough, and sufficiently well armed to give battle. The safety of fugitives while travelling by conveyance lay mainly in their concealment, and many were the stratagems employed. Characteristic of the service of the Underground Railroad were the covered wagons, closed carriages and deep-bedded farm-wagons that hid the passengers. There are those living who remember special day-coaches of more peculiar construction. Abram Allen, a Quaker of Oakland, Clinton County, Ohio, had a large three-seated wagon, made for the purpose of carrying fugitives. He called it the Liberator. It was curtained all around, would hold eight or ten persons, and had a mechanism with a bell, invented by Mr. Allen, to record the number of miles travelled.[1] A citizen of Troy, Ohio, a bookbinder by trade, had a large wagon, built about with drawers in such a way as to leave a large hiding-place in the centre of the wagon-bed. As the bookbinder drove through the country he found opportunity to help many a fugitive on his way to Canada.[2] Horace Holt, of Rutland, Meigs County, Ohio, sold reeds to his neighbors in southern Ohio. He had a box-bed wagon with a lid that fastened with a padlock. In this he hauled his supply of reeds; it was well understood by a few that he also hauled fugitive slaves.[3] Joseph Sider, of southern Indiana, found his pedler wagon well adapted to the transportation of slaves from Kentucky plantations.[4] William Still gives instances of negroes being placed in boxes, and shipped as freight by boat, and also by rail, to friends in the North. William Box Peel Jones was boxed in Baltimore and sent to Philadelphia by way of the Ericsson line of steamers, being seventeen hours on the way.[5] Henry Box Brown had the same thrilling and perilous experience. His trip consumed twenty-four hours, during which time he was in the care of the Adams Express Company in transit from Richmond, Virginia, to Philadelphia.[6]

Abolitionists that drove wagons or carriages containing refugees, "conductors" as they came to be called in the terminology of the Railroad service, generally took the precaution to have ostensible reasons for their journeys. They sought to divest their excursions of the air of mystery by seeming to be about legitimate business. Hannah Marsh, of Chester County, Pennsylvania, was in the habit of taking

[1] Judge R. B. Harlan and others, *History of Clinton County, Ohio*, pp. 380-383; letter of Seth Linton, Oakland, Clinton County, O., Sept. 4, 1892; Smedley, *Underground Railroad*, p. 187.

[2] The *Miami Union*, April 10, 1895, article entitled "A Reminiscence of Slave Times."

[3] Letter of Mrs. C. Grant, Pomeroy, Meigs Co., O.

[4] The *Republican Leader*, March 16, 1894, article, "Reminiscence of the Underground Railroad," by E. H. Trueblood.

[5] See *Underground Railroad Records*, pp. 46, 47.

[6] *Ibid.*, pp. 81-84; see also *Narrative of Henry Box Brown, who escaped from slavery enclosed in a box 3 feet long and 2 wide, written from a statement of facts made by himself,* 1849, by Charles Stearns.

garden produce to the Philadelphia markets to sell; when, therefore, she sometimes used her covered market-wagon, even in daytime, to convey fugitives, she attracted no attention, and made her trips without molestation.[1] Calvin Fairbank abducted the Stanton family, father, mother and six children, from the neighborhood of Covington, Kentucky, by packing them in a load of straw.[2] James W. Torrence, of Northwood, Ohio, together with some of his neighbors exported grain, and sometimes feathers, to Sandusky. These products were generally shipped when there were fugitives to go with the load. As the distance to Sandusky was a hundred and twenty miles, refugees who happened to profit by this arrangement were saved much time and no small amount of risk in getting to their destination.[3] Mr. William I. Bowditch, of Boston, used a two-horse carryall on one occasion to take a single fugitive to Concord.[4] Mr. John Weldon and other abolitionists, of Dwight, Illinois, took negroes to Chicago concealed in wagons loaded with sacks of bran.[5] Levi Coffin, of Cincinnati, Ohio, frequently received large companies for which safe transportation had to be supplied. On one occasion a party of twenty-eight negroes arrived, towards daylight, in the suburbs of Cincinnati, from Boone County, Kentucky, and it was necessary to send them on at once. Accordingly at Friend Coffin's suggestion a number of carriages were procured, formed into a long funeral-like procession and started solemnly on the road to Cumminsville.[6] An almost endless array of incidents similar to these can be given, but enough have been recited to illustrate the caution that prevailed in the transportation of fugitive slaves toward Canada.

The routes were very far from being straight. They are perhaps best described by the word zigzag. The exigencies

[1] Smedley, *Underground Railroad*, pp. 138, 139.
[2] *The Rev. Calvin Fairbank During Slavery Times*, pp. 24, 25; see also the *Chicago Tribune*, Jan. 29, 1893, p. 33.
[3] Conversation with James W. Torrence, Northwood, Logan Co., O., Sept. 22, 1894.
[4] Letter of William I. Bowditch, Boston, Mass., April 5, 1893.
[5] Letter of John Weldon, Dwight, Ill., Nov. 7, 1895.
[6] *History of Darke County, Ohio*, p. 332 et seq.

that determined in what direction an escaping slave should go during any particular part of his journey were, in the nature of the case, always local. The ultimate goal was Canada, but a safe passage was of greater importance than a quick one. When speed would contribute safety the guide would make a long trip with his charge, or perhaps resort to the steam railroad; but under ordinary circumstances, in those regions where the Underground Railroad was most patronized, a guide had almost always a choice between two or more routes; he could, as seemed best at the time, take the right-hand road to one station, or the left-hand road to another. In truth, the underground paths in these regions formed a great and intricate network, and it was in no small measure because the lines forming the meshes of this great system converged and branched again at so many stations that it was almost an impossibility for slave-hunters to trace their negroes through even a single county without finding themselves on the wrong trail. It was a common stratagem in times of special emergency to switch off travellers from one course to another, or to take them back on their track and then, after a few days of waiting, send them forward again. It is, then, proper to say that zigzag was one of the regular devices to blind and throw off pursuit. It served moreover to avoid unfriendly localities. It seems probable that the circuitous land route from Toledo to Detroit was an expedient of this sort, for slave-owners and their agents were often known to be on the lookout along the direct thoroughfare between the places named. The two routes between Millersburgh and Lodi in northern Ohio are explained by the statement that the most direct route, the western one, fell under suspicion for a while, and in the meantime a more circuitous path was followed through Holmesville and Seville.[1]

During the long process by which the slave with the help of friends was being transmuted into the freeman he spent much of his time in concealment. His progress was made in the night-time. When a station was reached he was provided

[1] Letter of Thomas L. Smith, Fredericksburg, Wayne Co., O., Oct. 6, 1894.

with a hiding-place, and he scarcely left it until his host decided it would be safe for him to continue his journey. The hiding-places the fugitive entered first and last were as dissimilar as can well be imagined. Slaves that crossed the Ohio River at Ripley, and fell into the hands of the Rev. John Rankin, were often concealed in his barn, which is said to have been provided with a secret cellar for use by the slaves when pursuers approached. The barn of Deacon Jirch Platt at Mendon, Illinois, was a haven into which many slaves from Missouri were piloted by way of Quincy. A hazel thicket in Mr. Platt's pasture-lot was sometimes resorted to,[1] as was one of his hayricks that was hollow and had a blind entrance.[2] Joshua R. Giddings, the sturdy antislavery Congressman from the Western Reserve, had an out-of-the-way bedroom in one wing of his house at Jefferson, Ohio, that was kept in readiness for fugitive slaves.[3] The attic over the *Liberator* office in Boston is said to have been a rendezvous for such persons.[4] A station-keeper at Plainfield, Illinois, had a woodpile with a room in the centre for a hiding-place.[5] The Rev. J. Porter, pastor of a Congregational church at Green Bay, Wisconsin, was asked to furnish a place of hiding for a family of fugitives, and at his wife's suggestion he put them in the belfry of his church, where they remained three days before a vessel came by which they could be safely transported to Canada.[6] Mr. James M. Westwater and other citizens of Columbus, Ohio, fitted up an old smoke-house standing on Chestnut Street near Fourth Street as a station of the Underground Railroad.[7] A fugitive reaching Canton, Washington County, Indiana, was secreted for a while in a low place in a thick, dark

---

[1] Letter of J. E. Platt, Guthrie, Ok., March 28, 1896. Mr. Platt is a son of Deacon Jirch Platt.
[2] Letter of William H. Collins, Quincy, Ill., Jan. 13, 1896.
[3] Conversation with J. Addison Giddings, Jefferson, O.
[4] Letter of Lewis Ford, Boston, Mass. See also *Reminiscences of Fugitive Slave Law Days in Boston*, by Austin Bearse, 1880, p. 12.
[5] Letter of John Weldon, Dwight, Ill., Jan. 10, 1896.
[6] Letter of the Rev. J. E. Roy, Chicago, Ill., April 9, 1896.
[7] W. G. Deshler and others, *Memorial on the Death of James M. Westwater*, pp. 14, 15.

woods; and afterwards in a rail pen covered with straw.[1] Eli F. Brown, of Amesville, Athens County, Ohio, writes: "I built an addition to my house in which I had a room with its partition in pannels. One pannel could be raised about a half inch and then slid back, so as to permit a man to enter the room. When the pannel was in place it appeared like its fellows. . . . In the abutment of Zanesville bridge on the Putnam side there was a place of concealment prepared."[2] "Conductors" Levi Coffin, Edward Harwood, and W. H. Brisbane, of Cincinnati, Ohio, had a number of hiding-places for slaves. "One was in the dark cellar of Coffin's store; another was at Mr. Coffin's out-of-the-way residence between Avondale and Walnut Hills; another was a dark sub-cellar under the rear part of Dr. Bailey's residence, corner of Sixth and College Streets."[3] The gallery of the old First Church at Galesburg, Illinois, was utilized as a place of concealment for refugees by certain members of that church.[4] Gabe N. Johnson, a colored man of Ironton, on the Ohio River, sometimes hid fugitives in a coal-bank back of his house.[5] This list of illustrations could be almost indefinitely continued. A sufficient number has been given to show the ingenuity necessarily used to secure safety.

In the transit from station to station some simple disguise was often assumed. Thomas Garrett, a Quaker of Wilmington, Delaware, kept a quantity of garden tools on hand for this purpose. He sometimes gave a man a scythe, rake, or some other implement to carry through town. Having reached a certain bridge on the way to the next station, the pretending laborer concealed his tool under it, as he had been directed, and journeyed on. Later the tool was taken back to Mr. Garrett's to be used for a similar purpose.[6] Valentine Nicholson, a station-keeper at Harveysburg, Warren County,

---

[1] Letter of E. H. Trueblood, Hitchcock, Ind.
[2] Letter of E. F. Brown, Amesville, O.
[3] *Cincinnati Commercial Gazette*, Feb. 11, 1894, article by W. Eldebe.
[4] Letter of Professor George Churchill, Galesburg, Jan. 29, 1896.
[5] Conversation with Gabe N. Johnson, Ironton, O., Sept. 30, 1894.
[6] Smedley, *Underground Railroad*, p. 242.

BARN OF SEYMOUR FINNEY, ESQ., DETROIT, MICHIGAN.
A shelter for fugitives in Detroit, formerly standing where the Chamber of Commerce Building now stands.

THE OLD FIRST CHURCH, GALESBURG, ILLINOIS.
Fugitive slaves were sometimes concealed in the gallery of this church.
(From a recent photograph.)

Ohio, concealed the identity of a fugitive, a mulatto, who was known to be pursued, by blacking his face and hands with burnt cork.[1] Slight disguises like these were probably not used as often as more elaborate ones. The Rev. Calvin Fairbank, and John Fairfield, the Virginian, who abducted many slaves from the South, resorted frequently to this means of securing the safety of their followers. Mr. Fairbank tells us that he piloted slave-girls attired in the finery of ladies, men and boys tricked out as gentlemen and the servants of gentlemen; and that sometimes he found it necessary to require his followers to don the garments of the opposite sex.[2] In May, 1843, Mr. Fairbank went to Arkansas for the purpose of rescuing William Minnis from bondage. He found that the slave was a young man of light complexion and prepossessing appearance, and that he closely resembled a gentleman living in the vicinity of Little Rock. Minnis was, therefore, fitted out with the necessary wig, beard and moustache, and clothes like those of his model; he was quickly drilled in the deportment of his assumed rank; and, as the test proved, he sustained himself well in his part. On boarding the boat that was to carry him to freedom he discovered his owner, Mr. Brennan, but so effectual was the slave's make-up that the master failed to penetrate the disguise.[3]

A similar story is told by Mr. Sidney Speed, of Crawfordsville, Indiana, when recalling the work of his father, John Speed, and that of Fisher Doherty. "In 1858 or 1859, a mulatto girl about eighteen or twenty years old, very good-looking and with some education, . . . reached our home. The nigger-catchers became so watchful that she could not be moved for several days. In fact, some of them were nearly always at the house either on some pretended business or making social visits. I do not think that the house was searched, or they would surely have found her, as during all this time she remained in the garret over the old log kitchen, where the fugitives were usually kept when there

---

[1] Letter of Valentine Nicholson, Indianapolis, Ind., Sept. 10, 1892.
[2] *The Rev. Calvin Fairbank During Slavery Times*, p. 10.
[3] *Ibid.*, p. 34 *et seq.*

was danger. Her owner, a man from New Orleans, had just bought her in Louisville, and he had traced her surely to this place; she had not struck the Underground before, but had made her way alone this far, and as they got no trace of her beyond here they returned and doubled the watches on Doherty and my father. But at length a day came, or a night rather, when she was led safely out through the gardens to the house of a colored man named Patterson. There she was rigged out in as fine a costume of silk and ribbons as it was possible to procure at that time, and was furnished with a white baby borrowed for the occasion, and accompanied by one of the Patterson girls as servant and nurse." Thus disguised, the lady boarded the train at the station. But what must have been her feelings to find her master already in the same car; he was setting out to watch for her at the end of the line. She kept her courage, and when they reached Detroit she went aboard the ferry-boat for Canada; her pretended nurse returned to shore with the borrowed baby; and as the gang-plank was being raised, the young slave-woman on the boat removed her veil that she might bid her owner good-by. The master's display of anger as he gazed at the departing boat was as real as the situation was gratifying to his former slave and amusing to the bystanders.[1]

John Fairfield, the Virginian, depended largely on disguises in several of his abducting exploits. At one time he was asked by a number of Canadian refugees to help some of their relatives to the North, and when he found that many of them had very light complexions, he decided to send them to Canada disguised as white persons. Having secured for them the requisite wigs and powder, he was gratified with the transformation in appearance they were able to effect. He therefore secured tickets for his party, and placed them aboard a night train for Harrisburg, where they were met by a person who accompanied them to Cleveland and saw them take boat for Detroit. Later Fairfield succeeded in aiding other companies of slaves to escape from Washington and

[1] Letter from Mr. Sidney Speed, Crawfordsville, Ind., March 6, 1896.

Harper's Ferry by resorting to similar means.[1] Among the Quakers the woman's costume was a favorite disguise for fugitives. No one attired in it was likely to be in the least degree suspicioned of being anything else than what the garb proclaimed. The veiled bonnet also was peculiarly adapted to conceal the features of the person disguised.[2] One incident will suffice to show the utility of the Quaker costume. One evening Joseph G. Walker, a Quaker of Wilmington, Delaware, was appealed to by a slave-woman, who was closely pursued. She was permitted to enter Mr. Walker's house, and a few minutes later, in the gown and bonnet of Mrs. Walker, she passed out of the front door leaning upon the arm of the shrewd Quaker.[3]

It is quite apparent that the Underground Railroad was not a formal organization with officers of different ranks, a regular membership, and a treasury from which to meet expenses. A terminology, it is true, sprang up in connection with the work of the Road, and one hears of station-keepers, agents, conductors, and even presidents of the Underground Railroad; but these titles were figurative terms, borrowed with other expressions from the convenient vocabulary of steam railways; and while they were useful among abolitionists to save circumlocution, they commended themselves to the friends of the slave by helping to mystify the minds of the public. The need of organization was not felt except in a few localities. It was only in towns and cities that the distinctions of "managers," "contributing members," and "agents" began to develop in any significant way, and even in the case of these places the distinctions must not be pushed far, for they indicate merely that certain men by their sagacious activity came to be called "managers," while others less bold, the contributing members, were willing to give money towards defraying the expenses of some trusty person, the agent, who would run the risk of piloting fugitives.

The first reference to an organization devoted to the busi-

---

[1] *Reminiscences of Levi Coffin*, pp. 439-442.
[2] M. G. McDougall, *Fugitive Slaves*, p. 61.
[3] Smedley, *Underground Railroad*, p. 244.

ness of aiding fugitive slaves occurs in a letter of George Washington, bearing date May 12, 1786. Washington speaks of a "society of Quakers in the city [Philadelphia], formed for such purposes. . . ."[1] We have no means of knowing how this body conducted its work, nor how long it continued to exist. It is sometimes stated that the formal organization of the Underground Road took place in 1838, but this is not an accurate statement. An organized society of the Underground Railroad was formed in Philadelphia about the year 1838. Mr. Robert Purvis, who was the president, has called this body the first of its kind, but this may be doubted in view of the quotation from Washington's letter above cited. The character of the organization appears from the following account of its methods given by Mr. Purvis:[2] "The funds for carrying on this enterprise were raised from our anti-slavery friends, *as the cases came up*,[3] and their needs demanded it; for many of the fugitives required no other help than advice and direction how to proceed. To the late Daniel Neall, the society was greatly indebted for his generous gifts, as well as for his encouraging words and fearless independence. . . . The most efficient helpers or agents we had, were two market-women, who lived in Baltimore. . . .

"Another most effective worker was a son of a slaveholder, who lived at Newberne, S.C. Through his agency, the slaves were forwarded by placing them on vessels. . . . Having the address of the active members of the committee, they were enabled to find us, when not accompanied by our agents. . . . The fugitives were distributed among the members of the society, but most of them were received at my house in Philadelphia, where . . . I caused a place to be constructed underneath a room, which could only be entered by a trap-door in the floor. . . ."

This account shows clearly that the organization of 1838 was limited; and while it was officered with a president, sec-

---

[1] Spark's *Washington*, IX, 158, quoted in *Quakers of Pennsylvania*, by Dr. A. C. Applegarth, *Johns Hopkins Studies*, X, 463.

[2] The letter from which this quotation is made will be found in *Underground Railroad*, by R. C. Smedley, pp. 355, 356.

[3] The italics are my own.

retary and committee, and had helpers at a distance called agents, it can scarcely be said that the plan of action of the society was different in essential points from that which developed without the formality of election of officers in many underground centres throughout the Northern states. Levi Coffin, by his devotion to the cause of the fugitive from boyhood to old age, gained the title of President of the Underground Railroad,[1] but he was not at the head of a formal organization. In northeastern Illinois, Peter Stewart, a prosperous citizen of Wilmington, who was a very active worker in the cause, was sometimes called President of the Underground Railroad,[2] but here again the distinction seems to have been complimentary and figurative. In truth the work was everywhere spontaneous, and its character was such that organization could have added little or no efficiency. Unfaltering confidence among members of neighboring stations served better than a code of rules; special messengers sent on the spur of the moment took the place of conferences held at stated seasons; supplies gathered privately as they were needed sufficed instead of regular dues; and, in general, the decision and sagacity of the individual was required rather than the less rapid efforts of an organization.

In a few centres where the amount of secret service to be done was large, a slight specialization of work is to be noticed. This division of labor consisted in the employment of a regular conductor or agent at these points to manage the work of transportation of passengers to points farther north; while the station-keepers attended more closely to the work of receiving and caring for the new arrivals. The special conductors chosen were men thoroughly acquainted with the different routes of their respective neighborhoods. At Mechanicsburg, Champaign County, Ohio, Udney Hyde, a fearless and well-known citizen, acted as agent between the local stations of J. R. Ware and Levi Rathbun, and stations to the northeast as far as the Alum Creek Quaker Settlement,

---

[1] Howe, *Historical Collections of Ohio*, Vol. II, pp. 103, 104; see also the *Reminiscences of Levi Coffin*.
[2] George H. Woodruff, *History of Will County, Illinois*, p. 268.

a distance of forty miles.[1] The stations at Mechanicsburg were among the most widely known in central and southern Ohio. They received fugitives from at least three regular routes, and doubtless had "switch connections" with other lines. Passengers were taken northward over one of the three, perhaps four roads, and as one or two of these lay through pro-slavery neighborhoods a brave and experienced agent was almost indispensable. George W. S. Lucas, a colored man of Salem, Columbiana County, Ohio, made frequent trips with the closed carriage of Philip Evans, between Barnesville, New Philadelphia and Cadiz, and two stations, Ashtabula and Painesville, on the shore of Lake Erie. Occasionally Mr. Lucas conducted parties to Cleveland and Sandusky and Toledo, but in such cases he went on foot or by stage.[2] His trips were sometimes a hundred miles and more in length. George L. Burroughes, a colored man of Cairo, Illinois, became an agent for the Underground Road in 1857, while acting as porter of a sleeping-car running on the Illinois Central Railroad between Cairo and Chicago.[3] At Albany, New York, Stephen Meyers, a negro, was an agent of the Underground Road for a wide extent of territory.[4] At Detroit there were several colored agents; among them George De Baptiste and George Dolarson.[5]

The slight approach to organization manifest in some centres in the division of labor between station-keepers and special

[1] Conversation with J. R. Ware, and with the daughter of Mr. Hyde, Mrs. Amanda Shepherd, Mechanicsburg, O., Sept. 7, 1895; conversation with Major Joseph C. Brand, Urbana, O., Aug. 13, 1894.

[2] Conversation with George W. S. Lucas, Salem, Columbiana Co., Aug. 14, 1892, when he was fifty-nine years old. He was remarkably clear and convincing in his statements, many of which have since been corroborated. Citizens of Salem referred to him as a reliable source of information.

[3] Letter from George L. Burroughes, Cairo, Ill., Jan. 6, 1896. Mr. Burroughes said that Mr. Robert Delany, a friend from Canada, proposed to him that they both take an agency for the Underground Railroad. Delany took the Rock Island route and Burroughes the Cairo route.

[4] Letter of Martin I. Townsend, Troy, N.Y., Sept. 4, 1896. Mr. Townsend was counsel for the fugitive, Charles Nalle, in the Nalle or Troy Rescue case. See the little book entitled, *Harriet, the Moses of Her People*, 2d ed., p. 146; see also *History of the County of Albany, New York, from 1609-1886*, p. 725.

[5] Conversation with Judge J. W. Finney, Detroit, Mich., July 27, 1897.

agents or conductors was caused by the large number of fugitives arriving at these points, and the extreme caution necessary. When, at length, indignation was aroused in the minds of Northern abolitionists by the passage of the Fugitive Slave Law, September 18, 1850, the determination to resist this measure displayed itself in certain localities in the formation of vigilance committees. Theodore Parker explains that it was in consequence of the enactment of this measure that "people held indignant meetings, and organized committees of vigilance whose duty was to prevent a fugitive from being arrested, if possible, or to furnish legal aid, and raise every obstacle to his rendition. The vigilance committees," he says, "were also the employees of the U. G. R. R. and effectively disposed of many a *casus belli* by transferring the disputed chattel to Canada. Money, time, wariness, devotedness for months and years, that cannot be computed, and will never be recorded, except, perhaps, in connection with cases whose details had peculiar interest, was nobly rendered by the true anti-slavery men."[1] Such committees of vigilance were organized in Syracuse, New York, Boston, Springfield and some of the smaller towns of Massachusetts, in Philadelphia and other places. New York City, like Philadelphia, had a Vigilance Committee as early as 1838. About this association of the metropolis there is scarcely any information.[2] We must be content then to confine our attention to the committees called into existence by the Fugitive Slave Law of 1850.

Eight days after the enactment of this law citizens of Syracuse, New York, issued a call through the newspapers for a public meeting, and on October 4 members of all parties crowded the city-hall to express their censure of the law. The meeting recommended "the appointment of a Vigilance Commitee of thirteen citizens, whose duty it shall be to see that no person is deprived of his liberty without 'due process of law.' And all good citizens are earnestly requested to aid

[1] Weiss, *Life and Correspondence of Theodore Parker*, Vol. II, pp. 92, 93.
[2] Frederick Douglass relates that when he escaped from Maryland to New York, in 1838, he was befriended by David Ruggles, the secretary of the New York Vigilance Committee; *Life of Frederick Douglass*, 1881, p. 205.

and sustain them in all needed efforts for the security of every person claiming the protection of our laws." This committee was appointed and an address and resolutions adopted.[1] At an adjourned meeting held on October 12 the assemblage voted to form an association, "pledged to stand by its members in opposing this law, and to share with any of them the pecuniary losses they may incur under the operation of this law." The determination shown in the organization of these two bodies was well sustained a year later when the attempt was made by officers of the law to seize Jerry McHenry as a fugitive slave. The Vigilance Committee decided to storm the court-house, where the colored man was confined under guard, and rescue the prisoner. This daring piece of work was successfully accomplished, and the government never again attempted to recover any slaves in central New York.[2]

The organization of the Vigilance Committee of Syracuse was closely followed by the organization of a similar committee in Boston. At a meeting in Faneuil Hall, October 14, 1850, resolutions were adopted expressing the conviction that no citizen would take part in reënslaving a fugitive, and pledging protection to the colored residents of the city. To make good this pledge a Vigilance Committee of fifty was appointed.[3] This body organized by choosing a president, treasurer, and secretary, a committee of finance, an executive committee, a legal committee and a committee of special vigilance and alarm. An appeal was then issued to the citizens of Boston calling their attention to the arrival of many destitute fugitives in Boston, and to the establishment of an agency

---

[1] The Rev. J. W. Loguen gives the names of the committee in his autobiography, p. 396.

[2] Samuel J. May, *Recollections of the Anti-Slavery Conflict*, pp. 349–364; Wilson, *Rise and Fall of the Slave Power in the United States*, Vol. II, pp. 305, 306.

[3] *Ibid.*, p. 308. The list of members of the Committee of Vigilance given by Austin Bearse, the doorkeeper of the Committee, contains two hundred and nine names. Among these are A. Bronson Alcott, Edward Atkinson, Henry I. Bowditch, Richard H. Dana, Jr., Lewis Hayden, William Lloyd Garrison, Samuel G. Howe, Francis Jackson, Ellis Gray Loring, James Russell Lowell, Theodore Parker, Edmund Quincy and others of distinction. See pp. 3, 4, 5, 6, in Mr. Bearse's *Reminiscences of Fugitive-Slave-Law Days in Boston*.

for the purpose of securing employment for fugitive applicants. Gifts of money and clothing were asked for. In response to a circular sent out by the finance committee to all the churches in 1851, a sum of about sixteen hundred dollars was raised. That there might be coöperation throughout the state notices were sent to all the towns in Massachusetts urging the formation of local vigilance committees; and as a result such committees were organized in some towns.[1]

The meeting-place of the Boston Committee was Meionaon Hall in Tremont Temple. Members were notified of an intended meeting personally, if possible, by the doorkeeper of the committee, Captain Austin Bearse.[2] The proceedings of the committee were secret, and comparatively little is now known about their work. It is, however, known that for ten years the organization was active, and that although it was not successful in rescuing Sims and Burns from a hard fate, it nevertheless secured the liberty of more than a hundred others.[3]

Soon after the Fugitive Slave Law was passed John Brown visited Springfield, Massachusetts, where he had formerly lived. The valley of the Connecticut had long been a line of underground travel, and citizens of Springfield, colored and white, had become identified with operations on this line. Brown at once decided that the new law made organization

[1] For much valuable material relating to the Vigilance Committee of Boston, see Theodore Parker's *Scrap-Book*, in the Boston Public Library.

[2] Mr. Bearse says: "There were printed tickets of notice which I delivered to each member in person, if possible, of which the following copies are specimens:

'BOSTON, June 7, 1854.

There will be a meeting of the Vigilance Committee at the *Meionaon* (Tremont Temple), on *Thursday evening*, June 8, at half-past seven.

Pass in by the *Office Entrance*, and through the *Meionaon Ante-Room*.

THEODORE PARKER, *Chairman of Executive Committees.*'

'VIGILANCE COMMITTEE! The members of the Vigilance Committee are hereby notified to meet at —— ——

By order of the Committee,

A. BEARSE, *Doorkeeper.*'"

— *Reminiscences of Fugitive-Slave-Law Days in Boston*, pp. 15, 16.

[3] *Ibid.*, p. 14.

necessary, and he formed, therefore, the League of Gileadites to resist systematically the enforcement of the law. The name of this order was significant in that it contained a warning to those of its members that should show themselves cowards. "Whosoever is fearful or afraid let him return and depart early from Mount Gilead."[1] In the "Agreement and Rules" that Brown drafted for the order, adopted January 15, 1851, the following directions for action were laid down: " Should one of your number be arrested, you must collect together as quickly as possible, so as to outnumber your adversaries. . . . Let no able-bodied man appear on the ground unequipped, or with his weapons exposed to view. . . . Your plans must be known only to yourselves and with the understanding that all traitors must die, wherever caught and proven to be guilty. . . . Let the first blow be the signal for all to engage, . . . make clean work with your enemies, and be sure you meddle not with any others. . . . After effecting a rescue, if you are assailed, go into the houses of your most prominent and influential white friends with your wives, and that will effectually fasten upon them the suspicion of being connected with you, and will compel them to make a common cause with you. . . . You may make a tumult in the court-room where a trial is going on by burning gunpowder freely in paper packages. . . . But in such case the prisoner will need to take the hint at once and bestir himself; and so should his friends improve the opportunity for a general rush. . . . Stand by one another, and by your friends, while a drop of blood remains; and be hanged, if you must, but tell no tales out of school. Make no confession." By adopting the Agreement and Rules forty-four colored persons constituted themselves "a branch of the United States League of Gileadites," and agreed "to have no officers except a treasurer and secretary pro tem., until after some trial of courage," when they could choose officers on the basis of "courage, efficiency, and general good conduct."[2] Doubtless the Gileadites of Springfield

[1] Judg. vii. 3; Deut. xx. 8; referred to by Brown in his "Agreement and Rules."
[2] F. B. Sanborn, in his *Life and Letters of John Brown*, pp. 125, 126,

WILLIAM STILL,

CHAIRMAN OF THE ACTING VIGILANCE COMMITTEE IN PHILADELPHIA,
PENNSYLVANIA, 1852–1860.

did efficient service, for it appears that the importance of the town as a way-station on the Underground Road increased after the passage of the Fugitive Slave Bill.[1]

We have already learned that Philadelphia had a Vigilance Committee before 1840. In a speech made before the meeting that organized the new committee, December 2, 1852, Mr. J. Miller McKim, the secretary of the Pennsylvania Anti-Slavery Society, gave the reasons for establishing a new committee. He said that the old committee "had become disorganized and scattered, and that for the last two or three years the duties of this department had been performed by individuals on their own responsibility, and sometimes in a very irregular manner." It was accordingly decided to form a new committee, called the General Vigilance Committee, with a chairman and treasurer; and within this body an Acting Committee of four persons, "who should have the responsibility of attending to every case that might require their aid, as well as the exclusive authority to raise the funds necessary for their purpose." The General Committee comprised nineteen members, and had as its head Mr. Robert Purvis, one of the signers of the Declaration of Sentiments of the American Anti-Slavery Society, and the first president of the old committee. The Acting Committee had as its chairman William Still, a colored clerk in the office of the Pennsylvania Anti-Slavery Society and a most energetic underground helper. The Philadelphia Vigilance Committee, thus constituted, continued intact until Lincoln issued the Emancipation Proclamation.[2] Some insight into the work accomplished by the Acting Committee can be obtained by an examination of the book compiled by William Still under the title *Underground Railroad Records*. The Acting Committee was required to keep a record of all its doings. Mr. Still's volume was evidently amassed by the

gives the agreement, rules, and signatures. See also R. J. Hinton's *John Brown and His Men*, Appendix, pp. 585, 588.

[1] Mason A. Green, *History of Springfield, Massachusetts, 1636-1886*, p. 506.

[2] Article, "Meeting to Form a Vigilance Committee," in the *Pennsylvania Freeman*, Dec. 9, 1852; quoted in *Underground Railroad Records*, by William Still, pp. 610-612.

transcription of many of the incidents that found their way under this order into the archives of the committee. The work was limited to the assistance of such needy fugitives as came to Philadelphia; and was not extended, except in rare cases, to inciting slaves to run away from their masters, or to aiding them in so doing.[1]

The relief of the destitution existing among the wayworn travellers was a matter requiring considerable outlay of time and money on the part of abolitionists. There was occasionally a fugitive or family of fugitives, that, having better opportunity or possessing greater foresight than others, made provision for the journey and escaped to Canada with little or no dependence on the aid of underground operators. Asbury Parker, of Ironton, Ohio, fled from Greenup County, Kentucky, in 1857, clad in a suit of broadcloth, alone befitting, as he thought, the dignity of a free man.[2] The brother of Anthony Bingey, of Windsor, Ontario, came unexpectedly into the possession of five hundred dollars. With this money he instructed a friend in Cincinnati to procure a team and wagon to convey the family of Bingey to Canada. The company arrived at Sandusky after being only three days on the road.[3]

But the mass of fugitives were thinly clad, and had only such food as they could forage until they reached the Underground Railroad. The arrival of a company at a station would be at once followed by the preparation, often at midnight, of a meal for the pilgrims and their guides. It was a common thing for a station to entertain a company of five or six; and companies of twenty-eight or thirty are not unheard of. Levi Coffin says, "The largest company of slaves ever seated at our table, at one time, numbered seventeen."[4] During one month in the year 1854 or 1855 there were sixty runaways at the house of Aaron L. Benedict, a station in the Alum

[1] Still's *Underground Railroad Records*, p. 177. References to the action of the committee of which Mr. Still was chairman will be found scattered through the *Records*. See, for example, pp. 70, 98, 102, 131, 150, 162, 173, 176, 204, 224, 274, 275, 303, 325, 335, 388, 412, 449, 493, 500.

[2] Conversation with Asbury Parker, Ironton, O., Sept. 30, 1894.

[3] Conversation with Anthony Bingey, Windsor, Ont., July 3, 1895.

[4] *Reminiscences*, p. 178.

Creek Quaker Settlement in central Ohio. On one occasion twenty sat down to dinner in Mr. Benedict's house.[1] It will thus be seen that the supply of provisions alone was for the average station-keeper no inconsiderable item of expense, and that it was one involving much labor.

The arrangements for furnishing fugitives with clothing, like much of the underground work done at the stations, came within the province of the women of the stations. While the noted fugitive, William Wells Brown, lay sick at the house of his benefactor, Mr. Wells Brown, in southwestern Ohio, the family made him some clothing, and Mr. Brown purchased him a pair of boots.[2] Women's anti-slavery societies in many places conducted sewing-circles, as a branch of their work, for the purpose of supplying clothes and other necessities to fugitives. The Woman's Anti-Slavery Society of Ellington, Chautauqua County, New York, sent a letter to William Still, November 21, 1859, saying: "Every year we have sent a box of clothing, bedding, etc., to the aid of the fugitive, and wishing to send it where it would be of the most service, we have it suggested to us, to send to you the box we have at present. You would confer a favor . . . by writing us, . . . whether or not it would be more advantageous to you than some nearer station. . . ."[3]

The Women's Anti-Slavery Sewing Society of Cincinnati maintained an active interest in underground work going on in their city by supplying clothing to needy travellers.[4] The Female Anti-Slavery Association of Henry County, Indiana, organized a Committee of Vigilance in 1841 "to seek out such colored females as are not suitably provided for, who may now be, or who shall hereafter come, within our limits, and assist them in any way they may deem expedient, either by advice or pecuniary means. . . ."[5]

[1] Conversation with M. J. Benedict, Alum Creek Settlement, Dec. 2, 1893. See also *Underground Railroad*, Smedley, pp. 56, 136, 142, 174.
[2] *Narrative of William W. Brown, A Fugitive Slave*, written by himself, 2d ed., 1848, p. 102.
[3] The letter is printed in full, together with other letters, in Still's *Underground Railroad Records*, pp. 590, 591.
[4] Levi Coffin, *Reminiscences*, p. 316.
[5] *Protectionist*, Arnold Buffum, Editor, New Garden, Ind., 7th mo., 1st, 1841.

In some of the large centres, money as well as clothing and food was constantly needed for the proper performance of the underground work. Thus, for example, at Cincinnati, Ohio, it was frequently necessary to hire carriages in which to convey fugitives out of the city to some neighboring station. From time to time as the occasion arose Levi Coffin collected the funds needed for such purposes from business acquaintances. He called these contributors "stock-holders" in the Underground Railroad.[1] After steam railroads became incorporated in the underground system money was required at different points to purchase tickets for fugitives. The Vigilance Committee of Philadelphia defrayed the travelling expenses of many refugees in sending some to New York City, some to Elmira and a few to Canada.[2] Frederick Douglass, who kept a station at Rochester, New York, received contributions of money to pay the railroad fares of the fugitives he forwarded to Canada and to give them a little more for pressing necessities.[3]

The use of steam railroads as a means of transportation of this class of passengers began with the completion of lines of road to the lakes. This did not take place till about 1850. It was, therefore, during the last decade of the history of the Underground Road that surface lines, as they were sometimes called by abolitionists, became a part of the secret system. There were probably more surface lines in Ohio than in any other state. The old Mad River Railroad, or Sandusky, Dayton and Cincinnati Railroad, of western Ohio, (now a part of the "Big Four" system), began to be used at least as early as 1852 by instructed fugitives.[4] The Sandusky, Mansfield and Newark Railroad (now the Baltimore and Ohio) from Utica, Licking County, Ohio, to Sandusky, was sometimes used by the same class of persons.[5] After

---

[1] *Reminiscences*, pp. 317, 321.
[2] Still's *Underground Railroad Records*, p. 613.
[3] *Ibid.*, p. 598. In the fragment of a letter from which Mr. Still quotes, Mr. Douglass says, "They [the fugitives] usually tarry with us only during the night, and are forwarded to Canada by the morning train. We give them supper, lodging, and breakfast, pay their expenses, and give them a half-dollar over."
[4] The *Firelands Pioneer*, July, 1888, p. 21.   [5] *Ibid.*, pp. 23, 57, 79.

the construction of the Cleveland, Columbus and Cincinnati Railroad [1] as far as Greenwich in northern Ohio, fugitives often came to that point concealed in freight-cars. In eastern Ohio there were two additional routes by rail sometimes employed in underground traffic: one of these appears to have been the Cleveland and Canton from Zanesville north,[2] and the other was the Cleveland and Western between Alliance and Cleveland.[3] In Indiana the Louisville, New Albany and Chicago Railroad from Crawfordsville northward was patronized by underground travellers until the activity of slave-hunters caused it to be abandoned.[4] Fugitives were sometimes transported across the State of Michigan by the Michigan Central Railroad. In Illinois there seems to have been not less than three railroads that carried fugitives: these were the Chicago, Burlington and Quincy,[5] the Chicago and Rock Island[6] and the Illinois Central.[7] When John Brown made his famous journey through Iowa in the winter of 1858–1859 he shipped his company of twelve fugitives in a stock car from West Liberty, Iowa, to Chicago, by way of the Chicago and Rock Island route.[8] In Pennsylvania and New York there were several lines over which runaways were sent when circumstances permitted. At Harrisburg, Reading and other points along the Philadelphia and Reading Railroad, fugitives were put aboard the cars for Philadelphia.[9] From Pennsylvania they were forwarded

[1] *Ibid.*, p. 74. The "Three C's" is now the Cleveland, Cincinnati, Chicago and St. Louis Railroad, or "Big Four" Route.
[2] Conversation with Thomas Williams, of Pennsville, O.; letter of H. C. Harvey, Manchester, Kan., Jan. 16, 1893.
[3] Letter of I. Newton Peirce, Folcroft, Pa., Feb. 1, 1893.
[4] Letter of Sidney Speed, Crawfordsville, Ind., March 6, 1896. Mr. Speed and his father were both connected with the Crawfordsville centre.
[5] *Life and Poems of John Howard Bryant*, p. 30; letter of William H. Collins, Quincy, Ill., Jan. 13, 1896; *History of Knox County, Illinois*, p. 211.
[6] Letter of George L. Burroughes, Cairo, Ill., Jan. 6, 1896.
[7] *Ibid.*; conversation with the Rev. R. G. Ramsey, Cadiz, O., Aug. 18, 1892.
[8] J. B. Grinnell, *Men and Events of Forty Years*, p. 216.
[9] Smedley, *Underground Railroad*, pp. 174, 176, 177, 365. The following letter is in point: —

"SCHUYLKILL, 11th Mo., 7th, 1857.

WILLIAM STILL, *Respected Friend*: —There are three colored friends at my house now, who will reach the city by the Philadelphia and Reading train this evening. Please meet them.
Thine, etc., E. F. PENNYPACKER."

by the Vigilance Committee over different lines, sometimes by way of the Pennsylvania Railroad to New York City; sometimes by way of the Philadelphia and Reading and the Northern Central to Elmira, New York, whence they were sent on by the same line to Niagara Falls. Fugitives put aboard the cars at Elmira were furnished with money from a fund provided by the anti-slavery society. As a matter of precaution they were sent out of town at four o'clock in the morning, and were always placed by the train officials, who knew their destination, in the baggage-car.[1] The New York Central Railroad from Rochester west was an outlet made use of by Frederick Douglass in passing slaves to Canada. At Syracuse, during several years before the beginning of the War, one of the directors of this road, Mr. Horace White, the father of Dr. Andrew D. White, distributed passes to fugitives. This fact did not come to the knowledge of Dr. White until after his father's demise. He relates: " Some years after . . . I met an old 'abolitionist' of Syracuse, who said to me that he had often come to my father's house, rattled at the windows, informed my father of the passes he needed for fugitive slaves, received them through the window, and then departed, nobody else being the wiser. On my asking my mother, who survived my father several years, about it, she said: 'Yes, such things frequently occurred, and your father, if he was satisfied of the genuineness of the request, always wrote off the passes and handed them out, asking no questions."[2]

In the New England states fugitives travelled, under the instruction of friends, by way of the Providence and Worcester Railroad from Valley Falls, Rhode Island, to Worcester, Massachusetts, where by arrangement they were transferred to the Vermont Road.[3] The Boston and Worcester Railroad between Newton and Worcester, Massachusetts, as also between Boston and Worcester, seems to have been used to some extent in this way.[4] The Grand Trunk, extending from Port-

[1] Letter of John W. Jones, Elmira, N.Y., Jan. 18, 1897.
[2] Letter of the Hon. Andrew D. White, Ithaca, N.Y., April 10, 1897.
[3] Mrs. Elizabeth Buffum Chace, *Anti-Slavery Reminiscences*, pp. 28, 38.
[4] Letter of William I. Bowditch, Boston, April 5, 1893. Mr. Bowditch says: "Generally I passed them (the fugitives) on to William Jackson, at

land, Maine, through the northern parts of New Hampshire and Vermont into Canada, occasionally gave passes to fugitives, and would always take reduced fares for this class of passengers.[1]

The advantages of escape by boat were early discerned by slaves living near the coast or along inland rivers. Vessels engaged in our coastwise trade became more or less involved in transporting fugitives from Southern ports to Northern soil. Small trading vessels, returning from their voyages to Norfolk and Portsmouth, Virginia, landed slaves on the New England coast.[2] In July, 1853, the brig *Florence* (Captain Amos Hopkins, of Hallowell, Maine) from Wilmington, North Carolina, was required, while lying in Boston harbor, to surrender a fugitive found on board. In September, 1854, the schooner *Sally Ann* (of Belfast, Maine), from the same Southern port, was induced to give up a slave known to be on board. In October of the same year the brig *Cameo* (of Augusta, Maine) brought a stowaway from Jacksonville, Florida, into Boston harbor, and, as in the two preceding cases, the slave was rescued from the danger of return to the South through the activity and shrewdness of Captain Austin Bearse, the agent of the Vigilance Committee of Boston.[3] The son of a slaveholder living at Newberne, North Carolina, forwarded slaves from that point to the Vigilance Committee of Philadelphia on vessels engaged in the lumber trade.[4] In November, 1855, Captain Fountain brought twenty-one fugitives concealed on his vessel in a cargo of grain from Norfolk, Virginia, to Philadelphia.[5]

The tributaries flowing into the Ohio River from Virginia and Kentucky furnished convenient channels of escape for

Newton. His house being on the Worcester Railroad, he could easily forward any one." Captain Austin Bearse, *Reminiscences of Fugitive-Slave Law Days in Boston*, p. 37.

[1] Letter of Brown Thurston, Portland, Me., Oct. 21, 1895.

[2] Mrs. Elizabeth Buffum Chace, *Anti-Slavery Reminiscences*, pp. 27, 30.

[3] Austin Bearse, *Reminiscences of Fugitive-Slave Law Days in Boston*, 1880, pp. 34–39.

[4] Smedley, *Underground Railroad*, letter of Robert Purvis, of Philadelphia, p. 335.

[5] Still, *Underground Railroad Records*, pp. 165–172. For other cases, see pp. 211, 379–381, 437, 558, 559–565.

many slaves. The concurrent testimony of abolitionists living along the Ohio is to the effect that streams like the Kanawha River bore many a boat-load of fugitives to the southern boundary of the free states. It is not a mere coincidence that a large number of the most important centres of activity lie along the southern line of the Western free states at points near or opposite the mouths of rivers and creeks. On the Mississippi, Ohio and Illinois rivers north-bound steamboats not infrequently provided the means of escape. Jefferson Davis declared in the Senate that many slaves escaped from his state into Ohio by taking passage on the boats of the Mississippi.[1]

Abolitionists found it desirable to have waterway extensions of their secret lines. Boats, the captains of which were favorable, were therefore drafted into the service when running on convenient routes. Boats plying between Portland, Maine, and St. John, New Brunswick, or other Canadian ports, often took these passengers free of charge.[2] Thomas Garrett, of Wilmington, Delaware, sometimes sent negroes by steamboat to Philadelphia to be cared for by the Vigilance Committee.[3] It happened on several occasions that fugitives at Portland and Boston were put aboard ocean steamers bound for England.[4] William and Ellen Craft were sent to England after having narrowly escaped capture in Boston.[5]

On the great lakes the boat service was extensive. The boats of General Reed touching at Racine, Wisconsin, received fugitives without fare. Among these were the *Sultana* (Captain Appleby), the *Madison*, the *Missouri*, the *Niagara* and the *Keystone State*. Captain Steele of the propeller *Galena* was a friend of fugitives, as was also Captain Kelsey of the *Chesapeake*. Mr. A. P. Dutton was familiar with these

---

[1] See p. 312, Chapter X.

[2] Letters of Brown Thurston, Portland, Me., Jan. 13, 1893, and Oct. 21, 1895.

[3] For letters from Mr. Garrett to William Still, of the Acting Committee of Vigilance of Philadelphia, notifying him that fugitives had been sent by boat, see Still's *Underground Railroad Records*, pp. 380, 387.

[4] Letter of S. T. Pickard, Portland, Me., Nov. 18, 1893.

[5] Still, *Underground Railroad Records*, p. 368 ; Wilson, *Rise and Fall of the Slave Power*, Vol. II, p. 325 ; *New England Magazine*, January, 1890, p. 580.

vessels and their officers, and for twenty years or more shipped runaway slaves as well as cargoes of grain from his dock in Racine.[1] The *Illinois* (Captain Blake), running between Chicago and Detroit, was a safe boat on which to place passengers whose destination was Canada.[2] John G. Weiblen navigated the lakes in 1855 and 1856, and took many refugees from Chicago to Collingwood, Ontario.[3] The *Arrow*,[4] the *United States*,[5] the *Bay City* and the *Mayflower* plying between Sandusky and Detroit, were boats the officers of which were always willing to help negroes reach Canadian ports. The *Forest Queen*, the *Morning Star* and the *May Queen*, running between Cleveland and Detroit, the *Phœbus*, a little boat plying between Toledo and Detroit, and, finally, some scows and sail-boats, are among the old craft of the great lakes that carried many slaves to their land of promise.[6] A clue to the number of refugees thus transported to Canada is perhaps given by the record of the boat upon which the fugitive, William Wells Brown, found employment. This boat ran from Cleveland to Buffalo and to Detroit. It quickly became known at Cleveland that Mr. Brown would take escaped slaves under his protection without charge, hence he rarely failed to find a little company ready to sail when he started out from Cleveland. "In the year 1842," he says, "I conveyed, from the first of May to the first of December, sixty-nine fugitives over Lake Erie to Canada."[7]

The account of the method of the Underground Railroad could scarcely be called complete without some notice of the rescue of fugitives under arrest. The first rescue occurred at the intended trial of the first fugitive slave case in Boston in 1793. Mr. Josiah Quincy, counsel for the fugitive, "heard

[1] Letter of A. P. Dutton, of Racine, Wis., April 7, 1896. As a shipper of grain and an abolitionist for twenty years in Racine, Mr. Dutton was able to turn his dock into a place of deportation for runaway slaves.
[2] A. J. Andreas, *History of Chicago*, Vol. I, p. 606.
[3] Letter of Mr. Weiblen, Fairview, Erie Co., Pa., Nov. 26, 1895.
[4] The *Firelands Pioneer*, July, 1888, p. 46.
[5] *Ibid.*, p. 50.
[6] The names of the last six boats given, as well as several of the others, were obtained from freedmen in Canada, who keep them in grateful remembrance.
[7] *Narrative of William W. Brown*, by himself, 1848, pp. 107, 108.

a noise, and, turning around, saw the constables lying sprawling on the floor, and a passage opening through the crowd, through which the fugitive was taking his departure without stopping to hear the opinion of the court." [1]

The prototype of deliverances thus established was, it is true, more or less deviated from in later instances, but the general characteristics of these cases are such that they naturally fall into one class. They are cases in which the execution of the law was interfered with by friends of the prisoner, who was spirited away as quickly as possible. The deliverance in 1812 of a supposed runaway from the hands of his captor by the New England settlers of Worthington, Ohio, has already been referred to in general terms.[2] But some details of the incident are necessary to bring out more clearly the propriety of its being included in the category of instances of violation of the constitutional provision for the rendition of escaped slaves. It appears that word was brought to the village of Worthington of the capture of the fugitive at a neighboring town, and that the villagers under the direction of Colonel James Kilbourne took immediate steps to release the negro, who, it was said, was tied with ropes, and being afoot, was compelled to keep up as best he could with his master's horse. On the arrival of the slave-owner and his chattel, the latter was freed from his bonds by the use of a butcher-knife in the hands of an active villager, and the forms of a legal dismissal were gone through before a court and an audience whose convictions were ruinous to any representations the claimant was able to make. The dispossessed master was permitted to continue his journey southward, while the negro was directed to get aboard a government wagon on its way northward to Sandusky. The return of the slave-hunter a day or two later with a process obtained in Franklinton, authorizing the retaking of his property, secured him a second hearing, but did not change the result. A fugitive, Basil Dorsey, from Liberty, Frederick County, Maryland, was seized in Bucks County, Pennsyl-

[1] Mr. Quincy's report of the case, quoted by M. G. McDougall, *Fugitive Slaves*, p. 35.
[2] See p. 38.

vania, in 1836, and carried away. Overtaken by Mr. Robert Purvis at Doylestown, he was brought into court, and the hearing of the case was postponed for two weeks. When the day of trial came the counsel for the slave succeeded in getting the case dismissed on the ground of certain objections. Thereupon the claimants of the slave hastened to a magistrate for a new warrant, but just as they were returning to rearrest the fugitive, he was hustled into the buggy of Mr. Purvis and driven rapidly out of the reach of the pursuers.[1] In October, 1853, the case of Louis, a fugitive from Kentucky on trial in Cincinnati, was brought to a conclusion in an unexpected way. The United States commissioner was about to pronounce judgment when the prisoner, taking advantage of a favorable opportunity, slipped from his chair, had a good hat placed upon his head by some friend, passed out of the court-room among a crowd of colored visitors and made his way cautiously to Avondale. A few minutes after the disappearance of the fugitive his absence was discovered by the marshal that had him in charge; and although careful search was made for him, he escaped to Canada by means of the Underground Railroad.[2] In April, 1859, Charles Nalle, a slave from Culpeper County, Virginia, was discovered in Troy, New York, and taken before the United States commissioner, who remanded him back to slavery. As the news of this decision spread, a crowd gathered about the commissioner's office. In the meantime, a writ of habeas corpus was served upon the marshal that had arrested Nalle, commanding that officer to bring the prisoner before a judge of the Supreme Court. When the marshal and his deputies appeared with the slave, the crowd made a charge upon them, and a hand-to-hand melée resulted. Inch by inch the progress of the officers was resisted until they were worn out, and the slave escaped. In haste the fugitive was ferried across the river to West Troy, only to fall into the hands of a constable and be again taken into custody. The mob had followed, however, and now stormed the door behind which the prisoner rested under guard. In the attack

---

[1] Smedley, *Underground Railroad*, pp. 356-361.
[2] Levi Coffin, *Reminiscences*, pp. 548-554.

the door was forced open, and over the body of a negro assailant, struck down in the fray, the slave was torn from his guards, and sent on his way to Canada.[1] Well-known cases of rescue, such as the Shadrach case, which occurred in Boston in January, 1851, and the Jerry rescue, which occurred in Syracuse nine months later, may be omitted here. They, like many others that have been less often chronicled, show clearly the temper of resolute men in the communities where they occurred. It was felt by these persons that the slave, who had already paid too high a penalty for his color, could not expect justice at the hands of the law, that his liberty must be preserved to him, and a base statute be thwarted at any cost.

[1] This account is condensed from a report given in the *Troy Whig*, April 28, 1859, and printed in the book entitled, *Harriet the Moses of Her People*, pp. 143–149.

Yours Truly
Levi Coffin

THE REPUTED PRESIDENT OF THE UNDERGROUND RAILROAD.
Mr. Coffin and his wife aided more than 3000 slaves in their flight.

CHAPTER IV

UNDERGROUND AGENTS, STATION-KEEPERS, OR CONDUCTORS

PERSONS opposed to slavery were, naturally, the friends of the fugitive slave, and were ever ready to respond to his appeals for help. Shelter and food were readily supplied him, and he was directed or conveyed, generally in the night, to sympathizing neighbors, until finally, without any forethought or management on his own part, he found himself in Canada a free man. These helpers, in the course of time, came to be called agents, station-keepers, or conductors on the Underground Railroad. Of the names of those that belonged to this class of practical emancipationists, 3,211 have been catalogued;[1] change of residence and death have made it impossible to obtain the names of many more. Considering the kind of labor performed and the danger involved, one is impressed with the unselfish devotion to principle of these emancipators. There was for them, of course, no outward honor, no material recompense, but instead such contumely and seeming disgrace as can now be scarcely comprehended.

Nevertheless, they were rich in courage, and their hospitality was equal to all emergencies. They gladly gave aid and comfort to every negro seeking freedom; and the numbers befriended by many helpers despite penalties and abuse show with what moral determination the work was carried on. It has been said that the Hopkins, Salsbury, Snediger, Dickey and Kirkpatrick families, of southern Ohio, forwarded more than 1,000 fugitives to Canada before the year 1817.[2] Daniel Gibbons, of Lancaster County, Pennsylvania, was engaged in helping fugitive slaves during a period of fifty-six years. "He did not keep a record of the number he passed until 1824.

---

[1] See Appendix E, pp. 403–439.
[2] William Birney, *James G. Birney and His Times*, p. 435.

But prior to that time, it was supposed to have been over 200, and up to the time of his death (in 1853) he had aided about 1,000."[1] It has been estimated that Dr. Nathan M. Thomas, of Schoolcraft, Michigan, forwarded between 1,000 and 1,500 fugitives.[2] John Fairfield, the abductor, "piloted not only hundreds, but thousands."[3] The Rev. Charles T. Torrey went to Maryland and "from there sent—as he wrote previous to 1844 —some 400 slaves over different routes to Canada."[4] Philo Carpenter, of Chicago, is reported to have escorted 200 fugitives to vessels bound for Canada.[5] In a letter to William Still, in November, 1857, Elijah F. Pennypacker, of Chester County, Pennsylvania, writes, "we have within the past two months passed forty-three through our hands."[6] H. B. Leeper, of Princeton, Illinois, says that the most successful business he ever accomplished in this line was the helping on of thirty-one men and women in six weeks' time.[7] Leverett B. Hill, of Wakeman, Ohio, assisted 103 on their way to Canada during the year 1852.[8] Mr. Van Dorn, of Quincy, in a service of twenty-five years, assisted "some two or three hundred fugitives."[9] W. D. Schooley, of Richmond, Indiana, writes, "I think I must have assisted over 100 on their way to liberty."[10] Jonathan H. Gray, Milton Hill and John H. Frazee were conductors at Carthage, Indiana, and are said to have helped over 150 fugitives.[11] "Thousands of fugitives found rest" at Ripley, Brown County, Ohio.[12] During the lifetime of General McIntire, a Virginian, who settled in Adams County, Ohio, "more than 100 slaves found a safe retreat under his roof." Other helpers in the same state

[1] Smedley, *Underground Railroad*, p. 56.
[2] Letter of Mrs. Pamela S. Thomas, Schoolcraft, Mich., March 25, 1896.
[3] Letter of Mrs. Laura S. Haviland, Englewood, Ill., June 5, 1893.
[4] Letter of M. M. Fisher, Medway, Mass., Oct. 23, 1893.
[5] E. G. Mason, *Early Chicago and Illinois*, 1890, p. 110.
[6] Letter of Sarah C. Pennypacker, Schuylkill, Pa., June 8, 1896.
[7] Letter of H. B. Leeper, Princeton, Ill., Dec. 19, 1895.
[8] Letter of E. S. Hill, Atlantic, Ia., Oct. 30, 1894.
[9] Wilson, *Rise and Fall of the Slave Power*, Vol. II, p. 67.
[10] Letter of W. D. Schooley, Nov. 15, 1893.
[11] Letter of James H. Frazee, Milton, Ind., Feb. 3, 1894.
[12] Henry Howe, *Historical Collections of Ohio*, Vol. I, p. 335. See also *History of Brown County, Ohio*, p. 443.

rendered service deserving of mention. Ozem Gardner, of Sharon Township, Franklin County, "assisted more than 200 fugitives on their way in all weathers and at all times of the day and night."[1] It is estimated by a friend of Dr. J. A. Bingham and George J. Payne, two operators of Gallia County, that the line of escape with which these men were connected was travelled by about 200 slaves every year from 1845 to 1856.[2] From 1844 to 1860 John H. Stewart, a colored station-keeper of the same county, kept about 100 fugitives at his house.[3] Five hundred are said to have passed through the hands of Thomas L. Gray, of Deavertown, in Morgan County.[4] Ex-President Fairchild speaks of the "multitudes" of fugitives that came to Oberlin, and says that "not one was ever finally taken back to bondage."[5] Many other stations and station-agents that were instrumental in helping large numbers of slaves from bondage to freedom cannot be mentioned here.

Reticent as most underground operators were at the time in regard to their unlawful acts, they did not attempt to conceal their principles. On the contrary, they were zealous in their endeavors to make converts to a doctrine that seemed to them to have the combined warrant of Scripture and of their own conscience, and that agreed with the convictions of the fathers of the Republic. The Golden Rule and the preamble of the Declaration of Independence they often recited in support of their position. When they had transgressed the Fugitive Slave Law of Congress they were wont to find their justification in what ex-President Fairchild of Oberlin has aptly called the Fugitive Slave Law of the Mosaic institutions:[6] "Thou shalt not deliver unto his master the servant which hath escaped unto thee; he shall dwell with thee, even among you, in that place which he shall

---

[1] *History of Franklin and Pickaway Counties, Ohio*, p. 424.
[2] Letter of Dr. N. B. Sisson, Porter, Gallia Co., O., Sept. 16, 1894.
[3] Letter of Gabe N. Johnson, Ironton, O., November, 1894.
[4] Article in the *New Lexington* (O.) *Tribune*, signed "W. A. D.," fall of 1885; exact date unknown.
[5] Henry Howe, *Historical Collections of Ohio*, Vol. II, p. 380.
[6] Fairchild, *The Underground Railroad*, Vol. IV; *Tract No. 87*, Western Reserve Historical Society, p. 97.

choose in one of thy gates where it liketh him best; thou shalt not oppress him."[1] They refused to observe a law that made it a felony in their opinion to give a cup of cold water to famishing men and women fleeing from servitude. Their faith and determination is clearly expressed in one of the old anti-slavery songs:—

> " 'Tis the law of God in the human soul,
> 'Tis the law in the Word Divine;
> It shall live while the earth in its course shall roll,
> It shall live in this soul of mine.
> Let the law of the land forge its bonds of wrong,
> I shall help when the self-freed crave;
> For the law in my soul, bright, beaming, and strong,
> Bids me succor the fleeing slave."

Theodore Parker was but the mouthpiece of many abolitionists throughout the Northern states when he said, at the conclusion of a sermon in 1850: "It is known to you that the Fugitive Slave Bill has become a law. . . . To law framed of such iniquity I owe no allegiance. Humanity, Christianity, manhood revolts against it. . . . For myself I say it solemnly, I will shelter, I will help, and I will defend the fugitive with all my humble means and power. I will act with any body of decent and serious men, as the head, or the foot, or the hand, in any mode not involving the use of deadly weapons, to nullify and defeat the operation of this law. . . ."[2]

Sentiments of this kind were cherished in almost every Northern community by a few persons at least. There were some New England colonies in the West where anti-slavery sentiments predominated. These, like some of the religious communities, as those of the Quakers and Covenanters, became well-known centres of underground activity. In general it is safe to say that the majority of helpers in the North were of Anglo-American stock, descendants of the Puritan and Quaker settlers of the Eastern states, or of Southerners that had moved to the Northern states to be rid of slavery. The

[1] Deut. xxiii, 15, 16.
[2] Delivered in Melodeon Hall, Boston, Oct. 6, 1850. The *Chronotype*, Oct. 7, 1850. See Vol. II, No. 2, of the *Scrap-book* relating to Theodore Parker, compiled by Miss C. C. Thayer, Boston Public Library.

many stations in the eastern and northern parts of Ohio and the northern part of Illinois may be safely attributed to the large proportion of New England settlers in those districts. Localities where the work of befriending slaves was largely in the hands of Quakers will be mentioned in another connection. Southern settlers in Brown County and adjoining districts in Ohio are said to have been regularly forwarding escaped slaves to Canada before 1817.[1] The emigration of a number of these settlers to Bond County, Illinois, about 1820, and the removal of a few families from that region to Putnam County in the same state about a decade later, helps to explain the early development of secret routes in the southern and north central parts of Illinois.[2]

In the South much secret aid was rendered fugitives, no doubt, by persons of their own race. Two colored marketwomen in Baltimore were efficient agents for the Vigilance Committee of Philadelphia.[3] Frederick Douglass's connection with the Underground Railroad began long before he left the South.[4] In the North, people of the African race were to be found in most communities, and in many places they became energetic workers. Negro settlements in the interior of the free states, as well as along their southern frontier, soon came to form important links in the chain of stations leading from the Southern states to Canada.

In the early days running slaves sometimes sought and received aid from Indians. This fact is evidenced by the introduction of fugitive recovery clauses into a number of the treaties made between the colonies and Indian tribes. Seven out of the eight treaties made between 1784 and 1786 contained clauses for the return of black prisoners, or of "negroes and other property."[5] A few of the colonies offered rewards to induce Indians to apprehend and restore runaways. In 1669 Maryland " ordered that any Indian who

[1] William Birney, *James G. Birney and His Times*, p. 435.
[2] Letter of H. B. Leeper, Princeton, Ill., Dec. 19, 1895.
[3] Smedley, *Underground Railroad*, p. 355.
[4] Letter of Frederick Douglass, Cedar Hill, Anacostia, D.C., March 27, 1893. Mr. Douglass escaped from slavery in 1839.
[5] M. G. McDougall, *Fugitive Slaves*, pp. 13, 104, 105.

shall apprehend a fugitive may have a 'match coate' or its value. Virginia would give '20 armes length of Roanake,' or its value, while in Connecticut 'two yards of cloth' was considered sufficient inducement."[1] The inhabitants of the Ottawa village of Chief Kinjeino in northwestern Ohio were kindly disposed towards the fugitive;[2] and the people of Chief Brant, who held an estate on the Grand River in Ontario west of Niagara Falls, were in the habit of receiving colored refugees.[3]

The people of Scotch and Scotch-Irish descent were naturally liberty loving, and seem to have given hearty support to the anti-slavery cause in whatever form it presented itself to them. The small number of Scotch communities in Morgan and Logan counties, Ohio, and in Randolph and Washington counties, Illinois, were centres of underground service.

The secret work of the English, Irish and German settlers cannot be so readily localized. In various places a single German, Irishman, or Englishman is known to have aided escaped slaves in coöperation with a few other persons of different nationality, but so far as known there were no groups made up of representatives of one or another of these races engaged in such enterprises. At Toledo, Ohio, the company of helpers comprised Congressman James M. Ashley, a Pennsylvanian by birth; Richard Mott, a Quaker; James Conlisk, an Irishman; William H. Merritt, a negro; and several others.[4] Lyman Goodnow, an operator of Waukesha, Wisconsin, says he was told that "in cases of emergency the Germans were next best to Quakers for protection."[5] Two German companies from Massachusetts enlisted for the War only when promised that they should not be required to restore runaways to their owners.[6]

[1] M. G. McDougall, *Fugitive Slaves*, pp. 7, 8, and the references there given.
[2] Letter of Colonel D. W. H. Howard, Wauseon, O., Aug. 22, 1894.
[3] See Chapter VII, p. 203.
[4] Conversation with the Hon. James M. Ashley, Toledo, O., August, 1894.
[5] Narrative of Lyman Goodnow in *History of Waukesha County, Wisconsin*, p. 462.
[6] See p. 355, Chapter XI.

Some religious communities and church societies were conservators of abolition ideas. The Quakers deserve, in this work, to be placed before all other denominations because of their general acceptance and advocacy of anti-slavery doctrines when the system of slavery had no other opponents. From the time of George Fox until the last traces of the evil were swept from the English-speaking world many Quakers bore a steadfast testimony against it.[1] Fox reminded slaveholders that if they were in their slaves' places they would consider it "very great bondage and cruelty," and he urged upon the Friends in America to preach the gospel to the enslaved blacks. In 1688 German Friends at Germantown, Pennsylvania, made an official protest "against the traffic in the bodies of men and the treatment of men as cattle." By 1772 New England Friends began to disown (expel) members for failing to manumit their slaves; and four years later both the Philadelphia and the New York yearly meetings made slaveholding a disownable offence. A similar step was taken by the Baltimore Yearly Meeting in 1777; and meetings in Virginia were directed, in 1784, to disown those that refused to emancipate their slaves.[2] Owing to obstacles in the way of setting slaves free in North Carolina, a committee of Quakers of that state was appointed in 1822 to examine the laws of some of the free states respecting the admission of people of color therein. In 1823 the committee reported that there was "nothing in the laws of Ohio, Indiana, and Illinois to prevent the introduction of people of color into those states, and agents were instructed to remove slaves placed in their care as fast as they were willing to go." These facts show the sentiment that prevailed in the Society of Friends. Many Southern Quakers moved to the North on account of their hatred of slavery, and established such important centres of underground work as Springboro and Salem, Ohio, and Spiceland and New Garden, Indiana. Quakers in New

---

[1] S. B. Weeks, *Southern Quakers and Slavery*, p. 198.

[2] *American Church History*, Vol. XII; see article on "The Society of Friends," by Professor A. C. Thomas, pp. 242-248; also Weeks, *Southern Quakers and Slavery*, pp. 198-219.

Bedford and Lynn, Massachusetts, and Valley Falls, Rhode Island, engaged in the service. The same class of people in Maryland coöperated with members of their society in the vicinity of Philadelphia. The existence of numerous Underground Railroad centres in southeastern Pennsylvania and in eastern Indiana is explained by the fact that a large number of Quakers dwelt in those regions.

The Methodists began to take action against slavery in 1780. At an informal conference held at Baltimore in that year the subject was presented in the form of a "Question, — Ought not this conference to require those travelling preachers who hold slaves to give promises to set them free?" The answer given was in the affirmative. Concerning the membership the language adopted was as follows: "We pass our disapprobation on all our friends who keep slaves; and advise their freedom." Under the influence of Wesleyan preachers, it is said, not a few cases of emancipation occurred. At a conference in 1785, however, it was decided to "suspend the execution of the minute on slavery till the deliberations of a future conference. . . ." Four years later a clause appeared in the Discipline, by whose authority is not known, prohibiting "The buying or selling the bodies or souls of men, women, or children, with an intention to enslave them." This provision evidently referred to the African slave-trade. In 1816 the General Conference adopted a resolution that "no slaveholder shall be eligible to any official station in our Church hereafter, where the laws of the state in which he lives will admit of emancipation, and permit the liberated slave to enjoy freedom." Later there seems to have been a disposition on the part of the church authorities to suppress the agitation of the slavery question, but it can scarcely be doubted that the well-known views of the Wesleys and of Whitfield remained for some at least the standard of right opinion, and that their declarations formed for these the rule of action. In 1842 a secession from the church took place, chiefly if not altogether on account of the question of slavery, and a number of abolitionist members of the uncompromising type founded a new church organization, which they called the "Wesleyan Methodist Connection of America." Slaveholders were excluded from fellowship in this body. Within two or three years the new organization had drawn away twenty thousand members from the old.[1] In 1844 a much larger secession took place on the same question, the occasion being the institution of proceedings before the General Conference against the Rev. James O. Andrew, D.D., a slaveholding bishop of the South. This so aggravated the Methodist Episcopal societies in the slave states that they withdrew and formed the Methodist Episcopal Church South. Among the members of the Wesleyan Methodist Connection and of the older society of the North there were a number of zealous underground operators. Indeed, it came to be said of the Wesleyans, as of the Quakers, that almost every neighborhood where a few of them lived was likely to be a station of the secret Road to Canada. It is probable that some of the Wesleyans at Wilmington, Ohio, coöperated with Quakers at that point. In Urbana, Ohio, there were Methodists of the two divisions engaged.[2] Service was also performed by Wesleyans at Tippecanoe, Deersville and Rocky Fort in Tuscarawas County,[3] and at Piqua, Miami County, Ohio.[4] In Iowa a number of Methodist ministers were engaged in the work.[5]

The third sect to which a considerable proportion of underground operators belonged was Calvinistic in its creed. All the various wings of Presbyterianism seem to have had representatives in this class of anti-slavery people. The sinfulness of slavery was a proposition that found uncompromising advocates among the Presbyterian ministers of the South in the early part of this century. In 1804 the Rev. James Gilliland removed from South Carolina to Brown County, Ohio, because he had been enjoined by his presbytery and synod "to be silent in the pulpit on the subject of the emancipation of the African."[6] Other ministers of prominence, like Thomas

[1] H. N. McTyeire, D.D., *History of Methodism*, 1887, pp. 375, 536, 601, 611.
[2] Conversation with Major J. C. Brand, Urbana, O., Aug. 13, 1894.
[3] Conversation with Thomas M. Hazlett, Freeport, Harrison Co., O., Aug. 18, 1895.
[4] Conversation with Mrs. Mary B. Carson, Piqua, O., Aug. 30, 1895.
[5] Letter of Professor F. L. Parker, Grinnell, Ia., Sept. 30, 1894.
[6] Wm. B. Sprague, D.D., *Annals of the American Pulpit*, Vol. IV, 1858, p. 137; Robert E. Thompson, D.D., *History of the Presbyterian Churches in the United States*, 1895, p. 122.

D. Baird, David Nelson and John Rankin, left the South because they were not free to speak against slavery. In 1818 the Presbyterian Church declared the system "inconsistent with the law of God and totally irreconcilable with the gospel of Christ." This teaching was afterwards departed from in 1845 when the Assembly confined its protest to admitting rather mildly that there was "evil connected with slavery," and declining to countenance "the traffic in slaves for the sake of gain; the separation of husbands and wives, parents and children, for the sake of filthy lucre or the convenience of the master; or cruel treatment of slaves in any respect." The dissatisfaction caused by this evident compromise led to the formation of a new church in 1847 by the "New School" Presbytery of Ripley, Ohio, and a part of the "Old School" Presbytery of Mahoning, Pennsylvania. This organization was called the Free Church, and by 1860 had extended as far west as Iowa.[1] It is not strange that the region in Ohio where the Free Presbyterian Church was founded was plentifully dotted with stations of the Underground Railroad, and that the house of the Rev. John Rankin, who was the leader of the movement, was known far and wide as a place of refuge for the fugitive slave.[2] At Savannah, Ashland County, Iberia, Morrow County, and a point near Millersburgh, Holmes County, Ohio, the work is associated with Free Presbyterian societies once existing in those neighborhoods.[3] In the northern part of Adams County, as also in the northern part of Logan County, Ohio, fugitives were received into the homes of Covenanters. Galesburg, Illinois, with its college was founded in 1837 by Presbyterians and Congregationalists, who united to form one religious society under the name of the "Presbyterian Church of Galesburg." Opposition to slavery was one of the conditions of membership in this organization from the beginning. This intense anti-slavery feeling caused the

---

[1] Robert E. Thompson, D.D., *History of the Presbyterian Churches in the United States*, 1895, pp. 136, 137.
[2] Address by J. C. Leggett, in a pamphlet entitled *Rev. John Rankin*, 1892, p. 9.
[3] Letter of Mrs. A. M. Buchanan, Savannah, O., 1893; conversation with Thomas L. Smith, Fredericksburg, Wayne Co., O., Aug. 15, 1895.

church to withdraw from the presbytery in 1855.[1] From the starting of the colony until the time of the War fugitives from Missouri were conducted thither with the certainty of obtaining protection. Thus Galesburg became, probably, the principal underground station in Illinois.[2] Joseph S. White, of New Castle, in western Pennsylvania, notes the circumstance that all the men with whom he acted in underground enterprises were Presbyterians.[3]

The religious centre in Ohio most renowned for the aid of refugees was the Congregational colony and college at Oberlin. The acquisition of a large anti-slavery contingent from Lane Seminary in 1835 caused the college to be known from that time on as a "hotbed of abolitionism." Fugitives were directed thither from points more or less remote, and during the period from 1835 to 1860 Oberlin was a busy station,[4] receiving passengers from at least five converging lines.[5] So notorious did the place become that a guide-board in the form of a fugitive running in the direction of the town was set up by the authorities on the Middle Ridge road, six miles north of Oberlin, and the sign of a tavern, four miles away, "was ornamented on its Oberlin face with a representation of a fugitive slave pursued by a tiger."[6] On account of the persistent ignoring of the law against harboring slaves by those connected with the institution, the existence of the college was put in jeopardy. Ex-President Fairchild relates that, "A Democratic legislature at different times agitated the question of repealing the college charter. The fourth and last attempt was made in 1843, when the bill for repeal was indefinitely postponed in the House by a vote of thirty-six to twenty-nine."[7] The anti-slavery influence of Oberlin went abroad with its

[1] Professor George Churchill, in *The Republican Register*, Galesburg, Ill., March 5, 1887.
[2] Charles C. Chapman & Co., *History of Knox County, Illinois*, p. 210.
[3] Joseph S. White, Note-book containing "Some Reminiscences of Slavery Times," New Castle, Pa., March 23, 1891.
[4] James H. Fairchild, D.D., *The Underground Railroad*, Vol. IV of publications of the Western Reserve Historical Society, Tract No. 87, p. 111.
[5] See the general map.
[6] James H. Fairchild, D.D., *Oberlin, the Colony and the College*, p. 117.
[7] *Ibid.*, p. 116. See also Henry Howe, *Historical Collections of Ohio*, Vol. II, p. 383.

students. Ex-President W. M. Brooks, of Tabor College, Iowa, a graduate of Oberlin, says, " The stations on the Underground Railroad in southwestern Iowa were in the region of Civil Bend, where the colony from Oberlin, Ohio, settled, which afterwards settled Tabor. . . . From this point (Civil Bend, now Percival) fugitives were brought to Tabor after 1852; here the entire population was in sympathy with the escaped fugitives; . . . there was scarcely a man in the community who was not ready to do anything that was needed to help fugitives on their way to Canada."[1] The families that founded Tabor were "almost all of them Congregationalists."[2] Professor L. F. Parker of Grinnell, Iowa, names Oberlin students in connection with Quakers as the chief groups in Iowa whose houses were open to fugitives.[3] Grinnell itself was first settled by people that were mainly Congregationalists.[4] From the time of its foundation (1854) it was an anti-slavery centre, "well known and eagerly sought by the few runaways who came from the meagre settlements southwest . . . in Missouri."[5]

There were, of course, members of other denominations that befriended the slave; thus, it is known that the Unitarian Seminary at Meadville, Pennsylvania, was a centre of underground work,[6] but, in general, the lack of information concerning the church connections of many of the company of persons with whom this chapter deals prevents the drawing of any inference as to whether these individuals acted independently or in conjunction with little bands of persons of their own faith.

There seems to have been no open appeal made to church organizations for help in behalf of fugitives except in Massachusetts. In 1851, and again in 1854, the Vigilance Committee of Boston deemed it wise to send out circulars to the clergymen of the commonwealth, requesting that contribu-

[1] Letter of President W. M. Brooks, Tabor, Ia., Oct. 11, 1894.
[2] I. B. Richman, *John Brown Among the Quakers, and Other Sketches*, p. 15.
[3] Letter of Professor L. F. Parker, Grinnell, Iowa, Sept. 30, 1894.
[4] J. B. Grinnell, *Men and Events of Forty Years*, p. 87.
[5] Letter of Professor L. F. Parker, Grinnell, Iowa, Sept. 30, 1894.
[6] Conversation with Professor Henry H. Barber, of Meadville, Pa., in Cambridge, Mass., June, 1897.

tions be taken by them to be applied in mitigation of the misery caused by the enactment of the Fugitive Slave Law. The boldness and originality of such an appeal, and more especially the evident purpose of its framers to create sentiment by this means among the religious societies, entitle it to consideration. The first circular was sent out soon after the enactment of the odious law, and the second soon after the passage of the Kansas-Nebraska Act. The results secured by the two circulars will be seen in the following letter from Francis Jackson, of Boston, to his fellow-townsmen and co-worker, the Rev. Theodore Parker.

BOSTON, Aug. 27, 1854.

THEODORE PARKER:

Dear Friend,— The contributions of the churches in behalf of the fugitive slaves I think have about all come in. I herewith inclose you a schedule thereof, amounting in all to about $800, being but *little more than half as much as they contributed in 1851.*

The Mass. Register published in January, 1854, states the number of Religious Societies to be 1,547 (made up of 471 Orthodox, 270 Methodist, and all others 239). We sent circulars to the whole 1,547; only 78 of them have responded — say 1 in 20 — from 130 Universalist societies, nothing, from 43 Episcopal $4, and 20 Friends $27 — the Baptists — four times as many of these societies have given now as gave in 1851, this may be because Brynes was a Baptist minister.

* * * * * * * *

The average amount contributed by 77 societies (deducting Frothingham of Salem) is $10 each; the 28th Congregationalist Church in this city did not take up a contribution, nevertheless, individual members thereof subscribed upwards of $300; they being *infidel* have not been reckoned with the churches.

Of the cities and large towns scarce any have contributed. Of the 90 and 9 in Boston all have gone astray but 2 — I have not heard of our circular being read in one of them; still it may have been. Those societies who have contributed, I judge were least able to do so.

FRANCIS JACKSON.[1]

The political affiliations of underground helpers before 1840 were, necessarily, with one or the other of the old

[1] Theodore Parker's *Scrap-book*, Boston Public Library.

parties — the Whig or the Democratic. As the Whig party was predominantly Northern, and as its sentiments were more distinctly anti-slavery than those of its rival, it is fair to suppose that the small band of early abolitionists were, most of them, allied with that party.[1] The Missouri Compromise in 1820, one may surmise, enabled those that were wavering in their position to ally themselves with the party that was less likely to make demands in the interests of the slave power. In 1840 opportunity was given abolitionists to take independent political action by the nomination of a national Liberty ticket. At that time, and again in 1844, many underground operators voted for the candidates of the Liberty party, and subsequently for the Free Soil nominees.[2]

But it is not to be supposed that all friends of the fugitive joined the political movement against slavery. Many there were that regarded party action with disfavor, preferring the method of moral suasion. These persons belonged to the Quakers, or to the Garrisonian abolitionists. The Friends or Quakers refused as far as possible to countenance slavery, and when the political development of the abolition cause came they regretted it, and their yearly meetings withheld their official sanction, so far as known, from every political organization. Nevertheless, there were some members of the Society of Friends that were swept into the current, and became active supporters of the Liberty party.[3] The most noted and influential of these was the anti-slavery poet, Whittier.[4] When, in 1860, the Republican party nominated Lincoln, "a large majority of the Friends, at least in the North and West, voted for him."[5]

The followers of Garrison that remained steadfast to the teachings and the example of their leader shunned all connection with the political abolitionist movement. Garrison

---

[1] This view agrees with the testimony gathered by correspondence from surviving abolitionists.

[2] This statement is based on a mass of correspondence.

[3] Professor A. C. Thomas on "The Society of Friends," in *American Church History*, Vol. XII, 1894, pp. 284, 285.

[4] Oliver Johnson, *William Lloyd Garrison and His Times*, 1879, p. 322.

[5] Professor A. C. Thomas, in *American Church History*, Vol. XII, p. 285.

never voted but once,[1] and by 1854 had gone so far in his denunciation of slavery that he burned the Constitution of the United States at an open-air celebration of the abolitionists at Framingham, Massachusetts.[2] To his dying day he seems to have believed "that the cause would have triumphed sooner, in a political sense, if the abolitionists had continued to act as one body, never yielding to the temptation of forming a political party, but pressing forward in the use of the same instrumentalities which were so potent from 1831 to 1840."[3]

The abolitionists were ill-judged by their contemporaries, and were frequently subjected to harsh language and occasionally to violent treatment by persons of supposed respectability. The weight of opprobrium they were called upon to bear tested their great strength of character. If the probity, integrity and moral courage of this abused class had been made the criteria of their standing they would have been held from the outset in high esteem by their neighbors. However, they lived to see the days of their disgrace turned into days of triumph. "The muse of history," says Rhodes, "has done full justice to the abolitionists. Among them were literary men, who have known how to present their cause with power, and the noble spirit of truthfulness pervades the abolition literature. One may search in vain for intentional misrepresentation. Abuse of opponents and criticism of motives are common enough, but the historians of the abolition movement have endeavored to relate a plain, honest tale; and the country has accepted them and their work at their true value. Moreover, a cause and its promoters that have been celebrated in the vigorous lines of Lowell and sung in the impassioned verse of Whittier will always be of perennial memory."[4]

Contempt was not the only hardship that the abolitionist had to face when he admitted the fleeing black man within his door, but he braved also the existing laws, and was some-

[1] *Life of Garrison*, by his children, Vol. I, p. 455.
[2] *Ibid.*, Vol. III, p. 412.
[3] Oliver Johnson, *William Lloyd Garrison and His Times*, p. 310.
[4] *History of the United States from the Compromise of 1850*, Vol. I, p. 75.

times compelled to suffer the consequences for disregarding the slaveholder's claim of ownership. In 1842 the prosecution of John Van Zandt, of Hamilton County, Ohio, was begun for attempting to aid nine slaves to escape. The case was tried first in the Circuit Court of the United States, and then taken by appeal to the Supreme Court. The suits were not concluded when the defendant died in May, 1847. The death of the plaintiff soon after left the case to be settled by administrators, who agreed that the costs, amounting to one thousand dollars, should be paid from the possessions of the defendant.[1] The judgments against Van Zandt under the Fugitive Slave Law amounted to seventeen hundred dollars.[2] In 1847 several members of a crowd that was instrumental in preventing the seizure of a colored family by the name of Crosswhite, at Marshall, Michigan, were indicted under the Fugitive Slave Law of 1793. Two trials followed, and at the second trial three persons were convicted, the verdict against them amounting, with expenses and costs, to six thousand dollars.[3] In 1848 Daniel Kauffman, of Cumberland County, Pennsylvania, sheltered a family of thirteen slaves in his barn, and gave them transportation northward. He was tried, and sentenced to pay two thousand dollars in fine and costs. Although this decision was reversed by the United States Supreme Court, a new suit was instituted in the Circuit Court of the United States and a judgment was rendered against Kauffman amounting with costs to more than four thousand dollars. This sum was paid, in large part if not altogether, by contributions.[4] In 1854 Rush R. Sloane, a lawyer of Sandusky, Ohio, was tried for enabling seven fugitives to escape after arrest by their pursuers. The two claimants of the slaves instituted suit, but one only obtained a judgment, which amounted to three thousand dollars and

[1] Letter of N. L. Van Sandt, Clarinda, Iowa. (Mr. N. L. Van Sandt is the son of John Van Zandt.) See also Wilson's *Rise and Fall of the Slave Power*, Vol. I, pp. 475, 476; T. R. Cobb, *Historical Sketches of Slavery*, p. 207; M. G. McDougall, *Fugitive Slaves*, p. 42.
[2] See pp. 274, 275, Chapter IX.
[3] Pamphlet proposing a "Defensive League of Freedom," signed by Ellis Gray Loring and others, of Boston, pp. 5, 6. See Chapter IX, p. 275.
[4] *Ibid.*

costs.[1] The arrest of the fugitive, Anthony Burns, in Boston, in the same year, was the occasion for indignation meetings at Faneuil and Meionaon Halls, which terminated in an attempt to rescue the unfortunate negro. Theodore Parker, Wendell Phillips and T. W. Higginson took a conspicuous part in these proceedings, and were indicted with others for riot. When the first case was taken up the counsel for the defence made a motion that the indictment be quashed. This was sustained by the court, and the affair ended by all the cases being dismissed.[2]

These and other similar cases arising from the attempted enforcement of the Fugitive Slave Act in various parts of the country led to the proposal of a Defensive League of Freedom. A pamphlet, issued soon after the rendition of Burns, by Ellis Gray Loring, Samuel Cabot, Jr., Henry J. Prentiss, John A. Andrew and Samuel G. Howe, of Boston, and James Freeman Clarke, of Roxbury, Massachusetts, stated the object of the proposed league to be "to secure all persons claimed as fugitives from slavery, and to all persons accused of violating the Fugitive Slave Bill the fullest legal protection; and also indemnify all such persons against costs, fines, and expenses, whenever they shall seem to deserve such indemnification." The league was to act as a "society of mutual protection and every member was to assume his portion of such penalties as would otherwise fall with crushing weight on a few individuals." Subscriptions were to be made by the members of the organization, and five per cent of these subscriptions was to be called for any year when it was needed.[3] How much service this association actually performed, or whether, indeed, it got beyond the stage of being merely proposed is not known; in any event, the fact is worth noting that men of marked ability, distinction and social connection

[1] 5 McLean's *United States Reports*, p. 64 *et seq.*; see also *The Firelands Pioneer*, July, 1888; account by Rush R. Sloane, pp. 47–49; account by H. F. Paden, pp. 21, 22; Chapter IX, pp. 276, 277.

[2] *Commonwealth*, June 28, 1854; M. G. McDougall, *Fugitive Slaves*, pp. 45, 46; Wilson, *Rise and Fall of the Slave Power*, Vol. II, pp. 443, 444. See Chapter X, pp. 331–333.

[3] Pamphlet proposing a "Defensive League of Freedom," pp. 1, 3, 11 and 12.

were forming societies, like the Defensive League of Freedom, and the various vigilance committees, for the purpose of defeating the Fugitive Slave Act.

Among the underground helpers there are a number of notable persons that have admitted with seeming satisfaction their complicity in disregarding the Fugitive Slave Law. A letter from Frederick Douglass, the famous Maryland bondman and anti-slavery orator, says: "My connection with the Underground Railroad began long before I left the South, and was continued as long as slavery continued, whether I lived in New Bedford, Lynn [both in Massachusetts], or Rochester, N.Y. In the latter place I had as many as eleven fugitives under my roof at one time."[1] In his autobiography Mr. Douglass declares concerning his work in this connection: "My agency was all the more exciting and interesting because not altogether free from danger. I could take not a step in it without exposing myself to fine and imprisonment, . . . but in face of this fact, I can say, I never did more congenial, attractive, fascinating, and satisfactory work."[2] Dr. Alexander M. Ross, a Canadian physician and naturalist, who has received the decorations of knighthood from several of the monarchs of Europe in recognition of his scientific discoveries, spent a considerable part of his time from 1856 to 1862 in spreading a knowledge of the routes leading to Canada among the slaves of the South.[3] Dr. Norton S. Townshend, one of the organizers of the Ohio State University and for years professor of agriculture in that institution, acted as a conductor on the Underground Railroad while he was a student of medicine in Cincinnati, Ohio.[4] Dr. Jared P. Kirtland, a distinguished physician and scientist of Ohio, kept a station in Poland, Mahoning County, where he resided from 1823 to 1837.[5]

Harriet Beecher Stowe gained the intimate knowledge of

[1] Letter of Frederick Douglass, Anacostia, D.C., March 27, 1893.
[2] *Life of Frederick Douglass*, 1881, p. 271.
[3] Ross, *Recollections and Experiences of an Abolitionist*, pp. 30–44, 67–71, 121–132; also letters of Alexander M. Ross, Toronto, Ont.
[4] Conversations with Professor N. S. Townshend, Columbus, O.
[5] Conversation with Miss Mary L. Morse, Poland, O., Aug. 11, 1892; letter of Mrs. Emma Kirtland Hine, Poland, O., Jan. 23, 1897.

FREDERICK DOUGLASS.

the methods of the friends of the slave she displays in *Uncle Tom's Cabin* through her association with some of the most zealous abolitionists of southern Ohio. Her own house on Walnut Hills, Cincinnati, was a refuge whence persons whose types are portrayed in George and Eliza, the boy Jim and his mother, were guided by her husband and brother a portion of the way towards Canada.[1] Colonel Thomas Wentworth Higginson, the essayist and author, while stationed as the pastor of a free church in Worcester, Massachusetts, from 1852 to 1858, often had fugitives directed to his care. In a recent letter he writes of having received on one occasion a "consignment of a young white slave woman with two white children" from the Rev. Samuel J. May, who had put her "into the hands, for escort, of one of the most pro-slavery men in Worcester." The pro-slavery man, of course, did not have a suspicion that he was acting as conductor on the Underground Railroad.[2]

Joshua R. Giddings, for twenty years in Congress an ardent advocate of the abolition of slavery, kept a particular chamber in his house at Jefferson, Ohio, for the use of refugees.[3] Sometimes when passing through Alliance, Ohio, Mr. Giddings found opportunity to call upon his friend, I. Newton Peirce, to whom he contributed money for the transportation of runaway slaves by rail from that point to Cleveland.[4] What his views were of the irritating law of 1850, he declared on the floor of the House of Representatives, February 11, 1852, in the following words: " . . . Let me say to Southern men; It is your privilege to catch your own slaves, if any one catches them. . . . When you ask us to pay the expenses of arresting your slaves, or to give the President authority to appoint officers to do that dirty work, give them power to compel our people to give chase to the panting bondman, you overstep the bounds of the Constitution, and there we meet you, and there we stand and there we shall remain. We shall protest

---

[1] See Chapter X, pp.
[2] Letter of T. W. Higginson, Dublin, N.H., July 24, 1896.
[3] Conversation with J. Addison Giddings, Jefferson, O., Aug. 9, 1892.
[4] Letter of I. Newton Peirce, Folcroft, Sharon Hill P.O., Pa., Feb. 1, 1893.

against such indignity; we shall proclaim our abhorrence of such a law. Nor can you seal or silence our voices."[1]

Thaddeus Stevens, a leading lawyer of Pennsylvania, who rendered the cause of abolition distinguished service in Congress, where he gained the title of the "great commoner," entered upon the practice of his profession at Gettysburg in 1816, and soon became known as a friend of escaping slaves. His removal to Lancaster in 1842 did not take him off the line of flight, and he continued to act as a helper. The woman that "kept house for him for more than twenty years, and nursed him at the close of his life, was one of the slaves he helped to freedom."[2]

James M. Ashley, member of Congress from Ohio for over nine years, and his successor in the House, Richard Mott, a Quaker, were confederates in their violation of the Slave Act at Toledo, Ohio. Mr. Ashley began his service in behalf of the blacks early in life. As a youth of seventeen in Kentucky, he helped two companies across the Ohio River, one company of seven persons, and the other of five.[3] Sidney Edgerton, who was elected to Congress from Ohio on the Free Soil ticket in 1858, and four years after was appointed governor of Montana Territory by President Lincoln, assisted his father in the befriending of slaves at Tallmadge, Summit County, Ohio.[4] Jacob M. Howard, afterwards United States senator from Michigan, was one of the principal operators at Detroit.[5] General Samuel Fessenden, of Maine, who received the nomination of the Liberty party for the governorship of his state, and later for Congress, and was during forty years the leading member of the bar in Maine, gave escaped bondmen reaching Portland a hearty welcome to his house on India Street.[6] In Vermont there were a number of men prominent in public affairs that were actively engaged in underground enterprises.

[1] George W. Julian, *The Life of Joshua R. Giddings*, 1892, p. 289.
[2] Smedley, *Underground Railroad*, pp. 36, 38, 46.
[3] Conversation with the Hon. James M. Ashley, Toledo, O., July, 1894.
[4] Conversation with ex-Governor Sidney Edgerton, Akron, O., Aug. 16, 1895.
[5] Conversation with Judge J. W. Finney, Detroit, Mich., July 27, 1895.
[6] Letter of S. T. Pickard, Portland, Me., Nov. 18, 1893.

Colonel Jonathan P. Miller, of Montpelier, who went to Greece, and assisted that country in its uprising in the twenties, served as a member of the Vermont legislature in 1833, and took part in the World's Anti-Slavery Convention in 1840, was among the early helpers in New England. Lawrence Brainerd, for several years candidate for governor of Vermont, and later chosen to the United States Senate as a Free Soiler, gave shelter to the wanderers at St. Albans, where they were almost within sight of "the Promised Land."[1] Others were the Rev. Alvah Sabin, elected to Congress in 1853, who kept a station at the town of Georgia, the Hon. Joseph Poland of Montpelier, the Hon. William Sowles of Swanton, the Hon. John West of Morristown and the Hon. A. J. Russell of Troy.[2]

Gerrit Smith, the famous philanthropist, kept open house for fugitives in a fine old mansion at Peterboro, New York. He was one of the prime movers in the organization of the Liberty party at Arcade, New York, in 1840, and was its candidate for the presidency in 1848 and in 1852. He was elected to Congress in 1853 and served one term. It is said that during the decade 1850 to 1860 he "aided habitually in the escape of fugitive slaves and paid the legal expenses of persons accused of infractions of the Fugitive Slave Law."[3] The Rev. Owen Lovejoy, brother of the martyr Elijah P. Lovejoy, served four terms in the national House of Representatives. On one occasion he was taunted by some pro-slavery members of the House with being a "nigger-stealer." In a speech made February 21, 1859, Mr. Lovejoy, referring to these accusations, said: "Is it desired to call attention to this fact — of my assisting fugitive slaves? . . . Owen Lovejoy lives at Princeton, Illinois, three-quarters of a mile east of the village, and he aids every fugitive that comes to his door and asks it. Thou invisible demon of slavery, dost thou think to cross my humble threshold, and forbid me to give bread to the hungry and shelter to the houseless! I bid you

---

[1] Letter of Aldis O. Brainerd, St. Albans, Vt., Oct. 21, 1895.
[2] Letter of Joseph Poland, Montpelier, Vt., April 7, 1897.
[3] O. B. Frothingham, *Life of Gerrit Smith; National Cyclopedia of American Biography*, Vol. II, pp. 322, 323.

defiance in the name of my God!"[1] Josiah B. Grinnell, who represented a central Iowa district in the Thirty-eighth and the Thirty-ninth congresses, had a chamber in his house at Grinnell that came to be called the "liberty room." John Brown, while on his way to Canada with a band of Missouri slaves, in the winter of 1858–1859, stacked his arms in this room, and his company of fugitives slept there.[2] Mr. Grinnell relates of the members of this party, "They came at night, and were the darkest, saddest specimens of humanity I have ever seen, glad to camp on the floor, while the veteran was a night guard, with his dog and a miniature arsenal ready for use on alarm. . . ."[3]

Thurlow Weed, the distinguished journalist and political manager, even in his busiest hours had time to afford relief to the underground applicant. One who knew Mr. Weed intimately relates the following incident: "On one occasion when several eminent gentlemen were waiting [to see the journalist] they were surprised and at first much vexed, by seeing a negro promptly admitted. The negro soon reappeared, and hastily left the house, when it was learned that he was a runaway slave, and had been aided in his flight for liberty by the man who was too busy to attend to Cabinet officers, but had time to say words of encouragement and present means of support to a flying fugitive."[4] Sydney Howard Gay, for several years managing editor of the *New York Tribune*, and subsequently on the editorial staff of the *New York Post* and the *Chicago Tribune*, was an efficient agent of the Underground Railroad while in charge of the *Anti-Slavery Standard*, which he conducted in New York City from 1844 to 1857.[5]

Among the clergymen that made it a part of their religious duty to minister to the needs of the exiles from the South, were John Rankin, Samuel J. May and Theodore Parker.

---

[1] Pamphlet of the Rev. D. Heagle, entitled *The Great Anti-Slavery Agitator, Hon. Owen Lovejoy*, pp. 16, 17, 34, 35.
[2] J. B. Grinnell, *Men and Events of Forty Years*, p. 207.
[3] *Ibid.*, pp. 217, 218.
[4] T. W. Barnes, *Life of Thurlow Weed*, 1884, Vol. II, p. 238.
[5] Wilson, *Rise and Fall of the Slave Power*, Vol. II, p. 52.

Mr. Rankin, a native of Tennessee, early developed his anti-slavery views in Kentucky, where from 1817 to 1821 he served as pastor of two Presbyterian churches at the town of Carlisle. During the next forty-four years he resided at Ripley, Ohio, in a neighborhood frequented by runaways.[1] Doubtless he became a patron of these midnight visitors at the time of his location in Ripley. In 1828 he established himself in a house situated upon the crest of a hill just back of the town and overlooking the Ohio River. For many years the lights beaming through the windows of this parsonage were hailed by slaves fleeing from the soil of Kentucky as beacons to guide them to a haven of safety.[2]

Samuel J. May, for many years a prominent minister in the Unitarian Church, writes: "So long ago as 1834, when I was living in the eastern part of Connecticut, I had fugitives addressed to my care. . . . Even after I came to reside in Syracuse [New York] I had much to do as a station-keeper or conductor on the Underground Railroad, until slavery was abolished by the proclamation of President Lincoln. . . . Fugitives came to me from Maryland, Virginia, Kentucky, Tennessee and Louisiana. They came, too, at all hours of day and night, sometimes comfortably, yes, and even handsomely clad, but generally in clothes every way unfit to be worn, and in some instances too unclean and loathsome to be admitted into my house."[3]

Theodore Parker, the learned theologian and iconoclast of Boston, often deserted his study that he might work in the cause of humanity. In his Journal, under the date October 23, 1850, Mr. Parker wrote: ". . . The first business of the anti-slavery men is to help the fugitives; we, like Christ, are to seek and save that which is lost."[4] In an unsigned note written in 1851 to his friend Dr. Francis, Mr. Parker says:—

. . . I have got some nice books (old ones) coming across the water. But, alas me! such is the state of the poor fugitive

---

[1] William Birney, *James G. Birney and His Times*, p. 435.
[2] J. C. Leggett, in a pamphlet entitled *Rev. John Rankin*, 1892, pp. 8, 9; see also *History of Brown County, Ohio*, p. 443.
[3] *Recollections of the Anti-Slavery Conflict*, p. 297.
[4] John Weiss, *Life and Correspondence of Theodore Parker*, 1864, p. 95.

slaves, that I must attend to living men, and not to dead books, and all this winter my time has been occupied with these poor souls. The Vigilance Committee appointed me spiritual counsellor of all fugitive slaves in Massachusetts while in peril. . . . The Fugitive Slave Law has cost me some months of time already. I have refused about sixty invitations to lecture and delayed the printing of my book — for that! Truly the land of the pilgrims is in great disgrace!

Yours truly.[1]

Among the underground workers there were two whose principal object in life seems to have been to assist fugitive slaves. These two organizers of underground travel were Levi Coffin, of Cincinnati, Ohio, and Thomas Garrett, of Wilmington, Delaware, both lifelong members of the Society of Friends, both capable business men, both able to number the unfortunates they had succored in terms of thousands.

Thomas Garrett was born in Pennsylvania in 1789, and espoused the cause of emancipation at the age of eighteen, when a colored woman in the employ of his father's family was kidnapped. He succeeded in rescuing the woman from the hands of her abductors, and from that time on made it his special mission to aid negroes in their attempts to gain freedom. In 1822 he removed to Wilmington, Delaware, and during the next forty years his efforts in behalf of fugitives were unremitting. He was not so fortunate as Levi Coffin in escaping the penalties of the Fugitive Slave Law; an open violation of the law got him into difficulty in 1848. He was tried on four counts before Judge Taney, and his entire property was swallowed up in fines amounting to eight thousand dollars. There is a tradition that the presiding judge admonished Garrett to take his loss as a lesson and in the future to desist from breaking the laws; whereupon the aged Quaker stoutly replied: "Judge, thou hast not left me a dollar, but I wish to say to thee, and to all in this court-room, that if any one knows of a fugitive who wants a shelter and a friend, send him to Thomas Garrett and he will befriend him."[2] Al-

[1] John Weiss, *Life and Correspondence of Theodore Parker*, 1864, p. 96.
[2] Lillie B. C. Wyman, in *New England Magazine*, March, 1896, p. 112; William Still, *Underground Railroad Records*, pp. 623-641; R. C. Smedley,

though sixty years of age when misfortune befel him, Mr. Garrett was successful in again acquiring a competence through the kindness of fellow-townsmen in advancing him capital with which to make a fresh start. Though satisfied, he was wont to think that his real work in life was never finished. "The war came a little too soon for my business. I wanted to help off three thousand slaves. I had only got up to twenty-seven hundred!"

Mr. Coffin was a native of North Carolina. Born in 1798, he was while still a boy moved to assist in the escape of slaves by witnessing the cruel treatment the negroes were compelled to endure. In 1826 he settled in Wayne County, Indiana, on the line of the Underground Road, and such was his activity that his house at New Garden (now Fountain City) soon became the converging point of three principal routes from Kentucky. In 1847 Mr. Coffin removed to Cincinnati for the purpose of opening a store where goods produced by free labor only should be sold. His relations with the humane work were maintained, and the genial but fearless Quaker came to be known generally by the fictitious but happy title, President of the Underground Railroad. It has been said of Mr. Coffin that "for thirty-three years he received into his house more than one hundred slaves every year."[1] In 1863 the Quaker philanthropist assisted in the establishment of the Freedmen's Bureau. In the following year and again in 1867, he visited Europe as agent for the Western Freedmen's Aid Commission. When the adoption of the Fifteenth Amendment of the Constitution was celebrated in Cincinnati by colored citizens and their friends, Mr. Coffin was one of those called upon by the chairman to address the great meeting. In response, the veteran station-keeper explained how he had obtained the title of President of the Underground Road. He said, "The title was given to me by slave-hunters, who could not find their fugitive slaves after they got into my hands. I accepted the office thus conferred upon me, and . . . endeavored to perform my

Underground Railroad, pp. 237-245; M. G. McDougall, *Fugitive Slaves*, p. 60.
[1] *Reminiscences of Levi Coffin*, 2d ed., p. 694.

duty faithfully. Government has now taken the work out of our hands. The stock of the Underground Railroad has gone down in the market, the business is spoiled, the road is now of no further use."[1] He then amid much applause resigned his office, and declared the operations of the Underground Railroad at an end.

[1] *Reminiscences of Levi Coffin*, p. 712.

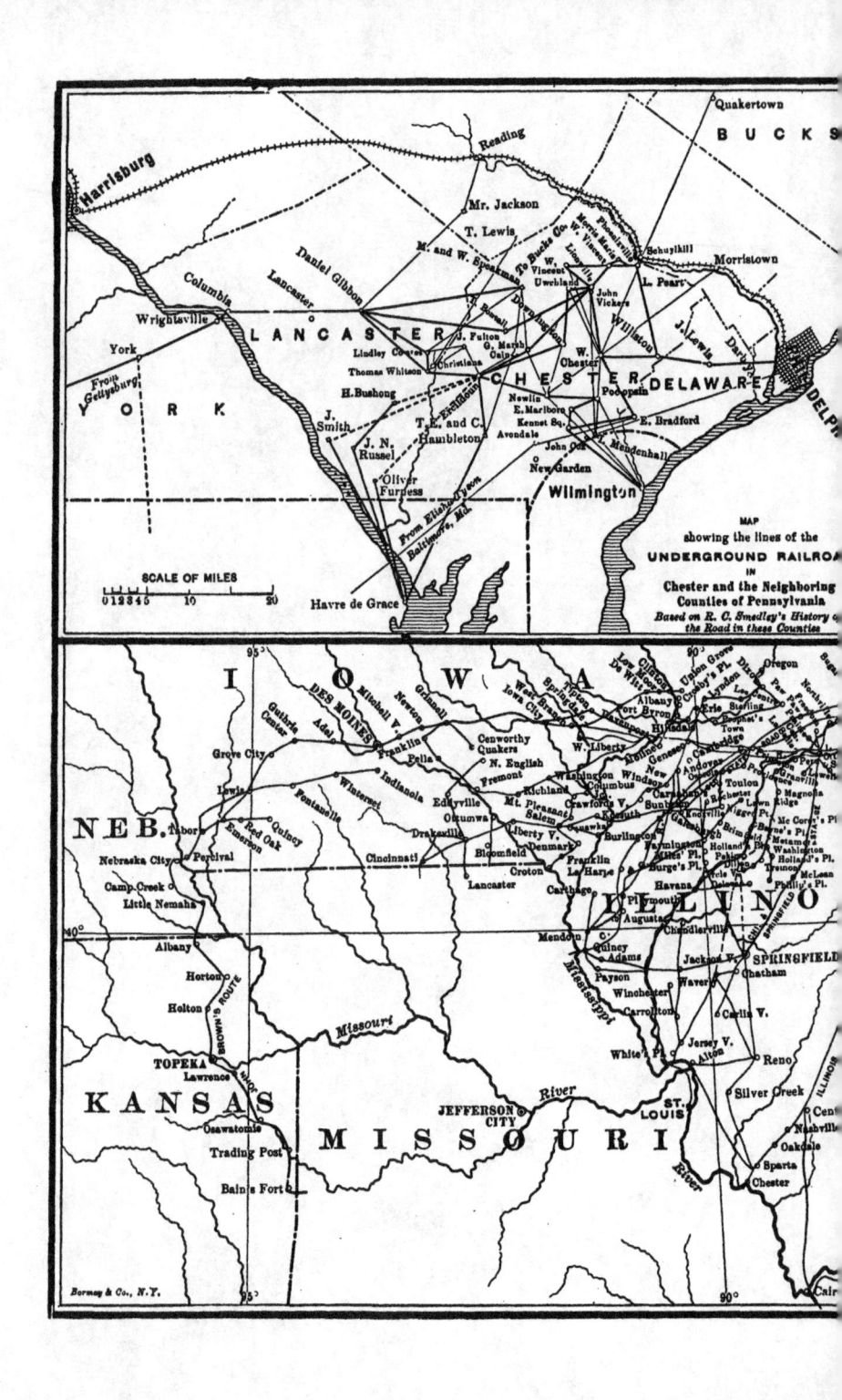

MAP
showing the lines of the
UNDERGROUND RAILROAD
IN
Chester and the Neighboring
Counties of Pennsylvania
Based on R. C. Smedley's History of
the Road in these Counties

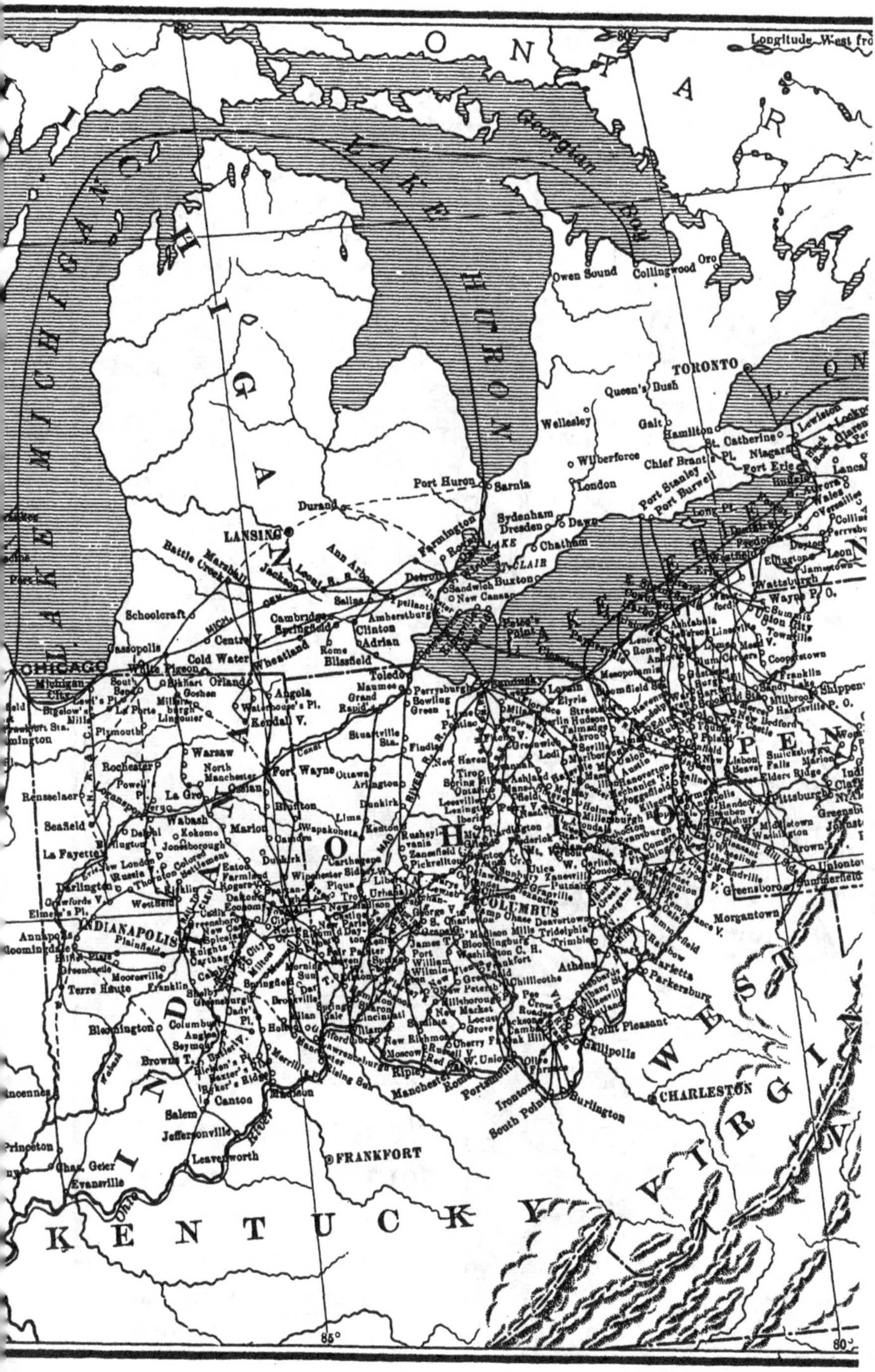

Longitude West fro
ONTARIO
LAKE HURON
Georgian Bay
LAKE MICHIGAN
MICHIGAN
INDIANA
OHIO
PEN
WEST VIRGINIA
KENTUCKY
Owen Sound
Collingwood
Oro
TORONTO
Queen's Bush
Wellesley
Galt
Hamilton
St. Catherine
Niagara
Chief Brant's Pl.
Wilberforce
London
Port Stanley
Port Burwell
Fort Erie
Port Huron
Sarnia
Sydenham
Dresden
Chatham
Buxton
Sandwich
New Canaan
Amherstburg
Durand
LANSING
Battle Creek
Marshall
Jackson
Ann Arbor
Farmington
Detroit
Schoolcraft
Cambridge
Springfield
Centre V.
Clinton
Adrian
Cassopolis
Cold Water
Wheatland
Rome
Blissfield
CHICAGO
White Pigeon
Orland
Michigan City
South Bend
Goshen
Angola
Toledo
Maumee
Perrysburgh
Grand Rapids
Bowling Green
Sandusky
Lorain
Elyria
La Porte
Plymouth
Kendall V.
Waterhouse's Pl.
Warsaw
Rochester
North Manchester
Fort Wayne
Ossian
Bluffton
Ottawa
Arlington
Findlay
Stuartville Sta.
Rensselaer
Logansport
Wabash
Kokomo
Jonesborough
Marion
Seafield
La Fayette
Darlington
Crawfords V.
Wapakoneta
Lima
Dunkirk
Kenton
Rushsylvania
Zanesfield
Pickrelltown
INDIANAPOLIS
Plainfield
Annapolis
Greencastle
Terre Haute
Mooresville
Franklin
Shelbyville
Greensburgh
Columbus
Seymour
Bloomington
Browns T.
Salem
Canton
Jeffersonville
Leavenworth
Evansville
Chas. Geier
Princeton
Madison
Rising Sun
Lawrenceburgh
Brookville
Springfield
Piqua
Troy
Urbana
Sidney
COLUMBUS
Chase
Deavertown
Tridelphia
Trimble
Athens
Washington C. H.
Bloomingburg
Chillicothe
Cincinnati
Hillsborough
New Market
Locust Grove
Ripley
Manchester
Portsmouth
Ironton
South Point
Burlington
Gallipolis
Point Pleasant
Parkersburg
Marietta
CHARLESTON
FRANKFORT
Morgantown
Greensboro
Uniontown
Summerfield
Pittsburgh
Washington
Middletown
Brownsville
Lisbon
Beaver
Elders Ridge
Mesopotamia
Bloomfield
Akron
Lodi
Wooster
Ashland
Mansfield
Mount Vernon
Zanesville
Cambridge
Sewickley
Meadville
Union City
Summit
Wattsburgh
Jamestown
Franklin
Sandy Lake
Shippen
Harrisville
Cooperstown
Townville
Linesville
Ashtabula
Dayton
Leon
Ellington
Westfield
Fredonia
Buffalo
Aurora
Wales
Lockport
Lewiston
Lancaster
Versailles
85°
80°

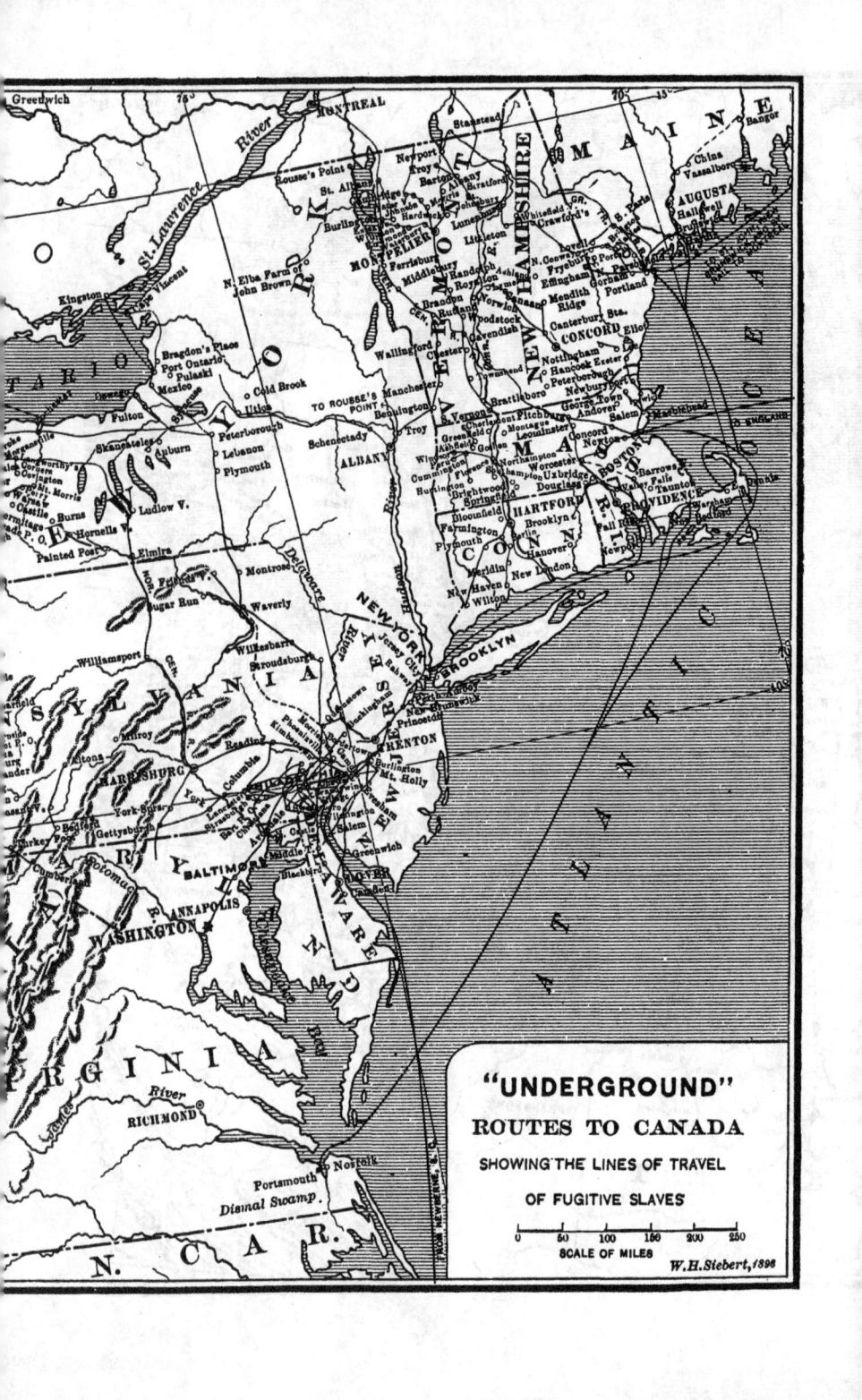

"UNDERGROUND" ROUTES TO CANADA

SHOWING THE LINES OF TRAVEL OF FUGITIVE SLAVES

0 50 100 150 200 250
SCALE OF MILES

W. H. Siebert, 1896

CHAPTER V

STUDY OF THE MAP OF THE UNDERGROUND RAILROAD SYSTEM

THERE are many features of the Underground Railroad that can best be understood by means of a geographical representation of the system. Such a representation it has been possible to make by piecing together the scraps of information in regard to various routes and parts of routes gathered from the reminiscences of a large number of abolitionists. The more or less limited area in which each agent operated was the field within which he was not only willing, but was usually anxious, to confine his knowledge of underground activities. Ignorance of one's accomplices beyond a few adjoining stations was naturally felt to be a safeguard. The local character of the information resulting from such precautions places the investigator under the necessity of patiently studying his materials for what may be called the cumulative evidence in regard to the geography of the system. It is because the evidence gathered has been cumulative and corroborative that a general map can be prepared. But a map thus constructed cannot, of course, be considered complete, for it cannot be supposed that after the lapse of a generation representatives of all the important lines and branches could be discovered. Nevertheless, however much the map may fall short of showing the system in its completeness, it will be found to help the reader materially in his attempt to realize the extent and importance of this movement.

The underground system, in accordance with the statement of James Freeman Clarke, is commonly understood to have extended from Kentucky and Virginia across Ohio, and from Maryland through Pennsylvania, New York and New England to Canada.[1] But this description is inadequate, for it fails to include the states west of Ohio. Henry Wilson extends the field westward by asserting that the "territory embraced by the Middle States and all the Western States east of the Mississippi . . . was dotted over with 'stations,'" and "covered with a network of imaginary routes, not found . . . in the railway guides or on the railway maps;"[2] and in another place he quotes the Rev. Asa Turner, a home missionary, who went to Illinois in 1830, who says: "Lines were formed through Iowa and Illinois, and passengers were carried from station to station . . . till they reached the Canada line."[3] The association of Kansas with the two states just named as a channel for the escape of runaways from the southwestern slave section, is made by Mr. Richard J. Hinton.[4] The addition of one other state, New Jersey, is necessary to complete the list of Northern states involved in the Underground Railroad system.[5] This region, which forms nearly one quarter of the present area of the Union, constituted the irregular zone of free soil intervening between Southern slavery and Canadian liberty.

The conditions that determined the number and distribution of stations throughout this region are clearly discernible even in the incomplete data with which we are forced to be content. It is safe to assert that in Ohio the conditions favorable to the development of a large number of stations, and the dissemination of these throughout the state, existed in a measure and combination not reproduced in the case of any other state. Ohio's geographical boundary gave it a long line of contact with slave territory. It bordered Kentucky with about one hundred and sixty miles of river frontage; and Virginia with perhaps two hundred and twenty-five miles or more, and crossings were made at almost any point. The character of the early settlements of Ohio is a factor that must not be overlooked. The northern and eastern parts of the

[1] *Anti-Slavery Days*, p. 81; M. G. McDougall, *Fugitive Slaves*, p. 61.
[2] *Rise and Fall of the Slave Power in America*, Vol. II, p. 66.
[3] *Ibid.*, p. 68.
[4] *John Brown and His Men*, p. 173.
[5] See pp. 123-125, this chapter.

state were dotted over with many little communities where
New England ideas prevailed; the southern and southwestern
parts came in time to be well sprinkled with the homes of
Quakers, Covenanters and anti-slavery Southerners and some
negroes; the central and southeastern portions contained a
number of Quaker settlements. The remote position and
sparse settlement of the northwestern section of the state
probably explain the failure to find many traces of routes in
that region. Family ties, church fellowship, an aggressive
anti-slavery leadership,— journalistic and political,— the leav-
ening influence of institutions like Oberlin College, Western
Reserve College and Geneva College, all contributed to propa-
gate a sentiment that was ready to support the fleeing slave;
and thus Ohio became netted over with a large number of
interlacing lines of escape for fugitive slaves. The western
portions of Pennsylvania and New York, and the eastern portion of Indiana shared with Ohio these favorable conditions,
and one is not surprised to find many stations in these regions.
The same is true of northern and west-central Illinois, where
many persons of New England descent settled. The few
lines known in southwestern Illinois were developed by a few
Covenanter communities. The geographical position of the
most southern portions of Illinois and Indiana determined the
character of the population settling there, and thus rendered
underground enterprises in those regions more than ordinarily
dangerous. There may have been stations scattered through
those parts, but if so, one can scarcely hope now to discover
them. The great number of routes in southeastern Pennsylvania, and the stream of slave emigration flowing through
New Jersey to New York are to be attributed largely to the
untiring activity of a host of Quakers, assisted by some
negroes. The coöperation of some zealous station-keepers
in the neighboring slave territory seems to account partly for
the multitude of stations that appear upon the map between
the lower Susquehanna and Delaware rivers. Whether there
was any underground work done in the central and northern
parts of Pennsylvania is not known; the indications are that
there was not much; the stations said to have existed at
Milroy, Altoona, Work's Place and Smicksburg probably

connected with lines running in a northwesterly direction to Lake Erie. This is known to have been true of the stations at Greensburg, Indiana, Clearfield and intermediate points, which were linked in with stations leading to Meadville and Erie. The remoteness of New York and of the New England states from the slaveholding section explains the comparatively small number of stations found in those states. Iowa, which bordered on slave territory, had only a small number of stations, for it was a new region, not long open to occupation; and only the southern part of the state was in the direct line of travel, which here was mostly eastward. There were a few places of deportation in southeastern Wisconsin for fugitives that had avoided Chicago, and followed the lake-shore or the Illinois River farther northward. A rather narrow strip of Michigan, adjoining Indiana and Ohio, was dotted with stations.

There were friends of the discontented slave in the South as well as in the North, although it cannot be said, upon the basis of the small amount of evidence at hand, that these were sufficient in number or so situated as to maintain regular lines of escape northward. Doubtless many acts of kindness to slaves were performed by individual Southerners, but those were not, in most of the cases, known as the acts of persons coöperating to help the slave from point to point until freedom and safety should be reached. That there were regular helpers in the South engaged in concerted action, Samuel J. May, a station-keeper of wide information concerning the Road, freely asserts. In 1869 he wrote, "There have always been scattered throughout the slaveholding states individuals who have abhorred slavery, and have pitied the victims of our American despotism. These persons have known, or have taken pains to find out, others at convenient distances northward from their abodes who sympathized with them in commiserating the slaves. These sympathizers have known or heard of others of like mind still farther north, who again have had acquaintances in the free states that they knew would help the fugitive on his way to liberty. Thus lines of friends at longer or shorter distances were formed from many parts of the South to the very borders of Canada. . . . "[1] It is not easy to substantiate this statement; and all that will be attempted here is the presentation of such examples as have been found of underground work on the part of persons living south of Mason and Dixon's line. Mr. Stephen B. Weeks is authority for the statement that "Vestal Coffin organized the Underground Railroad near the present Guilford College in 1819," and that "Addison Coffin, his son, entered its service as a conductor in early youth. . . ."[2] Levi Coffin, Vestal's cousin, helped many slaves from this region to reach the North before he moved to Indiana in 1826.[3] In Delaware there seems to have been a well-defined route upon which the houses of John Hunn, of Middletown,[4] Ezekiel Hunn, of Camden, and Thomas Garrett, of Wilmington,[5] were important stations. John Hunn speaks of himself as having been "superintendent of the Underground Railroad from Wilmington down the Peninsula."[6] Maryland also had its line — perhaps its lines — of Road. One route ran overland from Washington, D.C., to Philadelphia. Mr. W. B. Williams, of Charlotte, Michigan, throws some light on this route. He says, "My uncle, Jacob Bigelow, was for several years previous to the war a resident of Washington, D.C. He was an abolitionist, and general manager of the Underground Railway from Washington to Philadelphia. . . ."[7] Mr. Robert Purvis tells of two market-women that were agents of the Underground Road in Baltimore, forwarding fugitives to the Vigilance Committee with which he was connected in Philadelphia.[8] The Quaker City was also a central station for points still farther south. Vessels engaged in the lumber trade plying between Newberne, North Carolina, and Philadelphia, were often supplied with slave passengers by the son of a slaveholder living at Newberne.[9]

---

[1] *Recollections of the Anti-Slavery Conflict*, pp. 296, 297.
[2] *Southern Quakers and Slavery*, p. 242.
[3] *Ibid.*, p. 242. See also *Reminiscences of Levi Coffin*, pp. 12-31.
[4] Smedley, *Underground Railroad*, pp. 238, 244. [5] *Ibid.*, p. 326.
[6] Letter of John Hunn, Wyoming, Del., Sept. 16, 1893.
[7] In the *Key to Uncle Tom's Cabin* is the facsimile of a letter addressed to him by a slave, pp. 171, 172.
[8] R. C. Smedley, *Underground Railroad*, p. 355, letter from Robert Purvis printed therein. [9] Chapter III, p. 68.

A slave at Petersburg, Virginia, was agent for that section of country, directing fugitives to William Still in Philadelphia.[1] Eliza Bains, a slave-woman of Portsmouth, Virginia, sent numbers of her people to Boston and New Bedford by boat.[2] Frederick Douglass declared that his connection with the Underground Railroad began long before he left the South.[3] Harriet Tubman, the abductor, made use of stations at Camden, Dover, Blackbird, Middleton and New Castle in the State of Delaware on her way to Wilmington and Philadelphia.[4] The testimony of these various witnesses seems to show that underground routes existed in the South, but it is not sufficient in amount to enable one to trace extended courses of travel through the slaveholding states.

It is apparent from the map that the numerous tributaries of the Ohio and the great valleys of the Appalachian range afforded many tempting paths of escape. These natural routes from slavery have been recognized and defined by a recent writer.[5] "One," he says, " was that of the coast south of the Potomac, whose almost continuous line of swamps from the vicinity of Norfolk, Va., to the northern border of Florida afforded a refuge for many who could not escape and became 'marooned' in their depths, while giving facility to the more enduring to work their way out to the north star land. The great Appalachian range and its abutting mountains were long a rugged, lonely, but comparatively safe route to freedom. It was used, too, for many years. Doubtless a knowledge of that fact, for John Brown was always an active railroad man, had very much to do, strategically considered, with the Captain's decision to begin operations therein. Harriet Tubman . . . was a constant user of the Appalachian route in her efforts to aid escaping slaves.[6]

[1] Wm. Still, *Underground Railroad*, p. 41. "The Underground Railroad brought away large numbers of passengers from Richmond, Petersburg, and Norfolk, and not a few of them lived comparatively within a hair's breadth of the auction block." Wm. Still, *Underground Railroad Records*, p. 141.

[2] Conversation with Mrs. Elizabeth Cooley, a fugitive from Norfolk, Va., Boston, Mass., April 8, 1897.

[3] Letter of Frederick Douglass, Anacostia, D.C., March 27, 1893.

[4] Conversation with Mrs. Tubman, Boston, Mass., April 8, 1897.

[5] R. J. Hinton, *John Brown and His Men*, pp. 172, 173.

[6] Harriet Tubman has told the author that she did not travel by the

... Underground Railroad operations culminating chiefly at Cleveland, Sandusky, and Detroit, led by broad and defined routes through Ohio to the border of Kentucky. Through that State, into the heart of the Cumberland Mountains, northern Georgia, east Tennessee, and northern Alabama, the limestone caves of the region served a useful purpose. ... The Ohio-Kentucky routes probably served more fugitives than others in the North. The valley of the Mississippi was the most westerly channel, until Kansas opened a bolder way of escape from the southwest slave section." These were the main channels of flight from the slave states; but it must be remembered that escapes were continually taking place along the entire frontier between the two sections of the Union, the drift of travel being constantly towards those points where the homes of abolitionists or where negro settlements indicated initial stations on lines running north to freedom. The border counties of the slave states were thus subject to a steady loss of their dissatisfied bondmen. This condition is well represented in the case of several counties of Maryland, concerning which Mr. Smedley obtained information. He says, "The counties of Frederick, Carroll, Washington, Hartford and Baltimore, Md., emptied their fugitives into York and Adams counties across the line in Pennsylvania. The latter two counties had settlements of Friends and abolitionists. The slaves learned who their friends were in that part of the Free State; and it was as natural for those aspiring to liberty to move in that direction as for the waters of brooks to move toward larger streams."[1]

Along the southern margin of the free states began those well-defined trails or channels that have lent themselves to

mountain route. In his book entitled *The Underground Railroad* (p. 37), Mr. R. C. Smedley illustrates the value of the Alleghanies to the slaves of the regions through which they extend: "William and Phœbe Wright resided during their entire lives in a very old settlement of Friends, near the southern slope of South Mountain, a spur of the Alleghanies, which extends into Tennessee. This location placed them directly in the way to render great and valuable aid to fugitives, as hundreds, guided by that mountain range northward, came into Pennsylvania, and were directed to their home."

[1] *Underground Railroad*, p. 36.

representation upon the large map given herewith. In dealing with the tracings shown upon this map it will be best to consider the territory as divided into three regions, the first comprising the states of Pennsylvania, New Jersey and New York; the second, the New England states; and the third, the five states created out of the Northwest Territory. This arrangement will, perhaps, admit of the introduction of some system into the discussion of what might otherwise prove a complicated subject.

In point of time underground work seems to have developed first in eastern Pennsylvania.[1] Regular routes of travel began to be formed in the vicinity of Philadelphia about the middle of the first decade of the present century. It is said that "some cases of kidnapping and shooting of fugitives who attempted to escape occurred in Columbia, Pa., in 1804. This incited the people of that town, who were chiefly Friends or their descendants, to throw around the colored people the arm of protection, and even to assist those who were endeavoring to escape from slavery. . . . This gave origin to that organized system of rendering aid to fugitives which was afterward known as the 'Underground Railroad.'" Thus begun, the service rapidly extended, being greatly favored by the character of the population in southeastern Pennsylvania, which was largely Quaker, with here and there some important settlements of manumitted slaves. It was on account of the large number of runaways early resorting to Columbia that it became necessary to have an understanding with regard to places of entertainment for them along lines leading to the Eastern states and to Canada, whither most of the fugitives were bound.[2] There seems to have been scarcely any limitation upon the number of persons in Lancaster, Chester and Delaware counties willing to assume agencies for the forwarding of slaves; hence this region became the field through which more routes were de-

[1] See pp. 33 and 34, Chapter II.
[2] R. C. Smedley, *Underground Railroad*, pp. 26, 27, 28, 29, 30. For a description of the routes of this region, our dependence is almost wholly upon Mr. Smedley, whose intimate knowledge of them was obtained by conversation and correspondence with many of the operators. *Ibid.*, Preface, p. x.

veloped in proportion to its extent than any other area in the Northern states. It will be necessary to make use of a special map of the region in order to follow out the principal channels of escape and to discover the centres from which the Canada routes sprung.[1] West of the Susquehanna River Gettysburg and York were the stations chiefly sought by slaves escaping from the border counties of Maryland. Along the western shore of the Chesapeake runaways passed northward to Havre de Grace, where they usually crossed the Susquehanna, and with others from the Eastern Shore found their way to established stations in the southern part of Lancaster and Chester counties in Pennsylvania. From the territory adjacent to the Delaware the movement was to Wilmington, and thence north through Chester and Delaware counties. The routes developed in the three regions just indicated formed three systems of underground travel, the first of which may be called the western, the second, the middle, and the third, the eastern system. These systems comprised, besides the main roads indicated in heavy lines upon the map, numerous side-tracks and branches shown by the light lines. Their common goal was Phœnixville, the home of Elijah F. Pennypacker, and from here fugitives were sent to Philadelphia, Norristown, Quakertown, Reading and other stations as occasion required. While Phœnixville may be regarded as the central station for the three systems mentioned, it did not receive all the negroes escaping through this section, and Smedley says that "Hundreds were sent to the many branch stations along interlacing routes, and hundreds of others were sent from Wilmington, Columbia, and stations westward direct to the New England States and Canada. Many of these passed through the hands of the Vigilance Committee connected with the anti-slavery office in Philadelphia,"[2] From this point one outlet led overland across New Jersey to Jersey City and New York; another

[1] The special map of these counties will be found in a corner of the general map.
[2] *The Underground Railroad*, p. 209. For a description of the secret paths in southeastern Pennsylvania, see Smedley's book, pp. 30, 31, 32, 33, 34, 50, 53, 77, 85, 89, 90, 100, 132, 137, 142, 164, 172, 191, 192, 208, 217, 218, 219, etc.

outlet from Philadelphia, was the Reading Railroad, which also carried refugees from various stations along its course. How many steam railway extensions may have been connected with the underground tracks of southeastern Pennsylvania cannot be discovered. One such extension was the Northern Central Railroad from Harrisburg across the state to Elmira, New York.[1] Another trans-state route in eastern Pennsylvania appears to have had its origin at or near Sadsbury, Chester County, and to have run overland to Binghamton, New York.[2] The intermediate stations along this pathway are not known, although some disconnected places of resort in northeastern Pennsylvania[3] may have constituted a section of it. Lines of northern travel for fugitives also passed through Bucks County, but Dr. Edward H. Magill, formerly President of Swarthmore College, thinks these were "less clearly marked" than those running through Chester and Lancaster counties. He finds that friends of the slave in the middle section of Bucks County generally forwarded the negroes to Quakertown or even as far north, by stage or private conveyance, as Stroudsburg. From this point they sometimes went to Montrose or Friendsville, in Susquehanna County, near the southern boundary of the State of New York,[4] whence, together with fugitives from Wilkesbarre, and, perhaps, the Lehigh Valley, they were sent on to Gerrit Smith, at Peterboro in central New York, and thence to Canada.[5]

At the other end of Pennsylvania several routes and sections of routes have been discovered. The most important of these seem to have been the roads resulting from the convergence of at least three well-defined lines of escape at Uniontown in southwestern Pennsylvania from the neigh-

[1] Letters of Mrs. Susan L. Crane, Elmira, N.Y., Aug. 27, and Sept. 14 and 23, 1896; letters of John W. Jones, Elmira, N.Y., Dec. 17, 1896, and Jan. 16, 1897.
[2] Smedley, *Underground Railroad*, p. 91.
[3] See the general map.
[4] Article by Dr. Magill, entitled "When Men were Sold. The Underground Railroad in Bucks County," in *The Bucks County Intelligencer*, Feb. 3, 1898. Same article in the *Friends' Intelligencer*, Feb. 26, 1898.
[5] Letter of Horace Brewster, Montrose, Pa., March 20, 1898.

boring counties of Virginia and Maryland. A map drawn by Mr. Amos M. Jolliffe, of Uniontown, shows that there were two courses leading northward from his neighborhood, both of which terminated at Pittsburg.[1] From this point fugitives seem to have been sent to Cleveland by rail, or to have been directed to follow the Alleghany or the Ohio and its tributaries north. Investigation proves that friends were not lacking at convenient points to help them along to the main terminals for this region, namely, Erie and Buffalo, or across the border of the state to the much-used routes of the Western Reserve.[2] East of the Alleghany River significant traces of underground work are found running in a northeasterly direction from Greensburg through Indiana County to Clearfield,[3] a distance of seventy-five miles, and from Cumberland, Maryland, through Bedford and Pleasantville to Altoona,[4] about the same distance. These fragmentary routes may have had connections with some of the fragmentary lines of western New York. From Clearfield an important branch is known to have run northwest to Shippenville and Franklin, and so to Erie, a place of deportation on the lake of the same name.[5]

New Jersey was intimately associated with Philadelphia and the adjoining section in the underground system, and afforded at least three important outlets for runaways from the territory west of the Delaware River. Our knowledge of these outlets is derived solely from the testimony of the Rev. Thomas Clement Oliver, who, like his father, travelled the New Jersey routes many times as a guide or conductor.[6] Probably the most important of these routes was that leading

[1] Letter of Mr. Jolliffe, Nov. 17, 1895.
[2] Letter of John F. Hogue, Greenville, Pa., Nov. 25, 1895; letter of S. P. Stewart, Clark, Mercer Co., Pa., Dec. 26, 1895; letter of W. W. Walker, Makanda, Jackson Co., Ill., March 14, 1896; note-book of Joseph S. White, of New Castle, Pa., containing "Some Reminiscences of Slavery Times."
[3] Letters of C. P. Rank, Cush Creek, Indiana Co., Pa., Dec. 25, 1896, and Jan. 4, 1897; letter of William Atcheson, DuBois, Pa., Jan. 11, 1897.
[4] Letter of Wyett Perry, Bedford, Pa., Dec. 23, 1895; letter of John W. Rouse, Bedford, Pa., Nov. 25, 1895; letter of William M. Hall, Bedford, Pa., Nov. 30, 1895.
[5] Conversation with William Edwards, Amherstburg, Ont., Aug. 3, 1895.
[6] Conversation with Mr. Oliver, Windsor, Ont., Aug. 2, 1895.

from Philadelphia to Jersey City and New York. From Philadelphia the runaways were taken across the Delaware River to Camden, where Mr. Oliver lived, thence they were conveyed northeast following the course of the river to Burlington, and thence in the same direction to Bordentown. In Burlington, sometimes called Station A, a short stop was made for the purpose of changing horses after the rapid drive of twenty miles from Philadelphia. The Bordentown station was denominated Station B east. Here the road took a more northerly direction to Princeton, where horses were again changed and the journey continued to New Brunswick. Just east of New Brunswick the conductors sometimes met with opposition in attempting to cross the Raritan River on their way to Jersey City. To avoid such interruption the conductors arranged with Cornelius Cornell, who lived on the outskirts of New Brunswick, and, presumably, near the river, to notify them when there were slave-catchers or spies at the regular crossing. On receiving such information they took a by-road leading to Perth Amboy, whence their protégés could be safely forwarded to New York City. When the way was clear at the Raritan the company pursued its course to Rahway; here another relay of horses was obtained and the journey continued to Jersey City, where, under the care of John Everett, a Quaker, or his servants, they were taken to the Forty-second Street railroad station, now known as the Grand Central, provided with tickets, and placed on a through train for Syracuse, New York. The second route had its origin on the Delaware River forty miles below Philadelphia, at or near Salem. This line, like the others to be mentioned later, seems to have been tributary to the Philadelphia route traced above. Nevertheless, it had an independent course for sixty miles before it connected with the more northern route at Bordentown. This distance of sixty miles was ordinarily travelled in three stages, the first ending at Woodbury, twenty-five miles north of Salem, although the trip by wagon is said to have added ten miles to the estimated distance between the two places; the second stage ended at Evesham Mount; and the third, at Bordentown. The third route was called, from its initial station, the Greenwich line.

This station is vividly described as having been made up of a circle of Quaker residences enclosing a swampy place that swarmed with blacks. One may surmise that it made a model station. Slaves were transported at night across the Delaware River from the vicinity of Dover, in boats marked by a yellow light hung below a blue one, and were met some distance out from the Jersey shore by boats showing the same lights. Landed at Greenwich, the fugitives were conducted north twenty-five miles to Swedesboro, and thence about the same distance to Evesham Mount. From this point they were taken to Mount Holly, and so into the northern or Philadelphia route. Still another branch of this Philadelphia line is known. It constitutes the fourth road, and is described by Mr. Robert Purvis [1] as an extension of a route through Bucks County, Pennsylvania, that entered Trenton, New Jersey, from Newtown, and ran directly to New Brunswick and so on to New York.

Mr. Eber M. Pettit, for many years a conductor of the Underground Railroad in western New York,[2] asserts that the Road had four main lines across his state, and scores of laterals,[3] but he nowhere attempts to identify these lines for the benefit of those less well informed than himself. Concerning what may be supposed to have been one of the lines, he speaks as follows: " The first well-established line of the U. G. R. R. had its southern terminus in Washington, D.C., and extended in a pretty direct route to Albany, N.Y., thence radiating in all directions to all the New England states, and to many parts of this state. . . . The General Superintendent resided in Albany. . . . He was once an active member of one of the churches in Fredonia. Mr. T., his agent in Washington City, was a very active and efficient man ; the Superintendent at Albany was in daily communication by mail with him and other subordinate agents at all points along the line." [4] Frederick Douglass, who was familiar with this Albany route during the period of his residence in Rochester, describes it as running through Phil-

[1] Conversation with Mr. Purvis, Philadelphia, Dec. 23, 1895.
[2] *Sketches in the History of the Underground Railroad*, 1879, Preface, p. xvi.   [3] *Ibid.*, p. xiv.   [4] *Ibid.*, p. 34.

adelphia, New York, Albany, Rochester, and thence to Canada; and he gives the name of the person at each station that was most closely associated in his mind with the work of the station. Thus, he says that the "fugitives were received in Philadelphia by William Still, by him sent to New York, where they were cared for by Mr. David Ruggles, and afterwards by Mr. Gibbs, . . . thence to Stephen Myers at Albany; thence to J. W. Loguen, Syracuse; thence to Frederick Douglass, Rochester; and thence to Hiram Wilson, St. Catherines, Canada West."[1] Not all the negroes travelling by this route went as far as Rochester; some were turned north at Syracuse to the port of Oswego, where they took boat for Canada.[2] The Rev. Charles B. Ray, a member of the Vigilance Committee of New York City, and editor of *The Colored American*, has left some testimony which corroborates that just given. He knew of a regular route stretching from Washington, by way of Baltimore and Philadelphia, to New York, thence following the Hudson to Albany and Troy, whence a branch ran westward to Utica, Syracuse and Oswego, with an extension from Syracuse to Niagara Falls. New York was a kind of receiving point from which fugitives were assisted to Albany and Troy, or, as sometimes happened, to Boston and New Bedford, or, when considerations of safety warranted it, were permitted to pass to Long Island.[3] The lines that are said to have radiated from Albany are mentioned neither by Mr. Douglass nor by Mr. Ray, but we know from other witnesses that some of the fugitives sent to Troy found their way to places of refuge north and east. Mr. Martin I. Townsend, of Troy, writes that fugitives arriving at that city were supplied with money and forwarded either to Suspension Bridge, on the Niagara River, or by way of Vermont and Lake Champlain to Rouses Point.[4] It seems probable that another

[1] Letter of Frederick Douglass, Cedar Hill, Anacostia, D.C., March 27, 1893.
[2] Letter of Joseph A. Allen, Medfield, Mass., Aug. 10, 1896.
[3] Letter of Florence and Cordelia H. Ray, Woodside, L.I., April 12, 1897. See *Sketch of the Life of Rev. Chas. B. Ray*, written by the Misses Ray.
[4] Letters of Martin I. Townsend, Troy, N.Y., Sept. 4 and 15, 1896.

branch of the secret thoroughfare followed the valley of the Hudson from Troy to the farm of John Brown, near North Elba among the Adirondacks. Mr. Richard H. Dana visited this frontier home of Brown one summer, and was informed by his guide that the country about there belonged to Gerrit Smith; that it was settled for the most part by families of fugitive slaves, who were engaged in farming; and that Brown held the position of a sort of ruler among them. The view was therefore credited that this neighborhood was one of the termini of the Underground Railroad." [1]

Gerrit Smith, the friend and counsellor of Brown, lived at Peterboro, in central New York, where his house was an important station for runaway slaves. His open invitation to fugitives to come to Peterboro gave the post he maintained great publicity, and many negroes resorted thither. From Peterboro they were sent in Mr. Smith's wagon to Oswego.[2] A little to the east and north of this place of deportation there were what may perhaps be called emergency stations at or near Mexico, New Haven, Port Ontario [3] and Cape Vincent.[4] From the place last named, and perhaps also from Port Ontario, fugitives took boat for Kingston.[5] A route that came into operation much later than that with

[1] C. F. Adams, *Life of Richard Henry Dana*, Vol. I, p. 155; *History of Madison County, New York*, by Mrs. L. M. Hammond, p. 721.
[2] O. B. Frothingham, *Life of Gerrit Smith*, pp. 113, 114.
[3] Letter of O. J. Russell, Pulaski, N.Y., July 29, 1896.
[4] Mr. George C. Bragdon writes concerning the runaways harbored by his father, near Port Ontario: "I believe they usually went to Cape Vincent, near the mouth of the St. Lawrence, and were taken over to Canada from there. . . . I believe some of the slaves received by him were sent on from Peterboro by Gerrit Smith to *Asa S. Wing* or *James C. Jackson* (Mexico), and came from them to our house. They steered clear of the villages, as a rule. Our farm was favorably situated for concealing them and helping them on." Letter of George C. Bragdon, Rochester, N.Y., Aug. 11, 1896.

Mrs. Elizabeth Smith Miller, the daughter of Gerrit Smith, says that in October, 1839, the "White Slave, Harriet," was taken by Mr. Federal Dana from her father's house directly to Cape Vincent, and that Mr. Dana wrote from that point: "I saw her pass the ferry this morning into Canada." Letter received from Mrs. Miller, Peterboro, N.Y., Sept. 21, 1896.

[5] The fugitive Jerry McHenry, after his rescue in Syracuse, was hurried to Mexico, thence to Oswego, and from this point was transported across the lake to Kingston. May, *Some Recollections of Our Anti-Slavery Conflict*, pp. 378, 379.

which the Peterboro station was connected was the Elmira route. In 1844, John W. Jones, an escaped slave from Virginia, settled in Elmira, and began, together with Mr. Jervis Langdon, a prominent citizen of the town, to receive fugitives. A few years later the Northern Central Railroad was constructed, and supplied a means of travel through western New York to Niagara Falls. Underground passengers forwarded by rail from Philadelphia, Harrisburg and Williamsport were sent on via the Northern Central to Canada.[1] In the counties of New York west and south of the Elmira route the map shows some disconnected stations and sections of Road. Not enough is known about these to suggest with certainty their connections. It is, however, evident that their trend is toward the short arm of the Province of Ontario, which is separated from the United States only by the Niagara River, with crossings favorable for fugitives at Buffalo, Black Rock, Suspension Bridge and Lewiston. In the angle of southwestern New York there were two routes, the objective point of which was Buffalo. One of these, by way of Westfield and Fredonia, hugged closely the shore of Lake Erie;[2] the other, issuing by way of the Alleghany River from Franklin, Pennsylvania, ran through Jamestown and Ellington to Leon, where it branched, one division going to Fredonia and so on northward, whilst the other seems to have followed a more direct course to Buffalo.[3]

Notwithstanding the unfavorable position for this work of the New England states, a considerable number of fugitive slaves found their way through these states to Canada. A part of them came through Pennsylvania and New York. Smedley states, as already noted, that hundreds were sent from Wilmington, Columbia, and other points to the New

[1] Letters of Mrs. Susan L. Crane, Elmira, N.Y., Sept. 14 and 23, 1896. Mrs. Crane is a daughter of Mr. Jervis Langdon mentioned in the text; letter of John W. Jones, Elmira, N.Y., Dec. 14, 1896.

[2] A number of the stations along the lake shore are named in the sketches called "Romances and Realities of the Underground Railroad," by H. U. Johnson, printed in the *Lakeshore and Home Magazine*, 1885-1887.

[3] E. M. Pettit, in *Sketches in the History of the Underground Railroad*, pp. 30, 31, 32, gives an instance of the use of this route.

England states and Canada.[1] Another part came by boat from Southern ports to the shores of New England, landing at various places, chief among which seem to have been New Haven, New Bedford, Boston and Portland. Such was the number of arrivals and consequent demand for transportation to a place of safety, that these four places became the beginnings of routes, which it has been possible to trace on the map with more or less completeness.

The first of these may be called the Connecticut valley route. President E. B. Andrews, of Brown University, whose father was an active friend of slaves at Montague in western Massachusetts, describes this route as running from New York, New Haven, or New London up the Connecticut River valley to Canada.[2] This is corroborated by some writer in the *History of Springfield, Massachusetts*, where it is noted that there was a steady movement of parties of runaways up the valley on their way to the adjacent provinces.[3] Mr. Erastus F. Gunn, of Montague, Massachusetts, writes that the travel along this route was largely confined to the west side of the river, and was through Springfield, Northampton and Greenfield into the State of Vermont.[4] Fugitives disembarking at New Haven[5] went north through Kensington, New Britain and Farmington, and probably by way of Bloomfield or Hartford to Springfield. Sometimes they came up the river by steamboat to Hartford, the head of navigation, and continued their journey overland.[6] A trail probably much less used than the routes just mentioned, seems to have connected the southwestern part of Connecticut with the valley route.[7] In Massachusetts there were

---

[1] See p. 120, this chapter.
[2] Letter of Mr. Andrews, Providence, R.I., April, 1895.
[3] Pp. 470, 471.
[4] Letter of Mr. Gunn, Montague, Mass., Nov. 23, 1895.
[5] Letter of Simeon E. Baldwin, New Haven, Conn., Jan. 27, 1896; letter of Simeon D. Gilbert, New Haven, Conn., Feb. 27, 1896.
[6] Letter of D. W. C. Pond, New Britain, Conn. Mr. Pond is one of the surviving agents of New Britain.
[7] Letters of George B. Wakeman, Montour Falls, N.Y., April 21 and Sept. 26, 1896. Letter of the Rev. Erastus Blakeslee, Boston, Mass., Aug. 28, 1896.

ramifications from the valley route,[1] which may have terminated among the hills in the western part of the state, for all that one can now discover.

A line of Road originating at New Bedford in southeastern Massachusetts is mentioned in connection with the line up the Connecticut valley by the Hon. M. M. Fisher, of Medway, Massachusetts, as one of the more common routes.[2] Mrs. Elizabeth Buffum Chace says that slaves landing on Cape Cod went to New Bedford, whence under the guidance of some abolitionist they were conveyed to the home of Nathaniel P. Borden at Fall River. Between this station and the one kept by Mr. and Mrs. Chace at Valley Falls, Robert Adams acted as conductor; and from Valley Falls Mr. Chace was in the habit of accompanying passengers a short distance over the Providence and Worcester Railroad until he had placed them in the care of some trusted employee of that road to be transferred at Worcester to the Vermont Railroad.[3] The Rev. Joshua Young was receiving agent at Burlington, Vermont, and testifies that during his residence there he and his friend and parishioner, L. H. Bigelow, did "considerable business."[4] South of Burlington there was a series of stations not connected with the Vermont Central Railroad extension of the New Bedford route. The names of these stations have been obtained from Mr. Rowland E. Robinson, whose father's house was a refuge for fugitives at Ferrisburg, Vermont, and from the Hon. Joseph Poland, the editor of the first anti-slavery newspaper in his state, who was himself an agent of the Underground Road at Montpelier. The names are those of nine towns, which form a line roughly parallel to the west boundary of the state, namely, North Ferrisburg, Ferrisburg, Vergennes, Middlebury, Brandon, Rutland, Wallingford, Manchester and

[1] The stations, as indicated on the map, are named in letters from L. S. Abell and Charles Parsons, Conway, Mass.; C. Barrus, Springfield, Mass.; Judge D. W. Bond, Cambridge, Mass.; and Arthur G. Hill, Boston, Mass. See also article on "The Underground Railway," by Joseph Marsh, in the *History of Florence, Massachusetts*, pp. 165-167.
[2] Letter of Mr. Fisher, Oct. 23, 1893.
[3] *Anti-Slavery Reminiscences*, pp. 27, 28.
[4] Letter of Mr. Young, Groton, Mass., April 21, 1893.

CAVES IN SALEM TOWNSHIP, WASHINGTON COUNTY, OHIO.
The cave on the left was a rendezvous for fugitives.

HOUSE OF MRS. ELIZABETH BUFFUM CHACE,
A STATION OF THE UNDERGROUND RAILROAD, VALLEY FALLS, RHODE ISLAND.

Bennington.[1] They constituted what may be called the west Vermont route, Bennington being at the southern extremity, where escaped slaves were received from Troy, New York.[2] The terminal at the northern end of this route was St. Albans, whence runaways could be hastened across the Canadian frontier. The valley of the lower Connecticut seems to have yielded a sufficient supply of fugitive slaves to sustain a vigorous line of Road in eastern Vermont. It was over this line the travellers came that were placed in hiding in the office of Editor Poland at Montpelier, having made their way northward with the aid of friends at Brattleboro, Chester, Woodstock, Randolph and intermediate points. At Montpelier the single path divided into three branches, one extending westward and uniting with the west Vermont route at Burlington, another running northward into the Queen's dominions by way of Morristown and other stations, and the third zigzagging to New Port, where a pass through the mountains admitted the zealous pilgrims to the coveted possession of their own liberty.[3]

Having thus sketched in the Vermont lines of Underground Railroad, it is necessary for us to return to the consideration of the New Bedford route, which had some accessory lines near its source. One of these had stations at Newport and Providence, managed by Quakers — Jethro and Anne Mitchell with others in the former, and Daniel Mitchell in the latter.[4] Another was a short line through Windham County, in the northeastern part of Connecticut, to Uxbridge, where it joined the main line.[5] The Rev. Samuel J. May, who was a resident of Brooklyn, Connecticut, in the early thirties, had fugitives addressed to his care at that time, and he helped them on to Effingham L. Capron while he lived in Uxbridge, and after-

---

[1] Letter of Mr. Robinson, Ferrisburg, Vt., Aug. 19, 1896; letter of Mr. Poland, Montpelier, Vt., April 12, 1897.
[2] Letter of Mr. Brainerd, St. Albans, Vt., Oct. 21, 1895.
[3] Letters of Mrs. Abijah Keith, Chicago, Ill., March 28, and April 4, 1897; letters of Mr. Poland, April 7 and 12, 1897.
[4] Letter of James S. Rogers, Chicago, Ill., April 17, 1897.
[5] Letters of Joel Fox, Willimantic, Conn., July 30, 1896, and Aug. 3, 1896.

wards when he settled in Worcester.[1] From Boston [2] westward there were at least two paths to reach the New Bedford road, one of these was by way of Newton to Worcester, and the other through Concord to Leominster. Mr. William I. Bowditch generally passed on the fugitives received at his house to Mr. William Jackson, of Newton, thence they were sent by rail to Worcester.[3] Colonel T. W. Higginson writes that fugitives were sometimes sent from Boston to Worcester,[4] while he lived in the latter place, and that he has himself driven them at midnight to the farm of the veteran abolitionists, Stephen and Abby Kelley Foster, in the suburbs of the city.[5] All along the short route, from Boston to Leominster and Fitchburg, stations were systematically arranged, according to the statement of Mrs. Mary E. Crocker,[6] who was one of the helpers at Leominster.[7] This was the route taken by Shadrach, after his rescue in Boston.[8]

Boston was the starting-point of longer lines running north along the coast; one, so far as can now be made out, turning and passing obliquely across New Hampshire; the other following the shore into Maine. Mr. Simeon Dodge, of Marblehead, Massachusetts, who had intimate knowledge of the first of these courses, gives, in an illustrative case, the names of Marblehead, Salem and Georgetown as stations;[9] and Mr. G. W. Putnam, of Lynn, gives the names of persons harboring

[1] *Some Recollections of our Anti-Slavery Conflict*, p. 297.
[2] "In Boston there were many places where fugitives were received and taken care of. Every anti-slavery man was ready to protect them, and among these were some families not known to be anti-slavery." James Freeman Clarke, *Anti-Slavery Days*, p. 86.
[3] Letter of Mr. Bowditch, Boston, April 5, 1893.
[4] Letter of Mr. Higginson, Glimpsewood, Dublin, N.H., July 24, 1896.
[5] T. W. Higginson, *Atlantic Monthly*, March, 1897.
[6] Article on "The Fugitive Slave Law and Its Workings," in *Fitchburg Daily Sentinel*, Oct. 31, 1893.
[7] Letter of Mr. F. B. Sanborn, Concord, Mass., Feb. 1, 1896, states that "Concord was a place of resort for fugitives." Letter of Mr. S. Shurtleff, South Paris, Me., May 25, 1896, states that "The direct line of the Underground Railroad was from Boston through Vermont, via St. Albans."
[8] *Atlantic Monthly*, March, 1897, p. 345; *Fitchburg Daily Sentinel*, Oct. 31, 1893; letter of Mr. Sanborn, Concord, Mass., Feb. 1, 1896.
[9] Letter of Mr. Dodge, March, 1893.

slaves at two of these places.[1] A report of the Danvers Historical Society is authority for the statement that Mr. Dodge, together with some of the abolitionists of Salem, maintained a secret thoroughfare to Canada,[2] which passed through Danvers, and on through Concord, New Hampshire.[3] From Concord fugitives were sent north to Canterbury and Meredith Ridge[4] in two known instances, and more frequently, it appears, to Canaan and Lyme. James Furber, who lived in Canaan for several years, is said to have made trips to Lyme about once a fortnight with refugees received by him.[5] From Lyme they may have gone north by way of the Connecticut valley. At Salem the coast route parted company with the New Hampshire route, and ran on through Ipswich, Newburyport and Exeter[6] to Eliot, Maine, and perhaps farther.

Slaves sometimes reached Portland, Maine, travelling as stowaways on vessels from Southern ports. Consequently Portland became the centre of several hidden routes to Canada. Mr. S. T. Pickard, who lived in the family of Mrs. Oliver Dennett in Portland, says that Mrs. Dennett harbored runaway slaves, as did also Nathan Winslow and General Samuel Fessenden. The fugitives that came to Portland, he says, were on their way to New Brunswick and Lower Canada, and some were shipped directly to England.[7] Mr. Brown Thurston, the veteran abolitionist of Portland, is authority for the statement that routes extended from Portland to the provinces, by water to St. John, New Brunswick, and by rail to Montreal,[8] the road used being the Grand Trunk.[9] An important overland route also had its origin at Portland. Its two branches encircled Sebago Lake, united at Bridgton, and formed a single pathway to the northwest, and did not

[1] Letter of Mr. Putnam, Lynn, Mass., Feb. 14, 1894.
[2] *Old Anti-Slavery Days*, p. 150.
[3] Letter of David Mead, Davenport, Mass., Nov. 3, 1893.
[4] Letter of Judge Mellen Chamberlain, Chelsea, Mass., Feb. 1, 1896.
[5] Letter of C. E. Lord, Franklin, Pa., July 6, 1896.
[6] Letter of D. L. Brigham, Manchester, Mass., Nov. 16, 1893; letter of Professor Marshall S. Snow, Washington University, St. Louis, Mo., April 28, 1896.   [7] Letter of Mr. Pickard, Portland, Me., Nov. 18, 1893.
[8] Letter of Mr. Thurston, Jan. 13, 1893.
[9] Letter of Mr. Thurston, Oct. 21, 1895; letter of Aaron Dunn, South Paris, Me., April 9, 1896.

separate again until the eastern border of Vermont was reached. There, at Lunenburg, one branch took its course up the Connecticut valley to Stratford, and thence, probably, ran to Stanstead, Quebec; while the other, passing more to the westward, joined the easternmost of the branches from Montpelier, Vermont, at Barton, and so entered Canada.[1] Besides, there were at least two subsidiary routes, which were probably feeders of the "through line" just described. One of them ran to South Paris and Lovell;[2] the other, according to ex-President O. B. Cheney, of Bates College, who was privy to its operations, ran to Effingham, North Parsonsfield and Porter.[3] Both Lovell and Porter are within a few miles of several of the stations that form a part of the Maine section of this line, and could witnesses be found it is likely that their testimony would sustain the view that external evidence suggests.

In the free states included between the Ohio and the Mississippi rivers the number of underground trails was much greater than in the states farther east. Bordering on the slave states, Missouri, Kentucky and Virginia, with a length of frontier greatly increased by the sinuosities of the rivers, the states of Ohio, Indiana and Illinois were the most favorably situated of all the Northern states to receive fugitive slaves. Not only the bounding rivers themselves, but also their numerous tributaries, became channels of escape into free territory, and connected directly with many lines of Underground Railroad. These lines of Road are shown on the map as starting from the Ohio or the Mississippi, but they cannot be supposed to have abruptly originated there, for in some instances there were points south of these streams that formed an essential part of the system. It is impossible to bring together here the numerous bits of testimony through the correlation of which the multitude of lines within the old Northwest Territory has been traced. Only a general survey, therefore, of the Underground Railroad system in the Western states will be undertaken, while several smaller maps of limited

---

[1] Letter of J. Milton Hall, April 30, 1897.
[2] Letter of S. Shurtleff, May 25, 1896.
[3] Letter of Mr. Cheney, Pawtuxet, R.I., April 8, 1896.

areas will give the details of the multiple and complex routes found therein.

Concerning the number of paths there were in Ohio it is almost impossible to obtain a definite and correct idea. The location of the state was favorable to the development of new lines with the steady increase in the number of slaves fleeing across its southern borders; and, in the process of development, it was natural that the various branches should intertwine and form a great network. To disentangle the strands of this web and say how many there were is a thing not easy to accomplish, although an anonymous writer in 1842 seems to have found little or no difficulty in arriving at a definite conclusion. His estimate appeared in the *Experiment* of December 7, and is as follows: "It is evident from the statements of the abolitionists themselves, that there exist some eighteen or nineteen thoroughly organized thoroughfares through the State of Ohio for the transportation of runaway and stolen slaves, one of which passes through Fitchville, and which to my certain knowledge has done a 'land office business.'"[1] If the number of important initial stations fringing the southern and eastern boundaries of Ohio be counted as the points of origin of separate routes, it would be correct to say that there were not less than twenty-two or twenty-three routes in Ohio, but in a count thus made one would fail to note the instances in which, as in the case of Cincinnati, several lines sprang from one locality.

In the remaining portion of the Northwest Territory, the number of lines was relatively not so great; and extended areas, as in the western and northern parts of Indiana or the southeastern part of Illinois, contained few or no lines so far as can now be discovered. In western and northern Illinois the conditions were more favorable, and the multiplicity of routes is such that on account of the fusion, division and subdivision of roads it is impossible to say how many lines crossed the state. In Michigan the case is not so complicated, and one can trace with some clearness six or seven paths leading to Detroit. Iowa, not a part, however, of the old Northwest Territory, was traversed by lines terminating in Illinois, and

[1] The *Firelands Pioneer*, July, 1888, p. 67.

therefore deserves consideration here. In the southeastern part of the state there were several short routes with initial stations at Croton, Bloomfield, Lancaster and Cincinnati, all of which had terminals no doubt along the Mississippi, though it has been possible to complete but two of the routes. In southwestern Iowa, Percival and the three roads branching from it are said to have supplied means of egress for slaves from Missouri and Nebraska through three tiers of counties ranging across the state in lines parallel with the north boundary of Missouri. John Brown took the northernmost of these parallel roads in the winter of 1858 and 1859, when he led a company of twelve fugitives from Missouri through Kansas to Percival on their way to Chicago and Detroit.

UNDERGROUND LINES OF MORGAN COUNTY, OHIO.
Drawn by Thomas Williams.

Of the local maps, the first represents the lines passing through a portion of Morgan County, in the southeastern part of Ohio. It was drawn by Mr. Thomas Williams, whose services in behalf of runaways made him familiar with the location of operators in the western part of his county.[1] The area represented is twenty-five miles in length

---

[1] Corroborative evidence as regards the routes of Morgan County is found in letters from the following persons: E. M. Stanberry, McConnellsville, O.,

and sixteen in width at the widest part, and contains nineteen stations including the towns through which routes passed. The irregular distribution of these stations, and the way in which trips could be varied from one to another to suit the convenience of conductors or to elude pursuers is apparent. The fugitives that travelled over these routes crossed the Ohio River in the vicinity of Parkersburg and Point Pleasant, in what is now West Virginia, and proceeded north twenty or thirty miles by the help of abolitionists before reaching Morgan County. The southern part of this county was traversed by two parallel lines, one of which branched at Rosseau and ran on in parallels to the northern part of the county whence after sharp deflection to the west the branches converged at Deavertown; the other issued from its first station in three divergent lines, which rapidly converged at Pennsville and were united by a single course to the first route. In case of emergency a guide used his knowledge and discretion as to whether he should "cut across lots," skip stations, travel by the "longest way around," or go back on his track. The houses noted on the map as being off the regular routes appear to have been emergency stations and hence not so frequently used.

A special map of exceeding interest and importance is that drawn by Mr. Lewis Falley, of La Fayette, Indiana, showing the underground lines of Indiana and Michigan about 1848. Mr. Falley's acquaintance with the Road came about through the work of his father in the interest of fugitives in La Fayette after 1841. Subsequently Mr. Falley learned of the lines traversing his state through an itinerant preacher who sometimes stopped as a guest at his father's house. When Mr. Falley's map was received in March, 1896, the author himself had already plotted from other testimony a number of routes in southern and eastern Indiana and in Michigan, and a comparison of maps was made. On Mr. Falley's map three main roads appear, the eastern, middle and western routes. The first of these ran parallel, roughly speaking,

Nov. 1, 1892; T. L. Gray, Deavertown, O., Dec. 2, 1892; Martha Millions, Pennsville, O., March 9, 1892; E. R. Brown, Sugar Grove, O.; H. C. Harvey, Manchester, Kan., Jan. 16, 1893.

with the eastern boundary line of the state only a few miles from it, and took its rise from two lesser paths, which converged at Richmond from either side of the state line. The second or middle route sprang from three branches that crossed the Ohio at Madison, New Albany, and the neighborhood of Leavenworth, passed north through Indianapolis and Logansport, and entered Michigan a few miles east of Lake Michigan. The third or western route followed up the Wabash River to La Fayette, where it crossed the river, proceeded to Rensselaer, and thence northeasterly to the Michigan line, making its entrance to Michigan at the point where the middle route entered that state. From the two crossing-places on the Michigan border the northern extensions of the Indiana routes found their way to Battle Creek, from which station one trail led directly east to Detroit, and the other, by a more northerly course, to Port Huron. In southern Indiana the eastern route was connected with the middle route by a branch between Greensburg and Indianapolis, and the middle with the western by two branches, one between Salem and Evansville, and the other between Brownstown and Bloomingdale.

In the general map prepared by the author, the southern route through Michigan to Detroit, and the eastern, middle, and a portion of the western routes in Indiana on the map of Mr. Falley are duplicated with more or less completeness.

ROUTES THROUGH INDIANA AND MICHIGAN IN 1848.

As traced by Lewis Falley.

The initial stations along the Ohio River correspond in the two maps almost exactly, and many of the way-stations seen on the one map are to be found on the other. It is not to be expected that the two maps would agree in all particulars, and some stations occur on each that are not to be found on the other. Such differences are due to the development of new or the obliteration of old lines and the insufficient knowledge of the draughtsmen. It is not known that a map similar to Mr. Falley's has been devised for any other state or states among the many through which well-defined underground routes extended.

From a drawing made by Mr. W. B. Fyffe, an old-time station-agent of Ottawa, Illinois, the accompanying chart of a line of escape through Livingston and La Salle counties in Illinois is reproduced. The portion of the trail represented is about forty miles in length, and is remarkable for the directness of its course and the absence of interlacing lines. At Ottawa, the northernmost station shown, the trail loses these two characteristics, for it makes there a sharp turn on its way to the terminus, Chicago, and at Ottawa also it makes a junction with several other lines from the western part of the state.[1]

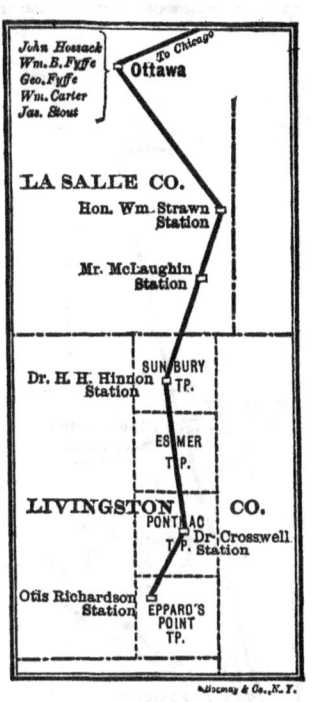

SIMPLE ROUTE THROUGH LIVINGSTON AND LA SALLE COUNTIES, ILLINOIS.

Drawn by William B. Fyffe.

A number of noteworthy features appear on the general map. The first deserving mention is the direction or trend of the underground lines. The region traversed by these lines may be described as an irregular crescent, the concavity

[1] For these features see the general map.

of which is in part filled by a portion of Ontario, Canada, which by reason of its proximity became the goal of the great majority of runaways. In the New England states the direction of the underground paths was, with perhaps an exception or two, from southeast to northwest, their objective point be-

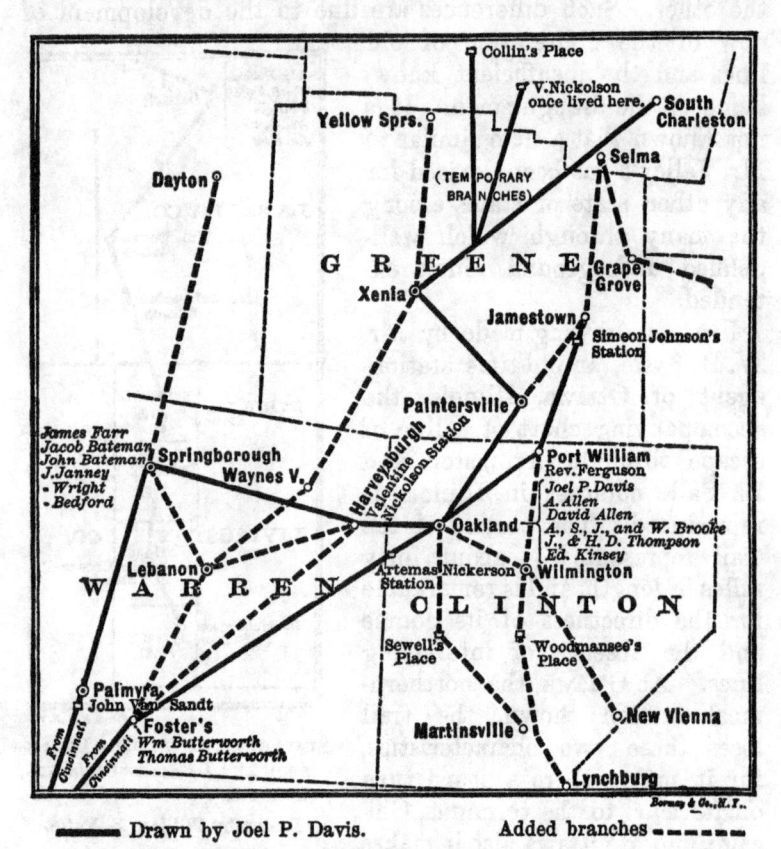

NETWORK OF ROUTES THROUGH GREENE, WARREN AND CLINTON COUNTIES, OHIO.

ing Montreal. The main lines of Pennsylvania and New York ran north until they reached the middle part of the latter state, and then veered off almost directly west to Canada. West of Pennsylvania the trend of the routes was in general to northeast, being in Ohio and Indiana to the shores of Lake

Erie, and in Illinois and Iowa to the southern extremity of Lake Michigan. Through central Iowa, northern Illinois and southern Michigan, the course of the routes was almost directly east.

It is not surprising that the regions through which the simplest and most direct routes passed should have been those at the two extremities of the great irregular crescent of free soil, where the number of routes was few and the activity of the stations limited. In the states that formed the middle portion of the crescent, it was natural that multiple and intricate trails should have been developed. The fact that slave-owners and their agents often sallied into this region in search of missing chattels was a consideration given due weight by the shrewd operators, who early learned that one of their best safeguards lay in complex routes, made by several lines radiating from one centre, or branch connections between routes, by paths that zigzagged from station to station. These features were characteristic, and serve to show that the safety of fugitives was never sacrificed by the abolitionists to any thoughtless desire for rapid transit. From Cincinnati, Ohio, not less than four branches of the Road radiated. One of these led to Fountain City, Indiana, where it was joined by two other important lines. From this point four lines diverged to the north. At Oberlin as many as five lines converged from the south. Quincy, Illinois, was the starting-point of four or five lines, and Knoxville, Ottawa and Chicago in the same state each received fugitives from several routes. The region in which the devices of multiple routes and cross lines were most highly developed is, as far as known, in southeastern Pennsylvania.

Some broken lines and isolated place-names occur upon the map. For example, in Iowa, branches of the system have been traced to Quincy, Indianola, North English and Ottumwa, but beyond these points the connections cannot be made. Examples of such incomplete sections will be found also in northern and central Illinois, in central Indiana, in western New York, in central and eastern Pennsylvania and in other states. It is not to be supposed that the routes represented by these fragmentary lines terminated abruptly without reaching a haven of safety, but only that the witnesses whose testimony is essential to complete the lines have not been discovered. In the case of the isolated place-names, a few of which occur in the New England states, in New York, Pennsylvania, Indiana and Illinois, the evidence at hand seemed to designate them as stations, without indicating in any definite way the neighboring stations with which they were probably allied.

On the general map may be noticed a few long stretches of Road that had apparently no way-stations. Such lines are usually identical with certain rivers, or canals, or railway systems. It has already been seen that the Connecticut River served to guide fugitives north on their way to Canada.[1] The Mississippi, Illinois, Ohio, Alleghany, and Hudson rivers united stations more or less widely separated.[2] The tow-paths of some of our western canals formed convenient highways to liberty for a considerable number of self-reliant fugitives, and were considered safer than public roads. A letter from E. C. H. Cavins, of Bloomfield, Indiana,[3] states that the Wabash and Erie Canal became a thoroughfare for slaves, who followed it from the vicinity of Evansville, Indiana, until they reached Ohio, probably in some instances going as far as Toledo, though usually, as the writer believes, striking off on one or another of several established lines of Underground Road in central and northern Indiana. James Bayliss,[4] of Massillon, in northeastern Ohio, states that fugitives sometimes came up the tow-path of the canal to Massillon, knowing that the canal led to Cleveland, whence a boat could be taken for Canada.[5]

The identity of a few of the tracings with steam railway lines signifies, of course, transportation by rail when the situation admitted of it. Sometimes, when there was not the usual eagerness of pursuit, and when the intelligence or the

[1] See p. 129, this chapter.
[2] See the language of Jefferson Davis, quoted on p. 312, Chapter X; letter of A. P. Dutton, Racine, Wis., April 7, 1896; E. M. Pettit, *Sketches in the History of the Underground Railroad*, pp. 29, 30, 31; letter of Florence and Cordelia H. Ray, referred to on p. 126, this chapter.
[3] Letter of Mr. Cavins, Dec. 5, 1895.
[4] Conversation with James Bayliss, Massillon, O., Aug. 15, 1895.
[5] Letter of Brown Thurston, Portland, Me., Oct. 21, 1895.

Caucasian cast of features of the fugitive warranted it, the traveller was provided with the necessary ticket and instructions, and put aboard the cars for his destination. The Providence and Worcester and the Vermont Central railroads furnished quick transportation from New Bedford, Massachusetts, to Canada.[1] In southeastern Pennsylvania the Philadelphia and Reading Railroad carried many slaves on their way to freedom, and according to Smedley, "All who took the trains at the Reading Railroad stations went directly through to Canada."[2] E. F. Pennypacker often forwarded negroes from Schuylkill to Philadelphia over this road, and William Still sent them on their northward journey.[3] Fugitives arriving at Harrisburg, Pennsylvania, sometimes took passage over the Northern Central Railroad to Elmira, New York. Mr. Jervis Langdon and John W. Jones, of Elmira, took care that underground passengers secured transportation from Elmira to their destination. The fugitives were always put in the baggage-car at four o'clock in the morning,[4] and went through without change to the Niagara River. The old Mad River Railroad bore many dark-skinned passengers from Urbana, if not also from Cincinnati and Dayton, Ohio, to Lake Erie.[5] In eastern Ohio the Cleveland and Western Railroad, from Alliance to Cleveland, was much patronized during several years by instructed runaways. Mr. I. Newton Peirce, then living in Alliance, had "an understanding with all the passenger-train conductors on the C. and W. R. R." that colored persons provided with tickets bearing the initials I. N. P. were to be admitted

[1] See p. 80, Chapter III.
[2] *Underground Railroad*, p. 174. See also pp. 176, 177.
[3] *Ibid.*, pp. 364, 365.
The following letter from Mr. Pennypacker to Mr. Still explains itself:
"SCHUYLKILL, 11th Mo., 7th, 1857.
WILLIAM STILL, *Respected Friend*, — There are three colored friends at my house now, who will reach the city by the Philadelphia and Reading train this evening. Please meet them.
Thine, etc., E. F. PENNYPACKER.
We have within the past two months passed forty-three through our hands, transported most of them to Norristown in our own conveyance. E. F. P."
[4] Letter of Mr. Jones, Elmira, N.Y., Jan. 16, 1897.
[5] See p. 78, Chapter III.

to the trains without question, unless slave-catchers were thought to be aboard the cars.[1] Indiana and Michigan are known to have had their steam railway lines in the secret service system: in the former state the Louisville, New Albany and Chicago Railroad was utilized by operators at Crawfordsville;[2] in the latter the Michigan Central supplied a convenient outlet to Detroit from stations along its course.[3] The Chicago and Rock Island Railroad from Peru, Lasalle County, Illinois, to Chicago was incorporated in the service, so also was the Illinois Central from Cairo and Centralia to the same terminus. The Chicago, Burlington and Quincy Railroad sometimes conveyed fugitives from Quincy on the Mississippi River to Chicago. Two men of prominence connected with this road, who secured transportation over its rails for many Canada-bound passengers, were Dr. C. V. Dyer, of Chicago, and Colonel Berrien, chief engineer of the road.[4]

Along the portion of the Atlantic coast shown on the map will be seen long lines connecting Southern with Northern ports. These represent routes to liberty by sea. It is reported by a station-keeper of Valley Falls, Rhode Island, that "Slaves in Virginia would secure passage either secretly or with the consent of the captains, in small trading vessels, at Norfolk or Portsmouth, and thus be brought into some port in New England, where their fate depended on circumstances;"[5] and the reporter gives several instances coming within her knowledge of fugitives that escaped from Virginia to Massachusetts as stowaways on vessels.[6] Boats engaged in the lumber trade sometimes brought refugees from Newberne, North Carolina, to Philadelphia.[7] Captain Austin Bearse, who was active in the rescue of stowaways from vessels arriving in Boston harbor from the South, cites two instances in which fugitives came by sea from Wilmington,

[1] Letter of Mr. Peirce, Folcroft, Delaware Co., Pa., Feb. 1, 1893.
[2] See p. 79, Chapter III. [3] *Ibid.*
[4] *Life and Poems of John Howard Bryant*, p. 30. Mr. Bryant made a practice of receiving fugitives in his house in Princeton, Ill.
[5] Mrs. Elizabeth Buffum Chace, *Anti-Slavery Reminiscences*, p. 27.
[6] *Ibid.*, pp. 28, 30.
[7] R. C. Smedley, *Underground Railroad*, p. 355.

North Carolina, and another from Jacksonville, Florida.[1] William Still gives a number of cases of escape by boat from Richmond and Norfolk, Virginia, and Wilmington, North Carolina, to the Vigilance Committee at Philadelphia.[2] Negroes arriving in New York City and coming within the horizon of Isaac T. Hopper's knowledge were often sent by water to Providence and Boston.[3]

Of the terminal stations or places of deportation along our northeastern boundary, there are not less than twenty-four, and probably many more. Three of them, Boston, Portland and St. Albans, were located in the New England states. Fugitives were probably less often sent directly to English soil from Boston than from the two other points, and in the few instances of which we have any hint, with perhaps one exception, the passengers so sent were put aboard vessels sailing for England. The boats running between Portland and the Canadian provinces were freely made use of to help slaves to their freedom, especially as the emigrants were often provided with passes. Sailing-vessels also furnished free passage, and carried the majority of the passengers that went from Portland.[4] St. Albans was the terminal of the Vermont line. Many fugitives were received and cared for here, and were sent on by private conveyance across the Canada border before the Vermont Central Railroad was built. Afterwards they were sent by rail, through the intervention of the Hon. Lawrence Brainerd, of St. Albans, who was one of the projectors of the steam railroad and largely interested in it financially.[5]

Along the northern boundary of New York and Pennsylvania there seem to have been not less than ten resorts facing the Canadian frontier. These were Ogdensburg,[6] Cape

[1] *Reminiscences of Fugitive-Slave Law Days in Boston*, pp. 34, 36, 37.
[2] William Still, *Underground Railroad Records*, pp. 77, 142, 151, 163, 165, 211, etc.
[3] Letter of James S. Rogers, Chicago, Ill., April 17, 1897.
[4] Letter of Brown Thurston, Portland, Me., Oct. 21, 1895.
[5] Letter of Aldis O. Brainerd, St. Albans, Vt., Oct. 21, 1895.
[6] "They crossed at Detroit and at Niagara and at Ogdensburg. Of those in New England, some went up through Vermont, some fled to Maine, and crossed over into New Brunswick." F. W. Seward, *Seward at Washington as Senator and Secretary of State*, Vol. I, p. 170.

Vincent, Port Ontario, Oswego, some port near Rochester, Lewiston, Suspension Bridge, Black Rock, Buffalo, Dunkirk Harbor and Erie. Doubtless the most important of these crossing-places were the four along the Niagara River, for here the most travelled of the routes in New York terminated. The harbors along Lake Ontario and the one on the St. Lawrence River appear to have been the terminals of side-tracks and branches rather than of main lines of Road.

Ohio may lay claim to eight terminal stations, all comparatively important. The best-known of these appear to have been Ashtabula Harbor, Painesville, Cleveland, Sandusky and Toledo, although the other three, Huron, Lorain and Conneaut, may be supposed, from their locations, to have done a thriving business. It is impossible to get now a measure of the efficiency of these various ports, for the period during which they were resorted to was a long one, and operators were obliged to work more or less independently, and obtained no adequate idea of the number emigrating from any one point. Custom-house methods were not followed in keeping account of the negroes exported across the Canada frontier. All that can be said in comparing these various ports is that Ashtabula Harbor, Cleveland and Sandusky, each seems to have been the terminus for four or five lines of Road, while perhaps only two or three lines ended at Toledo and Painesville, and one each at Huron, Lorain and Conneaut. Concerning the port at Huron we have a few observations, made by Mr. L. S. Stow, who lived a few miles from Lake Erie on the course of the Milan canal, and near one of the managers of the terminal, on whose premises fugitives often awaited the appearance of a Canada-bound boat. He says: "We used to see, occasionally, the fugitives, who ventured out for exercise while waiting for an opportunity to get on one of the vessels frequently passing down the canal and river from Milan, during the season of navigation. Many of these vessels passed through the Welland Canal on their way to the lower Lakes, and after leaving the harbor at Huron the fugitives were safe from the pursuit of their masters unless the vessels were compelled by stress of weather to return to harbor." [1]

[1] The *Firelands Pioneer*, July, 1888, pp. 80, 81.

THE DETROIT RIVER, AT DETROIT, MICHIGAN, IN 1850,
THE FAVORITE PLACE FOR FUGITIVES TO CROSS INTO CANADA.
(From an engraving in possession of C. M. Burton, Esq., of Detroit.)

HARBOR, ASHTABULA COUNTY, OHIO, IN 1860,
A PLACE OF DEPORTATION FOR FUGITIVES ON LAKE ERIE.
(From a photograph in possession of J. D. Hulbert, Esq., of Harbor, Ohio.)

Hundreds, nay, thousands of fugitives found crossing-places along the Detroit River, especially at the city of Detroit. The numerous routes of Indiana together with several of the chief routes of western Ohio poured their passengers into Detroit, thence to be transported by ferries and row-boats to the tongue of land pressing its shore-line for thirty miles from Lake Erie to Lake St. Clair upon the very borders of Michigan. The movement of slaves to this region was a fact of which Southerners early became apprised, and their efforts to recover their servants as these were about to enter the Canaan already within sight were occasionally successful, although the majority of the people of Detroit[1] and of the surrounding districts rejoiced to see the slave-catchers outwitted.

The places of deportation remaining to be mentioned are four, along the southwestern shore of Lake Michigan, namely, Milwaukee, Racine, South Port and Chicago. Of these the last-named was, doubtless, the most important, since through it chiefly were drained off the fugitives that came from Missouri over the routes of Iowa and Illinois. A single operator of Chicago, Mr. Philo Carpenter, is said to have guided not less than two hundred negroes to Canada-bound vessels.[2]

The lines of boat-service to the Canadian termini require a few words of comment. The longest line of travel on the lakes was that connecting the ports of Wisconsin and Illinois with Detroit or Amherstburg,[3] and was only approached in length by the route from Chicago to Collingwood, Ontario.[4] Five hundred miles would be a minimum statement of the distance refugees were carried by the boats of abolitionist captains from these westernmost ports to their havens of refuge. On Lake Erie the routes were, of course, much shorter, and ran up and down the lake, as well as across it. Important routes joined Toledo, Sandusky and Cleveland to Amherstburg and Detroit at one end of the lake, and Dunkirk, Ashtabula Harbor, Painesville and Cleveland with Buffalo and

---

[1] Silas Farmer, *History of Detroit and Michigan*, p. 346.
[2] Edward G. Mason, *Early Chicago and Illinois*, p. 110.
[3] See Chapter III, pp. 82, 83.
[4] Letter of John G. Weiblen, Fairview, Erie Co., Pa., Nov. 26, 1895.

Black Rock at the other end of the lake. Certain boats running on these routes came to be known as abolition boats, with ample accommodations for underground passengers. Thus, we are told, such passengers " depended on a vessel named the *Arrow*, which for many years plied between Sandusky and Detroit, but always touched first at Malden, Canada, where the fugitives were landed."[1] Frequent use was also made of scows, sail-boats and sharpies, with which refugees could be "set across" the lake, and landed at almost any point along the shore. Small vessels, a part of whose "freight" had been received from the Underground Railroad, were often despatched to Port Burwell in the night from the warehouse of Hubbard and Company, forwarding and commission merchants of Ashtabula Harbor.[2] Similar enterprises were carried on at various other points along the lake.[3] So far as known, Lake Ontario had only a few comparatively insignificant routes: at the upper end of the lake were two, one joining Rochester and St. Catherines, the other, St. Catherines and Toronto; at the lower end of the lake, Oswego, Port Ontario and Cape Vincent seem to have been connected by lines with Kingston.

It is impossible to tell how many cities, towns and villages in Canada became terminals of the underground system. Outside of the interlake region of Ontario it is safe to name Kingston, Prescott, Montreal, Stanstead and St. John, New Brunswick. Within that region the terminals were numerous, being scattered from the southern shore of Georgian Bay to Lake Erie, and from the Detroit and Huron rivers to the

[1] The *Firelands Pioneer*, July, 1888, p. 77.
[2] Conversation with Nelson Watrous, Harbor, O., Aug. 8, 1892; conversation with J. D. Hulbert, Harbor, O., Aug. 7, 1892.
[3] The following incident given by Mr. Rush R. Sloane will serve as an illustration: "In the summer of 1853, four fugitives arrived at Sandusky. . . . Mr. John Irvine . . . had arranged for a 'sharpee,' a small sail-boat used by fishermen, with one George Sweigels, to sail the boat to Canada with this party, for which service Captain Sweigels was to receive thirty-five dollars. One man accompanied Captain Sweigels, and at eight o'clock in the evening this party in this small boat started to cross Lake Erie. The wind was favorable, and before morning Point au Pelee Island was reached, and the next day the four escaped fugitives were in Canada." The *Firelands Pioneer*, July, 1888, pp. 49, 50.

Niagara. Owen Sound, Collingwood and Oro were the northernmost resorts, so far as now known. Toronto, Queen's Bush, Wellesley, Galt and Hamilton occupied territory south of these, and farther south still, in the marginal strip fronting directly on Lake Erie, there were not less than twenty more places of refuge. The most important of these were naturally those situated at either end of the strip, and along the shore-line, namely, Windsor, Sandwich and Amherstburg, New Canaan, Colchester and Kingsville, Gosfield and Buxton, Port Stanley, Port Burwell and Port Royal, Long Point, Fort Erie and St. Catherines. In the valley of the Thames also many refugees settled, especially at Chatham, Dresden and Dawn, and at Sydenham, London and Wilberforce. The names of two additional towns, Sarnia on the Huron River and Brantford on the Grand, complete the list of the known Canadian terminals. This enumeration of centres cannot be supposed to be exhaustive. A full record would take into account the localities in the outlying country districts as well as those adjoining or forming a part of the hamlets, towns and cities of the whites, whither the blacks had penetrated. The untrodden wilds of Canada, as well as her populous places, seemed hospitable to a people for whom the hardships of the new life were fully compensated by the consciousness of their possession of the rights of freemen, rights vouchsafed them by a government that exemplified the proud boast of the poet Cowper: —

> "Slaves cannot breathe in England; if their lungs
> Receive our air, that moment they are free!
> They touch our country and their shackles fall."

CHAPTER VI

ABDUCTION OF SLAVES FROM THE SOUTH

MOST persons that engaged in the underground service were opposed either to enticing or to abducting slaves from the South. This was no less true along the southern border of the free states than in their interior. The principle generally acted upon by the friends of fugitives was that which they held to be voiced in the Scriptural injunction to feed the hungry and clothe the naked. The quaking negro at the door in the dead of night seeking relief from a condition, the miseries of which he found intolerable and for which he was in no proper sense responsible, was a figure to be pitied, and to be helped without delay. Under such circumstances there was no room for casuistry in the mind of the abolitionist. The response of his warm nature was as decisive as his favorite passage of Scripture was imperative. The fugitive was fed, clothed if necessary, and guided to another friend farther on. But abolitionists were unwilling, for the most part, to involve themselves more deeply in danger by abducting slaves from thraldom. The Rev. John B. Mahan, one of the early anti-slavery men of southern Ohio, expressed this fact when he said, "I am confident that few, if any, for various reasons, would invade the jurisdiction of another state to give aid and encouragement to slaves to escape from their owners. . . ."[1] And in northern Ohio, in so radical a town as Oberlin, a famous station of the Underground Road, we are told that there was no sentiment in favor of enticing slaves away, and that this was never done except in one case — by Calvin Fairbank, a student.[2]

[1] *History of Brown County, Ohio*, p. 315.
[2] Conversation with ex-President James H. Fairchild, Oberlin, O., Aug. 3, 1892.

The general disinclination to induce escapes of slaves, either by secret invitation or by persons serving as guides, renders the few cases conspicuous, and gives them considerable interest. When instances of this kind became known to the slave-owners, as for example, by the arrest and imprisonment of some over-venturesome offender, the irritation resulting on both sides of Mason and Dixon's line was apt to be disproportionate to the magnitude of the cause. Nevertheless the aggravation of sectional feeling thus produced was real, and was valued by some Northern agitators as a means to a better understanding of the system of slavery.[1]

The largest number of abduction cases occurred through the activities of those well-disposed towards fugitives by the attachments of race. There were many negroes, enslaved and free, along the southern boundaries of New Jersey, Pennsylvania, Ohio, Indiana, Illinois and Iowa, whose opportunities were numerous for conveying fugitives to free soil with slight risk to themselves. These persons sometimes did scarcely more than ferry runaways across a stream or direct them to the homes of friends residing near the line of a free state. In the vicinity of Martin's Ferry, Ohio, there lived a colored man who frequented the Virginia shore for the purpose of persuading slaves to run away. He was in the habit of imparting the necessary information, and then displaying himself in an intoxicated condition, feigned or real, to avoid suspicion. At last he was found out, but escaped by betaking himself to Canada.[2] In the neighborhood of Portsmouth, Ohio, slaves were conveyed across the river by one Poindexter, a barber of the town of Jackson.[3] In Baltimore, Maryland, two colored women, who engaged in selling vegetables, were efficient in starting fugitives on the way to Philadelphia.[4] At Louisville, Kentucky, Wash Spradley, a shrewd negro, was instrumental in helping many of his enslaved brethren out of bondage.[5] These few instances

---

[1] See the Annual Reports of the Massachusetts Anti-Slavery Society.
[2] Conversation with Mrs. Joel Woods, at Martin's Ferry, Aug. 19, 1892.
[3] Conversation with Judge Jesse W. Laird, Jackson, O., June, 1895.
[4] Conversation with Mr. Robert Purvis, at Philadelphia, Dec. 23, 1895.
[5] Conversation with John Evans, at Windsor, Ont., C.W., Aug. 2, 1895;

will suffice to illustrate the secret enterprises conducted by colored persons on both sides of the sectional line once dividing the North from the South.

Another class of colored persons that undertook the work of delivering some of their race from the cruel uncertainties of slavery may be found among the refugees of Canada. Describing the early development of the movement of slaves to Canada, Dr. Samuel G. Howe says of these persons, "Some, not content with personal freedom and happiness, went secretly back to their old homes and brought away their wives and children at much peril and cost."[1] It has been stated that the number of these persons visiting the South annually was about five hundred.[2] Mr. D. B. Hodge, of Lloydsville, Ohio, gives the case of a negro that went to Canada by way of New Athens, and in the course of a year returned over the same route, went to Kentucky, and brought away his wife and two children, making his pilgrimage northward again after the lapse of about two months.[3] Another case, reported by Mr. N. C. Buswell, of Neponset, Illinois, is as follows: A slave, Charlie, belonging to a Missouri planter living near Quincy, Illinois, escaped to Canada by way of one of the underground routes. Ere long he decided to return and get his wife, but found she had been sold South. When making his second journey eastward he brought with him a family of slaves, who preferred freedom to remaining as the chattels of his old master. This was the first of a number of such trips made by the fugitive Charlie.[4] Mr. Seth Linton,[5] who was familiar with the work on a line of this Road running through Clinton County, Ohio, reports that a fugitive that had passed along the route returned after some months, saying he had come back to rescue his wife. His absence in the slave state continued so long that it was feared he had been captured, but after some weeks he reappeared, bringing

John Evans was a slave near Louisville, but was given his liberty in 1850, when his master became financially involved.

[1] Howe, *The Refugees from Slavery in Canada West*, p. 11.
[2] Redpath, *The Public Life of Captain John Brown*, p. 229.
[3] Letter from Mr. D. B. Hodge, Oct. 9, 1894.
[4] Letter from Colonel N. C. Buswell, March 13, 1896.
[5] Letter from Seth Linton.

his wife and her father with him. He told of having seen many slaves in the country and said they would be along as soon as they could escape. The following year the Clinton County line was unusually busy. A brave woman named Armstrong escaped with her husband and one child to Canada in 1842. Two years later she determined to rescue the remainder of her family from the Kentucky plantation where she had left them, and, disguised as a man, she went back to the old place. Hiding near a spring, where her children were accustomed to get water, she was able to give instructions to five of them, and the following night she departed with her flock to an underground station at Ripley, Ohio.[1]

Equally zealous in the slaves' behalf with the groups of persons mentioned in the last two paragraphs were certain individuals of Southern birth and white parentage, who found the opportunity to conduct slaves beyond the confines of the plantation states. Robert Purvis tells of the son of a planter, who sometimes travelled into the free states with a retinue of body-servants for the purpose of having them fall into the hands of vigilant abolitionists. The author has heard similar stories in regard to the sons of Kentucky slave-owners, but the names of the parties concerned were withheld for obvious reasons.

John Fairfield, a Virginian, devoted much time and thought to abducting slaves. Levi Coffin, who knew him intimately, describes him as a person full of contradictions, who, although a Southerner by birth, and living the greater part of the time in the South, yet hated slavery; a person lacking in moral quality, but devoted to the interests of the slave.[2] John Fairfield's ostensible business was, at times, that of a poultry and provision dealer; and his views, when he was among planters, were pro-slavery. Nevertheless his abiding interest seems to have been to despoil slaveholders of their human property. He made excursions into various parts of the South, and led many companies safely through to Canada. While Laura Haviland was serving as a mission teacher in Canada West (1852-1853), Fairfield arrived at Windsor,

[1] The *Firelands Pioneer*, July, 1888, p. 39.
[2] Coffin, *Reminiscences*, pp. 304, 305; letter of Miss H. N. Wilson, College Hill, O., April 14, 1892.

bringing with him twenty-seven slaves. Mrs. Haviland, who witnessed the happy conclusion of this adventure, testifies that it was but one of many, and that the abductor often made expeditions into the heart of the slaveholding states to secure his companies. On the occasion of the arrival of the Virginian with the twenty-seven a reception and dinner were given in his honor by appreciative friends in one of the churches of the colored people, and a sort of jubilee was celebrated. The ecstasies of some of the guests, among them an old negro woman over eighty years of age, touched the heart of their benefactor, who exclaimed, " This pays me for all dangers I have faced in bringing this company, just to see these friends meet."[1]

Northern men residing or travelling in the South were sometimes tempted to encourage slaves to flee to Canada, or even to plan and execute abductions. Jacob Cummings, a slave belonging to a small planter, James Smith, of southeastern Tennessee, was befriended by a Mr. Leonard, of Chattanooga, who had become an abolitionist in Albany, New York, before his removal to the South. Cummings was occasionally sent on errands to Mr. Leonard's store. This gave the Northerner the desired opportunity to show his slave customer where

[1] Laura S. Haviland, *A Woman's Life Work*, p. 199.
In a letter dated Lawrence, Kan., March 23, 1893, Mr. Fitch Reed gives some of the circumstances connected with the progress of this company through the last stages of its journey. He says: " In 1853, there came over the road twenty-eight in one gang, with a conductor by the name of Fairfield, from Virginia, who had aided in liberating all his father's and uncle's slaves, and there was a reward out for him of five hundred dollars, dead or alive. They had fifty-two rounds of arms, and were determined not to be taken alive. Four teams from my house [in Cambridge, Mich.] started at sunset, drove through Clinton after dark, got to Ypsilanti before daylight. Stayed at Bro. Ray's through the day. At noon, Bro. M. Coe, from our station, got on the cars and went to Detroit, and left Ray to drive his team. Coe informed the friends of the situation, and made arrangements for their reception. The friends came out to meet them ten miles before we came to Detroit, piloted us to a large boarding-house by the side of the river. Two hundred abolitionists took breakfast with them just before daylight. We procured boats enough for Fairfield and his crew. As they pushed off from shore, they all commenced singing the song, 'I am on my way to Canada, where colored men are free,' and continued firing off their arms till out of hearing. At eight o'clock, the ferry-boats started, and the station-keepers went over and spent most of the day with them."

Ohio and Indiana are on the map, and to advise him to go to Canada. As Cummings had a "hard master" he did not long delay his going.[1]

The risks and costs of a long trip were not too great for the enthusiastic abolitionist who felt that immediate rescue must be attempted. One remarkable incident illustrates the determination sometimes displayed in freeing a slave. Two brothers from Connecticut settled in the District of Columbia about the year 1848. They became gardeners, and employed among their hands a colored woman, who was hired out to them by her master. Soon after the passage of the Fugitive Slave Law (1850) she came weeping to her employers with the news that she was to be sold "down South." Stirred by her impending misfortune, one of the brothers had a large box made, within which he nailed the slave-woman and her young daughter. With the box in his market-wagon he set out on a long, arduous trip across Maryland and Pennsylvania into New York. After three weeks of travel he reached his journey's end at Warsaw. Here he delivered his charge to the care of friends, among whom they found a permanent home.[2]

There were ardent abolitionists living almost within sight of slave territory that had no scruples about helping slaves across the line and passing them on to freedom. In 1836, Dr. David Nelson, a Virginian, who had freed his slaves and moved to Marion County, Missouri, and had there founded Marion College, was driven into Illinois on account of his anti-slavery views. He settled at Quincy, and soon established the Mission Institute, which was chiefly a school for the education of missionaries. Mr. N. A. Hunt, now eighty-five years old but apparently of clear mind, was a student in Mission Institute in its early years. He relates an incident showing the spirit existing in the school, a spirit that manifested itself a little later in the actions of Messrs Burr, Work and Thompson. His story is that Dr. Nelson came to him one day in the

[1] Conversation with Jacob Cummings, Columbus, O., April, 1894.
[2] Conversation with the daughter mentioned, now the wife of William Burghardt, Warsaw, N.Y., June, 1894. Article on the Underground Railroad in the *History of Warsaw, New York*.

spring of 1839 or 1840, and asked him to go with another student across the Mississippi River and patrol the shore opposite Quincy. The students were to make signals at intervals by tapping stones together, and if their signals were answered they were to help such as needed help by conducting them to a place of safety, a station on the Underground Railroad, sixteen miles east of Quincy. The station could be easily recognized, for it was a red barn. The time chosen for crossing the river was always a Sunday night, a time known to be the best for the persons sometimes found waiting on the other side. This detailing of a watch from the school was regularly done, although with what results is not known.[1]

Among the students attending this Institute in 1841 were James E. Burr and George Thompson. These young men, together with a villager, Alanson Work, arranged with two slaves to convey them from bondage in Missouri. The abductors found themselves surrounded by a crowd of angry Missourians, and were speedily committed to jail in Palmyra. To insure the conviction of the prisoners three indictments were brought against them, one charging them with "stealing slaves, another with attempting to steal them, and the other with intending to make the attempt."[2] Conviction was a foregone conclusion. Work and his companions were pronounced guilty and sentenced to twelve years' imprisonment. These men were not required, however, to serve out their terms. Mr. Work was pardoned after three and a half years on the unjust condition that he return with his wife and children to the State of Connecticut, his former residence. Mr. Burr was released at the end of a little more than four years and six months, and Mr. Thompson after nearly five years' imprisonment. The anti-slavery character of Mission Institute at length brought down upon it the wrath of the Missourians. One winter night a party from Marion County crossed the Mississippi River on the ice, stealthily marched to the Institute, and set it on fire.[3]

[1] Letter from N. A. Hunt, of Riverside, Cal., Feb. 12, 1891.
[2] Quoted by Wilson, *Rise and Fall of the Slave Power in America*, Vol. II, p. 71.
[3] Asbury, *History of Quincy*, p. 74. The account of the Burr, Work and Thompson case occupies pp. 72, 73 and 74 of Asbury's volume.

In southern Indiana operations similar to those of the students of the Mission Institute were carried on by a supposedly inoffensive pedler of notions, Joseph Sider. With his large convenient wagon Sider traversed some of the border counties of Kentucky, supplying goods to his customers; one of his boxes was reserved for disguises for negroes that wished to cast off the garments of slavery. Sider's method involved the use of his vehicle for long trips to the Ohio River, where the passengers were conveyed by boat to a place of safety, and told to remain concealed until the wagon and team could be transported by ferry the following morning. So simple a plan did not excite suspicion, and served to carry fugitives rapidly forward to some line of underground traffic.[1]

Among those invasions of the South that caused considerable excitement at the time of their occurrence, the cases of Calvin Fairbank, Seth Concklin and John Brown are notable; and accounts of them cannot well be omitted from these pages, even though they may be more or less familiar to the reader. Mr. Calvin Fairbank came of English stock, and was born in Wyoming County, New York, in 1816. His home training as well as his attendance at Oberlin College furnished him with anti-slavery views, but the circumstance to which he traced his hearty hatred of the Southern institution arose by chance, when as a boy he was attending quarterly meeting with his parents. "It happened that my family was assigned," he relates, "to the good, clean home of a pair of escaped slaves. One night after service I sat on the hearthstone before the fire, and listened to the woman's story of sorrow. . . . My heart wept, my anger was kindled, and antagonism to slavery was fixed upon me."[2] In the spring of 1837 young Fairbank was sent by his father down the Ohio River in charge of a raft of lumber. A little below Wheeling he saw a large, active-looking, black man on the Virginia shore, going to the woods with his axe. He found

---

[1] E. Hicks Trueblood, "Reminiscences of the Underground Railroad," in the *Republican Leader*, Salem, Ind., March 16, 1894.

[2] *Rev. Calvin Fairbank During Slavery Times, or How the Way was Prepared.* Edited from his manuscript. Pp. 1-7.

the woodsman to be a slave, soon gained his confidence, and set him across the river on the raft. A few days later Mr. Fairbank moored his rude craft, and landed on the Kentucky shore opposite the mouth of the Little Miami River. Here he was approached by an old slave-woman, who sought the liberation of her seven children. The matter was easily arranged, and after dark the seven were speedily conveyed across the river.[1]

The rescue of Lewis Hayden and his family was the means of bringing Mr. Fairbank to the penitentiary, while it opened to his friend Hayden an honorable career in New England. Mr. Hayden became a respected citizen of Boston, and helped to organize the Vigilance Committee for the purpose of protecting the refugees that were settling in the city; in course of time he came to serve in the legislature of the State of Massachusetts. His wife, who survived him, made a bequest of an estate of about five thousand dollars to Harvard University to found a scholarship for the benefit of deserving colored students.[2] The story of Hayden's delivery and of his own imprisonment is best told in Mr. Fairbank's words: "Lewis Hayden . . . was, when a young man, . . . the property of Baxter and Grant, owners of the Brennan House, in Lexington. Hayden's wife, Harriet, and his son, a lad of ten years when I first knew them, were the slaves of Patrick Baine. On a September evening in 1844, accompanied by Miss D. A. Webster, a young Vermont lady, who was associated with me in teaching, I left Lexington with the Haydens, in a hack, crossed the Ohio River on a ferry at nine the next morning, changed horses, and drove to an Underground Railroad depot at Hopkins, Ohio, where we left Hayden and his family. . . . When Miss Webster and I returned to Lexington, after two days' absence, we were both arrested, charged by their master with helping Hayden's wife and son to escape. We were jointly indicted, but Miss Webster was tried first and sentenced to two years' imprisonment in the penitentiary at Frankfort. . . . While my case was still pending I learned that the governor was inclined to pardon Miss

---

[1] *Rev. Calvin Fairbank During Slavery Times*, pp. 12–14.
[2] *Boston Weekly Transcript*, Dec. 29, 1893.

Webster, but first insisted that I should be tried. When called up for trial in February, 1845, I pleaded guilty, and received a sentence of fifteen years. I served four years and eleven months, and then, August 23, 1849, was released by Governor John J. Crittenden, the able and patriotic man who afterwards saved Kentucky to the Union."[1]

In spite of his incarceration for aiding slaves to escape, and in the face of the heavier penalties laid by the new Fugitive Slave Law, passed shortly after his release from prison, Calvin Fairbank was soon engaged in similar enterprises. He declares, "I resisted its [the law's] execution whenever and wherever possible."[2] A little more than two years after his pardon Mr. Fairbank was again arrested, this time in Indiana, for carrying off Tamar, a young mulatto woman, who was claimed as property by A. L. Shotwell, of Louisville, Kentucky. Without process of law Mr. Fairbank was taken from the State of Indiana to Louisville, where he was tried in February, 1853. He was again sentenced to the state prison for a term of fifteen years, and while there was frequently subjected to the most brutal treatment. Altogether Mr. Fairbank spent seventeen years and four months of his life in prison for abducting slaves; he says that during his second term he received at the hands of prison officials thirty-five thousand stripes.[3] Having served more than twelve years of his second sentence, he was pardoned by acting Governor Richard T. Jacob. It was a singular occurrence that finally enabled Mr. Fairbank to regain his liberty. Among the friends upon whose favor he could rely was the lieutenant-governor of Kentucky, Richard T. Jacob, the son-in-law of Thomas H. Benton, of Missouri. Mr. Jacob was a man of strong anti-slavery tendencies, notwithstanding his political prominence and his private interests as a wealthy planter. The governor, Thomas E. Bramlette, was opposed to extending the executive clemency to so notorious an offender as Mr. Fairbank. Early in 1864 General Speed S. Fry was detailed by President Lincoln to enroll all the negroes of

---

[1] The *Chicago Tribune*, Sunday, Jan. 29, 1893.
[2] Ibid.
[3] *Rev. Calvin Fairbank During Slavery Times*, pp. 138, 144.

Kentucky, but he came into collision with Governor Bramlette, who sought to prevent General Fry from carrying out his orders. Upon receiving information to this effect the President summoned the executive of Kentucky to Washington to answer to charges; and thereupon Mr. Jacob became acting governor. On his first day in office the new executive of Kentucky was accosted by General Fry with the remark, " Governor, the President thinks it would be well to make this Fairbank's day." On the morning following, the prisoner received a full and free pardon.[1]

Mr. Fairbank gives many interesting devices that he employed in his work to throw off pursuit. " Forty-seven slaves I guided toward the north star, in violation of the state codes of Virginia and Kentucky. I piloted them through the forests, mostly by night; girls, fair and white, dressed as ladies; men and boys, as gentlemen, or servants; men in women's clothes, and women in men's clothes; boys dressed as girls, and girls as boys; on foot or on horseback, in buggies, carriages, common wagons, in and under loads of hay, straw, old furniture, boxes and bags; crossing the Jordan of the slave, swimming or wading chin deep; or in boats, or skiffs; on rafts, and often on a pine log. And I never suffered one to be recaptured."[2]

About 1850, Seth Concklin, a resident of Philadelphia, learned of the remarkable escape of Peter Still from Alabama to the Quaker City. Here the runaway was most happily favored in finding friends. William Still, his brother, from whom he had been separated by kidnappers long years before, was discovered almost immediately in the office of the Pennsylvania Anti-Slavery Society; and Seth Concklin soon proffered himself as an agent to go into the South and bring away Peter Still's family. The fugitive himself first visited Alabama to see what could be done for his wife and children; but failing to accomplish anything he gratefully accepted the offer of the daring Philadelphian. Mr. Concklin expected to assume the character of a slave-owner and

[1] *Rev. Calvin Fairbank During Slavery Times*, pp. 11, 104-143. See also the *Chicago Tribune*, Sunday, Jan. 29, 1893, p. 33.
[2] *Rev. Calvin Fairbank During Slavery Times*, pp. 10 and 11.

bring the Stills away as his servants; he found, however, that the steamboats on the Tennessee River were too irregular to be depended on. He therefore returned north to Indiana, and arranged for the escape of the slave family across that state to Canada. The story of his second attempt at the South has a tragic ending, notwithstanding its favorable beginning. Having made a safe start and a long journey of seven days and nights in a rowboat the whole party was captured in southwestern Indiana. A letter from the Rev. N. R. Johnston to William Still, written soon after the catastrophe, gives the following account of the affair: " On last Tuesday I mailed a letter to you, written by Seth Concklin. I presume you have received that letter. It gave an account of the rescue of the family of your brother. If that is the last news you have had from them I have very painful intelligence for you. They passed on (north) from near Princeton, where I saw them. . . . I think twenty-three miles above Vincennes, Ind., they were seized by a party of men, and lodged in jail. Telegraphic despatches were sent all through the South. I have since learned that the marshal of Evansville received a despatch from Tuscumbia to look out for them. By some means, he and the master, so says report, went to Vincennes and claimed the fugitives, chained Mr. Concklin, and hurried all off. . . ."[1] In a postscript, the same letter gave the rumor of Seth Concklin's escape from the boat on which he was being carried South; but the newspapers brought reports of a different nature. Their statements represented that the man " Miller " — that is, Concklin — " was found drowned, with his hands and feet in chains and his skull fractured."[2] The version of the tragedy given by the claimant of the fugitives, McKiernon, was as follows : " Some time last march a white man by the name of Miller appeared in the nabourhood and abducted the above negroes, was caught at vincanes, Indi. with said negroes and was thare convicted of steling and remanded back to Ala. to Abide the penalty of the law and on his return

[1] Letter dated Evansville, Ind., March 31, 1851. Printed in Still's *Underground Railroad Records*, pp. 30, 31.
[2] Still, *Underground Railroad Records*, p. 31.

met his Just reward by getting drowned at the mouth of cumberland River on the Ohio in attempting to make his escape."[1] Just how Concklin met his death will probably always remain a mystery. McKiernon's letter offered terms for the purchase of the poor slaves, but they were so exorbitant that they could not be accepted. Besides, it was not deemed proper to jeopardize the life of another agent on a mission so dangerous.

It is well known that John Brown aided fugitive slaves whenever the opportunity occurred, as did his Puritan-bred father before him. We have no record, however, of his abducting slaves from the South except in the case of his famous raid into Missouri in 1858. This exploit has a peculiar interest for us, not only as one of the most notable abductions, but as being, in a special way, the prelude of that great plan in behalf of the enslaved that he sought to carry out at Harper's Ferry. After Captain Brown's return from the Eastern states to Kansas in 1858, he and his men encamped for a few days at Bain's Fort. While here, Brown was appealed to by a slave, Jim Daniels, the chattel of one James Lawrence, of Missouri. Daniels had heard of Captain Brown, and, securing a permit to go about and sell brooms, had used it in making his way to Brown's camp.[2] His prayer was "For help to get away," because he was soon to be sold, together with his wife, two children and a negro man.[3] Such a supplication could not be made in vain to John Brown. On the following night (December 20) Brown's raid into Missouri was made. Brown himself gives the account of it:[4] "Two small companies were made up to go to Missouri and forcibly liberate the five slaves, together

[1] Still, *Underground Railroad Records*, p. 35. Letter dated South Florence, Ala., Aug. 6, 1851.

[2] Conversation with Samuel Harper and his wife, Jane Harper, the two surviving members of the company of slaves escorted to Canada by Brown in March, 1859. Their home since has been in or about Windsor. I found them there in the early part of August, 1895.

[3] Halloway, *History of Kansas*. Quoted from John Brown's letters, January, 1859 (pp. 539–545).

[4] In a letter written by Brown, January, 1859, to the *New York Tribune*, in which paper it was published. It was also published in the *Lawrence (Kansas) Republican*. See Sanborn's *Life and Letters of John Brown*, p. 481.

SAMUEL HARPER AND WIFE,
OF WINDSOR, ONTARIO,
the two survivors of the company of slaves abducted by John Brown from Missouri in the winter of 1858–1859.
(From a recent photograph.)

ELLEN CRAFT.
Disguised as a young planter, she escaped to Boston in 1848, bringing her husband with her as a valet.
(From a portrait in possession of the Hon. Simeon Dodge, of Marblehead, Mass.)

with other slaves. One of these companies I assumed to direct. We proceeded to the place, surrounded the buildings, liberated the slaves, and also took certain property supposed to belong to the estate.

"We, however, learned before leaving that a portion of the articles we had taken belonged to a man living on the plantation as a tenant, and who was supposed to have no interest in the estate. We promptly returned to him all we had taken. We then went to another plantation, where we found five more slaves; took some property and two white men. We moved all slowly away into the territory for some distance and then sent the white men back, telling them to follow us as soon as they chose to do so. The other company freed one female slave, took some property, and, as I am informed, killed one white man (the master) who fought against liberation. . . ."[1]

The company responsible for the shooting of the slave-owner, David Cruse, was in charge of Kagi and Charles Stephens, also known as Whipple. When this party came to the house of Mr. Cruse the family had retired. There was no hesitation, however, on the part of the strangers in requesting quarters for the night. Mrs. Cruse, her suspicions fully aroused, handed her husband his pistol. Jean Harper, the slave-woman that was taken from this house, asserts that her master would certainly have fired upon the intruders had not Whipple used his revolver first, with deadly effect. When the two squads came together the march back to Bain's Fort was begun. On the way thither Brown asked the slaves if they wanted to be free, and then promised to take them to a free country. Thus was Brown led to undertake one of his boldest adventures, one of the boldest indeed in the history of the Underground Road. With a mere handful of men he purposed to escort his band of freedmen on a journey of twenty-five hundred miles to Canada, in the dead of winter, and surrounded by the dangers that the publicity of his foray and the announcement of a reward of three thousand dollars for his arrest were likely to bring upon him. Brown and his

[1] Sanborn, *Life and Letters of John Brown*, pp. 482, 483; also Redpath, *The Public Life of Captain John Brown*, pp. 219, 220.

company tarried only one day at Bain's Fort; then proceeded northward by way of Topeka to the place of his friend, Dr. Doyle, five miles beyond, and then by way of Osawattomie, Holton and the house of Major J. B. Abbot near Lawrence, into Nebraska. Lawrence was reached January 24, 1859. At Holton a party of pursuers, two or three times as large as Brown's company, was dispersed in instant and ridiculous flight, and four prisoners and five horses were taken. The trip, after leaving Holton, was made amidst great perils. Under an escort of seventeen "Topeka boys" Brown pressed rapidly on to Nebraska City. At this point the passage of the Missouri was made on the ice, and the liberators with their charges arrived at Tabor in the first week of February. Here, Brown met with rebuff, "contrary to his expectation, and contrary to the whole former attitude of the people," we are told, "he was not welcomed, but, at a public meeting called for the purpose, was severely reprimanded as a disturber of the peace and safety of the village. Effecting a hasty departure from Tabor, and taking advantage of the protection offered by a few friendly families on the way, he and his party of fugitives came, on February 20, 1859, to Grinnell, Iowa, where they were cordially received by the Hon. J. B. Grinnell, who entertained them in his house. Brown's next stop was made at Springdale, which place he reached on February 25. Here the fugitives were distributed among the Quaker families for safety and rest before continuing the journey to Canada. But soon rumors were afloat of the coming of the United States marshal, and it became necessary to secure for the negroes railroad transportation to Chicago. Kagi and Stephens, disguised as sportsmen, walked to Iowa City, enlisted the services of Mr. William Penn Clark, an influential anti-slavery citizen of that place, and by his efforts, supplemented by those of Hon. J. B. Grinnell, a freight car was got and held in readiness at West Liberty. The negroes were then brought down from Springdale (distant but six miles) and, after spending a night in a grist-mill near the railway station, were ready to embark."[1] They were

[1] Irving B. Richman, *John Brown among the Quakers, and Other Sketches*, pp. 46, 47, 48.

stowed away in the freight-car by Brown, Kagi and Stephens, and the car was made fast to a train from the West on the Chicago and Rock Island Road. "On reaching Chicago, Brown and his party were taken into friendly charge by Allen Pinkerton, the famous detective, and started for Detroit. On March 10 they were in Detroit and practically at their journey's end."[1] On the twelfth the freedmen were, under Brown's direction, ferried across the Detroit River to Windsor, Canada.

The trip from southern Kansas to the Canadian destination had consumed three weeks. The restoration of twelve persons to "their natural and inalienable rights with but one man killed"[2] was a result which Brown seems to have regarded as justifiable, but one the tragedy of which he certainly deplored.[3] The manner in which this result had been accomplished was highly dramatic, and created great excitement throughout the country, especially in Missouri. Brown's biographer, James Redpath, writing in 1860, speaks thus of the consternation in the invaded state: "When the news of the invasion of Missouri spread, a wild panic went with it, which in a few days resulted in clearing Bates and Vernon counties of their slaves. Large numbers were sold south; many ran into the Territory and escaped; others were removed farther inland. When John Brown made his invasion there were five hundred slaves in that district where there are not fifty negroes now."[4] The success of the expedition just narrated was well fitted to increase confidence in John Brown's determination, and to arouse enthusiasm among his numerous refugee friends in Canada. The story of the adventure was not unlikely to penetrate the remote regions of the South, and perhaps find lodgment in the retentive memories of many slaves. The publication in the *New York Tribune* of his letter defending his abduction of the Missouri chattels just as he was begin-

---

[1] Irving B. Richman, *John Brown among the Quakers, and Other Sketches*, pp. 46, 47, 48.
[2] Sanborn, *The Life and Letters of John Brown*, p. 483. See the letter of "The Parallels."
[3] Hinton, *John Brown and His Men*, p. 221.
[4] Redpath, *The Public Life of Captain John Brown*, p. 221.

ning his journey east shows that Brown was not unwilling to have his act widely known. It was almost the middle of March when Brown arrived in Canada; his letter had been made public in January; it had had ample time for circulation. Before he left Kansas he said significantly, "He would soon remove the seat of the trouble elsewhere,"[1] and it was but six months after his arrival in Canada that the attack on Harper's Ferry was made.

For more than ten years John Brown had cherished a plan for the liberation of the slaves, in which abduction was to be in a measure employed. This plan he had revealed to Frederick Douglass as early as 1847. It is given in Douglass' words: "'The true object to be sought,' said Brown, 'is first of all to destroy the money value of slave property; and that can only be done by rendering such property insecure. My plan then is to take at first about twenty-five picked men, and begin on a small scale; supply them arms and ammunition; post them in squads of five on a line of twenty-five miles, the most persuasive and judicious of whom shall go down to the fields from time to time, as opportunity offers, and induce the slaves to join them, seeking and selecting the most restless and daring.' . . . With care and enterprise he thought he could soon gather a force of one hundred hardy men. . . . When these were properly drilled, . . . they would run off the slaves in larger numbers, retain the brave and strong ones in the mountains, and send the weak and timid to the North by the Underground Railroad: his operations would be enlarged with increasing numbers, and would not be confined to one locality. . . . 'If,' said Brown, 'we could drive slavery out of *one county*, . . . it would weaken the system throughout the state.' The enemy's country would afford subsistence, the fastnesses of the Alleghanies abundant protection, and a series of stations through Pennsylvania to the Canadian border a means of egress for timid slaves."[2]

The plot, as disclosed eleven years later to Richard J. Hinton (September, 1858) by Brown's lieutenant, Kagi, contains

[1] Hinton, *John Brown and His Men*, p. 222, note.
[2] *Life of Frederick Douglass*, 1881, pp. 280, 281 and 318, 319. Also Hinton, *John Brown and His Men*, pp. 30, 31, 32.

some additional details of interest. Hinton says: "The mountains of Virginia were named as the place of refuge, and as a country admirably adapted in which to carry on a guerilla warfare. In the course of the conversation, Harper's Ferry was mentioned as a point to be seized — but not held — on account of the arsenal. The white members of the company were to act as officers of different guerilla bands, which, under the general command of John Brown, were to be composed of Canadian refugees, and the Virginian slaves who would join them. . . . They anticipated, after the first blow had been struck, that, by the aid of the free and Canadian negroes who would join them, they could inspire confidence in the slaves, and induce them to rally. No intention was expressed of gathering a large body of slaves, and removing them to Canada. On the contrary, Kagi clearly stated, in answer to my inquiries, that the design was to make the fight in the mountains of Virginia, extending it to North Carolina and Tennessee, and also to the swamps of South Carolina, if possible. Their purpose was not the expatriation of one or a thousand slaves, but their liberation in the states wherein they were born, and were now held in bondage. . . . Kagi spoke of having marked out a chain of counties extending continuously through South Carolina, Georgia, Alabama, and Mississippi. He had traveled over a large portion of the region indicated, and from his own personal knowledge and with the assistance of the Canadian negroes who had escaped from those States, they had arranged a general plan of attack. . . . They expected to be speedily and constantly reinforced; first, by the arrival of those men who, in Canada, were anxiously looking and praying for the time of deliverance, and then by the slaves themselves. . . . The constitution adopted at Chatham [in the spring of 1858] was intended as the framework of organization among the emancipationists, to enable the leaders to effect a more complete control of their forces. . . ."[1] A comparison of these two versions of Brown's plan of liberation leads to the conclusion that the abduction of slaves to the North was a

[1] Hinton, *John Brown and His Men*, Appendix, pp. 673, 674, 675. Also Redpath, *The Public Life of Captain John Brown*, pp. 203, 204, 205.

measure to which the liberator never attached more importance than as a means of ridding his men of the care of helpless slaves; the brave he would use in organizing an insurrection amid the mountains of the Southern states that should wipe away the curse of slavery from the country.

It will be remembered that the occasion, if not the cause, of John Brown's raid into Missouri was the solicitation of aid by a slave for himself and companions. Such prayers for succor were not infrequently addressed to abolitionists by those in bonds or by their refugee friends. In the anti-slavery host there were many whose principles wavered not under any test applied to them, and whose impulses urged them upon humanitarian missions, however hemmed in by difficulties and dangers. Among those who heard and answered the cry of the slave were the Rev. Charles T. Torrey, Captain Jonathan Walker, Mrs. Laura S. Haviland, Captain Daniel Drayton, Richard Dillingham, William L. Chaplin and Josiah Henson.

The variety of persons represented in this short, incomplete list is interesting: Mr. Torrey was a Congregational clergyman of New England stock, and had been educated at Yale College; Messrs. Walker and Drayton were masters of sailing vessels, and came from the states of Massachusetts and New Jersey respectively; Mrs. Haviland was a Wesleyan Methodist, who founded a school or institute in southeastern Michigan for both white and colored persons; Richard Dillingham was a Quaker school-teacher in Cincinnati, Ohio; William L. Chaplin began his professional life as a lawyer in eastern Massachusetts, but soon became the editor of an anti-slavery newspaper; and Josiah Henson was a fugitive slave, one of the founders of the Dawn Institute in Canada West. With the exception of the last named they were white persons, whose sense of the injustice of slavery caused them to take a stand that shut them out of that conventionally respectable society to which their birth, education and talents would have admitted them.

In 1838 Charles T. Torrey resigned from the pastorate of a Congregational church in Providence, Rhode Island, and relinquished ease and quiet to engage in the anti-slavery struggle then agitating the country. He became a lecturer and a newspaper correspondent, and, early in the forties, the editor of a paper called *The Patriot*, at Albany, New York. While acting as Washington correspondent for several Northern papers he attended a convention of slave-owners at Annapolis, Maryland, in 1842, and was thrust into jail on the score of being an abolitionist. He was released after several days, having been placed under bonds to keep the peace. While in prison he solemnly reconsecrated himself to the work of freeing the slaves. Within a year from this time a refugee entreated Mr. Torrey to help him bring his wife and children from Virginia. The errand was undertaken, but came to a most mournful end. Arrested and imprisoned, Mr. Torrey with others attempted to break jail; he was betrayed, however, and at length, December 30, 1843, sentenced to the penitentiary for six years. Under the severities of prison life Mr. Torrey's health gave way. His pardon was sought by friends, but mercy was withheld from a man the depth of whose conviction made recantation impossible. In December, 1844, he wrote: "I cannot afford to concede any truth or principle to get out of prison. I am not rich enough." While his trial was pending he wrote his friend, Henry B. Stanton: "If I am a guilty man, I am a very guilty one; for I have aided nearly four hundred slaves to escape to freedom, the greater part of whom would probably, but for my exertions, have died in slavery." Concerning this confession Henry Wilson writes: "This statement was corroborated by the testimony of Jacob Gibbs, a colored man, who was Mr. Torrey's chief assistant in his efforts."[1] On May 9, 1846, Mr. Torrey died in prison. In death as in life, the lesson of the clergyman's career proclaimed but one truth, the injustice of slavery. When the remains of Mr. Torrey were conveyed to Boston for interment in the beautiful cemetery at Mt. Auburn, the use of Park Street Church, at first granted, was later refused to the brother-in-law of the dead minister, although as a worshipper he was entitled to Christian courtesy. Tremont Temple was procured for the funeral services, and was thronged by a multitude eager to

[1] Wilson, *Rise and Fall of the Slave Power in America*, Vol. II, p. 80.

do honor to a life of self-sacrifice, and show disapproval of the affront to the dead. A large meeting in Faneuil Hall on the evening of the funeral day paid tribute to the memory of the liberator. The occasion was made memorable by a poem by James Russell Lowell, and addresses by General Fessenden of Maine, Henry B. Stanton and Dr. Walter Channing. Whittier wrote: "His work for the poor and helpless was well and nobly done. In the wild woods of Canada, around many a happy fireside and holy family altar, his name is on the lips of God's poor. He put his soul in their soul's stead; he gave his life for those who had no claim on his love save that of human brotherhood."[1]

In 1844, the year after Mr. Torrey's disastrous attempt to abduct a slave-family, Captain Jonathan Walker was made a victim of the law on account of friendly offices undertaken in behalf of some trusting negroes. Once, while on the coast of Florida, Mr. Walker consented to ferry seven slaves from Pensacola to one of the neighboring Bahama Islands, where they might enjoy the freedom vouchsafed by English law. In the open boat used for the purpose Captain Walker suffered sunstroke, and on this account his craft was overhauled, and the escaping party was taken into custody. After two trials Captain Walker was condemned to punishments that remind one strongly of the barbarous penalties inflicted upon offenders in the reign of Charles the First of England: he was sentenced to stand in the pillory; to be branded on the hand with the letters S. S. (slave-stealer); to pay a fine and serve a term of imprisonment for each slave assisted; to pay the costs of prosecution; and to stand committed until his fines should be paid. His treatment in prison was brutal, but he was not obliged to endure it long, for, by the intervention of friends, his fines were paid, and he was released in the summer of 1848. Subjected to indignities and disgrace in the South, Captain Walker was the recipient of many demonstrations of approval on his return to the North. Whittier blazoned his stigmas into a prophecy

---

[1] Quoted by Wilson, in his *History of the Rise and Fall of the Slave Power in America*, Vol. II, p. 80.

of deliverance for the slave. In a poem of welcome the distinguished Quaker wrote:

" Then lift that manly right hand, bold ploughman of the wave,
Its branded palm shall prophesy 'Salvation to the Slave.'
Hold up its fire-wrought language that whoso reads may feel
His heart swell strong within him, his sinews change to steel."[1]

These words were set to music by Mr. George W. Clark, and sung by him with thrilling effect at many anti-slavery gatherings throughout New England. Mr. Walker became at once a conspicuous witness against the slave power in the great trial that was then going forward at the bar of public opinion. At Providence, Rhode Island, his return from the Florida prison was heralded, and a large reception was given him, attended by the Hon. Owen Lovejoy, brother of the martyr Lovejoy, Milton Clark, the white slave, and Lewis, his brother. It is said that three thousand people crowded the seats, aisles and doorways of the reception hall. In company with Mr. George W. Clark, Captain Walker was drafted into the work of arousing the masses, and the two agitators received a cordial hearing at many New England meetings. Doubtless the recital of the Captain's experiences intensified anti-slavery feeling throughout the Northern states.[2]

About 1847, Mrs. Laura S. Haviland accepted a mission to find the family of one John White, a slave, who had escaped from the South and was serving as a farm-hand in the neighborhood of Mrs. Haviland's school in southeastern Michigan. Mrs. Haviland went to Cincinnati where she consulted with the Vigilance Committee, and thence to Rising Sun, Indiana, to secure the services of several of John White's colored friends. Here a plan was formed for Mrs. Haviland to go into Kentucky to the plantation where the family lived, and, disguised as a berry picker, see the wife, inform her of her

[1] *Liberator*, Aug. 15, 1845, "The Branded Hand," quoted in part by Wilson, *History of the Rise and Fall of the Slave Power in America*, Vol. II, p. 83; Whittier's *Poetical Works*, Vol. III, Riverside edition, 1896, p. 114.
[2] Reminiscences written by George W. Clark, by request, have been used to secure an intimate acquaintance with some of the men engaged in the underground service.

husband's whereabouts, and offer to assist in her rescue. Accomplishing this errand and returning across the border into Indiana, Mrs. Haviland awaited the slave-woman's appearance; but her escape had been prevented by the vigilance evoked on account of the operations of counterfeiters in Kentucky. Then John White started South intent on saving his wife and children from slavery, but his efforts also were unsuccessful, and he was thrown into a Kentucky jail. However, he was soon released by Laura Haviland, who purchased him for three hundred and fifty dollars.[1]

In the summer of 1847, Captain Daniel Drayton sailed to Washington with a cargo of oysters, and while his boat was lying at the wharf he was cautiously approached by a negro, who wanted to get passage North for a woman and five children. The negro said the woman was a slave but that she had, under an agreement with her master, more than paid for her liberty, and when she asked for her "free papers" the master only answered by threatening to sell her South.[2] Captain Drayton allowed the woman and her children and a niece to stow themselves on board his vessel, and he soon landed them at Frenchtown, to the great joy of the woman's husband, who was awaiting them there.

It was by the suggestion of these fugitives that Captain Drayton undertook his important expedition with the schooner *Pearl* in 1848. On the evening of April 18 his boat was made fast at one of the Washington docks ready to receive a company of fugitives. The time seemed auspicious. The establishment of the new French Republic was being celebrated in the city by a grand torchlight procession, and slaves were left for the most part to their own devices. Thus favored, a large number escaped to the small craft of Captain Drayton and were carefully stowed away. The start was made without incident, and the vessel continued quietly on her course to the mouth of the Potomac; there, contrary winds were encountered, and the *Pearl* was brought to shelter in Cornfield Harbor, one hundred and forty miles from Washington. The disappearance of seventy-six slaves at one time caused

---

[1] Laura S. Haviland, *A Woman's Life Work*, pp. 91–110.
[2] *Personal Memoir of Daniel Drayton*, 1853, p. 23.

great excitement at the Capitol. The method of their departure was revealed by a colored hackman, who had driven two of the fugitives to the wharf. An armed steamer was sent in pursuit, and the *Pearl* was obliged to surrender. Her arrival under guard at Washington was the occasion for rejoicing to an infuriated mob of several thousand persons. The slaves were committed to jail as runaways; their helpers were with difficulty protected from murderous violence, and were escorted to the city prison. Under instructions from the district attorney twenty-four indictments were found against both Captain Drayton and his mate, Mr. Sayres. When the trial began in July, the list of indictments presented comprised forty-one counts against each of these prisoners. Three persons were prosecuted; and the aggregate amount of their bail was two hundred and twenty-eight thousand dollars. After two trials the accused were heavily sentenced, and remanded to jail until their fines should be paid. The sentence passed upon Captain Drayton required the payment of fines and costs together amounting to ten thousand and sixty dollars, and until paid the prisoner must remain in jail indefinitely.[1] His accomplices were treated with equal severity. Such penalties were accounted monstrous by the friends of the convicted, and efforts were constantly made to have the sentences mitigated or revoked. In 1852 Senator Sumner interested himself in behalf of the imprisoned liberators; and President Fillmore was induced to grant them an unconditional pardon.

The occurrence of these events at the national capital during a session of Congress, gave them a significance they would not otherwise have had. That they would become the subject of much fierce debate was assured by the presence in Congress of such champions as Messrs. Giddings and Hale for the antislavery party, and Messrs. Foote, Toombs, Calhoun and Davis for the pro-slavery party. Mr. Calhoun expressed the view of the South when, speaking upon a resolution brought before the Senate by Mr. Hale, April 20, he recorded himself as being in favor of an act making penal "these atrocities, these piratical attempts, these wholesale captures, these rob-

---

[1] *Personal Memoir of Daniel Drayton*, p. 102.

beries of seventy odd of our slaves at a single grasp." In this and in similar utterances made at the time, he foreshadowed the determination of the South to have a law that would restrain if possible from all temptations to aid or abet the escape of slaves. The result of this determination is seen in the Fugitive Slave Law of 1850.

This notable voyage of the *Pearl*, which caused so great an excitement at the time, has been frequently chronicled, while the experiences of the young Quaker, Richard Dillingham, have been seldom recounted, though marked by the same elements of daring and resignation. In December, 1848, the close of the year of the *Pearl's* adventure, Mr. Dillingham was solicited by some colored people in Cincinnati, Ohio, to go to Tennessee and bring away their relatives, who were slaves under a "hard master" at Nashville. He entered upon the project, made his way into the very heart of the South and arranged with the slaves for their escape. At the time appointed his three protégés were placed in a closed carriage and driven rapidly away, Mr. Dillingham following on horseback. The party got as far as Cumberland bridge, where they were betrayed by a colored man in whom confidence had been placed, and the fugitives and their benefactor were arrested. Mr. Dillingham was committed to jail, and his bail was fixed at seven thousand dollars. At his trial, which occurred April 12, 1849, Dillingham confessed, and asked for clemency, urging by way of explanation the dependence of his aged parents upon him as a stay and protection. As to the crime for which he was held he said frankly: "I have violated your laws. . . . But I was prompted to it by feelings of humanity. It has been suspected . . . that I was leagued with a fraternity who are combined for the purpose of committing such offences as the one with which I am charged. But . . . the impression is false, I alone am guilty, I alone committed the offence, and I alone must suffer the penalty. . . ." Yielding to his plea for clemency the jury returned a verdict for three years in the penitentiary, the mildest sentence allowed by the law for the offence. The *Nashville Daily Gazette* of April 13 did not conceal the fact that Mr. Dillingham belonged to a respectable family, and stated that he was not without the sympathy of those who attended the trial.[1] The prisoner himself was most grateful for the consideration shown him, and, in a letter to his betrothed written two days after his trial, he spoke of his short sentence with the deepest gratitude and thankfulness toward the court and jury and the prosecutors themselves. "My sentence," he added, "is far more lenient than my most sanguine hopes have ever anticipated."[2] The termination of the imprisonment of Dillingham was most melancholy. Separated from his aged parents, to whom he was devoted, and from the woman that was to have become his wife, his health soon proved unequal to the severe experiences of prison life; his keepers after nine months gave him respite from heavy work about the prison, and assigned him the place of steward in the hospital. He had not long been in his new station when cholera broke out among the convicts, and his services were in constant demand. His strength was soon exhausted, and about the first of August, 1850, he succumbed to the dread epidemic raging in the prison.[3]

It was the year in which young Dillingham came to his melancholy end that Mr. William L. Chaplin was found guilty of an offence similar to that for which Dillingham suffered.[4] When Mr. Charles T. Torrey, editor of the *Albany Patriot*, was sent to the Maryland penitentiary for aiding slaves to escape, Mr. Chaplin assumed control of Mr. Torrey's paper. Like his predecessor, Mr. Chaplin spent part of his time in the city of Washington reporting congressional proceedings for the *Patriot*, and like him could not be deaf to an entreaty in behalf of slaves. In 1850 Mr. Chaplin was prevailed upon to attempt the release from bondage of two

---

[1] A. L. Benedict, *Memoir of Richard Dillingham*, 1852, p. 18. Also Harriet Beecher Stowe, *A Key to Uncle Tom's Cabin*, pp. 58, 59.

[2] A. L. Benedict, *Memoir of Richard Dillingham*, p. 18.

[3] This account of Richard Dillingham is based on the *Memoir* written by his friend, A. L. Benedict, a Quaker, and published in 1852. Abridged versions of this memoir will be found in the *Reminiscences of Levi Coffin*, Appendix, pp. 713-718; and Howe's *Historical Collections of Ohio*, Vol. II, p. 590.

[4] Wilson, *History of the Rise and Fall of the Slave Power in America*, Vol. II, pp. 80-82.

negroes, one the property of Robert Toombs, the other, of Alexander H. Stephens. The sequel to this enterprise is thus recounted by Mr. George W. Clark, an intimate friend of General Chaplin's: "Suspicion was somehow awakened and watch set; the General was intercepted, arrested and imprisoned, and the attempt failed. The General gave bail, Secretary Seward being on his bond for five thousand dollars. While passing through Baltimore on his return home he was rearrested and put into . . . prison there, on a charge of aiding slaves to escape from that state. The bonds required were twenty thousand dollars. . . . It was arranged that William R. Smith, a noble and generous-hearted Quaker, and George W. Clark should traverse the State and appeal to the friends of humanity for contributions to save the General from the fate we feared awaited him, for if his case went to trial he would probably be sentenced to fifteen years in their State Prison, which would no doubt amount to a death sentence. William R. Smith and I went to work in live earnest. An abolition merchant, Mr. Chittenden of New York, gave us three thousand dollars, the always giving Gerrit Smith gave us five thousand, other friends gave us two thousand, but we still lacked ten thousand. . . . We were in great distress and anxiety over the extreme situation when the generous Gerrit Smith voluntarily came again to the rescue and advanced the other ten thousand dollars." It was in this way, through the most open-handed generosity of his friends, that Mr. Chaplin was enabled to go free after being in jail only five months. Prudence dictated the sacrificing of the excessive bail rather than the braving of fortune through a, trial certain to end in conviction.

We have thus far considered the recorded efforts toward the abduction of slaves made by six persons in response to the entreaty of the slaves concerned or of some of their friends. It is noteworthy that in the case of five of these persons their efforts, first or last, were calamitous, and that all were white persons. We come now to the case of Josiah Henson, exceptional in the series, by reason of the uniform success of his endeavors, and because of his race connections. Born and bred a slave, Henson at length resolved to extricate himself and family from the abjectness of their situation. "With a degree of prudence, courage and address," says Mrs. Harriet Beecher Stowe, "which can scarcely find a parallel in any history, he managed with his wife and two children to escape to Canada. Here he learned to read, and, by his superior talent and capacity for management, laid the foundation for the fugitive settlement of Dawn. . . ."[1] The possession of the qualities indicated in this characterization of Mr. Henson rendered him equal to such emergencies as arose in his missions to the South in search of friends and relatives of Canadian refugees.

Mr. Henson has left us the record of two journeys to the Southern states, made at the instance of James Lightfoot, a refugee of Fort Erie, Ontario.[2] Lightfoot had a number of relatives in slavery near Maysville, Kentucky, and was ready to use the little property he had accumulated during the short period of his freedom in securing the liberation of his family. Beginning the journey alone, Mr. Henson travelled on foot about four hundred miles through New York, Pennsylvania and Ohio, to his destination. The fact that the Lightfoots decided it to be unsafe to make their escape at this time did not prevent their visitor from agreeing to come a year later for them, nor did it prevent him from returning to Canada with companions. He went nearly fifty miles into the interior of Kentucky, where, as he learned, there was a large party eager to set out for a land of freedom, but waiting until an experienced leader should appear. In Bourbon County he found about thirty fugitives collected from different states, and with these he started northward. Mr. Henson gives his itinerary in the following words: "We succeeded in crossing the Ohio River in safety, and arrived in Cincinnati the third night after our departure. Here we procured assistance; and, after stopping a short time to rest, we started for Richmond, Indiana. This is a town which had been settled by Quakers, and there we found friends indeed, who at once helped us on our way, without loss of time; and after a difficult journey

[1] *A Key to Uncle Tom's Cabin*, 1853, Boston edition of 1896, pp. 274, 275; also *Father Henson's Story of His Own Life*, 1858, chaps. xii, xiii.
[2] *Father Henson's Story of His Own Life*, chaps. xvi, xvii.

of two weeks through the wilderness, reached Toledo, Ohio, . . . and there we took passage for Canada."[1] In the autumn of the year following this abduction Mr. Henson again visited Kentucky. This time several of the Lightfoots were willing to go North with him, and a Saturday night after dark was chosen as the time for setting out. In spite of some untoward happenings during the early part of the journey, and of pursuit even to Lake Erie, the daring guide and his party of four or five were put aboard a sailing-vessel and safely landed on Canadian soil. "Words cannot describe," writes Mr. Henson, "the feelings experienced by my companions as they neared the shore; their bosoms were swelling with inexpressible joy as they mounted the seats of the boat, ready eagerly to spring forward, that they might touch the soil of the freeman. And when they reached the shore they danced and wept for joy, and kissed the earth on which they first stepped, no longer the *Slave*, but the *Free*." Mr. Henson asserts, that "by similar means to those above narrated," he was "instrumental in delivering one hundred and eighteen human beings" from bondage.[2]

Important and interesting among the abductors are the few individuals that we must call, for want of a better designation, the devotees of abduction. We have already considered a person of this type in the odd character, John Fairfield, the Virginian. There are several other persons known to have been not less zealous than he in their violation of what were held in the South to be legitimate property rights. The names of these adventurous liberators are Rial Cheadle, Alexander M. Ross, Elijah Anderson, John Mason and Harriet Tubman.

Rial Cheadle appears to have been a familiar figure among the abolitionists of southeastern Ohio. Mr. Thomas L. Gray, a reputable citizen of Deavertown, Ohio, for many years engaged in underground operations in Morgan County, vouches for the extended and aggressive work of Cheadle, who frequently stopped at Mr. Gray's house for rest and refreshment

---

[1] *Father Henson's Story of His Own Life*, pp. 149, 150.
[2] *Ibid.*, pp. 162, 163.

on his midnight trips to Zanesville and stations farther on.[1] Cheadle seems to have been a man of eccentricities, if not of actual aberration of mind; or his oddities may have been assumed to prevent himself being taken seriously by those he wanted to despoil. He is said to have lived in Windsor Township, Morgan County, Ohio, on the site of the present village of Stockport, and to have engaged in teaching and other occupations for a time; finally, however, he devoted himself to the work of the Underground Road. He indulged himself in old-time minstrelsy, composing songs, which he sang for the entertainment of himself and others, and he thereby increased, doubtless, the reputation for harmless imbecility, which he seems to have borne among those ignorant of his purpose. He paid occasional visits to Virginia. "As a result it is said the slaves were frequently missing, but as his arrangements were carefully made the object of his visit was usually successful. . . . His habits were so well known to those who gave food and shelter to the negro that they were seldom unprepared for a nocturnal visit from him. . . . After the Emancipation, he said he was like Simeon of old, 'ready to depart.' He died in 1867." [2]

A man differing greatly from Rial Cheadle in all respects, save the intensity of his compassion for the slave, was the abductor Alexander M. Ross. Born in 1832 in the Province of Ontario, Canada, Mr. Ross sought, when a young man, to inform himself upon the question of American slavery, not only from the teachings of some of the foremost anti-slavery leaders of England and the United States, but also from the recital of their experiences by a number of fugitive slaves that had found an asylum in the province of his birth. While he was engaged in making inquiries among the refugees, *Uncle Tom's Cabin* was published, and brought conviction to many minds. "To me," writes Mr. Ross, "it was a command. A deep and settled conviction impressed

---

[1] The *New Lexington* (Ohio) *Tribune*, winter of 1885–1886. Some information in regard to Cheadle appears in a series of articles on the Underground Railroad contributed to this paper by Mr. Gray.

[2] *History of Morgan County, Ohio*, 1886, published by Charles Robertson, M.D., article on the Underground Railroad.

me that it was my duty to help the oppressed to freedom. . . . My resolution was taken to devote all my energies to let the oppressed go free."[1] In accordance with this resolution young Ross left Canada in November, 1856. He visited Gerrit Smith, at Peterboro, New York, who was ever ready to encourage the liberation of the slave, and who went with him to Boston, New York and Philadelphia, and westward into the states of Ohio and Indiana. The purpose of these travels was, evidently, to acquaint the intending liberator with the means to be employed by him in his new work, and with the persons in connection with whom he was to operate. Indeed, Mr. Ross distinctly says, in speaking of these visits, "I was initiated into a knowledge of the relief societies, and the methods adopted to circulate information among the slaves of the South; the routes to be taken by the slaves, after reaching the so-called free states; and the relief posts, where shelter and aid for transportation could be obtained."[2] His chief supporters, besides Gerrit Smith, were Theodore Parker and Lewis Tappan.[3]

During his expeditions Mr. Ross spread the knowledge of Canada among the slaves in the neighborhood of a number of Southern cities, such as Richmond, Virginia, Nashville, Tennessee, Columbus and Vicksburg, Mississippi, Selma and Huntsville, Alabama, Augusta, Georgia, and Charleston, South Carolina. His method of procedure was fixed in its details only after his arrival upon the scene of action; an ostensible interest or purpose was kept to the fore, and the real business of spreading the gospel of escape was reserved for clandestine conferences with slaves chosen on the score of intelligence and trustworthiness. These persons were informed how Canada could be best reached, and were told to spread with care the information among their fellows. If any decided within a few days that they would act upon the advice given them, explicit instructions were repeated to

[1] Dr. Alexander Milton Ross, *Recollections and Experiences of an Abolitionist; from 1855 to 1865*, 2d ed., 1876, p. 3. The first edition of this book was issued in 1867. For this and other works of Mr. Ross see *Prominent Men of Canada*, pp. 118, 119, 120.
[2] Ross, *Recollections and Experiences of an Abolitionist*, p. 5.
[3] *Ibid.*, p. 8.

DR. ALEXANDER M. ROSS,

AN ABDUCTOR OF SLAVES.

(His distinguished services as a naturalist are attested by his medals, bestowed by European princes.)

HARRIET TUBMAN,

"THE MOSES OF HER PEOPLE."

Herself a fugitive, she abducted more than 300 slaves, and also served as a scout and nurse for the Union forces.

them, and they were supplied with compasses, knives, pistols, money and such provisions as they needed. Thus equipped, they were started on their long and dangerous journey. Occasionally, when circumstances seemed to require it, Mr. Ross would personally guide the party to a station of the Underground Road, or even accompany it to Canada; otherwise he betook himself in haste to some new field of labor. The unimpeachable character of Mr. Ross, and the early appearance of the first edition of his *Recollections* make his reminiscences especially valuable and worth quoting. Mr. Ross began his work at Richmond early in the year 1857. His narrative of his first venture is as follows: "On my arrival in Richmond, I went to the house of a gentleman to whom I had been directed, and who was known at the North to be a friend of freedom. I spent a few weeks in quietly determining upon the best plans to adopt. Having finally decided upon my course, I invited a number of the most intelligent, active and reliable slaves to meet me at the house of a colored preacher, on a Sunday evening. On the night appointed for this meeting, forty-two slaves came to hear what prospect there was for an escape from bondage. . . . I explained to them my . . . purpose in visiting the slave states, the various routes from Virginia to Ohio and Pennsylvania, and the names of friends in border towns who would help them on to Canada. I requested them to circulate this information discreetly among all upon whom they could rely. . . . I requested as many as were ready to accept my offer, to come to the same house on the following Sunday evening, prepared to take the 'Underground Railroad' to Canada.

"On the evening appointed nine stout, intelligent young men declared their determination to gain their freedom, or die in the attempt. To each I gave a few dollars in money, a pocket compass, knife, pistol, and as much cold meat and bread as each could carry with ease. I again explained to them the route. . . . I never met more apt students than these poor fellows. . . . They were to travel only by night, resting in some secure spot during the day. Their route was to be through Pennsylvania, to Erie on Lake Erie, and from thence to Canada. . . . I learned, many months after, that they all had arrived safely in Canada. (In 1863 I enlisted three of these brave fellows in a colored regiment in Philadelphia, for service in the war that gave freedom to their race.)" [1]

Mr. Ross was a naturalist, and his tastes in this direction furnished him many good pretexts for excursions. A journey into the far South was made in the guise of an ornithologist. Describing his trip to the cotton states Mr. Ross says: " Finally my preparations were completed, and, supplied with a shot-gun and materials for preserving bird-skins, I began my journey into the interior of the country. . . . Soon after my arrival at Vicksburg I was busily engaged in collecting ornithological specimens. I made frequent visits to the surrounding plantations, seizing every favorable opportunity to converse with the more intelligent slaves. Many of these negroes had heard of Canada from the negroes brought from Virginia and the border slave states; but the impression they had was, that Canada being so far away, it would be useless to try and reach it. On these excursions I was usually accompanied by one or two smart, intelligent slaves, to whom I felt I could trust the secret of my visit. In this way I succeeded in circulating a knowledge of Canada, and the best means of reaching that country, to all the plantations for many miles around Vicksburg. . . . I continued my labors in the vicinity of Vicksburg for several weeks and then went to Selma, Alabama." [2]

In the ways described in these selections Mr. Ross induced companies of slaves to exchange bondage for freedom. How many he thus liberated we have, of course, no means of knowing. The risks he ran were such as to put his life in danger almost constantly. Betrayal would have ended, probably, in a lynching; and the disappearance simultaneously of a band of fugitives and the unknown naturalist was a coincidence not only sure to be noticed, but also widely published, thus increasing the dangers many fold. It is unnecessary to recount the occasions upon which the scientist found himself in danger of falling a victim to his zeal in

[1] Ross, *Recollections and Experiences of an Abolitionist*, pp. 10, 11, 12.
[2] *Ibid.*, pp. 37, 38, 39.

befriending slaves. Suffice it to say, his adventures all had a fortunate termination. Mr. Ross is best known by his numerous works relating to the flora and fauna of Canada, for which he received recognition among learned men, and decoration at the hands of European princes."[1]

Elijah Anderson, a negro, has been described by Mr. Rush R. Sloane, an underground veteran of northwestern Ohio, as the " general superintendent " of the underground system in this section of Ohio. Mr. Anderson's work began before the enactment of the Fugitive Slave Law of 1850, and continued until the time of his incarceration in the state prison at Frankfort, Kentucky, where he died in 1857. During this period his activity must have been unceasing, for he is quoted as having said in 1855 that he had conducted in all more than a thousand fugitives from slavery to freedom, having brought eight hundred away after the passage of the act of 1850. Not all of these persons were piloted to Sandusky, although that city was the point to which Anderson usually conveyed his passengers. After the opening of the Cleveland and Cincinnati Railroad he took many to Cleveland.[2]

The last two of the devotees of abduction to be considered in this chapter are persons that were themselves fugitive slaves, John Mason and Harriet Tubman.

Our only source of information about John Mason is an account printed in 1860, by the Rev. W. M. Mitchell, a colored missionary sent to minister to the refugees of Toronto by the American Baptist Free Mission Society.[3] This may be

---

[1] Mr. Richard J. Hinton in his book entitled *John Brown and His Men*, p. 171, while writing of Captain Brown's convention at Chatham, Canada West, mentions Mr. Ross in the following words: "Dr. Alexander M. Ross of Toronto, Canada, physician and ornithologist, who is still living, honored by all who know him, then a young (white) man who devoted himself for years to aiding the American slave, was a frequent visitor to this section (Chatham). He was a faithful friend of John Brown, efficient as an ally, seeking to serve under all conditions of need and peril."

More or less extended notices of Dr. Ross and his work have appeared during the past few years; for example, in the *Toronto Globe*, Dec. 3 and 10, 1892; in the *Canadian Magazine of Politics, Science, Art and Literature*, May, 1896; and in the *Chicago Daily Inter-Ocean*, March 18, 1896.

[2] The *Firelands Pioneer*, July, 1888, p. 44.   [3] See p. 3, Chapter I.

accepted as a credible source. The author has printed in the little book in which the account appears testimonials that serve to identify him, but better than these are the references found in the body of the book to underground matters pertaining to southern Ohio that have been made familiar through other channels of information. The statements of Mr. Mitchell, thus supported, lend the color of probability to other statements of his not corroborated by any information now to be obtained, especially since these are in keeping with known manifestations of liberating zeal. We may therefore use the narrative relating to John Mason with a certain degree of assurance as to its accuracy.

While engaged in Underground Railroad operations in Ohio Mr. Mitchell became acquainted with John Mason, a fugitive slave from Kentucky. He had obtained his liberty but was not content to see his fellows go without theirs, and "was willing," wrote Mr. Mitchell, "to risk the forfeiture of his own freedom, that he might, peradventure, secure the liberty of some. He commenced the perilous business of going into the State from whence he had escaped and especially into his old neighborhood, decoying off his brethren to Canada. . . . This slave brought to my house in nineteen months 265 human beings whom he had been instrumental in redeeming from slavery; all of whom I had the privilege of forwarding to Canada by the Underground Railroad. . . . He kept no record as to the number he had assisted in this way. I have only been able, from conversations with him on the subject, to ascertain about 1,300, whom he delivered to abolitionists to be forwarded to Canada. Poor man! he was finally captured and sold. He had been towards the interior of Kentucky, about fifty miles; it was while returning with four slaves that he was captured. . . . Daylight came on them, they concealed themselves under stacks of corn, which served them for food, as well as protection from the weather and passers-by. . . . Late in the afternoon of that day, in the distance was heard the baying of negro-hounds on their track; escape was impossible. . . . When the four slaves saw their masters they said, ' J. M., we can't fight.' He endeavored to rally their courage . . . but to no purpose. . . . Their leader resisted, but both his arms were broken, and his body otherwise abused. . . . Though he had changed his name, as most slaves do on running away, he told his master's name and to him he was delivered. He was eventually sold and was taken to New Orleans. . . . Yet in one year, five months, and twenty days, I received a letter from this man, John Mason, from Hamilton, Canada West. Let a man walk abroad on Freedom's Sunny Plains, and having once drunk of its celestial 'stream whereof maketh glad the city of our God,' afterward reduce this man to slavery, it is next to an impossibility to retain him in slavery."[1]

Harriet Tubman, like John Mason, did not reckon the value of her own liberty in comparison with the liberty of others who had not tasted its sweets. Like him, she saw in the oppression of her race the sufferings of the enslaved Israelites, and was not slow to demand that the Pharaoh of the South should let her people go. She was known to many of the anti-slavery leaders of her generation; her personality and her power were such that none of them ever forgot the high virtues of this simple black woman. Governor William H. Seward, of New York, wrote of her: "I have known Harriet long, and a nobler, higher spirit or a truer, seldom dwells in human form."[2] Gerrit Smith declared: "I am convinced that she is not only truthful, but that she has a rare discernment, and a deep and sublime philanthropy."[3] John Brown introduced her to Wendell Phillips in Boston, saying, "I bring you one of the best and bravest persons on this continent — General Tubman as we call her."[4] Frederick Douglass testified: "Excepting John Brown, of sacred memory, I know of no one who has willingly encountered more perils and hardships to serve our enslaved people than you have. Much that

---

[1] Mitchell, *The Underground Railroad*, p. 20 *et seq.*
[2] Sarah H. Bradford, *Harriet the Moses of Her People*, p. 76. See also Appendix, p. 137. These testimonials were given in 1868 and were printed in connection with a short biography of Harriet in the year mentioned. The first edition of this biography has not been accessible to me, but it is mentioned by the Rev. Samuel J. May in his *Recollections of the Anti-Slavery Conflict*, published the following year. The second edition of the book appeared in 1886.
[3] *Ibid.*, p. 139. [4] Hinton, *John Brown and His Men*, p. 173.

you have done would seem improbable to those who do not know you as I know you. . . ."[1] Mr. F. B. Sanborn said: "She has often been in Concord, where she resided at the houses of Emerson, Alcott, the Whitneys, the Brooks family, Mrs. Horace Mann, and other well-known persons. They all admired and respected her, and nobody doubted the reality of her adventures. . . ."[2] The Rev. S. J. May knew Harriet personally, and speaks with admiration, not only of the work she did in emancipating numbers of her own people, but also of the important services she rendered the nation during the Civil War both as a nurse and as "the leader of soldiers in scouting-parties and raids. She seemed to know no fear and scarcely ever fatigue. They called her their Moses."[3]

The name, Moses, was that by which this woman was commonly known. She earned it by the qualities of leadership displayed in conducting bands of slaves through devious ways and manifold perils out of their "land of Egypt." She first learned what liberty was for herself about the year 1849. She made her way from Maryland, her home as a slave, to Philadelphia, and there by industry gathered together a sum of money with which to begin her humane and self-imposed labors. In December, 1850, she went to Baltimore and abducted her sister and two children. A few months later she brought away another company of three persons, one of whom was her brother. From this time on till the outbreak of the War of the Rebellion her excursions were frequent. She is said to have accomplished nineteen such trips, and emancipated over three hundred slaves.[4] As may be surmised, she had encouragement in her undertakings; but her main dependence was upon her own efforts. All her wages were laid aside for the purpose of emancipating her people. Whenever she had secured a sufficient sum, she would disappear from her Northern home, work her passage South, and meet the band of expectant slaves, whom she had forewarned of her coming in some mysterious way.

[1] Mrs. Bradford, *Harriet the Moses of Her People*, p. 135.
[2] *Ibid.*, pp. 136, 137.   [3] *Ibid.*, p. 406.
[4] James Freeman Clarke, *Anti-Slavery Days*, pp. 81, 82. Also M. G. McDougall, *Fugitive Slaves*, p. 62.

Her sagacity was one of her most marked traits; it was displayed constantly in her management of her little caravans. Thus she would take the precaution to start with her pilgrims on Saturday night so that they could be well along on their journey before they were advertised. Posters giving descriptions of the runaways and offering a considerable reward for their arrest were a common means of making public the loss of slave property. Harriet often paid a negro to follow the man who posted the descriptions of her companions and tear them down. When there were babies in the party she sometimes drugged them with paregoric and had them carried in baskets. She knew where friends could be found that would give shelter to her weary freedmen. If at any stage of the journey she were compelled to leave her companions and forage for supplies she would disclose herself on her return through the strains of a favorite song: —

> Dark and thorny is de pathway,
> Where de pilgrim makes his ways;
> But beyond dis vale of sorrow,
> Lie de fields of endless days.

Sometimes when hard pressed by pursuers she would take a train southward with her companions; she knew that no one would suspect fugitives travelling in that direction. Harriet was a well-known visitor at the offices of the anti-slavery societies in Philadelphia and New York, and at first she seems to have been content if her protégés arrived safely among friends in either of these cities; but after she comprehended the Fugitive Slave Law she preferred to accompany them all the way to Canada. "I wouldn't," she said, "trust Uncle Sam wid my people no longer."[1] She knew the need of discipline in effecting her rough, overland marches, and she therefore required strict obedience of her followers. The discouragement of an individual could not be permitted to endanger the liberty and safety of the whole party; accordingly she sometimes strengthened the fainting heart by threatening to use her revolver, and declaring, "Dead niggers tell no tales, you go on or die." She was

[1] Mrs. Bradford, *Harriet the Moses of Her People*, p. 39.

not less lenient with herself. The safety of her companions was her chief concern; she would not allow her labors to be lightened by any course likely to increase the chances of their discovery. On one occasion, while leading a company, she experienced a feeling that danger was near; unhesitatingly she decided to ford a river near by, because she must do so to be safe. Her followers were afraid to cross, but Harriet, despite the severity of the weather (the month was March), and her ignorance of the depth of the stream, walked resolutely into the water and led the way to the opposite shore. It was found that officers were lying in wait for the party on the route first intended.

Like many of her race Harriet was a thorough-going mystic. The Quaker, Thomas Garrett, said of her: "... I never met with any person, of any color, who had more confidence in the voice of God, as spoken to her soul. She has frequently told me that she talked with God, and he talked with her, every day of her life, and she has declared to me that she felt no more fear of being arrested by her former master, or any other person, when in his immediate neighborhood, than she did in the State of New York, or Canada, for she said she never ventured only where God sent her. Her faith in the Supreme Power truly was great."[1] This faith never deserted her in her times of peril. She explained her many deliverances as Harriet Beecher Stowe accounted for the power and effect of *Uncle Tom's Cabin*. She insisted it was all God's doing. " Jes so long as he wanted to use me," said Mrs. Tubman, " he would take keer of me, an' when he didn't want me no longer, I was ready to go. I always tole him, I'm gwine to hole stiddy on to you, an' you've got to see me trou."[2]

In 1857, Mrs. Tubman made what has been called her most venturesome journey. She had brought several of her brothers and sisters from slavery, but had not hit upon a method to release her aged parents. The chief difficulty lay in the fact that they were unable to walk long distances. At length she devised a plan and carried it through. A home-

[1] Mrs. Bradford, *Harriet the Moses of Her People*, pp. 83, 84.
[2] *Ibid.*, p. 61.

made conveyance was patched together, and an old horse brought into use. Mr. Garrett describes the vehicle as consisting of a pair of old chaise-wheels, with a board on the axle to sit on and another board swinging by ropes from the axle on which to rest their feet. This rude contrivance Harriet used in conveying her parents to the railroad, where they were put aboard the cars for Wilmington; and she followed them in her novel vehicle. At Wilmington, Friend Garrett was sought out by the bold abductor, and he furnished her with money to take all of them to Canada. He afterwards sold their horse and sent them the money. Harriet and her family did not long remain in Canada; Auburn, New York, was deemed a preferable place; and here a small property was bought on easy terms of Governor Seward, to provide a home for the enfranchised mother and father.

Before Harriet had finished paying for her bit of real estate, the Civil War broke out. Governor Andrew of Massachusetts, appreciating the sagacity, bravery and kindliness of the woman, soon summoned her to go into the South to serve as a scout, and when necessary as a hospital nurse. That her services were valuable was the testimony of officers under whom she served; thus General Rufus Saxton wrote in March, 1868: "I can bear witness to the value of her services in South Carolina and Florida. She was employed in the hospitals and as a spy. She made many a raid inside the enemies' lines, displaying remarkable courage, zeal and fidelity." [1]

At the conclusion of the great struggle Harriet returned to Auburn, where she has lived ever since. Her devotion to her people has never ceased. Although she is very poor and is subject to the infirmities of old age, infirmities increased in her case by the effects of ill treatment received in slavery, she has managed to transform her house into a hospital, where she provides and cares for some of the helpless and deserving of her own race.[2]

[1] Mrs. Bradford, *Harriet the Moses of Her People*, Appendix, p. 142.
[2] Lillie B. C. Wyman, in the *New England Magazine*, March, 1876, pp. 117, 118. Conversation with Harriet Tubman, Cambridge, Mass., April 8, 1897.

CHAPTER VII

LIFE OF THE COLORED REFUGEES IN CANADA

THE passengers of the Underground Railroad had but one real refuge, one region alone within whose bounds they could know they were safe from reënslavement; that region was Canada. The position of Canada on the slavery question was peculiar, for the imperial act abolishing slavery throughout the colonies of England was not passed until 1833; and, legally, if not actually, slavery existed in Canada until that year. The importation of slaves into this northern country had been tolerated by the French, and later, under an act passed in 1790, had been encouraged by the English. It is a singular fact that while this measure was in force slaves escaped from their Canadian masters to the United States, where they found freedom.[1] Before the separation of the Upper and Lower Provinces in 1791, slavery had spread westward into Upper Canada, and a few hundred negroes and some Pawnee Indians were to be found in bondage through the small scattered settlements of the Niagara, Home and Western districts.

The Province of Upper Canada took the initiative in the restriction of slavery. In the year 1793, in which Congress provided for the rendition by the Northern states of fugitives from labor, the first parliament of Upper Canada enacted a

[1] "A case of this kind," says Dr. S. G. Howe, "was related to us by Mrs. Amy Martin. She says: 'My father's name was James Ford. . . . He . . . would be over one hundred years old, if he were now living. . . . He was held here (in Canada) by the Indians as a slave, and sold, I think he said, to a British officer, who was a very cruel master, and he escaped from him, and came to Ohio, . . . to Cleveland, I believe, first, and made his way from there to Erie (Pa.), where he settled. . . . When we were in Erie, we moved a little way out of the village, and our house was . . . a station of the U. G. R. R." *The Refugees from Slavery in Canada West*, by S. G. Howe, 1864, pp. 8, 9.

A GROUP OF REFUGEE SETTLERS, OF WINDSOR, ONTARIO.
MRS. ANNE MARY JANE HUNT, MANSFIELD SMITH, MRS. LUCINDA SEYMOUR, HENRY STEVENSON, BUSH JOHNSON.
(From a recent photograph.)

law against the importation of slaves, and incorporated in it a clause to the effect that children of slaves then held were to become free at the age of twenty-five years.[1] Nevertheless, judicial rather than legislative action terminated slavery in Lower Canada, for a series of three fugitive slave cases occurred between the first day of February, 1798, and the last day of February, 1800. The third of these suits, known as the Robin case, was tried before the full Court of King's Bench, and the court ordered the discharge of the fugitive from his confinement. Perhaps the correctness of the decisions rendered in these cases may be questioned; but it is noteworthy that the provincial legislature would not cross them, and it may therefore be asserted that slavery really ceased in Lower Canada after the decision of the Robin case, February 18, 1800.[2]

The seaboard provinces were but little infected by slavery. Nova Scotia, to which probably more than to any other of these, refugees from Southern bondage fled, had by reason of natural causes, lost nearly, if not quite all traces of slavery by the beginning of our century. The experience of the eighteenth century had been sufficient to reform public opinion in Canada on the question of slavery, and to show that the climate of the provinces was a permanent barrier to the profitable employment of slave labor.

During the period in which Canada was thus freeing herself from the last vestiges of the evil, slaves who had escaped from Southern masters were beginning to appeal for protection to anti-slavery people in the Northern states.[3] The arrests of refugees from bondage, and the cases of kidnapping of free negroes, which were not infrequent in the North, strengthened the appeals of the hunted suppliants. Under these circumstances, it was natural that there should have arisen early in the present century the beginnings of a movement on the northern border of the United States for the purpose of helping fugitives to Canadian soil.[4]

[1] Act of 30th Geo. III.
[2] See the article entitled "Slavery in Canada," by J. C. Hamilton, LL.B., in the *Magazine of American History*, Vol. XXV, pp. 233-236.
[3] M. G. McDougall, *Fugitive Slaves*, p. 20.
[4] *Ibid.*, p. 60; R. C. Smedley, *Underground Railroad*, p. 26.

Upon the questions how and when this system arose, we have both unofficial and official testimony. Dr. Samuel G. Howe learned upon careful investigation, in 1863, that the early abolition of slavery in Canada did not affect slavery in the United States for several years. "Now and then a slave was intelligent and bold enough," he states, "to cross the vast forest between the Ohio and the Lakes, and find a refuge beyond them. Such cases were at first very rare, and knowledge of them was confined to few; but they increased early in this century; and the rumor gradually spread among the slaves of the Southern states, that there was, far away under the north star, a land where the flag of the Union did not float; where the law declared all men free and equal; where the people respected the law, and the government, if need be, enforced it. . . . Some, not content with personal freedom and happiness, went secretly back to their old homes, and brought away their wives and children at much peril and cost. The rumor widened; the fugitives so increased, that a secret pathway, since called the Underground Railroad, was soon formed, which ran by the huts of the blacks in the slave states, and the houses of good Samaritans in the free states. . . . Hundreds trod this path every year, but they did not attract much public notice."[1] Before the year 1817 it is said that a single little group of abolitionists in southern Ohio had forwarded to Canada by this secret path more than a thousand fugitive slaves.[2] The truth of this account is confirmed by the diplomatic negotiations of 1826 relating to this subject. Mr. Clay, then Secretary of State, declared the escape of slaves to British territory to be a "growing evil"; and in 1828 he again described it as still "growing," and added that it was well calculated to disturb the peaceful relations existing between the United States and the adjacent British provinces. England, however, steadfastly refused to accept Mr. Clay's proposed stipulation for extradition, on the ground that the British government could not, "with respect to the British possessions where slavery is not admitted, de-

---

[1] S. G. Howe, *The Refugees from Slavery in Canada West*, pp. 11, 12.
[2] William Birney, *James G. Birney and His Times*, p. 435.

part from the principle recognized by the British courts that every man is free who reaches British ground."[1] During the decade between 1828 and 1838 many persons throughout the Northern states, as far west as Iowa, had coöperated in forming new lines of Underground Railroad with termini at various points along the Canadian frontier. A resolution submitted to Congress in December, 1838, was aimed at these persons, by calling for a bill providing for the punishment, in the courts of the United States, of all persons guilty of aiding fugitive slaves to escape, or of enticing them from their owners.[2] Though this resolution came to nought, the need of it may have been demonstrated to the minds of Southern men by the fact that several companies of runaway slaves were organized, and took part in the Patriot War of this year in defence of Canadian territory against the attack of two or three hundred armed men from the State of New York.[3]

Each succeeding year witnessed the influx into Canada of a larger number of colored emigrants from the South. At length, in 1850, the Fugitive Slave Law called forth such opposition in the North that the Underground Railroad became more efficient than ever. The secretary of the Massachusetts Anti-Slavery Society wrote in 1851 that, "notwithstanding the stringent provisions of the Fugitive Bill, and the confidence which was felt in it as a certain cure for escape, we are happy to know that the evasion of slaves was never greater than at this moment. All abolitionists, at any of the prominent points of the country, know that applications for assistance were never more frequent."[4] This statement is substantiated by the testimony of many persons who did underground service in the North.

---

[1] Mr. Gallatin to Mr. Clay, Sept. 26, 1827, *Niles' Register*, p. 290.

[2] *Congressional Globe*, Twenty-fifth Congress, Third Session, p. 34.

[3] The Patriot War defeated a foolhardy attempt to induce the Province of Upper Canada to proclaim its independence. The refugees were by no means willing to see a movement begun, the success of which might "break the only arm interposed for their security." *J. W. Loguen as a Slave and as a Freeman*, p. 344.

[4] *Nineteenth Annual Report of the Massachusetts Anti-Slavery Society*, January, 1851, p. 67.

From the other end of the line, the Canadian terminus, we have abundant evidence of the lively traffic both before and after the new act. Besides the later investigations of Dr. Howe we have the statement of a contemporary, still living. Anthony Bingey, of Windsor, Ontario, aided the Rev. Hiram Wilson and the Rev. Isaac J. Rice, two graduates of Hamilton College, in the conduct of a mission for refugees. Mr. Bingey first settled at Amherstburg, at the mouth of the Detroit River, where he kept a receiving station for fugitives, was in an excellent place for observation, and was allied with trained men, who gave themselves, in the missionary spirit, to the cause of the fugitive slave in Canada. When Mr. Bingey first went to Amherstburg, in 1845, it was a rare occurrence to see as many as fifteen fugitives arrive in a single company. In the course of time runaways began to disembark from the ferries and lake boats in larger numbers, a day's tale often running as high as thirty. Through the period of the Mexican War, and down to the beginning of Fillmore's administration, many of the fugitives from the South had settled in the States, but after 1850 many, fearing recapture, journeyed in haste to Canada, greatly increasing the number daily arriving there.[1] That there was no tendency towards a decline in the movement is suggested by two items appearing in the *Independent* during the year 1855. According to the first of these (quoted from the *Intelligencer* of St. Louis, Missouri): "The evil (of running off slaves) has got to be an immense one, and is daily becoming more aggravated. It threatens to subvert the institution of slavery in this state entirely, and unless effectually checked it will certainly do so. There is no doubt that ten slaves are now stolen from Missouri to every one that was 'spirited' off before the Douglas bill."[2] It is significant that the ardent abolitionists of Iowa and northwestern Illinois were vig-

---

[1] Interview with Elder Anthony Bingey, Windsor, Ontario, July 31, 1895. On this point Dr. S. G. Howe says: "Of course it [the Fugitive Slave Law] gave great increase to the emigration, and free born blacks fled with the slaves from a land in which their birthright of freedom was no longer secure." *Refugees from Slavery in Canada West*, p. 15.

[2] *Independent*, Jan. 18, 1855.

orously engaged in Underground Railroad work at this time. The other item declared that the number of fugitives transported by the "Ohio Underground Line" was twenty-five per cent greater than in any previous year; "indeed, many masters have brought their hands from the Kanawha (West Virginia), not being willing to risk them there."[1]

That portion of Canada most easily reached by fugitives was the lake-bound region lying between New York on the east and Michigan on the west, and presenting a long and inviting coast-line to northern Ohio, northwestern Pennsylvania and western New York. Lower Canada was often reached through the New England states and by way of the coast-line routes. The fugitives slaves entering Canada were principally from the border slave states, Missouri, Kentucky, Virginia, Maryland and Delaware. Some, however, favored by rare good fortune and possessed of more than ordinary sagacity or aided by some venturesome friend, had made their way from the far South, from the Carolinas, Alabama, Georgia and Tennessee, even from Louisiana.

The fugitives who reached Canada do not seem to have been notable; on the whole they were a representative body of the slave-class. An observer on a Southern plantation could hardly have selected out would-be fugitives, as being superior to their fellows. If he had questioned them all about their desire for liberty he would have found habitual runaways agreeing with their fellows that they were content with their present lot. The average slave was shrewd enough under ordinary circumstances to tell what he thought least likely to arouse suspicion. That such discretion did not signify lack of desire for freedom is shown not only by the numerous escapes, but by the narratives of fugitives. Said Leonard Harrod: "Many a time my master has told me things to try me; among others he said he thought of moving up to Cincinnati, and asked me if I did not want to go. I would tell him, 'No! I don't want to go to none of your free countries!' Then he'd laugh, but I did want to come — surely I did. A colored man tells the truth here, — there

[1] *Independent,* April 5, 1855; see also Von Holst's *Constitutional and Political History of the United States,* Vol. V, p. 63, note.

he is afraid to."[1] "I have known slaves to be hungry," said David West, "but when their master asked them if they had enough, they would through fear say, 'Yes.' So if asked if they wish to be free, they will say 'No.' I knew a case where there was a division of between fifty and sixty slaves among heirs, one of whom intended to set free her part. So wishing to consult them she asked of such and such ones if they would like to be free, and they all said 'No,' for if they had said yes, and had then fallen to the other heirs, they would be sold,—and so they said, 'No,' against their own consciences."[2] "From the time I was a little boy it always ground my feelings to know that I had to work for another man," said Edward Walker, of Windsor, Ontario.[3] When asked to help hunt two slave-women, Henry Stevenson, a slave in Odrain County, Missouri, at first declined, knowing that his efforts to find them would bring upon him the wrath of the other slaves. "I wouldn't go," he related; "the colored folks would 'a' killed me." In his refusal he was supported by a white man, who had the wisdom to observe that "'Twas a bad policy to send a nigger to hunt a nigger." Nevertheless, Stevenson's trustworthiness had been so often tested that he was taken along to help prosecute the search, and even accompanied the party of pursuers to Chicago, where he disappeared by the aid of abolitionists and was afterward heard of in Windsor, Ontario.[4] Elder Anthony Bingey, of the same place, said, "I never saw the day since I knew anything that I didn't want to be free. Both Bucknel and Taylor [his successive masters] liked to see their slaves happy and well treated, but I always wanted to be free."[5]

The manifestations of delight by fugitives when landed on the Canada shore is another part of the evidence of the sincerity of their aspirations for freedom. Captain Chapman,

[1] Drew, *A North-Side View of Slavery*, 1856, p. 340.
[2] *Ibid.*, p. 91.
[3] *Detroit Sunday News Tribune*, quoted by the *Louisville Journal*, Aug. 12, 1894.
[4] Conversation with Henry Stevenson, Windsor, Ont., July, 1895.
[5] Conversation with Elder Anthony Bingey, Windsor, Ont., July 31, 1895.

the commander of a vessel on Lake Erie in 1860, was requested by two acquaintances at Cleveland to put ashore on the Canada side two persons, who were, of course, fugitives, and he gives the following account of the landing: "While they were on my vessel I felt little interest in them, and had no idea that the love of liberty as a part of man's nature was in the least possible degree felt or understood by them. Before entering Buffalo harbor, I ran in near the Canada shore, manned a boat, and landed them on the beach. ... They said, 'Is this Canada?' I said, 'Yes, there are no slaves in this country'; then I witnessed a scene I shall never forget. They seemed to be transformed; a new light shone in their eyes, their tongues were loosed, they laughed and cried, prayed and sang praises, fell upon the ground and kissed it, hugged and kissed each other, crying, 'Bress de Lord! Oh! I'se free before I die!'"[1]

The state of ignorance in which the slave population of the South was largely kept must be regarded as the admission by the master class that their slaves were likely to seize the boon of freedom, unless denied the encouragement towards self-emancipation that knowledge would surely afford. The fables about Canada brought to the North by runaways well illustrate both the ignorance of the slave and the apprehensions of his owner. William Johnson, who fled from Hopkins County, Virginia, had been told that the Detroit River was over three thousand miles wide, and a ship starting out in the night would find herself in the morning "right whar she started from." In the light of his later experience Johnson says, "We knowed jess what dey tole us and no more."[2] Deacon Allen Sidney, an engineer on his master's boat, which touched at Cincinnati, had a poor opinion of Canada because he had heard that "nothin' but black-eyed peas could be raised there."[3] John Evans, who travelled through the Northern country, and even in Canada, with his Kentucky master, was insured against the

---

[1] E. M. Pettit, *Sketches in the History of the Underground Railroad*, pp. 66, 67. See also Chapter I, p. 14, and Chapter VI, p. 178.
[2] Conversation with William Johnson, at Windsor, Ont., July 31, 1895.
[3] Conversation with Allen Sidney, Windsor, Ont.

temptation to seize his liberty by the warning to let no
"British nigger" get near him lest he should be slain "jess
like on de battle-field."[1] John Reed heard the white people
in Memphis, Tennessee, talk much of Canada, but he adds
"they'd put some extract onto it to keep us from comin'."[2]

Although many disparaging things said about Canada at
the South were without the shadow of verity, there were
still hardships enough to be met by those who settled there.
The provinces constituted for them a strange country. Its
climate, raw, open and variable, and at certain periods of the
year severe, increased the sufferings of a people already destitute.
The condition in which many of them arrived beyond
the borders, especially those who migrated before the
forties, is vividly told by J. W. Loguen in his account of his
first arrival at Hamilton, Canada West, in 1835. Writing to
his friend, Frederick Douglass, under date of May 8, 1856,
he says: "Twenty-one years ago — I stood on this spot,
penniless, ragged, lonely, homeless, helpless, hungry and
forlorn. . . . Hamilton was a cold wilderness for the fugitive
when I came there."[3] The experience of Loguen corroborates
what Josiah Henson said of the general condition
of the fugitives as he saw them in 1830: "At that time they
were scattered in all directions and for the most part miserably
poor, subsisting not unfrequently on the roots and
herbs of the fields. . . . In 1830 there were no schools
among them and no churches, only occasionally preaching."[4]

The whole previous experience of these pioneers was a
block to their making a vigorous initiative in their own behalf.
Extreme poverty, ignorance and subjection were their
inheritance. Their new start in life was made with a
wretched prospect, and it would be difficult to imagine a
free lot more discouraging and hopeless. Yet it was brightened
much by the compassionate interest of the Canadian
people, who were so tolerant as to admit them to a share in

---

[1] Conversation with John Evans, Windsor, Ont., Aug. 2, 1895.
[2] Conversation with John Reed, Windsor, Ont.
[3] *The Rev. J. W. Loguen as a Slave and as a Freeman*, 1859, told by himself; chap. xxiv, pp. 338, 340.
[4] *Father Henson's Story of His Own Life*, 1858, p. 209.

the equal rights that could at that time be found in America only in the territory of a monarchical government. By the year 1838 the fugitive host of Canada West began to profit by organized efforts in its behalf. A mission of Upper Canada was established. It was described as including "the colored people who have emigrated from the United States and settled in various parts of Upper Canada to enjoy the inalienable rights of freedom."[1] During the winter of 1838-1839, this enterprise conducted four schools, while the Rev. Hiram Wilson, who seems to have been acting under other auspices, was supervising during the same year a number of other schools in the province.[2]

From this time on much was done in Canada to help the ransomed slave meet his new conditions. It was not long before the benevolent interest of friends from the Northern states followed the refugees to their very settlements as it had succored them on their way through the free states. In 1844 Levi Coffin and William Beard made a tour of inspection in Canada West. This was the first of several trips made by these two Quakers " to look after the welfare of the fugitives "[3] in that region. The Rev. Samuel J. May made two such trips, "the first time to Toronto and its neighborhood, the second time to that part of Canada which lies between Lake Erie and Lake Huron."[4] John Brown did not fail to keep himself informed by personal visits how the fugitives were faring there.[5] Men less prominent but not less interested among underground magnates were drawn to see how their former protégés were prospering; such were Abram Allen, a Hicksite Friend of Clinton County, Ohio, and Reuben Goens, a South Carolinian by birth, who became an enthusiastic coworker with the Quakers at Fountain City, Indiana, in aiding slaves to the Dominion.

These efforts were helpful to multitudes of negroes. Some insight into the work that was being accomplished is afforded

---

[1] *Mission of Upper Canada*, Vol. I, No. 17, Wed., July 31, 1839.
[2] *Ibid.*
[3] *Reminiscences of Levi Coffin*, p. 253.
[4] May, *Recollections of the Anti-Slavery Conflict*, p. 303.
[5] Hinton, *John Brown and His Men*, p. 175.

by Levi Coffin, who gives a valuable account of his Canadian trip, September to November, 1844. Among the first places he visited was Amherstburg, more commonly known at that time by the name of Fort Malden: " While at this place, we made our headquarters at Isaac J. Rice's missionary buildings, where he had a large school for colored children. He had labored here among the colored people, mostly fugitives, for six years. He was a devoted, self-denying worker, had received very little pecuniary help, and had suffered many privations. He was well situated in Ohio, as pastor of a Presbyterian church, and had fine prospects before him, but believed that the Lord called him to this field of missionary labor among the fugitive slaves who came here by hundreds and by thousands, poor, destitute, ignorant, suffering from all the evil influences of slavery. We entered into deep sympathy with him in his labors, realizing the great need there was here for just such an institution as he had established. He had sheltered at this missionary home many hundreds of fugitives till other homes for them could be found. This was the great landing-point, the principal terminus of the Underground Railroad of the West."[1] Later Mr. Coffin and his companion "visited the institution under the care of Hiram Wilson, called the British and American Manual Labor Institute for colored children."[2] "The school was then," he reports, "in a prosperous condition." Mr. Coffin continues: " From this place we proceeded up the river Thames to London, visiting the different settlements of colored people on our way, and then went to the Wilberforce Colony. . . . I often met fugitives who had been at my house ten or fifteen years before, so long ago that I had forgotten them, and could recall no recollection of them until they mentioned some circumstance that brought them to mind. Some of them were well situated, owned good farms, and were perhaps worth more than their former masters. . . . We found many of the fugitives more comfortably situated than we expected, but there was much destitution and suffering among those who had recently come in. Many fugitives arrived weary and footsore, with their clothing in rags, having been torn by

---

[1] Coffin, *Reminiscences*, pp. 249, 250.   [2] *Ibid.*, p. 251.

briers and bitten by dogs on their way, and when the precious boon of freedom was obtained, they found themselves possessed of little else, in a country unknown to them and a climate much colder than that to which they were accustomed. We noted the cases and localities of destitution, and after our return home took measures to collect and forward several large boxes of clothing and bedding to be distributed by reliable agents to the most needy." [1]

The government of Canada was not in advance of the public sentiment of the provinces when it gave the incoming blacks considerate treatment. It was early a puzzle in Mr. Clay's mind why Ontario and the mother country should yield unhindered entrance to such a class of colonists; his opinion of the character of the absconding slaves and of the unadvisability of their being received by Canada was expressed in a despatch of 1826 to the United States minister at London: "They are generally the most worthless of their class, and far, therefore, from being an acquisition which the British government can be anxious to make. The sooner, we should think, they are gotten rid of the better for Canada." [2] But the Canadians did not at any time adopt this view. Dr. Howe testified in 1863 that "the refugees have always received . . . from the better class of people, good-will and justice, and from a few, active friendship and important assistance." [3] The attitude of the Canadian government toward this class of immigrants was always one of welcome and protection. Not only was there no obstruction put in the way of their settling in the Dominion, but rather there was the clear purpose to see them shielded from removal and to foster among them the accumulation of property.

In the matter of the acquirement of land no discrimination was made by the Canadian authorities against the fugitive settlers. On the contrary these unpromising purchasers were encouraged to take up government land and become tillers of the soil. In 1844 Levi Coffin found that "Land had been easily obtained and many had availed themselves of this

---

[1] Coffin, *Reminiscences*, pp. 252, 253.
[2] *Niles' Register*, Vol. XXV, p. 289.
[3] Howe, *Refugees in Canada West*, p. 68.

advantage to secure comfortable homesteads. Government land had been divided up into fifty-acre lots, which they could buy for two dollars an acre, and have ten years in which to pay for it, and if it was not paid for at the end of that time they did not lose all the labor they had bestowed on it, but received a clear title to the land as soon as they paid for it."[1]

In 1848 or 1849 a company was formed in Upper Canada, under the name of the Elgin Association, for the purpose of settling colored families upon crown or clergy reserve lands to be purchased in the township of Raleigh. It was intended thus to supply the families settled with stimulus to moral improvement.[2] To whom is to be attributed the origin of this enterprise is not altogether clear; one writer ascribes it to the influence of Lord Elgin, Governor-General of Canada from 1849 to 1854, and asserts that a tract of land of eighteen thousand acres was allotted for a refugee settlement in 1848;[3] another says it was first projected by the Rev. William King, a Louisiana slaveholder, in 1849.[4] Mr. King's own statement is that a company of fifteen slaves he had himself emancipated became the nucleus of the settlement in 1849; and that under an act of incorporation procured by himself in 1850 an association was formed to purchase nine thousand acres of land and hold it for fugitive settlers.[5]

The Canadian authorities facilitated the efforts made by the friends of the fugitives to provide this class such supplies as could be gathered in various quarters, and they entered into an arrangement with the mission-agent, the Rev. Hiram Wilson, to admit all supplies intended for the refugees free of customs-duty. Mr. E. Child, a mission-teacher, educated at Oneida Institute, New York, received many boxes of such goods at Toronto;[6] and at a hamlet called "the Corners," a

---

[1] Levi Coffin, *Reminiscences*, pp. 252, 253.
[2] Benjamin Drew, *A North-Side View of Slavery*, p. 292.
[3] George Bryce, *Short History of the Canadian People*, p. 403.
[4] Benjamin Drew, *A North-Side View of Slavery*, p. 291.
[5] S. G. Howe, *Refugees from Slavery in Canada West*, pp. 107, 108.
[6] *History of Knox County, Illinois* (published by Charles C. Chapman and Co.), p. 203. Here it is stated: "Mr. Wilson arranged with the authorities to have all supplies for the fugitive slaves admitted free of customs duty.

few miles from Detroit, a Mr. Miller kept a depot for "fugitive goods." Supplies were also shipped to Detroit direct for transmission across the frontier.[1]

The circumstances attending the settlement of the refugees from slavery in Canada were favorable to their kindly reception by the native peoples. It was generally known that they had suffered many hardships on their journey northward, and that they usually came with nought but the unquenchable yearning for a liberty denied them by the United States. The movement to Canada had begun when the inter-lake portion of Ontario was largely an unsettled region; and indeed, during the period of the refugees' immigration, much of the interior was in the process of clearing. Moreover, the movement was one of small beginnings and gradual development. It brought into the country what it then needed — agricultural labor to open up government land and to help the native farmers.

In the elbow of land lying between Lake Ontario and Lake Erie, the fugitives were early received by the Indians under Chief Brant, having possessions along the Grand River and near Burlington Bay. Finding hospitality on these estates, the negroes not infrequently adopted the customs and mode of life of their benefactors, and remained among them.[2]

In the territory extending westward along the lake front white settlers were working their clearings, which were beginning to take on the aspect of cultivated farms. But farm hands were not plentiful, and the fugitive slaves were penniless, and eager to receive wages on their own account.

Many were the large well-filled boxes of what was most needed by the wanderer taken from the wharf at Toronto during that winter [1841] by E. Child, mission-teacher. He was then a student at Oneida Institute, N.Y., but for many years has resided in Oneida, this county. He went into Canada for the purpose of teaching the fugitives."

[1] Conversation with Jacob Cummings, a fugitive from Tennessee, now living in Columbus, O. Mr. Cummings was at one time a collecting agent for a settlement at Puce, Ont. He told the author, "While agent, I was sent to Sandusky. I would collect goods for the settlement, and ship it to Detroit, marked 'Fugitive Goods.' Brother Miller, at the Corners, a little place about fifteen miles from Detroit, would take care of these, and Canada wouldn't charge any duty on 'fugitive goods.'"

[2] J. C. Hamilton, *Magazine of American History*, Vol. XXV, p. 238.

Mr. Benjamin Drew, who made a tour of investigation among these people in 1855, and wrote down the narratives of more than a hundred colored refugees, gives testimony to show that in some quarters at least, as in the vicinity of Colchester, Dresden and Dawn, the number of laborers was not equal to the demand, and that the negroes readily found employment.[1] It was not to be expected that the field-hands and house-servants of the South could work to the best advantage in their new surroundings; a gentleman of Windsor told Mr. Drew that immigrants whose experience in agricultural pursuits had been gained in Pennsylvania and other free states were more capable and reliable than those coming directly to Canada from Southern bondage.[2] But such was the disposition of the white people in different parts of Canada, and such the demand for laborers in this developing section, that the Canada Anti-Slavery Society could say of the refugees, in its *Second Report* (1853): "The true principle is now to assume that every man, unless disabled by sickness, can support himself and his family after he has obtained steady employment. All that able-bodied men and women require is a fair chance, friendly advice and a little encouragement, perhaps a little assistance at first. Those who are really willing to work can procure employment in a short time after their arrival."[3]

The fact that there were large tracts of good land in the portion of Canada accessible to the fugitive was a fortunate circumstance, for the desire to possess and cultivate their own land was wide-spread among the escaped slaves. This eagerness drew many of them into the Canadian wilderness, there to cut out little farms for themselves, and live the life of pioneers. The extensive tract known as the Queen's Bush, lying southwest of Toronto and stretching away to Lake Huron, was early penetrated by refugees. William Jackson, one of the first colored settlers in this region, says that he entered it in 1846, when scarcely any one was to be found there, that other fugitive slaves soon followed in con-

[1] Drew, *A North-Side View of Slavery*, pp. 311, 368.
[2] *Ibid.*, p. 322.
[3] Quoted by Drew, p. 326.

REV. THEODORE PARKER,
A LEADING MEMBER OF THE VIGILANCE COMMITTEE OF BOSTON.

COL. T. W. HIGGINSON,
ONE OF THE PRIME MOVERS IN THE ATTEMPTED RESCUE OF BURNS.

DR. SAMUEL G. HOWE,
who made a valuable report on the life of fugitive settlers in Canada in behalf of the United States Freedman's Inquiry Commission in 1863.

BENJAMIN DREW,
who studied the condition of the colored refugees in Canada in 1855, and wrote an interesting book on the subject.

siderable numbers and cleared the land, and that in less than two years as many as fifty families had located there. The land proved to be good, was well timbered with hard wood, and farms of from fifty to a hundred acres in extent were soon put in cultivation.[1] In some other parts of Canada the same tendency to spread into the outlying districts and secure small holdings appeared among the colored people. Mr. Peter Wright, the reeve of the town of Colchester, noted this fact, and attributed the clearance of much land for cultivation to fugitive slaves.[2] That such land did not always remain in the possession of this class of pioneers was due to their ignorance of the forms of conveyancing, and doubtless sometimes to the sharp practices of unscrupulous whites.[3]

Encouragement was not lacking to induce refugees to take up land; several fugitive aid societies were organized for this purpose, and procured tracts of land and founded colonies upon them. The most important of the colonies thus formed were the Dawn Settlement at Dresden, the Elgin Settlement at Buxton and the Refugees' Home near Windsor.[4] These three communities deserve special consideration, inasmuch as they illustrate an interesting movement in which benevolent persons in Canada, England and the United States coöperated to improve the condition of the refugees.

The Dawn Settlement, the first of the three established, may be said to have had its beginning in the organization of a school called the British and American Institute.[5] The purpose to found such a school seems to have been cherished by the missionary, the Rev. Hiram Wilson, and his coworker, Josiah Henson, as early as 1838; but the plan was not undertaken until 1842.[6] In that year a convention of colored persons was

[1] Drew, *A North-Side View of Slavery*, p. 190.
[2] *Ibid.*, p. 367.
[3] *Ibid.*, pp. 367, 369; Austin Steward, *Twenty-two Years a Slave, and Forty Years a Freeman*, p. 272.
[4] Howe, *Refugees from Slavery in Canada West*, pp. 68, 69.
[5] Drew, *A North-Side View of Slavery*, p. 308.
[6] *The Life of Josiah Henson, formerly a Slave, as narrated by Himself*, 1852, p. 115. See also *Father Henson's Story of His Own Life*, 1858, p. 171. Mr. Drew ascribes the honor of the original conception of this Institute to the Rev. Hiram Wilson. (See *A North-Side View of Slavery*, p. 311.) Mr. Henson, after asserting that he and Mr. Wilson called the convention of 1838,

called to decide upon the expenditure of some fifteen hundred dollars collected in England by a Quaker named James C. Fuller; and they decided, under suggestion, to start "a manual-labor school, where children could be taught those elements of knowledge which are usually the occupations of a grammar-school; and where the boys could be taught, in addition, the practice of some mechanic art, and the girls could be instructed in those domestic arts which are the proper occupation and ornament of her sex." [1] It was decided to locate the school at Dawn, and accordingly three hundred acres of land were purchased there, upon which were erected log buildings and schoolhouses, and soon the work of instruction was begun. It was "an object from the beginning, of those who . . . managed the affairs of the Institute, to make it self-supporting, by the employment of the students, for certain portions of their time, on the land." [2] The advantages of schooling on this basis attracted many refugee settlers to Dresden and Dawn. The Institute also gave shelter to fugitive slaves "until they could be placed out upon the wild lands in the neighborhoods to earn their own subsistence."

The Rev. Mr. Wilson served the Institute during the first seven years of its existence, teaching its school, and ministering to such refugees as came. The number of "boarding-scholars" with which he began was fourteen, and at that time "there were no more than fifty colored persons in all the vicinity of the tract purchased." [3] In 1852 there were about sixty pupils attending the school, and the settlers on the land of the Institute had increased to five hundred; [4] while other colonies in the same region had, collectively, a population of

---

continues, "I urged the appropriation of the money to the establishment of a manual-labor school. . . ." (*Father Henson's Story of His Own Life*, p. 169.) It appears that both Wilson and Henson were placed on the committee on site. As they were friends and coworkers, it is safe to accord them equal shares in the undertaking.

[1] *Father Henson's Story of His Own Life*, p. 169.

[2] *The Life of Josiah Henson, formerly a Slave, as narrated by Himself*, p. 115.

[3] Drew, *A North-Side View of Slavery*, p. 311.

[4] *First Annual Report of the Anti-Slavery Society of Canada*, p. 17. See also Drew's *North-Side View*, p. 311.

between three thousand and four thousand colored people.[1] From what has been said it is easy to see that the influence of Dawn Institute was considerable; its managers were not content that it should instruct the children of colored persons only; they extended the advantages of the school to the children of whites and Indians as well. Adult students were also admitted, and varied in number from fifty-six to one hundred and sixteen.[2] The good results of the policy thus pursued are apparent in the character and habits of the communities that developed under the influence of the Institute.

Concerning these communities Mr. Drew observed: "The colored people in the neighborhood of Dresden and Dawn are generally prosperous farmers — of good morals. . . . But here, as among all people, are a few persons of doubtful character, who have not been trained 'to look out for a rainy day,' — and when these get a little beforehand they are apt to rest on their oars. . . . Some of the settlers are mechanics, — shoemakers, blacksmiths and so forth. About one-third of the adult settlers are in possession of land which is, either in whole or in part, paid for."[3] In 1855, the year in which these observations were made, the Institute had already passed the zenith of its usefulness, and its buildings were fast falling into a state of melancholy dilapidation. The cause of this decline is probably to be found in the bad feeling, neglect and failure arising out of a divided management.[4]

The origin of the Elgin Settlement is discussed above; whether or not it was projected by Lord Elgin in 1848, it is certain that in 1849 the Rev. William King, a Presbyterian clergyman from Louisiana, had manumitted and settled slaves on this tract. This company, fifteen in number, formed the nucleus of a community named Buxton, in honor of Thomas Fowell Buxton, the philanthropist, and the rapid growth of the settlement thus begun seems to have led to the incorporation of the Elgin Association in August, 1850. It is prob-

[1] *Life of Josiah Henson, formerly a Slave, as narrated by Himself*, p. 118.
[2] *Ibid.*, p. 117.
[3] *A North-Side View of Slavery*, p. 309.
[4] *Father Henson's Story of His Own Life*, pp. 182–186.

able that Mr. King early became the chief agent in advancing the interests of the settlers, his support being derived mainly from the Mission Committee of the Presbyterian Church of Canada. The plan that was carried out under his management provided for the parcelling of the land into farms of fifty acres each, to be had by the colonists at the government price, two dollars and fifty cents per acre, payable in twelve annual instalments. No houses inferior to the model of a small log house prescribed by the improvement committee were to be erected,[1] although settlers were permitted to build as much better as they chose. A court of arbitration was established for the adjudication of disputes, and a day-school and Sunday-school gave much needed instruction.

The growth of the Elgin Settlement is set forth in a series of reports, which afford many interesting facts about the enterprise. The number of families that entered the settlement during the first two years and eight months is given as seventy-five;[2] a year later this number was increased to one hundred and thirty families, comprising five hundred and twenty persons;[3] the year following there were a hundred and fifty families in Buxton;[4] and eight years later, in 1862, when Dr. Howe visited Canada, he was informed by Mr. King that the population of the settlement was "about one thousand,—men, women and children," and that two thousand acres had been deeded in fee simple to purchasers, one-third of which had been paid for, principal and interest. The impressions of Dr. Howe are well worth quoting: " Buxton is certainly a very interesting place. Sixteen years ago it was a wilderness. Now, good highways are laid out in all directions through the forest; and by their side, standing back thirty-three feet from the road, are about two hundred cottages, all built on the same pattern, all looking neat and comfortable. Around each one is a cleared

---

[1] The dimensions of the model house were twenty-four by eighteen feet, and twelve feet high.
[2] *Third Annual Report*, September, 1852, quoted by Drew in *North-Side View of Slavery*, p. 293.
[3] *Fourth Annual Report*, September, 1853. See Drew's work, p. 294.
[4] *Fifth Annual Report*, September, 1854; Drew's work, p. 295.

place, of several acres, which is well cultivated. The fences are in good order, the barns seem well-filled; and cattle and horses, and pigs and poultry, abound. There are signs of industry and thrift and comfort everywhere; signs of intemperance, of idleness, of want, nowhere. There is no tavern, and no groggery; but there is a chapel and a schoolhouse.

"Most interesting of all are the inhabitants. Twenty years ago most of them were slaves, who owned nothing, not even their children. Now they own themselves; they own their houses and farms; and they have their wives and children about them. They are enfranchised citizens of a government which protects their rights. . . . The present condition of all these colonists, as compared with their former one is very remarkable."[1] Mr. King told Dr. Howe that only three of the whole number that settled in the colony had their first instalment on their farms paid for them by friends;[2] and he summed up his experience as follows: "This settlement is a perfect success. . . . Here are men who were bred in slavery, who came here and purchased land at the government prices, cleared it, bought their own implements, built their own houses after a model, and have supported themselves in all material circumstances, and now support their schools, in part. . . . I consider that this settlement has done as well as a white settlement would have done under the same circumstances."[3]

The colony known as Refugees' Home was the outgrowth of a suggestion of Henry Bibb, who was himself a fugitive slave. Soon after the passage of the Fugitive Slave Law of 1850, he proposed the formation of "a society which should 'aim to purchase thirty thousand acres of government land . . . in the most suitable sections of Canada . . . for the homeless refugees from American slavery to settle upon.'" The association, organized in the summer of 1852, set about carrying out Bibb's plan and accomplishing a work similar to the objects of the Elgin Association. The money required for the purchase of land was to be obtained partly through contributions and partly through sales of the farms first

---

[1] Howe, *Refugees from Slavery in Canada West*, pp. 70, 71.
[2] *Ibid.*, p. 108. [3] *Ibid.*, p. 110.

marketed. Each family of colonists was to have twenty-five acres, "five of which" it was to "receive free of cost, provided" it should "within three years from the time of occupancy, clear and cultivate the same." For the remaining twenty acres the original price — two dollars an acre — was to be paid in nine equal annual payments. Those obtaining land from the Association, whether by purchase or gift, were to hold it for fifteen years before having the right to dispose of it.

In the first year of the association's existence forty lots of twenty-five acres each were taken up, and arrangements were made for a school and church. Mrs. Laura S. Haviland was employed as a teacher in the fall of 1852, and at once opened both a day-school and a Sunday-school. She also organized an unsectarian or Christian Union Church, which later entered the Methodist Episcopal denomination. The material condition of the settlers Mrs. Haviland describes for us in a few words. She says: "They had erected a frame-house for school and meeting purposes. The settlers had built for themselves small log houses, and cleared from one to five acres each on their heavily timbered land, and raised corn, potatoes and other garden vegetables. A few had put in two and three acres of wheat, and were doing well for their first year."[1]

The three colonies described in the foregoing pages are typical of a number of communities settled upon lands purchased in Canada for their use, and regulated by rules drawn up by the associations that had sprung into existence for the benefit of the homeless refugees. The assumption upon which these associations proceeded was that they were to deal with a class of persons who, notwithstanding their present destitution, were desirous of living worthily in the state of freedom to which they had just attained, a class needing direction, instruction and opportunity for self-help rather than sustained charity. It was intended that fugitives should not be left to work out alone their own salvation, but that the deficiencies of ignorance and inexperience should be mitigated for those willing to profit by the good offices of the

[1] Laura S. Haviland, *A Woman's Life Work*, pp. 192, 196, 201.

missions. The fugitive aid society did not, as we have already seen, try to prevent the fugitives from settling together in the form of communities; on the contrary, such colonization was the inevitable result of their procedure, and doubtless to them it seemed desirable. Such is the suggestion contained in the arrangement under which farms were sold to purchasers by the Elgin and Refugees' Home associations: settlers on the tract of the former agreed to hold their farms for at least ten years without transferring their rights; settlers on the land of the latter were to keep their holdings for a minimum of fifteen years without transfer. In the dealings of the Home Association this restriction, we are told, caused some dissatisfaction.

Whether this segregation of the colored people in localities more or less apart from the white population of Canada was a good thing for the refugees has been questioned. Dr. S. G. Howe studied the life of this class in Canada in 1862 as the representative of the United States Freedman's Inquiry Commission, and wrote a report which is indispensable for a knowledge of the conditions surrounding the colored settlers in the provinces. He summarizes his judgment as follows:

"The negroes, going into an inhabited and civilized country, should not be systematically congregated in communities. Their natural affinities are strong enough to keep up all desirable relations without artificial encouragement. Experience shows that they do best when scattered about, and forming a small proportion of the whole community.

"Next, the discipline of the colonies, though it only subjects the negroes to what is considered useful apprenticeship, does prolong a dependence which amounts almost to servitude; and does not convert them so surely into hardy, self-reliant men, as the rude struggle with actual difficulties, which they themselves have to face and to overcome, instead of doing so through an agent.

"Taken as a whole, the colonists have cost to somebody a great deal of money and a great deal of effort; and they have not succeeded so well as many who have been thrown entirely upon their own resources. . . .

"It is just to say that some intelligent persons, friends of the colored people, believe that in none of the colonies, not even in Buxton, do they succeed so well, upon the whole, as those who are thrown entirely upon their own resources."[1]

Upon examination, these objections do not seem to be well grounded. It is noteworthy that of the prime movers in the organization of the three colonies we have considered, two, Josiah Henson and Henry Bibb, were themselves fugitive slaves; the third, the Rev. William King, had been at one time a slave-owner, and the fourth, the Rev. Hiram Wilson, was a missionary among the refugees for many years. These men were persons of wide observation and experience among fugitive slaves. It is safe to say that there were no men in Canada that knew better the disadvantages under which the average fugitive, just arrived from the South, was called upon to begin the struggle for a livelihood. And it will be admitted that there were none in or out of Canada more zealous and self-sacrificing in promoting the refugee's interests. These men evidently believed that the fugitive was not in a condition to do the best for himself upon his first arrival on free soil, that he needed to be delivered in some degree from the weight of his ignorance, and guided in his wholesome ambition to secure a home.

To the eyes of some Canadian observers those runaways who had lingered a while in the Northern states before crossing the border into Canada appeared to be more vigorous, independent and successful in all undertakings than their less experienced brethren. Whatever superiority they may have possessed that is not assignable to natural endowment, cannot safely be set down to the unchecked play upon them of rough experiences, or to their facing and vanquishing great discouragements unaided. The runaway slaves that lived in the free states were not as a class left to fight their way to attainable success alone. They settled among friends in anti-slavery neighborhoods, whether in city or country, and were stimulated by the practical interest manifested by these persons in their welfare. They were thus enabled to benefit by those educative influences that the missions of Canada were organized to supply. It is not improbable that

---

[1] *The Refugees from Slavery in Canada West*, pp. 69, 70.

some of the refugees whose self-reliant behavior called out the approval of Dr. Howe and others belonged to this group of partly disciplined fugitives. Dr. Howe must have seen many such persons, for his journey in Canada West was not made until 1862, after the Fugitive Slave Law of 1850 had driven many of them from the states into the provinces. Drew remarks pertinently: "The Fugitive Slave Bill drove into Canada a great many who had resided in the free states. These brought some means with them, and their efforts and good example have improved the condition of the older settlers."[1]

The other group of Canadian refugees — those whose passage had been direct from the condition of abject dependence, where the whole routine of life had been determined by the master or overseer, to the condition of active independence and responsibility, where the readiness to take hold and to care for one's own interests were required — this group doubtless contained persons of ability and energy; but they must have been in the minority. During the later years of its history the Underground Railroad made flight comparatively easy for all who once got out of the slave states, so that frail women and young children often went through to Canada with little or no difficulty. There were of course many individuals of extraordinary ability, who had enjoyed in slavery a wider range of experience than was vouchsafed the average slave; but such people could take care of themselves anywhere. Here we are concerned with the large number that needed to have the way pointed out to them if they were ever to become the possessors of their own homes; they were not sufficiently informed to originate and carry on successful building and loan associations for themselves, but they certainly could profit by an institution devised to serve the same purpose. If it be admitted that ownership of land and all that that implies was a good thing for the refugee, then it is difficult to see how that idea could have been better inculcated far and wide than through the methods employed by the Canadian organizations.

Besides enabling refugees to secure homes for themselves

[1] *A North-Side View of Slavery*, p. 367.

there were other offices the associations conceived to be a part of their duty, and the performance of which is set forth in their records. The first and most urgent of these was to supply immediate relief to the wayworn travellers continually arriving; with this was combined the necessity of helping these persons to find employment. The British and American Institute at Dawn was obliged to conduct, as part of its work, what would now be called perhaps a supply and employment bureau. Josiah Henson, one of the founders of the Institute, describing this branch of the work, says: "Many of these poor creatures arrive destitute of means, and often in want of suitable clothing, and these, as far as possible, have been supplied them. Since the passage of the late Fugitive Slave Bill, . . . they have arrived in large numbers at the Institute, and have been drafted off among their brethren who had been previously settled, and who are now making every effort and sacrifice to meet their destitute circumstances."[1] Henry Bibb, of the Refugees' Home, as early as 1843 saw the need of maintaining a stock of supplies at Windsor out of which to relieve the immediate necessities of fugitives.[2] The missionary, Isaac J. Rice, kept a similar supply room at Amherstburg.[3] It appears from all this that the recognition of the deplorable destitution of arriving fugitives was general among the aid societies and their representatives, and that prompt action was taken to meet wants that could brook no delay.

Another service performed by these colonization societies was that of providing superior schools for the colored people; education for all that could take it was one of the cardinal features of their programme. The state of public sentiment in some places in Canada was such that colored children were either altogether excluded from the public schools, or, if allowed to enter, they were annoyed beyond endurance by the rude behavior of their fellow-pupils. In some places they braved the prejudice against them, but the numbers courageous enough to do this were insignificant. Under

---

[1] *The Life of Josiah Henson, as narrated by Himself*, p. 117.
[2] Conversation with the Rev. Jacob Cummings, a refugee now living at Columbus, O.   [3] *Ibid.*

such circumstances the best that could be done by the friends of the black race was to open schools under private management. That the societies were not averse to mixed schools is shown by the fact that white pupils were admitted in various instances to classes formed primarily for colored children.[1] This need of schools did not appeal alone to the colonization societies. It was seen and responded to by other organizations; thus the English Colonial Church and School Society thought it advisable to locate schools at London,[2] Amherstburg,[3] Colchester[4] and perhaps other places; and certain religious bodies of the United States felt it incumbent on them to support school-teachers (ten or more) in different parts of Canada.[5] Besides the schools thus provided a few were conducted by individuals; as examples of this latter class may be named a private school at Chatham taught by Alfred Whipper,[6] a colored man, and another at Windsor managed by Mrs. Mary E. Bibb, the wife of Henry Bibb mentioned above.[7]

The supervision of the colonies maintained by their respective associations does not appear to have been unduly strict. Occasionally controversies came up over what was thought by the refugees to be improper assumption of authority by some agent or representative of the association, but an examination of the terms under which land was taken by the intending settlers brings to light only such rules as were meant to foster intelligence, morality and sobriety among the colonists. The aid societies were not only zealous for education. They also provided against those evil influences to which they thought the negroes were most likely to succumb. Thus, for example, in the case of the Buxton[8] and Refugees' Home settlements the manufacture and sale of intoxicants were forbidden. Such regulations seem to have been sus-

[1] *First Annual Report of the Anti-Slavery Society of Canada*, 1852, Appendix, p. 22.
[2] Drew, *A North-Side View of Slavery*, p. 148.
[3] *Ibid.*, p. 349.
[4] *Ibid.*, p. 369.
[5] *First Annual Report of the Anti-Slavery Society of Canada*, 1852, p. 22.
[6] Drew, *A North-Side View of Slavery*, p. 236.
[7] *Ibid.*, p. 322.
[8] *Ibid.*, pp. 294, 325.

tained by the sentiment of the communities for which they were made, and are not known to have been the source of opposition. Indeed, the directors of Buxton specially commended the habits of sobriety prevalent among the people whose best interests they were striving to promote,[1] and the Rev. William King found satisfaction in the fact that a saloon opened on the borders of that settlement could not find customers enough to support it, and closed its doors within a twelvemonth. His testimony relating to the standard of social purity mantained by the colonists was creditable in its showing, and indicated a high sense of morality scarcely to be expected among a people stained by the gross practices of slave-life.[2] Of the colored people in the neighborhood of Dawn Institute the reports were equally good. Mr. Drew found them to be " generally very prosperous farmers — of good morals, and mostly Methodists and Baptists."[3] Mr. Henson related with evident pride that out of the three thousand or four thousand colored people congregated in the settlements about Dawn not one had "been sent to jail for any infraction of the laws during the last seven years (1845–1852)."[4]

The widest range of dissatisfaction appeared at the Refugees' Home, where the fugitives are reputed to have been unduly burdened. Thomas Jones, not a colonist, and without any personal grievances to complain of, voiced the feeling to Mr. Drew. After relating some annoying changes made in the regulations as to the time in which clearings were to be made, as to the size of the houses to be erected and so forth, he declared that the settlers "doubt about getting deeds, . . . The restrictions in regard to liquor, and not selling [their land] under so many years, nor the power to will . . . property to . . . friends, only to children if . . . [they] have any, make them dissatisfied. They want to do as they please." From this it appears that the population of

[1] *Third Annual Report* (1852), quoted by Drew, p. 293.
[2] Howe, *Refugees from Slavery in Canada West*, pp. 109, 110.
[3] Drew, *A North-Side View of Slavery*, p. 309.
[4] *The Life of Josiah Henson, formerly a Slave, as narrated by Himself*, p. 118.

Refugees' Home was not altogether content with the local government under which it lived, but apparently the complaints made were to be attributed more to the unjust changes in the charter of the colony than to the moral régime the Home Association sought to enforce.

In general we may say, then, that in so far as the three colonies considered were typical of the whole class, there was nothing inherent in the provisions of their constitutions or in the nature of their organizations to place their members in a kind of servitude. As property owners, these citizens became subject to legitimate obligations, which might have been differently arranged, but could scarcely have been less onerous or of better intention. The requirement that ownership should be for a period of ten or fifteen years, made by the Elgin and Refugees' Home societies, was perhaps annoying; but the explanation, if not the full justification, of such a demand lay in the evident desire of the societies to give all purchasers ample time in which to make their payments, and in the irresponsibility of the class with which they were dealing.

It is impossible to tell how many landed colonies there were in Canada. Dr. Howe, perhaps the best contemporary observer, speaks indefinitely of benevolent persons that formed organizations at various periods for the relief and aid of the refugees, and says that these organizations generally took the form of societies for procuring tracts of land and settling colonies upon them, but he gives no further details.[1] Whatever their number, it is quite certain that these colonies comprised but a small part of the refugee population. The natural tendency was for fugitives to drift at once to the towns, where there was immediate prospect of relief and employment. In this way many of the Canadian centres came to have an increasing proportion of colored inhabitants. The towns first receiving such additions were naturally those of mercantile importance in the lake traffic of the decades before the Civil War. Thus, Amherstburg and Windsor, Port Stanley and Port Burwell, St. Catherines, Hamilton and

---

[1] Howe, *Refugees from Slavery in Canada West*, p. 69.

Toronto, and Kingston and Montreal, early became important places of resort for escaped slaves.

The movement was normally from these and other centres on the lake shore, or near it, to the interior. How rapid it was we can only judge by the few chance indications that remain. During Drew's travels in Canada West he learned that in 1832 the town of Chatham was a mere hamlet comprising a few houses and two or three shops, although the oldest deed of the place on record is dated 1801. Steamboats did not begin to ply on the river Sydenham between Chatham and Detroit until 1837. But long before this year, and, in fact, at the first settlement of the town, colored people began to come in.[1] When Levi Coffin made his first trip to Canada, in 1844, he visited a number of settlements of colored people scattered along the river Thames north of Dawn, and found the colony at Wilberforce already established.[2] This colony had been founded as early as 1830, and because it was originally settled by a group of emancipated slaves, it soon began to attract new settlers from the incoming stream of runaways. By 1846 the more distant interior was invaded. In that year the long strip of country stretching from the western extremity of Lake Ontario across to Lake Huron, and designated on the general map as Queen's Bush, was entered by pioneers who had escaped from slavery. This region was not surveyed until about 1848, and by that time there were as many as fifty families located there.[3] Some time during the years 1845 to 1847, the Rev. R. S. W. Sorrick went as far north as Oro, where he found "some fifty persons settled, many comfortable and doing well, but many [suffering] a great deal from poverty."[4] The surveying of the tract called Queen's Bush, and the subsequent arranging of the terms of payment for land already occupied, caused a number of colored settlers to sell their clearings in "the Bush" and move away. Some of these, it appears, went south to Buxton, but some went north to the shores of Georgian Bay and

---

[1] *A North-Side View of Slavery*, p. 235.
[2] *Reminiscences of Levi Coffin*, p. 521.
[3] Drew, *A North-Side View of Slavery*, p. 189.
[4] *Ibid.*, p. 190.

located at Owen Sound.[1] From this testimony it is certain that by 1850 fugitive slaves had found their way in considerable numbers throughout the inter-lake portion of Canada West.

Farther east, the Province of Quebec attracted negroes from the Southern states as early as the thirties; and they began to make pilgrimages northward by way of secret lines of travel through New England. By 1850, there were at least five or six of these lines, all well patronized, considering their remoteness from slaveholding territory. Maritime routes, by way of ports along the New England coast to New Brunswick, Nova Scotia, and even Cape Breton Island, seem also to have existed. A case is cited by the Rev. Austin Willey in his book, entitled *Anti-Slavery in the State and Nation*, in which more than twenty colored refugees were sent from Portland to New Brunswick at one time, soon after the rescue of Shadrach in Boston, in 1851. It is reported that there are still settlements of ex-slaves in Nova Scotia, near Halifax;[2] and the statement has recently been made that "there are at least two negro families living in Inverness County, Cape Breton, who are, in all probability, the descendants of fugitive slaves."[3]

As regards this movement into the Eastern provinces, no detailed information can be had. Even in the Western lake-bound region, it was the towns that were the most accessible for the traveller desirous of studying the condition of fugitives; most visitors contented themselves with the briefest memorials of their visits; and those whose accounts are at the same time helpful and extended, describe or even mention only a limited number of abiding-places of escaped slaves. Though Drew notices in his book but thirteen communities, and Dr. Howe refers to eleven only, numerous other places are mentioned by other observers. Sketching his first visit to Canada, Mr. Coffin writes: "Leaving Gosfield County,

[1] Drew, *North-Side View of Slavery*, p. 190.
[2] A statement to this effect, which appeared in the *Marine Journal* of New York, is quoted in *McClure's Magazine* for May, 1897, p. 618.
[3] See the letter signed "D. F.," printed in *McClure's Magazine*, May, 1897, p. 618.

we made our way to Chatham and Sydenham, *visiting the various neighborhoods of colored people*. We spent several days at the settlement near Down's Mills, and visited the institution under the care of Hiram Wilson, called the British and American Manual Labor Institute. . . . From this place we proceeded up the river Thames to London, *visiting the different settlements of colored people on our way*, and then went to the Wilberforce colony."[1] After naming a list of twelve towns near which refugees had settled, Josiah Henson says: "Others are scattered in small numbers in different townships, and at Toronto there are about four hundred or five hundred variously employed. . . ."[2] Such testimony goes to show that the refugee population of Canada was widely distributed, both in the cities and towns and in the country.

If the information at hand in regard to the distribution of the refugees is unsatisfactory, it can hardly be expected that the numbers can now be ascertained. The official figures of the successive Canadian censuses are untrustworthy. Dr. Howe, who studied them, concluded that, "It is impossible to ascertain the number of exiles who have found refuge in Canada since 1800. . . . It is difficult, moreover, to ascertain the present number (1862). The census of 1850 is confused. It puts the number in Upper Canada at 2,502 males and 2,167 females. But in a note it is stated, '*there are about 8,000 colored persons in Western Canada.*' This word "about" is an admission of the uncertainty; and as if to make that uncertainty greater, the same census in another part puts the number in Western Canada at 4,669." The census of 1860 Dr. Howe found to be equally unreliable. In giving the colored population as 11,223, it underrated the number greatly, as he discovered by looking into the records of several cities and by making inquiry of town officers. In this manner he learned that the number of colored people living in St. Catherines was about 700, although the census showed only 472; in Hamilton, probably more than

---

[1] *Reminiscences of Levi Coffin*, p. 251. The italics are my own.
[2] *The Life of Josiah Henson, formerly a Slave, as narrated by Himself*, p. 100.

500, despite the government showing of only 62; in Toronto, 934, although the census gave but 510; in London, Canada West, as the mayor estimated, there were 75 families of colored people, whereas the census showed only 36 persons. "There has been no movement of the colored population," Dr. Howe tells us, "sufficient to explain such discrepancies; and the conclusion is that the census of 1850, and that of 1860, included some of the colored people in the white column."[1]

If the information contained in the census reports of the Canadas relating to the refugee population of the provinces is misleading, so also is it true that little value can be attached to the estimates made at various times by visitors to the communities of fugitives, most of whom had inadequate data upon which to base their conclusions. These estimates not only differ widely, but sometimes leave room for doubt as to what geographical area and period of time they are intended to cover. Coffin in 1844 was told that there were about forty thousand fugitives in Canada;[2] but eight years later Henson estimated the number at between twenty thousand and thirty thousand, and daily increasing.[3] In the same year (1852) the Anti-Slavery Society of Canada in its *First Annual Report* stated that there were about thirty thousand colored residents in Canada West.[4] The Rev. Hiram Wilson said from the lecture platform that there were sixty thousand fugitives in Canada, and Elder Anthony Bingey, a coworker with Mr. Wilson, who heard this estimate given by his friend, informed the writer that Mr. Wilson had travelled over the country from Toronto westward and was as competent a judge as could be found in Ontario.[5] John Brown attended a conference at Chatham in the spring of 1858, and his biographer, Mr. R. J. Hinton, thinks there were probably not less than seventy-five thousand fugitives

[1] Howe, *The Refugees from Slavery in Canada West*, pp. 15, 16.
[2] *Reminiscences of Levi Coffin*, p. 253.
[3] *The Life of Josiah Henson, formerly a Slave, as narrated by Himself*, Appendix, p. 99.
[4] Quoted by Howe in *The Refugees from Slavery in Canada West*, p. 17.
[5] Conversation with Mr. Bingey, Windsor, Ont., July 31, 1895.

living in Canada West at that time.[1] The Rev. W. M. Mitchell, a negro missionary writing in 1860, was of the opinion that there were sixty thousand colored people in Upper Canada, that fifteen thousand of these were free-born, and that the remaining forty-five thousand were fugitive slaves from the United States.[2] The Rev. Dr. Willes, Professor of Divinity in Toronto College, is quoted as having said that there were about sixty thousand emancipated slaves in Canada, the most of whom had escaped from bondage.[3] Dr. Howe came to the conclusion in 1863 that the whole number of slaves enfranchised by residence in the provinces was between thirty and forty thousand. He thought that at the time of his visit the population did not fall below fifteen thousand nor exceed twenty thousand; although other observers, he said, estimated it as ranging from twenty thousand to thirty thousand.[4]

Besides the diversity of the figures here presented, it should be noted that most of the estimates refer only to Canada West; and further that they take no account of the losses under a high death-rate, due to the action of the new climatic conditions upon the settlers. Travellers were not in possession of the elements necessary for a computation, the resident missions were tempted to overstate, and the Canadian officials did not know how to secure data, and, perhaps, did not try to secure them fully. One can only say that the numerous lines of Underground Railroad would not have been taxed beyond their capacity to convey a number of refugees equal to the highest estimate given above during the period these lines are known to have been active.

The great majority of escaped slaves were possessed of but little more than the boon of freedom when they arrived in what was for them "the promised land." Church missions, anti-slavery societies and colonies found in them worthy subjects for their benefactions, which were intended to put the recipients in the way of earning their own livelihood.

---

[1] *John Brown and His Men*, p. 171.
[2] *The Underground Railroad*, p. 127.
[3] *Ibid.*, p. 166.
[4] *The Refugees from Slavery in Canada West*, pp. 15, 17.

The need of clothing, shelter and employment was provided for as promptly as circumstances would allow, and the fugitives soon came to realize that the efforts made in their behalf were to help them attain that independence of which they had been so long deprived.

As the region to which the refugees had recourse in largest numbers was well covered with forests, and was beginning to be cleared for tillage, a common occupation among them was that of the woodsman. Many were able to hire themselves to the native farmers to cut timber, while many others, who arranged to lease or buy land, went to work to clear garden patches and little farms for themselves. Josiah Henson sought to develop a lumber industry in the neighborhood of Dawn by setting up a sawmill on the farm of the British and American Institute, and shipping its products to Boston and New York.[1] Such work, in a climate to which they were unaccustomed, was an experience beyond the strength of some of the fugitives; and their exposure to the cold of the Canadian winter sowed the seeds of consumption in many.[2]

Farming appears to have been the occupation naturally preferred by the refugees, and probably the majority of them looked forward to owning farms.[3] It was the pursuit their masters followed, and for which they themselves were best adapted. The way to it was open through the demand for farm-hands on the part of many white settlers, and the special encouragement frequently needed was supplied by the example and aid of one or another of the colonies.

It is not surprising that a considerable number of the fugitives contented themselves with the present enjoyment of their newly acquired liberty, and neglected to make provision for the future. Such persons were quite ready to work, but were slow to understand how they could acquire land in time, and secure the full profits of their labor to themselves. The weight of enforced ignorance, dependence and poverty was upon them. Not infrequently they entered

[1] *Father Henson's Story of His Own Life*, p. 173 et seq.
[2] This is substantiated by the testimony of various Canadian refugees.
[3] *First Annual Report of the Anti-Slavery Society of Canada*, p. 15.

into profitless bargains, leasing wild lands on short terms, and finding themselves dispossessed when their clearings were about ready for advantageous cultivation.[1] Their knowledge of agriculture was scanty, and their planting, in consequence, often injudicious. They were, however, zealous to learn. The Rev. R. S. W. Sorrick, who gave some instruction to the settlers at Oro in the art of farming, declared them to be a most teachable people.[2] The refugees at Colchester appear to have been equally openminded to the practical suggestions given them in a series of lectures on "crops, wages and profit" delivered before them by Mr. Henson.

It is well known that among the slave-owners of the border states the practice existed widely of entrusting some of their negroes with the responsibilities of farm management; and that in the same portion of the South slaves were often permitted to hire their own time for farm labor; thousands of runaways also had gathered experience in the free states before their emigration to Canada; hence one is prepared in a measure to understand the rapid strides made by a large class of the negro population in the country of their adoption. Many of these people already had a gauge of their ability, and were not afraid to go forward in the acquirement of lands and homes of their own. To the advancement made by this numerous class is due the favorable comment called forth from observing persons, both Canadians and visiting Americans. Dr. Howe has left us some interesting information concerning the condition of refugee farmers in Canada. He found some cultivating small gardens of their own near large towns, where they had a ready market for the produce they raised; others, more widely scattered, tilled little farms, which for the most part were clear of encumbrance; these farms were "inferior to the first-class farms of their region in point of cultivation, fences, stock and the like," but were "equal to the average of second-class farms"; their owners lacked the capital, intelligence and skill of the best farmers,

[1] *Father Henson's Story of His Own Life*, pp. 165, 166; Drew, *A North-Side View of Slavery*, pp. 196, 369.
[2] Drew, *A North-Side View of Slavery*, p. 120.

but, far from being lazy, stupid or thriftless, supported themselves in a fair degree of comfort, and occupied houses not easily distinguishable in appearance from the farmhouses of their white neighbors. The miserable hut of the worthless negro squatter was occasionally to be seen, but usually the rude cabin and small clearing marked the spot where a newly arrived fugitive had begun his home, which in due course was to pass through successive stages until it should become a well-cleared farm, with good buildings and a large stock of animals and tools.[1]

A fact deplored by some friends of the refugees was the inclination to congregate in towns and cities.[2] A committee of investigation appointed by the Anti-Slavery Society of Canada reported in 1852 that, although many fugitives were scattered through the various districts, the larger number was massing in certain localities, those named being Elgin, Dawn and Colchester village settlements, Sandwich, Queen's Bush, Wilberforce, Hamilton and St. Catherines, together with the Niagara district and Toronto.[3] According to Josiah Henson the towns about which these people were gathering were Chatham, Riley, Sandwich, Anderton (probably Anderson), Malden, Colchester, Gonfield (doubtless Gosfield), London, Hamilton and the colonies at Dawn and Wilberforce.[4] Other centres undoubtedly existed, though no exhaustive list of such places could be made from the meagre accounts left us.

The movement to the towns was natural, for friends and employment were more easily to be found there than elsewhere. Certain parts or quarters of the towns rapidly filled up with the negroes, and the bonds of race and sympathy came into full play, causing constant accretions of new settlers. This was especially true of Fort Malden or Amherstburg, for years the principal port of entry for fugitives landing from the Michigan and Ohio borders. The

[1] *The Refugees from Slavery in Canada West*, pp. 65, 66. See also Drew, *A North-Side View of Slavery*, p. 368.
[2] Mitchell, *The Underground Railroad*, p. 128.
[3] *First Annual Report of the Society*, pp. 16, 17.
[4] *The Life of Josiah Henson, formerly a Slave, as narrated by Himself*, p. 100.

result in this and similar cases was unsatisfactory; the people seemed not to do as well as in other places.[1] In Hamilton and Toronto, we are told, the dwellings of the blacks were scattered among those of the whites, instead of being crowded together in a single suburban locality more or less distinct from the city of which it formed a part.[2] However, local conditions existing in Toronto, such as rent charges, tended to confine the colored people to the northwest section of the city.[3]

A wide range of occupations was open to the refugees in the towns; besides the lighter kinds of service about hotels and other public houses, and the work of plastering and whitewashing, often performed by negroes, various trades were followed, such as blacksmithing, carpentering, building, painting, mill-work and other handicrafts. There were good negro mechanics in Hamilton, Chatham, Windsor, Amherstburg and other places. A few were engaged in shopkeeping, or were employed as clerks, while a still smaller number devoted themselves to teaching and preaching.

As a class the fugitives in the towns, as in the country, were accounted steady and industrious, and their dwellings were said to be "generally superior to those of the Irish, or other foreign emigrants of the laboring class," and "far superior to the negro huts upon slave plantations, which many of them formerly inhabited."[4] Dr. J. Wilson Moore, of Philadelphia, visited the refugee communities in various Canadian towns, for example at Chatham, London and Wilberforce, and was favorably impressed with what he saw; with the orderly deportment of the crowds of colored peo-

[1] Dr. Howe quotes the following statement from Mr. Brush, town clerk of Malden: "A portion of them (the colored people) are pretty well behaved, and another portion not. . . . A great many of these colored people go and sail (are sailors) in the summer-time, and in the winter lie around, and don't do much. . . . We have to help a great many of them, more than any other class of people we have here. I have been clerk of the council for three years, and have had the opportunity of knowing. I think the council have given more to the colored people than to any others." See also *A North-Side View of Slavery*, p. 58.

[2] *A North-Side View of Slavery*, p. 62.

[3] *Ibid.*, p. 94.

[4] Howe, *The Refugees from Slavery in Canada West*, p. 63.

ple at Chatham while returning from a celebration of the anniversary of the West Indian emancipation, with the air of neatness and comfort displayed by the homes of the fugitives at London, with the advance from log cabins to brick and frame-houses made by the settlers at Wilberforce.[1] The weight of evidence supplied by Mr. Drew was unquestionably favorable to the view that the refugees were making substantial progress. He found the condition of the colored people in Toronto such as to be a proper cause of satisfaction for the philanthropist; many men in Hamilton were well-to-do; concerning those living in London he learned that some were highly intelligent and respectable, but that others wasted their time and neglected their opportunities; he noted that there was great activity among the negroes at Chatham, where they engaged in a large variety of manual pursuits; at Windsor, almost all the members of this class had comfortable homes, and some owned neat and handsome houses; at Sandwich a few were house-owners, the rest were tenants; in Amherstburg the assurance was given that the colored people of Canada were doing better than the free negroes in the United States; the settlers at New Canaan were reported to be making extraordinary progress, considering the length of time they had lived there; and out of a colored population of seventy-eight at Gosfield all of the heads of families, with two or three exceptions, were freeholders.[2] Dr. Howe, who visited the houses of the colored people in the outskirts of Chatham and other large places, described them as being for the most part small and tidy two-story houses with garden lots about them, neatly furnished, the tables decently spread and plentifully supplied. He was convinced that the fugitive slaves lived better than foreign immigrants in the same region, and clothed their children better.[3]

The relation of the slave to his wife and children was a

[1] Still, *Underground Railroad Records*, p. xvii.
[2] *A North-Side View of Slavery*, pp. 94, 119, 147, 234, 321, 344, 348, 376, 378.
[3] *The Refugees from Slavery in Canada West*, pp. 63, 64. See also Mitchell's *Underground Railroad*, pp. 130, 131, 133, 135, 137–139, 142–144, 146, 148 *et seq.*

precarious one in the South, especially in the border region from which most of the Canadian exiles came. Slave-breeding for the Southern market was extensively carried on in Virginia, Kentucky and other border states; slave-traders made frequent trips through this section; and their coming brought consternation, distress and separation to many a slave-family. These and other violations of the domestic ties might be expected to react on the home life of the slave-family, tending to discourage regard for the forms of family life, and to take away incentive to constancy. In view of such degradation it is surprising to note the care taken by many refugees for the formal legitimation of the alliances made by them in slavery. Once secure in their freedom and in their domestic relations, they began to substitute for the marriage after " slave fashion " the legal form of marriage, which they saw observed about them in Canada. Dr. Howe noticed that the fugitives settled themselves in families, respected the sanctity of marriage, and showed a general improvement in morals.[1]

This recognition of a new standard of social virtue signifies a great gain on the part of the refugees. As the withholding of any real instruction from the slaves in the South helped to brutalize them, so their moral elevation in Canada went hand in hand with their enlightenment through schools and religious teaching. What advantages were afforded them in the way of education in their new abiding-place, and what measure of benefit did they derive from these opportunities?

It appears that under the Canadian law colored people were permitted either to send their children to the common schools or to have separate schools provided from their proportionate share of the school funds. In some districts, however, local conditions stood in the way of the education of colored children. Many of the parents did not appreciate the need of sending their children to school regularly; it often happened that they were too destitute to take advan-

---

[1] *The Refugees from Slavery in Canada West*, pp. 95, 101, Appendix, pp. 109, 110. In her book, *A Woman's Life Work*, p. 193, Mrs. Laura S. Haviland reports some interesting cases of this sort.

tage of these opportunities; again, they were unaccustomed to the enjoyment of equal privileges with the whites and were timid about assuming them. The children, unused to the climate of the new country, perhaps also thinly clad, were sickly and often unable to go to school.[1]

Prejudice was also not wanting in some quarters among the whites. In the town of Sandwich, on the Detroit River, in 1851 or 1852, the feelings of the two people were much agitated over the question of mixed schools.[2] The towns of Chatham, London and Hamilton appear also to have been more or less affected by prejudice against the negro.[3] Partly owing to this prejudice, and partly to their own preference, the colored people, acting under the provision of the law that allowed them to have separate schools, set up their own schools in Sandwich and in many other parts of Ontario.[4] Drew incidentally noted the existence of separate schools at Colchester, Amherstburg, Sandwich, Dawn and Buxton; the existence of private schools at London, Windsor and perhaps one or two other places; and the presence of an extremely small number of colored children in the common schools at Hamilton and London. Concerning Toronto, he tells us that no distinction existed there in regard to school privileges. Such figures as Drew supplies show the separate, private and mission schools to have been more numerously attended than the public or common schools. The former furnished the conditions under which whatever appreciation of education there was native in a community of negroes, or whatever taste for it could be awakened there, was free to assert itself unhindered by real or imagined opposition. That the refugees were capable of a genuine interest in the schools provided for them, even under the most disheartening circumstances, appears from the fact that "many of the colored settlers were attracted to Dresden and Dawn by the preferred advantages of education on the industrial plan in the Dawn Institute."[5] Adults and children both attended; the schools of the mission-workers were intended to reach as many as possible

---

[1] Mitchell, *The Underground Railroad*, pp. 140, 164, 165.
[2] Drew, *A North-Side View of Slavery*, pp. 341, 342.
[3] *Ibid.*, pp. 118, 147, 235.   [4] *Ibid.*, p. 341.   [5] *Ibid.*, p. 308.

of a constituency made up largely of grown persons. An evening school for adults was established in Toronto, and had a good attendance.[1] Sunday-schools were an important accessory, furnishing, as they did, opportunities to many whose week days were full of other cares. Mrs. Haviland's experience was probably that of mission-teachers in other parts of Canada. On Sundays her schoolhouse was filled to overflowing, many of her congregation coming five or six miles to get to the meeting. The Bible was read with eagerness by those whose ignorance required prompting at every word. The oppression of past years was forgotten, for the hour, in the pleasure of learning to read the Word of God. An aged couple, past eighty, were among the most regular attendants.[2] The spread of the earnest desire for knowledge shown in these meetings would suffice to explain an observation made by Dr. Howe in 1863 to the effect that a surprisingly large number could then read and write.[3]

An agency illustrative of the refugees' desire for self-improvement was the association made up of local societies called "True Bands." The first of these clubs was organized at Amherstburg or Malden in September, 1854, and in less than two years there were fourteen such societies in various parts of Canada West. The total membership of the association is not known, but the True Band of Malden comprised six hundred persons, and that of Chatham, on the first enrolment, three hundred and seventy-five. Persons of both sexes were admitted to membership, and a small monthly payment was required. The objects of the association were comprehensive; they included the improvement of the schools, the increase of the school attendance among the colored people, the abatement of race prejudice, the arbitration of disputes between colored persons, the employment of a fund for aiding destitute persons just arriving from slavery, the suppression of begging in behalf of refugees by self-appointed agents, and so forth. The True Band at Malden did much good work; and in all other places where the societies

[1] *First Annual Report of the Anti-Slavery Society of Canada*, p. 15.
[2] *A Woman's Life Work*, pp. 192, 193.
[3] *The Refugees from Slavery in Canada West*, p. 77.

were formed it is reported that excellent results were secured. These clubs demonstrated their ability by concerted action to care for numerous strangers as they arrived in Canada after their long pilgrimage.[1]

Another object of the True Band association was to prevent divisions in the church, and as far as possible to heal those that had already occurred. This provision was apparently intended to serve as a check on the disposition of the refugees to multiply churches. "Whenever there are a few families gathered together," wrote one observer, "they split up into various sects and each sect must have a meeting-house of its own. . . . Their ministers have canvassed the United States and England, contribution-box in hand; and by appealing to sectarian zeal, got the means of building up tabernacles of brick and wood, trusting to their own zeal for gathering a congregation. . . ."[2] This eagerness to build churches has been criticised as consuming much of the time and substance of the exiles, and causing division where union was desirable. But if this side of the religious life and activities of the refugees calls for condemnation, another side, which was fostered by the new conditions, was the more marked manifestation of the religious nature of the blacks in what has been well called in contrast with their emotionalism the higher forms of conscience, morality and good works.[3]

The minds of many of the Canadian exiles were ever going back to the friends and loved ones they had left behind them on the plantations of the South. Each new band of pilgrims as it came ashore at some Canadian port was scanned by little groups of negroes eagerly looking for familiar faces. Strange and solemn reunions after years of separation and of hardship took place along the friendly shores of Canada. But the fugitive that was safe in the promised land was anxious to assist fortune, and as soon as he had learned to write or could find an acquaintance to write for him, was likely to send a letter to some trusted agent of the Underground Railroad for advice or assistance in an attempt to release some slave

[1] Drew, *A North-Side View of Slavery*, pp. 236, 237.
[2] Howe, *The Refugees from Slavery in Canada West*, p. 92.
[3] *Ibid.*

or family of slaves from their thraldom. Many, we know, took a more dangerous method than this, and went personally to seek their relatives in the South, and piloted them safely back to English soil; but the appeal to anti-slavery friends in the States, while probably less effective, sometimes secured the desired results. William Still, the chairman of the Acting Vigilance Committee of Philadelphia, — a position that brought him in contact with hundreds of escaped slaves as they were being sent beyond our northern frontier, — was the recipient of numerous letters entreating his aid for the deliverance of the kinsmen of refugees.[1]

Fugitive slaves were admitted to citizenship in the provinces on the same terms as other immigrants. Many of them became property owners in the course of time, paid their allotted share of the taxes, and thus gained the franchise; Dr. Howe examined the records of several towns in 1862 and made comparisons of the amount of taxable property owned by whites and blacks. According to his statement the proportion of white rate or tax payers to the white population of Malden was in the ratio of one to three and one-third; that of the colored ratepayers of the town to the colored population, one to eleven. The average amount paid by the whites was $9.52, while that paid by the blacks was $5.12. In Chatham the white ratepayers were "about one to every three and one-half of the white population, and the colored about one to every thirteen of the colored population." The average tax paid by white and black was $10.63 and $4.98 respectively. At Windsor it appears that the proportion of ratepayers among the whites was as one to seven and one-fourth, and among the blacks it was as one to five. Here the per capita average was $18.76 for the former, and $4.18 for the latter.[2] These towns, it is to be noted, were not colonies; and in them the fugitives were offered no peculiar inducements to become the owners of property. All things considered, the showing is highly creditable for the negroes.

[1] Still, *Underground Railroad Records*, 2d ed., pp. 59, 65, 105, 137, 193, 249, 263, 291, 293, 337, 385, 448, 490.
[2] *The Refugees from Slavery in Canada West*, pp. 61, 62.

The fact that they had been slaves did not debar the refugees from the exercise of whatever political rights they had acquired. The negro voters used their privilege freely in common with the native citizens, allying themselves with the two regular parties of Canada, the Conservative and the Reform.[1] In some communities negroes were elected to office. The Rev. William King, head of the Buxton Settlement, has mentioned the offices of pathmasters, school trustees, and councillors as those to which colored men were chosen within his knowledge. These, he said, were as high as the negro had then attained, and he thought that white men would refuse to vote for a black running for Parliament.[2] Dr. J. Wilson Moore, a friend of the refugees, said of them in 1858 that their standing was fair, and that the laws of the land made no distinction. He observed that they did jury duty with their white neighbors, and served as school directors and road commissioners. On the whole, he thought, they were as much respected as their intelligence and virtue entitled them to be.[3]

In view of the remarkable progress made by the refugees and of their general serviceableness as settlers in the provinces, it is easy to understand why the Canadian government maintained its favorable attitude towards them to the end of the long period of immigration. In 1859 the Governor-General testified to the favorable opinion the central government entertained of the fugitives as settlers and citizens by assuring the Rev. W. M. Mitchell that "We can still afford them homes in our dominions"; and the Parliament of Ontario manifested its interest in their continued welfare by voting to incorporate the Association for the Education and Elevation of the Colored People of Canada upon the showing that the association would thereby be enabled to extend its philanthropic labors among the blacks.[4] The Canadian authorities seem to have become established in the view reached after a candid and prolonged investigation by Dr.

[1] Still, *Underground Railroad Records*, p. xxvii.
[2] Howe, *The Refugees from Slavery in Canada West*, Appendix, p. 108.
[3] Still, *Underground Railroad Records*, p. xvii.
[4] Mitchell, *The Underground Railroad*, pp. 155, 156.

Howe, that the refugees "promote the industrial and material interests of the country and are valuable citizens."[1]

[1] *The Refugees from Slavery in Canada West*, p. 102. William Still, who made a trip through Canada West in 1855, expressed a view similar to that above quoted, and added the words: "To say that there are not those amongst the colored people in Canada, as every place, who are very poor, . . . who will commit crime, who indulge in habits of indolence and intemperance, . . . would be far from the truth. Nevertheless, may not the same be said of white people, even where they have had the best chances in every particular?" *Underground Railroad Records*, p. xxviii.

CHURCH OF THE FUGITIVE SLAVES IN BOSTON

This church once stood near the house of Lewis Hayden, 66 Phillips Street, Boston, Massachusetts.

(From an old engraving.)

CHAPTER VIII

FUGITIVE SETTLERS IN THE NORTHERN STATES

THERE were many fugitives from bondage that did not avail themselves of the protection afforded by the proximity of Canadian soil. For various reasons these persons remained within the borders of the free states; some were drawn by the affinities of race to seek permanent homes in communities of colored people; some, keeping the stories of their past lives hidden, found employment as well as oblivion among the crowds in cities and towns; some, choosing localities more or less remote from large centres of population, settled where the presence of Quakers, Wesleyan Methodists, Covenanters or Free Presbyterians gave them the assurance of safety and assistance; and some, after a severe experience of pioneer life in the woods of Canada, preferred to run their chances on the southern shores of the lakes, where it was easier to gain a livelihood, and whence escape could be made across the line at the first intimation of danger.

As one would suppose, it is impossible to determine with any accuracy how many fugitive settlers there were in the North at any particular time. Estimates both local and general in character have come down to us, and, naturally enough, one is inclined to attach greater value to the former than to the latter, on the score of probable correctness, but here the investigator is met by the extreme paucity of examples, which, as it happens, are confined to two towns in eastern Massachusetts, namely, Boston and New Bedford. In October, 1850, the Rev. Theodore Parker stated publicly that there were in Boston from four hundred to six hundred fugitives.[1] Concerning the refugee population of New Bedford our information is much less definite, for it is

---

[1] *Chronotype*, Oct. 7, 1850.

reported that in that place there were between six hundred and seven hundred colored citizens, many of whom were fugitives.[1] Nevertheless one cannot doubt that the representatives of this class were numerous and widely scattered throughout the whole territory of the free zone, for reference is made by many surviving abolitionists not only to individual refugees or single families of refugees that dwelt in their neighborhood, but even to settlements a considerable part of whose people were runaway slaves. Where conditions were peculiarly favorable it was not an unknown thing for runaways to conclude their journeys when scarcely more than within the borders of free territory. The Rev. Thomas C. Oliver, of Windsor, Canada, is authority for the statement that fugitive settlers swarmed among their Quaker protectors at Greenwich, New Jersey, on the very edge of a slave state.[2] In communities situated at greater distance from the sectional line, like Columbus[3] and Akron,[4] Ohio, Elmira[5] and Buffalo,[6] New York, and Detroit, Michigan, many fugitives are known to have lived. The Rev. Calvin Fairbank relates that, while visiting Detroit in 1849, he discovered several families he had helped from slavery living near the city. He went to see these families, and afterward wrote concerning them: "Living near the Johnsons, and like them contented and comfortable, I found the Stewart and Coleman families, for whom I had also lighted the path of freedom."[7] In the vicinity of Sandy Lake, in the northwestern part of Pennsylvania, there was a colony of colored people, most of whom were runaway slaves.[8]

Such evidence, which is local in its nature, should be considered in conjunction with the general estimates of those persons that expressed opinions after wide observation in regard to the whole number of fugitive settlers in the North.

[1] Clipping from the *Commonwealth*, preserved in a scrap-book relating to Theodore Parker, Boston Public Library.
[2] Conversation with Mr. Oliver, Windsor, Ont., Aug. 2, 1895.
[3] Conversation with the Rev. James Poindexter, Columbus, O., summer of 1895.   [4] *History of Summit County, Ohio*, pp. 579, 580.
[5] Letters of Mrs. Susan L. Crane, Elmira, N.Y.
[6] See p. 250, this chapter.   [7] *The Chicago Tribune*, Jan. 29, 1893.
[8] Letter of John F. Hogue, Greenville, Pa., Nov. 25, 1895.

The most indefinite of these contemporary opinions is that of the veteran underground helper, Samuel J. May, who states that "hundreds ventured to remain this side of the Lakes."[1] Other judges attempt to put their estimates into figures; thus, Henry Wilson thinks that by 1850 twenty thousand had found homes in the free states;[2] Mr. Franklin B. Sanborn, admitting the inherent difficulty of the calculation, places the number at from twenty-five thousand to fifty thousand;[3] and the Canadian refugee, Josiah Henson, wrote in 1852: "It is estimated that the number of fugitive slaves in the various free states . . . amounts to 50,000."[4]

Fugitives that thus dwelt in the Northern states for a longer or shorter period did so at their own risk, and in general against the advice of their helpers. Their reliance for safety was altogether upon their own wariness and the public sentiment of the communities where they lived, and until slavery perished in the Civil War they were subjected to the fear of surprise and seizure. The Southern people apparently regarded their right to recover their escaped slaves as unquestionable as their right to reclaim their strayed cattle, and they were determined to have the former as freely and fully recognized in the North as the latter;[5] and it might be added that there were not a few people in the North quite willing to admit the slaveholder's right freely to reclaim his human property, and to aid him in doing so. What the sentiment was that prevailed in the North during the twenties and thirties of the present century is evidenced in certain laws enacted by the legislatures of some of the states in line with the Federal Slave Law of 1793. Thus, in an act passed by the assembly of Pennsylvania, March 25, 1826, provision was made for the issuance by courts of record of the commonwealth of certificates or warrants

[1] *Some Recollections of our Anti-Slavery Conflict*, p. 297.
[2] *Rise and Fall of the Slave Power*, Vol. II, p. 304; see also E. B. Andrews' *History of the United States*, Vol. II, p. 36.
[3] Conversation with Mr. Sanborn, Cambridge, Mass., March, 1897.
[4] *The Life of Josiah Henson, formerly a Slave, as narrated by Himself*, p. 97.
[5] James H. Fairchild, *The Underground Railroad*, Tract No. 87, in Vol. IV, Western Reserve Historical Society, p. 106.

of removal for negroes or mulattoes, claimed to be fugitives from labor;[1] and in a law enacted by the legislature of Ohio, February 26, 1839, it was provided that any justice of the peace, judge of a court of record, or mayor should authorize the arrest of a person claimed as a fugitive slave on the affidavit of the claimant or his agent, and that the judge of a court of record before whom the fugitive was brought should grant a certificate of removal upon the presentation of satisfactory proof.[2]

Among those that paid homage to such laws as these, and thus made the North an unsafe refuge for slaves, were to be found representatives of all classes of society. Samuel J. May opens to view the convictions of some of the most cultured people of his day by the following incidents related concerning two well-known New England clergymen. "The excellent Dr. E. S. Gannett, of Boston, was heard to say, more than once, very emphatically, and to justify it, 'that he should feel it to be his duty to turn away from his door a fugitive slave, — unfed, unaided in any way, rather than set at naught the law of the land.'

"And Rev. Dr. Dewey, whom we accounted one of the ablest expounders and most eloquent defenders of our Unitarian faith, — Dr. Dewey was reported to have said at two different times, in public lectures or speeches during the fall of 1850 and the winter of 1851, that 'he would send his *mother* into slavery, rather than endanger the Union, by resisting this law enacted by the constituted government of the nation.' He has often denied that he spoke thus of his 'maternal relative,' and therefore I allow that he was misunderstood. But he has repeatedly acknowledged that he did say, 'I would consent that my own brother, my own son, should go, *ten times rather* would I go myself into slavery, than that this Union should be sacrificed.'"[3] After the occurrence of the famous Jerry rescue at Syracuse, October 1, 1851, many newspapers representing both political parties

---

[1] G. M. Stroud, *A Sketch of the Laws Relating to Slavery*, 2d ed., 1856, pp. 281, 282.
[2] *Statutes of the State of Ohio*, 1841, collated by J. R. Swan, pp. 595-600.
[3] *Some Recollections of our Anti-Slavery Conflict*, p. 367.

emphatically condemned the successful resistance made to the law by the abolitionists as " a disgraceful, demoralizing and alarming act." [1]

There were not wanting in almost every community members of the shiftless class of society that were always ready to obstruct the passage of fugitive slaves to the North, and whose most vigorous exercise was taken in the course of some slave-hunting adventure. The Rev. W. M. Mitchell, who had had this class to contend with in the performance of his underground work during a number of years in Ohio, characterized it in a description, penned in 1860, in which he sets forth one of the conditions that made the Northern states an unsafe refuge for self-liberated negroes. "The progress of the Slave," he wrote, "is very much impeded by a class of men in the Northern States who are too lazy to work at respectable occupations to obtain an honest living, but prefer to obtain it, if possible, whether honestly or dishonestly, by tracking runaway slaves. On seeing advertisements in the newspapers of escaped slaves, with rewards offered, they, armed to the teeth, saunter in and through Abolition Communities or towns, where they are likely to find the object of their pursuit. They sometimes watch the houses of known Abolitionists. . . . We are hereby warned, and for our own safety and that of the Slave, we act with excessive caution. The first discoverer of these bloody rebels communicates their presence to others of our company, that the entire band in that locality is put on their guard. If the slave has not reached us, we are on the lookout, with greater anxiety than the hunters, for the fugitive, to prevent his falling into the possession of those demons in human shape. On the other hand should the Slave be so fortunate as to be in our possession at the time, we are compelled to keep very quiet, until the hunter loses all hopes of finding him, therefore gives up the search as a bad job, or

---

[1] *Some Recollections of Our Anti-Slavery Conflict*, p. 380. The newspapers named by Mr. May are, *The Advertiser* and *The American* of Rochester, *The Gazette* and *Observer* of Utica, *The Oneida Whig*, *The Register*, *The Argus* and *The Express* of Albany, *The Courier* and *Inquirer* and *The Express* of New York.

moves on to another Abolition Community, which gives us an opportunity of removing the Fugitive further from danger, or sending him towards the North Star. . . ."[1]

It is not to be supposed, of course, that the business of slave-hunting was carried on mainly by the persons here described in such uncomplimentary terms. Persons of this type contented themselves generally, no doubt, with acting as spies and informers, and rarely engaged in the excitement of a slave-hunt except as the aids of Southern planters or their agents. If it is true that there was a sentiment averse to slavery prevailing through many years in the North, it is also true that the residents of the free states for the most part conceded the right of Southerners to pursue and recover their fugitives without hindrance from their Northern neighbors. The free states thus became what the abolitionists called the "hunting-ground" of the South, and as early as 1830 or 1835 the pursuit of slaves began to attract wide attention. During the years following many localities, especially in the middle states, were visited from time to time by parties on the trail of the fleeing bondman, or seeking out the secluded home of some self-freed slave; and after the enactment of the Fugitive Slave Law of 1850 Southerners became more energetic than before in pushing the search for their escaped chattels. It has been recorded that "more than two hundred arrests of persons claimed as fugitives were made from the time of the passage of the Bill to the middle of 1856. About a dozen of these were free persons, who succeeded in establishing the claim that they never had been slaves; other persons, equally free, were carried off. Half a dozen rescues were made, and the rest of these cases were delivered to their owners. These arrests took place more frequently in Pennsylvania than in any other Northern state. Many fugitives were caught and carried back, of whom we have no accounts, save that they were seen on the deck of some river steamboat, in the custody of their owners, without even passing through the formality of appearing before a commissioner. About two-thirds of the persons arrested as above had trials. When the arrests to the number of two hundred, at least, can be traced,

[1] *The Underground Railroad*, pp. 13, 14.

and their dates fixed, during six years, we may suppose that the Bill was not, as some politicians averred, practically of little consequence."[1]

Concerning the efficiency of the new law there is a difference of opinion among the contemporary writers that commented upon it; but there could be no disagreement as to the distress into which it plunged some of the refugees long resident in the free states. In not a few instances these persons had married, acquired homes, and were rearing their families in peace and happiness. Under the Fugitive Slave Act some of these settlers were seized upon the affidavit of their former owners, and with the sanction of the federal authority were carried back into slavery. Among the many cases that might be cited the following will serve to illustrate the misfortunes ever ready to be precipitated upon fugitive settlers in the Northern states. In 1851 John Bolding, claimed as the property of a citizen of Columbia, South Carolina, was arrested in Poughkeepsie, New York, and taken back to the South. Bolding was a young man of good character, recently married, and the possessor of a small tailor shop in Poughkeepsie.[2] In August, 1853, George Washington McQuerry, of Cincinnati, was remanded to slavery in Kentucky. He had lived several years in Ohio, had married a free woman, and they had three children.[3] In September, 1853, a family of colored persons at Uniontown, Pennsylvania, were claimed as slaves by a Virginian. Their statement that they had been permitted by their master to visit friends in Fayette County did not prevent their immediate restoration to him.[4] In May, 1857, Addison White, a runaway from Kentucky, was found living near Mechanicsburg, Ohio, where he had been at work about six months earning means to send for his wife and children. Some of the abolitionists of the neighborhood prevented his reclamation.[5] In three of these cases at least the reënslavement of the refugees was prevented by an abolition sentiment locally

---

[1] Weiss, *Life and Correspondence of Theodore Parker*, Vol. II, p. 93.
[2] *The Fugitive Slave Law and Its Victims*, by Samuel May, Jr., 1861, p. 19.
[3] *Ibid.*, p. 31. See Appendix B, p. 374.   [4] *Ibid.*, p. 68 *et seq.*
[5] See Appendix B, p. 375.

strong enough to lead to the purchase of the slaves from their claimants; but it is noteworthy that public opinion in the neighborhoods where these runaways lived was unable to shield them from capture.

The refugees that preferred to settle in the Northern states rather than in Canada naturally made homes for themselves in anti-slavery communities among tried friends. Here they could rest with some assurance upon the benevolence of these localities and feel safe, although their liberty was still in danger. A slave-hunter in entering such neighborhoods was obliged to move with great caution; he was in the midst of strangers, with few allies, and his scheme was likely to fail if his presence became known. Sometimes, when he was in the very act of leading the captive back to the South in bonds, he would find his progress interrupted by a crowd, his authority questioned, his return to the office of a magistrate insisted upon, and ultimately, perhaps, his prisoner released by a procedure more or less formal. The slave-hunter that incautiously flourished weapons and made threats was likely to be arrested and subjected to such additional delays and inconveniences as would render his undertaking expensive as well as vexatious. There can be no doubt that this was the experience of many slave-owners that sought to recover their servants in the free states. Mr. Clay touched on this point, April 22, 1850, in presenting petitions to the United States Senate from four citizens of Kentucky. These persons, he said, "state that each of them has lost a slave. . . . That these slaves have taken refuge in the state of Ohio, and that it is in vain for them to attempt to recapture them; that they cannot go there and attempt to recover their property without imminent hazard to their lives."[1] This statement, reiterating the idea contained in the petitions themselves, namely, that the danger attending pursuit was great, is too strong in reference to a large number of the abolition communities in the Northern states, in many of which non-resistance principles were advocated. At the same time it must be remembered that the usual methods of slave-catchers were not conciliatory to the people

[1] *Congressional Globe*, New Series, Vol. XXII, Part I, p. 793.

among whom they went, and that their bravado sometimes secured for them rough treatment at the hands of a mob, especially if the number of colored people present was large enough to warrant their venting their outraged feelings.

The difficulty of recovering slave property in the North had been considerable for some years, and it was steadily growing greater. The uncertainty of reclamation in the large number of cases made the whole business unprofitable and undesirable for slave-owners. A writer in the *North American Review* for July, 1850, says, "Though thousands of slaves have escaped by crossing the Ohio River, or Mason and Dixon's line, during the last five years, no attempt has been made to reclaim them in more than one case out of a thousand."[1] If one takes this statement as meant to convey merely the idea that the number of pursuits was extremely small in proportion to the number of escapes there will be no difficulty in accepting it, for probably this was the fact down to 1850; and the explanation of it, so far as can be gathered from the lips of Southern men, is to be found in the strong probability of failure in undertaking these costly enterprises. Thus Mr. Mason, of Virginia, in his argument in favor of a new fugitive slave law, declared that, under the existing conditions, "you may as well go down into the sea and endeavor to recover from his native element a fish which has escaped from you, as expect to recover a . . . fugitive. Every difficulty is thrown in your way by the population. . . . There are armed mobs, rescues. This is the real state of things."[2]

The law of 1850 was intended to remove the occasion for such complaints on the part of slaveholders, and secure them in the recovery and possession of their property. The effect of its provisions upon the South was to arouse slave-owners to greater activity in the pursuit of their chattels, while in the North the effect was to increase greatly the determination in the minds of many to resist the enforcement of the law. Despite the severe penalties it levelled

[1] F. Bowen on "Extradition of Fugitive Slaves," Vol. LXXI, p. 252 *et seq.*
[2] *Congressional Globe*, Thirty-first Congress, First Session, p. 1583; also M. G. McDougall, *Fugitive Slaves*, p. 31.

against those that should be guilty of shielding the refugee, the expression of sympathy for fugitive settlers was open and hearty in many quarters; and public meetings were held by abolitionists to proclaim defiance to the law and protection to the fugitive. At Lowell, Massachusetts, an immense Free Soil meeting adopted resolutions inviting former residents of the city to return from Canada, where they had taken refuge;[1] at Syracuse, New York, a gathering of all parties declared its abhorrence of the Fugitive Slave Law, and formed an association or vigilance committee "so that the Southern oppressors may know that the people of Syracuse and its vicinity are prepared to sustain one another in resisting the encroachments of despotism";[2] at Boston an indignation meeting was held "for the denunciation of the law and the expression of sympathy and coöperation with the fugitive." Among the resolutions adopted at this meeting, one advised "the fugitive slaves and colored inhabitants of Boston and the neighborhood to remain with us, for we have not the smallest fear that any one of them will be taken from us and carried off to bondage; and we trust that such as have fled in fear will return to their business and homes"; another resolution proposed the appointment of a vigilance committee "to secure the fugitives and colored inhabitants of Boston and vicinity from any invasion of their rights by persons acting under the law."[3] In Ashtabula County, Ohio, a meeting at Hartsgrove resolved, "that we hold the Fugitive Slave Law in utter contempt . . . and that we will not aid in catching the fugitive, but will feed him, and protect him with all the means in our power, and that we will pledge our sympathy and property for the relief of any person in our midst who may suffer any penalties for an honorable opposition . . . to the requirements of this law."[4] In other portions also of the free states meetings were held in which the purpose was avowed to protect fugitive slaves.[5]

[1] Wilson, *Rise and Fall of the Slave Power in America*, Vol. II, p. 306.
[2] Samuel J. May, *Some Recollections of Our Anti-Slavery Conflict*, p. 353.
[3] John Weiss, *Life and Correspondence of Theodore Parker*, Vol. II, p. 94.
[4] Article by the Rev. S. D. Peet, in *History of Ashtabula County, Ohio*, pp. 33, 34.
[5] "No sooner was the deed done, the Fugitive Slave Act sent forth to be

The change of sentiment in the North from passive acquiescence in the law to active resistance to it is best seen, perhaps, in the history of the so-called personal liberty laws. The real object of these statutes was to impair the operation of the national Fugitive Slave Law, although their proposed object was in most cases to prevent the removal of free colored citizens to the South under the claim that they were fugitive slaves. These statutes were passed by the legislatures of various states during the period of a little more than thirty years from 1824 to 1858, the greater number being enacted after the repeal of the Missouri Compromise in 1854. The first two in the series were those enacted by Indiana and Connecticut in 1824 and 1838 respectively, and provided that on appeal fugitives might have a trial by jury. In 1840 Vermont and New York framed laws granting jury trial, and also providing attorneys to defend fugitives. In 1842 the Prigg decision gave the occasion for a new class of statutes; the release of state authorities from the execution of the Slave Law by the opinion handed down by Justice Story was taken advantage of in Massachusetts, Vermont, Pennsylvania and Rhode Island, and the officers of the states were forbidden from performing the duties imposed by the law of 1793. The decade from 1850 to 1860 is marked by a fresh crop of these personal liberty acts, due to the sentiment aroused by the law of 1850 and aggravated by the repeal of the Missouri Compromise. As the new national law avoided the employment of state officers, state legislation was now directed in the main to limiting the powers of the executors of the laws as far as possible, and depriving them of the facilities of action. Thus, the new laws generally provided counsel for any one arrested as a fugitive; secured to him a trial surrounded by the usual safeguards; prohibited the use of state jails; and forbade state officers to issue writs or give aid to the claimant. The penalty for the violation of these

the law of the land, than outcries of contempt and defiance came from every free state, and pledges of protection were given to the colored population. It is not within the scope of my plan to attempt an account of the indignation meetings that were held in places too numerous to be even mentioned here." S. J. May, *Some Recollections of the Anti-Slavery Conflict*, p. 349.

provisions was a heavy fine and imprisonment. "Such acts," it is said, "were passed in Vermont, Connecticut and Rhode Island, in Massachusetts, Michigan and Maine. Later, laws were also enacted in Wisconsin, Kansas, Ohio and Pennsylvania. Of the other Northern States, two only, New Jersey and California, gave any official sanction to the rendition of fugitives. In New Hampshire, New York, Indiana, Illinois, Iowa and Minnesota, however, no full personal liberty laws were passed."[1]

Notwithstanding the disposition shown in many parts of the free states to protect fugitive settlers, the Slave Law of 1850 spread consternation and distress among them, and caused numbers to leave the little homes they had established for themselves, and renew their search for liberty. Perhaps in no community of the North did fugitive settlers feel themselves more secure than in Boston, the city of Garrison, Phillips and Parker; here they were gathered together by the Rev. Leonard B. Grimes, a colored man, who soon organized a church of fugitive slaves, and such was the feeling of confidence among them that in 1849 a building was begun for this unique congregation. Within a few months, however, the new Slave Law was enacted, and wrung from this band of runaways a cry of anguish that may be justly regarded as expressing the distress of the people of this class in all quarters of the free states. At a meeting of the Boston refugees, held October 5, 1850, an appeal to the clergy of Massachusetts was issued, in the preamble of which was embodied the slaves' view of their own situation, and their pitiful entreaty for help. As "trembling, proscribed and hunted fugitives . . . now scattered through the various towns and villages of Massachusetts, and momentarily liable to be seized by the strong arm of government, and hurried back to stripes, tortures and bondage . . ." they implored the clergy to "'lift up (their) voices like a trumpet' against the Fugitive Slave Bill, recently adopted by Congress. . . ."[2] The church building of the

[1] M. G. McDougall, *Fugitive Slaves*, pp. 65–70, and the references there given.
[2] Scrap-book of clippings, circulars, etc., presented to the Boston Public Library by Mrs. L. L. Parker.

fugitive settlers "was arrested midway towards its completion, and the members were scattered in wild dismay. More than forty fled to Canada. One of their number, Shadrach, was seized, but more fortunate than the hapless Sims, who had no fellowship with them, he succeeded in making his escape."[1] An individual case that illustrates the sudden disaster experienced by numerous households throughout the North was recorded by the Rev. J. S. C. Abbott, in January, 1852. The case occurred in Boston in 1851 : "A colored girl, eighteen years of age, a few years ago escaped from slavery at the South. Through scenes of adventure and peril she found her way to Boston, obtained employment, secured friends, and became a consistent member of a Methodist church. She became interested in a very worthy young man, of her own complexion, who was a member of the same church. They were soon married. Their home, though humble, was the abode of piety and contentment. . . . Seven years passed away; they had two little boys, one six and the other four years of age. These children, the sons of a free father, but of a mother who had been a slave, by the laws of our Southern states were doomed to their mother's fate. These Boston boys, born beneath the shadow of Faneuil Hall, the sons of a free citizen of Boston, and educated in the Boston free schools, were, by the compromises of the Constitution, admitted to be slaves, the property of a South Carolinian planter. The Boston father had no right to his own sons. The law, however, had long been considered a dead letter. The Christian mother, as she morning and evening bowed with her children in prayer, felt that they were safe from the slave-hunter, surrounded as they were by the churches, the schools, and the free institutions of Massachusetts.

"The Fugitive Slave Law was enacted. It revived the hopes of the slave-owners. A young, healthy, energetic mother, with two fine boys, was a rich prize. . . . Good men began to say : 'We must enforce this law ; it is one of the compromises of the Constitution.' Christian ministers began to preach: 'The voice of the law is the voice of God.

[1] C. E. Stevens, *Anthony Burns, A History*, 1856, p. 208.

There is no higher rule of duty.' . . . The poor woman was panic-stricken. Her friends gathered around her and trembled for her. Her husband was absent from home, a seaman on board one of our Liverpool packets. She was afraid to get out of doors lest some one from the South should see her and recognize her. One day, as she was going to the grocery for some provisions, her quick and anxious eye caught a glimpse of a man prowling around, whom she immediately recognized as from the vicinity of her old home of slavery. Almost fainting with terror, she hastened home, and, taking her two children by the hand, fled to the house of a friend. She and her trembling children were hid in the garret. In less than one hour after her escape, the officer with a writ came for her arrest.

". . . At midnight, her friends took her in a hack, and conveyed her, with her children, to the house of her pastor. A prayer-meeting had been appointed there, at that hour, in behalf of the suffering sister. A small group of stricken hearts were assembled. . . . Groanings and lamentations filled the room. No one could pray. . . . Other fugitives were there, trembling in view of a doom more dreadful to them than death. After an hour of weeping . . . they took this Christian mother and her children in a hack, and conveyed them to one of the Cunard steamers, which fortunately was to sail for Halifax the next day. . . . Her brethren and sisters of the church raised a little money from their scanty means to pay her passage, and to save her for a few days from starving, after her first arrival in the cold land of strangers. Her husband soon returned to Boston, to find his home desolate, his wife and his children exiles in a foreign land.

"I think that this narrative may be relied upon as accurate. I received the facts from the lips of one, a member of the church, who was present at that midnight 'weeping-meeting,' before the Lord. Such is slavery in Boston, in the year 1852. Has the North nothing to do with slavery?"[1]

[1] Quoted by F. B. Sanborn, in his *Life of Dr. S. G. Howe, the Philanthropist*, pp. 237, 238, 239. Similar stories are related by Lydia Maria Child, in her *Life of Isaac T. Hopper*, pp. 455–458.

In localities nearer to slave territory than Boston, and in places where anti-slavery sentiment was perhaps less pronounced, it may be supposed that terror was not less prevalent among fugitive settlers. The members of the colored community near Sandy Lake in northwestern Pennsylvania, many of whom had purchased small farms and had them partly paid for, sold out or gave away their farms and went to Canada in a body.[1] The sudden disappearance of refugees from their habitations in various other places as soon as the character of the new law became noised abroad was a phenomenon the cause of which was unmistakable. Of the many that thus vanished from their accustomed haunts,[2] Josiah Henson, writing in 1852, said: "Some have found their way to England, but the mass are flying to Canada, where they feel themselves secure. Already several thousands have gone thither, and have added considerably to the number already settled, or partially settled, in that part of the British dominions. . . ."[3] As Mr. Henson was a worker among the refugees in Canada he was in a position to speak from his personal knowledge, and his testimony is sustained by that of the Rev. Anthony Bingey, an escaped slave, who helped receive fugitives at Amherstburg, Ontario, one of the chief landing-places of the negro emigrants from the United States. Mr. Bingey states that after the Fugitive Slave Law took effect the runaways came there " by fifties every day, like frogs in Egypt." Before that time " many had settled in the States, but after the Fugitive Slave Law they could be taken, so they came in from all parts."[4] Sumner estimated that, altogether, " as many as six thousand Christian men and women, meritorious persons, — *a larger band than that of the escaping Puritans*, — precipitately fled from homes which they had established" to British soil. The Liberator published a statement, made in February, 1851,

[1] Letter of John F. Hogue, Greenville, Pa., Nov. 25, 1895; letter of the Rev. James Lawson, Franklin, Pa., Nov. 25, 1895.
[2] *Life of William Lloyd Garrison*, Vol. III, p. 302. See also Rhodes's *History of the United States*, Vol. I, p. 198.
[3] *The Life of Josiah Henson, formerly a Slave, as narrated by Himself*, pp. 97, 98, 99.
[4] Conversation with Mr. Bingey, Windsor, Ont., July 31, 1896.

that the African Methodist and Baptist churches of Buffalo, New York, had both lost a large number of members, the loss of the former being given as one hundred. The Baptist church of the colored people of Rochester, in the same state, out of a membership of one hundred and fourteen, lost one hundred and twelve, including the pastor. The African Baptist church of Detroit lost eighty-four members at this time.[1]

One must not imagine, however, that all the fugitives migrated beyond the borders of the free states. No doubt a considerable number, more daring than the rest,[2] or in some way favored by circumstances, chose to remain and run the risk of discovery. Colonel Thomas Wentworth Higginson asserts that "For many years fugitive slaves came to Massachusetts and remained, this lasting until the Fugitive Slave Law was passed in 1850, and longer. Even after that period we tried to keep them in Worcester, where I then lived, it being a strong anti-slavery place, and they often stayed."[3] Some of the fugitives that were induced to move by the Slave Law only passed from one state into another, instead of continuing their journey to regions beyond the jurisdiction of a United States commissioner. Of a company of blacks dwelling near the home of Elijah F. Pennypacker in Chester County, Pennsylvania, at the time of the enactment of the law of 1850, it is said that while some went to Canada, some went to New York and some to Massachusetts.[4] It was noted above that the new church of the fugitives of Boston was stopped midway in the process of building by the promulgation of the act, but it is significant that the structure was completed soon after. Evidently not all of the refugees departed from the city of their adoption. It is related that "When the first fury of the storm had blown over, Mr. Grimes set himself with redoubled energy to repair the

---

[1] *Life of Garrison*, Vol. III, p. 302; also foot-note, pp. 302, 303.
[2] "Some of the boldest chose to remain, and armed themselves to defend their freedom, instinctively calculating that the sight of such an exigency would make the Northern heart beat too rapidly for prudence!" Weiss, *Life and Correspondence of Theodore Parker*, Vol. II, p. 92.
[3] Letter of Mr. Higginson, Cambridge, Mass., Feb. 5, 1894.
[4] R. C. Smedley, *History of the Underground Railroad*, p. 210.

wastes that had been made. He collected money from the charitable, and purchased the members of his church out of slavery, that they might return without fear to the fold. He made friends among the rich, who advanced funds for the completion of his church. At length it was finished, and, as if for an omen of good, was dedicated on the first day when Burns stood for trial before Commissioner Loring."[1] Runaways entering the free states for the first time after the subsidence of the paroxysm of fear among their fellows sometimes remained in neighborhoods where the conditions were supposed to be favorable to their safety. Some of these were never disturbed, and consequently never went to Canada at all.

Among the fugitive settlers in the Northern states there were some at least that became widely known among abolitionists and others as active agents of the Underground Railroad. Frederick Douglass was one of these, and during his residence in New Bedford, Massachusetts, and later during his residence in Rochester, New York, he was able to help many runaways. The Rev. J. W. Loguen, who became a bishop of the African Methodist Church about 1869, settled in Syracuse, New York, in 1841, and became immediately one of the managers of secret operations there. In his hospitable home, Samuel J. May relates, was fitted up an apartment for fugitive slaves, and, for years before the Emancipation Act, scarcely a week passed without some one, in his flight from slavedom to Canada, enjoyed shelter and repose at Elder Loguen's."[2] Lewis Hayden, for many years a prominent citizen of Boston, who owed his liberty to the self-sacrificing efforts of the Rev. Calvin Fairbank and Miss Delia Webster in September, 1844,[3] made a practice of harboring slaves in his house, number 66 Phillips

[1] C. E. Stevens, *Anthony Burns, A History*, p. 208. In a foot-note it is said, "The church is a neat and commodious brick structure, two stories in height, and handsomely finished in the interior. It will seat five or six hundred people. The whole cost, including the land, was $13,000, of which, through the exertion of Mr. Grimes, $10,000 have already (1856) been paid. . . ."

[2] *Some Recollections of our Anti-Slavery Conflict*, pp. 202, 203.

[3] *Rev. Calvin Fairbank During Slavery Times*, pp. 46, 48, 49.

Street. "Some there are," a recent writer declares, "who well remember when William Craft was in hiding here from the slave-catchers, and how Lewis Hayden had placed two kegs of gunpowder on the premises, resolved to blow up his house rather than surrender the fugitive. The heroic frenzy of the resolute black face, as with match in hand Hayden stood waiting the man-stealers, those who saw it declare that they can never forget."[1]

William Wells Brown, who distinguished himself as an anti-slavery lecturer in this country and England, rendered considerable service to fellow-fugitives shortly after his escape from Missouri about 1840.[2] Securing employment on a Lake Erie steamboat, he was able to provide the means of transportation for many runaways across the lake. As the boat frequently touched at Cleveland on its trips to and fro between Buffalo and Detroit, Mr. Brown made an arrangement with some Cleveland friends to furnish transportation, which was done without charge, for any negroes they might wish to send to Canada. The result was that delegations of anxious refugees were often taken aboard at the Cleveland wharf. Brown engaged in this service in the early forties, and his companies were therefore small, but he sometimes gave passage to four or five at one time. "In the year 1842," he says, "I conveyed, from the first of May to the first of December, sixty-nine fugitives over Lake Erie to Canada. In 1843 I visited Malden, in upper Canada, and counted seventeen in that small village whom I had assisted in reaching Canada."[3] John W. Jones, a respected citizen of Elmira, New York, made his way in 1844 from Virginia to the city where he still lives. During the following year he succeeded in aiding two younger brothers to join him, and thereafter he continued, in coöperation with Mr. Jervis Langdon and other abolitionists of Elmira, to succor his brethren in their search for places of refuge. After the construction of the Northern Central Railroad

---

[1] Article by A. H. Grimké, on "Anti-Slavery Boston," in *The New England Magazine*, December, 1890, p. 458.

[2] S. J. May, *Some Recollections of our Anti-Slavery Conflict*, p. 289.

[3] *Narrative of William W. Brown, A Fugitive Slave*, pp. 106, 107, 108.

through Elmira, Mr. Jones effected an arrangement with some of the employees of that road by which his friends could be carried through to the Canadian border in baggage-cars. At the same time he was in regular correspondence with William Still, the agent of the central underground station at Philadelphia, who frequently sent him companies of passengers requiring immediate transportation.[1] John H. Hooper, a fugitive from the Eastern Shore of Maryland and an acquaintance there of Fred Douglass, kept a station at Troy, New York, where he settled.[2] Louis Washington, who fled from Richmond, Virginia, to Columbus, Ohio, became a conductor of the Underground Road at that point. Mr. James Poindexter, a well-known colored clergyman of Columbus, knew Washington intimately, and testifies that he had teams and wagons with which he conveyed the midnight pilgrims on their way.[3] There are other cases of fugitive settlers that became members of the large company of underground operators. But a sufficient number have been mentioned to indicate that they were not rare. The first and the last of the seven named did not continue long in the status of escaped slaves. Frederick Douglass secured his liberty in a legal way through the payment by English friends of the sum of $750 to his master. Louis Washington purchased his own freedom. The other five, so far as known, were never relieved by the payment of money from the claims of their masters. Most, if not all, of these men remained in the Northern states after the passage of the Fugitive Slave Law of 1850.

[1] Letters of Mrs. Susan Crane, Elmira, N.Y.; letters of John W. Jones, Elmira, N.Y.; see also Still, *Underground Railroad Records*, p. 530.

[2] Letters of Mr. Martin I. Townsend, Troy. N.Y., Sept. 4, 1896, and April 3, 1897.

[3] Conversation with Mr. Poindexter, Columbus, O., in the summer of 1895.

CHAPTER IX

PROSECUTIONS OF UNDERGROUND RAILROAD MEN

THE aversion to a law for the rendition of fugitive slaves that early manifested itself in the North was perhaps foreshadowed in the hesitating manner in which the question was dealt with by Congress. The original demand for legislation was caused by the activity of kidnappers in Pennsylvania; but the first bill, reported from committee to the House in November, 1791, was dropped for some reason not now discoverable. At the end of March in the following year a committee of the Senate was appointed to consider the matter, but it accomplished nothing. At the beginning of the next session a second Senate committee was chosen, and from this body a bill emanated. This bill proved to be unsatisfactory, however, and after the committee had been remodelled by the addition of two new members the bill was recommitted with instructions to amend. With some slight change the measure proposed by the committee was adopted by the Senate, January 18; and after an interval of nearly three weeks the House passed it with little or no debate, by a vote of forty-eight to seven. Thus for nearly a year and a quarter the subject was under the consideration of Congress before it could be embodied in a bill and sent to the executive for his signature. On February 12, 1793, President Washington signed this bill and it became a law.[1]

The object of the law was, of course, to enforce the constitutional guarantee in regard to the delivery of fugitives from service to their masters. An analysis of the law will show that forcible seizure of the alleged fugitive was authorized; that the decision of the magistrate before whom he was to be taken was allowed to turn on the testimony of the master, or

---

[1] M. G. McDougall, *Fugitive Slaves*, pp. 17, 18.

SALMON P. CHASE,

OF OHIO,

known as "attorney-general for fugitive slaves," on account of his frequent appearance as counsel in fugitive slave cases.

THOMAS GARRETT,

OF WILMINGTON, DELAWARE,

who aided 2700 runaways, and paid $8000 in fines for his violations of the slave laws.

the affidavit of some magistrate in the state from which he came; and that trial by jury was denied. Persons attempting to obstruct the law by harboring or concealing a fugitive slave, resisting his arrest, or securing his rescue, were liable to a fine of five hundred dollars for the benefit of the claimant, and the right of action on account of these injuries was reserved to the claimant.[1]

The exclusive regard for the rights of the owner exhibited in these provisions was fitted to stir the popular sense of justice in the Northern states, most of which had already ranged themselves by individual action on the side of liberty. Persons moved by the appeals of the hunted negro to transgress the statute would naturally try to avoid its penalties by concealment of their acts, and this we know was what they did. The whole movement denominated the Underground Railroad was carried on in secret, because only thus could the fugitives, in whose behalf it originated, and their abettors, by whom it was maintained, be secure from the law. When through mischance or open resistance, as sometimes happened, an offender against the law was discovered and brought to trial, the case was not allowed to progress far before the Fugitive Recovery Act itself was assailed vigorously by the counsel for the defendant. The grounds of attack included the absence of provision for jury trial, the authority of the claimant or his agent to arrest without a warrant, the antagonism between state and federal legislation, the supposed repugnancy of the law of 1793 to the Ordinance of 1787, the denial of the power of Congress to legislate on the subject of fugitive slaves, and the question as to the responsibility for the execution of the law. Nearly if not all of these disputed points were involved in the great question as to the constitutionality of the congressional act, a question that kept working up through the successive decisions of the courts to irritate and disturb the peace between the sections, that the fugitive clause in the federal Constitution, the act of 1793 itself, and the judicial affirmations following in their train were intended to promote.

The omission of a provision from the law of Congress secur-

[1] *Statutes at Large*, I, 302-305.

ing trial by jury to the alleged fugitive was at once remarked by the friends of the bondman, and caused the law to be denounced in the court-room as worthy only of the severest condemnation.[1] As early as 1819, in the case of Wright *vs.* Deacon, tried before the Supreme Court of Pennsylvania, it was urged that the supposed fugitive was entitled to a jury trial, but the arguments made in support of the claim have not been preserved.[2] The question was presented in several subsequent cases of importance arising under the law of 1793, namely, Jack *vs.* Martin, in 1835,[3] Peter, *alias* Lewis Martin, about 1837,[4] and State *vs.* Hoppess, in 1845.[5] From the reports of these cases one is not able to gather much in the way of direct statement showing what were the grounds

[1] Professor Eugene Wambaugh, of the Law School of Harvard University, in a letter to the author, comments as follows on the source of the injustice wrought by the Fugitive Slave acts: "The difficulty lay in the initial assumption that a human being can be property. Grant this assumption, and there follow many absurdities, among them the impossibility of framing a Fugitive Slave Law that shall be both logical and humane. Human beings are entitled to a trial of the normal sort, especially in a case involving the liability of personal restraint. Chattels, however, are entitled to no trial at all; and if a chattel be lost or stolen, the owner may retake it wherever he finds it, provided he commits no breach of the peace. (3 Blackstone's *Commentaries*, 4.) If slaves had been treated as ordinary chattels, there could have been no trial as to the ownership of them, unless, indeed, there were a dispute between competing claimants. There would have been, however, the fatal objection that thus a free man — black, mulatto, or white — might be enslaved without a hearing. Here, then, is a puzzle. If the man is a slave, he is entitled to no trial at all. If he is free, he is entitled to a trial of the most careful sort, surrounded with all the safeguards that have been thrown up by the law. When there is such a dilemma, is it strange that there should be a compromise? The Fugitive Slave Laws really were a compromise; for in so far as they provided for an abnormal and incomplete trial, a hearing before a United States Commissioner, simply to determine rights as between the supposed slave and the supposed master, they conceded the radical impossibility of following out logically the supposition that human beings can be chattels, and, in so far as they denied to the supposed slave the normal trial, they assumed in advance that he was a slave. I need not write of the dilemma further. A procedure intermediate between a formal trial and a total denial of justice was probably the only solution practicable in those days; but it was an illogical solution, and the only logical solution was emancipation."

[2] 5 *Sergeant and Rawle's Reports*, 63. See Appendix B, p. 368.

[3] 14 *Wendell's Reports*, 514. See Appendix B, p. 368.

[4] In the Circuit Court of the United States for the Southern District of New York, 2 *Paine's Reports*, 352. [5] 2 *Western Law Journal*, 282.

taken for the advocacy of trial by jury in such cases, but the indications that appear are not to be mistaken. In all of these cases it seems to have been insisted that the law of 1793 failed to conform to the constitutional requirement on this point; and in State vs. Hoppess it is distinctly stated that the law provided for a trial of the most important right without a jury, contrary to the amendment of the Constitution declaring that "In suits at common law, where the value shall exceed twenty dollars, the right of trial by jury shall be preserved . . . .";[1] and that the act also authorized the deprivation of a person of his or her liberty contrary to another amendment, which declares that no person shall be "deprived of life, liberty, or property, without due process of law."[2] In Jack vs. Martin, as probably in the other cases, the obvious objection seems to have been made that the denial of the jury contributed to make easy the enslavement of free citizens. The courts, however, did not sustain these objections; thus, for example, in the last case named, Judge Nelson, while admitting the defect of the law, decided in conformity with it,[3] and the claims upon the constitutional guarantees, asserted in behalf of the supposed fugitive, were also overruled, a reason given in the case of Wright vs. Deacon being that the evident scope and tenor of both the Constitution and the act of Congress favored the delivery of the fugitive on a summary proceeding without the delay of a formal trial in a court of common law. Another reason offered by the court in this case, and repeated by the Circuit Court of the United States for the Southern District of New York in the matter of Peter, *alias* Lewis Martin, was that the examination under the federal slave law was only preliminary, its purpose being merely to determine the claimant's right to carry the fugitive back to the state whence he had fled, where the question of slavery would properly be open to inquiry.

The mode of arrest permitted by the law was a cause of irritation to the minds of abolitionists throughout the free states, and became one of the points concerning which they joined issue in the courts. The law empowered the claimant

---

[1] Amendments, Article VII.   [2] *Ibid.*, Article V.
[3] 12 *Wendell's Reports*, 315–324.

to seize the fugitive wheresoever found for the purpose of taking him before an officer to prove property. The circumstances that quickened the sympathy of a community into active resistance to this feature of the law are fully illustrated in one of the earliest cases coming before a high court, in which the question of seizure was brought up for determination. The case is that of Commonwealth *vs.* Griffith, which was tried in the Supreme Judicial Court of Massachusetts, at the October term in 1823. From the record of the matter appearing in the law-books, one gathers that a slave, Randolph, who had fled from his master in Virginia, found a refuge in New Bedford about 1818, where by his thrift he acquired a dwelling-house. After several years he was discovered by Griffith, his owner's agent, and was seized without a warrant or other legal process, although the agent had taken the precaution to have a deputy sheriff present. The agent's intention was to take the slave before a magistrate for examination, pursuant to the act of 1793.[1] New Bedford was a Quaker town, and the slave seems not to have lacked friends, for the agent was at once indicted for assault and battery and false imprisonment. The action thus begun was prosecuted in the name of the state, under the direction of Mr. Norton, the attorney-general. As against the act of Congress the prosecution urged that the Constitution did not authorize a seizure without some legal process, and that such a seizure would manifestly be contrary to the article of the amendments of the Constitution that asserted the right of the people to be secure in their persons, houses, papers and effects, against unreasonable searches and seizures.[2] The protest that if the law was constitutional any citizen's house might be invaded without a warrant under pretence that a negro was concealed there called forth the interesting remark from Chief Justice Parker that a case arising out of a constable's entering a citizen's house without warrant in search of a slave had come before him in Middlesex, and that he had held the act to be a trespass. Nevertheless, the court sustained the law

[1] 2 *Pickering's Reports*, 12. See Appendix B, p. 368.
[2] Amendments, Article IV; 2 *Pickering's Reports*, 15, 16.

on the ground that slaves were not parties to the Constitution, and that the amendment referred to had relation only to the parties.[1]

The question of arrest without warrant emerged later in several other cases; for example, Johnson vs. Tompkins (1833),[2] the matter of Peter, *alias* Lewis Martin (1837),[3] Prigg vs. Pennsylvania (1842),[4] and State vs. Hoppess (1845).[5] The line of objection followed by those opposing the law in this series will be sufficiently indicated by the arguments presented in the Massachusetts case of 1823, treated above. The tribunals before which the later suits were brought did not depart from the precedent set in the early case, and the act of 1793 was invariably justified. In Johnson vs. Tompkins the court pointed out that under the law the claimant was not only free to arrest his fugitive without a warrant, but that he was also free to do this unaccompanied by any civil officer, although, as was suggested, it was the part of prudence to have such an officer to keep the peace.[6] In the famous case of Prigg vs. Pennsylvania, the Supreme Court of the United States went back of the law of Congress to the Constitution in seeking the source of the master's right of recaption, and laid down the principle that "under and in virtue of the Constitution, the owner of a slave is clothed with entire authority, in every state in the Union, to seize and recapture his slave, whenever he can do it without any breach of the peace, or any illegal violence. In this sense and to this extent this clause of the Constitution may properly be said to execute itself, and to require no aid from legislation, state or national."[7]

For many years before Prigg's case various states in the North had considered it to be within the province of their

[1] 2 *Pickering's Reports*, 19.
[2] In the Circuit Court of the United States for the Eastern District of Pennsylvania. 1 *Baldwin's Circuit Court Reports*, p. 571 et seq. See Appendix B, p. 368. [3] 2 *Paine's Reports*, 350. See Appendix B, p. 369.
[4] 16 *Peters' Reports*, 613.
[5] 2 *Western Law Journal*, 282. See Appendix B, p. 371.
[6] 1 *Baldwin's Circuit Court Reports*, 571; Hurd, *Law of Freedom and Bondage*, Vol. II, p. 444.
[7] 16 *Peters' Reports*, 613.

legislative powers to enact laws dealing with the subject of fugitive slaves. It would be beside our purpose to enter here upon an examination of these statutes, but it is proper to say that the variety of particulars in which these differed from the law concerning the same subject enacted by Congress prepared the way for a series of legal contests in regard to the question, whether the power to legislate in relation to fugitive slaves could be exercised properly by the states as well as by the federal government. This issue presented itself in at least three notable cases under the law of 1793: these were Jack *vs.* Martin (1835), Peter, *alias* Lewis Martin (1837), and Prigg *vs.* Pennsylvania (1842). The decisions reached in the first and last cases are of especial significance, because, in the first, the question of concurrent jurisdiction constituted the subject of main interest for the Supreme Court of New York, the court to which the case had been taken from an inferior tribunal; while in the last case, the importance attaches to the conclusive character of an adjudication pronounced by the most exalted court of the nation.

In Jack *vs.* Martin the action was begun under the New York law of 1828 for the recovery of a fugitive from New Orleans. Notwithstanding the fact that this law authorized the seizure and return of fugitives to their owners, and that in the case before us, as occurred also in the case of Peter, *alias* Lewis Martin, the negro was adjudged to his claimant, the law of the state was considered invalid, because the right of legislation on the subject was held to belong exclusively to the national government.[1]

In Prigg's case[2] a statute of Pennsylvania, passed in 1826, and bearing the suggestive title, "An act to give effect to the provisions of the Constitution of the United States relative to fugitives from labor, for the protection of free people of color, and to prevent kidnapping," was violated by Edward Prigg in seizing and removing a fugitive slave-woman and her children from York County, Pennsylvania, into Maryland, where their mistress lived. In the argument made before the Supreme Court in support of the state law, the authority of the state to legislate was urged on the ground that

[1] 12 *Wendell's Reports*, 311, 316-318.   [2] See Appendix B, p. 370.

such authority was not prohibited to the states nor expressly granted "in terms" to Congress;[1] that the statute of Pennsylvania had been enacted at the instance of Maryland, and with a view to giving effect to the constitutional provision relative to fugitives;[2] that the states could best determine how the duty of delivery enjoined upon them should be performed so as to be made acceptable to their citizens;[3] and that the act of Congress was silent as to the rights of negroes wrongfully seized and of the states whose territory was entered and laws violated by persons acting under pretext of right.[4] The Supreme Court did not sustain these objections. A majority of the judges agreed with Justice Story in the view that Congress alone had the power to legislate on the subject of fugitive slaves. The reasons given for this view were two: first, the constitutional source of the authority, by virtue of which the force of an act of Congress pervades the whole Union uncontrolled by state sovereignty or state laws, and secures rights that otherwise would rest upon interstate comity and favor; and, secondly, the necessity of having a uniform system of regulations for all parts of the United States, by which the differences arising from the varieties of policy, local convenience and local feelings existing in the various states can be avoided. The right to retake fugitive slaves and the correlative duty to deliver them were to be " coextensive and uniform in remedy and operation throughout the whole Union." While maintaining that the right of legislation in this matter was exclusively vested in Congress, the court insisted that it did not thereby interfere with the police power of the several states, and that by virtue of this power the states had the authority to arrest and imprison runaway slaves, and to expel them from their borders, just as they might do with vagrants, provided that in exercising this jurisdiction the rights of owners to reclaim their slaves secured by the Constitution and the legislation of Congress were not impeded or destroyed.[5]

As the friends of runaway slaves sometimes sought to oppose to the summary procedure of the federal law the

[1] 16 *Peters' Reports*, 579. [2] *Ibid.*, 588–590. [3] *Ibid.*, 595.
[4] *Ibid.*, 602. [5] *Ibid.*, 612–617.

processes provided by state laws in behalf of fugitives, so in their endeavor to overthrow the act of 1793, they occasionally appealed to the Ordinance for the government of the Northwest Territory. The Ordinance, it will be remembered, contained a clause prohibiting slavery throughout the region northwest of the Ohio River, and another authorizing the surrender of slaves escaping into this territory.[1] The abolitionists took advantage of these provisions under certain circumstances, in the hope of securing the release of those that had fallen into the eager grasp of the congressional act, and at the same time of proving the incompatibility of this measure with the Ordinance. The attempt to do these things was made in three well-known cases, which came before the courts about 1845. The first of these was State vs. Hoppess, tried before the Supreme Court of Ohio on the circuit, to secure the liberation of a slave that had fled from his keeper, but was afterwards recaptured;[2] the second was Vaughan vs. Williams, adjudicated in the Circuit Court of the United States for the District of Indiana, a case originating in an action against the defendant for rescuing certain fugitives;[3] and the third was Jones vs. Van Zandt, which was carried to the Supreme Court of the United States and there decided. This last case grew out of the aid given nine runaways by Mr. Van Zandt, through which one of them succeeded in escaping.[4] The arguments, based upon the Ordinance, that were advanced in these cases are adequately set forth in the report of the first case, a report prepared by Salmon P. Chase, subsequently Chief Justice of the Supreme Court of the United States. These arguments, two in number, were as follows: first, the Ordinance expressly prohibited slavery, and thereby effected the immediate emancipation of all slaves in the Territory; and, secondly, the clause in the Ordinance providing for the surrender of fugitives applied only to persons held to service in the *original* states.[5]

[1] See Chap. II, pp. 28, 32. [2] 2 *Western Law Journal*, 279-293.
[3] 3 *Western Law Journal*, 65-71; also, 3 *McLean's Reports*, 530-538.
[4] 5 *Howard's Reports*, 215 et seq.
[5] 2 *Western Law Journal*, 281, 283; 3 *McLean*, 530.

The opinions given by the courts in the cases under consideration failed to support the idea of the irreconcilability existing between the law of 1793 and the Ordinance. The Supreme Court of Ohio declared that under the federal Constitution the right of recaption of fugitive slaves was secured to the new states to the same extent that it belonged to the original states.[1] The Circuit Court of the United States took virtually the same stand by pointing out that a state carved from the Northwest Territory assumed the same constitutional obligations by entering the Union that the original thirteen states had earlier assumed, and that where a conflict occurred the Constitution was paramount to the Ordinance.[2] Finally, the Supreme Court at Washington declared that the clause in the Ordinance prohibiting slavery applied only to people living within the borders of the Northwest Territory, and that it did not impair the rights of those living in states outside of this domain. Wheresoever the Ordinance existed the states preserved their own laws, as well as the Ordinance, by forbidding slavery; the provision of the Constitution and the act of Congress looking toward the delivery of fugitive slaves did not interfere with the laws of the free states as to their own subjects. The court therefore held that there was no repugnance between the act and the Ordinance.[3]

Among the various objections raised in the court-room against the law of 1793, the denial of the power of Congress to legislate on the subject of fugitive slaves was one that should not be overlooked. It commanded the attention of the bench in at least two important cases, both of which have been mentioned in other connections, namely, Peter, *alias* Lewis Martin (1837), and State *vs.* Hoppess (1845). In both of these cases the denial of legislative authority was based upon the doctrine that there had been no delegation of the necessary power to Congress by the Constitution. The fugitive slave clause in the Constitution, it was said in the report of the second case, prepared by Mr. Chase,

[1] 2 *Western Law Journal*, 288.
[2] 3 *McLean's Reports*, 532; 3 *Western Law Journal*, 65.
[3] 5 *Howard's Reports*, 230, 231.

granted no power at all to Congress, but was "a mere clause of compact imposing a duty on the states to be fulfilled, if at all, by state legislation."[1] However prevalent this view may have been in the Northern states,—and the number of state laws dealing with the subject of fugitive slaves indicates that it predominated,—neither the Circuit Court of the United States for the Southern District of New York in the earlier case, nor the Supreme Court of Ohio in the later, were willing to subscribe to the doctrine. On the contrary, both asserted the power of Congress to pass laws for the restoration of runaway slaves, on the ground that the creation of a duty or a right by the Constitution is the warrant under which Congress necessarily acts in making the laws needful to enforce the duty or secure the right.[2]

The outcome of the judicial examination in the high courts of the various points thus far considered was wholly favorable to the constitutionality of the law of 1793. The one case within the category of great cases in which that law was decided to be unconstitutional in any particular was that of Prigg vs. Pennsylvania. By the law of 1793 state and local authorities were empowered to take cognizance of fugitive slave cases together with judges holding their appointments from the federal government.[3] In the hearing given the case before the Supreme Court at Washington, in 1842, Mr. Johnson, the attorney-general of Pennsylvania, cited former decisions of the Supreme Court to show that in so far as the congressional law vested jurisdiction in state officers it was unconstitutional and void.[4] The court's answer was momentous and far-reaching. While the law was declared to be constitutional in its essential features, it was asserted that it did not point out any state functionaries, or any state actions, to carry its provisions into effect. The states could not, therefore, so the court decided, be compelled to enforce them; and any insistence that the states were bound to provide means for the

---

[1] 2 *Paine's Reports*, 354; 2 *Western Law Journal*, 282.
[2] 2 *Paine's Reports*, 354, 355; also, 2 *Western Law Journal*, 289.
[3] See Section 3 of the act, *Statutes at Large*, I, 302-305.
[4] 16 *Peters' Reports*, 598.

performance of the duties of the national government, nowhere delegated or entrusted to them by the Constitution, would bear the appearance of an unconstitutional exercise of the interpretative power.[1] As the decision in the Prigg case carried the weight of great authority, and became a precedent for all future judgments,[2] the relief it afforded state officers from distasteful functions was soon accepted by many states, and they enacted laws forbidding their magistrates to issue warrants for the arrest or removal of fugitive slaves.[3] In consequence of this manifest disinclination on the part of the Northern states to restore to Southern masters their escaped slaves, the federal government was induced to make more effective provision for the execution of the Constitution in this particular. Such provision was embodied in the second Fugitive Slave Law, passed as a part of the Compromise of 1850.

That the new law was not intended to extinguish the old is apparent from the title assigned it, which read : " An Act to amend, and supplementary to, the Act entitled ' An Act respecting Fugitives from Justice, and Persons escaping from the service of their Masters, . . ."[4] Its evident purpose was to increase the facilities and improve the means for the recovery of fugitives from labor. To this end it created commissioners, who were to have authority, like the judges of the circuit and district courts of the United States, to issue warrants for the apprehension of runaway slaves, and to grant certificates for the removal of such persons back to the state or territory whence they had escaped. All cases were to be heard in a summary manner ; the testimony of the alleged fugitive could not be received in evidence ; and the fee of the commissioner or judge was to be ten dollars when the decision was in favor of the claimant, but only five dollars when it was unfavorable. The penalties created by the new law were more rigorous than those

[1] 16 *Peters' Reports*, 608, 622. See also Marion G. McDougall's *Fugitive Slaves*, pp. 108, 109.
[2] M. G. McDougall's *Fugitive Slaves*, p. 28.
[3] See Chap. IX, pp. 245, 246, and Chap. X, p. 337.
[4] *Statutes at Large*, IX, 462.

imposed by the old. A fine not to exceed a thousand dollars and imprisonment not to exceed six months constituted the punishment for harboring a runaway or aiding in his rescue, and the party injured could bring suit for civil damages against the offender in the sum of one thousand dollars for each fugitive lost through his interference. If the claimant apprehended a rescue, the officer making the arrest could be required to retain the fugitive in his custody for the purpose of removing him to the state whence he had fled. The refusal of the officer to obey and execute the warrants and precepts issued under the provisions of the law laid him liable to a fine of a thousand dollars for the benefit of the claimant; and the escape of a fugitive from his custody, whether with his assent or without it, made him liable to a prosecution for the full value of the labor of the negro thus lost. Ample security from such disaster was intended to be provided for the marshal and his deputies by the clause authorizing them to summon to their aid the bystanders, or posse comitatus, when necessary, and all good citizens were commanded to respond promptly with their assistance. In removing a fugitive back to the state from which he had escaped, when an attempt at rescue was feared, the marshal in charge was commanded to employ as many persons as he deemed necessary to resist the interference. The omission of the new law to mention any officers appointed by the states is doubtless traceable, as is the clause establishing commissionerships, to the ruling in the decision of Prigg's case that state officers could not be forced to execute federal legislation.

It will be remembered that the decision in the Prigg case also contained a ruling that acknowledged the right of the claimant to seize and remove the alleged fugitive, wheresoever found, without judicial process. It has been suggested recently that this part of the decision, denominated the most obnoxious part, was avoided in the law of 1850.[1] But the language of the new law no more denied this right than

---

[1] Henry W. Rogers, Editor, *Constitutional History of the United States as seen in the Development of American Law*, Lecture III, by George W. Biddle, p. 152.

the language of the old bestowed it. In both cases equally the claimant seems to have enjoyed the right of private seizure and arrest without process, but for the purpose of taking the supposed fugitive before the proper official.[1] So far as the language of the statute was concerned the Prigg decision was quite as possible under the later as under the earlier law. It was the language of the Constitution upon which this part of the famous decision was made to rest, and that, it needs scarcely be said, continued unchanged during the period with which we are concerned.

It is not to be supposed, of course, that the law of 1850 was found to be intrinsically less objectionable to abolitionists than the measure it was intended to supplement. On the contrary, it soon proved to be decidedly more objectionable. The features of the first Slave Act that were obnoxious to the Northern people, and had been subjected to examination in the courts, were retained in the second act, where they were associated with a number of new features of such a character that they soon brought the new law into the greatest contempt. While, therefore, the records of the trials of the chief cases arising under the later law are found to contain arguments borrowed from the contentions made in the cases

[1] Section 3 of the law of 1793 provided that "the person to whom such labour or service may be due, his agent or attorney, is hereby empowered to seize and arrest such fugitive from labour, and to take him or her before any judge of the circuit or district courts of the United States, . . . within the state, or before any magistrate of a county (etc.) . . . wherein such seizure . . . shall be made, and upon proof to the satisfaction of such judge or magistrate . . . it shall be the duty of such judge or magistrate to give a certificate thereof . . . which shall be a sufficient warrant for removing the said fugitive . . . to the state or territory from which he or she fled."

Section 6 of the act of 1850 provides that "the person or persons to whom such service or labour may be due, or his, her, or their agent or attorney . . . may pursue and reclaim such fugitive person, either by procuring a warrant . . . or by seizing and arresting such fugitive, where the same can be done without process, and by taking, or causing such person to be taken, forthwith before such court, judge or commissioner, whose duty it shall be to hear and determine the case . . . in a summary manner; and upon satisfactory proof . . . to make out and deliver to such claimant, his or her agent or attorney, a certificate . . . with authority . . . to use such reasonable force . . . as may be necessary . . . to take and remove such fugitive person back to the State or Territory whence he or she may have escaped as aforesaid."

already discussed, it is interesting to note that they afford proof that new arguments were also brought to bear against the act of 1850. As with the first Fugitive Slave Law, so also with its successor, fault was found on account of the absence of any provision for jury trial;[1] the authority of a claimant or his agent to arrest without legal process;[2] the opposition alleged to exist between the law and the Ordinance of 1787;[3] and the power said to be improperly exercised by Congress in legislating upon the subject of fugitive slaves.[4] It is unnecessary to introduce here a study of these points as they presented themselves in the various cases arising, for a discussion of them would lead to no principles of importance other than those discovered in the cases already examined.[5]

In some of the cases that were tried under the act of 1850, however, new questions appeared; and in some, where the questions were perhaps without novelty, the circumstances were such that the cases cannot well be passed over in silence.

If, as was freely declared by the abolitionists, it was possible for free negroes to be abducted from the Northern states under the form of procedure laid down by the act of 1793, there can be little reason to doubt that the same thing was equally possible under the procedure established by the act

---

[1] Sims' case, tried before the Supreme Judicial Court of Massachusetts, March term, 1851. See 7 *Cushing's Reports*, 310.

Miller *vs.* McQuerry, tried before the Circuit Court of the United States, in Ohio, 1853. See 5 *McLean's Reports*, 481–484.

Ex parte Simeon Bushnell, etc., tried before the Supreme Court of Ohio, May, 1859. See 9 *Ohio State Reports*, 170.

[2] Norris *vs.* Newton *et al.*, tried before the Circuit Court of the United States, in Indiana, May term, 1850. See 5 *McLean's Reports*, 98.

Ex parte Simeon Bushnell, etc. See 9 *Ohio State Reports*, 174.

United States *vs.* Buck, tried before the District Court of the United States for the Eastern District of Pennsylvania, 1860. See 8 *American Law Register*, 543.

[3] Booth's case, tried before the Supreme Court of Wisconsin, June term, 1854. See 3 *Wisconsin Reports*, 3.

Ex parte Simeon Bushnell, and *ex parte* Charles Langston, tried before the Supreme Court of Ohio, May, 1859. See 9 *Ohio State Reports*, 111, 114–117, 124, 186.

[4] Sims' case. See 7 *Cushing's Reports*, 290. Booth's case. See 3 *Wisconsin Reports*.

[5] For the text of the Slave Laws, see Appendix A, pp. 359–366.

of 1850. Certain it is that the anti-slavery people were not dubious on this point, but they had scarcely had time to formulate their criticisms of the new law when the first case under it of which there is any record demonstrated the ease with which this legislation could be taken advantage of in the commission of a foul injustice. The case occurred September 26, only eight days after the passage of the act. A free negro, James Hamlet, then living in New York, was arrested as the slave of Mary Brown, of Baltimore. The hearing took place before a United States commissioner and the negro's removal followed at once. The community in which Hamlet was living was greatly incensed when the facts concerning his disappearance became known, and the sum of money necessary for his redemption was quickly contributed. Before a fortnight had elapsed he was brought back from slavery.[1]

The summary manner in which this case was disposed of had prevented a defence being made in behalf of the supposed fugitive. In the next case, however, that of Thomas Sims, which was tried before the Supreme Judicial Court of Massachusetts in 1851, the negro was represented by competent counsel, who brought forward objections against the second Fugitive Slave Law. Almost the first of these was directed against the power of the special officers, the commissioners, created by the new law. It was insisted that the authority with which these officers were invested was distinctly judicial in character, despite the constitutional provision limiting the exercise of the judicial power of the United States to organized courts of justice, composed of judges, holding their offices during good behavior, and receiving fixed salaries for their services.[2] The same argument seems to have been adduced in Scott's case, tried before the District Court of the United States in Massachusetts in 1851; in the case of Miller *vs.* McQuerry, tried before the

---

[1] Marion G. McDougall, *Fugitive Slaves*, pp. 43 and 44, with the references there given; Wilson, *Rise and Fall of the Slave Power*, Vol. II, pp. 304, 305. See Appendix B, p. 372.

[2] 7 *Cushing's Reports*, 287. The constitutional requirement will be found in Article III, Section 1, of the Constitution of the United States.

Circuit Court of the United States in Ohio in 1853;[1] in Booth's case, argued in the Supreme Court of Wisconsin in 1854;[2] in the case known as *ex parte* Robinson, adjudicated by the Circuit Court of the United States for the Southern District of Ohio at its April term, 1855;[3] and in the case *ex parte* Simeon Bushnell, argued and determined in the Supreme Court of Ohio in 1859.[4] The court met this argument by a direct answer in four of the cases mentioned, namely, those of Sims, Scott, Booth and *ex parte* Robinson. In the first, Sims' case, Chief Justice Shaw pointed out that under the Slave Law of 1793 the jurisdiction over fugitive slave cases had been conferred on justices of the peace and magistrates of cities and towns corporate, as well as on judges of the United States circuit and district courts, and that evidently, therefore, the power bestowed had not been deemed judicial in the sense in which it was urged that the functions of the commissioners were judicial. At the same time the judge admitted that the "argument from the limitation of judicial power would be entitled to very grave consideration" if it were without the support of early construction, judicial precedent and the acquiescence of the general and state governments. In the trial of James Scott, on the charge of aiding in the rescue of Shadrach (May or June, 1851), Judge Sprague, of the United States District Court, held that the legal force of the certificate issued by a commissioner lay merely in the authority it conveyed to remove the person designated from one state to another, and that the disposition made of the person removed depended solely upon the laws of the state to which he was taken. The facts set down in the certificate were not, therefore, to be considered as matters judicially established, but as facts only in the opinion of the commissioner. In Booth's case, the opinion of the Supreme Court of Wisconsin contained a reference to the legality of the power of the commissioners and sustained the objection to their authority on the ground of unconstitutionality.[5] In *ex parte* Robinson, Judge McLean admitted

[1] 5 *McLean's Reports*, 481.
[2] 3 *Wisconsin Reports*, 39.
[3] 6 *McLean's Reports*, 359.

9 *Ohio State Reports*, 176.
3 *Wisconsin Reports*, 64.

that the inquiry made by the commissioner was "somewhat in the nature of judicial power," but that the same remark applied to all the officers of the accounting departments of the government, as, for example, the examiners in the Patent Office. He also remarked that the Supreme Court had always treated the acts of the commissioners, in the cases that had come before it, as possessed of authority under the law.[1]

The uncertainty as to the precise character of the commissioners' power displayed in the different views of the courts before which the question was brought marks the observations of the commissioners themselves in regard to their authority. Examples will be found in Sims' and Burns' cases. In the former, Mr. George T. Curtis declared that claims for fugitive slaves came within the judicial power of the federal government, and that, consequently, the mode and means of the application of this power to the cases arising were properly to be determined by Congress. In the latter, Mr. Edward G. Loring asserted that his action was not judicial at all, but only ministerial.

An additional ground of objection to the commissioners was found in the provision made in the law of 1850 for their remuneration. When one of these officers issued a certificate authorizing the removal of a runaway to the state whence he had escaped, he was legally entitled to a fee of ten dollars; when, however, he withheld the warrant he could receive but five dollars. Abolitionists took much offence at this arrangement, and sometimes scornfully denominated the special appointees under the law the "ten-dollar commissioners," and insisted that the difference between the fees was in the nature of a bribe held out to the officers to induce them to decide in favor of the claimant. Considering the prevalence of this feeling outside of the courts, it is not surprising that objections to the section of the act regulating the fees of commissioners should have been taken within the court-room.[2] Such objection was raised in McQuerry's case, and was answered by Judge McLean.

[1] 6 *McLean's Reports*, 359, 360.
[2] Hurd, *Law of Freedom and Bondage*, Vol. II, p. 747.

This answer is probably the only one judicially declared, and is worth quoting: "In regard to the five dollars, in addition, paid to the commissioner, where the fugitive is remanded to the claimant," the judge explained, "in all fairness it cannot be considered as a bribe, or as so intended by Congress; but as a compensation to the commissioner for making a statement of the case, which includes the facts proved, and to which the certificate is annexed. In cases where the witnesses are numerous and the investigation takes up several days, five dollars would scarcely be a compensation for the statement required. Where the fugitive is discharged, no statement is necessary."[1]

The fees paid to commissioners were, as indicated in the remarks just quoted, by way of remuneration for services rendered in inquiries relative to the rights of ownership of negroes alleged to have escaped from the South. These inquiries, together with similar inquiries that arose under the act of 1793, constitute a group by themselves. Another group is made up of the cases growing out of the prosecution under the two acts of persons charged with harboring fugitive slaves, or aiding in their rescue. The secrecy observed by abolitionists in giving assistance to escaping bondmen shows that the evils threatening, if a discovery occurred, were constantly kept in mind. After the passage of the second act, public denunciation of the measure was indulged in freely, and open resistance to its provisions, whether these should be considered constitutional or not, was recommended in some quarters. Such remonstrances seem to have early disturbed the judicial repose of the courts, for, six months after the new Fugitive Slave Bill had become a law, Justice Nelson found occasion in the course of a charge to the grand jury of the Circuit Court of the United States for the Southern District of New York to deliver a speech on sectional issues in which he gave an exposition of the new law, "so that those, if any there be, who have made up their minds to disobey it, may be fully apprised of the consequences."[2] The severer penalties of the law of 1850 had

[1] 5 *McLean's Reports*, 481.
[2] 1 *Blatchford's Circuit Court Reports*, 636.

PENALTIES FOR AIDING FUGITIVES 273

no deterrent effect upon those who were determined to resist its enforcement. The fervor displayed in harboring runaways increased rather than diminished throughout the free states, and the spirit of resistance thus fostered broke out in daring and sometimes successful attempts at rescue. Through the activity of slave-owners in seeking the recovery of their lost property, and the support afforded them by the government in the strict enforcement of the new law, a number of offenders were brought to trial and subjected to punishments inflicted under its provisions.

Among the prosecutions arising under the two congressional acts the following cases are offered as typical. The number has been limited by choosing in general from among such as came before supreme courts of the states, or before circuit and district courts of the United States.

One of the earliest cases of which we have record was brought before the Circuit Court of the United States for the Eastern District of Pennsylvania on writ of error, in 1822. The action was for the penalty under the law of 1793 for obstructing the plaintiff, a citizen of Maryland, in seizing his escaped slave in Philadelphia for the purpose of taking him before a magistrate there to prove property. The trial in the United States District Court had terminated in a verdict of $500 for the slave-owner. Judge Washington, of the Circuit Court, decided, however, that there was an error in the judgment of the lower court, that the judgment must be reversed with costs, and the cause remitted to the District Court in order that a new trial might be had. This case is known in the law books as the case of Hill *vs.* Low.[1]

Occasionally an attempt at rescue ended in the arrest and imprisonment of the slave-catchers, as well as the release of the captured negro. When a party of rescuers went to such a length as here indicated it laid itself liable to an action for damages on the ground of false imprisonment, as well as to prosecution for the penalty under the Fugitive Slave Law. This is illustrated in the case of Johnson *vs.*

---

[1] 4 *Washington's Circuit Court Reports*, 327–331.

Tomkins, a case belonging to the year 1833.[1] It was the outgrowth of the attempt of a master to reclaim his slave from the premises of a Quaker, John Kenderdine, of Montgomery County, Pennsylvania. Before the slave-owner could return to New Jersey, the state of his domicile, he and his party were overtaken, and after violent handling in which the master was injured, they were taken into custody, and were forthwith prosecuted. The trial ended in the acquittal of the company from New Jersey, whose seizure of the negro was found to be justifiable. Then followed the prosecution of some of the Pennsylvania party for trespass and false imprisonment, before the Circuit Court of the United States. The fact that the defendants were all Quakers was noted by the judge, who found it "hard to imagine" the motives by which these persons, "members of a society distinguished for their obedience and submission to the laws" were actuated. The question of damages was left exclusively to the jury. The verdict rendered was for $4,000, and the court gave judgment on the verdict.[2]

The law of 1793 provided a double penalty for those guilty of transgressing its provisions: first, the forfeiture of a sum of $500 to be recovered for the benefit of the claimant by action of debt; secondly, the payment of such damages as might be awarded by the court in an action brought by the slave-owner on account of the injuries sustained through the loss, or even the temporary absence, of his property. In the famous case of Jones vs. Van Zandt, which was pending before the United States courts, in Ohio and at Washington, for five years, from 1842 to 1847, the defendant was compelled to pay both penalties. In April, 1842, Mr. Van Zandt, an anti-slavery Kentuckian, who had settled at Springdale, a few miles north of Cincinnati, Ohio, was caught in the act of conveying a company of nine fugitives in his market-wagon at daybreak one morning, and, notwithstanding the efforts of the slave-catchers, one of the negroes escaped. The trial was held before the United States Circuit Court at its July term, 1843. The jury gave

---

[1] 4 *Baldwin's Circuit Court Reports*, 571–605.
[2] *Washington's Circuit Court Reports*, 327–331.

a verdict for the claimant of $1,200 in damages on two counts.[1] Besides the suit for damages, an action was brought against Van Zandt for the penalty of $500. In this action, as in the other, the verdict was for Jones, the plaintiff. The matter did not end here, however, and was carried on a certificate of division in opinion between the judges to the Supreme Court of the United States. The decision of this court was also adverse to Van Zandt, and final judgment was entered against him for both amounts. This settlement was reached at the January term in 1847.[2]

The successful rescue of a large company of slaves was likely to make the adventure a very expensive one for the responsible persons that took part in it. Such was the experience of the defendants in the case of Giltner *vs.* Gorham and others, determined in 1847. Six slaves, the chattels of Mr. Giltner, a citizen of Carroll County, Kentucky, were discovered and arrested in Marshall, Michigan, by the agents of the claimant, but through the intervention of the defendants were set at liberty. Action was brought to recover the value of the negroes, who were estimated to be worth $2,752. In the first trial the jury failed to agree. At the succeeding term of court, however, a verdict for the value of the slaves was found for the plaintiff.[3]

The value of four negroes was involved in the case of Norris *vs.* Newton and others. These negroes were found in September, 1849, after two years' absence from Kentucky, living in Cass County, Michigan. Here they had taken refuge among abolitionists and people of their own color. They were at once seized by their pursuers and conveyed across the line into Indiana, but had not been taken far when their progress was stopped by an excited crowd with a sheriff at its head. The officer had a writ of habeas corpus, and the temper of the crowd would admit of no delay in securing a hearing for the fugitives. The court-house at South Bend, whither the captives were now taken, was at

[1] 2 *McLean's Reports*, 612.
[2] 5 *Howard's Reports*, 215-232; see also Schuckers, *Life and Public Services of S. P. Chase*, 53-66; Warden, *Private Life and Public Services of S. P. Chase*, 296-298. [3] 4 *McLean's Reports*, 402-426.

once crowded with spectators, and the streets around it filled with the overflow. The negroes were released by the decision of the judge, but were rearrested and placed in jail for safe-keeping. On the following day warrants were sworn out against several members of the Kentucky party, charging them with riot and other breaches of the peace, and civil process was begun against Mr. Norris, the owner of the slaves, claiming large damages in their behalf. Meanwhile companies of colored people, some of whom had firearms and others clubs, came tramping into the village from Cass County and the intermediate country. Fortunately a demonstration by these incensed bands was somehow avoided. Two days later the fugitives were released from custody on a second writ of habeas corpus, and, attended by a great bodyguard of colored persons, were triumphantly carried away in a wagon. The slave-owner, the charges against whom were dropped, had declined to attend the last hearing accorded his slaves, declaring that his rights had been violated, and that he would claim compensation under the law. Suit was accordingly brought in the Circuit Court of the United States in 1850, and the sum of $2,850 was awarded as damages to the plaintiff.[1]

Another case in which large damages were at stake was that of Oliver *vs.* Weakley and others, tried in the United States Circuit Court for the Western District of Pennsylvania, in October term, 1853. It was alleged and proved that Mr. Weakley, one of the defendants, had given shelter in his barn to several slaves of the plaintiff, who was a citizen of Maryland. The jury failed to agree on the first trial. A second trial was therefore held, and this time a verdict was reached; one of the defendants was found guilty, and damages to the amount of $2,800 were assessed upon him; the other defendants were declared "not guilty."[2]

The dismissal without proper authority of seven fugitives from the custody of their captors at Sandusky, Ohio, by Mr. Rush R. Sloane, a lawyer of that city, led to the institution of two suits against him by Mr. L. F. Weimer, the claimant of three of the slaves. The suits were tried before

[1] 5 *McLean's Reports*, 92–106.   [2] 2 *Wallace Jr.'s Reports*, 324–326.

the District Court of the United States at Columbus, Ohio, in 1854, and a verdict for $3,000 and costs was returned in favor of the slaveholder. The costs amounted to $330.30, and the defendant had also to pay $1,000 in attorneys' fees. Some friends of Mr. Sloane in Sandusky formed a committee and collected $393, an amount sufficient to pay the court and marshal's costs, but the judgment and the other expenses were borne by the defendant individually.[1]

The burden of the penalty, of which, as we have just seen, a small fraction was assumed by sympathizers with the offender in the case of Mr. Sloane, was altogether removed by friendly contributors in the case of another citizen of Sandusky. Two negroes from Kentucky, who were being cared for at the house of Mr. F. D. Parish, were protected from arrest by their benefactor in February, 1845. As Parish was a fearless agent of the Underground Road, the fugitives were not seen afterwards in northern Ohio. The result was that Parish was required to undergo three trials, and in the last, in 1849, the Circuit Court of the United States for the District of Ohio fined him $500, the estimated value of the slaves at the time. This sum, together with the costs and expenses, amounting to as much more, was paid by friends of Mr. Parish, who made up the necessary amount by subscriptions of one dollar each.[2]

[1] 6 *McLean's Reports*, 259–273. Mr. Sloane's account of the case will be found in *The Firelands Pioneer* for July, 1888, pp. 46–49. A copy of the certificate of the clerk of court there given is here reproduced : —

"Louis F. Weimer *vs.* Rush R. Sloane. United States District of Ohio, in debt.

OCTOBER TERM, 1854.
Judgment for Plaintiff for $3000 and costs.

Received July 8th, 1856, of Rush R. Sloane, the above Defendant, a receipt of Louis F. Weimer, the above Plaintiff, bearing date Dec. 14th, 1854, for $3000, acknowledging full satisfaction of the above judgment, except the costs; also a receipt of L. F. Weimer, Sr., per Joseph Doniphan, attorney, for $85, the amount of Plaintiff's witness fees in said case; also certificates of Defendant's witnesses in above case for $162; also $20 in money, the attorney's docket fees attached, which, with the clerk and marshal's fees heretofore paid, is in full of the costs in said case.

(Signed)   WILLIAM MINER, *Clerk.*"

[2] For the first trial (1845), see 3 *McLean's Reports*, 631; *s. c.* 5 *Western Law Journal*, 25; 7 *Federal Cases*, 1100; for the second trial (1847), see

It will have been noticed that the Van Zandt and Parish cases were in litigation for about five years each. A famous Illinois case, that of Dr. Richard Eells, occupied the attention of the courts and of the public more or less during an entire decade. The incidents that gave rise to this case occurred in Adams County, Illinois, in 1842. In that year Mr. Eells was indicted for secreting a slave owing service to Chauncey Durkee, of Missouri, and was convicted and sentenced to pay a fine of $400 and the costs of the prosecution. The case was taken on writ of error first to the Supreme Court of the state, and after the death of Mr. Eells to the Supreme Court of the United States. In both instances the judgment of the original tribunal was confirmed. The decision of the federal court was reached at its December term for 1852.[1]

It was sometimes made clear in the courts that the defendants in cases arising under the Fugitive Slave laws were persons in the habit of evading the requirements of these laws. This is true of the case of Ray *vs.* Donnell and Hamilton, which was tried before the United States Circuit Court in Indiana, at the May term, 1849. A slave woman, Caroline, and her four children fled from Kemble County, Kentucky, and found shelter in a barn near Clarksburg, Indiana. Here they were discovered by Woodson Clark, a farmer living in the neighborhood, who took measures immediately to inform their master, while the slaves were removed to a fodder-house for safe-keeping. In some way Messrs. Donnell and Hamilton learned of the capture of the negroes by Mr. Clark, and secured a writ of habeas corpus in their behalf; but, if the testimony of Mr. Clark's son, supported by certain circumstantial evidence, is to be credited, the blacks were released from custody by the personal efforts of the defendants, and not by legal process. Considerable evidence conflicting with that just mentioned appears to have

---

10 *Law Reporter*, 395; s. c. 5 *Western Law Journal*, 206; 7 *Federal Cases*, 1093; for the third trial (1849), see 5 *McLean's Reports*, 64; s. c. 7 *Western Law Journal*, 222; 7 *Federal Cases*, 1095. See also *The Firelands Pioneer*, July, 1888, pp. 41, 42.

[1] 5 *Illinois Reports*, 498–518; 14 *Howard's Reports*, 13, 14.

had little weight with the jury, for it gave a verdict for the claimant and assessed his damages at $1,500.[1]

In the trial of Mitchell, an abolitionist of the town of Indiana, Pennsylvania, in 1853, for harboring two fugitives, some of the evidence was intended to show that he was connected with a "regularly organized association," the business of which was "to entice negroes from their owners, and to aid them in escaping to the North." The slaves he was charged with harboring had been given employment on his farm in the country, where, as it was thought, they would be secure. After remaining about four months they were apprised of danger and escaped. Justice Grier charged the jury to "let no morbid sympathy, no false respect for pretended 'rights of conscience,' prevent it from judging the defendant justly." A verdict of $500 was found for the plaintiff.[2]

Penalties for hindering the arrest of a fugitive slave were imposed in two other noted cases, which deserve mention here, although they are considered at length in another connection. One of these was Booth's case, with which the Supreme Court of Wisconsin, and the District and Supreme Courts of the United States dealt between the years 1855 and 1858. The sentence pronounced against Mr. Booth included imprisonment for one month and a fine of $1,000 and costs —$1,451 in all.[3] The other case was what is commonly known as the Oberlin-Wellington case, tried in the United States District Court at Cleveland, Ohio, in 1858 and 1859. Only two out of the thirty-seven men indicted were convicted, and the sentences imposed were comparatively light. Mr. Bushnell was sentenced to pay a fine of $600 and costs and to be imprisoned in the county jail for sixty days, while the sentence of the colored man, Langston, was a fine of $100 and costs and imprisonment for twenty days.

In all of the cases thus far considered the charges upon which the transgressors of the Fugitive Slave laws were

---

[1] 4 *McLean's Reports*, 504-515.
[2] 2 *Wallace Jr.'s Reports*, 313, 317-323.
[3] 21 *Howard's Reports*, 510; *The Fugitive Slave Law in Wisconsin, with Reference to Nullification Sentiment*, by Vroman Mason, p. 134.

prosecuted were, in general terms, harboring and concealing runaways, obstructing their arrest, or aiding in their rescue. There was, however, one case in which the crime alleged in the indictment was much more serious, being nothing less than treason against the United States. This was the famous Christiana case, marked not only by the nature of the indictment, but by the organized resistance to arrest made by the slaves and their friends, and by the violent death of one of the attacking party. The frequent abduction of negroes from the neighborhood of Christiana, in southeastern Pennsylvania, seems to have given occasion for the formation, about 1851, of a league for self-protection among the many colored persons living in that region.[1] The leading spirit in this association was William Parker, a fugitive slave whose house was a refuge for other runaways. On September 10, Parker and his neighbors received word from the Vigilance Committee of Philadelphia that Gorsuch, a slaveholder of Maryland, had procured warrants for the arrest of two of his slaves, known to be staying at Parker's house. When, therefore, Gorsuch with his son and some friends appeared upon the scene about daybreak on the morning of the 11th, and, having broken into the house, demanded the fugitives, the negroes lost little time in sounding a horn from one of the upper-story windows to summon their friends. From fifty to one hundred men, armed with guns, clubs and corn-cutters, soon came up. Castner Hanway and Elijah Lewis, two Quakers, who had been drawn to the place by the disturbance, declined to join the marshal's posse and help arrest the slaves; but they advised the negroes against resisting the law, and warned Gorsuch and his party to depart if they would prevent bloodshed. Neither side would yield, and a fight was soon in progress. In the course of the conflict the slave-owner was killed, his son severely wounded, and the fugitives managed to escape.

The excitement caused by this affair extended throughout the country. The President of the United States placed a company of forty-five marines at the disposal of the United

[1] Smedley, *Underground Railroad*, pp. 107, 108; 2 *Wallace Jr.'s Reports*, 159.

States marshal, and these proceeded under orders to the place of the riot. A large number of police and special constables made search far and wide for those concerned in the rescue. Their efforts were rewarded with the arrest of thirty-five negroes and three Quakers, among the latter Hanway and Lewis, who gave themselves up. The prisoners were taken to Philadelphia and indicted by the grand jury for treason. Hanway was tried before the Circuit Court of the United States for the Eastern District of Pennsylvania in November and December, 1851. In the trial it was shown by the defence that Mr. Hanway was a native of a Southern state, had lived long in the South, and, during his three years' residence in Pennsylvania, had kept aloof from anti-slavery organizations and meetings; his presence at the riot was proved to be accidental. Under these circumstances the charge of Justice Grier to the jury was a demonstration of the unsoundness of the indictment: the judge asked the jury to observe that a conspiracy to be classed as an act of treason must have been for the purpose of effecting something of a public nature; and that the efforts of a band of fugitive slaves in opposition to the capture of any of their number, even though they were directed by friends and went the full length of committing murder upon their pursuers, was altogether for a private object, and could not be called "levying war" against the nation. It did not take the jury long to decide the case. After an absence of twenty minutes the verdict "not guilty" was returned. One of the negroes was also tried, but not convicted. Afterward a bill was brought against Hanway and Lewis for riot and murder, but the grand jury ignored it, and further prosecution was dropped.[1]

One cannot examine the records of the various cases that have been passed in review in the preceding pages of this chapter without being struck in many instances by the character of the men that served as counsel for fugitive slaves and

[1] Still's *Underground Railroad Records*, pp. 348-368; Smedley, *Underground Railroad*, pp. 107-130; 2 *Wallace Jr.'s Reports*, pp. 134-206; M. G. McDougall, *Fugitive Slaves*, pp. 50, 51; Wilson, *Rise and Fall of the Slave Power*, Vol. II, pp. 328, 329.

their friends. It not infrequently happens that one comes upon the name of a man whose principles, ability and eloquence won for him in later years positions of distinction and influence at the bar and in public life. In the Christiana case, for example, Thaddeus Stevens was a prominent figure; in the Van Zandt case Salmon P. Chase and William H. Seward presented the arguments against the Fugitive Slave Law before the United States Supreme Court;[1] Mr. Chase also appeared in Eells' case, and in the case known as *ex parte* Robinson, besides others of less judicial importance. Rutherford B. Hayes took part in a number of fugitive slave cases in Cincinnati, Ohio. A letter written by the ex-President in 1892 says: " As a young lawyer, from the passage of the Fugitive Slave Law until the war, I was engaged in slave cases for the fugitives, having an understanding with Levi Coffin and other directors and officers of the U. R. R. that my services would be freely given."[2] John Jolliffe, another lawyer of Cincinnati, less known than the anti-slavery advocates already mentioned, was sometimes associated with Chase and Hayes in pleading the cause of fugitives.[3] The Western Reserve was not without its members of the bar that were ready to display their legal talent in a movement well grounded in the popular mind of eastern Ohio. An illustration is afforded by the trial of the Oberlin-Wellington rescuers, when four eminent attorneys of Cleveland offered their services for the defence, declining at the same time to accept a fee. The event shows that the political aspirations of these men were not injured by their procedure, for Mr. Albert G. Riddle, who spoke first for the defence, was elected to Congress from the Cleveland district the following year, and Mr. Rufus P. Spalding, one of his associates, was similarly honored by the same district in 1862.[4] In November, 1852, the legal firm of William H. West and James Walker, of Bellefontaine, Ohio, attempted to release from custody several

---

[1] Wilson, *Rise and Fall of the Slave Power*, Vol. I, p. 477.
[2] Letter of Mr. Hayes, Fremont, O., Aug. 4, 1892.
[3] *Reminiscences of Levi Coffin*, pp. 548, 549.
[4] Rhodes, *History of the United States*, Vol. II, p. 364. The others representing the rescuers were Franklin T. Backus and Seneca O. Griswold. See J. R. Shipherd's *History of the Oberlin-Wellington Rescue*, p. 14.

RUSH R. SLOANE,
OF SANDUSKY, OHIO,
fined $3000 and costs for assisting runaways to Canada.

THADDEUS STEVENS, M.C.,
who befriended fugitives in southeastern Pennsylvania, and appeared for them in court.

J. R. WARE,
OF MECHANICSBURG, OHIO,
a station-keeper, in a centre receiving fugitives from several converging routes.

EX-PRESIDENT R. B. HAYES,
who, as a young lawyer in Cincinnati, Ohio, served as counsel in fugitive slave cases.

negroes belonging to the Piatt family of Kentucky, before their claimants could arrive to prove property. The attempt was successful, and, by prearrangement, the fugitives were taken into a carriage and driven rapidly to a neighboring station of the Underground Railroad. The funds to pay the sheriff, the court expenses and the livery hire were borne in part by Messrs. West and Walker.[1]

Among the names of the legal opponents of fugitive slave legislation in Massachusetts, that of Josiah Quincy, who gained distinction in public life and as President of Harvard College, is first to be noted. Mr. Quincy was counsel for the alleged runaway in one of the earliest cases arising under the act of 1793.[2] In some of the well-known cases that were tried under the later act Richard H. Dana, Robert Rantoul, Jr., Ellis Gray Loring, Samuel E. Sewell and Charles G. Davis appeared for the defence. Sims' case was conducted by Robert Rantoul, Jr., and Mr. Sewell; Shadrach's by Messrs. Davis, Sewell and Loring; and Burns' case by Mr. Dana and others.[3]

Instances gathered from other Northern states seem to indicate that information of arrests under the Fugitive Slave acts almost invariably called out some volunteer to use his legal knowledge and skill in behalf of the accused, and that in many centres there were not lacking men of professional standing ready to give their best efforts under circumstances that promised, in general, little but defeat. Owen Lovejoy, of Princeton, Illinois, was arrested on one occasion for aiding fugitive slaves, and was defended by James H. Collins, a well-known attorney of Chicago. Returning from the trial of Lovejoy, Mr. Collins learned of the arrest of Deacon Cushing, of Will County, on a similar charge, and together with John M. Wilson he immediately volunteered to conduct the new case.[4] At the hearing of Jim Gray, a runaway from Missouri, held before Judge Caton of the State Supreme Court at Ottawa, Illinois, Judge E. S. Leland, B. C. Cook,

[1] Conversation with Judge William H. West, Bellefontaine, O., Aug. 11, 1894.
[2] M. G. McDougall, *Fugitive Slaves*, p. 35.
[3] *Ibid.*, pp. 44, 46, 47.
[4] G. H. Woodruff, *History of Will County, Illinois*, p. 264.

O. C. Gray and J. O. Glover appeared voluntarily as counsel for the negro.[1] As a result of the hearing it was decided by the court that the arrest was illegal, since it had been made under the state law; the negro was, therefore, discharged from the arrest, but could not be released by the judge from the custody of the United States marshal. However, the bondman was rescued, and thus escaped. Eight men were indicted on account of this affair, prominent among whom were John Hossack and Dr. Joseph Stout, of Ottawa. Mr. Hossack, who was tried first, had an array of six of the leading lawyers of Chicago to present his side of the case; they were the Hons. Isaac N. Arnold, Joseph Knox, B. C. Cook, J. V. Eustace, E. Leland and E. C. Larnard. Mr. Stout had three of these men to represent him, namely, Messrs. Eustace, Larnard and Arnold.[2] Early in March, 1860, two citizens of Tabor, Iowa, Edward Sheldon and Newton Woodford, were captured while conducting four runaways from the Indian Territory to a station of the Underground Railroad. At the trial they were ably defended by James Vincent, Lewis Mason and his brother, and were acquitted. It may be added that the trial closed at nine o'clock in the evening, and before daybreak the negroes had been rescued and sent forward on their way to Canada.[3]

In Philadelphia there were several lawyers that could always be depended on to resist the claims of the slave-owner to his recaptured property in the courts. William Still mentions two of these, namely, David Paul Brown and William S. Pierce, as "well-known veterans" ready to defend the slave "wherever and whenever called upon to do so."[4] Robert Purvis relates an incident of David Paul Brown that will be recognized as characteristic of the spirit in which the class of advocates to which he belonged rendered their services for the slave. A case growing out of the capture of a

[1] The *Ottawa Republican*, Nov. 9, 1891. The hearing occurred Oct. 20, 1859.
[2] The *Pontiac* (Ill.) *Sentinel*, 1891-1892.
[3] The *Tabor* (Ia.) *Beacon*, 1890-1891, Chap. XXI of a series of articles by the Rev. John Todd, on "The Early Settlement and Growth of Western Iowa."
[4] *Underground Railroad Records*, p. 367.

negro by his pursuers occupied the attention of Mr. Purvis for a season in 1836, and he desired to engage Mr. Brown for the defence ; he accordingly presented the matter to the distinguished attorney, offering him a fee of fifty dollars in advance. Mr. Brown promptly undertook the case, but refused the money, saying : "I shall not now, nor have I ever, accepted fee or reward, other than the approval of my own conscience, and I respectfully decline receiving your money."[1]

In what was, so far as known, the last case under the Slave Law of 1850, Mr. John Dean, a prominent lawyer of Washington, D.C., displayed noteworthy zeal in the interest of his client, a supposed fugitive. The affair occurred in June, 1862, and came within the cognizance of the United States courts. Mr. Dean, who had just obtained the discharge of the colored man from arrest, interfered to prevent his seizure a second time as the slave of a Virginian. The claimant, aided by other persons, sought to detain the black until a civil officer should arrive to take him into custody, but the attorney's surprising play at fisticuffs defeated the efforts of the assailing party and the black got away. He soon enlisted in one of the colored regiments then forming in Washington, and it is to be surmised that all question concerning his status was put to rest by this step. Mr. Dean was indicted for aiding in the escape of a fugitive slave, and although the affair is said to have caused great excitement in the Capital, especially in the two Houses of Congress, it never reached a legal decision, but lapsed through the progress of events that led rapidly to the Emancipation Proclamation and the repeal of the Fugitive Slave laws.[2]

In the crisis that was reached with the beginning of the new decade, the question of the rendition of fugitives from service was by no means lost sight of. As in 1850, so in 1860 a measure for the more effective protection of slave property appears to have been a necessary condition in any plan of compromise that was to gain Southern support. President Buchanan sought to meet the situation by pro-

---

[1] Smedley, *Underground Railroad*, p. 359.
[2] This case is given by Mr. Noah Brooks, in his *Washington in Lincoln's Time*, 1895, pp. 197, 198.

posing, in his message of December 4, 1860, the adoption of "explanatory" amendments to the Constitution recognizing the master's right of recovery and the validity of the Fugitive Slave Law; he also recommended a declaration against the so-called personal liberty laws of the states as unconstitutional, and therefore void. This produced, within three months, in the House, a crop of more than twenty resolutions relative to fugitive slaves; the deliberations of that body issued at length, March 1, 1861, in the passage of a bill to make more effective the law of 1850. The new measure provided for an appeal to the Circuit Court of the United States, where cases were to be tried by jury. But in the Senate this bill never got beyond the first reading.

That the people of the Northern states would have acquiesced in a new law for the surrender of runaway negroes was certainly not to be expected. Both the law of 1793 and that of 1850 had been systematically evaded as well as frequently denounced, and now memorials were being sent to Congress praying for the repeal of the despised legislation.[1] A bill for this purpose was introduced into the House by Mr. Blake, of Ohio, in 1860, but was smothered by the attempt to amend the existing law. A similar measure was introduced into the Senate in December, 1861, by Mr. Howe, of Wisconsin, who prefaced its presentation by declaring that the Fugitive Slave Law "has had its day. As a party act it has done its work. It probably has done as much mischief as any other one act that was ever passed by the national legislature. It has embittered against each other two great sections of the country."[2] The bill was referred to a committee, where it was kept for some time, and at length was reported adversely in February, 1863.

In the meantime slavery was subjected to a series of destructive attacks in Congress, despite the views of some, who held that the institution was under constitutional protection. The passions and exigencies of the War, together with the humane motives from which the anti-slavery movement had sprung, did not leave these assaults without justification.

[1] Wilson, *Rise and Fall of the Slave Power*, Vol. III, p. 395.
[2] *Congressional Globe*, Thirty-seventh Congress, First Session, 1356.

In August, 1861, a law was enacted providing for the emancipation of negroes employed in military service against the government; in April, 1862, slavery was abolished in the District of Columbia; in May, army officers were forbidden to restore fugitives to their owners; in June slavery was prohibited in the territories; and in July an act was passed granting freedom to fugitives from disloyal masters that could find refuge with the Union forces.

In the train of these measures, and in September of the same year in which most of them were enacted, President Lincoln issued his proclamation of warning to the South declaring that all persons held as slaves in the states continuing in rebellion on the 1st of January, 1863, should be "thenceforth and forever free." When the warning was carried into effect on the first day of the new year by the famous Proclamation of Emancipation, ownership of slave property in the border states was not abolished. The loyalty of these states was their protection against interference. As the Fugitive Slave Law was not yet repealed opportunity was still afforded to civil officers to enforce its provisions both north and south of Mason and Dixon's line. North of the line there was, however, no disposition to enforce the law. South of it wandering negroes were sometimes arrested by the civil authorities for the purpose of being returned to their masters. The following advertisement, printed two months and a half after the final proclamation went into effect, illustrates the method pursued in dealing with supposed fugitives: —

"There was committed to the jail in Warren County, Kentucky, as runaway slave, on the 29th September, 1862, a negro man calling himself Jo Miner. He says he is free, but has nothing to show to establish the fact. He is about thirty-five years of age, very dark copper color, about five feet eight inches high, and will weigh one hundred and fifty pounds. The owner can come forward, prove property, and pay charges, or he will be dealt with as the law requires.

R. J. POTTER, J. W. C.
March 16, 1863. 1 m."[1]

[1] *Liberator*, May 1, 1863. Extract from the *Frankfort Commonwealth*, quoted by M. G. McDougall, *Fugitive Slaves*, p. 80.

Although the proposition to repeal the Fugitive Slave Law of 1850 had been made in Congress in 1860, and repeated in 1861 and 1862, no definite and conclusive action was taken until 1864. During the session of 1863–1864 five bills were introduced into the House looking toward the repeal of the law. In the discussion of the subject the probable effect of revocation upon the border states was frequently dwelt upon, and it was urged by many members that the loyal slave states would consider repeal as "insult and outrage." Mr. Mallory, of Kentucky, was one of those that took this view. He therefore demanded that the law "be permitted to remain on the statute-book," urging, "If you say it will be a dead letter, so much less excuse have you for repealing it, and so much more certainly is the insult and wrong to Kentucky gratuitous." In reply to this and other arguments the need of enlisting negro soldiers was pressed on the attention of the House, and it was said by Mr. Hubbard, of Connecticut, "You cannot draft black men into the field while your marshals are chasing women and children in the woods of Ohio with a view to render them back into bondage. The moral sense of the nation, ay, of the world, would revolt at it."[1] The conclusion that slavery was already doomed to utter destruction could not be avoided. The House therefore decided to throw away the empty guarantee of the institution, and June 13 the vote on the bill for repeal was taken. It resulted in the measure being carried by a vote of 82 to 57. When the bill from the House came before the Senate the question of repeal was already under consideration, and, indeed, had been for three months and a half. Nevertheless, the House measure was at once referred to committee and was reported back June 15. It was then discussed by the Senate for several days and voted on on June 23, the result being a vote of 27 in favor of repeal to 12 against it. Two days later President Lincoln affixed his signature to the bill, and the Fugitive Slave laws were thereby annulled June 25, 1864. The constitutional provision for the recovery of runaways, which had been

---

[1] *Congressional Globe*, Thirty-eighth Congress, First Session, 2913. See also M. G. McDougall, *Fugitive Slaves*, p. 85.

judicially declared in the decision of Prigg's case to be self-executing was not cancelled until December 18, 1865, when the Secretary of State proclaimed the adoption of the Thirteenth Amendment to the Constitution by the requisite number of states.

CHAPTER X

THE UNDERGROUND RAILROAD IN POLITICS

To set forth the political aspect of the Underground Railroad is not easy. Yet this side must be understood if the Underground Railroad is to appear in its true character as something more than a mere manifestation of the moral sentiment existing in the North and in some localities of the South. The romantic episodes in the fugitive slave controversy have been frequently described; but it has altogether escaped the eye of the general historian that the underground movement was one that grew from small beginnings into a great system; that it must be reckoned with as a distinct causal factor in tracing the growth of anti-slavery opinion; that it furnished object lessons in the horrors of slavery without cessation during two generations to communities in many parts of the free states; that it was largely serviceable in developing, if not in originating, the convictions of such powerful agents in the cause as Harriet Beecher Stowe and John Brown; that it alone serves to explain the enactment of that most remarkable piece of legislation, the Fugitive Slave Law of 1850; and, finally, that it furnished the ground for the charge brought again and again by the South against the North of injury wrought by the failure to execute the law, a charge that must be placed among the chief grievances of the slave states at the beginning of the Civil War.

Even in colonial times there was difficulty in recovering fugitive slaves, because of the aid rendered them by friends, as is apparent from an examination of some of the regulations that the colonies began to pass soon after the introduction of slavery in 1619. The Director and Council of New Netherlands enacted an ordinance as early as 1640,

GERRIT SMITH, M.C.,
the multi-millionnaire, whose mansion in Peterboro, New York, was a station.

JOSHUA R. GIDDINGS, M.C.,
who kept a room in his house in Jefferson, Ohio, for fugitives

CHARLES SUMNER,
THE CHAMPION OF THE FUGITIVE SLAVE IN THE SENATE OF THE UNITED STATES.

RICHARD H. DANA, JR.,
COUNSEL FOR COLORED REFUGEES IN BOSTON, MASSACHUSETTS.

one of the provisions of which forbade all inhabitants of New Netherlands to harbor or feed fugitive servants under a penalty of fifty guilders, "for the benefit of the Informer; ⅓ for the new Church and ⅓ for the Fiscal."[1] Other regulations for the same colony contained clauses prohibiting the entertainment of runaways; such are the laws of 1642,[2] 1648,[3] 1658,[4] and, after the Dutch had been supplanted by English control, those of 1702[5] and 1730.[6] An act of Virginia that went into force in 1642 was attributed to the complaints made at every quarter court "against divers persons who entertain and enter into covenants with runaway servants and freemen who have formerly hired themselves to others, to the great prejudice if not the utter undoing of divers poor men, thereby also encouraging servants to run from their masters and obscure themselves in some remote plantation." By way of penalty, to break up the practice of helping runaways, this law provided that persons guilty of the offence were to be fined twenty pounds of tobacco for each night's hospitality.[7] That the law was ineffectual is indicated by the increase of the penalty in 1655 by the addition to the twenty pounds of tobacco for each night's entertainment of forty pounds for each day's entertainment.[8] Similar acts were passed by Virginia in 1657,[9] 1666,[10] and 1726.[11] The last act required masters of vessels to swear that they would make diligent search of their craft to prevent the stowing away of servants or slaves eager to escape from their owners. An act of Maryland passed in 1666 established a fine of five hundred pounds of casked tobacco for the first night's hospitality, one thousand pounds for the second, and fifteen hundred pounds for each succeeding night.[12] A law of New Jersey in 1668 laid a penalty of

[1] *Laws and Ordinances of New Netherlands*, 32.
[2] *Ibid.* [3] *Ibid.*, 104.
[4] *Laws of New Netherlands*, 344.
[5] *Acts of Province of New York from 1691 to 1718*, p. 58.
[6] *Ibid.*, 193.
[7] *Statutes at Large*, Hening, *Laws of Virginia*, I, 253.
[8] *Ibid.*, I, 401. [10] *Ibid.*, II, 239.
[9] *Ibid.*, I, 439. [11] *Ibid.*, IV, 168.
[12] *Maryland Archives, Assembly Proceedings*, 147.

five pounds in money and such damages as the court should adjudge upon any one transporting or contriving the transportation of an apprentice or servant;[1] while another law, enacted seven years later, declared that every inhabitant guilty of harboring an apprentice, servant or slave, should forfeit to his master or dame ten shillings for every day's concealment, and, if unable to pay this amount, should be liable to the judgment of the court.[2] Provisions are also to be found in the regulations of Massachusetts Bay,[3] Rhode Island,[4] Connecticut,[5] Pennsylvania[6] and North Carolina,[7] clearly intended to discourage the entertainment or the transportation of fugitives. It is interesting to note that in these early times Canada was a refuge for fugitives. In 1705 New York passed a law, which was reënacted ten years later, to prevent the escape of negro slaves from the city and county of Albany to the French in Canada. The reason given for the law was the necessity of keeping from the French in time of war knowledge that might prove serviceable for military purposes.[8]

The group of enactments just considered together with many other early measures relating to the subject of fugitives makes it clear that the question of extradition of runaway slaves had also arisen in colonial times. A stipulation for the return of fugitives had been inserted in the formal agreement entered into by Plymouth, Massachusetts, Connecticut and New Haven at the time of the formation of the New England Confederation in 1643,[9] and may be supposed to

[1] *New Jersey Laws*, 82.
[2] *Ibid.*, 109.
[3] *Charters and General Laws of the Colony and Province of Massachusetts Bay*, 386, 750 (1707 and 1718 respectively).
[4] *Proceedings of General Assembly, Colony of Rhode Island and Providence Plantations*, Providence, 177; *Records of Colony of Rhode Island*, 177.
[5] *Acts and Laws of His Majestie's Colony of Connecticut*, 229 (1730 probably).
[6] *Province Laws of Pennsylvania*, Philadelphia, 1725; *Province Laws of Pennsylvania*, 325.
[7] *Laws of North Carolina*, 89 (1741); *Ibid.*, 371 (1779).
[8] *Acts of Province of New York*, 77 (1705); *Laws of Province of New York*, 218 (1715); Marion G. McDougall, *Fugitive Slaves*, 8.
[9] *Plymouth Colony Records*, IX, 5; Marion G. McDougall, *Fugitive Slaves*, 7.

have remained in force for a period of forty years. In the first national constitution, the Articles of Confederation adopted in 1781, no such provision was made. This omission soon became serious through the action of the states of Vermont, Pennsylvania, Massachusetts, Connecticut and Rhode Island between 1777 and 1784 in taking steps toward immediate or gradual emancipation; for the first time the question of the status of fugitives in free regions was now raised.

When, in 1787, the question arose of providing a government for the territory northwest of the Ohio River, the difficulty was felt; and the Northwest Ordinance included a clause for the reclamation of fugitives from labor. A proposition made by Mr. King in 1785 to prohibit slavery in this region without any provision for reclaiming fugitives had gone to committee, but was never afterwards called up in Congress. In the discussion of 1787 an amendment was offered by Nathan Dane, of Massachusetts, the first clause of which excluded slavery from the territory, and the second clause provided for the rendition of fugitives. The previous delay and the prompt and unanimous approval of the compromise measure of Mr. Dane give force to the contention of a special student of the Ordinance, that the stipulation forbidding slavery could not have been adopted without the provision for the recovery of runaways.[1]

About six weeks after the incorporation, by the Continental Congress, of the fugitive slave clause in the Northwest Ordinance, a similar provision was made a part of the Constitution of the United States by the vote of the Federal Convention at Philadelphia.[2] In the case of the Constitution, as of the Ordinance, the clause was probably necessary for the acceptance and adoption of the instrument, and the action of the legislative body was unanimous.[3]

[1] Peter Force, on the Ordinance of 1787, in the *National Intelligencer*, 1847. See also E. B. Chase's volume, entitled *Teachings of Patriots and Statesmen, or the "Founders of the Republic" on Slavery*, 1860, pp. 155, 160, 161, 169.
[2] E. B. Chase, *Teachings of Patriots and Statesmen . . . on Slavery*, p. 9.
[3] Alexander Johnston's careful survey of the subject in the *New Princeton Review*, Vol. IV, p. 183; J. H. Merriam, *Legislative History of the Ordinance of 1787*, Worcester, 1888; M. G. McDougall, *Fugitive Slaves*, p. 64.

The settlement reached in regard to fugitives appears to have excited little comment in the various state conventions called to ratify the work of the Philadelphia Convention. It would be interesting to know what was the nature of the discussion on the point in the North. In the South the tone of sentiment concerning the matter is illustrated by the remarks of Madison in the Virginia convention, and of Iredell and Pinckney in the conventions of North and South Carolina respectively.[1] Madison asserted of the fugitive clause that it "secures to us that property which we now possess." Iredell explained that "In some of the Northern states they have emancipated all their *slaves*. If any of our slaves go there and remain there a certain time, they would, by the present laws, be entitled to their freedom, so that their masters could not get them again. This would be extremely prejudicial to the inhabitants of the Southern states; and to prevent it this clause is inserted in the Constitution. Though the word *slave* is not mentioned, this is the meaning of it." Pinckney declared: "We have obtained a right to recover our slaves, in whatever part of America they may take refuge, which is a right we had not before. In short, considering the circumstances, we have made the best terms for the security of this species of property it was in our power to make. We would have made better if we could; but, on the whole, I do not think them bad."[2]

The constitutional provision was, of course, general in its terms, and, although mandatory in form, did not designate any particular officer or branch of government to put it into execution. Accordingly the law of 1793 was enacted. This law, however, was of such a character as to defeat itself from the beginning. Before the close of the year in which the measure was passed a case of resistance occurred, which showed that adverse sentiment existed in Massachusetts,[3]

---

[1] These views are quoted by E. B. Chase, in his *Teachings of Patriots and Statesmen . . . on Slavery*.

[2] *Ibid.* See also Elliot's *Debates*, Vol. III, 182, 277.

[3] Appendix B, p. 367, 6. First recorded case of rescue (Quincy's case, Boston).

and three years later another case — especially interesting because it concerned an escaped slave of Washington — demonstrated to the first President that there was strong opposition in New Hampshire to the law.[1] The method of proof prescribed by the measure was intended to facilitate the recovery of fugitives, but it was so slack that it encouraged the abduction of free negroes from the Northern states,[2] and thus, by the injustice it wrought, stirred many to give protection and assistance to negroes.[3] The number of cases of kidnapping that occurred along the southern border of the free states between 1793 and 1850 helps doubtless to explain the development of numerous initial stations of the Underground Railroad during this period.

The inefficiency of the first Fugitive Slave Act was early recognized, and the period during which it was in existence witnessed many attempts at amendment. It is possible that the failure of Washington to recover his slave in 1796 furnished the occasion for the first of these.[4] A motion was made, December 29, 1796, looking toward the alteration of the law.[5] Apparently nothing was done at this time, and the matter lapsed until 1801, when it came up in January and again in December of that year.[6] In the month last named a committee was appointed in the House, which reported a bill that gave rise to considerable debate. This bill provided that employing a fugitive as well as harboring one should be punishable; and that those furnishing employment to negroes must require them to show official certificates and must publish descriptions of them. It is reported that Southern members "considered it a great injury to the owners of that species of property, that runaways were employed in the Middle and Northern states, and even assisted in pro-

---

[1] Appendix B, p. 367. Washington's fugitive, October, 1796.
[2] Chapter II, p. 22; Chapter V, p. 120.
[3] *Ibid.*
[4] William Goodell, *Slavery and Anti-Slavery*, pp. 231, 232.
[5] *House Journal*, Fourth Congress, Second Session, p. 65; *Annals of Congress*, pp. 1741, 1767.
[6] *House Journal*, Sixth Congress, Second Session, p. 220; *Annals of Congress*, p. 1053; *House Journal*, Seventh Congress, First Session, p. 34; *Annals of Congress*, p. 317.

curing a living. They stated that, when slaves ran away and were not recovered, it excited discontent among the rest. When they were caught and brought home, they informed their comrades how well they were received and assisted, which excited a disposition in others to attempt escaping, and obliged their masters to use greater severity than they otherwise would. It was, they said, even on the score of humanity, good policy in those opposed to slavery to agree to this law."[1] Northern members did not accept this view of the fugitive slave question, and when the proposed bill was put to vote January 18, 1802, it failed of passage.[2] The division on the measure took place on sectional grounds, all the Northern members but five voting against it, all the Southern members but two for it.[3]

For the next fifteen years Congress appears to have given no consideration to the propriety of amending the law of 1793. Its attention was mainly occupied by the abolition of the slave-trade, the agitation preliminary to the War of 1812, and the events of that War.[4] At length, in 1817, a Senate committee reported a bill to revise the law, but it was never brought up for consideration. In the same year a bill was drafted and presented to the House, on account of the need of a remedy for the increased insecurity of slave property in the border slave states. Pindall, of Virginia, seems to have been its originator; at any rate he was the chairman of the committee that reported the proposition. The interest in the discussion that resulted was increased, doubtless, by two petitions, one from the Pennsylvania Abolition Society, asking for a milder law than that in existence, the other from the Baltimore Quakers, seeking some security for free negroes against kidnapping.

The House bill as presented in 1817 secured to the claimant of a runaway the right to prove his title before the courts

[1] *House Journal*, Seventh Congress, First Session, p. 125; *Annals of Congress*, pp. 422, 423.
[2] The vote stood 46 to 43.
[3] *House Journal*, Seventh Congress, First Session, pp. 125, 128; *Annals of Congress*, pp. 423, 425.
[4] W. E. B. Du Bois, *The Suppression of the American Slave Trade*, pp. 105–109.

of his own state, and thus to reclaim his human property through requisition upon the governor of the state in which it had taken refuge; it was further provided that the writ of habeas corpus was to have no force as against the provisions of the proposed act. The objections made to the measure are worth noting. Mr. Holmes, of Massachusetts, disapproved of the effort to dispense with the writ of habeas corpus, stating that such action would remove a safeguard from the liberty of free colored people. Mr. Mason, of the same state, declared against trial by jury, which somebody had proposed, insisting that "juries in Massachusetts would in ninety-nine cases out of one hundred decide in favor of fugitives, and he did not wish his town (Boston) infected with the runaways of the South." Mr. Sergeant, of Pennsylvania, sought to amend the bill by making the judges of the state in which the arrest occurred the tribunal to decide the fact of slavery. And, last of all, Mr. Whitman, of Massachusetts, opposed the provision making it a penal offence for a state officer to decline to execute the act; a point, it should be remarked, that came into prominence in the famous case of Prigg vs. Pennsylvania in 1842. Notwithstanding these efforts to modify the bill, it was carried without change, January 30, 1818, by a vote of 84 to 69. In the Senate the bill was not passed without alteration. After a vote to limit the act to four years, the upper House made amendments requiring some proofs of the debt of service claimed other than the affidavit of the claimant, and then passed the act on March 12. The lower House did not find the modified bill to its liking, and therefore declined to consider it further.[1]

This failure to secure a new general fugitive slave act by no means prevented those interested from renewing their

[1] *House Journal*, Fifteenth Congress, First Session, pp. 50, 86, 182, 186, 189, pp. 193, 198; *Annals of Congress*, pp. 446, 447, 513, 829-831, 838, 840, 1339, 1393. *Senate Journal*, Fifteenth Congress, First Session, pp. 128, 135, 174, 202, 227, 228, 233; *House Journal*, p. 328; *Annals of Congress*, pp. 165, 210, 259, 262, 1339, 1716; T. H. Benton, *Abridgment of the Debates of Congress*, Vol. VI, pp. 35, 36, 37, 110; M. G. McDougall, *Fugitive Slaves*, pp. 21-23; Lalor's *Cyclopædia*, Vol. II, pp. 315, 316; Schouler, *History of the United States*, Vol. III, p. 144.

endeavors in that direction. Before the close of the year the House was prompted to bestir itself again by a resolution of the Maryland legislature asking protection against citizens of Pennsylvania who were charged with harboring and protecting fugitive slaves.[1] That the allegation was well founded cannot be doubted. Evidence has already been adduced to show that numerous branches of the Underground Railroad had begun to develop in southeastern Pennsylvania as early at least as the year 1800.[2] A month after the presentation of the Maryland resolution a committee of the House was appointed. This committee reported a bill without delay, but again nothing was accomplished. The framing of the Missouri Compromise at the next session of Congress, in 1820, gave opportunity for the incorporation of a fugitive recovery clause, to enable Southern settlers in Missouri and other slave states to recapture their absconding slaves from the free territory north of the new state.[3] The fugitive clause in the Ordinance of 1787 had insured the same right for slave-owners taking land along the western frontier of Illinois.

But of what utility were such provisions unless they could be carried into effect? Immediately after the Missouri Compromise became a law, propositions for new fugitive slave acts were again offered in both the House and the Senate.[4] A later attempt was made in the winter of 1821-1822, when another resolution of the Maryland legislature similar to the one mentioned above was presented. These efforts, like the earlier ones, failed to secure the desired legislation.[5]

[1] McDougall, *Fugitive Slaves*, p. 23.
[2] Chapter II, pp. 21, 22.
[3] *Annals of Congress*, Sixteenth Congress, First Session, pp. 1469, 1587. McDougall, *Fugitive Slaves*, p. 23. It will be remembered that according to the compromise Missouri was to be admitted into the Union as a slave state, while slavery was to be prohibited in all other territory gained from France north of 36 degrees 30 minutes. See Appendix A, p. 361.
[4] *House Journal*, Sixteenth Congress, First Session, p. 427.
[5] *Senate Journal*, Sixteenth Congress, First Session, pp. 319, 326; *Annals of Congress*, p. 618; *House Journal*, Seventeenth Congress, First Session, p. 143; *Annals of Congress*, pp. 553, 558, 710. *Annals of Congress*, Seventeenth Congress, First Session, pp. 1379, 1415, 1444; Benton, *Abridgment*

The last petition of Maryland to Congress for the redress of her grievance due to the underground operations of anti-slavery Pennsylvanians was made December 17, 1821. The month of January of the same year had witnessed the presentation in Congress of a resolution from the general assembly of Kentucky, protesting against Canada's admission of fugitives to her domain, and requesting negotiation with Great Britain on the subject. In 1826, during the administration of John Quincy Adams, negotiations were at length opened. Henry Clay, then Secretary of State, instructed Mr. Gallatin, the American Minister at the Court of St. James, to propose an agreement between the two countries providing for "mutual surrender of all persons held to service or labor, under the laws of either party, who escape into the territory of the other." His purpose in urging such a stipulation was, he declared, "to provide for a growing evil which has produced some, and if it be not shortly checked, is likely to produce much more irritation." He also stated that Virginia and Kentucky were particularly anxious that an understanding should be reached.

In February, 1827, Mr. Clay again communicated with Mr. Gallatin on the subject, being led to do so by another appeal made to the general government by the legislature of Kentucky. At this time he mentioned the fact that a provision for the restoration of fugitive slaves had been inserted in the treaty recently concluded with the United Mexican States, a treaty, it should be added, that failed of confirmation by the Mexican Senate. About five months later the American Minister sent word to the Secretary of State that the English authorities had decided that "It was utterly impossible for them to agree to a stipulation for the surrender of fugitive slaves," and this decision was reaffirmed in September, 1827.

The positive terms in which this conclusion was announced by the representative of the British government might have been accepted as final at this time had not further consideration of the question been demanded by the House of Rep-

of the Debates of Congress, Vol. VI, p. 296; McDougall, *Fugitive Slaves*, pp. 23, 24.

resentatives. On May 10, 1828, that body adopted a resolution "requesting the President to open a negotiation with the British government in the view to obtain an arrangement whereby fugitive slaves, who have taken refuge in the Canadian provinces of that government, may be surrendered by the functionaries thereof to their masters, upon their making satisfactory proof of their ownership of said slaves." This resolution was promptly transmitted to Mr. Barbour, the new Minister, with the explanation before made to Gallatin, that the evil at which it was directed was a growing one, well calculated to disturb "the good neighborhood" that the United States desired to maintain with the adjacent British provinces. But as in the case of the former attempts to secure the extradition of the refugee settlers in Canada, so also in this, the advances of the American government were met by the persistent refusal of Great Britain to make a satisfactory answer.[1]

The agitation in Congress for a more effective fugitive slave law, and the diplomatic negotiations for the recovery of runaways from Canadian soil, which have been recounted in the preceding pages, must be regarded as furnishing evidence of the existence in many localities in the free states of a strong practical anti-slavery sentiment. This evidence is reënforced by the facts presented in the earlier chapters of this volume. The escape of slaves from their masters into the free states and their simple but impressive appeals for liberty were phenomena witnessed again and again by many Northern people during the opening as well as the later decades of the nineteenth century; and deepened the conviction in their minds that slavery was wrong. Thus for years the runaway slave was a missionary in the cause of freedom, especially in the rapidly settling Western states. His heroic pilgrimage, undertaken under the greatest difficulties, was calculated to excite active interest in his behalf. Persons living along the border of the slave states, whose sympathies were stirred to action by their personal know-

---

[1] Niles' *Weekly Register*, Vol. XXXV, pp. 289–291; S. G. Howe, *The Refugees from Slavery in Canada West*, pp. 12–14; William Goodell, *Slavery and Anti-Slavery*, p. 264; M. G. McDougall, *Fugitive Slaves*, p. 25.

ledge of the hardships of slavery, became the promoters of lines of Underground Railroad, sending or taking fugitives northward to friends they could trust. It was not an infrequent occurrence that intimate neighbors were called in to hear the thrilling tales of escape related in the picturesque and fervid language of negroes that valued liberty more than life. The writer, who has heard some of these stories from the lips of surviving refugees in Canada, can well understand the effect they must have produced upon the minds of the spectators. Many children got their lasting impression of slavery from the things they saw and heard in homes that were stations on the Underground Road. John Brown was reared in such a home. His father, Owen Brown, was among the earliest settlers of the Western Reserve in Ohio that are known to have harbored fugitives, and the son followed the father's example in keeping open house for runaway slaves.[1] As early as 1815 many blacks began to find their way across the Reserve,[2] and it is stated that even before this year more than a thousand fugitives had been assisted on their way to Canada by a few antislavery people of Brown County in southwestern Ohio.[3] It is probable that numerous escapes were also being made thus early through other settled regions. The cause for this early exodus is not far to seek. The increase of the domestic slave-trade from the northern belt of slaveholding states to the extreme South, due to the profitableness of cotton-raising, and stimulated by the prohibition of the foreign slave-trade in 1807, aroused slaves to flight in order to avoid being sold to unknown masters in remote regions. The slight knowledge they needed to guide them in a northerly course was easily obtainable through the rumors about Canada everywhere current during the War of 1812.[4] The noticeable political effects of the straggling migration that began under these circumstances is seen in the renewed agitation by Southern members of Congress during the years 1817 to 1822 for a more stringent Fugitive Slave Law, and

[1] Chapter II, p. 37.   [2] *Ibid.*, pp. 37, 38.
[3] William Birney, *James G. Birney and His Times*, p. 435.
[4] Chapter II, p. 27.

the negotiations with England several years later looking toward the restoration to the South of runaways who had found freedom and security on Canadian soil.

The influence of the Underground Road in spreading abroad an abiding anti-slavery sentiment was, of course, greatly restricted by the caution its operators had to observe to keep themselves and their protégés out of trouble. The deviating secret routes of the great system were developed in response to the need of passengers that were in constant danger of pursuit. It is this fact of the pursuit of runaways into various communities where they were supposed to be in hiding, together with the harsh scenes enacted by hireling slave-catchers in raiding some station of the Underground Road, that gave to the operations of the Road that publicity necessary to make converts to the anti-slavery cause. During the earlier years of the Road's development the pursuit of runaways was not so common as it came to be after 1840, and later, after the passage of the second Fugitive Slave Law in 1850; but cases are recorded, as already noted, in 1793 in Boston, 1804 in eastern Pennsylvania, 1818 in New Bedford, Massachusetts, and elsewhere. These are but illustrations of a class of early cases that brought the question of slavery home to many Northern communities with such force as could not have been done in any other way. These cases, like the numerous cases of kidnapping that occurred during the same period, contributed not a little to keep alive a sentiment that was steadily opposed to slavery, and that expressed and strengthened itself in the practice of harboring and protecting fugitives. The great effect upon public opinion of these cases, and such as these, appears from the sad affair of Margaret Garner, a slave-woman who escaped from Boone County, Kentucky, late in January, 1856, and found shelter with her four children in the house of a colored man near Cincinnati, Ohio. Rather than see her offspring doomed to the fate from which she had hoped to save them, she nerved herself to accomplish their death. While her master, successful in his pursuit, was preparing to take them back across the river, she began the work of butchery by killing her favorite child. Before she could finish her awful task she was interrupted and put in prison. The efforts to prevent her return to Southern bondage proved unavailing, and she was at length delivered to her master, together with the children she had meant to kill. President R. B. Hayes, who was practising law in Cincinnati at the time, and lived on a pro-slavery street, told Professor James Monroe, of Oberlin College, that the tragedy converted "the whole street," and that the day after the murder "a leader among his pro-slavery neighbors" called at his house, and declared with great fervor, "Mr. Hayes, hereafter I am with you. From this time forward, I will not only be a black Republican, but I will be a *damned abolitionist!*"[1]

That the doctrine of immediate abolition should find expression during the years in which the underground movement was in its initial stage of development, is a fact the importance of which should be given due recognition in tracing the growth of anti-slavery sentiment to 1830, and in showing thus what was the preparation of the North for the advent of Garrison and his followers, and for the party movements in opposition to slavery. It is surely worthy of remark in this connection that, of the three men that promulgated the idea of immediate abolition before 1830, one published a book, containing, besides other things, an argument in support of the assistance rendered to fugitive slaves, while another was known both in Ohio and in the Southern states as an intrepid underground operator.

Of the trio the first in point of time as also in pungency of statement was the Rev. George Bourne, who went to live in Virginia about 1809 after several years residence in Maryland. Mr. Bourne's acquaintance with slavery impressed him deeply with the evils of the system, and he accordingly felt constrained to preach and also to publish some vehement protests against it. For this he was persecuted and driven from Virginia, and, like a hunted slave, he found his way in the night into Pennsylvania, where he settled with his family. Among his writings is a small volume entitled *The Book and Slavery Irreconcilable*, published in 1816 and addressed to all that

[1] James Monroe, *Oberlin Thursday Lectures, Addresses, and Essays*, 1897, p. 116. See Appendix B, pp. 367-377, for cases under the Slave laws.

professed to be members of Christian churches. In it the author vigorously and repeatedly urged the "immediate and total abolition" of slavery, and warned his contemporaries of the consequences of continuing the system until by its growth it should endanger the Union. He could discover no palliative suitable to the evil. "The system is so entirely corrupt," he said, "that it admits of no cure but by a total and immediate abolition. For a gradual emancipation is a virtual recognition of the right, and establishes the rectitude of the practice. If it be just for one moment, it is hallowed forever; and if it be inequitable, not a day should it be tolerated."[1]

Eight years after the appearance of the book containing these uncompromising views, a treatise was published at the town of Vevay on the Ohio River in southeastern Indiana by the Rev. James Duncan. This small work was entitled *A Treatise on Slavery, in which is shown forth the Evil of Slaveholding, both from the Light of Nature and Divine Revelation.* The purpose of the work as set forth by the author was to persuade all slaveholders that they were "guilty of a crime, not only of the highest aggravation, but one that, if persisted in," would "inevitably lead them to perdition."[2] He therefore assailed the principle of slavery, denying the argument admitted by some of the apologists for slavery among his contemporaries, namely, "that the emancipation of slaves need not be sudden, but gradual, lest the possessors of them should be too much impoverished, and lest the free inhabitants might be exposed to danger, if the blacks were all liberated at once." This doctrine of the inexpediency of immediate abolition Mr. Duncan denied, taking the position that such excuses would "go to justify the practice of slaveholding, because the only motive that men can have to practise slavery is that it may be a means of preventing poverty and other penal evils. If the fear of poverty or any penal

---

[1] These quotations are taken from the summary of Bourne's *The Book and Slavery Irreconcilable*, given in the *Boston Commonwealth*, July 25, 1885, since the original was inaccessible to the present writer. The summary is known to be trustworthy. See *The Life of Garrison*, by his children, Vol. I, postscript to the Preface, and the references to the original there given.

[2] Preface, p. viii.

sufferings will exculpate the possessors of slaves from blame for a few months or years, it will do it for life; and if some may be lawfully held to labor without wages, all may be held the same way; and if the principle of slavery is morally wrong, it ought not to be practised to avoid any penal evil, but if just, even the cruel treatment of slaves would not condemn the practice."[1] He maintained that, although the different sections of the country were not equally guilty of the sins of slaveholding, yet the nation as a whole was responsible for the evil,—on account of the number in the free states that were friendly to slavery, on account also of the advocacy by Northern representatives of the policy of slavery extension, and, finally, on account of the slack zeal of some of those inimical to the institution.[2] He proposed that Christians should have no church fellowship with slaveholders; he urged political action against slavery; and he supplemented the assertion that it was the duty of slaves to escape if they could, by the statement that it was impossible for any one to hinder or prevent their escape without flying in the face of the moral law.[3] As regards gradualism, which was practised in some states, he said: "If it is lawful to hold a man in bondage until he is twenty-eight years of age, it must be equally lawful to hold him to the day of his death; and if it is sinful to hold him to the day of his death, it must partake of the same species of crime to hold him until he is

[1] Preface, pp. vii, viii.
[2] *A Treatise on Slavery*, reprinted by the American Anti-Slavery Society, 1840, p. 59.
[3] *Ibid.*, p. 107. In advocating political action Mr. Duncan said, "The practice of slaveholding in a slave state need not deter emancipators or others from the privilege of voting for candidates to the legislative bodies, or from using their best endeavors to have men placed in office that would be favorable to the cause of freedom, and who may be best qualified to govern the state or commonwealth, but it ought to prevent any from officiating as a magistrate, when his commission authorizes him to issue a warrant to apprehend the slave when he is guilty of no other crime than that of running away from unmerited bondage." This was not the first time political action was proposed, for Mr. Bourne declared in his work (*The Book and Slavery Irreconcilable*): "Every voter for a public officer who will not destroy the system, is as culpable as if he participated in the evil, and is responsible for the protraction of the crime." See the *Boston Commonwealth*, July 25, 1885.

twenty-eight."[1] The arguments in support of his position he based largely upon the Decalogue, the Golden Rule and other scriptural injunctions, as well as upon the Declaration of Independence and the Constitution of the United States.[2] Underground operators always justified themselves on these grounds; and their motives in joining the Liberty and Free Soil parties later — as many of them did — appear not to have been other than the motives of Bourne and Duncan in advocating political action against slavery.

The last member of the trio who complained of delay in granting freedom to the enslaved was the Rev. John Rankin, the pastor of a Presbyterian church in the town of Ripley on the Ohio River in southwestern Ohio. Long residence in Tennessee and Kentucky had filled him with hatred of slavery, and for this hatred he gave his reasons in a series of thirteen vigorous letters addressed to his brother Thomas, a merchant at Middlebrook, Augusta County, Virginia, who had recently become a slave-owner. The letters were written in 1824, and were collected in a little volume in 1826. In the preface, Mr. Rankin said that the safety of the government and the happiness of its subjects depended upon the extermination of slavery,[3] and in the letters themselves he attacked the system of American slavery in unmistakable language. In principle he stood clearly with Bourne and Duncan, as he afterwards came to the support of Garrison, although he did not use the words "immediate abolition." He held that "Avarice tends to enslave, but justice requires emancipation."[4] He heard with impatience the excuse for continued slaveholding that freedom would ruin the blacks because they were not capable of doing for themselves, and must, therefore, either all starve or steal. With sarcasm he exclaimed, "Immaculate tenderness! Astonishing sympathy! But what is to be dreaded more than such tenderness and sympathy? Who would wish to have them exercised upon

---

[1] *A Treatise on Slavery*, p. 123.
[2] *Ibid.*, pp. 21, 32–40, 82, 84, 87–94, 96, 107. Mr. Duncan held that slavery was "directly contrary to the Federal Constitution." See pp. 110, 111.
[3] *Letters on American Slavery*, Preface, p. iii. [4] *Ibid.*, p. 20.

REV. JOHN RANKIN.
(From a bust by Ellen Rankin Copp, of Chicago, Illinois.)

himself? . . . And have not many of those [slaves] who have been emancipated in America become wealthy and good citizens? . . . We are commanded to 'do justly and love mercy,' and this we ought to do without delay, and leave the consequences attending it to the control of Him who gave the command."[1] It has been noted in another place that Mr. Rankin was for years an active agent of the Underground Railroad, in association with a number of abolitionists of his neighborhood, among whom he was a recognized leader.[2]

The idea has somehow gained credence in the general accounts of the anti-slavery movement that the Garrisonian movement was one that could scarcely be said to have had precursors in the earlier agitation; and the pre-Garrison abolitionists have been thought of, apparently, as marked by mild philanthropy, adherence to law and tolerance. It has been supposed that an interval of inactivity followed upon the earlier movements, and that the later movement was thus a thing apart, radically different in its character from anything that had gone before. In view of the evidence brought together in this volume it is perhaps not too much to say that a real continuity of development is traceable through the period with which we have had to do, and that many little communities throughout the country, under the influences always at work, had germinated the idea of immediate abolition, in support of which texts were easily found in the Bible; and that thus the way had been prepared for the anti-slavery ideas and activities of 1830 and the subsequent years. Mr. Garrison himself "confessed his indebtedness for his views" of slavery to Bourne's *The Book and Slavery Irreconcilable*, next after the Bible itself,[3] and in Number 17 of the first volume of the *Liberator* appears an extract quoted from Bourne's work.[4] It is certain that Garrison was familiar with the work as early as September 13, 1830,[5] and he may have been so earlier. He arrived at the doctrine during the

[1] *Letters on American Slavery*, pp. 104, 107.
[2] Chapter IV, p. 109.
[3] *The Life of Garrison*, by his children, Vol. I, p. 306.
[4] *Ibid.*, postscript to Preface. [5] *Ibid.*, p. 207.

summer of 1829, before his association with Lundy at Baltimore.[1] It cannot be determined when Garrison first became acquainted with the *Letters on Slavery* of the Rev. John Rankin, but they seem to have had a wide circulation, for about the year 1825 they had fallen into the hands of the Rev. Samuel J. May, living at the time in Brooklyn, Connecticut, and he had read them with interest.[2] In the second volume of the *Liberator* Garrison republished these letters, and in after years, on more than one occasion, he acknowledged himself the "disciple" of their author.[3]

The outspoken courage characteristic of the new phase into which the anti-slavery cause passed in 1830 helped to increase the resistance made in the North to the law for the rendition of fugitive slaves. The sympathy with the slave now became vocal in various centres, and made itself heard among the blacks of the South through the passionate and unguarded utterances of their masters. The evidence gathered from surviving abolitionists in the states adjacent to the lakes shows an increased activity of the Underground Road during the decade 1830-1840. The removal of the Indians from the Gulf states and the consequent opening of vast cotton-fields during the period named led many slaves to flee from the danger of transportation to the far South.[4] Under these circumstances pursuits of runaways became more frequent, and were often marked by a display of anger on the part of the pursuing party easily accounted for by the anti-slavery agitation in the free states. Open interference and rescues in which both negroes and whites took part became more common.[5] Many persons of respectability, more courageous than the great majority of their class at that time, not only enrolled themselves in the new anti-slavery societies, but made it a part of their duty to engage in the defence of fugitive slaves. Salmon P. Chase often served as counsel for

---

[1] *The Life of Garrison*, Vol. I, p. 140.
[2] *Memoir of S. J. May*, by George B. Emerson and others, pp. 76, 78, 87, 139, 140. See also *Life of Garrison*, Vol. I, p. 213, foot-note.
[3] *Life of Garrison*, Vol. I, pp. 305, 306; Vol. III, pp. 379, 380.
[4] G. M. Weston, *Progress of Slavery in the United States*, p. 22.
[5] McDougall, *Fugitive Slaves*, pp. 38, 39.

the captured runaway during this period, and soon gained for himself the unenvied title of "attorney-general for fugitive slaves."[1] Other men of talents, position and education were not behind the rising Ohioan in their protection of the refugee. A formal organization of Underground Railroad workers, with Robert Purvis as president, was effected at Philadelphia in 1838. It is evident that the Underground Railroad was now developing with rapidity. The conditions prevailing in the North and South during the decade 1840-1850 were not less favorable to the escape of slaves, and, in one particular, were more favorable; the decision in the Prigg case in 1842 took away much of the effectiveness of the Fugitive Slave Act of 1793, and thus made pursuit little less than useless.

About four years before this historic decision was declared, that is to say, in December, 1838, John Calhoun, of Kentucky, sought to introduce a resolution in the House looking towards an enactment making it unlawful for any person to aid fugitive slaves in escaping from their owners, and another making it unlawful for any person in the non-slaveholding states to entice slaves from their owners, the prosecution of offenders against these proposed laws to take place in the courts of the United States. Objections were made to the introduction of these resolutions, and Mr. Calhoun was prevented from getting a reference of the matter to the Committee on the Judiciary by a vote of 107 to 89.[2] When the Prigg decision came, its political significance was quickly shown in the passage of laws by various Northern states forbidding their officers from performing the duties imposed by the act of 1793. From 1842 to 1850, Massachusetts, Vermont, Pennsylvania and Rhode Island passed such laws, and Connecticut, while repealing an earlier law on her statute books as being at the time unconstitutional, retained the portion of it that restrained state officers from assisting in the execution of the act.

In the meantime the Southern leaders did not fail to note the progress of anti-slavery sentiment north of Mason and

[1] J. W. Schuckers, *The Life and Public Service of Samuel Portland Chase*, p. 52. For portrait see plate facing p. 254.
[2] *Congressional Globe*, Twenty-fifth Congress, Third Session, p. 34.

Dixon's line. This was not less manifest in the formation of the Liberty party in the early years of the decade 1840-1850, than in the legislative and other opposition to the Fugitive Slave Law. Indeed, so marked an impression had been made upon the minds and sympathies of anti-slavery men by the brave and successful flight of slaves, that a Liberty convention at Peterboro, New York, in January, 1842, issued an address to slaves, declaring that slavery was to be "tortured even unto death," advising them to seek liberty by flight, and assuring them that the abolitionist knew no more grateful employment than that of helping escaping slaves to Canada. In August of the following year the national convention of the new party, comprising nearly a thousand delegates from all the free states except New Hampshire, made the disavowal of the fugitive recovery clause of the Constitution a part of the party platform, voting by a decisive majority " to regard and treat the third clause of the Constitution, whenever applied to the case of a fugitive slave, as utterly null and void; and consequently as forming no part of the Constitution of the United States whenever we are called upon or sworn to support it."[1] About the time of the announcement of this principle, Mr. Garrison issued in behalf of the American Anti-Slavery Society an address to the bondmen of the South, in which they were promised deliverance from their chains, and were encouraged to run away from their masters. "If you come to us, and are hungry," ran the address, "we will feed you; if thirsty, we will give you drink; if naked, we will clothe you; if sick, we will minister to your necessities; if in prison, we will visit you; if you need a hiding-place from the face of the pursuer, we will provide one that even bloodhounds will not scent out."[2]

Such open attacks upon the property rights of planters and slave-traders must have been extremely aggravating to Southerners, and, of course, contributed to bring the question of a more effective Fugitive Slave Law again under the consideration of Congress, notwithstanding the fact that a large share of that body's attention was occupied during the period from

[1] Wilson, *Rise and Fall of the Slave Power*, Vol. I, pp. 552, 553.
[2] *Ibid.*, p. 563.

1844 to 1848 with matters connected with the annexation of Texas, the Mexican War and the settlement of the Oregon boundary dispute. In 1847 the legislature of Kentucky presented a petition to Congress urging the importance of new laws so framed as to enable the citizens of slaveholding states to reclaim their negroes when they had absconded into the free states. This resulted in a bill reported in the Senate, but the bill never got beyond its second reading. Two years later an attempt was made in the House to secure legislation for the same object, but the committee to whom the matter was referred seems never to have reported.

At intervals more or less frequent, during a period of more than fifty years, the South had been demanding of Congress adequate protection for its human property against the depredations of those Northerners who rejoiced in the work of secret emancipation. The efforts of the slaveholding section for a stricter fugitive recovery law had uniformly failed down to 1850, and it seems altogether likely that the success won in the year named would not have been realized,[1] if a bill intended to meet the needs of slave-owners had not been made an essential part of the great scheme of compromise for the adjustment of the differences threatening the perpetuity of the Union at the time.[2] The measure that was finally adopted, as a part of the programme of compromise, was one introduced into the Senate by Mr. Mason, of Virginia, in the early part of the first session of the Thirty-first Congress. It

[1] "The wonder is how such an Act came to pass, even by so lean a vote as it received; for it was voted for by less than half of the Senate, and by six less than the number of senators from the slave states alone. It is a wonder how it passed at all; and the wonder increases on knowing that, of the small number that voted for it, many were against it, and merely went along with those who had constituted themselves the particular guardians of the rights of the slave states, and claimed a lead in all that concerned them. These self-instituted guardians were permitted to have their own way, some voting with them unwillingly, others not voting at all. It was a part of the plan of 'compromise and pacification' which was then deemed essential to save the Union; under the fear of danger to the Union on one hand, and the charms of pacification and compromise on the other, a few heated spirits got the control and had things their own way." Benton's *Thirty Years' View*, Vol. II, p. 780.

[2] See Rhodes' *History of the United States*, Vol. I, pp. 130–136, for a discussion of the question whether the Union was in danger in 1850.

was aimed, said its author, at evils "more deeply seated and widely extended than those" his colleague recognized. "The state from whence I came," continued Mr. Mason, "and the states of Kentucky and Maryland, being those states of the Union that border on the free states, have had ample experience, not only of the difficulties, but of the actual impossibility of reclaiming a fugitive when he once gets within the boundaries of a non-slaveholding state."[1] Henry Clay, the author of the Compromise, whose disposition had been to lean to the Northern rather than to the Southern side of the general controversy, expressed the irritation of his own state, Kentucky, when he said concerning the question of fugitive slaves: "Upon this subject I do think that we have just and serious cause of complaint against the free States. I think they have failed in fulfilling a great obligation, and the failure is precisely upon one of those subjects which in its nature is most irritating and inflammatory to those who live in slave States. . . . It is our duty to make the law more effective; and I shall go with the senator from the South who goes furthest in making penal laws and imposing the heaviest sanctions for the recovery of fugitive slaves and the restoration of them to their owners."[2] Delaware and Missouri had grievances similar to those of Kentucky and other border states. The region constituted by these states suffered heavy losses through the operations of the Underground Railroad.[3]

That the cotton states also lost considerable property every year by the escape of slaves to the North appears from a statement of Senator Jefferson Davis, of Mississippi: "Negroes do escape from Mississippi frequently," he said, "and the boats constantly passing by our long line of river frontier furnish great facility to get into Ohio; and when they do escape it is with great difficulty that they are recovered; indeed, it seldom occurs that they are restored. We, though

---

[1] *Congressional Globe*, Thirty-first Congress, First Session, Appendix, p. 1583.

[2] *Life and Speeches of Henry Clay*, Vol. II, pp. 641, 643. The speech from which the above quotations are made was delivered Feb. 5 and 6, 1850.

[3] *Congressional Globe*, Thirty-first Congress, Second Session, Appendix, p. 1051; McDougall, *Fugitive Slaves*, p. 31.

less than the border states, are seriously concerned in this question. . . . Those who, like myself, live on that great highway of the West — the Mississippi River — and are most exposed, have a present and increasing interest in the matter. We desire laws that shall be effective, and at the same time within the constitutional power of Congress; such as shall be adequate, and be secured by penalties the most stringent which can be imposed."[1] Calhoun admitted that discontent was universal in the South, and declared that conciliation could only come when the North consented to meet certain conditions, one of which was the restoration of fugitive slaves.

Many of the speeches contained suggestions and prophecies of disunion. One of these, made by Pratt, of Maryland, called the attention of the Senate to a recent address delivered by Mr. Seward, of New York, before an assembly of Ohioans, in which he urged them to "extend a cordial welcome to the fugitive who lays his weary limbs at your door, and *defend him as you would your household gods.*"[2] Another made by Yulee, of Florida, informed the Senate of a convention then sitting at Cazenovia, New York, attended by more than thirty runaway slaves, and held for the purpose of devising ways and means of escape for blacks. The language of the address to slaves issued by the convention was not calculated to reassure slave-owners. In part it ran: "Including our children, we number here in Canada 20,000 souls. The population in the free States are, with few exceptions, the fugitive slave's friends.

"We are poor. We can do little more for your deliverance than pray to God for it. We will furnish you with pocket compasses, and in the dark nights you can run away. We cannot furnish you with weapons; some of us are not inclined to carry arms; but if you can get them, take them, and, before you go back into bondage, use them, if you are obliged to take life. The slaveholders would not hesitate to kill you, rather than not take you back into bondage.

"Numerous as the escapes from slavery are, they would still be more so, were it not for the master's protection of the

---

[1] *Congressional Globe*, Thirty-first Congress, First Session, Appendix, p. 1615.   [2] *Ibid.*, p. 1592.

rights of property. You even hesitate to take the slowest of his horses; but we say take the fastest. Pack up provisions and clothes; and either get a key, or force the lock, and get his money and start."[1] In view of such proceedings, openly conducted without hindrance, the Senator appealed to his auditors and to the country to consider whether "this Union can long continue?"[2]

In his famous 7th-of-March speech, Webster freely admitted that the complaints of the South in regard to the non-rendition of fugitive slaves were just, and that the North had fallen short of her duty. He therefore decided to support Mason's Fugitive Slave Bill, although he wanted it amended in certain particulars, and sought especially to have in it a clause securing trial by jury to the refugee in case he denied owing service to the claimant. He criticised the abolition societies of the North, and said he thought their operations for the last twenty years had produced "nothing good or valuable." The press of the South he found to be as violent as that of the other section. There was, he decided, "no solid grievance presented by the South within the redress of the government, . . . but the want of a proper regard to the injunction of the Constitution for the delivery of fugitive slaves."[3]

Under the combined championship of Webster, Clay and Calhoun, and to bring about better feeling between the two parts of the country, which in the eyes of many contemporaries seemed on the verge of splitting asunder, the new Fugitive Slave Law was passed by the Senate, August 26, 1850, and by the House a few days later. By the signature of President Fillmore the measure became a law, September 18.

The vote by which the new law had been passed through the two Houses of Congress did not betoken a disposition at the North to meet the obligations it imposed upon that section. Only three of the senators representing free states voted for the measure. These were Dodge and Jones, of Indiana, and Sturgeon, of Pennsylvania. Among the one

---

[1] *Congressional Globe*, Thirty-first Congress, First Session, Appendix, pp. 1622, 1623.
[2] *Ibid.*   [3] *Webster's Works*, Vol. V, pp. 354, 355, 357, 358, 361.

hundred and thirty-six members from the Northern states in the House, only thirty-one voted with the slaveholders. Three of the thirty-one were Whigs, the rest Democrats.[1] Jefferson Davis showed that he comprehended the true situation when he said, during the following session of Congress, that the history of the law proved that it would not furnish the needed security, because the Northern majority did not pass the bill, but merely allowed the Southern minority to pass it, and because the measure had to be executed in the North.[2] This view of the case seems not to have been taken by those representing the border slave states. The comprehensive character of Clay's scheme was favorable to the incorporation in it of a measure stringent enough to suit the most aggrieved without exciting the opposition such a measure would have called out if presented by itself.

Whatever the expectations of the various slaveholding states with regard to the recovery of their runaways under the new law, Joshua R. Giddings, himself an enthusiastic agent of the Underground Railroad and a better judge of the real convictions of the North than Webster, took the earliest occasion to give utterance to the sentiments of the people upon whom depended the success or failure of the law of 1850. Giddings did not delay, nor did he mince matters. In the earliest days of the session following that in which the compromise had been passed he denounced the Fugitive Slave Law and predicted its failure. Concerning the citizens of his own state, he said: "The freemen of Ohio will never turn out to chase the panting fugitive. They will never be metamorphosed into bloodhounds, to track him to his hiding-place, and seize and drag him out, and deliver him to his tormentors. Rely upon it they will die first. . . . Let no man tell me there is no higher law than this fugitive bill. We feel there is a law of right, of justice, of freedom, implanted in the breast of every intelligent human being, that

---

[1] Von Holst, *Constitutional and Political History of the United States*, Vol. IV, pp. 18, 19. The hundred and thirty-six Northern members comprised seventy-six Whigs and fifty Democrats.

[2] *Congressional Globe*, Thirty-first Congress, Second Session, Appendix, p. 324. See also Von Holst's work, Vol. IV, p. 27.

bids him look with scorn upon this libel on all that is called law." [1]

That slave-owners counted on deriving benefits from the law appears from the great number of attempts at once made to reclaim runaways, and the frequent prosecutions of those guilty of facilitating their escape. The period sometimes designated the "era of slave-hunting" began in the North. Slave-owners and their agents entered vigorously upon the chase, and a larger number of communities in the free states than ever before were invaded by men engaged in the disgusting business of capturing blacks, intelligent and ambitious enough to seek their own liberty. Villages, towns and cities from Iowa to Maine, but especially in the middle states, witnessed scenes calculated to awaken the popular detestation of slavery as it had never been awakened before. Pitiable distress fell upon the fugitive settlers in the North and did much to quicken consciences everywhere. The capture of a fugitive in the place where he had been living invariably caused an outburst of indignation; and if the victim were not rescued before his removal by his captors a sum of money was raised if possible, and his freedom was purchased if that could be done. All of these circumstances contributed to increase the traffic along the numerous and tortuous lines of the Underground Railroad, which, according to the testimony of surviving abolitionists, did its most thriving business in all parts of the North during the decade from 1850 to 1860. The marked increase in the number of negroes seeking aid on their way to Canada at the outset of this period was due to the flight of many of the fugitive settlers from their accustomed haunts in the free states; but the supply later on must be attributed to the ease of communication through various channels by which slaves were every day learning of the body of abolitionists eager to help them to freedom. The readiness of the Northern people to act in opposition to the law arose from their abhorrence of a measure that they considered unrighteous and cruel, and from their resentment

---

[1] *Congressional Globe*, Thirty-first Congress, Second Session, pp. 15, 16. Von Holst, *Constitutional and Political History of the United States*, Vol. IV, p. 15.

at the requirement that they must join in the hunt, so that the fugitive might be promptly enslaved.[1] The wide-spread opposition to the law led to prosecutions of underground workers in various places, and these prosecutions greatly helped to keep the slavery question before the attention of the country, despite the wishes and endeavors of the politicians who strove to silence the issue.[2]

The record of the year 1851 illustrates the character of the general contest, which had already set in before the enactment of the new law, but which assumed thenceforth an importance it had never had before. Early in the year Shadrach was seized in Boston, carried before the commissioner, and remanded to custody, but was rescued by a crowd of negroes and hurried off to Canada. Later Sims was caught and confined in the court-house until he was marched to Long Wharf under guard of three hundred policemen. William and Ellen Craft, fugitives from Georgia, were tracked to Boston, but, aided by Theodore Parker and other faithful friends, succeeded in escaping to England. Other notable instances of pursuit occurred at Chicago, Illinois, Poughkeepsie, New York, and Westchester and Wilkesbarre, Pennsylvania. At Philadelphia a free negro was arrested, proved a slave by perjured testimony and taken to Maryland; fortunately he gained his liberty again by the refusal of the planter to whom he was delivered to identify him as his lost property. At Buffalo an alleged fugitive was released on writ of habeas corpus by Judge Conkling. At the hearing that followed the lack of evidence caused the judge to discharge the prisoner, and he was soon in Canada. In the attempt of the Maryland slave-owner, Gorsuch, and his party, to recover certain runaway slaves from Christiana, Pennsylvania, Gorsuch was killed and his son seriously wounded, while the fugitives managed to escape. This affair caused intense excitement, not only in Pennsylvania, but through-

[1] McDougall, *Fugitive Slaves*, p. 53.
[2] "These prosecutions attracted more attention to the slavery question in a few months than the abolitionists had been able to arouse in twenty years." Professor Edward Channing, *The United States of America, 1765–1865*, p. 241.

out the country. Another case resulting in the death of one of the parties concerned grew out of the kidnapping of a free negro girl from the house of a Mr. Miller, in Nottingham, Pennsylvania; Miller succeeded in rescuing the girl, but he was mysteriously murdered before he reached home. Near the close of the year 1851 Jerry McHenry was arrested in Syracuse, New York, while an agricultural fair and a convention of the Liberty party were in progress in that city. The attempted escape and the recapture of the negro wrought up the crowd to a state of intense feeling, which was not relieved until the fugitive was rescued and sent to Canada.[1] There were many other instances in which communities were given the opportunity to show their spirit in the defence of helpless bondmen.

The political leaders and the administration, who were responsible for the enactment of the Fugitive Slave Law, were not willing to see its provisions thus trampled under foot. Upon the reassembling of Congress in December, 1850, President Fillmore expressed himself in his message as pleased with the compromise measures, although, he admitted, they had not yet realized their purpose fully. "It would be strange," he said, "if they had been received with immediate approbation by people and states prejudiced and heated by the exciting controversies of their representatives." He nevertheless had faith that the various enactments would be generally sustained. The tinge of doubt in the communication of the President pretty certainly referred to the fierce denunciations of the Fugitive Slave Law recently uttered by mass-meetings in various parts of the Northern states, and to several cases of resistance where the execution of the law had been attempted. His reassuring expressions voiced his own hope and that of the political magnates; and he meant also, perhaps, to carry assurance to the South. Some balm seemed necessary, for the Georgia convention in accepting the compromise as a "permanent adjustment of the sectional controversy," voted, "That it is the deliberate opinion of this convention that upon the faithful execution of the Fugitive

---

[1] F. W. Seward, *Seward at Washington as Senator and Secretary of State*, 1891, Vol. I, pp. 169, 170. McDougall, *Fugitive Slaves*, pp. 44, 47–51, 58, 59.

Slave Bill by the proper authorities depends the preservation of our much-loved Union."[1]

The open resistance to the law upon several occasions in 1851 brought opportunities to the administration to exert itself in favor of the faithful execution of the law. After the rescue of Shadrach from the United States marshal on February 15, much excitement existed, especially at the centre of government. The President immediately issued a proclamation commanding all civil and military officers, and calling on all good citizens, to "aid in quelling this and similar combinations" and to assist in capturing the persons that had set the law at defiance. The Senate, after debate, adopted a resolution requesting the President to lay before it information relating to the rescue, and inquiring whether further legislation was desirable. This request was promptly complied with by the executive. Then Clay, the author of the resolution, urged that the President be invested with extraordinary power to enforce the law, but failed to gain substantial support for his proposition. In the meantime five of the rescuers of Shadrach were indicted and tried, but owing to the disagreement of the jury none of them were convicted. The energetic action of the administration and its supporters had apparently accomplished no result, except to demonstrate the difficulties with which the enforcement of the Fugitive Slave Act was encompassed.

The same lesson was taught in two important instances toward the end of this year, when the government undertook to carry the law into effect. The Gorsuch tragedy at Christiana, Pennsylvania, led the President to order the United States marshal, district attorney and commissioner from Philadelphia, with forty-five United States marines from the navy-yard, to assist in arresting those supposed to have been engaged in the fight. The fugitives had escaped and could not be recovered, but a number of other persons, most of whom were colored, were arrested, taken to Philadelphia, and indicted for treason. But the efforts of the authorities to convict were unavailing, and the prisoners went scot free.[2]

[1] *Boston Atlas*, Dec. 17, 1850.
[2] For references see Appendix B, 53, Christiana case, p. 373.

Within a few days after the passage of the Fugitive Slave Law in September of the previous year, the spirit of resistance in Syracuse, New York, had manifested itself in public meetings at which the law was denounced and a Vigilance Committee organized.[1] In the early part of June following, Daniel Webster, who was travelling extensively through the Northern states and exerting his personal and official influence to secure obedience to the law, visited Syracuse and made a speech. In the course of his remarks he insisted in no conciliatory terms that the law must be enforced. He said, "Those persons in this city who mean to oppose the execution of the Fugitive Slave Law are traitors! traitors!! traitors!!! This law ought to be obeyed, and it will be enforced — yes, it shall be enforced, and that, too, in the midst of the next anti-slavery convention, if then there shall be any occasion to enforce it."

As if in fulfillment of this prediction of the Secretary of State, on October 1, 1851, a day when a convention of the Liberty party was in progress, an attempt was made to capture one Jerry McHenry, an undoubted fugitive; but the Vigilance Committee, under efficient leadership, succeeded in rescuing him out of the hands of his captors. At this outcome there was much exultation among the anti-slavery people, as also when later the prosecution instituted against eighteen of the rescuers ended in a failure to convict. It is worthy of note that Seward was the first to sign the bond of those indicted; and that Gerrit Smith, then a member of Congress, made a defiant speech in the fall of 1852 in Canandaigua, where the trial of one of the rescuers was going on.[2]

Such incidents, together with the aggravation caused by the removal of fugitives successfully seized, made it plain that the compromise was not the "finality" that the politicians declared it to be; and that the Whig and Democratic parties chose to decree it in their national platforms in the summer of 1852. The principles of political opposition

---

[1] S. J. May, *Some Recollections of our Anti-Slavery Conflict*, p. 349.
[2] *Ibid.*, pp. 373-384; Frothingham, *Life of Gerrit Smith*, p. 117; McDougall, *Fugitive Slaves*, pp. 48, 49; Wilson, *Rise and Fall of the Slave Power*, Vol. II, pp. 327, 328.

HARRIET BEECHER STOWE.

determined by the conditions of the time were uttered by the convention of the Free Soil party, with which many of the underground operators were now allied, in the words: "No more slave states, no more slave territories, no nationalized slavery, and no national legislation for the extradition of slaves." The issue of the presidential campaign in the election of Pierce, a compromise Democrat, marks only a temporary disturbance in the progress of sentiment, due to the desire of the country to have rest, the disinclination of many Whigs to support their own candidate, General Winfield Scott, and the policy of acquiescence he represented; and the solidarity of action among the Democrats, who were generally satisfied both with their principles and their candidate.

As it was the Fugitive Slave Law that brought the North face to face with slavery nationalized, so it was the Fugitive Slave Law that occasioned, in the spring of 1852, the production of *Uncle Tom's Cabin*, a novel the great political significance of which has been generally acknowledged. The observations and experience that made possible for Mrs. Harriet Beecher Stowe the writing of this remarkable book were gained by her while living at Cincinnati, where she was enabled to study the effects of slavery. While thus a resident on the borders of Kentucky, she numbered among her friends slaveholders on the one side of the Ohio River and abolitionists on the other. At the time of her first trip across the Ohio in 1833, she visited an estate, which is described as that of Colonel Shelby in *Uncle Tom's Cabin*.[1] Her associations and sympathies brought home to her the personal aspects of slavery, and her house on Walnut Hills early become a station on the Underground Railroad, remaining so doubtless till 1850, when she removed with her husband, Professor Calvin Stowe, to Brunswick, Maine.

During the intervening years she was unconsciously gleaning incidents and scenes and discovering characters for her future book. The woful experiences of her midnight visitors, whose hunger for freedom rose superior to every other need, awoke her deepest compassion, and the neighbor-

[1] C. E. Stowe, *Life of Harriet Beecher Stowe*, pp. 71, 72.

hood in which she lived, nay, even her own household, supplied the circumstances and adventures depicted in the lives of some of her most admirable characters. Mrs. Stowe herself declared *Uncle Tom's Cabin* to be "a collection and arrangement of real incidents, — of actions really performed, of words and expressions really uttered, — grouped together with reference to a general result, in the same manner that the mosaic artist groups his fragments of various stones into one general picture."[1] For example she points out that the service of Senator Bird in the incident of the novel in which Eliza escapes from her pursuers Tom Locker and Marks had its counterpart in the service rendered a negro girl in her own employ by Professor Stowe and his brother-in-law, Henry Ward Beecher, in 1839. This girl was secretly conveyed northward by her escorts a distance of twelve miles to the house of John Van Zandt, another station-keeper of the Underground Road; and Van Zandt it was who "performed the good deed which the author in her story ascribes to Van Tromp."[2] Concerning the leading Quaker character in her book Mrs. Stowe says: "The character of Rachel Halliday was a real one, but she has passed away to her reward. Simeon Halliday, calmly risking fine and imprisonment for his love to God and man, has had in this country many counterparts among the sect. The writer had in mind, at the time of writing, the scenes in the trial of Thomas Garet, of Wilmington, Delaware, for the crime of hiring a hack to convey a mother and four children from Newcastle jail to Wilmington, a distance of *five* miles."[3] The thrilling adventures of Eliza in escaping across the Ohio River with her child in her arms as the ice was breaking up was an actual occurrence that took place fifty miles above Cincinnati, at Ripley, an initial station of an important underground route.[4]

---

[1] *A Key to Uncle Tom's Cabin*, p. 5; Charles Dudley Warner in *The Atlantic Monthly*, September, 1896, p. 312.

[2] *A Key to Uncle Tom's Cabin*, p. 23; C. E. Stowe, *Life of Harriet Beecher Stowe*, p. 93; *Uncle Tom's Cabin;* Howe, *Historical Collections of Ohio*, Vol. II, pp. 102, 103; J. W. Shuckers, *Life of Chase*, p. 53.

[3] *A Key to Uncle Tom's Cabin*, p. 54.

[4] *Reminiscences of Levi Coffin*, pp. 147-151; Howe, *Historical Collections*

By the combination of such elements under the crystallizing influence of the Fugitive Slave Law of 1850, Mrs. Stowe made her story. Intent on having the people of the North understand what the "system" was, about which so many seemed apathetic, she set to work in response to appeals to her to take up her pen. The result, wholly unexpected, was the production of a book that did for the whole population of the free states what the Underground Railroad had been doing for a part only : the author made real the sin of slavery to the consciences of freemen, by an object-lesson in the possible evils of slavery and the desire of the slave to be free. In Harriet Beecher Stowe the thousands of fugitive slaves that had been unwittingly acting as missionaries in the cause of freedom through the earlier years found at last a champion whose words carried their touching story to the multitudes. The disheartening circumstances under which her novel had been composed and the exhausted condition in which the author found herself at its conclusion did not permit her to look for anything but the failure of her undertaking. As she finished the last proof-sheets " it seemed to her that there was no hope; that nobody would hear, nobody would read, nobody would pity; that this frightful system, which had already pursued its victims into the free States, might at last even threaten them in Canada."[1] But the success of the book was immediate. Three thousand copies were sold on the first day of publication, and more than three hundred thousand in this country within the year.[2]

The political effect of the novel has been disparaged by a few writers, because it did not cause anti-slavery gains in the national election occurring in the fall of 1852. Thus George Ticknor wrote in December of that year, " It deepens the horror of servitude, but it does not affect a single vote."[3]

---

of *Ohio*, Vol. II, p. 104 ; see also article on "Early Cincinnati," by Judge Joseph Cox in the *Cincinnati Times-Star*, Feb. 6, 1891 ; a report of "The Story of Eliza," as told by the Rev. S. G. W. Rankin, printed in the *Boston Transcript*, Nov. 30, 1895, an article on Harriet Beecher Stowe, in the *Cincinnati Enquirer*, Nov. 3, 1895, p. 17.

[1] Quoted by Charles Dudley Warner in *The Atlantic Monthly*, September, 1896, p. 315.

[2] *Ibid.*   [3] *Life of George Ticknor*, Vol. I, p. 286.

This was certainly true, for the mass of Northerners were resting in the belief that a substantial political settlement had been reached in the great compromise. It was not to be expected that this belief, which was the outcome of weeks of strenuous discussion, was to be easily tossed aside under the emotional stimulus of a novel. The immediate effect of *Uncle Tom's Cabin* as a political agency lay in the renewal on a vast scale of the consideration of the question of slavery, which the compromise had been thought by so many to have settled. Its remote effect, which did not show itself until the latter part of the decade 1850–1860 has been best explained by the historian, James Ford Rhodes. This writer says, "The mother's opinion was a potent factor in politics between 1852 and 1860, and boys in their teens in the one year were voters in the other. It is often remarked that previous to the war the Republican party attracted the great majority of school-boys, and that the first voters were an important factor in its final success; . . . the youth of America whose first ideas on slavery were formed by reading *Uncle Tom's Cabin* were ready to vote with the party whose existence was based on opposition to an extension of the great evil."[1] They were also ready to fight for the cause of union and of freedom in 1861.

Soon after the publication of Mrs. Stowe's book, Sumner began his movement in the Senate to secure the repeal of the Fugitive Slave Law. In May, 1852, he presented a memorial from the Society of Friends in New England, asking for its repeal;[2] in July he offered a resolution instructing the Committee on Judiciary to report a bill for this purpose;[3] and in August he sought to secure his end by proposing an amendment to the civil and diplomatic appropriations bill.[4] In the speech made at the time he presented this amendment, a speech said to rank with that of Webster on the Compromise in 1850 in the popular interest it aroused, Sumner pointed to the example of Washington, who let one of his slaves remain unmolested in New Hampshire rather than "excite a

---

[1] *History of the United States*, Vol. I, pp. 284, 285.
[2] Peirce, *Life of Sumner*, Vol. III, p. 283.
[3] *Ibid.*, p. 289.   [4] *Ibid.*, p. 292.

mob or riot, or even uneasy sensations in the minds of well-disposed citizens." The execution of the Fugitive Slave Law, he asked Congress to note, involved mobs, cruelty and violence everywhere its enforcement was tried. The wonderful reception given *Uncle Tom's Cabin* was, he thought, an expression of the true public sentiment. "A woman, inspired by Christian genius, enters the lists, like another Joan of Arc, and with marvellous powers sweeps the chords of the popular heart. Now melting to tears, and now inspiring to rage, her work everywhere touches the conscience, and makes the slave-hunter more hateful."[1] He saw the import of the appeal of fugitive slaves to Northern communities for protection and liberty. "For them every sentiment of humanity is aroused. Rude and ignorant they may be, but in their very efforts for freedom they claim kindred with all that is noble in the past. Romance has no stories of more thrilling interest; classical antiquity has preserved no examples of adventure and trial more worthy of renown. They are among the heroes of our age. Among them are those whose names will be treasured in the annals of their race. By eloquent voice they have done much to make their wrongs known, and to secure the respect of the world. History will soon lend her avenging pen. Proscribed by you during life, they will proscribe you through all time. Sir, already judgment is beginning; a righteous public sentiment palsies your enactment."[2]

Through his denunciation of the law, his justification of those who aided the fugitive, and his recognition of the power of the fugitive's appeal, Sumner may be said to have become the representative and spokesman in the Senate of fugitive slaves and their Northern friends. How closely he identified himself with their cause is indicated by his determined efforts

[1] Peirce, *Life of Sumner*, Vol. III, pp. 296, 297; *Congressional Globe*, Vol. XXV, p. 1112.
[2] *Congressional Globe*, Vol. XXV, p. 1112; Peirce, *Life of Sumner*, Vol. III, p. 297.
In a public speech made in 1850 Mr. Garrison had this to say, "Who are among our ablest speakers? Who are the best qualified to address the public mind on the subject of slavery? Your fugitive slaves, — your Douglasses, Browns and Bibbs, — who are astonishing all with the cogency of their words and the power of their reasoning." *Life of Garrison*, Vol. III, p. 311.

to secure the repeal of the obnoxious law, efforts repeated in July, 1854, and February, 1855, and carried by him to a successful issue in 1864.[1]

The action of public sentiment in the Northern states, which, he said, palsied the Fugitive Slave Law, was accompanied, during the decade from 1850 to 1860, by tokens of open violation of the law, defiant resolutions adopted by mass-meetings, and obstructional legislation passed by various free states; the spirit of nullification was thus aroused in many localities north of Mason and Dixon's line. The demands of character and humanity had long been obeyed by many men and women for whom any compromise involving the continuance in slavery of their fellow-men was a dreadful crime. These persons had refused to yield obedience to that statute which in their belief was subversive of the "higher law." Under the action of causes that have been discussed in earlier chapters, the sentiment that had developed the secret and illicit traffic along numerous lines of the Underground Railroad became more obtrusive and less regardful of congressional legislation. Besides participating in the public and legitimate activities of anti-slavery societies, and sharing in the organization of the Liberty and Free Soil parties, the abolitionists formed vigilance committees in various communities, the avowed purpose of which was to thwart the Fugitive Slave Act; and while these bodies held their meetings in secret and guarded the names of their members, it was often a matter of common report in those localities that certain well-known men of the neighborhood were active members. It was the Vigilance Committee of Syracuse that rescued Jerry McHenry from custody of the officers, in the presence of a great crowd; and the leaders in the affair, Gerrit Smith, Charles A. Wheaton and Samuel J. May, far from seeking oblivion, published an acknowledgment in the newspapers that they had aided all they could in the rescue of Jerry, were ready for trial, and would rest their defence on the "unconstitutionality and extreme wickedness" of the Fugitive Slave Law. None of these men were tried. The citizens

---

[1] Peirce, *Life of Sumner*, Vol. III, p. 309, foot-note; Vol. IV, pp. 71, 175–177.

of Onondaga County held a mass-convention in approval of the liberation of the negro, and unanimously adopted resolutions justifying and applauding the act.[1]

From this time on till the outbreak of the Civil War bold and open opposition to the authority of the federal law is a purpose not to be mistaken or overlooked. The state reports of the Pennsylvania and Massachusetts Anti-Slavery societies boasted of the steadily increasing numbers of fugitives aided by abolitionists at many centres, and heaped reproaches on the judges and commissioners that gave decisions adverse to runaways.[2] Fugitive slave cases were stubbornly contested in the courts on the ground that the law of 1850 was unconstitutional. The series of cases in which the law was subjected to the penetrating criticism of some of the ablest lawyers in the country is a long and interesting one; nothing in the history of the times more clearly shows the effect of the Underground Railroad in rousing ever-widening indignation at the hunt for fugitives.[3]

In the spring of 1854 two cases, one in Wisconsin and the other in Massachusetts, served to show the pitch to which the spirit of resistance among the most responsible citizens could rise in both the West and the East. On March 10, 1854, Joshua Glover, who was living near Racine, Wisconsin, was arrested as a fugitive slave by United States deputy marshals and the claimant, B. W. Garland, of St. Louis. After a severe struggle Glover was knocked down, placed in a wagon, driven to Milwaukee, and there lodged in jail. The news of the capture reached Racine in a few hours, and a popular meeting, larger than ever before held in the town, assembled on the court-house square to take action. At this meeting it was resolved to secure Glover a fair trial in Wisconsin; and it was voted, "That inasmuch as the Senate of the United States has repealed all compromises adopted by the Congress of the United States,[4] we, as citizens of Wis-

[1] S. J. May, *Some Recollections of our Anti-Slavery Conflict*, pp. 380, 381. Mr. May says another convention was held ten days later to condemn the action of the rescuers, and did so, but not without dissent.
[2] See the reports after 1850.   [3] For selected cases see Appendix B, p. 372.
[4] The Kansas-Nebraska legislation, repealing the Missouri Compromise of 1820, which was at this time before Congress, is here referred to.

consin, are justified in declaring, *and do declare, the slave-catching law of 1850 disgraceful and also repealed.*" This was but one of many nullifying resolutions adopted about this time in various parts of the North, although most of the resolutions were somewhat less extreme in statement.[1]

At an afternoon meeting the deliberations ended in the decision of about a hundred citizens of Racine to take boat at once for Milwaukee. Upon arrival this delegation found the latter city in an uproar. A meeting of five thousand persons had already appointed a Committee of Vigilance to see that Glover had a fair trial, and this demonstration had led the authorities to call for the local militia to preserve order; but the militia did not appear. Such was now the temper of the crowd that it could be satisfied with nothing less than the immediate release of the prisoner. Glover was therefore demanded, but, as he was not forthcoming, the jail door was battered in, the negro brought out, placed in a wagon and forwarded to Canada by the Underground Railroad. The act of the rescuers was indorsed by the public sentiment of the state; with but few exceptions justified by the newspapers. Among the resolutions passed by mass-meetings held to take action against the Kansas-Nebraska bill, then pending in Congress, there was usually one thanking the rescuers for their conduct.

Remembering with satisfaction the deliverance of Jerry, a special convention assembled at Syracuse, New York, on March 22, 1854, and sent a congratulatory message to Milwaukee and Racine, offering to join them and all the sister cities of the North in a "holy confederacy, which . . . shall swear that no broken-hearted fugitive shall ever again be consigned to slavery from the North, under the accursed act of 1850." A state convention met at Milwaukee, April 13 and 14, which was attended by delegates from all the populated districts. This assembly adopted a number of resolutions, several of which were quotations from the Virginia and Kentucky resolutions, including the famous one

[1] Vroman Mason on "The Fugitive Slave Law in Wisconsin, with Reference to Nullification Sentiment," in the *Proceedings of the State Historical Society of Wisconsin*, 1895, pp. 122, 123.

declaring "that, as in other cases of compact among parties having no common judge, each party has an equal right to judge for itself, as well of infractions, as of the mode and measure of redress." The Fugitive Slave Law was pronounced unconstitutional, and aid was promised the rescuers of Glover.

It is interesting to note that at this convention a state league was also formed, which has been called a forerunner of the Republican party in Wisconsin.

The Supreme Court of the state was soon given an opportunity to place itself on record with regard to the validity of the federal law. The case of one of the rescuers, Sherman M. Booth, came before it for decision. In passing judgment the court showed itself to be in line with the sentiment of the state, for it declared the act of 1850 unconstitutional; the principal grounds assigned were the absence of congressional power to legislate on the subject of the surrender of fugitives from labor, the improper conferring of judicial authority upon commissioners, and the viciousness of depriving a person of his liberty 'without due process of law.' Booth was, of course, discharged. But the matter was not dropped here. The United States District Court now obtained jurisdiction of the case; the jury found the prisoner guilty, and the judge sentenced him to imprisonment for one month, and to pay a fine of $1,000 and the costs of prosecution — in all, $1,451. The news of the conviction caused great excitement; denunciatory meetings were again the order of the day; and money was subscribed for the further defence of the prisoners. Some of the resolutions passed at this time did not stop short of asserting the readiness of the people to maintain their cause with the bayonet. Application was made to the Supreme Court of the state for a writ of habeas corpus, and Booth, together with a colleague, Rycraft, was again released.

The controversy now came before the Supreme Court at Washington, and on petition of the Attorney-General a writ of error was granted by that tribunal to be served on the Supreme Court of Wisconsin. The state court, however, refused to obey this writ. At length, on March 6, 1857, the United States Supreme Court assumed jurisdiction, in an unusual way, acting on the basis of a certified copy of proceedings, which did not appear upon the official record. At the December term, 1858, the judgment of the Supreme Court of Wisconsin was reversed, and that court was directed to return Booth into federal custody. Again the state court would not yield obedience. Booth was therefore rearrested by the United States marshal, March 1, 1860, and was confined in the custom-house at Milwaukee. The friends of the prisoner once more applied to the state Supreme Court for a writ of habeas corpus, but, failing to get it on account of a change in the personnel of the court, they did not rest until they had rescued him from the government prison five months later. On October 8 Booth was again arrested, and this time he remained in prison until, under the pressure brought to bear upon President Buchanan, he was pardoned just before Lincoln's inauguration.[1]

Notwithstanding the obstinacy of the highest state court in refusing to carry out the commands of the highest United States court, the decision rendered by the latter in Booth's case was of great importance. It clearly defined for the first time the limits of state authority and disclosed the powerlessness of state courts to override the jurisdiction granted to the federal courts by the Constitution of the United States.

The people of Wisconsin, however, were unwilling to recognize this fact. Having enacted a personal liberty law in 1857, they made Byron Paine, a young lawyer, who had taken a prominent part in the defence of Booth, their candidate in 1859 for associate justice of the Supreme Court, and elected him on a combined anti-slavery and state rights issue. Thus the state maintained its ground until the eve of the Civil War. Then it relinquished it to assist in coercing South Carolina and other Southern states from their secession, the right of which these states defended by the same doctrine of state sovereignty.[2]

[1] Ableman *vs.* Booth ; for references see Appendix B, 62, Glover rescue case, p. 374.
[2] This account of Booth's case is in the main a condensation of the excel-

The Glover rescue occurred while the Kansas-Nebraska Act was pending in Congress. The attempted rescue of Burns came just after this piece of legislation, already passed by the Senate, had been voted by the House. This measure, which set aside the Missouri Compromise prohibiting slavery from all the Louisiana territory lying north of 36° 30' north latitude, except that included within the State of Missouri, deeply stirred public feeling in the free states: thus the violence of the demonstrations in the Booth and Burns cases was in some measure a protest against Douglas legislation. Burns was arrested in Boston on May 24, 1854, under a warrant granted by the United States commissioner. He felt his case to be hopeless, and so told Richard H. Dana, Jr., and Theodore Parker; but they urged him to make a defence, and prevailed on the commissioner to postpone the hearing. Boston was soon ablaze with indignation kindled in part by the inflammatory handbills scattered broadcast by members of the Vigilance Committee. These handbills contained invectives against the "kidnapper," and expressed a sentiment prevalent in New England, as in other parts of the North, when they declared "the compromises trampled upon by the slave power when in the path of slavery are to be crammed down the throat of the North."

In response to messages from the Vigilance Committee Thomas Wentworth Higginson, A. Bronson Alcott and others hurried to Boston to consult with the leaders there on what was best to be done. A mass-meeting had been called for Friday evening, the 26th, to be held in Faneuil Hall, and it was now planned to make an attack, at the height of this meeting, on the court-house, where Burns was in durance, and "send the whole meeting pell-mell to Court Square, ready to fall in behind the leaders and bring out the slave."

---

lent and exhaustive discussion given by Mr. Vroman Mason in the *Proceedings of the State Historical Society*, 1895, pp. 117-144. Other material will be found in *The Story of Wisconsin*, 1890, by R. G. Thwaites, pp. 247-254; *A Complete Record of the John Olin Family*, 1893, by C. C. Olin, pp. liii-lxxiv; the *Liberator*, April 7 and 24, 1854; 3 *Wisconsin Reports*, pp. 1-64; 21 *Howard's Reports*, p. 506 et seq.; Wilson, *Rise and Fall of the Slave Power*, Vol. II, pp. 444-446.

The city was in a state of wild excitement when the time for action came, and it was natural that in the confusion existing some of the arrangements should miscarry. The crowd that filled Faneuil Hall was so dense as to cut off all communication with the speakers on the platform, and prevented concerted action. When, under the impassioned oratory of Phillips, Parker and others, the audience had given evidences of its readiness to undertake the rescue, the announcement that an attack upon the court-house was about to begin was made from the rear of the hall, and it was proposed that the meeting should adjourn to Court Square. Phillips had not received notice of the project, and the other speakers had not fully comprehended it. The alarm was thought to be a scheme to break up the meeting and was not followed by the decisive action necessary to success.

Arriving at the court-house the crowd found a small party under the lead of Higginson, Stowell and a negro battering in a door with a stick of timber. Entrance was gained by a few only, — who found themselves in the hands of the police, — while the concourse outside was daunted at the outset by the mysterious killing of one of the marshal's deputies. The arrest of several of Higginson's companions followed, and a renewal of the assault, if there was any danger of such a thing, was prevented by the approach of two companies of artillery and two more of marines ordered out by the mayor to preserve the peace. Troops were retained at the court-house during the examination of Burns, and it is reported by an eye-witness that the seat of justice "had the air of a beleaguered fortress." On the 2d of June Commissioner Loring remanded the fugitive to slavery.

The presence in Boston of a multitude of visitors attracted thither by the annual meeting of the New England Anti-Slavery Society, the state convention of the Free Soil party, and the spring meetings of the religious bodies, as well as by the arrest of the negro, led the authorities to take all precautions to forestall any fresh attempt at rescue when the fugitive should be sent out of the city. Accordingly, over a thousand soldiers with loaded muskets, and furnished with a cannon loaded with grape-shot, were detailed to assist the city police and a large number of deputy marshals to carry out the law. In the procession that accompanied Burns to the United States revenue cutter, by which he was to be carried back to Virginia, there were four platoons of marines and a battalion of artillery, besides the marshal's civil posse of one hundred and twenty-five men. Fifty thousand people lined the streets along which this procession passed, and greeted it with hisses and groans, while over their heads were displayed many emblems of mourning and shame. It is little wonder that the *Enquirer* of Richmond, Virginia, commenting with satisfaction on the rendition of Burns, was led to add, "but a few more such victories and the South is undone."[1] Such was the state of public opinion in Massachusetts that the Board of Overseers of Harvard College declined to confirm the election of Commissioner Loring as a member of the Harvard faculty; and the people petitioned, until their request was granted, for his removal from the office of judge of probate.

Similar hostility to the Fugitive Slave Law existed in Illinois. John Reynolds, who had been governor of the state, wrote about 1855 that when President Jackson issued his proclamation in December, 1832, condemning nullification in South Carolina, the legislature of Illinois hailed it with gratification and pledged the state to sustain the executive in his purpose to enforce the federal laws at all hazards. Jackson's proclamation, he said, had a strong tendency to suppress the spirit of nullification throughout the Union. The law of 1850 had been framed in pursuance of the Constitution, and was hailed as the foundation of sectional peace and happiness, but "within a few years, a section of the State of Illinois, the city of Chicago, is not disposed to execute this act of Congress. The opposition in Illinois to this law is not extensive, but confined to a single city, so far as I know. Yet in that disaffected district the act is a dead letter. . . ."[2] The number of centres in Illinois in which the act was disapproved

---

[1] T. W. Higginson in *The Atlantic Monthly*, for March, 1897, p. 349-354; Rhodes, *History of the United States*, Vol. I, pp. 500-506; Wilson, *Rise and Fall of the Slave Power*, Vol. II, pp. 434, 444.

[2] John Reynolds' *History of Illinois*, 1855, pp. 269-271.

and violated was far beyond the knowledge of ex-Governor Reynolds.

In Ohio incidents arising out of the operations of the Underground Railroad became the occasions for serious contests between the state and federal authorities. On May 15, 1857, the United States deputy marshal for southern Ohio, with nine assistants, entered the house of Udney Hyde, near Mechanicsburg, Champaign County, in pursuit of a fugitive slave. The approach of the posse had been observed by the negro, who took refuge in Hyde's garret. Some firing was done by both the negro and the marshal, with the result that the officer and his party were glad to take their positions outside of the house. Here they were soon found by a crowd of citizens from the neighboring town, whose sympathies were so unmistakably with the fugitive that the pursuers decided to leave without delay. Returning twelve days later, they were told that the fugitive, Addison White, had gone to Canada. Thereupon they arrested several persons in the neighborhood on the charge of aiding a slave to escape, and set off with these persons ostensibly for Urbana, where the examination was to be held.

Instead of going to Urbana, the party took a southern course through Clark and Green counties. The sheriff of Clark County, who organized a company to give chase, overtook the marshal and his men, and received at their hands a severe beating. Bands of angry citizens now scoured the country, and, at length, after a skirmish locally known as "the battle of Lumbarton," captured the marshal's posse. On the charge of assault with intent to kill, the prisoners were placed in jail at Springfield. This action occasioned a serious clash between the United States District Court for the southern district of Ohio and the state courts; and the federal tribunal asserted its jurisdiction by releasing the marshal's posse, although in the decision rendered it was admitted that there "was a question whether the marshal had not exceeded authority in the use of unnecessary force."

So critical had the situation now become that Governor Chase determined to have a personal conference with President Buchanan and the Secretary of State, General Cass. The

Governor therefore sent an officer of his staff to Washington to arrange for the meeting, and to say to the Secretary of State that Mr. Chase "was as earnest in support of the authority of the federal government, legitimately exercised, as he was in support of the authority of the state; but that he should feel compelled to protect the state officials in the exercise of their duties, and the state courts in the exercise of their legitimate functions, if it took every man in the state to do it." In order to adjust the existing differences before they culminated in open hostility between the two governments, it was proposed on the part of Mr. Chase that the United States district attorney at Cincinnati be instructed to drop all suits against citizens of the state, with the understanding that a similar course be followed by the state with regard to the marshal and his deputies. At the formal meeting this was the plan adopted. Thus the affair was amicably settled, although it did not fail to leave a deep impression on the public mind, and to evoke comments from the press indicative of the restiveness of the abolitionists under the jurisdiction of United States courts in fugitive slave cases.[1]

Another example of open violation of the Slave Law, which resulted in conflict between the federal and state courts, exists in the famous Oberlin-Wellington rescue case. On September 13, 1858, two slave-catchers, provided with the necessary papers, and accompanied by the proper officers, arrested a runaway near the town of Oberlin, in which he had been living for more than two years. News of the capture

[1] The *Cincinnati Enquirer*, the leading Democratic paper of southern Ohio at the time, said of the contention arising out of the attempted arrest of Addison White: "The designation of the attorney-general by Governor Chase to aid the lawyer retained by the sheriff of Clark County, is equivalent to a declaration of war on the part of Chase and his abolition crew against the United States Courts. Let war come, the sooner the better." Quoted in the *Life of Chase*, by J. W. Schuckers, p. 179, foot-note. Material relating to the Addison White case will be found in Shuckers, *Life of Chase*, pp. 177–182; Warden, *Life of Chase*, pp. 350, 351; Beer, *History of Clark County, Ohio;* the same quoted by Henry Howe in his *Historical Collections of Ohio*, Vol. I, pp. 384–386. The writer has also had the advantage of a conversation with Mrs. Amanda Shepherd (the daughter of Udney Hyde), who was an eye-witness of the attempts to capture White at her father's house.

was brought to Oberlin by two young men, who saw the negro in the hands of his captors as they were proceeding toward Wellington. A large crowd of men, among whom were several students and a professor of Oberlin College, took the trail of the slave-catchers, found them at Wellington, and without violence freed the slave. The arrest of a large number of the rescuers followed, and their arraignment took place before the United States District Court at Cleveland. Public sentiment was clearly with the prisoners, and their counsel were men of high rank in their profession. Two of the offenders were tried and convicted. On account of the state of feeling at the time, the legal proceedings were denounced as political trials. Mass-meetings were held throughout eastern Ohio to express the sympathy of the people with the rescuers, and to cast odium on the federal courts. The Dred Scott decision, recently rendered by the Supreme Court at Washington, called down upon that tribunal much condemnation. At an immense mass-convention held in Cleveland, May 24, 1859, resolutions were adopted, which accepted the compact theory of government voiced in the Virginia and Kentucky resolutions, declared the equal right of each party to the compact "to judge for itself, as well of infractions, as of the mode and measure of redress," and declared the Fugitive Slave Law of 1850 to be void because, "in the opinion of this assembly, passed by Congress in the exercise of powers improperly assumed."[1] A fund denominated "the Fund of Liberty" was created, to be applied in defence of the Oberlin rescuers, and a committee was appointed to take action for the release of those persons.

Meanwhile the grand jury of Lorain County — the county in which the fugitive had been seized — had indicted four of the slave-catchers under a personal liberty law passed by Ohio in 1857.[2] This procedure led to negotiations, which finally terminated in a compromise between the executors and the opponents of the Fugitive Slave Act. On the one hand the United States authorities agreed to stop prosecution in

[1] J. R. Shipherd, *History of the Oberlin-Wellington Rescue.* The resolutions appear at pp. 253, 254.
[2] *Ibid.*, pp. 231-235.

the remaining rescue cases, while on the other hand the Lorain County people consented to dismiss the suits against the so-called kidnappers. This conclusion of the matter was regarded as a victory for the "higher law" by the friends of the Oberlin parties, and the release of the prisoners was heralded in Cleveland by the firing of a hundred guns. Their return to Oberlin was signalized by a celebration in their honor. The *Cleveland Plain Dealer* said the government had been "beaten at last with law, justice, and facts all on its side, and Oberlin with its rebellious Higher Law creed is triumphant."[1]

That these events were not without their political influence is apparent from the adoption of a resolution at the great Cleveland convention above mentioned asserting that the chief reliance of freedom in the United States rested in the Republican party.[2] It is worthy of note also that this party at its state convention, held in June, demanded the repeal of the Fugitive Slave Act.[3] It has been already pointed out that some of the counsel of the Oberlin rescuers early received places of political preferment, partly at least in consequence of distinction won by them in the defence of those known to be guilty of violating the law of 1850.[4]

The enactment of personal liberty laws by various Northern states, with the purpose of impairing the efficiency of the Fugitive Slave laws, is characteristic of the period during which the underground system had its most rapid expansion, namely, the two decades from 1840 to 1860. These laws may be fairly considered as the palpable but guarded expression of an opposition that was free to go to the full length in its midnight operation of the Underground Road. During the period indicated occurred the series of celebrated fugitive slave cases, beginning with the Latimer case in 1842; and the precautions, rarely neglected by the friend of the slave, were often forgotten or spurned in the excitement of the instant or in the exaltation of wrath. The rigorous character of the law of 1850 acted in two ways north of Mason and Dixon's line:

[1] The *Plain Dealer*, July 6, 1859, quoted by Shipherd, p. 267.
[2] Shipherd, *History of the Oberlin-Wellington Rescue*, pp. 253, 254.
[3] The *Cleveland Herald*, June 3, 1859.   [4] Chapter IX, p. 282.

first, it created a reaction against slavery and brought many recruits into underground work to aid the rapidly increasing number of escaping slaves; second, in connection with the repeal of the Missouri Compromise, it led public sentiment in many states to provide additional safeguards in the form of personal liberty bills for the protection of fugitives and their helpers.[1] These bills ran counter in spirit if not always in letter to legislation that was held by the United States Supreme Court to be in keeping with the constitutional clause providing for the recovery of fugitive slaves. In principle they were, therefore, like the nullification ordinance of 1832.[2]

While the system of the Underground Railroad was thus expanding and pressing everywhere against legislative restraints, there arose a man who sought to solve the whole slavery problem in his own rash way. When John Brown led a company of slaves from Missouri to Canada despite the attempts to prevent him; and when soon thereafter he attempted to execute his plan for the general liberation of slaves, he showed the extreme to which the aid to fugitives might lead. The influence of Brown's training in Underground Railroad work is plain in the methods and plans he followed, which have given him a place in American history. Early convinced that action was the thing needed to help the bondman, he set himself to find a way of effecting the destruction of slavery. In devising his scheme he seems to have considered an underground channel of escape as a necessary feature of it for those lacking the courage to join a move-

[1] Joel Parker, *Personal Liberty Laws and Slavery in the Territories*, 1861, pp. 10, 11.

[2] J. B. Robinson, *Pictures of Slavery and Anti-Slavery*, 1863, pp. 332, 333; M. G. McDougall, *Fugitive Slaves*, p. 70; Rhodes, *History of the United States*, Vol. II, p. 74. Mr. Rhodes says of the personal liberty bills: "They were dangerously near the nullification of a United States law, and had not the provocation seemed great, would not have been adopted by people who had drunk in with approval Webster's idea of nationality. . . . While they were undeniably conceived in a spirit of bad faith towards the South, they were a retaliation for the grossly bad faith involved in the repeal of the Missouri Compromise. Nullification cannot be defended, but in a balancing of the wrongs of the South and the North, it must be averred that in this case the provocation was vastly greater than the retaliation."

CAPTAIN JOHN BROWN.
(From a photograph in the possession of the Kansas State Historical Society.)

ment sure to involve them in armed conflict with their masters. This feature was designated the "Subterranean Pass Way." The varying character of the testimony in regard to this feature, as well as the natural change of view that took place in Brown's mind with the passage of the years, does not permit one to say definitely what importance was attached by the liberator to the Pass Way as a part of his plan, but its utility in reducing the value of slaves must have been apparent to him. That the whole movement he contemplated would have the effect of making slave property unstable he showed when speaking of the initiative of the movement in Virginia. Brown said: "If the slaves could in this way be driven out of the county, the whole system would be weakened in that State."[1] In this matter the judgment of the liberator was not at fault, for it has been estimated that his attack on Harper's Ferry caused the value of slave property in Virginia to decline to the extent of $10,000,000.[2] That Brown had the sympathy of a large number of persons in the North, including some public men, was a circumstance calculated to make a deeper impression on the minds of the Southern men generally than this decline in the price of Virginia slaves.

[1] Hinton, *John Brown and His Men*, pp. 31, 32.
[2] *Ibid.*, p. 30.

CHAPTER XI

EFFECT OF THE UNDERGROUND RAILROAD

The effect of Underground Railroad operations in steadily withdrawing from the South some of its property and thus causing constant irritation to slave-owners and slave-traders has already been commented upon. The persons losing slaves of course regarded their losses as a personal and undeserved misfortune. Yet, considering the question broadly from the standpoint of their own interests, the work of the underground system was a relief to the masters and to the South. The possibility of a servile insurrection was a dreadful thing for Southern minds to contemplate; but they could not easily dismiss the terrible scenes enacted in San Domingo during the years 1791 to 1793 and the three famous uprisings of 1800, 1820 and 1831, in South Carolina and Virginia. The Underground Railroad had among its passengers such persons as Josiah Henson, J. W. Loguen, Frederick Douglass, Harriet Tubman, William Wells Brown and Henry Bibb; it therefore furnished the means of escape for persons well qualified for leadership among the slaves, and thereby lessened the danger of an uprising of the blacks against their masters. The negro historian, Williams, has said of the Underground Road that it served as a "safety-valve to the institution of slavery. As soon as leaders arose among the slaves, who refused to endure the yoke, they would go North. Had they remained, there must have been enacted at the South the direful scenes of San Domingo."[1]

It is difficult to arrive at any satisfactory idea of the actual loss sustained by slave-owners through underground channels. The charges of bad faith against the free states made in Congress by Southern members were sometimes accompanied

[1] *History of the Negro Race in America*, Vol. II, pp. 58, 59.

LOSS SUSTAINED BY SLAVE-OWNERS

by estimates of the amount of human property lost on account of the indisposition of those living north of Mason and Dixon's line to meet the requirements of the fugitive slave legislation. Thus as early as 1822, Moore, of Virginia, speaking in the House in favor of a new fugitive recovery law, said that the district he represented lost four or five thousand dollars worth of runaway slaves annually.[1] In August, 1850, Atchison, of Kentucky, informed the Senate that "depredations to the amount of hundreds of thousands of dollars are committed upon the property of the people of the border slave states of this Union annually."[2] Pratt, of Maryland, said that not less than $80,000 worth of slaves was lost every year by citizens of his state.[3] Mason, of Virginia, declared that the losses of his state were already too heavy to be borne, that they were increasing from year to year, and were then in excess of $100,000 per year.[4] Butler, of South Carolina, reckoned the annual loss of the Southern section at $200,000.[5] Clingman, of North Carolina, said that the thirty thousand fugitives then reported to be living in the North were worth at current prices little less than $15,000,000.[6] Claiborne, the biographer of General John A. Quitman, who was at one time governor of Louisiana, indicated as one of the defects of the second Fugitive Slave Law its failure to make "provision for the restitution to the South of the $30,000,000, of which she had been plundered through the 100,000 slaves abducted from her in the course of the last forty years" (1810-1850);[7] and the same writer stated that slavery was rapidly disappearing from the District of Columbia at the time of the enactment of the new law, the number of slaves "having been reduced since 1840 from

[1] Benton's *Abridgment of the Debates of Congress*, Vol. VII, p. 296.
[2] *Congressional Globe*, Thirty-first Congress, First Session, Appendix, p. 1601.
[3] *Ibid.*, p. 1603.
[4] *Ibid.*, p. 1605.
[5] Von Holst, *Constitutional and Political History of the United States*, Vol. III, p. 552.
[6] *Congressional Globe*, Thirty-first Congress, First Session, p. 202. See also Von Holst's work, Vol. III, p. 552, foot-note.
[7] J. F. H. Claiborne, *Life and Correspondence of John A. Quitman*, Vol. II, p. 28.

4,694 to 650, by 'underground railroads' and felonious abductions."[1]

The wide divergences among the estimates here given, as well as the obvious difficulty of getting reliable information in regard to the number of runaway slaves, renders these figures of little use in determining the loss of human property by the slaveholding states. Nevertheless, the estimates are valuable in illustrating the character of the complaints that were made in Congress, and in enabling one to realize that the tenure of slave property in the border states was rendered precarious by the operations of the Underground Railroad. Can it be thought strange that the disappearance week by week and month by month of valuable slaves over the unknown routes of the underground system should have produced wrath, suspicion and hostility in the minds of people who could justly claim to have a constitutional guarantee, the laws of Congress, and the decisions of the highest courts on their side?

In the compendiums of the United States Census for 1850 and 1860 are some statistics on fugitive slaves, which fall far short of the most moderate estimates of the Southerners, and flatly disagree with the testimony gathered from all other quarters. The official reports appear to show that the number of slaves escaping from their masters was small and inconsiderable, that it rapidly decreased, and that it was independent of proximity to a free population. But the censuses are not only opposed to the evidence, they are on their face inadequate.

If, as those tables indicate, only 1,011 slaves escaped from their masters in 1850, and only 803 in 1860, and in the latter year only 500 escaped from the border slave states, then it becomes impossible to understand the emphasis laid by Southern men upon the value of their runaway slaves, the steady pressure made by the border states for a more stringent law that resulted in the Fugitive Slave Act of 1850, and the allegation of bad faith on the part of the North put

---

[1] J. F. H. Claiborne, *Life and Correspondence of John A. Quitman*, Vol. II, p. 30. His figures are, of course, not correct.

forth by the Southern states as a reason for secession.[1] In considering the weight to be ascribed to the figures on fugitive slaves supplied by the census compendiums, it is proper to set over against them the showing afforded by the same compendiums relative to the decline of the slave population in the border slave states during the decade 1850–1860; for it is to be noted that the compendiums show a marked decline in these states, that they show a greater percentage of decline in the northernmost counties of these states than in the states as a whole, and, what is even more remarkable, that the loss appears to have been still greater during this time in the four "pan-handle" counties of Virginia than in any of the other states referred to, or in the border counties of any one of them.[2] It can scarcely be suggested that the relatively rapid decline of the slave population in the border counties was due to larger shipments of slaves to the far South from these marginal regions without at the same time suggesting that the explanation for such shipments lay in the proximity of a free population and the numerous lines of Underground Railroad maintained by it. The concurrence of evidence from sources other than the census reports, and the agreement therewith of part of the evidence gathered from these reports themselves, constrains one to say that those who compiled the statistics on fugitive slaves did not secure the facts in full; and that the complaints of large losses sustained by slave-owners through the befriending of fugitive slaves by Northern people, frequently made by Southern representatives in Congress and by the South generally, were not without sufficient foundation.

It is natural that there should be great variation among the guesses made as to the total number of those indebted for liberty to the Underground Road. Very few of the persons that harbored runaways were so indiscreet as to keep a register of their hunted visitors. Their hospitality was equal to all possible demands, but was kept strictly secret. Under these circumstances one should handle all numerical generalizations with caution.

[1] Census of 1860, pp. 11, 12. See Table A, Appendix C, p. 378.
[2] See Tables B and C, Appendix C, p. 379.

344 UNDERGROUND RAILROAD

4 mo. 14 — 1844 — John Osborn and wife and two children from Maysville Kentucky — 0 = 4

5 mo 8 A colored man and wife from Mason Co. Kentucky Ls - 2

5 mo 10 A colored man from Winchester Kentucky

5 mo. 25 = 4 colored men from Mason Co. Kentucky, one of them taken in Woodbury by the tobacco pedler — see R. 4   4

5 mo. 27 3 colored men — D. W. from Mason Co Kentucky   3

6 mo 3 2 colored men from Hunter Co. Kentucky — 0 2

6 mo 4 3 colored men from Tremble Co. Kentucky and 1 white man from Vixburg Mississippi 0. 4

6 mo. 15 A colored man from Kentucky driving carriage for an Oberlin Lady   1
see R.
3 months 21

8 mo 12 A colored man and boy from Kentucky, boy stoped at J. S. Hockins Ls.   2

RECORD OF FUGITIVES AIDED DURING FIVE MONTHS.

FACSIMILE OF OSBORN'S RECORD

8 mo 16 A colored man and wife and one child, 12 months old, and wife's sister from Kentucky — the man having been back from Gilead for them   4

8 mo. 21 A colored woman from Kentucky said she came all the way alone   1

8 mo 24 A colored woman who had been to Canada and went back and got four of her children and one grandchild, and a man and wife from Kentucky. D. B.   7

8 mo 25 five colored men from Kentucky   5

8 mo 28 A colored man from Kentucky   F.   1

9 mo 2 A colored man from Kentucky — M. D.

9 mo 4 two colored boys from Virginia L. 2

9 mo. 8 two colored boys from Kentucky L. 2

9 mo 10 one yellow man from Kentucky caught near Crotty's and carried back

KEPT BY DANIEL OSBORN, OF ALUM CREEK SETTLEMENT, OHIO.

By rare good fortune the writer has found a single leaf of a diary kept by Daniel Osborn, a Friend or Quaker, of Alum Creek Settlement, Delaware County, Ohio, which gives a record of the blacks passing through that neighborhood during an interval of five months, from April 14 to September 10, 1844. The accompanying facsimiles, which reproduce the two sides of the leaf, show that the number is forty-seven. The year in which this memorandum was made may be fairly taken as an average year, and the line on which this Quaker settlement was a station as a representative underground route in Ohio. Now, along Ohio's southern boundary there were the initial stations of at least twelve important lines of travel, some of which were certainly in operation before 1830. Let us consider, as we may properly, that the period of operation continued from 1830 to 1860. Taking these as the elements for a computation, one may reckon that Ohio may have aided not less than 40,000 fugitives in the thirty years included in our reckoning.[1] That the number of refugees after 1844 did not decrease is indicated by the statement that during one month in the year of 1854–1855 sixty were harbored by one member of the Alum Creek Settlement. It is to be remembered that several families of the settlement were engaged in this work.[2]

An illustration of underground activity in the East may be ventured. Mr. Robert Purvis, of Philadelphia, states that he kept a record of the fugitives that passed through the hands of the Vigilance Committee of Philadelphia for a long period, till the trepidation of his family after the passage of the Fugitive Slave Bill in 1850 caused him to destroy it. His record book showed, he says, an average of one a day sent northward. In other words, between 1830 and 1860 over 9,000 runaways were aided in Philadelphia. But we know that the Vigilance Committee did not begin this sort of work in the Quaker City, and that underground activities there date back at least to the time of Isaac T. Hopper's earliest efforts, that

[1] This computation was first printed by the writer in the *American Historical Review*, April, 1896, pp. 462, 463.
[2] Conversation with M. J. Benedict, L. A. Benedict and others, Alum Creek Settlement, Ohio, Dec. 2, 1893.

is, 1800 and before. We also know that there were many centres round about Philadelphia, some of whose work was certainly done independently of that place.

That the resources of some of the operators in centres in the West were being drained almost to exhaustion by the demands of the heavy traffic towards the close of the underground period, distinctly appears in the following letter from Col. J. Bowles, of Lawrence, Kansas, to Mr. F. B. Sanborn: —

LAWRENCE *April 4th* 1859

MR. F. B. SANBOURN

Dear Sir at the suggestion of friend Judge Conway I address you these few hastily written lines. I see I am expected to give you some information as to the present condition of the U. G. R. R. in Kansas or more particularly at the Lawrence depot. In order that you may fully understand the present condition of affairs I shall ask your permission to relate a small bit of the early history of this, the only *paying*, R. R. in Kansas.

Lawrence has been (from the first settlement of Kansas) known and cursed by all slave holders in and out of Mo. for being an abolition town. Missourians have a peculiar faculty for embracing every opportunity to denounce, curse, and *blow* every thing they dislike. This peculiar faculty of theirs gave Lawrence great notoriety in *Mo.* especially among the negroes to whom the principal part of their denunciations were directed and on whom they were intended to have great effect. I have learned from negroes who were *emigrating* from *Mo.* that they never would have known anything about a land of freedom or that they had a friend in the world only from their master's continual abuse of the Lawrence abolits. Slaves are usually very cunning and believe about as much as they please of what the master is telling him (thoug of course he must affect to believe every word) knowing it is to the master's interest to keep him ignorant of every thing that would make him likely or even wish to be free.

One old fellow said "when he started to come to Lawrence he didn't know if all de peoples in disha town war debbils as ole massa had said or not, but dis he did know if he could get dar safe old massa was fraid to come arter him, and if dey all should prove to be bad as ole massa had said he could lib wid dem bout as well as at home." Some few of them were unavoidably taken back to Mo. after leaving here for Iowa. Many of them found an opportunity to make their escape and bring others with them and none ever failed to be a successful missionary in the cause, telling every one he had a chance to converse with of the land of freedom, and the friends he found in Lawrence. One man I know well who has been captured twice and was shot each time in resisting his captors (one of whom he killed) told me that he was confident he had assisted in the escape of no less than twenty five of his fellow beings, and that he had also given information or sown the seed that would make a hundred more free men. He is now with some others in or about Canada. The last and successful escape was made from western Texas where he was sent for safe keeping. You can see from the above why L—— has had more than would seem to be her share of this good work to do. At first our means were limited and of course could not do much but then we were not so extensively known or patronized. As our means increased we found a corresponding increase in opportunity for doing good to the white man as well as the black. Kansas has been preëminently a land of charity. The friends in the East have helped such objects liberally yet Kansas has had much to do for herself in that line. To give you an idea of what has been done by the people of this place in U. G. R. R. I'll make a statement of the number of fugitives who have found assistance here. In the last four years I am personally known to [cognizant of] the fact of nearly three hundred fugitives having passed through and received assistance from the abolitionists here at Lawrence. Thus you see we have been continually strained to meet the heavy demands that were almost daily made upon us to carry on this (not very) *gradual emancipation.* I usually have assisted in collecting or begging money for the needy of either class. Many of the most zealous in the cause of humanity complained (as they had good cause to) that this heavy (and continually increasing) tax was interfering with their business to such a degree that they could not stand it longer and that other provisions must be made by which they would be relieved of a portion of a burden they had long bourn. This was about the state of affairs last Christmas when as you are aware the slaves have a few days holiday. Many of them chose this occasion to make a visit to Lawrence and during the week some twenty four came to our town, five or six of the number brought means to assist them on their journey. These were sent on, but the remainder must be kept until money could be raised to send them on. $150 was the am't necessary to send them to a place of safety. Under the circumstances it necessarily took some time to raise that am't, and a great many persons had to be applied to. It was not enough that the sympathies and love for the cause of humanity was appealed to in order to raise money, many had to be argued with and shown that the cause was actually in a suffering condition and the fugitives were then in town and the number must also be made known in order that the person might give liberally. Lawrence like most all towns has her bad men pimps and worst of all a few democrats, all of whom will do *anything* for money. Somewhere in the ranks of the intimate friends to the cause these traitors to God and humanity found a judas who for thirty pieces of silver did betray our cause. This was not suspected until after the capture of Dr Day. . . . Every thing goes to prove that the capture of Day's party was the work of a traitor who though suspected has not yet been fairly tried and *dealt* with as will be done as soon as Day is bailed out which will be done [in] a few days.

* * * * * * * * *

We would like . . . that you plead our cause with those of our friends who are disposed to censure us and convince them we are still worthy and in great need of their respect and coöperation. I am sorry to say (but tis true) that many of the most zealous in the cause of humanity have become somewhat discouraged by the hard times and the lamentable capture of Day and party and cannot be induced to take hold of it and lend a willing hand. Never the less the work has went slowly but surely on, until very recently. Those who have persevered like many others, have found *their* bottom dollar also of the money so generously contributed by persons of your notable society. This is partialy owing to heavy expenses of the trial of Dr Day and son which has been principally borne by the society here and has amounted to near $300. Now seems to be our dark day and we are casting about to see what can be done. We have some eight or ten fugitives now on hand who cannot be sent off until we get an addition to our financial department. This statement of facts has been made with a full knowledge of the many calls that is made upon your generosity in that quarter. Nothing shall be urged as an alternative for we feel confident the case here presented will meet with merited assistance sympathy or advice, as you may deem best. One word of old Brown and his movement in the emancipation cause, and I will have done. I understand from some parties who have been corresponding with some persons in Boston and other places in behalf of our cause that we could and would receive material aid only they are holding themselves in readiness to assist Brown. Such men I honor and they show themselves worthy the highest regard yet I assure them they do not understand Brown's plans for carrying out his cause. I have known Brown nearly four years, he is a bold cool calculating and far seeing man who is as consciencious as he is smart. He "knows the right and dare maintain it." I have talked confidentially with him on the subject. I know he expressed himself in this way as to the effects that he intended to make the master pay the way of the slave to the land of freedom. That is he intended to take property enough with the slaves to pay all expenses. So you see there is not fear of a large demand from that quarter. By no means would I be understood as counciling not to assist him. No indeed if I counciled at all it would be to this effect, render him all the assistance he ever asks for he is worthy and his cause is a good one. *Others* would have been with him only they had all they could do in another quarter. I feel myself highly honored to be placed where I can with propriety communicate with a society whom I have only known to admire. Hoping what I have written (disconnectedly and badly written as it is) may be acceptable and that I may hear from you soon. I am very respectfully Your obedient servant

J. Bowles
Lawrence

F. B. Sanbourn
Concord.

The success of the Underground Road in transporting negroes beyond the limits of the Southern states was long ago commented upon as standing in marked contrast with that of the American Colonization Society. This association was organized in 1816, and soon had auxiliary societies in most of the states. Its object was to remove the free blacks and such as might be made free from the South, and colonize them on the coast of Africa. By 1857, after an existence of forty years, the Colonization Society had sent to Africa 9,502 emigrants, of whom 3,676 were free-born, 326 self-purchased, and 5,500 emancipated on condition of being transported. That the informal method of the abolitionists was many times as efficient as that adopted by the organization mentioned, with its treasury and its board of officers, cannot be denied.[1]

By actual count it is found that the number of persons within the limits of Ohio named as underground workers in the collections upon which this book is based, is about 1,540; in all other states taken together the number found is 1,670. It is proper to observe that these figures are minimum figures. Death and infirmity, as well as removal, have carried many unknown operators beyond the chance of discovery.

It is not surprising that the secret enterprises of this determined class of people — so effectual as to make rare the pursuit of a fugitive during the last years of the decade preceding the War[2] — should have become the ground of an important charge against the North in the crisis of 1860. The violation of the Fugitive Slave Law was an accusation upon which Southern members of Congress rang all the changes in the course of the violent debates of the sessions of 1860–1861. Thus Jones, of Georgia, said in the House in April, 1860: "It is a notorious fact that in a good many of the non-slaveholding states the Republican party have regularly organized societies — underground railroads — for the avowed purpose of stealing the slaves from the border States, and carrying them off to a free State or to Canada. These predatory bands are kept up by private and public subscriptions among the Abolitionists; and in many of the States, I am sorry to say, they receive the sanction and protection of the law. The border States lose annually thousands and millions of dollars' worth of property by this system of larceny that has been carried on for years." Polk, of Missouri, whose state had suffered not a little through the flight and abduction of slaves, made the same complaint in the Senate in January, 1861: "Underground railroads are established," said he, "stretching from the remotest slaveholding States clear up

---

[1] E. M. Pettit, *Sketches in the History of the Underground Railroad*, Introduction, p. xi. Wilson gives an account of the American Colonization Society in his *Rise and Fall of the Slave Power*, Vol. I, pp. 208–222; see also the *Life of Garrison*, by his children, Index.

[2] McDougall, *Fugitive Slaves*, p. 71.

to Canada. Secret agencies are put to work in the very midst of our slaveholding communities to steal away slaves. The constitutional obligation for the rendition of the fugitive from service is violated. The laws of Congress enacted to carry this provision of the Constitution into effect are not executed. Their execution is prevented. Prevented, first, by hostile and unconstitutional state legislation. Secondly, by a vitiated public sentiment. Thirdly, by the concealing of the slave, so that the United States law cannot be made to reach him. And when the runaway is arrested under the fugitive slave law — which, however, is seldom the case — he is very often rescued. . . . This lawlessness is felt with special seriousness in the border slave States. The underground railroads start mostly from these States. Hundreds of thousands of dollars are lost annually. And no State loses more heavily than my own. Kentucky, it is estimated, loses annually as much as $200,000. The other border States no doubt lose in the same ratio, Missouri much more. But all these losses and outrages, all this disregard of constitutional obligation and social duty, are as nothing in their bearing upon the Union in comparison with the animus, the intent and purpose of which they are at once the fruit and the evidence. . . ."[1] Of this animus the election of Lincoln was regarded as the crowning proof; and it became, as is well known, the signal for secession.

In December, 1860, the very month in which South Carolina chose to withdraw from the Union, the arrest of a runaway negro in Canada gave rise to an extradition case that became an additional cause of excitement. The negro was William Anderson, who in 1853 had been caught without a pass in Missouri, and had killed the man that tried to capture him. In 1860 he was recognized in Canada by a slave-catcher from Missouri, was arrested on the charge of murder, and thrown into jail at Toronto. As the Ashburton treaty contained an article providing for the extradition of slaves guilty of crimes committed in the United States, the American government sought to secure the surrender of

[1] *Congressional Globe*, Thirty-sixth Congress, Second Session, p. 356; see also *ibid.*, Appendix, p. 197.

Anderson for punishment. Lord Elgin, Governor-General of Canada at the time, was appealed to in the fugitive's behalf by Mrs. Laura S. Haviland. He made a spirited reply to the effect that "in case of a demand for William Anderson, he should require the case to be tried in their British court; and if twelve freeholders should testify that he had been a man of integrity since his arrival in their dominion, it should clear him." Nevertheless, the case was twice decided against the defendant, first by the common magistrate's court, then by the Court of Error and Appeal, to which it had been carried on a writ of habeas corpus. But this did not end the matter. Through the efforts of the fugitive's friends application was made for a writ of habeas corpus to the English Court of the Queen's Bench, and the writ was granted. Anderson was defended by Gerrit Smith, whose eloquent speech produced a profound impression in Canada, and did not fail to attract considerable notice in all parts of the United States.[1]

During the month of December, in which the Anderson case came into prominence, the example of secession set by South Carolina was followed by five other cotton states. Meantime Congress was giving unmistakable evidence of the importance attaching to the fugitive slave question. In his message of December 4, President Buchanan gave serious consideration to this question, although he insisted that the Fugitive Slave Law had been duly enforced in every contested case during his administration.[2] He recommended an "explanatory amendment" to the Constitution affording "recognition of the right of the master to have his slave who has escaped from one state to another restored and 'delivered up' to him, and of the validity of the Fugitive Slave Law enacted for this purpose, together with a declaration that all State laws impairing or defeating this right, are violations of

[1] Accounts of Anderson's case will be found in a collection of pamphlets in the Boston Public Library; in the *Liberator*, Dec. 3, 1860 and Jan. 22, 1861; in *A Woman's Life Work*, by Laura S. Haviland, pp. 207, 208; in the *History of Canada*, by J. M. McMullen, Vol. II, p. 259; in the *History of Canada*, by John MacMullen, p. 553; and in *Fugitive Slaves*, by M. G. McDougall, pp. 25, 26.

[2] *Journal of the Senate*, Thirty-sixth Congress, Second Session, p. 10.

the Constitution, and are consequently null and void."[1] On December 12 not less than eleven resolutions were introduced into the House on this subject, and on December 13, 18 and 24 other resolutions followed. Resolutions of a similar nature continued to be presented in both Houses during January and February of the succeeding year, ceasing only with the end of the session.[2]

These efforts on the part of the national legislature to appease the spirit of secession in the South were paralleled by efforts equally futile on the part of various Northern state legislatures during the same period. It was reported that towards the close of the year 1860 a caucus of governors of seven Republican states was held in New York City, and decided to recommend to their legislatures "the unconditional and early repeal of the personal liberty bills passed by their respective states." As a matter of fact this recommendation was made by the Republican governors of four states, Maine, Massachusetts, New York and Illinois, and the Democratic governors of Rhode Island and Pennsylvania. Rhode Island repealed her personal liberty law in January, 1861; Massachusetts modified hers in March; and was followed by Vermont, which took similar action in April. Ohio had repealed her act in 1858, but her legislature seized this opportunity to urge her sister states to cancel any of their statutes "conflicting with or rendering less efficient the Constitution or the laws."[3] The conciliation of the South was clearly the purpose of these measures, but action came too late, for confidence between the sections had already been destroyed.

The fact that the border slave states, with the exception of Virginia, remained in the Union, must not be interpreted as indicating small losses of human property by these states. The strong ties existing between the states lying on either side of the sectional line, the presence of a rigorous Union sentiment in Kentucky, western Virginia and the slaveholding regions lying east and west of these, together with the hope

---

[1] *Journal of the Senate*, Thirty-sixth Congress, Second Session, p. 18.
[2] For a complete list of these resolutions see Mrs. McDougall's monograph on *Fugitive Slaves*, Appendix, pp. 117-119.
[3] Rhodes, *History of the United States*, Vol. III, pp. 252, 253.

of a new compromise entertained by these states, tended to keep them in their places in the Union. The prospect of a stampede of slaves, in case they should join the secession movement, was a consideration that may be supposed to have had some weight in fixing the decision of the border slave states. Certainly it was one to which Northern men attached considerable importance at the time in explaining the steadfast position of these states; and the impossibility of recovering even a single fugitive from the free states in case of a disruption of the Union along Mason and Dixon's line was a thing of which Southern members of the national House were duly reminded by their Northern colleagues.

The retention of the loyalty of the border slave states was a matter of grave concern to President Lincoln, who sought first of all the preservation of the Union. In his inaugural address Lincoln had declared his purpose to see to it that the Fugitive Slave Law was executed, and when a few months later an opportunity presented itself he kept his promise. Congress also realized the need of caution on account of the border states, and moved slowly in framing general enactments. The changed conditions surrounding the slaves, due to the marshalling of forces for the War and the advance of Northern troops into the enemy's country, multiplied the chances for escape throughout the South, and removed the necessity for a long and perilous journey by the slaves to find friends. Negroes from the plantations of both loyal and disloyal masters flocked to the camps of Union soldiers, and could not be separated. Under such circumstances the need of uniformity of method in dealing with cases early became apparent. The War had scarcely more than commenced when protests began to be made against the employment of Northern troops as slave-catchers. A letter read in the Senate by Mr. Sumner, in December, 1861, made inquiry, "Shall our sons, who are offering their lives for the preservation of our institutions, be degraded to slave-catchers for any persons, loyal or disloyal? If such is the policy of the government, I shall urge my son to shed no more blood for its preservation."[1] Two German companies in one of the Massachusetts regi-

[1] *Congressional Globe*, Thirty-seventh Congress, First Session, p. 30.

ments also entered protest, making it a condition of their enlistment that they should not be required to perform such discreditable service. "They complained, and with them the German population generally throughout the country." [1] The inexpediency of the return of fugitives by the army was recognized by Congress in the early part of 1862, and a bill forbidding officers from restoring them under any consideration was signed by the President on May 14, 1862.[2]

The various acts of Congress and the President relative to fugitive slaves down to the Proclamation of Emancipation, practically circumscribed the legal effect of the Fugitive Slave laws to the border states, for in the free states the laws had not been observed for a long time. It was not until June, 1864, that these measures were swept from the statute-book of the nation, notwithstanding the insistence of Kentucky and the other loyal states of the South that a constitutional obligation rested upon the government to retain them. The repeal act did not remove this obligation. Such a result could come only with the extinction of slavery, and the last vestige of slavery did not disappear until the adoption of the Thirteenth Amendment to the Constitution in 1865. The Amendment provides: "Neither slavery nor involuntary servitude, except as a punishment for crime, whereof the party shall have been duly convicted, shall exist within the United States or any place subject to their jurisdiction."

The general significance of the long controversy in regard to fugitive slaves can best be understood by tracing the development as a sectional issue of the question at the bottom of it, namely, the obligation to restore fugitives to their masters. The creation of a line dividing the free North from the slaveholding South in the early years of our national history, and the enactment of the first Fugitive Slave Law, by which the general government assumed a certain responsibility for runaways, led to the opening of the question. From that time

---

[1] *Congressional Globe*, Thirty-seventh Congress, First Session, p. 30; see also M. G. McDougall's *Fugitive Slaves*, p. 79.

[2] *House Journal*, Thirty-seventh Congress, Second Session, p. 265; *Senate Journal*, Thirty-seventh Congress, Second Session, p. 285; *Congressional Globe*, Thirty-seventh Congress, Second Session, p. 1243.

on, the steadily increasing number of escapes, together with the spread of the underground system, which made these escapes almost uniformly successful, kept the question open. Operations along the secret lines constantly caused aggravation in the South; and the pursuit of passengers, mobs and violence were results widely witnessed in the North. The other questions between the sections were subject to compromise, but party action could not control the workings of the Underground Railroad. The stirring sights and affecting stories with which the North became acquainted through the stealthy migration of slaves were well adapted to make abolitionists rapidly, and the consequence was more aggravation on both sides. The practice of midnight emancipation in Northern states during the early years was accompanied, not unnaturally, with the formulation and statement of the principle of immediatism in neighborhoods where underground methods were familiar. Thus the way was prepared for Garrison and his talented coworkers, whose eloquent tongues and pens could no more be controlled by pro-slavery forces than could the Underground Railroad itself. Agitation reacted upon the Road and increased its activity; this caused counter agitation by Southerners in and out of Congress until a more rigorous Fugitive Slave Law was secured.

The Compromise of 1850 failed to reconcile the sections: Northern men despised the Fugitive Slave Law, and displayed greater zeal than ever before in aiding runaway slaves. Thus, in the later stages of the controversy, as from its beginning, the fugitive was a successful missionary in the cause of freedom. Personal liberty laws were passed by the free states to defend him; *Uncle Tom's Cabin* was written to portray to the world his aspirations for liberty and his endeavors to secure it; John Brown devised a "subterranean pass way" to assist him, as a part of the great scheme of liberation that failed at Harper's Ferry. One of the chief reasons for withdrawing from the Union assigned by the seceding states was the bad faith of the North in refusing to surrender fugitives. At the outbreak of the Civil War large numbers of slaves sought refuge with the Union forces, the government soon found it impracticable to restore them, and disavowed all responsibility for them in 1862. By the Proclamation of Emancipation slavery was abolished within the area of the disloyal states, and the controversy became merely formal, the loyal slave states striving to maintain an abstract right based by them upon the Constitution. In 1864, however, they were forced to yield, and the fugitive slave legislation was repealed. The year following witnessed the cancellation of the fugitive slave clause in the Constitution by the amendment of that instrument. In view of all this it is safe to say that the Underground Railroad was one of the greatest forces which brought on the Civil War, and thus destroyed slavery.

APPENDIX A

CONSTITUTIONAL PROVISIONS AND NATIONAL ACTS RELATIVE TO FUGITIVE SLAVES, 1787-1850

Fugitive Clause in Northwest Ordinance of 1787. [Chapter II, p. 20.]

1787, July 13. Art. VI. " There shall be neither slavery nor involuntary servitude in the said Territory, otherwise than in the punishment of crimes, whereof the party shall have been duly convicted; *provided*, always, that any person escaping into the same, from whom labor or service is lawfully claimed in any one of the original States, such fugitive may be lawfully reclaimed and conveyed to the person claiming his or her labor or service aforesaid." Read first time, July 11, 1787. Passed July 13, 1787. — *Journals of Congress*, XII, 84, 92.

Fugitive Clause in the Constitution. [Chapter II, p. 20.]

1787, Sept. 13. Art. IV, § 2. "No person held to service or labor in one State, under the laws thereof, escaping into another, shall, in consequence of any law or regulation therein, be discharged from such service or labor, but shall be delivered up on claim of the party to whom such service or labor may be due." — *Revised Statutes of the United States*, I, 18.

First Fugitive Slave Act. [Chapter II, p. 21.]

1793, Feb. 12. *An Act respecting fugitives from justice and persons escaping from the service of their masters.*

" SECTION 1. *Be it enacted by the Senate and House of Representatives of the United States of America in Congress assembled,* That whenever the executive authority of any state in the Union, or of either of the territories northwest or south of the river Ohio, shall demand any person as a fugitive from justice, of the executive authority of any such state or territory to which such person shall have fled, and shall moreover produce the copy of an indictment found, or an affidavit made before a magistrate of any state or territory as aforesaid, charging the person

359

so demanded, with having committed treason, felony or other crime, certified as authentic by the governor or chief magistrate of the state or territory from whence the person so charged fled, it shall be the duty of the executive authority of the state or territory to which such person shall have fled, to cause him or her to be arrested and secured, and notice of the arrest to be given to the executive authority making such demand, or to the agent of such authority appointed to receive the fugitive, and to cause the fugitive to be delivered to such agent when he shall appear: But if no such agent shall appear within six months from the time of the arrest, the prisoner may be discharged. And all costs or expenses incurred in the apprehending, securing, and transmitting such fugitive to the state or territory making such demand, shall be paid by such state or territory.

"SEC. 2. *And be it further enacted*, That any agent, appointed as aforesaid, who shall receive the fugitive into his custody, shall be empowered to transport him or her to the state or territory from which he or she shall have fled. And if any person or persons shall by force set at liberty, or rescue the fugitive from such agent while transporting, as aforesaid, the person or persons so offending shall, on conviction, be fined not exceeding five hundred dollars, and be imprisoned not exceeding one year.

"SEC. 3. *And be it also enacted*, That when a person held to labour in any of the United States, or in either of the territories on the northwest or south of the river Ohio, under the laws thereof, shall escape into any other of the said states or territory, the person to whom such labour or service may be due, his agent or attorney, is hereby empowered to seize or arrest such fugitive from labour, and to take him or her before any judge of the circuit or district courts of the United States, residing or being within the state, or before any magistrate of a county, city or town corporate, wherein such seizure or arrest shall be made, and upon proof to the satisfaction of such judge or magistrate, either by oral testimony or affidavit taken before and certified by a magistrate of any such state or territory, that the person so seized or arrested, doth, under the laws of the state or territory from which he or she fled, owe service or labour to the person claiming him or her, it shall be the duty of such judge or magistrate to give a certificate thereof to such claimant, his agent or attorney, which shall be sufficient warrant for removing the said fugitive from labour, to the state or territory from which he or she fled.

"SEC. 4. *And be it further enacted*, That any person who shall knowingly and willingly obstruct or hinder such claimant, his agent or attorney, in so seizing or arresting such fugitive from labour, or shall rescue such fugitive from such claimant, his agent or attorney, when so arrested pursuant to the authority herein given or declared; or shall harbour or conceal such person after notice that he or she was a fugitive from labour, as aforesaid, shall, for either of the said offences, forfeit and pay the sum of five hundred dollars. Which penalty may be recovered by and for the benefit of such claimant, by action of debt, in any court proper to try the same; saving moreover to the person claiming such labour or service, his right of action for or on account of the said injuries or either of them."— *Statutes at Large*, I, 302–305.

Fugitive Slave Clause in the Missouri Compromise.
[Chapter X, p. 298.]

1820, March 19. The Missouri Compromise provided "that any persons escaping into the same, from whom labor or service is lawfully claimed in any State or Territory of the United States, such fugitive may be lawfully reclaimed, and conveyed to the person claiming his or her labor, or service, as aforesaid." — *Annals of Congress*, 16 *Cong.* 1 *Sess.*, 1469, 1587.

Second Fugitive Slave Act. [Chapter II, p. 22.]

1850, Sept. 18. *"An Act to amend, and supplementary to, the Act entitled 'An Act respecting Fugitives from Justice, and Persons escaping from the Service of their Masters,' approved February twelfth, one thousand seven hundred and ninety-three.*

" Be it enacted by the Senate and House of Representatives of the United States of America in Congress assembled, That the persons who have been, or may hereafter be, appointed commissioners, in virtue of any act of Congress, by the Circuit Courts of the United States, and who, in consequence of such appointment, are authorized to exercise the powers that any justice of the peace, or other magistrate of any of the United States, may exercise in respect to offenders for any crime or offence against the United States, by arresting, imprisoning, or bailing the same under and by virtue of the thirty-third section of the act of the twenty-fourth of September, seventeen hundred and eighty-nine, entitled 'An Act to establish the judicial courts of the United States,' shall be, and are hereby, authorized and required to exercise and discharge all the powers and duties conferred by this act.

"Sec. 2. *And be it further enacted*, That the Superior Court of each organized Territory of the United States shall have the same power to appoint commissioners to take acknowledgments of bail and affidavits, and to take depositions of witnesses in civil causes, which is now possessed by the Circuit Court of the United States; and all commissioners who shall hereafter be appointed for such purposes by the Superior Court of any organized Territory of the United States, shall possess all the powers, and exercise all the duties, conferred by law upon the commissioners appointed by the Circuit Courts of the United States for similar purposes, and shall moreover exercise and discharge all the powers and duties conferred by this act.

"Sec. 3. *And be it further enacted*, That the Circuit Courts of the United States, and the Superior Courts of each organized Territory of the United States, shall from time to time enlarge the number of commissioners, with a view to afford reasonable facilities to reclaim fugitives from labor, and to the prompt discharge of the duties imposed by this act.

"Sec. 4. *And be it further enacted*, That the commissioners above named shall have concurrent jurisdiction with the judges of the Circuit and District Courts of the United States, in their respective circuits and districts within the several States, and the judges of the Superior Courts of the Territories, severally and collectively, in term-time and vacation; and shall grant certificates to such claimants, upon satisfactory proof being made, with authority to take and remove such fugitives from service or labor, under the restrictions herein contained, to the State or Territory from which such persons may have escaped or fled.

"Sec. 5. *And be it further enacted*, That it shall be the duty of all marshals and deputy marshals to obey and execute all warrants and precepts issued under the provisions of this act, when to them directed; and should any marshal or deputy marshal refuse to receive such warrant, or other process, when tendered, or to use all proper means diligently to execute the same, he shall, on conviction thereof, be fined in the sum of one thousand dollars, to the use of such claimant, on the motion of such claimant by the Circuit or District Court for the district of such marshal; and after arrest of such fugitive, by such marshal or his deputy, or whilst at any time in his custody under the provisions of this act, should such fugitive escape, whether with or without the assent of such marshal or his deputy, such marshal shall be liable, on his official bond, to be prosecuted for the benefit of such claimant, for the full value of the service or labor of said fugitive in the State, Territory, or District whence he escaped: and the better to enable the said commissioners, when thus appointed, to execute their duties faithfully and efficiently, in conformity with the requirements of the Constitution of the United States and of this act, they are hereby authorized and empowered, within their counties respectively, to appoint, in writing under their hands, any one or more suitable persons, from time to time, to execute all such warrants and other process as may be issued by them in the lawful performance of their respective duties; with authority to such commissioners, or the persons to be appointed by them, to execute process as aforesaid, to summon and call to their aid the bystanders, or *posse comitatus* of the proper county, when necessary to insure a faithful observance of the clause of the Constitution referred to, in conformity with the provisions of this act;

and all good citizens are hereby commanded to aid and assist in the prompt and efficient execution of this law, whenever their services may be required, as aforesaid, for that purpose; and said warrants shall run, and be executed by said officers, anywhere in the State within which they are issued.

"SEC. 6. *And be it further enacted,* That when a person held to service or labor in any State or Territory of the United States, has heretofore or shall hereafter escape into another State or Territory of the United States, the person or persons to whom such service or labor may be due, or his, her, or their agent or attorney, duly authorized, by power of attorney, in writing, acknowledged and certified under the seal of some legal officer or court of the State or Territory in which the same may be executed, may pursue and reclaim such fugitive person, either by procuring a warrant from some one of the courts, judges, or commissioners aforesaid, of the proper circuit, district, or county, for the apprehension of such fugitive from service or labor, or by seizing and arresting such fugitive, where the same can be done without process, and by taking, or causing such person to be taken, forthwith before such court, judge, or commissioner, whose duty it shall be to hear and determine the case of such claimant in a summary manner; and upon satisfactory proof being made, by deposition or affidavit, in writing, to be taken and certified by such court, judge, or commissioner, or by other satisfactory testimony, duly taken and certified by some court, magistrate, justice of the peace, or other legal officer authorized to administer an oath and take depositions under the laws of the State or Territory from which such person owing service or labor may have escaped, with a certificate of such magistracy or other authority, as aforesaid, with the seal of the proper court or officer thereto attached, which seal shall be sufficient to establish the competency of the proof, and with proof, also by affidavit, of the identity of the person whose service or labor is claimed to be due as aforesaid, that the person so arrested does in fact owe service or labor to the person or persons claiming him or her, in the State or Territory from which such fugitive may have escaped as aforesaid, and that said person escaped, to make out and deliver to such claimant, his or her agent or attorney, a certificate setting forth the substantial facts as to the service or labor due from such fugitive to the claimant, and of his or her escape from the State or Territory in which such service or labor was due, to the State or Territory in which he or she was arrested, with authority to such claimant, or his or her agent or attorney, to use such reasonable force and restraint as may be necessary, under the circumstances of the case, to take and remove such fugitive person back to the State or Territory whence he or she may have escaped as aforesaid. In no trial or hearing under this act shall the testimony of such alleged fugitive be admitted in evidence; and the certificates in this and the first [fourth] section mentioned, shall be conclusive of the right of the person or persons in whose favor granted, to remove such fugitive to the State or Territory from which he escaped, and shall prevent all molestation of such person or persons by any process issued by any court, judge, magistrate, or other person whomsoever.

"SEC. 7. *And be it further enacted*, That any person who shall knowingly and willingly obstruct, hinder, or prevent such claimant, his agent or attorney, or any person or persons lawfully assisting him, her, or them, from arresting such a fugitive from service or labor, either with or without process as aforesaid, or shall rescue, or attempt to rescue, such fugitive from service or labor, from the custody of such claimant, his or her agent or attorney, or other person or persons lawfully assisting as aforesaid, when so arrested, pursuant to the authority herein given and declared; or shall aid, abet, or assist such person so owing service or labor as aforesaid, directly or indirectly, to escape from such claimant, his agent or attorney, or other person or persons legally authorized as aforesaid; or shall harbor or conceal such fugitive, so as to prevent the discovery and arrest of such person, after notice or knowledge of the fact that such person was a fugitive from service or labor as aforesaid, shall, for either of said offences, be subject to a fine not exceeding one thousand dollars, and imprisonment not exceeding six months, by indictment and conviction before the District Court of the United States for the district in which such offence may have been committed, or before the proper court of criminal jurisdiction, if committed within any one of the organized Territories of the United States; and shall moreover forfeit and pay, by way of civil damages to the party injured by such illegal conduct, the sum of one thousand dollars, for each fugitive so lost as aforesaid, to be recovered by action of debt, in any of the District or Territorial Courts aforesaid, within whose jurisdiction the said offence may have been committed.

"SEC. 8. *And be it further enacted*, That the marshals, their deputies, and the clerks of the said District and Territorial Courts, shall be paid, for their services, the like fees as may be allowed to them for similar services in other cases; and where such services are rendered exclusively in the arrest, custody, and delivery of the fugitive to the claimant, his or her agent or attorney, or where such supposed fugitive may be discharged out of custody for the want of sufficient proof as aforesaid, then such fees are to be paid in the whole by such claimant, his agent or attorney; and in all cases where the proceedings are before a commissioner, he shall be entitled to a fee of ten dollars in full for his services in each case, upon the delivery of the said certificate to the claimant, his or her agent or attorney; or a fee of five dollars in cases where the proof shall not, in the opinion of such commissioner, warrant such certificate and delivery, inclusive of all services incident to such arrest and examination, to be paid, in either case, by the claimant, his or her agent or attorney. The person or persons authorized to execute the process to be issued by such commissioners for the arrest and detention of fugitives from service or labor as aforesaid, shall also be entitled to a fee of five dollars each for each person he or they may arrest and take before any such commissioner as aforesaid, at the instance and request of such claimant, with such other fees as may be deemed reasonable by such commissioner for such other additional services as may be necessarily performed by him or them; such as attending at the examination, keeping the fugitive in custody, and providing him with food and lodging during his detention, and until the final determination of such commissioner; and, in general, for performing such other duties as may be required by such claimant, his or her attorney or agent, or commissioner in the premises, such fees to be made up in conformity with the fees usually charged by the officers of the courts of justice within the proper district or county, as near as may be practicable, and paid by such claimants, their agents or attorneys, whether such supposed fugitives from service or labor be ordered to be delivered to such claimants by the final determination of such commissioners or not.

"SEC. 9. *And be it further enacted*, That, upon affidavit made by the claimant of such fugitive, his agent or attorney, after such certificate has been issued, that he has reason to apprehend that such fugitive will be rescued by force from his or their possession before he can be taken beyond the limits of the State in which the arrest is made, it shall be the duty of the officer making the arrest to retain such fugitive in his custody, and to remove him to the State whence he fled, and there to deliver him to said claimant, his agent, or attorney. And to this end, the officer aforesaid is hereby authorized and required to employ so many persons as he may deem necessary to overcome such force, and to retain them in his service so long as circumstances may require. The said officer and his assistants, while so employed, to receive the same compensation, and to be allowed the same expenses, as are now allowed by law for transportation of criminals, to be certified by the judge of the district within which the arrest is made, and paid out of the treasury of the United States.

"SEC. 10. *And be it further enacted*, That when any person held to service or labor in any State or Territory, or in the District of Columbia, shall escape therefrom, the party to whom such service or labor shall be due, his, her, or their agent or attorney, may apply to any court of record therein, or judge thereof in vacation, and make satisfactory proof to such court, or judge in vacation, of the escape aforesaid, and that the person escaping owed service or labor to such party. Whereupon the court shall cause a record to be made of the matters so proved, and also a general description of the person so escaping, with such convenient certainty as may be; and a transcript of such record, authenticated by the attestation of the clerk and of the seal of the said court, being produced in any other State, Territory, or district in which the person so escaping may be found, and being exhibited to any judge, commissioner, or other officer authorized by the law of the United States to cause persons escaping from service or labor to be delivered up, shall be held and taken to be full and conclusive evidence of the fact of escape, and that the service or labor of the person escaping is due to the party in such record mentioned. And upon the production by the said party of other and further evidence if necessary, either oral or by affidavit, in addition to what is contained in the said record of the identity of the person escaping, he or she shall be delivered up to the claimant. And the said court, commissioner, judge, or other person authorized by this act to grant certificates to claimants of fugitives, shall, upon the production of the record and other evidences aforesaid, grant to such claimant a certificate of his right to take any such person identified and proved to be owing service or labor as aforesaid, which certificate shall authorize such claimant to seize or arrest and transport such person to the State or Territory from which he escaped: *Provided*, That nothing herein contained shall be construed as requiring the production of a transcript of such record as evidence as aforesaid. But in its absence the claim shall be heard and determined upon other satisfactory proofs, competent in law.

"Approved, September 18, 1850."— *Statutes at Large*, IX, 462–465.

APPENDIX B

LIST OF IMPORTANT FUGITIVE SLAVE CASES

THE following list is not intended to be exhaustive: it by no means includes all the cases illustrative of the work of the Underground Road, but it represents fairly well the various phases of that work, and does not intentionally omit any of the famous cases. Less than one half of the list here given will be found in Mrs. McDougall's *Fugitive Slaves*, Appendix D, pp. 124-128.

1. Early escape to Canada.

1748. Negro servant escapes from the English to Canada: *New York Colonial Manuscripts*, X, 209.

2. Case of ship *Friendship*.

1770. Harbored a slave: Moore, *Slavery in Massachusetts*, 117.

3. Somersett case.

1772. England refuses to return a fugitive slave: Moore, *Slavery in Massachusetts*, 117; Cobb, *Historical Sketch of Slavery*, 163; Goodell, *Slavery and Anti-Slavery*, 44-52; Hurd, *Law of Freedom and Bondage*, I, 189-193; Broom, *Constitutional Law*, 6-119; Howells, *State Trials*, XX, 1; Taswell-Langmead, *English Constitutional History*, 300, n.

4. Dalby's fugitive.

1786. Aided by Quakers in Philadelphia: Sparks, *Washington*, IX, 158; Applegarth, *Quakers of Pennsylvania*, 463.

5. Slave escaped from Drayton.

1786. Difficult to apprehend because, as Washington declared, there were "numbers who would rather facilitate the escape of slaves than apprehend them when runaways." Lund, *Origin of the Late War*, I, 20.

6. First recorded case of rescue. (Quincy's case.)

1793. Alleged fugitive rescued from the court-room in Boston: Edw. C. Learned, *Speech on the New Fugitive Slave Law*, Chicago, Oct. 25, 1850; Whittier, *Prose Works*, II, 129, "A Chapter of History"; Goodell, *Slavery and Anti-Slavery*, 232; *Boston Atlas*, Oct. 15, 1850; McDougall, *Fugitive Slaves*, 35.

7. Washington's fugitive.

1796, October. Public sentiment in Portsmouth, New Hampshire, prevents the return of a fugitive slave to President Washington: *Maga-*

zine of American History, December, 1877, p. 759; Charles Sumner, *Works*, III, 177; McDougall, *Fugitive Slaves*, 35.

8. Columbia case.

1804. General Boude defends a runaway: Smedley, *Underground Railroad*, 26.

9. Case of Wright *vs.* Deacon.

1819. Trial before Supreme Court of Pennsylvania to determine status of an alleged runaway: 5 Sergeant and Rawle's *Reports*, 63.

10. Case of Hill *vs.* Low.

1822. Action brought in Circuit Court of the United States for the Eastern District of Pennsylvania for penalty under the law of 1793 for obstructing arrest of a fugitive: 4 Washington's *Circuit Court Reports*, 327.

11. Case of Commonwealth *vs.* Griffith.

1823. Prosecution in Supreme Judicial Court of Massachusetts of a slave-catcher for seizing without a warrant a runaway in New Bedford: 2 Pickering's *Reports*, 15.

12. Escape of Tice Davids.

1831. Mysterious disappearance of a slave at Ripley, Ohio, leads to the naming of the Underground Railroad: Rush R. Sloane, *Firelands Pioneer*, July, 1888, p. 35.

13. Dayton (Ohio) case.

1832, January. Rendition of the fugitive, Thomas Mitchell, at Dayton, Ohio, followed by the suicide of the negro, at Cincinnati, when on his way back to slavery: Howe, *Historical Collections of Ohio*, II, 554, 555.

14. Case of Johnson *vs.* Tompkins.

1833. Prosecution of a claimant for seizure and removal of his escaped slave from Pennsylvania to New Jersey; followed by counter prosecution of the abolitionists before Circuit Court of the United States: 1 Baldwin's *Circuit Court Reports*, 571; 13 *Federal Cases*, 840.

15. Case of Jack *vs.* Martin.

1835. Action under New York law for recovery of a fugitive from New Orleans: 12 Wendell's *Reports*, 311.

16. Basil Dorsey case.

1836. Trial and rescue of Dorsey in Bucks County, Pennsylvania: Smedley, *Underground Railroad*, 356–361; E. H. Magill, "When Men were Sold. The Underground Railroad in Bucks County," in *The Bucks County Intelligencer*, Feb. 3, 1898.

17. Matilda case.

1837, March. Rescue of a slave at Cincinnati, Ohio, on her way from Virginia to Missouri with her master. Later she was found in the employ of James G. Birney, who was tried for harboring the fugitive, while Matilda was remanded to her master: Schuckers, *Life and Public Services of S. P. Chase*, 41-44; Warden, *Private Life and Public Services of S. P. Chase*, 282-284; 8 *Ohio Reports*.

18. Schooner *Boston* case. (Georgia and Maine controversy.)

1837. Controversy between Georgia and Maine over a stowaway on the schooner *Boston*, who escaped through Maine to Canada: Wilson, *Rise and Fall of the Slave Power*, I, 473; Niles's *Register*, LIII, 71, 72, LV, 356; *Senate Journal*, 1839-40, pp. 235-237; *Senate Doc.*, 26 Cong., 1 Sess., Vol. V, Doc. 273; McDougall, *Fugitive Slaves*, 41.

19. Case of Peter, *alias* Lewis Martin.

1837. Fugitive adjudged to his claimant by Circuit Court for the Southern District of New York: 2 Paine's *Reports*, 350; 16 *Federal Cases*, 881.

20. Philadelphia case.

1838. Attempted rescue of a captured fugitive by a crowd of colored people: *Liberator*, March 16, 1838.

21. Marion (Ohio) case.

1838. Rescue of a fugitive at Marion, Ohio, from the hands of his claimant, who sought to detain him after the decision of the court in the slave's favor: Aaron Benedict, *The Sentinel*, Mt. Gilead, Ohio, July 13, 1893.

22. Escape of Douglass.

1838. Escape of Frederick Douglass from Baltimore to New York: *Life and Times of Douglass;* Williams, *Negro Race in America*, II, 59, 422; Wilson, *Rise and Fall of the Slave Power*, I, 501, 502.

23. Isaac Gansey case. (Virginia and New York controversy.)

1839. Controversy between Virginia and New York over extradition of three negroes demanded by Virginia for aiding a slave to escape: *U. S. Gazette*, "Case of Isaac," Judge Hopkinson's Speech; Wilson, *Rise and Fall of the Slave Power*, I, 474; Seward, *Works*, II, 449-518; Von Holst, *Constitutional History*, II, 538-540: *Senate Documents*, 27 Cong., 2 Sess., Vol. II, Doc. 96; McDougall, *Fugitive Slaves*, 41.

24. Granville (Ohio) rescue case.

1841. Discharge of fugitive, John, after a hearing obtained through a writ of habeas corpus; follqwed by the departure of the negro over an underground route: Bushnell, *History of Granville*, Licking County, Ohio, 307, 308.

25. Burr, Work and Thompson case.

1841. Prosecution for aiding fugitive slaves in western Illinois: Wilson, *Rise and Fall of the Slave Power*, II, 71; Goodell, *Slavery and Anti-Slavery*, 440; Thompson, *Prison Life and Reflections;* Asbury, *History of Quincy, Illinois*, 74.

26. Van Zandt case. (Jones *vs.* Van Zandt.)

1842–1847. Prosecution for aiding runaways in southwestern Ohio: 5 Howard's *Reports*, 215; Letter of N. L. Van Sandt, Clarinda, Iowa; Wilson, *Rise and Fall of the Slave Power*, I, 475, 476; Cobb, *Historical Sketches of Slavery*, 207; 2 McLean's *Reports*, 612; Schuckers, *Life and Public Services of S. P. Chase*, 53–66; Warden, *Private Life and Public Services of S. P. Chase*, 296.

27. Prigg case. (Prigg *vs.* the Commonwealth of Pennsylvania.)

1842. Prosecution for causing arrest and removal of a runaway contrary to provisions of a state law. Decision of the Supreme Court of the United States frees state officers from taking part in fugitive slave cases: 16 Peters' *Reports*, 539; *Report of Case of Edward Prigg*, Supreme Court, Pennsylvania; Cobb, *Historical Sketch of Slavery*; Bledsoe, *Liberty and Slavery*, 355; Clarke, *Anti-Slavery Days*, 69; Hurd, *Law of Freedom and Bondage*, II, 456–492; Wilson, *Rise and Fall of the Slave Power*, I, 472, 473; Von Holst, *Constitutional History*, III, 310–312.

28. Latimer case.

1842. Famous fugitive slave case in Boston. Fugitive released by purchase: *Liberator*, Oct. 25, Nov. 11, Nov. 25, 1842, Feb. 3, 7, 17, 1843, and Aug. 16, 1844; *Law Reporter*, Latimer Case, March, 1843; *Eleventh Annual Report of Mass. Anti-Slavery Society; Mass. House Journal*, 1843, pp. 72, 158; *Mass. Senate Journal*, 1843, p. 232; Wilson, *Rise and Fall of the Slave Power*, I, 477; McDougall, *Fugitive Slaves*, 39, 40.

29. Milton Clark rescue case.

1842, September. Release of the fugitive, captured in Lake County, Ohio, by writ of habeas corpus in Ashtabula County, Ohio, followed by his disappearance by way of the Underground Railroad: *Geneva* (Ohio) *Times*, Sept. 14, 1892.

30. Eells case.

1842–1852. Prosecution for harboring a slave in Adams County, Illinois: 5 *Illinois Reports*, 498; 14 Howard's *Reports*, 13.

31. Case of Charles T. Torrey.

1843. Prosecution for attempt to abduct slaves from Virginia: Wilson, *Rise and Fall of the Slave Power*, II, 80.

32. Case of Delia A. Webster.

1844. Prosecution for attempt to abduct slaves from Kentucky: *Rev. Calvin Fairbank During Slavery Times; Chicago Tribune*, Jan. 29, 1893.

33. Case of Calvin Fairbank.

1844. Prosecution for attempt to abduct slaves from Kentucky: *Rev. Calvin Fairbank During Slavery Times; Chicago Tribune*, Jan. 29, 1893.

34. Marysville (Ohio) rendition case.

1844, September 10. Rendition of two fugitives captured on the Scioto River, near Marysville, Union County, Ohio: *Marysville Tribune*, May 17, 1893; Letter of Mahlon Pickrell, Zanesfield, Ohio, March 25, 1893.

APPENDIX B 371

35. Walker case.

1844. Prosecution for attempt to abduct slaves from Florida: Trial and Imprisonment of Jonathan Walker, *Liberator*, Aug. 16, 31, Sept. 6, 13, Oct. 18, 25 and Dec. 27, 1844, Aug. 8, 15, and July 18, 1845; Wilson, *Rise and Fall of the Slave Power*, 83; McDougall, *Fugitive Slaves*, 42.

36. Case of State vs. Hoppess. (Watson case.)

1845. Action before the Supreme Court of Ohio on the circuit to secure the liberation of a recaptured slave: 2 *Western Law Journal*, 279; Schuckers, *Life and Public Services of S. P. Chase*, 74–77; Warden, *Private Life and Public Services of S. P. Chase*, 309.

37. Case of Vaughan vs. Williams.

1845. Prosecution before the Circuit Court of the United States for the District of Indiana for rescuing fugitive slaves: 3 *Western Law Journal*, 65; 8 *Law Reporter*, 375; 28 *Federal Cases*, 1115; 3 McLean's *Reports*, 530.

38. Parish case. (Jane Garrison case.)

1845–1849. Prosecution of F. D. Parish for aiding fugitives at Sandusky, Ohio: *Firelands Pioneer*, July, 1888; Warden, *Private Life and Public Services of S. P. Chase*, 310; A. E. Lee, *History of Columbus, Ohio*, I, 598.

39. Toledo (Ohio) rescue case.

1847, February. Rescue of a fugitive from custody while his captor was being tried on a charge of assault and battery before a justice of the peace: Conversation with James M. Ashley, Toledo, Ohio, July, 1895, and with Mavor Brigham, Toledo, Ohio, Aug. 4, 1895.

40. Crosswhite rescue case. (Case of Giltner vs. Gorham.)

1847. Prosecution for obstructing arrest of fugitives at Marshall, Michigan: Pamphlet proposing a "Defensive League of Freedom," by E. G. Loring, and others, pp. 5, 6; 4 McLean's *Reports*, 402.

41. Kauffman case.

1848. Prosecution of Daniel Kauffman, of Cumberland County, Pennsylvania, for aiding fugitives: E. G. Loring and others, Pamphlet proposing a "Defensive League of Freedom," pp. 5, 6.

42. Garrett case.

1848. Prosecution of Thomas Garrett, of Wilmington, Delaware, for aiding fugitive slaves: Still, *Underground Railroad Records*, 623–641; Smedley, *Underground Railroad*, 237–245; McDougall, *Fugitive Slaves*, 60; Wyman, *New England Magazine*, March, 1896.

43. Case of Drayton and Sayres. (Case of the schooner Pearl.)

1848, April 18. Prosecution for attempting abduction of slaves from Washington, D.C.: *Personal Memoir of Daniel Drayton;* Wilson, *Rise and Fall of the Slave Power*, II, 104; McDougall, *Fugitive Slaves*, 42.

44. Ohio and Kentucky controversy.

1848. Controversy on account of extradition of fifteen persons, charged with aiding fugitives, demanded by Kentucky: *Liberator*, July 14, 1848.

45. Craft escape.

1848. Escape of William and Ellen Craft: *Liberator*, Nov. 1, 1850; Still, *Underground Railroad*, 368; Clarke, *Anti-Slavery Days*, 83; Wilson, *Rise and Fall of the Slave Power*, II, 325; *New England Magazine*, January, 1890; McDougall, *Fugitive Slaves*, 59.

46. Case of Richard Dillingham.

1848, December. Prosecution for attempting to abduct slaves from Nashville, Tennessee: Benedict, *Memoir of Richard Dillingham;* Stowe, *Key to Uncle Tom's Cabin*, 58, 59; *Reminiscences of Levi Coffin*, 713–718; Howe, *Historical Collections of Ohio*, II, 590.

47. Clarksburgh (Indiana) case. (Case of Ray *vs.* Donnell and Hamilton.)

1849, May. Prosecution for aiding fugitive slave: 4 McLean's *Reports*, 504.

48. Case of Norris *vs.* Newton and others.

1849, September. Fugitives captured in Cass County, Michigan, discharged on trial at South Bend, Indiana, prosecution of those who interfered following: 5 McLean's *Reports*, 92.

49. First case under the Fugitive Slave Law of 1850. (Hamlet "kidnapping" case.)

1850, September 26. Rendition of James Hamlet, a free negro, living in New York City: *Fugitive Slave Bill, its History and Unconstitutionality, with an Account of the Seizure of James Hamlet*, 3; Wilson, *Rise and Fall of the Slave Power*, II, 304; McDougall, *Fugitive Slaves*, 43, 44.

50. Chaplin case.

1850. Prosecution of William L. Chaplin for attempting to abduct slaves of Robert Toombs and Alexander H. Stephens from Washington, D.C.: Wilson, *Rise and Fall of the Slave Power*, II, 80–82; *Case of William R. Chaplin*, etc. (Boston, 1851), p. 54.

51. Sims case.

1851. Rendition in Boston: *Liberator*, April 17 and 18; *Daily Morning Chronicle*, April 26, 1851; *Twentieth Annual Report of Mass. Anti-Slavery Society*, 1855, p. 19; *Trial of Sims, Arguments by R. Rantoul, Jr., and C. G. Loring;* C. F. Adams, *Life of Richard Henry Dana*, I, 185–301; 7 Cushing's *Reports*, 287; Wilson, *Rise and Fall of the Slave Power*, II, 333; *New England Magazine*, June, 1890; McDougall, *Fugitive Slaves*, 44.

52. Shadrach case.

1851, February. Rescue in Boston: *Liberator*, Feb. 21, May 30, 1851; *Boston Traveller*, Feb. 15, 1851; *Boston Courier*, Feb. 17, 1851; *Washington National Era*, Feb. 27, 1851; *Cong. Globe*, 31 Cong., 2 Sess., Appendix,

238, 295, 510; May, *Fugitive Slave Law and its Victims*, 10; Wilson, *Rise and Fall of the Slave Power*, II, 329; Von Holst, III, 21; *Statesman's Manual*, III, 1919; *New England Magazine*, May, 1890; McDougall, *Fugitive Slaves*, 47, 48; Rhodes, *History of the United States*, I, 209, 210, 290.

53. Christiana case.

1851, September. Riot in Christiana, Pennsylvania, caused by attempt to arrest and remove fugitives, followed by trial on the charge of treason of the persons alleged to have prevented the arrest: 2 Wallace Jr.'s *Reports*, 159; 9 *Legal Intelligencer*, 22; 4 *American Law Journal*, n. s., 458; 9 *Western Law Journal*, 103; 26 *Federal Cases*, 105; Still, *Underground Railroad*, 348–368; "Parker's account," "The Freedman's Story," T. W. Higginson, *Atlantic Monthly*, Feb. and March, 1866; *U. S. vs. Hanway, Treason*, 247; May, *Fugitive Slave Law and its Victims*, 14; *History of the Trial of Castner Hanway and others for Treason; N. Y. Tribune*, Sept. 12, 1851, and Nov. 26 to Dec. 12; *Boston Daily Traveller*, Sept. 12, 1851; *National Anti-Slavery Standard*, Sept. 18, 1851; *Lowell Journal*, Sept. 19, 1851; Smedley, *Underground Railroad*, 107–130; Wilson, *Rise and Fall of the Slave Power*, II, 328, 329; McDougall, *Fugitive Slaves*, 50, 51; Rhodes, *History of the United States*, I, 222–224.

54. Jerry rescue.

1851, October. Rescue of Jerry McHenry in Syracuse, New York: *Liberator*, Oct. 10–17, 1851; S. J. May, *Recollections of the Anti-Slavery Conflict*, 349–364; *Life of Gerrit Smith*, 117; *Trial of H. W. Allen*, 3; Wilson, *Rise and Fall of the Slave Power*, II, 305, 306; E. W. Seward, *Seward at Washington as Senator and Secretary of State*, I, 169, 170; McDougall, *Fugitive Slaves*, 44, 47–51.

55. Parker rescue.

1851, December 31. Rescue by Mr. Miller: Wilson, *Rise and Fall of the Slave Power*, II, 324; May, *Fugitive Slave Law and its Victims*, 15; *Liberator*, 1853, Feb. 4; *Lunsford Lane*, 113.

56. Brig Florence rescue.

1853. Rescue of a slave on board by Capt. Austin Bearse: Bearse, *Reminiscences of Fugitive Slave-Law Days in Boston*, 34.

57. Case of Oliver *vs.* Weakley and others.

1853. Prosecution before the United States Circuit Court for the Western District of Pennsylvania in October term for harboring fugitives: 2 Wallace Jr.'s *Reports*, 324.

58. Louis case.

1853, October. Escape of the fugitive, Louis, from the court-room while on trial in Cincinnati: *Liberator*, Oct. 28, 1853; *Reminiscences of Levi Coffin*, 548–554.

59. Bellefontaine (Ohio) rescue case.

1852, November. Discharge of the Piatt slaves from custody by the probate judge of Logan County, followed by their escape over the Underground Railroad: *Logan County Gazette*, November, 1852; Letter of the Hon. Robert T. Kennedy, Bellefontaine, Jan. 22, 1893; Conversation with Judge Wm. H. West, Bellefontaine, Aug. 11, 1894; Letter of R. H. Johnston, Belle Centre, Ohio, Sept. 22, 1894.

60. Case of Miller *vs.* McQuerry.

1853, August. Rendition of a fugitive, for several years a resident near Troy, Ohio, by the Circuit Court of the United States at Cincinnati, Ohio: 5 McLean's *Reports*, 481; 10 *Western Law Journal*, 528; 17 *Federal Cases*, 335; May, *The Fugitive Slave Law and its Victims*, 28; *History of Darke County, Ohio*, 324, 325.

61. Mitchell's case.

1853. Prosecution of Mitchell, an abolitionist of Indiana, Pennsylvania, for harboring slaves: 2 Wallace Jr.'s *Reports*, 313; *Pittsburgh Dispatch*, Feb. 13, 1898.

62. Glover rescue case. (Case of Ableman *vs.* Booth.)

1854, March 10. Rescue of Joshua Glover by a mob at Milwaukee; followed by the prosecution of Sherman M. Booth, one of the rescuers, and a conflict between the Supreme Court of Wisconsin and the Supreme Court of the United States: *Liberator*, April 7, 24, 1854; Wilson, *Rise and Fall of the Slave Power*, II, 444; Mason, *The Fugitive Slave Law in Wisconsin with Reference to Nullification Sentiment*, 1895; C. C. Olin, *A Complete Record of the John Olin Family*, 1893; Byron Paine and A. D. Smith, *Unconstitutionality of the Fugitive Slave Act. Argument of A. D. Smith*, Milwaukee, 1854. Wisconsin Supreme Court, *Unconstitutionality of the Fugitive Slave Act, Decision in case of Booth and Rycraft.*

63. Burns case.

1854, May 24. Rendition of Anthony Burns in Boston: *Liberator*, May, June, 1854, Aug. 22, 1861; *Kidnapping of Burns*, Scrapbook collected by Theodore Parker; Personal Statement of Mr. Elbridge Sprague, N. Abington; Accounts in *Boston Journal*, May 27, 29, 1854; *Daily Advertiser*, May 26, 29, June 7, 8, July 17; *Traveller*, May 27, 29, June 2, 3, 6, 10, July 15, 18, Oct. 3, Nov. 29, Dec. 5, 7, 1854, April 3, 4, 10, 11, 1855; *Evening Gazette*, May 27, 1854; *Worcester Spy*, May 31; Argument of Mr. R. H. Dana; May, *Fugitive Slave Law and its Victims*, 256; Stevens, *History of Anthony Burns; New York Tribune*, May 26, 1854; Clarke, *Anti-Slavery Days*, 87; Greeley, *American Conflict*, I, 218; Wilson, *Rise and Fall of the Slave Power*, II, 435; Von Holst, VI, 62; Garrisons' *Garrison*, II, 201, III, 409; C. F. Adams, *Dana*, I, 262–330; Rhodes, *History of the United States*, I, 500–506; T. W. Higginson, *Atlantic Monthly*, March, 1897, 349–354; McDougall, *Fugitive Slaves*, 45; Lillie B. C. Wyman, *New England Magazine*, July, 1890.

64. Sloane case.

1854. Prosecution of Rush R. Sloane before the District Court of the United States at Columbus, Ohio, for dismissing fugitives from the custody of their captors at Sandusky, Ohio: 5 McLean's *United States Reports*, 64; Rush R. Sloane and H. F. Paden, *Firelands Pioneer*, 47–49, 21–22.

65. Rosetta case.

1855, March. Release of the slave girl, Rosetta, by writ of habeas corpus from the possession of her master, who brought her voluntarily to Columbus, Ohio; followed some time later by the seizure and removal of the girl, and the pursuit of her captors to Cincinnati, where they were compelled by legal process to give her up: Warden, *Private Life and Public Services of S. P. Chase*, 344, 345; A. E. Lee, *History of Columbus, Ohio*, I, 602, 603.

66. Erican case.

1855, May 28. Unsuccessful attempt at Columbus, Ohio, to persuade two slave girls to leave their master, P. Erican, a Frenchman from New Orleans, *en route* with his family to Europe: Lee, *History of Columbus, Ohio*, 603.

67. Margaret Garner case.

1856, January. Rendition of Margaret Garner at Cincinnati, Ohio, after she had killed one of her children to prevent its return to bondage: *Liberator*, Feb. 8, 22, 29, 1856; May, *Fugitive Slave Law and its Victims*, 37; *Lunsford Lane*, 119; Greeley, *American Conflict*, I, 219; Lalor's *Cyclopaedia*, I, 207; Wilson, *Rise and Fall of the Slave Power*, II, 446, 447; James Monroe, *Oberlin Thursday Lectures, Addresses and Essays*, 116; Schuckers, *Life and Public Services of S. P. Chase*, 171–176; Warden, *Private Life and Public Services of S. P. Chase*, 346–350.

68. Williamson case.

1856, January. Prosecution for aiding fugitives: *Narrative of the Facts in the Case of Passmore Williamson*, Pennsylvania Anti-Slavery Society; *Annual Report of the American Anti-Slavery Society*, New York, May 7, 1856, p. 24; May, *Fugitive Slave Law and its Victims*, 9, 34; Wilson, *Rise and Fall of the Slave Power*, II, 448.

69. Johnson rescue case.

1856, July 16. Rescue of slave on ship from Mobile: *Liberator*, July 18, 1856.

70. Gatchell case.

1857, January. Rendition of Philip Young: Chambers, *Slavery and Color; Fugitive Slave Law*, Appendix, 197.

71. Addison White case.

1857, May 15. Prosecution of Udney Hyde and others for aiding the fugitive, Addison White, at Mechanicsburg, Champaign County, Ohio: Beer, *History of Clark County, Ohio*; Howe, *Historical Collections of*

Ohio, I, 384–386; Schuckers, *Life and Public Services of S. P. Chase*, 177–182; Warden, *Private Life and Public Services of S. P. Chase*, 350, 351.

72. Oberlin-Wellington rescue case.

1858, September 13. Rescue of the boy, John, at Wellington, Ohio, followed by the prosecution of two rescuers, and the indictment of four of the slave-catchers: Shipherd, *History of the Oberlin-Wellington Rescue; Liberator*, Jan. 28, April 29, May 6, June 3, 10, 1859; Cleveland (Ohio) *Plain Dealer*, July 6, 1859; *Lunsford Lane*, 179; *Anglo-African Magazine* (Oberlin-Wellington Rescue), 209; May, *Fugitive Slave Law and its Victims*, 108; *New Englander*, XVII, 686.

73. Nuckolls case.

1858, December. Prosecution of Nuckolls of Nebraska City, Nebraska, for injuring a person who remonstrated against his search for fugitives: Rev. John Todd, Tabor (Iowa) *Beacon*, 1890–91, Chapter XXI, of a series of articles entitled " The Early Settlement and Growth of Western Iowa."

74. John Brown's raid.

1858, December 20. Abduction of twelve slaves from Missouri, who were conducted directly through to Canada: Sanborn, *Life and Letters of John Brown*, 480–483; Redpath, *Public Life of Capt. John Brown*, 219–221; Hinton, *John Brown and His Men*, 30–32, 221, 222; Von Holst, *John Brown*, 104; I. B. Richman, *John Brown among the Quakers, and Other Sketches*, 46–48; *Life of Frederick Douglass*, 1881, 280, 281, 318, 319; McDougall, *Fugitive Slaves*, 51, 52.

75. Charles Nalle case. (Troy, New York, rescue case.)

1859, April 28. *Troy Whig*, April 28, 1859; Bradford, *Harriet, the Moses of Her People*, 143–149; *History of the County of Albany, N. Y., from 1609–1886*, p. 765; *Liberator*, May 4, 1860.

76. Jim Gray case.

1859, October 20. Dismissal of fugitive from arrest by decision of State Supreme Court at Ottawa, Illinois, followed by the rescue of the slave from the custody of the United States marshal, and the prosecution of several of the rescuers: *Ottawa* (Ill.) *Republican*, Nov. 9, 1891; *Pontiac* (Ill.) *Sentinel*, 1891–92; Speech of John Hossack, convicted of violation of the Fugitive Slave Law, before Judge Drummond of the United States District Court, Chicago, Ill. (New York, 1860.)

77. Sheldon and Woodford case.

1860, March. Prosecution of Edward Sheldon and Newton Woodford, of Tabor, Iowa, for aiding fugitives: Rev. John Todd, *Tabor* (Iowa) *Beacon*, 1890–91, Chapter XXI, of series of articles on " The Early Settlement and Growth of Western Iowa."

78. Anderson case.

1860. Extradition case between United States and Canada: *Pamphlets on Anderson Case*, Boston Public Library; *Life of Gerrit Smith*, 15; *Liberator*, Dec. 3, 1860, Jan. 22, 1861; *British Documents*, Parliament of Great Britain, " Correspondence Respecting Case of Fugitive Slave, Anderson," London, 1861.

79. Cleveland (Ohio) rendition case.

1861. Rendition of the fugitive slave, Lucy, in Cleveland, Ohio, to her master, Wm. S. Goshorn, of Wheeling, West Virginia: *Cleveland Herald*, date unknown.

80. Iberia (Ohio) whipping case.

1861, November. Prosecution of the Rev. George Gordon, Principal of Iberia College, for "resisting process" in the hands of a United States deputy marshal, who was endeavoring to capture a fugitive slave on the night of Sept. 20, 1860. The deputy and his assistants were caught, disarmed, taken to the woods and whipped. Principal Gordon witnessed without protest the last ten or fifteen lashes, and for so doing was sentenced to six months' confinement in the county jail, to pay a fine of $300, and the costs of prosecution — $1000 or $1500 more: Rev. George Gordon in the *Principia*, Nov. 29, 1861.

81. John Dean case.

1862, June. Prosecution of John Dean, a prominent lawyer of Washington, D.C., for protecting his client, an alleged fugitive just released, from a second arrest: Noah Brooks, *Washington in Lincoln's Time*, 197, 198.

APPENDIX C

FIGURES FROM THE UNITED STATES CENSUS REPORTS RELATING TO FUGITIVE SLAVES

TABLE A

	\multicolumn{4}{c}{Census of 1850}	\multicolumn{4}{c}{Census of 1860}
	Slaves	Fugitives	Ratio of Fugitives to Slaves	Per Cent of Loss	Slaves	Fugitives	Ratio of Fugitives to Slaves	Per Cent of Loss
Alabama	342,844	29	11,822	.0084	435,080	36	12,086	.0082
Arkansas	47,100	21	2,242	.0445	111,115	28	3,968	.0252
Delaware	2,290	26	88	1.1352	1,798	12	150	.6674
Florida	39,310	18	2,184	.0457	61,745	11	5,613	.0177
Georgia	381,682	89	4,288	.0233	462,198	23	20,096	.0049
Kentucky	210,981	96	2,198	.0455	225,483	119	1,895	.0527
Louisiana	244,809	90	2,720	.0366	331,726	46	7,211	.0138
Maryland	90,368	279	324	.3088	87,189	115	758	.1318
Mississippi . . .	309,878	40	7,558	.0132	436,631	68	6,422	.0155
Missouri	87,422	60	1,457	.0686	114,931	99	1,161	.0860
North Carolina . .	288,548	64	4,508	.0222	331,059	61	5,262	.0184
South Carolina . .	384,984	16	24,061	.0041	402,406	23	17,501	.0057
Tennessee	239,459	70	3,421	.0292	275,719	29	9,509	.0105
Texas	58,161	29	2,005	.0498	182,566	16	11,410	.0087
Virginia	472,528	82	5,693	.0175	490,865	117	4,194	.0238
	3,200,364	1,011	3,165	.0315	3,950,511	803	4,919	.0203

TABLE B

Showing that the Percentage of Decline of the Slave Population from 1850-1860 was Greater in the Northernmost Counties of the Border Slave States than in these States as a Whole

State	Counties Bordering on the States	Ratio between White and Slave Population in the Counties Bordering on the Free States 1850	Ratio between White and Slave Population in the Counties Bordering on the Free States 1860	Ratio between White and Slave Population in Whole State 1850	Ratio between White and Slave Population in Whole State 1860	Per Cent of Decline of Slave Population in Counties in 10 Years	Per Cent of Decline of Slave Population in States in 10 Years
Kentucky	Ill., O., Ind.	.20	.11	.27	.24	45	11
Virginia	Pa., O.	.018	.0089	.53	.47	55	11
Missouri	Ia., Ill.	.11	.081	.15	.108	25	28
Maryland	Pa.	.058	.032	.201	.16	33	20.4
					Average	39.5	17.6

TABLE C

Showing the Percentage of Decline of the Slave Population in the "Pan Handle" Counties of Virginia from 1850-1860

State	"Pan Handle" Counties Bordering Pa. and O.	White Population 1850	Slave Population 1850	White Population 1860	Slave Population 1860	Ratio between White and Slave Population 1850	Ratio between White and Slave Population 1860	Per Cent of Decline of Slave Population in 10 Years
Virginia	Hancock	4,040	3	4,442	2	.00074	.00045	39
"	Brooke	4,923	100	5,425	18	.0203	.0033	83
"	Ohio	17,612	164	22,196	100	.0093	.0045	51
"	Marshall	10,050	49	12,911	29	.0048	.0022	54
"	Wetzel	3,319	32	6,691	10	.0096	.0015	84
For all the Counties		39,944	348	51,665	159	.0089	.0030	56

APPENDIX D

BIBLIOGRAPHY

1. Unpublished Reminiscences

The materials upon which in large measure this book is based are reminiscences gathered by correspondence and conversation with more than a thousand persons, many of whom were old-time abolitionists, while the remainder included the families and intimate friends of abolitionists, and a number of fugitive slaves. It was discovered by the author after only a short search for published sources that little was to be gleaned in the libraries and that information sufficient in amount for an extended study could be obtained only by what geologists and botanists call fieldwork. The collection of materials went on as time could be spared for this purpose until a great mass of letters and notes had been brought together, and then the work of sorting, arranging and classifying began. The reminiscences were grouped by states and counties, so as to bring out as far as possible the coincident and confirmatory character of evidence relating to the same neighborhood or district; and the value of the materials appeared in the tracings of underground lines the author was able to make, county by county and state by state, throughout the region of the free states from Iowa to Maine. For the purpose of showing the extent and importance of the underground movement these unpublished reminiscences have proved to be invaluable.

2. Printed Collections of Underground Railroad Incidents

There are a few volumes that supply us with numerous illustrations of the Underground Railroad in operation. These books are not general treatises on the underground system, but give us an insight into the clandestine work of several limited localities; they are important because they exhibit the methods and devices of operators, show the sacrifices made by them in behalf of the midnight seekers after liberty, and supplement with valuable matter the unpublished reminiscences. In addition to the well-known books of Still, Smedley and Coffin, the author has found the three smaller, and hitherto unquoted books by W. M. Mitchell, E. M. Pettit and H. U. Johnson, to be useful.

APPENDIX D 381

3. PERSONAL RECOLLECTIONS

A few of those who were active in aiding slaves to escape to Canada have published volumes of personal recollections, in which, among other things, they tell more or less about their connection with the humane but illegitimate work of the abolitionists, and give vivid sketches of some of their associates, as well as of some of their dark-skinned protégés. Such books are the Rev. James Freeman Clarke's *Anti-Slavery Days*, the Rev. Samuel J. May's *Recollections of our Anti-Slavery Conflict*, J. B. Grinnell's *Men and Events of Forty Years*, Mrs. Laura S. Haviland's *A Woman's Life Work* and Mrs. E. B. Chace's *Anti-Slavery Reminiscences*. A small class of books, of which the *Personal Memoirs* of Daniel Drayton, and the books by Dr. A. M. Ross and the Rev. Calvin Fairbank are representatives, are indispensable as sources of information relating to the abduction of slaves from the South. The little book entitled *Harriet, the Moses of her People*, in which that remarkable guide of fugitives, Harriet Tubman, relates her exploits through the pen of her friend, Mrs. S. H. Bradford, properly belongs to this group.

4. LETTERS, DIARIES AND SCRAP-BOOKS

The liability of Underground Railroad operators to severe penalties for harboring runaways explains the dearth of evidence in the form of letters, diaries and scrap-books they have left behind; such evidence would have been incriminating. It is known that a few abolitionists kept diaries and scrap-books and even wrote letters in regard to the business of the Road, but most of these records appear to have been destroyed before the beginning of the Civil War. The author has been able to secure only two or three letters and the single leaf of a diary in centres where much work was done. Three scrap-books in the Boston Public Library, containing memoranda, clippings, handbills, etc., that refer in particular to the experiences of Theodore Parker, shed much light on the work of the Vigilance Committee of Boston, and supply important information in regard to the famous case of Anthony Burns.

5. BIOGRAPHIES AND MEMOIRS

Biographies and memoirs of anti-slavery men not infrequently contain references to aid rendered to fugitives, explain the motives of the philanthropists, and give their versions of the fugitive slave cases that came within their immediate knowledge; such books are often indices of the public sentiment of the localities in which their subjects lived, and when read in conjunction with the biographies of pro-slavery advocates help us to realize the conflicting interests that expressed themselves in the slavery controversy. Lydia Maria Child's *Life of Isaac T. Hopper* has preserved to us the record of one of the pioneers of the underground movement, while the biographies of *Gerrit Smith* and *James and Lucretia Mott*, show these persons to have been worthy successors of the benign and shrewd Hopper. In the biographies of John Brown by Redpath, Hinton and Sanborn, and in the *Life of Harriet Beecher Stowe*, by her son, Charles E. Stowe, we have proofs of the deep and enduring impression made by underground experiences upon strong characters capable of assimilating and transforming these into forces of historical moment. Chase, Seward and Sumner were among our public men who acted as counsel for fugitive slaves; it is not surprising therefore that their biographers have given considerable space to the consideration of cases with which these men were connected. The prominence of the statesmen just named and others of their class as party leaders makes their biographies indispensable in tracing the political history of the antebellum period. Claiborne's *Life and Correspondence of John A. Quitman* may properly be named as an excellent and valuable example of the class of biographies of prominent men of the South.

A few obituary pamphlets have been gathered, which have proved to be of some service: such are A. L. Benedict's *Memoir of Richard Dillingham*, and pamphlets relating to Mr. John Hossack, of Ottawa, Illinois, and Mr. James M. Westwater, of Columbus, Ohio.

6. Slave Biographies and Autobiographies

A recital of the life and sufferings of many colored refugees in books written by themselves or by sympathetic friends, and published in various free states during the two or three decades preceding 1860, tended to increase the Northern feeling against slavery and doubtless also to carry to many minds convictions that found a partial expression in underground efforts. These books contain descriptions of slave life on the plantation and tell with the omission of particulars, which it would have been imprudent at the time to relate, the story of the escape to liberty. The omission of these particulars renders these sources of little use in tracing the secret routes to Canada followed by the refugees, or in confirming, in part or in whole, the routes of others. In the case of Frederick Douglass, the gaps and omissions appearing in the first autobiography are filled with much valuable information in the second, written after slavery was abolished. The books by Josiah Henson, the Rev. J. W. Loguen and Austin Steward are interesting as the narratives of negroes of superior ability who spent a part at least of their time after self-emancipation in Canada, and could therefore write intelligently on the condition of their people there.

7. MATERIALS RELATING TO SLAVERY AND FUGITIVE SLAVES IN CANADA

There is but little material in regard to slavery and fugitive slaves in Canada. The question of slavery in the provinces is clearly presented in a few pages of Vol. XXV of the *Magazine of American History*, while the life of the colored refugees in Canada during the period of immigration and settlement can only be seen in anything like a sufficient light in Benjamin Drew's *North-Side View of Slavery*, and Dr. S. G. Howe's *Refugees from Slavery in Canada West*.

8. STATE, COUNTY AND LOCAL HISTORIES

Many contributions on the Underground Railroad appear in the collections of historical, biographical and other materials that make up a large number of our state, county and local histories so-called. Accounts, which when taken by themselves are fragmentary and therefore of little importance, have been brought to light by searching through these histories; and not unnaturally, perhaps, the largest number have been found in the county histories of Ohio. Six or seven of these histories afford articles relating to the Underground Railroad; and characteristic items and incidents have been printed in both state and local histories besides. Illinois comes next in the number of contributions preserved in its local histories. The utmost diligence of the student in the library alcoves devoted to Indiana, Iowa, Massachusetts, Michigan, New York, Pennsylvania and Wisconsin, will result in the finding of from one to three contributions only, as the case may be; while from the shelves given to Maine, Vermont, New Hampshire and New Jersey, he is not likely to secure anything to his purpose.

9. REPORTS OF SOCIETIES

The reports of anti-slavery societies, especially those of Massachusetts and Pennsylvania, are rich in comments upon the prosecutions in the South of abductors of slaves, and do not fail to show the effect of the Fugitive Slave Law of 1850 upon the activity of Underground Railroad lines. They also tell something of the missionary work done among the refugees in Canada. In the last-named respect they are secondary to the *Reports of the Anti-Slavery Society of Canada*, the *Refugees' Home Society*, and the *Canada Mission*.

Within the past ten years various societies of the historical type have been instrumental, directly or indirectly, in the publication of addresses bearing upon the violation of the Fugitive Slave laws. A series of lectures before the Political Science Association of the University of Michigan, several of which involve this theme, were published in 1889 under the general title, *Constitutional History of the United States as seen in the Development of American Law*. A collection of letters and addresses commemorative of the anti-slavery movement and some of its leaders was printed in 1893 in a book, called *Old Anti-Slavery Days*, by the Danvers (Mass.) Historical Society. An address on "The Underground Railroad" by ex-President James H. Fairchild, of Oberlin College, forms *Tract No. 87* in Vol. IV. of the publications of the Western Reserve Historical Society. The best account of the Glover rescue case will be found in a pamphlet by Mr. Vroman Mason on the *Fugitive Slave Law in Wisconsin, with Reference to Nullification Sentiment*, issued in 1895 by the State Historical Society of Wisconsin.

10. Records of Trials

The reader who acquaints himself even superficially with John Codman Hurd's two volumes, entitled the *Law of Freedom and Bondage in the United States*, can not fail to be impressed with the value of legal reports for the study of the great contention over slavery. Hurd's pages are full of descriptions and discussions of cases in their judicial bearing, and his foot-notes are largely made up of references to the published reports of trials.

In the series of these records of trials, one may trace the history of legal opposition to the enforcement of the Fugitive Slave laws, note the decision in the Prigg case, by which the efficiency of the law of 1793 was destroyed, and the Southern demand for a new law made imperative, mark the clash of state and federal jurisdictions, and see the growth of the spirit of nullification in the North. For these purposes, one should consult not only the records of the Supreme Court and the lower courts, such as *Federal Cases*, Howard's *Reports*, McLean's *Reports*, *Ohio State Reports*, *Wisconsin Reports*, etc., but also the various law periodicals, for example, the *American Law Register*, the *Legal Intelligencer*, and the *Western Law Journal*. Some important cases have been published in pamphlet form, while two at least are more minutely set forth in books; a volume is devoted to the Oberlin-Wellington rescue case, and several relate to the trial of Anthony Burns.

11. Periodicals and Newspapers

In marked contrast with the legal reports and law periodicals, little can be gleaned from the popular magazines of fugitive slave days. The ethics of resistance to the laws for the recovery of runaways is discussed in the *North American Review* for July, 1850, and in the *Democratic Review*, Vol. V, 1851, and incidents typical of the experience of the underground operator and his confederates are recited in *Once a Week* for June, 1862. Careful and extended search has revealed nothing in the better known periodicals published during the War and the two decades following. Recently, however, abolitionists have become retrospective and reminiscent, and the tales of their midnight adventures in contravention of those laws of their country which they deemed subversive of the "higher law" begin to appear in periodicals and newspapers. For example, the first of a series of stories, which are founded upon facts, was printed in the *Lake Shore and Home Magazine* for July, 1887, an article on the Underground Railroad appeared in the *Magazine of Western History* for March, 1887, and a "symposium" of reminiscences was published in the *Firelands Pioneer* for July, 1888. Articles of a miscellaneous nature, in which points of interest are brought out, have been appearing in some of the monthly magazines within more recent years, for instance, in the *Atlantic Monthly*, the *Century Magazine*, and the *New England Magazine*.

Only vague and rare references to the Underground Railroad and its workings are made in the newspapers of ante-bellum days, and these are of little value. The *Liberator* was fierce in its opposition to the Fugitive Slave Laws, and contains many stories of fugitives, but in this, as in less radical newspapers, the editor observed a discreet silence concerning the secret efforts of his colaborers in emancipating the bondman. It is necessary, therefore, to rely upon the long delayed accounts contributed by operators now advanced in years to the columns of the press. In 1885, interesting articles were printed in the *Western Star*, of Indiana, and the *New Lexington* (Ohio) *Tribune*, and since then, especially since 1890, many others have been published. These have been patiently gathered, and form a part of the author's collections.

12. Histories of Religious Societies

Materials relative to the attitude of various religious denominations towards slavery are to be found in the histories of the different church organizations, such as William Hodgson's *The Society of Friends in the Nineteenth Century*, Dr. H. N. McTyeire's *History of Methodism*, and Dr. R. E. Thompson's *History of the Presbyterian Churches in the United States*.

Other works, for example A. C. Applegarth's *Quakers in Pennsylvania* and S. B. Weeks' *Southern Quakers and Slavery*, which, while dealing with a single denomination, are not to be regarded as denominational histories in any strict sense, contain points of interest and value.

13. MATERIALS BEARING ON LEGISLATION

The study of our colonial legislation supplies ample proof that the harboring of the hunted slave early became a source of annoyance to slave-owners. Laws against this misdemeanor, with curious penalties attached, are included in the collections of statutes of various colonies, for example, in the *Laws and Ordinances of New Netherlands*, the *Maryland Archives* (Assembly Proceedings), the *Acts of the Province of New York*, the *Province Laws of Pennsylvania*, the *Laws of Virginia*, etc. These statutes have been made accessible through their publication in series of volumes, a good collection of which may be found in the State Library in Boston. Among the most important editions are Leaming and Spicer's collection for New Jersey, Hening's series of Virginia Statutes at Large, Bacon's collection for Maryland, and Iredell's edition of South Carolina Statutes.

The history of our national legislation respecting fugitive slaves may be traced in outline in the *Journals of the Senate and House*. For the voicing of the need of this legislation, which one would naturally expect to find in the speeches of members from the Southern states, one must turn to the *Annals of Congress*, covering the period from 1789 to 1824, the *Congressional Debates*, for the period from 1824 to 1837, and the *Congressional Globe* from 1833 to 1864. The provisions of the Fugitive Slave laws one may find, of course, in the *Statutes at Large*, and some of the effects of the law of 1850 may be studied in a pamphlet entitled *The Fugitive Slave Law and Its Victims*, compiled by Samuel May, Jr., and first published in 1856. An enlarged edition of this pamphlet was issued in 1861.

14. CONTEMPORANEOUS AND MODERN BOOKS ON SLAVERY.

Under this heading are brought for convenience several different classes of books on slavery. The first of these classes comprises the three small volumes, published during the interval from 1816 to 1826, in which immediate emancipation was advocated by the Rev. George Bourne, the Rev. James Duncan, and the Rev. John Rankin. Our interest here in the teaching of these men arises primarily from the circumstance that two of them, at least, are known to have done what they could to advance the work of the Underground Railroad, while all of them lived, at the time of the appearance of their books, on or near the border line over which came the trembling fugitive in search of freedom.

Another class is made up of volumes descriptive of slavery. Such are Mrs. Frances A. Kemble's *Journal of a Residence on a Georgian Plantation in 1836-1839*, Frederick Law Olmsted's *Cotton Kingdom*, G. M. Weston's *Progress of Slavery in the United States*, and a book that has but recently come from the press, Edward Ingle's *Southern Sidelights*.

In a third class must be grouped such recent monographs as Mrs. Marion G. McDougall's *Fugitive Slaves*, and Miss Mary Tremaine's *Slavery in the District of Columbia*. The former has been found to be especially serviceable, not only because of its subject matter, but also because of its numerous and accurate references and its long list of notable fugitive slave cases.

15. Secondary Works

One will seek in vain in the secondary works for an adequate account of the Underground Railroad, or a proper estimate of its importance, whether one looks in the general histories of the United States, such as the works of Von Holst, Schouler, and Rhodes, the more condensed books of which we have an example in Prof. J. W. Burgess's *The Middle Period*, or the histories of slavery, like Wilson's *Rise and Fall of the Slave Power in America*, Greeley's *American Conflict*, Williams' *History of the Negro Race*, and Willey's *History of the Anti-Slavery Cause in State and Nation*. These works are important for their discussions from different points of view of the political forces and constitutional questions involved in the struggle for emancipation, and in general they present descriptions of the famous contested fugitive slave cases and cases of rescue, but they have failed, on account of the small amount of evidence hitherto available, to arrive at a proper view of the political significance of the underground system.

16. Libraries

While the great mass of evidence that has made this volume possible was collected by field work, the author did not neglect to search libraries, both public and private, in the prosecution of his undertaking. He was able to make use of the public libraries of Cincinnati, besides the private library of Major E. C. Dawes of that city, the state library, and the library of Ohio State University at Columbus, the library of C. M. Burton, Esq., of Detroit, Michigan, and during two years' residence in Cambridge, Massachusetts, he was able to avail himself of the splendid collections of anti-slavery books and pamphlets to be found in the Boston Public Library and the library of Harvard University. The materials for the chapter on "Prosecutions of Underground Railroad Men" were gathered in the Harvard Law Library.

PRINTED COLLECTIONS OF UNDERGROUND RAILROAD INCIDENTS

LEVI COFFIN. Reminiscences of Levi Coffin, the Reputed President of the Underground Railroad; being a Brief History of the Labors of a Lifetime in Behalf of the Slave, with the Stories of Numerous Fugitives, who gained their Freedom through his Instrumentality; and Many Other Incidents. Second Edition. Cincinnati, 1880.

ASCOTT R. HOPE (a *nom de plume* for Robert Hope Moncrieff). Heroes in Homespun, 1894.

H. U. JOHNSON. From Dixie to Canada. Romances and Realities of the Underground Railroad. (Reprinted from the Lake Shore and Home Magazine.) Vol. I. Orwell, Ohio, 1894.

REV. W. M. MITCHELL. The Underground Railroad. London, 1860.

EBER M. PETTIT. Sketches in the History of the Underground Railroad; comprising Many Thrilling Incidents of the Escape of Fugitives from Slavery, and the Perils of those who aided them. Fredonia, N.Y., 1879.

R. C. SMEDLEY. History of the Underground Railroad in Chester and the Neighboring Counties of Pennsylvania. Lancaster, Pa., 1883.

WILLIAM STILL. Underground Railroad Records. Revised Edition. With a Life of the Author. Narrating the Hardships, Hairbreadth Escapes, and Death Struggles of the Slaves in their Efforts for Freedom. Together with Sketches of Some of the Eminent Friends of Freedom, and Most Liberal Aiders and Advisers of the Road. Hartford, Conn., 1886.

PERSONAL RECOLLECTIONS

AUSTIN BEARSE. Remembrances of Fugitive Slave Days in Boston. Boston, 1880. (Pamphlet.)

HENRY THOMAS BUTTERWORTH. Reminiscences and Memories of Henry Thomas Butterworth and Nancy Irwin Wales, His Wife, with Some Account of their Golden Wedding. Nov. 3, 1880. Lebanon, Ohio, 1886. (Pamphlet.)

ELIZABETH BUFFUM CHACE. Anti-Slavery Reminiscences. Central Falls., R.I., 1891. (Pamphlet.)

JAMES FREEMAN CLARKE. Anti-Slavery Days. A Sketch of the Struggle which ended in the Abolition of Slavery in the United States. New York, 1883.

DANIEL DRAYTON. Personal Memoirs, etc., including a Narrative of the Voyage and Capture of the Schooner *Pearl*. Published by the American and Foreign Anti-Slavery Society. Boston and New York, 1855.

The Rev. Calvin Fairbank. During Slavery Times. How he "Fought the Good Fight" to Prepare "the Way." Edited from his Manuscript. Chicago, 1890.

Josiah Bushnell Grinnell. Men and Events of Forty Years. Autobiographical Reminiscences of an Active Career from 1850 to 1890. Boston, 1891.

Laura S. Haviland. A Woman's Life-work: Labors and Experiences of Laura S. Haviland. Fourth Edition. Chicago, 1889.

Samuel J. May. Some Recollections of our Anti-Slavery Conflict. Boston, 1869.

Joseph Morris. Reminiscences. Richland Township, Marion Co., Ohio. Date unknown.

A. G. Riddle. Recollections of War Times. New York, 1873.

George W. Julian. Political Recollections. 1840-1872. Chicago, 1884.

Dr. Alexander Milton Ross. Recollections and Experiences of an Abolitionist. Second Edition. Toronto, 1876.

BIOGRAPHIES AND MEMOIRS

Charles Francis Adams. Richard Henry Dana. A Biography. 2 Vols. Vol. I. Boston, 1890.

George E. Baker, Editor. The Life of William H. Seward, with Selections from his Works. 3 Vols. New York, 1853, 1861, 1864.

A. L. Benedict. Memoir of Richard Dillingham. Philadelphia, 1852. (Pamphlet.)

William Birney. James G. Birney and his Times. The Genesis of the Republican Party, with Some Account of Abolition Movements in the South before 1828. New York, 1890.

John Howard Bryant. Life and Poems. 1894.

Lydia Maria Child. Isaac T. Hopper: A True Life. Twelfth Thousand. Boston, 1854.

J. F. H. Claiborne. Life and Correspondence of John A. Quitman. 2 Vols. New York, 1860.

W. G. Deshler and Others. Memorial on the Death of James M. Westwater. Published by the Board of Trade, Columbus, Ohio, 1894. (Pamphlet.)

O. B. Frothingham. Life of Gerrit Smith. New York, 1878.

Wendell Phillips Garrison and Francis Jackson Garrison. William Lloyd Garrison, 1805-1879: The Story of his Life, told by his Children. 4 Vols. 8vo. New York, 1885.

Mrs. Anna D. Hallowell. James and Lucretia Mott. Life and Letters. Boston, 1884.

Rev. D. Heagle. The Great Anti-Slavery Agitator, Hon. Owen Lovejoy as a Gospel Minister, with a Collection of his Sayings in Congress. Princeton, Ill., 1886. (Pamphlet.)

Richard J. Hinton. John Brown and his Men, with Some Account of the Roads they traveled to reach Harper's Ferry. New York, 1894.

In Memoriam. John Hossack. Deceased Nov. 8, 1891. (Reprinted from the Republican Times,) Ottawa, Ill., 1892. (Pamphlet.)

Oliver Johnson. William Lloyd Garrison and his Times. Boston, 1880.

George W. Julian. Life of Joshua R. Giddings. Chicago, 1892.

Memoir of Jervis Langdon, Elmira, N.Y. (Pamphlet.)

J. C. Leggett. Oration. Ceremonies attendant upon the Unveiling of a Bronze Bust and Granite Monument of Rev. John Rankin. (Ripley, Ohio), 1892. (Pamphlet.)

Thomas J. Mumford, Editor. Memoir of S. J. May. Boston, 1873.

John G. Nicolay and John Hay. Abraham Lincoln. A History. Vol. III. New York, 1890.

C. C. Olin. A Complete Record of the John Olin Family. Indianapolis, 1893.

Mrs. L. D. Parker. Scrap-book containing Newspaper Clippings, etc., relating to Theodore Parker and Others. Boston Public Library.

Theodore Parker. Scrap-book collection, with Hand-bills and his own Manuscript relating to Anthony Burns. Boston Public Library.

E. L. Pierce. Memoir and Letters of Charles Sumner. 4 Vols. Vols. III and IV. Boston, 1877–1893.

Florence and H. Cordelia Ray. Sketch of the Life of Rev. Charles B. Ray. New York, 1887. (?)

James Redpath. The Public Life of Captain John Brown, with an Autobiography of his Childhood and Youth. Boston, 1860.

F. B. Sanborn. The Life and Letters of John Brown, Liberator of Kansas, and Martyr of Virginia. Boston, 1885.

——— ———. Dr. S. G. Howe, The Philanthropist. New York, 1891.

J. W. Schuckers. The Life and Public Services of Salmon Portland Chase, United States Senator, and Governor of Ohio; Secretary of the Treasury, and Chief Justice of the United States. New York, 1874.

F. W. Seward. Seward at Washington, as Senator and Secretary of State. 2 Vols. New York, 1891.

C. E. Stowe. Life of Harriet Beecher Stowe: compiled from her Letters and Journals. Boston, 1889.

Miss C. C. Thayer. Two Scrap-books relating to Theodore Parker. Boston Public Library.

ROBERT B. WARDEN. An Account of the Private Life and Public Services of Samuel Portland Chase. Cincinnati, 1874.

JOHN WEISS. Life and Correspondence of Theodore Parker. 2 Vols. New York, 1864.

SLAVE BIOGRAPHIES AND AUTOBIOGRAPHIES

W. I. BOWDITCH. The Rendition of Anthony Burns. Boston, 1850.

* SARAH H. BRADFORD. Harriet, The Moses of Her People. New York, 1886.

Boston Slave Riot and Trial of Anthony Burns. Boston, 1854.

* WILLIAM W. BROWN. Narrative of William W. Brown. A Fugitive Slave. Second Edition. Boston, 1848.

* FREDERICK DOUGLASS. My Bondage and My Freedom. Part I. — Life as a Slave. Part II. — Life as a Freeman. With an Introduction by Dr. James M'Cune Smith. New York and Auburn, 1855.

——— ———. Life and Times of Frederick Douglass, Written by himself. His Early Life as a Slave, His Escape from Bondage, and His Complete History to the Present Time. With an Introduction by Mr. George L. Ruffin, of Boston. Hartford, Conn., 1881.

* JOSIAH HENSON. Life of Josiah Henson, formerly a Slave, now an Inhabitant of Canada, as narrated by himself. Preface by T. Binney. Boston, 1849.

——— ———. Story of His Own Life with an Introduction by Mrs. H. B. Stowe. Boston, 1858.

REV. J. W. LOGUEN. As a Slave and as a Freeman. Syracuse, N.Y., 1859.

MRS. K. E. R. PICKARD. The Kidnapped and Ransomed. Personal Reflections of Peter Still and his Wife Vina after Forty Years of Slavery. Syracuse, N.Y., 1856.

CHARLES STEARNS. Narrative of Henry Box Brown, who escaped from Slavery enclosed in a Box 3 feet long and 2 wide, written from a Statement of Facts made by Himself. 1849.

CHARLES EMERY STEVENS. Anthony Burns. A History. Boston. 1856.

* AUSTIN STEWARD. Twenty-two Years a Slave, and Forty Years a Freeman; Embracing a Correspondence of Several Years, While President of Wilberforce Colony, London, Canada West. Rochester, N.Y., 1857.

---

* Available from Dover Publications. Visit www.doverpublications.com for price and availability.

MATERIALS RELATING TO SLAVERY AND FUGITIVE SLAVES IN CANADA

GEORGE BRYCE. Short History of the Canadian People. London, 1887.

JOHN CHARLES DENT. The Last Forty Years, Canada Since the Union of 1841. Vol. I, 1881.

* BENJAMIN DREW. A North-Side View of Slavery: The Refugee, or the Narratives of Fugitive Slaves in Canada related by Themselves, with an Account of the History and Conditions of the Colored Population of Upper Canada. Boston, 1856.

J. C. HAMILTON. Slavery in Canada. Magazine of American History, Vol. XXV.

SAMUEL G. HOWE. The Refugees from Slavery in Canada West. Report to Freedman's Inquiry Committee. Boston, 1864.

JOHN M. MCMULLEN. History of Canada. 2 Vols. Vol. II, 1892.

STATE, COUNTY, AND LOCAL HISTORIES

Illinois.

A. T. ANDREAS. History of Chicago from the Earliest Period to the Present Time. Chicago, 1884.

S. J. CLARKE. History of McDonough County, Ill. Springfield, Ill., 1878.

History of Knox County, Ill.; with Record of its Volunteers in the late War, Portraits, Biographical Sketches, History of Illinois, etc. Chicago, 1878.

EDWARD G. MASON. Early Chicago and Illinois. Chicago, 1890.

GEORGE H. WOODRUFF. Forty Years Ago. A Contribution to the Early History of Joliet, and Will County, Ill. 1874.

——— ———. History of Will County, Ill. 1878.

Indiana.

History of Henry County, Ind.

History of Wayne County, Ind., from its First Settlement to the Present Time; with numerous Biographical and Family Sketches. Cincinnati, 1872.

Iowa.

L. P. ALLEN and Others. The History of Clinton County, Iowa, containing a History of the County, its Cities, Towns, etc. Chicago, 1879.

---

* Available from Dover Publications. Visit www.doverpublications.com for price and availability.

Massachusetts.

LEONARD BOLLES ELLIS. History of New Bedford and its Vicinity, 1602–1892. Syracuse, N.Y., 1892.

MASON A. GREEN. Springfield, (Mass.) 1636–1886. History of Town and City, including an Account of the Quarter-Millennial Celebration. Issued by the Authority and Direction of the City. Springfield, 1888.

JOSEPH MARSH. Article on "The Underground Railway," in the History of Florence, Mass.

Michigan.

SILAS FARMER. Article on "Slavery and the Colored Race," in the History of Detroit and Michigan. Detroit, 1884.

E. G. RUST. Calhoun County (Mich.) Business Directory. For 1869–1870. Together with a History of the County. Battle Creek, Mich., 1869.

New York.

GEORGE ROGERS HOWELL and JONATHAN TENNY, Editors, assisted by Local Writers. Bi-Centennial History of Albany, N.Y., with Portraits and Biographies and Illustrations. New York, 1886.

BENSON JOHN LOSSING. The Empire State. A Compendious History of the Commonwealth of New York. Hartford, Conn., 1888.

ANDREW W. YOUNG. History of the Town of Warsaw, New York. Buffalo, 1869.

Ohio.

History of Ashtabula County, Ohio; with Illustrations and Biographical Sketches of its Pioneers and Most Prominent Men. Philadelphia, Williams Bros., 1878. Article on the Underground Railroad contributed by S. D. Peet.

ALEXANDER BLACK. The Story of Ohio. Boston, 1888.

REV. HENRY BUSHNELL. The History of Granville, Licking Co., Ohio. Columbus, 1889.

JAMES H. FAIRCHILD. Oberlin — The Colony and the College. Oberlin, Ohio, 1883.

History of Franklin and Pickaway Counties, Ohio.

History of Geauga and Lake Counties, Ohio, with Illustrations and Biographical Sketches of its Pioneers and Most Prominent Men. Philadelphia, Williams Bros., 1878.

HENRY HOWE. Historical Collections of Ohio. 3 Vols. Columbus, 1891.

RUFUS KING. Ohio, First Fruits of the Ordinance of 1787. Boston and New York, 1888.

ALFRED E. LEE. History of the City of Columbus. New York and Chicago, 1892. Chapter XXXI, by Leander J. Critchfield, on "Bench and Bar."

W. H. MCINTOSH and Others. The History of Darke County, Ohio: containing a History of the County; its Cities, Towns, etc. Chicago, 1880.

WILLIAM T. MARTIN. History of Franklin County. Columbus, Ohio, 1858.

History of Medina County, Ohio.

J. R. SHIPHERD. History of the Oberlin-Wellington Rescue, with an Introduction by Prof. Henry C. Peck and Hon. Ralph Plum. Boston, 1859.

JACOB H. STUDER. Columbus, Ohio; Its History, Resources, and Progress. Columbus, 1873.

History of Summit County, Ohio.

History of Washington County, Ohio, with Illustrations and Biographical Sketches. H. Z. Williams and Bros., Publishers. Cleveland, Ohio, 1881.

Pennsylvania.

J. SMITH FUTHEY and GILBERT COPE. History of Chester County, Pa., with Genealogical and Biographical Sketches. Philadelphia, 1881.

Wisconsin.

C. W. BUTTERFIELD and Others. History of Waukesha County, Wis.; preceded by a History of Wisconsin. Chicago, 1880.

R. G. THWAITES. The Story of Wisconsin. Boston, 1891.

PERIODICALS

F. BOWEN. Extradition of Fugitive Slaves. North American Review, Vol. LXXI, July, 1850.

S. E. B. Fugitive Slaves in Ohio. Once a Week, Vol. VI, June 14, 1862.

RICHARD BURTON. The Author of Uncle Tom's Cabin. Century Magazine, 1896.

THOMAS E. CHAMPION. The Underground Railroad and One of its Operators. The Canadian Magazine of Politics, Science, Art and Literature, May, 1895.

GEORGE WILLIS COOKE. Article on Harriet Beecher Stowe. New England Magazine, September, 1896.

Fugitive Slave Law; Shall it be Enforced? The Democratic Review, Vol. V, 1851.

ARCHIBALD H. GRIMKE. Anti-Slavery Boston. New England Magazine, December, 1890.

THOMAS WENTWORTH HIGGINSON. Cheerful Yesterdays. Atlantic Monthly, March, 1897.

G. W. E. HILL. Underground Railroad Adventures. The Midland Monthly Magazine, Des Moines, Iowa, 1895.

JOHN HUTCHINS. The Underground Railroad. Magazine of Western History, Cleveland, Ohio, March, 1887.

H. U. JOHNSON. Romances and Realities of the Underground Railroad. Lake Shore and Home Magazine, July, 1885 to May, 1888.

LIDA ROSE MCCABE. The Oberlin-Wellington Rescue. Godey's Magazine, October, 1896.

H. F. PADEN. Underground Railroad Reminiscences. Firelands Pioneer, Norwalk, Ohio, July, 1888.

WILBUR H. SIEBERT. The Underground Railroad for the Liberation of Fugitive Slaves. Annual Report of the American Historical Association for 1895.

—— ——. Light on the Underground Railroad, with Map. American Historical Review, April, 1896.

RUSH R. SLOANE. The Underground Railroad of the Firelands. Firelands Pioneer, July, 1888.

G. T. STEWART. The Ohio Fugitive Slave Law. Firelands Pioneer, July, 1888.

NINA MOORE TIFFANY. Stories of the Fugitive Slaves. New England Magazine, (William and Ellen Craft) January, 1890; (Shadrach) May, 1890; (Sims) June, 1890; (Anthony Burns) July, 1890.

CHARLES DUDLEY WARNER. The Story of Uncle Tom's Cabin. Atlantic Monthly, September, 1896.

LILLIE B. C. WYMAN. Black and White [Margaret Garner]. New England Magazine, N. S., Vol. V; Harriet Tubman. *Ibid.*, March, 1896.

CAPTAIN C. WOODRUFF. Some Experiences in Abolition Times. Firelands Pioneer, July, 1888.

NEWSPAPERS

Andover Old and New. Boston *Evening Transcript*, May 16, 1896.

PHILIP ATKINSON. Anecdotes of Owen Lovejoy. New York *Weekly Witness*, Oct. 2, 1895.

AARON BENEDICT. The Underground Railroad. *Sentinel*, Mt. Gilead, Ohio, July 13, 20, 27, Aug. 3, 10, 1893.

ROBERT W. CARROLL. An Underground Railway. Cincinnati *Times-Star*, Aug. 19, 1890.

The Cleveland Fugitive Slave Case. Cleveland *Herald*, 1861.

NATHAN COGGESHALL. Reminiscences of the "Underground R. R." *Leader*, Marion, Ind., Feb. 15, 1896.

JUDGE JOSEPH COX. Early Cincinnati. Cincinnati *Times-Star*, Feb. 6, 1891.

MARY E. CROCKER. The Fugitive Slave Law and its Workings. Fitchburg (Mass.) *Daily Sentinel*, Oct. 31, 1893.

E. C. DAWES. Some Local History. Marietta (Ohio) *Tri-Weekly Register*, Aug. 30, 1890.

TERESA DEAN. White City Chips. *Daily Inter-Ocean*, Chicago, 1893.

J. M. DONNOHUE. The Underground Railroad. *Banner Times*, Greencastle (Ind.), Dec. 16, 1895.

Exploits of Calvin Fairbank. *Illustrated Buffalo Express*, Jan. 29, 1893.

Fight for Freedom. *Pittsburgh Dispatch*, Feb. 13, 1898.

MRS. J. M. FITCH. The Rescue of a Slave [Oberlin-Wellington Rescue Case]. New York *Sun*, April 7, 1895.

W. B. FYFFE. A History of Anti-Slavery Days and Afterwards. Pontiac (Ill.) *Sentinel*, 1890-1891.

WILLIAM LLOYD GARRISON. *The Liberator*.

MARIANNA GIBBONS. In Slavery Days. Lewiston *Gazette*, reprinted in Bedford (Pa.) *Enquirer*. Date unknown.

Glorious Old Thief [Calvin Fairbank]. Chicago *Tribune*, Jan. 29, 1893.

THOMAS L. GRAY. Underground Railroad. New Lexington (Ohio) *Tribune*, October, 1885, February 1886.

JOSIAH HARTZELL. And Milly and Martha were Free; a True Story of the Underground Railway of Later Slavery Days. Cleveland *Leader*, Feb. 16, 1896.

Helped Many Slaves; William Cratty talks of Underground Railroad Days. Chicago *Evening Post*, July 18, 1893.

E. HUFTELEN. Local History; The Underground Railroad of Forty Years Ago. *Spirit of the Times*, Batavia, Genesee County, N.Y., Feb. 8, 1896.

—————— ——————. The Underground Railroad. Some of its Early History, by a Le Roy Man. (Same as the preceding article.) Le Roy *Gazette*, Genesee County, N.Y., Feb. 26, 1896.

M. E. H. A Reminiscence of Slave Times. Miami (Ohio) *Union*, April 10, 1895.

WILLIAM T. KELLEY. Underground R. R. Reminiscences. *Friends' Intelligencer and Journal*, Fourth Month 2, 9, Fifth Month 28, 1898.

JOHN KENNEDY. Local History. Batavia *Times*, Genesee County, N.Y., Feb. 15, 1896.

GEORGE S. MCDOWELL. Uncle Tom's Cabin; Originals of Some of

the Characters in the Great Book. Cincinnati *Commercial Gazette*. Date unknown.

DR. EDWARD H. MAGILL. When Men Were Sold; the Underground Railroad in Bucks County. *The Bucks County* (Pa.) *Intelligencer*, Feb. 3, 1898. The same in *Friends' Intelligencer and Journal*, Second Month 19, 26, Third Month 5, 12, 1898.

——— ———. Underground Railroad Additions. *Friends' Intelligencer and Journal*, Fourth Month 16, 1898.

CHARLES MERRICK. Reminiscences of the Jerry Rescue. *Northern Christian Advocate*, Nov. 15, 1893.

J. B. NAYLOR. A Spike From the Underground Railway. *Ohio Farmer*, Aug. 1, 8, 1895. Signed, S. Q. Lapius.

DAVID NEWPORT. Fugitive Slaves. *Friends' Intelligencer and Journal*, Sixth Month 11, 1898.

MRS. J. F. NICHOLSON. Memoirs of Long Ago. *Western Star* (Ind.), Dec. 10, 1885.

An Old House with a Wonderful History. Marysville (Ohio), *Tribune*, May 17, 1893.

DOUGLAS P. PUTNAM. A Station on the Old Underground Railroad. Marietta (Ohio) *Register*, Oct. 25, 1894.

Recollections of the "Underground Railroad" of Antebellum Days. Felicity (Ohio) *Times*, July 6, 1893.

Reminiscences of Slavery. Marietta (Ohio) *Daily Register*, Jan. 12, 1895.

CARLTON RICE. Reminiscent. *Oneida*, Madison County, N.Y., May 16, 20, 23, 1896.

L. L. RICE. Lewis and Milton Clark. Geneva (Ohio) *Times*, Sept. 14, 1892.

A. M. Ross. A Democratic Abolitionist. Somerset (Pa.) *Standard*, Jan. 31, 1896.

The Semi-Centennial of the First Church. Galesburg (Ill.) *Republican Register*, March 5, 1887.

JOHN SHEARER. Old Uncle Joe Mayo. Marysville (Ohio) *Tribune*, April 27, 1881.

Sketches of the Life of Carver Tomlinson; assisted in the Great "Underground Railroad." *Lostant Reporter* (La Salle Co., Ill.), Aug. 10, 1896.

Slavery Days Recalled. Detroit *Free Press*, Jan. 24, 1893.

In Slavery Days. New Castle (Ind.) *Daily News*, March 5, 1897.

Slave Raid. Story of the *Pearl* Expedition. Interesting Episode of Antebellum Days. The Failure of the Affair. Some Very Exciting Scenes. From the Washington *Post*, reprinted in the Cincinnati *Enquirer*, Sept. 14, 1895.

GILES B. STEBBINS. Thomas Garrett. Detroit *Post,* 1871.

Stories of Runaway Slaves. Detroit *Sunday News-Tribune,* Aug. 12, 1894.

Stories of Runaway Slaves. From Detroit *Sunday News-Tribune,* reprinted in Louisville (Ky.) *Sunday Morning Journal,* Aug. 12, 1894.

Story of Calvin Fairbank. Cincinnati *Commercial Gazette,* March 18, 1893.

JAMES STOUT. A Bit of History; the Rescue of the Slave, Jim Gray, in 1859. Pontiac *Sentinel,* Livingston Co., Ill., 1890.

REV. JOHN TODD. Reminiscences of the Early Settlement and Growth of Western Iowa. Tabor (Iowa) *Beacon,* 1890–1891.

E. HICKS TRUEBLOOD. Reminiscences of the Underground Railroad. *Republican Leader,* Salem, Ind., Nov. 17, Dec. 1, 1893, Jan. 26, Feb. 2, 23, March 2, 16, 23, April 6, 27, 1894.

JOHN W. TUTTLE and F. P. AMES. Reminiscences of Slavery. Marietta (Ohio) *Register,* 1893–1894. Four articles.

Two Good Men. Sketch of the Lives of John B. Tolman and S. Silsbee; Reminiscences of the Underground Railroad. Lynn (Mass.) *Daily Evening Item,* Dec. 19. Year unknown.

The Underground Railroad. Chicago *Inter-Ocean Curiosity Shop,* 1881, 1884.

The Underground Railroad. From a History of Hancock County, dated 1880. *La Harper,* Hancock Co., Ill., April 3, 1896.

The Underground Railroad. Ohio *State Journal,* Nov. 14, 1894.

James M. Westwater, Pioneer Merchant and Friend of the Oppressed. Columbus (Ohio) *Dispatch,* Feb. 21, 1894.

Where Harriet Beecher Stowe witnessed the Scenes depicted in her Uncle Tom's Cabin. Cincinnati *Enquirer* (Supplement), Nov. 3, 1895.

RUFUS R. WILSON. Exploits of Calvin Fairbank. *Illustrated Buffalo Express,* Jan. 29, 1893.

Joel Wood. Noticed in the Martin's Ferry (Ohio) *Evening Times,* May 2, 1892.

MATERIALS BEARING ON LEGISLATION

Acts and Laws of His Majestie's Colony of Connecticut, 239 (1730?).

Maryland Archives, Assembly Proceedings, 147, May, 1666.

Charters and Laws of the Colony and Province of Massachusetts Bay, 750, October, 1718.

New Jersey Laws, 82, May 30, 1668.

Laws and Ordinances of New Netherlands, 32, Aug. 7, 1640; 32, April 13, 1642; 104, Oct. 6, 1648.

Laws of New Netherlands, 344, April 9, 1658.

Acts of Province of New York from 1691 to 1718; 58, 1702.
Acts of Province of New York, 77, 1705; 218, 1715.
Laws of North Carolina, 89, 1741; 371, 1779.
Province Laws of Pennsylvania, Philadelphia, 1725; Province Laws of Pennsylvania, 325 (1726?).
Plymouth Colony Records, IX, 5, Aug. 29, 1643. (Fugitive Slave Clause of the Articles of Confederation.)
Records of Colony of Rhode Island, 177, Oct. 27, 1714.
Hening, Laws of Virginia, I, 401, March, 1655-1656; II, 239, October, 1666; II, October, 1705; IV, 168, May, 1726.
Annals of Congress, 1789-1824.
THOMAS HART BENTON. Abridgment of the Debates of Congress from 1789 to 1856. 16 Vols. Washington, 1857-1861.
Congressional Debates, 1824-1837.
Congressional Globe, 1833-(1873).
Journals (House and Senate).
SAMUEL MAY, JR. The Fugitive Slave Law and Its Victims. New York, 1856. Enlarged Edition, N.Y., 1861.
J. H. MERRIAM. Legislative History of the Ordinance of 1787. Worcester, 1888.
Niles' Weekly Register, September, 1828, to March, 1829. Vol. XXXV.
JOEL PARKER. Personal Liberty Laws, and Slavery in the Territories (pamphlet). Boston, 1861.
Statutes at Large.
GEORGE M. STROUD. A Sketch of the Laws relating to Slavery in the Several States of America. Second Edition with Alterations and Considerable Additions. Philadelphia, 1856.
HENRY WILSON. History of the Antislavery Measures of the Thirty-seventh and Thirty-eighth United States Congresses, 1861-1864. Boston, 1864.

CONTEMPORANEOUS AND MODERN BOOKS ON SLAVERY

REV. GEORGE BOURNE. The Book and Slavery Irreconcilable. Philadelphia, 1816.— A summary of this book by Wm. Orland Bourne, under the title "Anti-Slavery Leaders; the Pioneer Abolitionist." *Boston Commonwealth*, July 25, 1885.
WILLIAM CHAMBERS. American Slavery and Colour. London, 1857.
EZRA B. CHASE. Teachings of Patriots and Statesmen, or the "Founders of the Republic" on Slavery. Philadelphia, 1860.
JOHN NELSON DAVIDSON. Negro Slavery in Wisconsin. Address delivered before the State Historical Society of Wisconsin, December, 1892.

Rev. James Duncan. A Treatise on Slavery, in which is shown forth the Evil of Slaveholding, both from the Light of Nature and Divine Revelation. Vevay, Ind., 1824.

William Goodell. Slavery and Anti-Slavery; a History of the Great Struggle in Both Hemispheres; with a view of the Slavery Question in the United States. New York, 1852.

Edward Ingle. Southern Sidelights; a Picture of Social and Economic Life in the South a Generation before the War. New York, 1896.

Francis Anne Kemble. Journal of a Residence on a Georgian Plantation in 1836-1839. New York, 1863.

Marion Gleason McDougall. Fugitive Slaves (1619-1865). Fay House Monographs, No. 3. Boston, 1891.

Frederick Law Olmsted. The Cotton Kingdom. 2 Vols. New York, 1861.

Rev. John Rankin. Letters on American Slavery addressed to Mr. Thomas Rankin, Merchant at Middlebrook, Augusta County, Virginia. (First published in 1826.) Fifth edition. Boston, 1838.

J. B. Robinson. Pictures of Slavery and Anti-Slavery; Advantages of Negro Slavery and the Benefits of Negro Freedom. Philadelphia, 1863.

Harriet Beecher Stowe. A Key to Uncle Tom's Cabin, presenting the Original Facts and Documents upon which the Story is founded, together with Corroborative Statements verifying the Truth of the Work. Boston, 1853.

Mary Tremain. Slavery in the District of Columbia; the Policy of Congress and the Struggle for Abolition. New York, 1892.

G. M. Weston. Progress of Slavery in the United States. Washington, D.C., 1858.

REPORTS OF SOCIETIES

Annual Reports presented to the Massachusetts Anti-Slavery Society by its Board of Managers. See Reports 13, 15, 18, 19.

Annual Reports of the Pennsylvania Anti-Slavery Society.

Danvers Historical Society. Old Anti-Slavery Days. Proceedings of the Commemorative Meeting held by the Danvers Historical Society at the Town Hall, Danvers, April 26, 1893; with Introduction, Letters, and Sketches. Danvers, Mass., 1893.

James H. Fairchild. The Underground Railroad. Tract No. 87 in Vol. IV. Western Reserve Historical Society. An Address delivered for the Society in Association Hall, Cleveland, Ohio, Jan. 24, 1895.

First Annual Report presented to the Anti-Slavery Society of Canada by its Executive Committee. Toronto, March 24, 1852.

VROMAN MASON. The Fugitive Slave Law in Wisconsin, with Reference to the Nullification Sentiment. State Historical Society of Wisconsin, 1895.

REFUGEES' HOME SOCIETY. Report of Committee. Winsor, 1852.

HENRY WADE ROGERS, Editor. Constitutional History of the United States as seen in the Development of American Law. Lectures before the Political Science Association of the University of Michigan. New York, 1889.

Seventh Annual Report of the Canada Mission. Rochester, N.Y.

HISTORIES OF RELIGIOUS SOCIETIES

A. C. APPLEGARTH, Ph.D. Quakers in Pennsylvania. Baltimore, 1892.

WILLIAM HODGSON. The Society of Friends in the Nineteenth Century; a Historical View of the Successive Convulsions and Schisms during the Period. Vol. II. Philadelphia, 1875.

HOLLAND N. MCTYEIRE, D.D. History of Methodism; with some Account of the Doctrine and Polity of the Episcopal Methodism in the United States down to 1884. Nashville, Tenn., 1887.

WILLIAM B. SPRAGUE, D.D. Annals of the American Pulpit.

PROFESSOR A. C. THOMAS. The Society of Friends. In Vol. XII of the American Church History Series. 1894.

ROBERT E. THOMPSON, D.D. History of the Presbyterian Churches in the United States. American Church History Series, New York, 1895.

STEPHEN B. WEEKS, Ph.D. Southern Quakers and Slavery; a Study in Institutional History. Baltimore, 1896.

SECONDARY WORKS

JOHN W. BURGESS. The Middle Period, 1817–1858. New York, 1897.

JAMES FORD RHODES. History of the United States from the Compromise of 1850. 3 Vols. New York, 1893.

JAMES SCHOULER. History of the United States under the Constitution. Vols. III, IV, V. Washington, 1880. New York, 1880–1891.

H. E. VON HOLST. Constitutional and Political History of the United States. Chicago, 1877–1892.

REV. AUSTIN WILLEY. The History of the Anti-Slavery Cause in State and Nation. Portland, Maine, 1886.

GEORGE W. WILLIAMS. History of the Negro Race in America from 1619 to 1880. 2 Vols. New York, 1883.

HENRY WILSON. History of the Rise and Fall of the Slave Power in America. 3 Vols. Boston, 1872–1877.

J. S. WALTON and M. G. BRUMBAUGH. Stories of Pennsylvania. New York, 1897.

WOODROW WILSON. Division and Reunion, 1829–1889. New York, 1893.

IMAGINATIVE WORKS

HARRIET BEECHER STOWE. Uncle Tom's Cabin.

J. M. C. SIMPSON. The Emancipation Car, being an Original Composition of Anti-Slavery Ballads, composed exclusively for the Underground Railroad. Janesville, Ohio, 1874.

CHARLES HUMPHREY ROBERTS. Down the Ohio (a work of fiction, containing scenes from the Underground Railroad). Chicago, 1891.

JOHN GREENLEAF WHITTIER. Poetical Works (anti-slavery poems printed in Vol. III of the Riverside edition). Boston, 1896.

APPENDIX E

DIRECTORY OF THE NAMES OF UNDERGROUND RAILROAD OPERATORS

ARRANGED ALPHABETICALLY BY STATES AND COUNTIES [1]

CONNECTICUT
Fairfield
Daskam, Benjamin Jas.

Litchfield
Blakeslee, Dea. Joel.
Bull, Wm.
Dunbar, Dea. Ferrand.

Middlesex
Reed, Dea. George.

Windham
Alexander, Prosper.
Brown, Benjamin.
Brown, John.
Conant, J. A.
Fox, Joel.
Griffin, Ebeneser.
Lewis, J. A.
Pearl, Phillips.

DELAWARE
Queen Anne
Hardcastle, Wm.

Wilmington
Flint, Isaac S.
Garrett, Thomas.
Hunn, John.
Walker, Joseph G.
Webb, Benjamin.
Webb, Thomas.
Webb, Wm.

ILLINOIS
Adams
Andrew, Lewis.
Baldwin, Eben.
Ballard, Dea.
Barnet, Berryman.
Bartholomew, Darwin.
Battell, Wm.
Benton, Erastus.
Brown, Dea.
Burns, Capt. John.
Burr.
Chapin, John.
Chittenden, Henry.
Clark, Nathan.
Eells, Dr. Richard.
Fowler. W. E.
Griffin, Ed.
Hammond, Julius.
Hart, Martin.
Hubbard, Jonathan.
Hunter, Andrew.
Hunter, George.
Kirby, Rev. Wm.
Mullen, Wm.
Nelson, Dr. David.
Platt, Dea. Josiah.
Platt, Enoch.
Platt, H. D.
Platt, I.
Reynard, John.
Reynolds, L. E.
Safford.
Sartle, Rasselas.
Stillman, Henry.
Stillman, Levi.

[1] The names of colored operators are marked with a †.

Stillman, S. O.
Thompson, George.
Turner, Edward.
Van Dorn, John K.
Van Dorn, Wm.
Weed, Dea. L. A.
Wickwire, James.
Wilcox, L. H.
Work, Alanson.

Alexander

Burroughs, George L.

Bond

Davis, Bloomfield.
Harnard, Rev.
Hunt, N. A.
Leeper, John.
McCord, David.
McCord, Robert.
McLain.
Rosber, Ed.
Rosebrough, James.
Wafer.
Wood, Charles.

Bureau

Bryant, Arthur.
Bryant, Cyrus.
Bryant, John Howard.
Clark, Daniel.
Clark, Seth C.
Collins.
Cook, Dea. Caleb.
Foster.
Frary, Roderick B.
Hall, George.
Hall, John.
Hart, Dr. Langley.
Holbrook, Dea. J. T.
Lovejoy, Owen G.
Mather, Benj.
Phelps, Charles.
Pilkerton, Wm.
Reeve, Dea.
Stannard.
Weldon, John.
Wells, Dea.
Wilson.

Cook

Blanchard, President.
Bliss.
Carpenter, Philo.

Collins, James H.
Crandall.
Dyer, Dr. C. V.
Eastman, Hon. Z.
Farnsworth, Col.
Johnson. J.
Kellogg, H. H.
Paine, Seth.
Phillips, W. I.
Pinkerton, Allen.
Stoddard, J. P.
Webster, Prof.
Weiblen, John G.

Dupage

Fowler, Dea.

Fulton

Birge, Luther.
Dobbins.
Field, H. H.
Lyman, Dea.
Marsh, Rev. M.
Miles, Freeman.
Thomas, A. B.
Wickwire.
Wilson, Eli.

Hancock

Adkins family.
Austin, Strong.
Burton, Dea.
Cook, L. A.
Cook, Marcus.
Maynard, Louis Calvin.
Wilcox, L. L.

Henderson

Thomson, John.

Henry

Allen, James M.
Allen, Wm. S.
Allen, Wm. T.
Bernard.
Buck, Dea.
Jones, Elder.
McFarlane.
Pomeroy, Dr.
Stewart, E. M.
Stewart, Roderick R.
Ward, Dea.
Wilcox.

APPENDIX E

Jersey
Carter, Ebenezer.
French, Josiah.
Garesche.
Henderson, Ben.
Snedeker.
White, Hiram.
Wolcott, Elihu.

Kane
Fitch, Ira H.
Johnson, Dea. Reuben.
Mighels, Ezekiel.
Pierce, Thomas.
Root, Dr.
Strong, Dea.
Wagner, John.

Kendall
Whitney, Dea. Isaac.

Knox
Blanchard.
Camp, C. F.
Child, E.
Cross, Rev. John.
Davis, George.
Hitchcock, Samuel.
Kimball, Solon.
Neeley.
Powell, Hod.
West, John.
West, Nehemiah.

La Salle
Brown.
Butler, Benj.
Campbell.
Carter, Wm.
†Freeman.
Fyfe, George.
Gooding, Dr.
Hard, Dr. Chester.
Hart.
Hossack, H. L.
Hossack, John.
Kelsy, Levi.
King, Claudius B.
Lewis, Samuel R.
McLaughlin.
Stout, James.
Stout, Joseph.
Strawn, Hon. Wm.

Lee
Towne.

Livingston
Croswell, Dr. James.
Fyfe, W. B.
Hinman, Rev. H. H.
Richardson, Otis.

McDonough
Blazer, John.

McHenry
Russel.

McLean
Moss, Dea.

Marshall
Bell, John.
Ranney, Joel.
Stone.

Mercer
Carnahan, David.
Carnahan, John.
Carnahan, Wm. M.
Cowden, John.
Graham, J. C.
Higgins, Dr.
Hill, James.
Hoagland, Henry.
Markham, S. A.
Sample, John.

Montgomery
Bryce, Robert.
Merritt, W. W.

Morgan
Chamberlain, Timothy.
Jackson, Rev. Andrew W.
Miller, Henry M.

Ogle
Bogue, Virgil A.
Gammell, Rev. George.
Perkins, Dea. Timothy.
Shaver, Solomon.
Waterbury, Dea. John.

Peoria
Brown, Edwin R.
Huey, Virgil.

Pratts, Jonathan.
Webster, W. W.
Wright, S. G.

Putnam
Childs.
Lewis, Wm.
Willes, Stephen.

Randolph
Breath, Samuel.
Chambers, Mathew.
Crawford, Bryce.
Crawford, James.
Davis, I. B.
East, Henry.
Gault, Hugh C.
Harshaw, Rev.
Hayes, Wm.
Hill, Anthony.
Hood.
Lippincott, Charles.
McLain, Thomas.
McLurkins family.
Milligan, Rev. Jas.
Moore family.
Morrison, Daniel.
Ramsey, Robert.
Sloane, Rev. Wm.
Todd family.
Wafer, Thomas.
Wilson.
Wylie, Adam.

Rock Island
Delany, Robert.

Sangamon
Stevenson, James.
Webster.
Wyckoff.

Stark
Buswell, James.
Dunn, Agustus.
Hall, Dr. Thomas.
Hall, Wm.
Hodgson, Jonathan.
Rhodes, Hugh.
Rhodes, Joseph.
Stone, Liberty.
Winslow, Calvin.
Wright, Rev. S. W.

Tazewell
Dillon, Ellis.
Holland.
Holton.
Mathews.
Mickle.
Phillips.
Woodron, Samuel.

Vermilion
Harper.

Washington
Henry, John.
McClurken, John.

Wayne
Ambler.

Whiteside
Hamilton, Dea.
Millikin, Dea.

Will
Beach, Dea.
Cushing, Dea.
Denny, Allen.
Goodhue.
Haven, Samuel.
Stewart, Col. Peter

Woodford
Bayne, James G.
Drennan, Thomas.
Kern, George.
McCoy, John.
Morse, Joseph T.
Morse, Levi P.
Morse, Dea. Mark.
Morse, Parker, Jr.
Morse, Captain Parker.
Piper, James A.
Ranney, James.
Whitemire, Dr. James.
Work, James.
Work, Samuel.

Miscellaneous
Turner, Asa.
Lukins.

INDIANA

Bartholomew
Hall, John.
Newsom, Willis.
Parker.
Parks, Willis.
Thomas, John.
Wears.

Bond
Douglass, James.
Hill, Anthony.
McFarland, Robert.
McLain, John A.
Rosbrough, James.
Wafer, James.

Boone
Johns, Samuel.

Carroll
Montgomery, Robert.

Cass
Crain, J. E.
Faber, Dr. Ruel.
†Hill, Jim.
Keep, Barton R.
Kreider, Wm. M.
Manly, W. T. S.
Patterson, Joseph.
Powell, Jeptha.
Powell, Josiah G.
Powell, Lemuel.
Powell, Lycurgus.
Powell, Wm.
Tomlinson, Thomas T.
Turner.
Vigus, Capt.
White, Batley.

Dearborn
Collier, John.
Collier, Ralph.
Hansell, John.
Smith, Thomas.

Decatur
Cady.
Capen.
Donnell, Luther.
Knapp, A. W.
Taylor.

Delaware
Swain.

Elkhart
Matchett, Dr.

Gibson
McCormack, Rev.

Grant
Baldwin, Charles.
Coggeshall, Nathan.
Hill, Aaron.
Jay, David.
Ratliff, John.
Shugart, John.

Hendricks
Harvey, Harlan.
Harvey, Dr. T. B.
Harvey, Dr. Wm. F.
Hobbs, Elisha.

Henry
Adamson, Isaac.
Bales, John.
Bond, Jonathan.
Burley, Charles.
Charuness, Wm., Jr.
Edgerton, Roger.
Hinshaw, Seth.
Iddings, Dr.
Jessup, Jesse.
Jessup, Tidaman.
Macy, Enoch.
Macy, Jonathan.
Macy, Lilburne.
Macy, Phebe.
Macy, Wm.
Saint, Alpheus.
Schooley, W. D.
Small, Mrs. Jane.
Wickersham, Caleb.

Howard
Jones, Daniel.

Jackson
Cox, Richard.
†Parks, Willis.

Jefferson
Baxter, James.
Carr, John.

Eliott, Robert.
Hickland, Louis.
Stephens, Judge.
Stephenson, Rev. Robert.
Waggner, Isaac.
Wagner, Jacob.

Jay
Baird.
Brown family.
Gray, Thomas.
Haines family,
Hopkins family.
Ira, Jonah.
Lewis, Enos.
Mendenhall family.
Puxon, Joshua.
Williams family.
Wright family.

Jennings
Bland.
Deney, Aaron.
Deney, Thomas.
Hale, Jacob.
Hicklen, Felix.
Hicklen, James.
Hicklen, Dr. John.
Hicklen, Louis.
Hicklen, Thomas.
Marshall.
Stanley, Eli.
Stott, James.
Stott, Samuel.

Kosciusko
Gordon.
Harpers, Thomas.
Hurlburts, Chauncey.

La Porte
Dakin, Dr. George M.
Harper.
Williams, Rev. W. B.

Montgomery
Clarke, Samuel.
Doherty, Fisher.
Elmers.
Emmons.
Speed, John.

Morgan
Williams.

Noble
Waterhouse.
Whitford, Stutely.

Parke
Hadley, Alfred.
Stanley, W. P.

Putnam
Browder, Parker S.
Hillis, "Singing" Joe.

Randolph
Alexanders.
Bond, Amos.
Bond, John H.
Clayton, John.
Crane, Willis.
Diggs, Bury, Jr.
Jones, Daniel.
Moorman, John A.
Rinard, Solomon.
Smith, Samuel.
Wiggins, Lemuel.
Worth, A.
Wright, Solomon.
Zimri.

Ripley
Bland, James.
Cady, Dr. A. P.
Dautherd.
Holton, Francis.
Hughes, Henry.
Hulse, Walter.
King, Henry.
McDowell, Duncan.
McDowell, Washington.
Merrell, F. M.
Neil, Willett.
Passmore, George.
Passmore, Joseph H.
Queer, Ervin.
Smith, Hiram.
Van Cleave, John S.
Van Cleave, Jared.
Waddle, Henry.
Waggoner, James.

Rush
Cogeshall, Tristan.
Frazee, John H.
Gray, Jonathan H.
Henley, Henry.

Hill, Milton.
Jessop, Sidiman.
Macy, Henry.
Patterson, Robert.
Small, Zachareal.
Smawl, Abraham.
White, Elisha B.

Steuben

Barnard, Lewis.
Barry, Capt.
Butler, Henry P.
Butler, M. B.
Butler, Seymour S.
Clark, S. W.
Fox, Allen.
Fox, Denison.
Fox, J. A.
Gale, Judge.
Hendry.
Jackson, Samuel.
Kimball, Augustus.
McGowan, S.
Newton, Nelson.
Spear, Rev. E. R.
Waterhouse.

Tippecanoe

Falley, Lewis.
Hockett, Moses.
Hollingsworth, Benjamin.
Hollingsworth, John.
Robinson, John.

Union

Beard, Wm.
Casterline, Dr.
Elliott, J. P.
Gardner, Edwin.
Hayworth, Joel.
Huddleson, Wm.
Maxwell, John.
Smith, Gabriel.

Vermilion

Beard, Wm.

Wabash

Brace, Avery.
Hayward, Wm.
Place, Maurice.

Washington

Thompson, James L.
Trueblood, Wm. Penn.

Wayne

Charles, John.
Charnnese, Wm.
Clark, Daniel.
Coe, John.
Coffin, Levi.
Cogshalls.
DeBaptiste, George.
Edgerton, Thomas.
Frazier, Thomas.
Goems, Reuben.
Haddleson, Jonathan.
Harris.
Hayworth, James.
Hill, Daniel.
Hough, Wm.
Huff, Daniel.
Huff, Zimri.
Johnson, Dr.
Lewis.
Malsbys.
Mareys.
Maxwell family.
Moore, Samuel.
Nixon, Samuel.
Overman.
Puckett, Daniel.
Roberst, Able.
Stanton, Dr. Benj.
Stanley, Ira.
Thomas, Luke.
Thornburg, Lewis.
Unthank, Jonathan.
Way, Dr. Henry H.
Whippo, John.
Wilcuts, David.
Williams, John F.
Wooton, Martha.

White

Lawrie, James.

Miscellaneous

Brandt, Hon. Isaac.
Maxwell.
Smith, Dr. A. J.
Talberts.

IOWA

Appanoose

Adamson, H.
Armstrong.
Calverts.
Fulcher, John.

Gilbert, Josiah.
Green, Jacob.
Hedgecock, Wm.
Hollbrook, Luther R.
McDonald, D.
Martin, Wesley.
Robinson, Moses.
Root, George.
Stanton, Nathan.
Stanton, Seth B.
Tulcher, John.

Cass

Coe, J. N.
Grindley, Amos.
Hitchcock, Rev. George B.
Mills, Hon. Oliver.

Cedar

Maxon, Wm.

Clinton

Bather, Andrew.
Bather, J. R.
Brindell, G. W.
Burdette, Capt.
Campbell, C. B.
Gleason, Abel B.
Graham, Judge.
Jones, J. B.
Leslie, H.
Mix, Lawrence.
Olin, Nelson.
Palmer, B. R.
Savage, T.
Star, W. B.
Stillman, Mrs. J. D.
Weston, George W.

Davis

Corner, Albert.
Corner, Arthur.
Conner, W. E.
Elliott, George.
Elliott, John.
Hardy, David.
Hardy, James.
Klingler, Wm.
Paggett, Hiram.
Stanton, Seth B.
Truit, Adbell.

Fremont

Adams, S. H.
Avery, E.

Blanchard, Dr. Ira D.
Bottsford, Rev.
Brooks, Wm. M.
Case, Cephas.
Clark, Wm. L.
Cummings, Origin.
Dea, S. D.
Gaston, A. C.
Gaston, George B.
Gaston, James K.
Hallam, John.
Horton, H. B.
Hill, Rev. E. S.
Hill, L. B.
Hunter, George.
Irish, Henry.
Jones, Jonas.
Lambert, Mrs. Lydia Blanchard.
Lane, William.
Lawrence, Charles F.
Mason.
Platt, Mrs. E. G.
Platt, Lester.
Platt, Rev. M. F.
Sheldon, Hon. E. T.
Shepardson, Mrs. S. R.
Smith, James L.
Todd, Rev. John.
Williams, Reuben.
Williams, Hon. Sturgis.
Woods, D.
West, Jesse.

Henry

Armstrong, J. H. B.
Corey, Benj.
Edwards, James.
Holbrake, L.
Howe, Prof. S. L.
Pickering, John H.

Johnson

Clark, Wm. Penn.

Keokuk

Durfee family.

Lee

Adamson, Brown.

Madison

Roberts, Hon. B. F.
Scott, Dr. John.

Mahaska
Hockett, Isaac.
McCormick, Mathew.
Montgomery, Wm.

Mills
Bradburgh.
Bradshaw.
Briggs, Daniel.
Morse.
Tolles, C. W.
Wing.
Woodford, Newton.

Pottawattamie
Bradway, Calvin.

Poweshiek
Bailey, John F.
Bixby, Amos.
Bliss, Harvey.
Brande, Elder T.
Cooper, Col. S. F.
Grinnell, Hon. J. B.
Hamlin, Homer.
Harris family.
Parker, Prof. L. F.
Parks, Philo.

Wapello
English.
Wilson.

Washington
Rankin, Samuel.

KANSAS
Bowles, Col. J.
Brown, John, and his men.
Gossard, Rev. S. J.

KENTUCKY
Fee, Rev. John Grigg.
Fee, John S.
Jones.

MAINE
Androscoggin
Cheney, Rev. O. B.

Cumberland
Appleton, Gen.
Dennet, Oliver.

Fessenden, Gen. Samuel.
Hall, Col. Levi.
Hussey, Samuel F.
Morrill, Peter.
Packard, Prof. A. S.
Parsons, A. F.
Parsons, Dr. C. G.
Pease, Dr.
Smyth, Wm.
Thomas, Mrs. Elias.
Thurston, Brown.
Winslow, Nathan.
Woodman, Hon. J. C.

Kennebec
Chadwick, Abel.

Oxford
Blago.
Morse, Capt. Seth.
Moulton, Col. John.

MARYLAND
Hubbard, Daniel.
Kelly, Jonah.
Leaverton, Jacob and Hannah.
Tyson, Elisha.

MASSACHUSETTS
Bristol
Adams, Robert.
Bailey, John.
Torrey, Rev. Charles T.

Essex
Bibb, Henry.
Bingham, D. L.
†Brown, Henry Box.
†Brown, Wm. Wells.
Buffum, Jonathan.
Coffin, Joshua.
Crocker, Samuel.
Dodge, Simeon.
Goodwin, Hooper R.
Goodwin, John.
Goodwin, Samuel.
Hathaway, Benjamin G.
Innis, John A.
Orne, A. C.
†Redmond, Chas. Lennox.
Silsbee, S.
Tolman, John B.
Ware, Erastus.
Young, Dr. Samuel.

Franklin

Andrews, Erastus.
Blake, Hosea.
Craft.
Fisk, Dr. C. L.
Leavitt, Hart.
Monson, Osee.

Hampden

Buell, Joseph C.
Church, Dr. Jefferson.
Coolidge, Jonas.
Elmer, Rufus.
Howland, John.
Osgood, Dr. Samuel.
Woods, John M.

Hampshire

Abel, George.
Breck, Moses.
Critchlow, A. P.
Fairbank, Rev. Calvin.
Hammond.
Hill, Arthur G.
Hill, Samuel L.
Hingman.
Lyman.
Ross, Austin.
Williston, J. Payson.

Middlesex

Bigelow, Mrs. Francis E.
Brooks, Mrs. Mary M.
Farnsworth, Dr. Amos.
White, Wm. S.

Norfolk

Fisher, Hon. Milton M.
Southwick, Miss Sarah.

Suffolk

Andrew, Hon. John A.
Apthorp, Robert E.
Atkinson, Edward (?).
Bearse, Capt. Austin.
Bowditch, Henry I.
Bowditch, Wm. I.
Browne, John W.
Davis, Chas. G.
Gilbert, Timothy.
†Hayden, Lewis.
Hilliard, Mrs. Geo. S.
Jackson, Edmund.
Jackson, Francis.

Kemp, Henry.
List, Charles.
Loring, Ellis Gray.
Marjoram, Wm. W.
Morris, Robert.
Parker, Theodore.
Phillips, Wendell.
Scott, James.
Sewall, Samuel E.
Smith, Joshua B.
Southwick, Joseph.
Spear, John M.
Waugh, Rev. George.
Whipple, Charles K.
Whitmore, Joseph Benj.
Wright, Elizur.

Worcester

Capron, Effingham L.
Crocker, S. S.
Drake, Jonathan.
Earle, Edward.
Everett, Joshua T.
Hadwin, Charles.
Higginson, Col. T. W.
Smith, Joel.
Snow, Benj.
Ward, Alvin.

Miscellaneous

Jackson, Dr. James Caleb.

MICHIGAN
Calhoun

Fitch, Jabez.
Hussey, Erastus.
McMahon, Edward.
Muzzy.

Cass

Bogue, Steven.
Bonine, Isaac.
Shugart, Zachariah.

Genesee

Northrop, Rev. H. H.

Kalamazoo

Thomas, Dr. N. M.

Kalkaska

Gillett, Amasa.

Lenawee
Carpenter.
Chandler, Thomas.
Coe, John M.
Dolbear, F.
Gilbert, Warren.
Haviland, Laura S.
Horkney, Richard.
Mason, Joseph.
Moore, Samuel.
Owen, Dr. Woodland.
Reed, Fitch.
Wells, James B.

Oakland
Frost, A. P.
Powers, Nathan.

St. Joseph
Clarke, Rev. Chas. G.
Cleveland, Rev. John P.
Gurney, Chester.
Kanouse, Rev. John S.
Mills, Rev. Louis.
Northrop, H. H.
Weed, Rev. Ira M.

Washtenaw
Bartlett, Moses.
Beckley, Guy.
Camp, Ira.
Fowler, Joseph.
Goodell, Jotham.
Harwood.
Lowy, John.
Ray.

Wayne
†De Baptiste, George.
†Dolarson, George.
Finney, Seymour.
Foote, Rev. C. C.
Howard, Jacob M.
Sheeley, Alanson.
Tyler, Capt. Elisha.
Watson, Walter.

NEW JERSEY
Burlington
†Coleman, John.
Evans, Robert.
Middleton, Enoch.
†Stevens, Samuel.

Cumberland
Bond, Leven.
Cooper, Ezekial.
Murry, Nathaniel.
Sheppard, J. R.
Sheppard, Thomas R.
Stanford, Alges.
Stanford, Julia.

Gloucester
Douden, Wm.
†Louis, Pompey.
†Sharper, Jubilee.

Hudson
Everett, John.
Mott, Dr. James.
Phillips, Peter James.

Mercer
Conove, Elias.
Earl, J. J.
Plumly, B. Rush.

Middlesex
Freedlyn, Jonathan.
Sickler, Adam.

Salem
Goodwin, Abigail.
†Oliver, Rev. Thomas Clement.

Union
Garrison, Joseph.

Miscellaneous
Reeve, Wm.

NEW HAMPSHIRE
Belknap
Chamberlain, Wm.

Carroll
Dearborn.

Coos
Chase, Hon. Aurin M.
Colby, Col. Joseph.

Grafton
Furber, James.
Harris, James.
Hughes.

Hillsboro
Cheney, Dea. Moses.
Wilson, Hon. James.
Wood, James.
Wood, Moses.

Merrimack
Brooks, Mrs.
Chamberlain, John A.
Chamberlain, Moses.
Rice, Miss.

Rockingham
Philbrick.
Snow, Solomon P.

Strafford
Cartland, Jonathan.
Cartland, Joseph.
Thompson, S. Millett.

NEW YORK
Albany
Chaplin, Gen. Wm. L.
Delavan, E. C.
Goodwin.
Jackson, Dr. J. C.
Mott, Abigail.
Mott, Lydia.
†Myers, Stephen.
Williams.

Allegany
Case, Dea.

Cattaraugus
Chapman, Capt.
Cooper, Wm.
Welles.

Chautauqua
Andrew.
Cranston.
Frink, Rev.
Knowlton.
Little, John.
Pettit, Dr. J.
Pettit, Eber M.

Chemung
†Jones, John W.
Langdon, Jervis.

Chenango
Berry, Col.

Erie
Aldrich.
Barker, Gideon.
Haywood, Hon. Wm.
Johnson, Geo. W.
Moore, Dea. Henry.
Williams.

Genesee
Brewster, Judge.
Comstock, Dea.
Huftelen, E.
McDonald, Daniel.

Livingston
Sleeper, Col. Reuben.

Madison
Jarvis, Dr.
Smith, Hon. Gerrit.

Monroe
Anthony, Asa.
Anthony, Daniel.
Anthony, Mary.
Avery, Geo. A.
Bishop, W. G.
Bloss, Wm. C.
Bostwick, Nelson.
Carpenter.
Croffts, Mrs.
Degarmo.
Dolley, Dr.
Douglass, Frederick.
Doy, Dr. John.
Falls, Wm. S.
Fish, Benj.
Fish, Mrs. Sarah.
Gibbs, Isaac.
Gilbert, Grove S.
Hallowell, Mary.
Hallowell, Wm.
Humphry, Geo. H.
Husbands, J. D.
James, Thomas.
Kedzie, John.
Marsh, Joseph.
Moore, Lindley Murray.
Morris, J. P.
Porter, Samuel D.
Post, Amy.

Post, Isaac.
Quinby, Henry.
Sampson, A. S.
Sherman, Dr.
Thayer, George.
Williams, Capt.
Williams, E. C.

New York
Briggs.
Downing, George T.
Gibbs.
Hopper, Isaac T.
Johnson, Oliver.
†Pennington.
Ray, Rev. Chas. B.
†Ruggles, David.
†Smith, Dr. McCune.

Niagara
Binmore, Thomas.
Childs, W. H.
Richardson, M. C.
Spauling, Lyman.

Oneida
Stewart, Alvan.

Onondaga
Barbour.
Bates, Abner.
Carson.
Lee, Rev. Luther.
†Loguen, Rev. J. W.
May, Rev. Samuel J.
Minor, Rev. Ovid.
Wheaton, Charles.

Oswego
Bragdon, George L.
Fox, Edward.
French.
Jackson, James C.
Salmon, George.
Salmon, Wm. Lyman.
Stevens, Ard. H.
Wing, Asa S.

Rensselaer
†Hooper, John H.
Shipherd, Rev. Fayette.

Steuben
Balcom, Judge.
Thacher, Judge Otis.

Ulster
Chase.
Colby, Col.

Wyoming
Andrews, Josiah.
Breck, Allen Y.
Chapin, Willard J.
Frank, Dr. Augustus.
Galusha, Rev. Ellin.
Gates, Seth M.
Lyman, R. W.
McKay, F. C. D.
Miller, Frank.
Poenix, Samuel F.
Shepard, Col. Chas. O.
Waldo, H. N.
Young, Andrew W.

NORTH CAROLINA
Coffin, Vestal.

OHIO
Adams
Baldridge, Samuel T.
Blackstone, Benj. D.
Burgess, Rev. Dyer.
Cannon, Edward.
Cannon, Urban.
Caskey, James.
Caywood, John.
Cooley.
Copples, Daniel.
Hollingsworth, Abraham.
Kirker.
Kirkpatrick, Nathaniel.
Lafferty, Absolem.
McClanahan.
McIntire, General.
McKinley, Charles.
McKinley, David.
McKinley, John.
McKinley, Wm.
Nobles, Dr.
Ourslers.
Puntenney.
Ralston, Robert.
Ralston, Thomas.
Rothrock, Joseph.
Stroups, Wm.
Taber, Oliver.
Taylor, James.
Torrence, James W.

Vandermans.
Waites.
Wickersham.
Wilson, John T.

Ashland

Garrett, Ezra.
Gordon, James.
Lawson, John.
Rose.
Stott, George.
Talentire, John.
Wilson, Robert.
Woods, John.

Ashtabula

Austin, Aaron C.
Austin, Eliphalet.
Austin, Joab.
Austin, L. B.
Bartlett, Dea.
Bigelow, Capt. Saxton.
Bissell, L.
Brown, Alex.
Brown, James.
Bushnell.
Carpenter, Jehaziel.
Coleman, Alby.
Conklin, Rev.
Cowles, Miss Betsey.
Cowles, Miss Martha.
Culbertson, Jacob.
Denny, Judge Wm. S.
Edwards, Lawrence.
Edwards, Smith.
Edwards, T. S.
Farrington, Dr. S. H.
Fisk, Amos.
Garlic, A. K.
Giddings, Hon. Joshua R.
Hall, James.
Hancock, Capt. Wm.
Harris, Dr. Henry.
Hawley.
Hezlet, George.
Hubbard, Henry.
Hubbard, Wm.
Hylop, George.
Jones, Lynds.
King, Alexander.
King, Edward.
McDonald, James.
McDonald, Jesse.
McDonald, Lyman.
Nellis, J. I. D.

Parsons, Wm. Henry.
Peck, Lyman.
Plumb, Ralph.
Plumb, Samuel.
Savage, Amasa.
Shipman, Amos.
Terrell, Rev. Sherman.
Tinan, Joseph.
Trescott, Samuel.
Wick, C. C.
Wilson, Wm.
Wing, J. K.

Athens

Alderman, Hosea.
Barker, Judge Isaac.
Beaton, T. A.
Blake, Edward.
Brown, Eli F.
Brown, John.
Brown, Leonard.
Day, Artemus.
Glazier, Abel.
Glazier, Walter.
Harold, Joseph.
Hibbard, Elausome.
Hibbard, Elisha.
Hibbard, J. S.
Hibbard, John M.
Jewett, Dr. Leonard.
Kessinger, Joseph C.
Lewis, John.
McCoy, Rev. J. C.
Moore, David.
Moore, Eliakim H.
Morse, Peter.
Newton, Solomon.
Potter, Orville.
Smith, Hon. Lot L.
Vorhes, Albert.
Vorhes, John.
Winn, John T.

Belmont

Bailey, Dr. Jesse.
Branson, Isaiah.
Campbell.
Cope, Joshua.
Cottrell, Robert.
Dickens, John.
Dillon, Wm.
George, Travis.
Halper, Sandy.
Hargrave, Joseph.
Holloway, Isaac.

Howard, Horton.
Kirk, Robert.
Nichols, Eli.
Palmer, Wm.
Reynolds, John.
Rivers, James L.
Schoolies, Dr.
Smith, John W.
Wood, Joel.
Wright, Charles.
Wright, John.
Wright, Nehemiah.
Wright, Wm.

Brown

Baird, Wm.
Beasley, Dr. Alfred.
Beck, Dr. Isaac M.
Borroughs, Dr.
Bowers, Robert.
Brown, Isaac H.
Bull, Kirby.
Campbell, Dr. Alex.
Collins, Eli C.
Collins, James.
Collins, Theodore.
Collins, Thomas.
Concade.
Crane, A. B.
Crosby, Robert.
Dunlap, Wm.
Frazier, Wm.
Gilliland, S. W.
Graham.
Heinman.
Hopkins, Godin.
Hopkins, Thomas.
Hudson, John D.
Huggins, Amzi.
Huggins, J. E.
Huggins, J. N.
Huggins, M. H.
Huggins, R. I.
Huggins, Robert.
Huggins, W. D.
Huggins, Wm.
Johnson, Alex.
Kincaid.
Kirker, Thomas.
Mace, Richard.
Macklem, Wm.
McCague, Thomas.
McCoy, James.
McCoy, Kenneth.
McCoy, Wm.

McFerson, James.
McGee, Isaiah.
McKegg, George.
McMaken, Mark Campbell.
McVey.
Mahan, Rev. John.
Mathews, George.
Menaugh, Wm.
Miller, R. S.
Miller, Scott.
Minnaw, Wm.
Moore.
Norton, Dr. Greenleaf.
Pangburn.
Patton, Joseph.
Pettijohn.
Pogue, Mary.
Porter, John.
Rankin, Rev. John, and sons.
Rice, Benj.
Robinson, John R.
Saulsbury, Thomas.
Scott, James.
Shepard, John.
Simpson, John.
Snedigher, John.
Turney, Alston.
Turney, David.
Wilson, Alexander.

Butler

Elliott, Wm.
Falconer, Dr.
Lewis, Jane.
Marshall, Samuel.
Rigden, Dr.
Scobey, Dr. Wm. H.
Woods, John.

Carroll

Campbell, Wm.
Farmer, Dr. Wm.
George, J. D.
George, Robert.
Holmes.
McLaughlin, John.
McLaughlin, Wm.
Palmer, John.
Rutan, Daniel.
Thompson, Hance.

Champaign

Adams, Lewis.
Atkinson, Cephas.

Baldwin, Thomas.
Baldwin, Wm. H.
†Bird, Owen.
Boucher, Joshua.
Brand, Maj. Joseph C.
Butcher, Dr. J. M.
†Byrd, Peter.
Corwin, Moses B.
Cowgill, Henry.
Cowgill, Dr. Thomas.
Davenport, Dr.
Hitt, John W.
Howard, Anson.
Hyde, Udney.
Jamison, Wm.
Lewis, Griffith.
McCoy, George.
Pierce, Jonathan.
Rathburn, Levi.
Reno, Frank.
Reno, Joseph.
Reno, Lewis.
Stanton, Benjamin.
Ware, J. R.
Winder, Abner.
Winder, Edward.
Winder, Henry.
Winder, James.
Winder, Joshua.
Winder, Levi.
Winder, Moses.
Winder, Thomas.
Winslow, S. A.

Clarke

Anderson, Abijah.
Borton, Thomas.
† Delaney, Henry.
Dudale, Joseph.
Dugglas, Joseph A.
Face, Chauncey.
Farr, James.
†Fields, George.
†Fields, Jacob.
†Gazway, John W.
†Guy, Henry.
Heiskell, D. O.
Howell, Samuel C.
†Martin, Henry.
Newcomb, Isaac.
Nichols, John D.
†Nutter, Abraham.
†Nutter, Henry.
Pierce, Jacob.
Pierce, Jonathan.

Pierce, Wm.
†Piles, Robert.
Smith, Seth.
Stanton, Benjamin.
†Stanup, Levi.
Stout, Charles.
Stout, James.
Thomas, Pressly.
Thorne, Thomas.
Thorne, Wm.
Van Meter, Joel.
Wildman, John.
Wilson, Daniel.
Wright, Richard.

Clermont

Barber, W. S.
Brown, Isaac H.
Buntin, James.
Burrows, Salathiel F.
†Davis, Sandy.
Ebersole, Jacob.
Edwards, Fred.
Fee, Enos.
Fee, Lee.
Fee, M. T.
Fee, Oliver Perry Spencer.
Fee, Robert E.
Gibson, Dr. M.
Hayden, James.
Hayden, Joseph.
Hoover.
House, David.
Huber, Boerstler.
Huber, Charles B.
Larkin, Moses.
Mace, Richard.
Melvin, "Jack."
Miller, Lewis.
Morris, Thomas.
Parrish, Joseph, Sr.
Pease, Dr. L. T.
Pettijohn, Rev. John.
Poage, Rev. Smith.
Powell, Andrew L.
Reese, Wm. J.
Reilley, Jeret.
Rice, Benjamin.
South, James W.
Sowards, James.
Utter, Hon. Dowty.
Waite, Deloss S.

Clinton

Allen, Abram.
Allen, David.

APPENDIX E

Bales, Isaac.
Betts, Aaron.
Brooke, Dr. Abram.
Brooke, Edward.
Brooke, James B.
Brooke, Samuel.
Brooke, Wm.
Dakin, Dr. George M.
Dakin, Perry.
Davis, Isaac.
Davis, Joel P.
Furguson, Samuel.
Hadley, John.
Haines, Mark.
Haines, Samuel.
Haynes, Wright.
Hiatt, Christopher.
Hibben, Thomas.
Johnson.
King, D. S.
Linton, Seth.
Nicholson, Artemas.
Oren, Elihu.
Osburn, Wm.
Sewell, David.
Strickle, Andrew.
Thompson, H. B.
Waln, W. M.
Woodmansee, Thomas.

Columbiana

Bonsall, Daniel.
Bowen, Benj. F.
Bronson, Daniel.
Brooks, Samuel.
Carey, Dr.
Cattell.
Coppoc.
Davis, Benj. B.
Evans, Philip.
Farmer, Dr. James.
French, Thomas.
French, Esther.
Galbraith, David.
Galbraith, James.
Galbraith, Nathan.
Galbraith, Thomas.
Garretson.
George, "Squire."
Heaton, Jacob.
Hise, Howell.
Irish, Wm. B.
Irwin, Malon.
Irwin, Samuel.
†Lucas, George W. S.

McMillan, Joel.
Myers, Samuel.
Negus, West.
Robinson, Marius Racine.
Smith, David J.
Stanley, Jonathan.
Street, John.
Street, Zadock.
Trescott, Isaac.
West.

Coshocton

Boyd, James.
Boyd, Luther.
Boyd, Wm. Miller.
Campbell, Alexander.
Elliott, Wm.
Foster, Prior.
Lawrence, Solon.
Nichols, Eli.
Powell, Thomas.
Seward, Ebenezer.
Shannon, John P.
Shannon, Isaac.
Wier, Samuel.
White, Benj.

Crawford

Quaintance, Fisher.
Roe, Joseph.

Cuyahoga

Adams, Ezekiel.
Atkins, Quintus F.
Bell, John.
Cady, Asa.
Cay, Capt.
Ford, Cyrus.
Ford, Frank.
Ford, Horace.
Mackelwrath, Michael.
Paine, Robert.
Wade, Edward.

Darke

Clemens.
Gilpatrick, Dr. Rufus.
Hanway, James.
Spencer, Anderson.

Delaware

Benedict, Aaron.
Benedict, Aaron L.
Benedict, Cyrus.

Benedict, Daniel.
Benedict, G. G.
Benedict, M. J.
Cratty, John.
Cratty, Robert.
Cratty, Wm.
Dillingham, Micajah.
Dodds, Wm.
Flannigan, Dea.
Levering, Griffith.
Lewis, John.
Mosher, Joseph.
Osborn, Aaron L.
Osborn, Daniel.
Osborn, Wm.
Ream, Samuel.
Wood, Daniel.

Erie

Alsdorf, Col. V. B.
Anderson, Elijah.
†Anderson, Peter.
Barber, Rev. Eldad.
Barney, George.
Beatty, John.
†Boston, Rev. Thomas.
Brainard.
†Brown, Bazel.
†Brown, Isaac.
†Butler, Thomas.
†Butler, Wm.
†Carr, Samuel.
Clark, Wm. H., Jr.
Clark, Wm. H., Sr.
Darling, Isaac.
Davidson, J. N.
Drake, Thomas.
†Floyd, Samuel.
Goodwin, Homer.
Hadley, Clifton.
†Hamilton, Andrew.
†Hamilton, John.
†Hampton, John.
Hathaway, Peter.
Hitchcock, S. E.
†Holmes, Robert.
Irvine, John.
Irvine, Samuel.
†"Black Jack."
†Jackson, John.
Jennings, R. J.
†Johnson, Benjamin.
†Jones.
Keech, C. C.
Lewis, L. H.

Lockwood, George.
Lockwood, Henry.
†Loot, John B.
McGee, Thomas C.
McLouth, O. C.
Merry, H. F.
Nugent, Capt. James.
Parish, F. D.
Peck, Otis L.
Pool, John G.
Reynolds, Geo. J.
†Ritchie, Grant.
†Robertson, George.
†Robinson, Andy.
Root, J. M.
Ruess, Herman.
Scott, Lyman.
Sloane, Hon. Rush R.
Starr, Perez.
Thorpe, Rev. John.
Tillinghast, O. C.
Walker, Samuel.
Williams, H. C.
†Wilson, Wm.
†Winfield, Alfred.
†Winfield, John.

Fayette

Atkins, Isaac.
Browder, Fletcher.
Connor, James.
Dickey, Rev. Wm.
Eastman, David.
Edwards, Wm.
Elliott, Wilson.
Eustick, Robert.
Eustick, Wm.
Gillespie, Dr.
Gillespie, George.
Hopkins, Jerry.
Larmour, James.
Larmour, Thomas.
McNara, James.
Orcutt, Barrack.
Pinkerton, Wm.
Puggsly, Jacob.
Rodgers, Thomas.
Roeback, Hugh.
Steele, Adam.
Steele, Robert.
Steward, Dr. Hugh.
Steward, Col. James.
Stewart, George.
Wilson, Samuel.

APPENDIX E   421

Franklin

Alexander, Shepherd.
Black, George W.
Bookel, John.
Bull, Jason.
Clarke.
Coulter, Dr.
Dickerman, Benonah.
Ferguson, Wm.
Freeland, Jeremiah.
Gardner, Ozem.
Gardner, Wilson.
Graham, David.
Hambleton, Isaac H.
Hambleton, Thomas.
Hoffman, John.
Jenkins, David.
Kline, Jacob.
Kilbourne, Col. James.
Kline, Thomas.
Mattoon, Ansel.
Patterson, David.
Park, James.
Pettibone.
†Poindexter, Rev. James.
Rees, John.
Rollison, L.
Sebring, Edward L.
Sharp, Garrett.
Smith, Dr. Samuel.
Thompson, Daniel.
Thompson, John W.
†Ward, John.
†Washington, Lewis, Sr.
†Washington, Thomas.
†Washington, Wm.
Westwater, James M.
Wilson, James.

Gallia

Allen, Richard.
Audrey, James P.
Bingham, Dr. Julius A.
Blodgett, Reuben.
†Chavis, John.
Clark, Daniel.
Clark, Wm.
†Cousins, Joseph.
†Crossland, Chas.
Davis, Hiram.
Eaton, Dr. Henry.
Eblen, James.
†Ellison, Wm.
Glenn, Andrew.
Glenn, Curry.

Glenn, James.
Glenn, M. K.
Hanger, Frederick.
Hanger, George.
†Harvey, Henry.
Heacock, J. D.
†Hocks, Wm.
Holcomb, A. J.
Holcomb, E. J.
Holcomb, E. T.
Holcomb, J. E.
Holcomb, Hon. Samuel R.
†James, Caliph.
†James, Howell.
Jarrett, Gabriel.
Kent, Abel.
Payne, George J.
Porter, John D.
Porter, Marshall.
Porter, Sumner.
Ross, N. D.
Sisson, N. B.
†Stewart, Isaac.
†Stewart, Jacob.
†Stewart, James W.
†Stewart, John J.
†Stewart, John S.
†Stewart, T. N.
Symmes, Wm.
Tate, David.

Green

Arnett, James H.
Atkinson, Thomas.
Barrett, James.
†Bell, John H.
Beven, Abel.
Clemons, James.
Coates, Lindley.
Coat, Joseph.
Compton, John.
†Conway.
†Davis, James.
Fletcher, Robinson.
Fletcher, Wm.
†Gillingham, Wm.
†Johnson, Hezekiah.
Johnson, Simeon.
Little, Cyrus.
Little, Robert.
†Lucas, Wm.
†McAllister, John.
†Martin, Harry.
Martin, Dr.
Monroe, David.

Orcutt, Barach.
†Overton, Lewis.
†Shelton, Walter.
†Sloan, Frederick.
†Washington, Henry.
Watson, Dr.
Whitney, Wm.
Wynins, Judge.

Guernsey
Boyd, James.
Broom, Daniel.
Brown, Thomas.
Craig, John.
Craig, Samuel.
Crooks, John.
Green, John.
Hall, Edward.
Leeper, John.
McCracken, Alex.
McCracken, Wm.
Miller, Adam.
Miller, Joseph.
Oldham, M.
Patterson, Samuel.
Reed, Judge.
Richey, Andrew.
Swayne, Samuel.
Thompson, Ebenezer.
Thompson, Eleazer.
Thompson, Rev. Evan.
White, P. H.

Hamilton
Aten, Adrian.
Bailey, Dr. Gamaliel.
Bales, Asa.
Birney, Wm.
Ball, Flamen.
Brisbane, Dr. Benj. Lawton.
Brisbane, Rev. Wm. Henry.
Burgoyne, Judge.
Burnett, Cornelius.
Burnett, Thomas.
Bushnell, Horace.
Butterworth, Wm.
Cable, Rev. Jonathan.
Carey, Wm.
Chase, Salmon P.
Cheney, Charles.
Coffin, Addison.
Coffin, Levi.
Colby, Dr.
Coleman, Mrs. Elizabeth.
Coleman, John H.

Donaldson, A.
Donum, Thomas.
Fairfield, John.
Franklin, Thomas.
Glenn, Edward R.
Harwood, Dr. Edward.
†Hatfield, John.
Hayes, Rutherford B.
Hogans, Judge.
Jolliffe, John.
Lewis, Henry.
Lewis, Rev. Samuel.
Lindley, Aaron.
Mussey, Dr. W. H.
Pennington, Levi.
Pfaff, Dr. J. L.
Pugh, A. M.
Pyle, Mrs. M. J.
Reynolds, Samuel.
Roberts, Hansel.
Roberts, Wade.
Robinson, Mrs. Emily.
Rusk, Rev.
Schooley, Nathaniel.
Stowe, Professor Calvin E.
Stowe, Harriet Beecher.
Townshend, Dr. Norton S.
Van Zandt, John.
White, Micajah.
Williams, Hatfield.
Wilson, Rev. D. M.
Wilson, J. G.
Wilson, Samuel.

Hancock
Adams, David.
Ardinger, P. D.
Beach, Dr. Belizur.
Bigelow, Henry.
Brown, Ezra.
Bushon, A.
Chadwick, C.
Cory, David J.
Cox, Hiram.
Cox, John.
Engleman, John.
Haglar, E.
Henderson, Fred.
Huber, Benjamin.
Hurd, R. B.
King, John, Sr.
Markle, Joel.
Morall, Joseph.
McCaughey, W.
Newell, Hugh.

Parker, Jonathan.
Porch, Henry.
Strothers, Robert.
Wheeler, Jesse.

Hardin

†Bray, Tapler.
Edgars, David H.
Elder, Culbertson.
†Harris, Henry.
†Hunster, Wm.
McConnell, Isaiah.
Newcomb, Cromwell.
†Newlan, Henry.
†Newlan, John A.
Watson, John.
Williams, Obadiah H.

Harrison

Carnehan, John.
Clarke, George P.
Cope, Jacob.
Cope, John.
Cope, Joseph.
Goff, J. H.
Hammond, Richard.
Hanna, Wilson.
Hazlett, John.
Huggins, Henry M.
Hunt, John.
Johnson, Micajah T.
†Johnson, West.
Lee, Rev. J. B.
Lee, Judge Thomas.
Lucas, Henry.
Lucas, Edward.
McFaddin, Wm.
McFarland.
McNealy, Cyrus.
Mead, Joseph.
Paul, Samuel.
Rogers, Wm.
Steele, Dr.
Swain, Thomas.
Walker, Rev. John.
†Willis, Lot.
Wilson, Dr. Martin.
Wilson, Wm.
Work, Alexander.
Work, David.

Highland

Bales, W.
Beatty, Alexander.
Brooks, Wm.

Campbell, Richard.
Cowgill, Benjamin.
Cowgill, John.
Doster, Henry.
Douglas, Wm.
Dunlap, Dr. Milton.
Evans, Noah.
Fullerton, George.
Ghormley, David.
Ghormley, Wm.
Gillispie.
Hibben, Samuel.
Hunter, John V.
Keys, Wm.
Lucas, Richard.
McClure, "Squire."
McElroy, Ebenezer.
McElroy, Thomas.
Nelson, John.
Nelson, Wm.
Parker, Samuel.
Patterson, Alexander.
Rodgers, Col. Thomas.
Sewell, David.
Smith, Wm.
Somers, Absalom.
Strain, John R.
Strickel, Stephen.
Sumner, Robert.
Templeton, Robert.
Templeton, Wm.
Thuma, Peter.
Tomlinson, Jacob.
Tomlinson, Moses.
Ustick, W. A.
Van Pelt, Jonathan.
Williams, Nat.
Wilson, Adam R.
Wilson, Thomas.
Wilson, Wm.
Young.

Holmes

Bell, Alexander.
Bigham, Ebenezer.
Bigham, J. C.
Crocko, John.
Crocko, Kieffer.
Finney, John.
Fleming, James.
Johnson, Andrew.
Johnson, James.
McClellan, Andrew.
McClellan, Samuel.
McClure, John.
Whitten, Rev.

Huron

Adams, Henry.
Bly, Rouse.
Buckingham, Henry.
Healy, Jacob.
Healy, Joseph.
Palmer, Rundell.
Palmer, Samuel.
Palmer, Seeley.
Parker, "Elder" Benj.
Parker, Nelson.
Parker, Rev. Seth C.
Sherman, Lemuel.
Smith, Willis R.
Strong, Abner.
Townsend, Hiram.
†Wilson, Wm.
Wright, Judge Jabez.

Jackson

Bingham, Julius A.
Crookham, George L.
Ford, Rev. I. N.
Isham, Asa W.
†Janes.
Montgomery, Samuel G.
†Nooks, Noah.
†Steward family.
†Woodson family.

Jefferson

Clarke, Samaria.
Clark, Wm.
Cope, Joseph H.
Crab, Henry.
Crab, John.
†Davis, John.
George, A. W.
George, David.
George, James.
George, Robert.
George, Judge Thomas.
Griffith, John.
Hammond, Alexander.
Hammond, Hon. John.
Hammond, Joseph.
Herford family.
Holloway, Jacob.
Jenkins, George K.
Ladd, Benj.
Ladd, James D.
Ladd, James L.
Ladd, Wm. H.
Lindsay, Dr.
Lukens.
McGrew, Finley B.
McGrew, J. C.
Mendenhall, Cyrus.
Orr, George.
Orr, John.
†Pointer, Thomas.
Powell, John.
†Ray, Wm.
Roberts, Ezekiel.
Robinson, Wm.
Stanton, Dr. Benj.
Tetirick, Elias.
Tomlinson, Carver.
Updegraff, David.
Underwood, Johnson.
Watson, John M.
Watson, Mathew.
Wolcott, C. C.

Knox

Delanow.
Frederick.
Townsend, Thomas.

Lake

Butler, Samuel.
Howe, Mrs. Sophia Hull.
Marshall, Seth.
Pepoon, A. C.
Pepoon, Benjamin.
Perkins.
Root, Phineas.

Lawrence

Beaman, Rev.
Campbell, Hiram.
Campbell, John.
Chester, Rev. Joseph.
†Coker, Tolliver.
Cratoff.
Creighton, Rev. Joseph H.
†Dicher, James.
Hall, Dr. Cornelius.
†Holly, Benjamin.
†Johnson, Gabe N.
Leete, Ralph.
†Lynch, Philip.
McGugin, Wm.
†Mathews, John.
Reckard, Judge Wm.
Wilgus, Chas.
Wilson, Stephen.

Licking

Bancroft, Dr. W. W.
Cane, Norton.

APPENDIX E

Dunlop, Wm.
Green.
Hillyer, Justin.
Howe, Curtis.
Knowlton, L. W.
Linnel, Joshua.
Rees, John.
Rose, Lamuel.
Whiting, Christopher L.
Wright, E. C.
Wright, Wm. S.

Logan

Aiken, James.
Aiken, Joseph.
Barnet, James.
†Bird, Erasmus.
†Bird, Redmond.
Boyd, David.
Boyd, Robert.
†Day, John.
†Day, Solomon.
Dickinson, Robert.
Elliot.
Forsyth, J. M.
Fulton, James.
Fulton, Thomas.
George, Henry.
†Hicks, John.
Hunt, David.
†Hunt, Howell.
Jameson, Cornelius.
Jeffers, Dr.
Johnston, J. B.
Johnston, Renwick.
Johnston, Samuel P.
McAyral, Dr. R. A.
McRaille, George.
McWelly, Paul.
Milligan, J. C. K.
Milligan, J. S. T.
Mitchell, Mathew.
†Mocksley, Wm.
†Overly, Barney.
Patterson, Abraham.
Patterson, David.
Patterson, Isaac.
Pickerell, Henry.
Pickerell, Mahlon.
Pickerell, Wm.
Rankin, James.
Richie, Jonathan.
†Scott, Henry A.
Scott, Thomas.
Sloane, J. R. W.

†Sprague, Esau.
Stanton, Benjamin.
†Tabor, Allen.
Townsend, Levi.
Trumbull, James.
Trumbull, John.
Walker, Judge James.
†White, Henry.
Williams, Asa.
Williams, Silas.
Young, John.

Lorain

Boise, Eli.
Brooks, Samuel.
Bushnell, Simeon.
†Cox, Sabraham.
DeWolf, Mathew.
Fitch, J. M.
Gillet, Mathew.
Hewes, Lewis.
Langston, Chas. H.
Loveland, Abner.
Manderville, John.
Niles, Henry.
Siples, Wm.
Soules, Walter.
Wadsworth, Loring.
Warren, Luther.

Lucas

Anderson, David.
Ashley, James M.
Brigham, Mavor.
Conlisk, James.
Mott, Richard.
Scott, Dr. H.

Madison

Allen, Wm. V.
Baskerville, James.
Baskerville, Marshall Pinkerton.
Baskerville, Richard A.
Baskerville, Samuel.
Baskerville, Wm. B.
Byers, Moses.
Byers, Newton.
Creamer.
Orcutt, Daniel.
Rapp, Jonah.
Slagle, Christian K.

Mahoning

Adair, James.
Andrews, Chauncey.

Bailey, David.
Barnes, Jacob.
Bousell, Daniel.
Burnet, Henry.
Eaton, Daniel.
Garlic, Dr. Theodatus.
Hart, Ambrose.
Henry, Francis.
Hoge, Wesley.
Holcombe, John R.
Holland, Richard,
Kidwalader, Edward.
Kidwalader, Eli.
Kirk, John.
Kirtland, Dr. Jared Potter.
Laughridge, John.
Moore, Sampson.
Morse, Elkinch.
Sharp, Thomas.
Squires, John.
Thorn, Wilson.
Truman, Daniel.
Van Fleet, John.
Wells, John.

Marion

Ashbaugh, Arminens.
Ashbaugh, Frederick.
Botsford, Wm. Hiram.
Clark, Enoch.
Clements, Anson.
David.
Dudley, Moses.
Fisher, Wm.
Morris, Joseph.
Petus, Nathan.
Spelman, E. G.

Medina

Burr, Timothy.
Hulburt, Halsey.
Matteson, Cyrus.

Meigs

Barrets family.
Holt, Horace.
Jiles, Cyrus.
Milles family.
Rathbon family.
Simpson family.

Miami

Abbott, Dr. N.
Brandriff, Rev. Richard.

Clyde, George C.
Coate, Elijah.
Coates, Jonathan.
Coates, Joshua.
Davis, Henry.
Dooling, Dr. Wm.
Fairfield, Mikey P.
Green, Wm.
Hutchins, Josiah.
Jay, Denny.
†Lawrence, Henry.
McCampbell, John Milton.
McMurd, Robert T.
Miles, Ephraim.
Miles, John.
Miles, Samuel.
†Nelson, John.
Pearson, Isaac.
Pemberton, Jesse.
Pickering, Burrell.
Scudder, James.
Smith, Lester.
Stevens, Andrew.
Stevens, Samuel.
Tullis, John T.

Morgan

Adams, James.
Arkins, E. W.
Bagley, Samuel.
Beckwith, David.
Beckwith, Solomon.
Bundy, Wm.
Byers, Thomas.
Cheadle, Rial.
Coldasure, Mrs.
Cope, Charles.
Cope, Nathan P.
Cope, Wm.
Corner, Arthur.
Corner, Edward.
Corner, Wm.
Coulson, Jehu.
Deaver, David H.
Deaver, Jonas.
Deaver, Mrs. Affadilla.
Dennis, Adam.
Devore, John.
Doudna, Joseph.
Dunlap, Adam.
Everett, John.
Eves, James.
Folk, Wm.
Gift, Mrs. Jane.
Glendenon, David.

APPENDIX E

Glendenon, Isaac.
Glines, Wm.
Graham, Benjamin.
Gray, Thomas L.
Guthrie, Erastus.
Hambleton, James.
Hambletou, John.
Harrison, Wm.
Hart, James W.
Harvey, John.
Hughes, Edward.
Jones, J. K.
Lavery, Joseph.
Lee, Dr. John.
Little, Dr. H. H.
Mariam, Cyrus.
Martin, George.
Matson, Enoch.
Millhouse, Wm.
Millions, Daniel.
Millions, Robert.
Millions, Wm.
Multon, James.
Nowlton, George.
Penrose, Thomas.
Porter, Ralph.
Reese, Mrs. Rhoda.
Sheppard, Isaiah.
Smith, Humphrey.
Smith, Thomas K.
Stanbery, Elias.
Stanbery, Jacob.
Stanbery, Perly.
Stokely, Mrs. Lydia.
Stone, John B.
Weller, Henry.
Williams, Enoc.
Williams, Isaac.
Williams, Jno. Thos.
Wood, John.
Wood, Joshua.
Woodward, Joseph.
Woodward, William.

Morrow

Andrews, Samuel.
Auld, James.
Benedict, Wm.
Brownlee, Archy.
Dillingham, Richard.
Eaton, Joseph.
Ford, Gen. Henry.
Gordon, Rev.
Hammond, John.
Hammond, Richard.

Hindman, Rev. Samuel.
Hughes, Benjamin.
Hull, George.
Keese, John.
Luke, Thomas.
McClaren, Robert.
McGinnis.
McKibben, James.
McNeal, Allen.
McNeal, J. F.
Mosher, Asa.
Mosher, John.
Oshel, James.
Patent, Mark.
Preshaw, Wm.
Roberts, Dr. Reuben L.
Steele, Wm.
Tabor, Wm.
Taylor, James.
Walker, Andrew.
Walker, John.
Willets, Joel.
Wood, David.
Wood, Israel.
Wood, Jonathan.

Montgomery

Aughey, John.
Bruen, Luther.
Coates, David.
Coates, Henry.
Herrman, Henry.
Jay, Denny.
Jay, Samuel.
Jewett, Dr. Adams.
Jewett, Dr. Hibbard.
Shedd, James A.

Muskingum

Bells.
Brown family.
Buckingham.
Elliot family.
Emerson family.
Gillespie, Mathew.
Gutherie, Austin Albert.
Hodly family.
Harmon family.
McAtier family.
Marlow.
Nye, Maj. Horace.
Pennock, Elwood.
Speer, Robert.
Stitt, James, Sr.
Terrell, Adam.

Terrell, Marlow.
Wallace, David.
Ward, Hudson Champlin.
Whipple, Levi.

Noble

Calland, Robert.
Cleveland, Timothy.
Garner, Peter M.
Horton, Richard.
Horton, Thomas.
Leeper, Rev. Wm.
Lingo, Achilles.
Phillips, Rev.
Steele, Wm.
Tuttles, Church B.

Perry

Burrell, Almond Hervey.

Pickaway

Doddridge, Wm.
Drisback, Jonathan.
Hanby, Rev. Wm.

Pike

†Barretts family.
†Munces family.

Portage

Case, Truman.
Folgier, Wm.
Frazer.
Hutton, Mrs. Massey.
Keen, Greenbury.
Quier, A. C.
Sloane, John.
Steadman, General.

Preble

Brown, Rev. Jas. R.
Brown, Nathan, Jr.
Elliott, Hugh.
Geeding, Adam H.
Gifford.
Graves.
Kinnelly, Daniel.
Maddock, John.
Mitchel.
Silvers, Samuel.
Stubbs, Jesse.
Stubbs, John W.
Stubbs, Newton.
Talberts.

Richland

Blymyers.
Craig, Dr. I. U.
Finney, James.
Finney, John P.
Gass, Benjamin.
McClure, Benjamin.
McClure, James.
McClure, John.
McClure, Samuel.
McClure, Wm.
Martin, Isaac.
Martin, James.
Mitchell, George.
Reed, John.
Robbins.
Roe, Joseph.
Sandersall, Thomas.
Wood, James.

Ross

Anderson, James.
Chancelor, Richard.
Chancelor, Robert.
Claypool, Isaac.
Fidler, Jesse.
Fidler, John.
Fullerton, Rev. Hugh S.
Galbraith, Robert.
†Green.
Harmon, John.
Jackson, James.
Langstren, Chas. H.
Lunbeck, Joseph.
†Mitchell, Rev. W. M.
Prizer, David.
Redmond, Andrew.
Sample, John.
Scott, Sutterfield.
†Skillgess, Joseph.
Steward, Col. Robert.
Tulley, Erasmus.

Sandusky

Bidwell, Iberias.
La Fever, John.
Paden, Hon. H. F.

Scioto

Ashton, Joseph.
Kennedy, Milton.
†Love, Joseph.
†Lucas, Dan.
McClain, Capt.

APPENDIX E

Seneca
Grimes family.
Whetsels family.

Shelby
Bennet, John S.
Ogden, Pharaoh A.
Roberts, James M.

Stark
Austin, James.
Blakesley, Jonathan.
Bowman, Isaac.
Brooks, Dr. Abram.
Brooks, Edward.
Brooks, James.
Brooks, Samuel.
Coates, Isaac.
Coffin, Chas.
Cole, Dr. Joseph.
Cope, Hiram.
Cope, Mary Ann.
Edgerton, Gov. Sidney.
Erwin, Mahlon.
Folger, Capt. Robert H.
Fox, Jehial.
Gaskin.
Gilbert, Barclay.
Grant, Chas.
Hall, John.
Johnson, Ellis.
Lukens, Joseph.
Macy, Mathew.
Macy, Samuel.
Marshall, Benj.
Mead, Abner.
Peirce, I. Newton.
Purdy, Fitch.
Purdy, Gerden.
Quier, Arome.
Quier, Mary.
Rockhill, Samuel.
Rotch, Thomas.
Sperry, I. P.
Stout, Zebbes.
Williams, Irvine.
Williams, Richard.
Wright, Alpha.
Wright, Dr. Amos.
Wright, Clement.

Summit
Brown, Jason.
Brown, John.

Clarke, Ezra.
Hudson, David.

Trumbull
Braden, John.
Brown, Col.
Brown, Ephraim.
Bushnell, Gen. Andrew.
Coon.
Douglass, Thomas.
Fenn, Benjamin.
Fuller, Samuel.
Green, Cyrel.
Haines, Acyel.
Harris, Milo.
Hart, Ambrose.
Hayes, Col.
Hayes, Seth.
Hoffman, B. F.
Hutchins, John.
Jenkins.
King, Judge Leicester.
Stewart, Charles.
Sutliff, Judge Levi.
Tracy, Azel.
Weed, John.

Tuscarawas
Craig, Wm. H.
Fox, J. W.
Lindsey, Samuel.
McClain, Edward.
McClain, Wm.
Meek, Robert.
Powell, F. W.
Powell, Thomas.

Union
Carroll, Asa.
Cherry, Samuel A.
Ferris, Herman.
Kinney, Dr. S. M.
†Mayo, Joe.
Rathbon, Dr. Charles.
Skinner, Aaron.
Skinner, W. H.
Wood, Judge Wm. W.

Vinton
Brown, Henry.
Castor, James.
Fogg, Thomas P.
Hawk, Benjamin.
Hudson, S.

Morris, Abram.
Ogle, Henry.

Warren

Allen, Abram.
Allen, David.
Bateman, Jacob.
Bateman, John.
Bateman, Warner M.
Bedford, Wm.
Brooks, Dr.
Butterworth, Henry T.
Butterworth, Samuel.
Butterworth, Wm. B.
Carr, Job.
Corwin, R. G.
Evans, Joseph.
Farr, Angelina.
Farr, Franklin.
Hopkins, Thomas.
Miller.
Mullin, Isaac.
Mullin, Job.
Nicholson, Valentine.
Potts, Edward.
Potts, John.
Potts, Samuel.
Pugh, Achilles.
Thomas, Jonah D.
†Wilson, Fred.
Wilson, Jesse.
Wright, Jonathan.

Washington

Bailey, Uriah.
Cottle, Hamilton.
Curtis, Liberty.
Curtis, Eli.
Dufer, Abe.
Eastman, Adoniram.
Fairchild, Hiram.
Fairchild, Joseph.
Fulcher, Andrew.
Garner, Peter M.
Gould, Ephraim.
Hale, Smith.
Hale, Levi.
Harris, Asa.
†Harrison, Geo. Wm.
Heald, Wm. S.
Hibbard, T. B.
Hovey, Harvey.
Hughes, Benjamin.
Jones, Jerry.

Lawton, James.
Lee, Jonathan.
Loraine, Craton.
Lund, Isaac.
McCoy, Rev. J. C.
Mallett, Albert.
Morris, Andrew.
†Norman, Frank.
Norton, Rev. Richard.
Porter, Thomas.
Powells, Washington.
Preston, Col.
Price, Abraham.
Putnam, David.
Rice, James.
Ridgeway, Thomas.
Shepard, Courtland.
Shotwell, Isaac.
Shotwell, Titus.
Smith, Harvey.
Smith, Wm. Joseph.
Steel, Wm.
Stephenson, Dr.
Stanton, Burdin.
Stanton, Nathan.
Stone, Frank.
Stone, Col. John.
Tuttle, C. B.
Vickers, Dr.
Wilson, Thomas.

Wayne

Battles, Thomas S.
Bell, Charity.
Burr, Timothy.
Clark, David.
Cheney, Hibben.
Daniels, Isaac.
Degarmon, Dr. Joseph.
Ladd, Benjamin W.
McClelland, H. R.
May, Daniel.
Oldroyd, Charles.
Perdu.
Rose, James.
Seibert, Samuel.
Smith, Thomas L.
Taggart, Robert.

Western Reserve

Brown, Owen.
King, Leicester.
Perkins, Gen.
Wright, Elizur.

Wood

Merriton, Wm.
Moore, Lee.

Miscellaneous

Cross, Joseph.
Fulcher, John.
Heberling, A.
Palmer, Rundell.

PENNSYLVANIA

Adams

Everett, Hamilton.
Stevens, Thaddeus.
Walker, Benjamin.
Wright, Wm.

Allegheny

Taylor, Charles.

Beaver

Brown, Rev. Abel.
Gilbert, Joshua.
Rakestraw.

Bedford

†Crawley, Joseph.
†Fidler, Rev. John.
Perry, Wyett.
†Rouse, Rev. Elias.

Berks

Lewis, Thomas.
Scarlett, Joseph P.

Blair

Nesbet, Wm.

Bucks

Atkinson family.
Beause family.
Blackfan family.
Brown family.
Buckman family.
Burgess, William.
Corson, George.
Fell, Joseph.
Heston, Jacob.
Ivins, Barclay.
Jackson, Wm.
Janney, Richard.
Johnson, Wm. H.
Kenderdine, John E.

Linton, Mahlon B. and wife.
Lloyd, William.
Longshore, Jolly.
Magill, Jonathan P.
Moore, Richard.
Palmer, Jonathan.
Paxson family.
Pierce family.
Price, Kirk J.
Schofield, Benjamin.
Simpson family.
Smith, Chas. and Martha.
Swain family.
Trego family.
Twining family.
Warner, Isaac.
Williams, Edward.

Butler

Brown.
McGee, John.
McGee, George.

Chester

Agnew, Allen.
Agnew, Maria.
Barnard, Eusebius.
Barnard, Sarah D.
Barnard, Sarah Marsh.
Barnard, Simon.
Barnard, Wm.
Bonsall, Abram.
Bonsall, Thomas.
Carson, Charles.
Cain, Dr. Augustus W.
Coates, Levi.
Corson.
Cox, John.
Cox, Hannah.
Darlington, Chandler.
Darlington, Hannah M.
Darlington sisters.
Evans, Nathan.
Fulton, James, Jr.
Fulton, Joseph.
Fussell, Dr. Bartholomew.
Fussell, Dr. Edwin.
Fussell, Wm.
Groff, John A.
Haines, Joseph.
Hambleton, Charles.
Hambleton, Eli.
Hambleton, Thomas.
Hamer, Jesse.
Hayes, Esther.

Hayes, Mordecai.
Haynes, Jacob.
Hopkins, Thomas.
Jackson, Wm.
Kent, Benj.
Kent, Hannah.
Kimber, Emmor.
Kirk, Isaiah.
Lewis, Elizabeth.
Lewis, Esther.
Lewis, Grace Anna.
Lewis, Marianne.
Lindley, Jacob.
Maris, Morris.
Marsh, Gravner.
Mendenhall, Dinah.
Mendenhall, Isaac.
Meredith, Isaac.
Meredith, Thamazine.
Moore, Charles.
Moore, Joseph.
Painter, Samuel M.
Peart, Lewis.
Pennypacker, Elijah F.
Pierce, Benjamin.
Pierce, Gideon.
Price, George D.
Preston, Amos.
Preston, Mahlon.
Richards, Henry.
†Shadd, Abraham D.
Speakman, Micajah.
Speakman, Wm. A.
Sugar, John.
Sugar, Wm.
Taylor, Wm. W.
Thomas, Zebulon.
Thorne, J. Williams.
Trimble, Wm.
Vickers, John.
Vickers, Paxson.
Vickers, Thomas.
Walton.
Walker, Enoch.
Whitson, Moses.
Williams, James.
Williamson, Seymour C.
Wood, James.

Clearfield

Atcheson, George.
Atcheson, Wm.
Cochran, Isaac.
Gallaker, James.

Kirk, Jason, and sons.
Westover, Wm.

Crawford

Benn, Jonathan.
Brown, M. M.
Churchill.

Dauphin

Lewis, Dr.

Delaware

Dannaker, James T.
Garrett, Isaac.
Garrett, Philip.
Garrett, Samuel.
Jackson, John.
Lewis, James.
Price, Benjamin.
Price, Philip.
Truman, George S.

Erie

Henry, Frank.
Judson, Dr.
Towner, Jehiel.
Reeder, James.
Reeder, Job.

Fayette

Benson, Joe.
†Black, Joe.
Chalfant, Mathew.
Jackson, John.
Jackson, Joseph.
McClure, Potan.
Miller, Jacob B.
Waller, Thomas.
Wares, Joe.
Webster, Cato.

Hampden

Osgood, Dr.

Indiana

Baker, James.
Baker, John.
Campbell, Joseph.
Dixon.
Gamble, George.
Hamilton, James.
Henry.
Huston, John.
Huston, Robert.

APPENDIX E

Mitchell, Dr.
Mitchell, Robert.
Morehead, James.
Park, James L.
Powell, Wilson.
Rank, C. R.
Rank, George.
Rank, Samuel.
Rank, S. K.
Rank, Zenas.
Spaulding, George.
Swispelm, Jane G.
Thomas, Jesse.
White, S. P.
White, Wm., and three sons.
Work, the brothers.

Lancaster

Bessick, Thomas.
Bond, Samuel.
Brinton, Joseph.
Brinton, Joshua.
Brown, Ellwood.
Bushong, Henry.
Carter, Henry.
Coates, Lindley.
Eshelman, Dr. J. K.
Furniss, Oliver.
Gibben, Daniel.
Gibbons, Joseph.
Haines, Joseph.
Hood, Caleb C.
Hood, Joseph.
Jackson, Thomas.
Mifflin, Jonathan.
Mifflin, Samuel W.
Moore, James.
Moore, Jeremiah.
Peart, Thomas.
Russell, John Neal.
Smith, Allen.
Smith, Joseph.
Smith, Stephen.
Thorne, I. Wm.
Webster, George.
Whipper, Wm.
Whitson, Micah.
Whitson, Thomas.
Wright, Wm.

Lawrence

Anderson, Alex.
Bradford, A. B.
Bushnell, Rev. Wells.
Cadwalader.

Enwer, Daniel.
Enwer, John N.
Hart, Dr. A. G.
McKeever, Judge.
McKeever, Mathew.
McMillen, White.
Minich, James.
Mitchell, S. W.
Semple, Amzi C.
Semple, Eli.
Sharpless, Benjamin.
Stevenson, E. M.
Walker, W. W.
White, Joseph S.
Wright, Alexander.
Young, David.
Young, John.
Young, William.

Luzerne

Gildersleeve.

Mercer

Bishop.
Gilbert, John.
Gordon, Rev. George.
Grierson, Robert.
Hogue, John I.
Hogue, Wesley.
Jansan, Mathew.
Minich, James.
Squires, John.
Thorn, Wilson.
Travis, Richard.
Ward.
Wilson, George.
Young, John.

Mifflin

Johnston, Wm. B.
Maclay, Dr. Samuel.
Nourse, Rev. Joseph.
Thompson, James.
Thompson, Samuel.

Monroe

Singmaster, Jacob.
Vail family.

Montgomery

Aaron, Rev. Samuel.
Corson, E. Hick.
Corson, George.
Corson, Lawrence E.
Corson, Dr. Wm.

Garrigues, Benjamin.
Newport, David.
Paxson, Dr. Jacob I.
Pierce, Eli D.
Read, Thomas.
Roberts, Isaac.
Roberts, John.
Ross, Daniel.
Warner.

Philadelphia

Aaron, Rev. Samuel.
Bias, James Gould.
Brown, David Paul.
Burr, John P.
†Burris, Sam'l D.
Coates, Edwin H.
Davis, Edward M.
†Depee, N. W.
Earle, Hon. Thomas.
Elder, Dr.
Fortune, James.
Furness, Rev. Wm. H.
†Garnet, Henry Highland.
Harrison, Benj.
Harrison, Thomas.
Hastings, Samuel D.
Johnson, Wm. H.
Lambson, Capt.
McKim, J. Miller.
Moore, Esther.
Mott, James.
Mott, Lucretia.
Purvis, Robert.
Rhoads, Samuel.
†Ruggles, David.
†Still, Wm.
Smith, Stephen.
†Tubman, Harriet.
Twining, Henry M.
Ware, Isaiah.
Whildon, Capt.
†White, Jacob C.
Williamson, Hon. Passmore.
Wise, Charles.

Somerset

†Smith.
Willey, Wm.

Susquehanna

Bard, Sam'l.
Brewster, Horace.
Carmalt, Caleb.
Foster, Wm.

Lyons, B. R.
Post, Albert.
Post, Isaac.
Warner, Sam'l.

Venango

Conley.
Clapp, B. Ralph.
Howe, John W.
Hughes, John.
Kingsley, James.
†Lawson, James.
†Lawson, Job.
McDowell, Alex.
Raymond, Wm.
Rodgers, James.
Small, S. H.
Travis, Rich.

Washington

Lemoin, Dr.
McKeever, Mathew.

Wyoming

Drake, Jonathan.
Overfield, Nicholas.

York

Fisher, Joel.
Goodrich, Wm. C.
Jourdon, Cato.
Loney, Robert.
Mifflin, Jonathan.
Mifflin, Susan.
Mifflin, Sam'l.
Wallace.
Wierman, Joel.
Willis, Samuel.
Wright, Wm.

RHODE ISLAND

Newport

Mitchell, Jethro.
Mitchell, Anne.

Providence

Adams, Robert.
Buffum, Arnold.
Buffum, Wm.
Chace, Mrs. Elizabeth Buffum.
Chace, Samuel B.
Mitchell, Daniel.
Walker, Capt. Jonathan.

VIRGINIA
Brock
Bryant, Joseph.

Wheeling
†Naler, Dick.
Steele, Joshua.

Miscellaneous
Smith, Samuel A.

VERMONT
Addison
Barber, E. D.
Barker, Samuel.
Fuller, R. L.
Gordon, Joseph.
Robinson, Rowland T.
Rogers, Joseph.
Wicker, Cyrus W.

Bennington
Robert, Daniel, Jr.
Wilcox, Dr. S.

Caledonia
Bailey, Rev. Kiah.

Chittenden
Bigelow, L. G.
Briggs, Wm. P.
Byington, Anson.
Dean, Professor.
French, Wm. H.
Hoag, Nathan C.
Lovely, Noble.
McNeil.
Stansbury, E. A.
Young, Rev. Joshua, D.D.

Franklin
Brainerd, Hon. Lawrence.
Comings, Andrew.
Felton, Charles.
Green, Rev.
Kendall, Col. Samuel.
Martin, Jefferson.
Sanborn, E. S.
Sabin, Hon. Alvah.

Lamoille
Caldwell, A. W.
Dodge, Jonathan.

Gleed, Rev. John.
Hotchkiss, J. M.
Safford, Madison.
West, Hon. John.

Orange
Griswold, Howard.
Kimball, F. W.
Moore, Dr. L. C.
Putnam, Rev. George.
Rowell, Hon. A. J.

Rutland
Marsh, R. V.
Nicholson, D. E.
Ranney, E. S.
Rogers, Aaron.
Rogers, Dinah.
Thrall, R. R.

Washington
Arms, Dr.
Butler, Dea.
Miller, Col. J. P.
Parker, Dea.
Stows, Stephen F.

Windham
Frost, Willard.
Shafter, Oscar L.
Shafter, Wm. R.

Windsor
Fletcher, Ryland.
Hutchinson, Ozamel.
Hutchinson, Hon. Titus.
Morris, Dea. Sylvester.
Woodward, Daniel.

WISCONSIN
Racine
Bartlett, J. O.
Bunce, Charles.
Dutton, A. P.
Fitch, "Elder."
Peffer.
Pick, S. B.
Reed, Gen.
Secor, Dr.
Steel, Capt.
Utley, W. L.
Waterman, W. H.
Wright, George S.

Waukesha
Brown, Samuel.
Chandler, Daniel.
Clinton, Dea. Allen.
Dougherty.
Goodnow, Lyman.
Mendall, Dea.

Walworth
Thompson, Charles.

WASHINGTON, D.C.
Bigelow, Jacob.
Drayton, Capt. Daniel.

MEMBERS OF THE VIGILANCE COMMITTEE OF BOSTON, MASSACHUSETTS[1]

(Organized October 14, 1850)

Adams, Charles B.
Adams, George.
Alcott, A. Bronson.
Allen, Ephraim.
Allyne, Joseph W.
Andrew, John A.
Andrews, Erastus.
Apthorp, Robert E.
Atkinson, Edward.
Atkinson, William P.
Augustus, John.
Ayres, John.
Barker, Rensalaer.
Baxter, Thompson.
Bearse, Austin.
Bigelow, Dennis.
Bishop, Joel P.
Blakemore, William.
Blanchard, Joshua P.
Bolles, John A.
Botume, John, Jr.
Bouve, Thomas T.
Bowditch, Henry I.
Bowditch, William I.
Bramhall, Cornelius.
Bridge, Jonathan D.
Brimblecom, F.
Brimblecom, F. A.
Browne, John W.
Bryant, David.
Bruce, Jeptha C.
Burlingame, Anson.
Burrage, Alvah A.
Cabot, Fred. S.

Capen, Lemuel.
Carew, Thomas.
Carnes, George W.
Caswell, Lewis E.
Channing, William F.
Channing, William H.
Chase, L. G.
Cheever, George F.
Child, Alfred A.
Child, Daniel F.
Colver, Nathaniel.
Cornell, William M.
Cowing, Cornelius.
Crosby, Robert R.
Curtis, John, Jr.
Cushing, Henry D.
Cutter, Abraham E.
Dana, Richard H., Jr.
Danforth, John C.
Davie, Johnson.
Davis, Charles G.
Denio, Sylvanus A.
Dodge, George.
Dodge, Joshua G.
Downer, Samuel, Jr.
Edmunds, Edward.
Eldridge, John S.
Ellis, Charles.
Ellis, Charles M.
Emmons, John L.
Fay, Emery B.
Fillebrown, Edward.
Fisher, George J.
Fitch, Jonas.

[1] This list of names is taken from Bearse's *Reminiscences of Fugitive-Slave Law Days in Boston*, pp. 3, 4, 5, 6.

APPENDIX E

Fuller, Richard F.
Gage, Benjamin W.
Garrison, William Lloyd.
Gibbs, John B.
Gilbert, Timothy.
Gore, John C.
Gove, John.
Gooch, Daniel W.
Greene, Benjamin H.
Hamlet, William.
Hanscom, Simon P.
Hanson, Moses P.
†Hayden, Lewis.
Hayes, Joseph K.
Hersey, Nathan W.
Hildreth, Richard.
Hilton, John T.
Holman, Joshua B.
Holmes, Richard.
Holmes, William H.
Hood, Richard.
Houghton, George W.
Howe, Samuel G.
Howland, David.
Hovey, Charles F.
Hoxie, Timothy W.
Hunt, Ebenezer.
Hunter, Thomas.
Jackson, Edmund.
Jackson, E. W.
Jackson, Francis.
Jameson, William H.
Jenkins, William H.
Jewett, John P.
Kemp, Henry.
Kendall, Stephen B.
Kimball, John S.
Kimball, Peter.
King, John G.
King, T. Starr.
Knapp, Frederick N.
Lawton, John T.
Layton, Joseph J.
Lewis, Enoch.
Lewis, Joel W.
Lincoln, Henry W.
List, Charles.
Lloyd, Samuel H.
Locke, Amos W.
Loring, Ellis Gray.
Lowell, James Russell.
Mackay, T. B.
Manley, John R.
Marjoram, William W.
Marsh, Bela.

Marston, Russell.
May, Frederick W. G.
May, Samuel, Jr.
McCrea, J. B.
McPhail, Andrew M., Jr.
Merriam, E. S.
Merrill, George.
Minot, George.
Mitchell, George H.
Moody, Loring.
Morris, Robert.
Mussey, Benjamin B.
Nichols, Henry P.
Nash, Nathaniel C.
Nell, William C.
Orne, Otis.
Osgood, Isaac.
Parker, Henry T.
Parker, Theodore.
Parkman, John.
Parks, Luther, Jr.
Perkins, Thomas C.
Phelps, Sylvester.
Phillips, Wendell.
Pratt, J.
Prentiss, Henry J.
Putnam, Joseph H.
Quimby, J. P.
Quincy, Edmund.
Raymond, William T.
Richards, James B.
Ritchie, Uriah.
Rogers, George M.
Rogers, John S.
Rogers, Robert B.
Russell, George R.
Russell, Thomas, Jr.
Sargent, John T.
Sawyer, William N.
Sewall, Samuel E.
Shaw, Francis G.
Slack, Charles W.
Smilie, J. H.
Smith, Chauncey.
Smith, Joshua B.
Smith, J. W.
Smith, Stephen.
Snowden, Isaac H.
Southwick, Joseph.
Sporrell, William.
Spear, John M.
Spooner, Lysander.
Spooner, William B.
Steele, William M.
Stone, James W.

Stone, Milton J.
Storrs, Amariah.
Sullivan, John W.
Swift, John L.
Taft, A. C.
Talbot, S. D.
Tappan, Charles.
Thayer, David.
Thompson, John.
Tolman, James.
Towne, William B.
Treanor, Barnard S.
Trafton, Mark.
Trask, Henry P.
Wakefield, Enoch H.

Wallcutt, Robert F.
Walker, Dana D.
Warren, Washington.
Waters, Edwin F.
Waterston, Robert C.
Webb, Seth, Jr.
Whipple, Charles K.
White, William A.
Whitman, William H.
Wilson, Alexander.
Withington, Oliver W.
Wright, Elizur.
Yerrington, J. M. W.
York, Jasper H.

MEMBERS OF THE "LEAGUE OF GILEADITES" OF SPRINGFIELD, MASSACHUSETTS [1]

(Organized among the negroes by John Brown, January 15, 1851)

Addams, Joseph.
Burns, William.
Chandler, Samuel.
Dowling, B. C.
Fowler, Jane.
Gazam, C. A.
Gordon, William.
Green, Eliza.
Green, William.
Hector, Henry.
Holmes, G. W.
Howard, J. N.
Johnson, Ann.

Johnson, Henry.
Johnson, Reverdy.
Jones, H. J.
Montague, William H.
Odell, Charles.
Robinson, Henry.
Rollins, Charles.
Smith, John.
Strong, John.
Thomas, Cyrus.
Wallace, L.
Webb, Scipio.
Wicks, Jane.

And seventeen others, whose names are unknown.

MEMBERS OF THE VIGILANCE COMMITTEE OF SYRACUSE, NEW YORK [2]

(Organized October 4, 1850)

Agan, P. H.
Barnes, George.
Bates, Abner.

Clary, Lyman.
Levenworth, C. W.
†Loguen, J. W.

[1] Sanborn, in his *Life and Letters of John Brown*, pp. 125 and 126, prints this roll of members.

[2] This list will be found in the *Autobiography of the Rev. J. W. Loguen*, p. 396.

Putnam, H.
Raymond, R. R.
Sedgwick, C. B.
Smith, V. W.

Thomas, John.
Wheaton, C. A.
Wilkinson, John.

MEMBERS OF THE GENERAL VIGILANCE COMMITTEE OF PHILADELPHIA, PENNSYLVANIA [1]

(Organized December 2, 1852)

Asher, J.
Burr, J. P.
Bustill, Charles H.
Depee, Nathaniel.
Goines, B. N.
Gordon, Henry.
Hall, Morris.
M'Kim, J. M.
Nickless, Samuel.

Oliver, John D.
Purvis, Robert.
Reason, Prof. C. L.
Riley, W. H.
Still, William.
Wears, Josiah C.
White, Jacob C.
Whitson, Cyrus.
Wise, Charles.

[1] These names are given in Still's *Underground Railroad Records*, pp. 610, 611, 612.

INDEX

ABBOT, Major J. B., host of John Brown, 164.

Abbot, Rev. J. S. C., on effect of Fugitive Slave Law of 1850, on family of fugitives, 247, 248.

Abduction, Harriet Tubman, a practitioner in, 6; of slaves from Missouri by John Brown, 8, 9, 338; Rufus King on, 29 n.; of abolitionists, rewards for, 52, 53; of slaves from Covington, Ky., by Fairbank, 61; of slaves by John Fairfield, the Virginian, 66, 67; methods of, employed by Dr. A. M. Ross, 104; Still on abductions through agency of the U. G. R. R., 118 n.; sentiment of abolitionists against, 150; by negroes, 151; by refugees of Canada, 152, 153; by Southern whites, 153, 154; by Northern whites, 154, 155; by Burr, Work and Thompson, 155, 156; by Joseph Sider, 157; by Calvin Fairbank, 157-160; by Seth Concklin, 160-162; by John Brown, 162-165; in Brown's plan of liberation, 166, 167; by Charles T. Torrey, 168-170; by Capt. Jonathan Walker, 170, 171; by Laura S. Haviland, 171, 172; by Capt. Daniel Drayton, 172, 173; by Richard Dillingham, 174, 175; by Wm. L. Chaplin, 175, 176; by Josiah Henson, 176-178; by Rial Cheadle, 178, 179; by Dr. A. M. Ross, 179-182; by Elijah Anderson, 183; by John Mason, 183, 184; by Harriet Tubman, 185-189; of friends from the South planned by Canadian exiles, 231, 232; of a free negro from New York in 1850, 269; of negroes from southeastern Pennsylvania, 280; of free negroes from Northern state under law of 1793, 295; failure of Fugitive Slave Law of 1850 to recompense South for losses through, 341; disappearance of slavery from District of Columbia attributed to the U. G. R. R. and, 341, 342.

Abolition, gradual, 17; boats, 148; in Canada, 190, 191; sentiment of, in Northern states prevents reclamation of fugitives, 241-243; immediate, before Garrison, advocated by Bourne in 1816, 303, 304; immediate, advocated by Duncan in 1824, 304-306; immediate, advocated by Rankin in 1824, 306-308; immediate, germination of idea of, 307; immediate, formulation of the principle of, in U. G. R. R. neighborhoods, 357.

Abolitionists, hidden methods of, 2; recollections of, main source of history of Underground Railroad, 11; characterization of, 12; convictions of, 17; Fugitive Slave Law of 1850 detested by, 24; in Iowa, 43; testimony of, regarding activity of the U. G. R. R. (1830-1840), 44, 308; social disdain borne by, 48-50; espionage endured by, 50-54; rewards for abduction of, 52, 53; known as "conductors," 60; destitution of fugitives relieved by expenditures of, 76-78; waterway extensions of U. G. R. R. established by, 82; temper of, shown in rescue of fugitives under arrest, 86; political affiliations of, 99-101; United States Constitution burned at meeting of, 101; treated with justice in history, 101; penalties paid by, 102, 103; settlements of, in Maryland, 119; Brown Thurston of Portland, Me., a veteran, 133; on number of U. G. R. R. lines in Ohio, 135; devices of, to secure safety of fugitives, 141; sentiment of, against abduction, 150; dine with Fairfield the abductor, 154 n.; risks taken by an, in abducting a slave, 155; abductions by, along the borders of slave territory, 155; appeals

441

442   INDEX

of fugitives to, for aid for friends in bondage, 168; arrest of Charles T. Torrey for being an, 169; number of fugitives early aided by, in southern Ohio, 192; testimony of, on the effects of the Fugitive Slave Law of 1850, 193; underground work in Iowa and Illinois by, 194, 195; Canadian refugees visited by, 199-201; refuge found by runaway slaves among, in Northern states, 212, 213, 275; visitation of communities of, by slave hunters, 239, 240; prevent reclamation of fugitives, 241, 242; irritated by mode of arrests under Slave Law of 1793, 259; efforts to use Northwest Ordinance in defeat of law of 1793, 262, 263; law of 1850 objectionable to, 267-273; possibility of abduction of free negroes from the North under law of 1850, declared by, 268, 269; on commissioners' fees under law of 1850, 271, 272; secrecy observed by, 272; characteristics of pre-Garrisonian, 307; grateful employment of, in helping slaves, 310; societies of, criticised by Webster, 314; information about, among slaves, 316; exultation of, over rescue of Jerry McHenry, 320; residence of Harriet Beecher Stowe among, in Cincinnati, O., 321; various activities of, 326; increasing number of fugitives aided by, 327; restiveness of, under jurisdiction of United States Courts in fugitive slave cases, 335; of Lawrence, Kan., abused by Missourians, 347; aid rendered fugitives by, at Lawrence, Kan., 348; efficiency of underground work of, compared with work of American Colonization Society, 350, 351; support of U. G. R. R. by, alleged, 351; multiplication of, due to the U. G. R. R., 357.

Adams, Robert, 130.

Agents of the U. G. R. R., significance of the name, 67; in Baltimore, 68; employment of regular, 69, 70; number of, 87; hospitality of, 87-89; admitted principles of, 89, 90; nationality of, 90-92; church connections of, 93-98; churches of Massachusetts appealed to by, 99; political affiliations of, 99-101; character of, 101; penalties suffered by, 102, 103; Defensive League of Freedom for payment of fines of, proposed in Boston, 103, 104; notable persons among, 104-112; limited area of operation of, 113; in Pennsylvania, 121; in New York, 122-127; in New Jersey, 123, 124; in Massachusetts, 129, 130; in Vermont, 130, 131; devices of, 137; work of abduction by Seth Concklin as one of the, 160; fearless work of, at Sandusky, O., 276, 277; Harriet B. Stowe and John Brown as, 290; Rev. John Rankin, active in ranks of, 307; J. R. Giddings one of the most enthusiastic of, 315; appealed to by Canadian refugees for abduction of friends, 231, 232; among fugitive settlers in the North, 251-253.

Alabama, purchase of slaves by, 26; underground line from northern, 119; Canadian refugees from, 195; attempted abduction of Peter Still's family from, 160; operations in, planned by Brown, 167.

Alcott, A. B., friend of Harriet Tubman, 186; part of, in the Burns case, 331.

Alleghanies, the use to be made of, in Brown's plan of liberation, 166.

Allen, Abram, special conveyance of, for fugitives, 59, 60; visit of, to Canada, 199.

Alum Creek Quaker Settlement, leaf from diary of station-keeper in, 10; activity of station in, 76, 77; facsimile of record kept by Daniel Osborn of, 344, 345.

American Baptist Free Mission Society, ministrations to refugees in Toronto, Canada, 3, 183.

American Colonization Society, objects and work of, compared with those of U. G. R. R., 350, 351.

American Historical Review, on Underground Railroad, 5.

Amherstburg, Canada West as a receiving depot for fugitives, 194; visit of Levi Coffin to, 200; supplies for Canadian refugees in, 214; congregation of fugitives in, 225; negro mechanics in, 226; Dr. Howe on condition of colored people in, 226 n.; Drew on condition of refugees in, 227; separate schools for negroes in, 229; first "True Band" organized in, 230; comparison of amounts of property owned by whites and blacks in, and in other places, 232.

INDEX

Anderson, Elijah, abductor, 183.
Anderson, William, extradition of the fugitive, from Canada refused, 352, 353.
Andrew, Bishop James O., church proceedings against, 95.
Andrew, John A., 103; appreciation of Harriet Tubman, 189.
Andrews, Ex-Pres. E. Benjamin, on route in Massachusetts, 129.
"Anti-Slavery Days, History of," in Illinois, 6.
Anti-Slavery in the State and Nation, on refugees forwarded to Brunswick, 219.
Anti-slavery men, Theodore Parker on the first duty of, 109; meetings of, in New England, 171. *See* Abolitionists.
Anti-slavery movement, Chas. T. Torrey engages in, 168, 169; humane motives of, 286; U. G. R. R., a causal factor in development of, 290, 302; character of pre-Garrisonian, 307; continuity of development of, 307, 308; failure of *Uncle Tom's Cabin* to produce election gains for, 323.
Anti-slavery sentiment, among people from the Southern states, 31, 32, 41; revenge on Mission Institute for, 156; in Congress, 173; settlement of fugitives in communities characterized by, 212, 242; proof of early, in free states, 300; influence of U. G. R. R. in spreading, 302; in the North, 309, 310.
Anti-Slavery Society, of Philadelphia, of New York, Harriet Tubman a well-known visitor of the, 189; of Massachusetts, 193; of Canada, 204; benefactions of, for fugitive slaves, 222, 223; persons of respectability in societies, 308; encouragement given by, to bondmen to flee, 310; reports of Pennsylvania and Massachusetts societies on increasing number of fugitives after 1850, 327; of New England, meeting of, at time of rendition of Burns, 332.
Appalachian route of escape for slaves, 118.
Appleby, Capt., master of lake boat carrying fugitives, 82.
Arkansas, abducting trip of Fairbank into, 65.
Armstrong, abductor, 153.

Armstrong, J. H. B., operator, 42, 43.
Arnold, Hon. Isaac N., counsel in fugitive slave case, 284.
Arrest, of abductor Calvin Fairbank, 158, 159; of abductor Charles T. Torrey, 169; of abductor Capt. Walker, 170; of abductors Drayton and Sayres, 173; of abductor Dillingham, 174; of abductor Chaplin, 176; of fugitive slaves in the North between 1850-1856, 240, 241; mode of, under law of 1793, 257-259; right of private, under law of 1850, 267; of fugitive slave, penalties for hindering, 279; of operators, 283; of negroes in the South during the War, 287; of free negro in Philadelphia, 317; of Jerry McHenry in Syracuse, 318; of rescuers in Christiana case, 319; of Burns in Boston, 331.
Articles of Confederation (1643), clause for rendition of fugitives quoted, 19; absence of provision for return of fugitives in, 293.
Ashburton Treaty, extradition of the fugitive Anderson from Canada sought under, 352, 353.
Ashley, Congressman James M., operator, 92, 106.
Association for the Education and Elevation of the Colored People of Canada, 233.
Atchison, of Kentucky, on loss sustained by slave-owners of border states, 341.

Baine, Patrick, owner of Harriet Hayden, 158.
Bains, Eliza, operator in Portsmouth, Va., 118.
Baird, Thomas D., 96.
Baltimore, fugitive shipped in a box from, 60; agents in, 68, 91, 117, 151; anti-slavery sentiment in Friends' Yearly Meeting of, 93; abductions of Harriet Tubman from, 186; petition of Quakers of, against kidnapping, 296.
Baptist Church, appeal to societies of, in Massachusetts, 99.
Barbour, American Minister, on negotiations with England concerning fugitive slaves, 300.
Baxter and Grant, owners of Lewis Hayden, 158.
Bayliss, James, on canal route, 142.

Beacon, the, reminiscences of "Early Settlement and Growth of Western Iowa," in, 7.

Beard, William, visit of, to Canadian refugees, 199.

Bearse, Capt. Austin, doorkeeper of Boston Vigilance Committee, 73; rescues from vessels by, 81; on stowaways from the South, 144.

Beck, Dr. Isaac M., brief mention of, 32 *n.*; reward for abduction of, 53.

Beecher, Henry Ward, counterpart of, in *Uncle Tom's Cabin*, 322.

Benedict, Aaron, reminiscences of U. G. R. R., 6.

Benedict, Aaron L., runaways entertained by, 76, 77.

Benezet, Anthony, precepts of, 49.

Benton, Thomas H., 159; on passage of Fugitive Slave Law of 1850, 311 *n.*

Berrien, Col., conductor, 144.

Bibb, Henry, projector of Refugees' Home, 209; stock of supplies maintained by, 214; passenger on U. G. R. R., 340.

Bibb, Mrs. Mary E., school-teacher among Canadian refugees, 215.

Bigelow, Jacob, operator, 117.

Bigelow, L. H., 130.

Bingey, Anthony, on escape of his family to Canada, 76; on increase of fugitives arriving in Canada, 194; desire for freedom of, 196; on refugee population of Ontario, 221; on effects of Slave Law of 1850, 249.

Bingham, Dr. J. A., 89.

Blake, Capt., fugitives carried by boat of, 83.

Blake, of Ohio, bill of, for repeal of Fugitive Slave laws, 286.

Boat service for transportation of absconding slaves, 81-83; 118, 145-148, 219, 252.

Bolding, John, seizure of, under Slave Law of 1850, 241.

Booth, Sherman M., power of commissioners questioned in case of, 270; penalty imposed in case of, 279; case of, before the courts in Wisconsin, 329; limits of state authority defined in case of, 330; protest against Douglas legislation in case of,

Borden, Nathaniel P., 130.

Boston, conveyance of fugitives by William I. Bowditch of, 61; Vigilance Committee of, 71-73; escapes by vessel to, 81; early rescue in, 83, 84; rescue of Shadrach in, 86; appeal of Vigilance Committee of, for aid, 98, 99; attempted rescue of Burns in, 103, 330-332; aid rendered fugitives by Theodore Parker in, 109, 110; slaves sent to New Bedford and, from Virginia, 118; James Freeman Clarke on protection of fugitives in, 132; refugees sent from New York to, 145; to England from, 145; estimate of fugitives in, 235; law of 1850 denounced by meeting in, 244; consternation among fugitives in, 246-248; continued residence of refugees in, after 1850, 250, 251; Lewis Hayden in, 251, 252; early pursuit of fugitives in, 302; Shadrach, Sims, and Craft cases in, 317.

Boston and Worcester Railroad, 80.

Boston Public Library, scrap-book of Theodore Parker in, 8.

Bourne, Rev. George, early advocate of immediate abolition, 303, 304, 306; political action against slavery proposed by, 305 *n.*

Bowditch, William I., 61, 132.

Bowles, Col. J., letter of, on U. G. R. R. depot at Lawrence, Kan., 347-350.

Brace, Avery, 16.

Bragdon, George C., on stations on the St. Lawrence, 127 *n.*

Brainerd, Hon. Lawrence, 107; fugitives shipped by rail by, 145.

Bramlette, Gov. Thomas E., opposed to pardon of Fairbank, 159, 160.

Brant, Chief, fugitives received by people of, 92, 203.

Brennan, Mr., escape of slave from, 65.

Brisbane, W. H., hiding-places provided by, 64.

British and American Manual Labor Institute, colored children, 200; origin of Dawn Settlement, 205; work of, for Canadian refugees, 214; visited by Levi Coffin, 220; lumber industry established at, 223; colored settlers attracted by, 229, 230.

Brooks, Prof. W. M., on stations in southwestern Iowa, 33, 98.

Brooks family, of Concord, Mass., friends of Harriet Tubman, 186.

Brown, David Paul, counsel for fugitive slaves, 284, 285.

INDEX 445

Brown, Eli F., hiding-place provided by, 64.
Brown, Henry Box, shipment of, in a box, 60.
Brown, John, notes of, relating to his raid, 8; father of, a friend of fugitives, 37; League of Gileadites organized by, 73, 74; transportation of party of, through Iowa, 79; entertained by J. B. Grinnell, 108; strategy of, 118; North Elba home of, a terminus of the U. G. R. R., 127; route followed by, with his abducted slaves, 136, 164, 165; Missouri raid of, 162, 163; effect of his raid, 165; plan of liberation of, 166-168, 357; Dr. A. M. Ross, a friend of, 183 n.; on Harriet Tubman, 185; concern of, for fugitive settlers in Canada, 199; influence of U. G. R. R. upon, 290, 301, 338, 339; Col. J. Bowles on, 349, 350.
Brown, Mary, owner of James Hamlet, 269.
Brown, Owen, father of John Brown, early operations of, 37, 301.
Brown, Wells, befriends the fugitive William Wells Brown, 77.
Brown, William Wells, befriended, 77; conveyance of fugitives to Canada by, 83, 252; qualities of leadership in, 340.
Buchanan, James, amendments to Constitution in regard to fugitive slaves recommended by, 286; Booth pardoned by, 331; appealed to in Addison White case, 334; on enforcement of Fugitive Slave law during his administration, 353.
Bucknel and Taylor, slave-owners, 196.
Buffalo, boat service to, 83; release of alleged fugitives in, 317.
Burns, Anthony, Theodore Parker's memoranda on rendition of, 8; Vigilance Committee fails to rescue, 73; attempt to rescue, 103; case of, 251, 271, 283; rendition of, 331-333.
Burr, James E., one of abducting party of, Work and Thompson, 155, 156.
Burroughes, George L., agent of Underground Road, 70.
Bushnell, Simeon, case of, 270; penalty paid by, 279.
Buswell, N. C., on abduction by Canadian refugee, 152.
Butler, of South Carolina, on loss sustained by slave-owners, 341.

Buxton Settlement in Canada. See Elgin Association.
Buxton, Thomas Fowell, 207.

CABOT, Samuel, Jr., 103.
Calhoun, on Drayton's expedition with the *Pearl*, 173, 174; on an enactment making it unlawful to aid fugitives, 309; on the need of a new fugitive slave law, 313; championship of the Slave Law of 1850, 314.
California, sanction of, to Slave Law of 1850, 246.
Calvinists. See Presbyterian Church.
Campbell, C. B., 58.
Campbell, Dr. Alexander, reward for abduction of, 53.
Canada, escapes from the American colonies to, 20, 292; Clay's negotiations for extradition of fugitive slaves from, 22, 299, 300; knowledge of, among slaves, 27-30, 180, 182, 197, 198; underground routes through New York to, 35; early arrival of fugitives in, 43, 44; entered from Detroit, 66; number of fugitives forwarded to, by one abolitionist neighborhood before 1817, 87; number sent to, by Chas. T. Torrey before 1844, 88; fugitives received by people of Chief Brant in, 92; terminals in, 127, 133, 134; route to, via Portland, Me., 133; Ontario, the goal of the great majority of runaways, 140, 148; extent of the region in, settled by refugees, 148, 149; hospitality of, 149; abductions by refugees of, 152; excursions of the abductor Fairfield to, 153, 154; reception given Fairfield and his protégés on their arrival in, 154; enthusiasm in, over John Brown's Missouri raid, 165; part to be taken by refugees of, in Brown's plan of liberation, 167; Dawn Institute in, 168; delight of fugitives on reaching, 178, 196, 197; ministrations of American Baptist Free Mission Society among refugees at Toronto, 183; number assisted to, by abductor John Mason, 184; trips of abductor Harriet Tubman to, 187, 189; position of Canada on slavery question, 190, 191; early arrival of fugitive slaves in, 192; increased influx of fugitives, 193, 194; refugees in, a representative body of the slave

class, 195, 196; severity of conditions in, 198; treatment of refugee settlers in, 199, 200; attitude of government of, toward refugees, 201-203; conditions favorable to settlement of fugitives in, 203-205; fugitive aid societies in, 204, 205; Dawn Settlement, 205-207; Elgin Settlement, 207-209; Refugees' Home Settlement, 209, 210; objects of the colonies, 210, 211; Dr. Howe's criticism of the colonies, 211, 212: defence of the colonies, 212, 213; services of the colonization societies, 213-215; conclusions concerning the colonies, 216, 217; fugitive settlers in towns of, 217, 218; movement of fugitives to the interior of, 218, 219; refugees in the eastern provinces of, 219; refugee population in, 220-224, 313; occupations of refugees in, 223; congregation of refugees in towns of, 225, 226; prosperity of refugees in, 226, 227; their domestic life in, 227, 228; their school opportunities in, 228, 229; their societies for self-improvement in, 230, 231; their efforts for the rescue of friends from slavery, 231, 232; their taxable property in, 232; their political privileges in, 232; their value as citizens, 233, 234; return of many from, 235; increased influx of fugitives into, after passage of law of 1850, 246-250, 316; escape of Shadrach and Jerry McHenry to, 317, 318; Glover forwarded to, 328; escape of Addison White to, 334; extradition of Anderson refused by, 352, 353.

Canadian Anti-Slavery Society, on employment for Canadian refugees, 204; on refugee population in Canada West, 221; on congregation of Canadian refugees in towns, 225.

Canadian Magazine of Politics, Science, Art, and Literature, on Underground Railroad, 5.

Canal routes, 142.

Cape Breton Island, sea routes to, 219.

Capron, Effingham L., operator, 131, 132.

Capture, of fugitive slaves thwarted, 83-86; under Slave Law of 1850, 240-242; of fugitive settlers in the North, 316; of Sims in Boston, 317; of boy John near Oberlin, 335, 336.

Carpenter, Philo, operator, 88, 147.

Carpenter, slave-hunter, 53, 54.

Cass, Gen., Secretary of State, appealed to in the Addison White case, 334.

Caton, Judge, 283.

Cavins, E. C. H., on route through Indiana, 142.

Censor, the, containing "Sketches in the History of the Underground Railroad," 4.

Census reports of Canada, on refugee population, 220.

Census reports of United States, on fugitive slaves, 26, 44, 342, 343.

Chace, Mrs. Elizabeth Buffum, 49; on New Bedford route, 130.

Chamberlain, Hon. Mellen, 36.

Channing, Dr. Walter, 170.

Channing, Prof. Edward, on prosecutions of anti-slavery men, 317 n.

Chaplin, William L., abductor, 168, 175, 176.

Chapman, Capt., on delight of slaves reaching Canada, 196, 197.

Charles, John, 53.

Chase, Salmon P., on the Ordinance of 1787, 262; on the fugitive slave clause in the Constitution, 263, 264; in the Van Zandt case, 282; counsel for fugitive slaves, 308, 309; in the Addison White case, 334, 335.

Cheadle, Rial, abductor, 178, 179.

Cheney, Rev. O. B., 37, 134.

Chicago, a place of deportation, 83, 88, 147; terminus for line through Livingston and La Salle counties, Ill., 139; multiple routes of, 141; hostility of, to law of 1850, 333.

Chicago and Rock Island Railroad, 79, 144, 165.

Chicago, Burlington, and Quincy Railroad, 79, 144.

Child, E., receiver of goods for Canadian refugees at Toronto, 202.

Chittenden, subscription of, for release of W. L. Chaplin, 176.

Christiana case, 280, 281, 317; Thaddeus Stevens in, 282; effort of the government to enforce the law of 1850 in, 319.

Church connection of U. G. R. R. helpers or agents, 93-99; of Canadian refugees, 216.

Church of fugitives, in Boston, 246; in Buffalo, Rochester, Detroit, and Boston, 250.

INDEX

Cincinnati *Enquirer*, the, on contention over Addison White case, 335 *n.*
Cincinnati, supplies for fugitives provided by Woman's Anti-Slavery Sewing Society of, 77; Dr. N. S. Townshend conductor in, 104; home of Harriet Beecher Stowe a station in, 105; work of Levi Coffin in, 110-112; multiple routes in, 135, 141; appeal of colored people in, to Mr. Dillingham, 174; seizure of McQuerry in, 241; counsel for fugitive slave cases in, 282; effect of the Margaret Garner case in, 302, 303; observations used in *Uncle Tom's Cabin* made in, 321.
Civil War. *See* War of Rebellion.
Claiborne, on loss sustained by slaveowners from 1810-1850, 341.
Clark, George W., coöperation of, with Capt. Walker in anti-slavery work, 171; on the abductor Wm. L. Chaplin, 176.
Clark, Lewis, 171.
Clark, Milton, 171.
Clark, Wm. Penn, friend of John Brown, 164.
Clark, Woodson, informed against slaves, 278.
Clarke, Rev. James Freeman, on northern opposition to rendition, 25, 103; on extent of U. G. R. R. system, 113, 114; on protection of fugitives in Boston, 132 *n.*
Clay, Henry, negotiations of, with England for extradition of fugitives, 22, 44, 299; flight of slave of, 27; on the execution of the law of 1850 in Indiana, 48; on the escape of slaves to Canada, 192; on the Canadian refugees, 201; on the difficulty of recapturing fugitives, 242; championship of new Fugitive Slave Law by, 312, 314; compromise of, 315; proposition of, that the President be invested with power to enforce the law of 1850, 319.
Cleveland, boat service for fugitives from, 83, 252; deportation station, 146; eminent attorneys of, in Oberlin-Wellington case, 282; trial of Oberlin-Wellington rescuers at, 336; celebration in, over victory of abolitionists in Oberlin-Wellington case, 337.
Cleveland and Canton Railroad, 79.
Cleveland and Western Railroad, 79, 143.

Cleveland, Columbus and Cincinnati Railroad, 79, 183.
Cleveland *Plain Dealer*, on results in Oberlin-Wellington case, 337.
Clingman, of North Carolina, on value of fugitive settlers in Northern states, 341.
Coffin, Addison, early operator in North Carolina, 40, 117.
Coffin, Levi, author of *The Reminiscences of*, 2, 4; early service in North Carolina and Indiana, 40, 117; methods of, 61, 64; reputed president of the U. G. R. R., 69; largest company of fugitives entertained by, 76; devotee of underground work, 78, 110-112; on John Fairfield the abductor, 153; visit of, to Canadian refugees, 199-201, 218-220; on acquisition of land by Canadian refugees, 201, 202; on the number of Canadian refugees, 221; association of, with R. B. Hayes, 282.
Coffin, Vestal, organizer of U. G. R. R. near Guilford College, N.C., 1819, 117.
Coleman, family of refugees near Detroit, 236.
Collins, James H., counsel in defence of Owen Lovejoy, 283.
Colonies, fugitive slave clause in treaties between Indian tribes and, 91, 92; of fugitive slaves in Canada, 205; Dawn Settlement, 205-207; Elgin Settlement, 207-209; Refugees' Home Settlement, 209, 210; Dr. S. G. Howe on refugee, 211, 212; his criticism of, answered, 213, 214, 217; services of, 215, 216; conclusions concerning, 217; question of extradition between American, 290.
Commissioners, duties of, under the second Fugitive Slave Law, 265; creation of, due to decision in Prigg's case, 266; surrender of James Hamlet by one of, 269; power of, questioned, 269-271; observations of, regarding their own authority, 271; remuneration of, 271.
Committees of Vigilance. *See* Vigilance Committees.
Communication, methods of, 56; facsimile and other illustrations of messages, 10, 57, 58, 59, 79 *n.*; use of signals across Delaware River, 125; ease of, contributes to swell number of fugitives, 316.

Compromise of 1850, relation of second Fugitive Slave Law to, 265, 311; repetition of, with modifications, proposed in 1860, 285, 286; not a finality, 320; how regarded by Northern people, 324; failure of, 357

Concklin, Seth, abductor, 157, 160–162.

Conductors, methods of, 60, 61, 64; significance of the title, 67; regularly employed, 69, 70; number of, 87; their hospitality, 88, 89; their principles, 89, 90; their nationality, 90, 91; their church connections, 93–98; political affiliations of, 99–101; character of, 101; penalties suffered by, 102; proposed Defensive League of Freedom in behalf of, 103, 104; notable persons among, 105–112.

Confederation, New England (1643), provision in, for delivery of fugitives, 19; Articles of, quoted, 19.

Congregational Church, operators among members of, 96–98, 168; abductor Charles T. Torrey, clergyman of, 168.

Congress, speech of J. R. Giddings in lower House on fugitive slaves, 105; speech of Owen Lovejoy in lower House on fugitive slaves, 107; the expedition of the *Pearl* subject of debate in, 173, 174; resolution of 1838 in, providing for punishment of persons aiding fugitives, 193; petitions presented by Kentuckians in upper House declaring danger of slave-hunting in Ohio, 242; Fugitive Slave Law of 1793 in, 254; power of, to legislate on subject of fugitive slaves, 255, 263, 264, 268; cases growing out of differences between slave laws of the state and of, 260, 261; counsel for fugitives elected to, 282; excitement in, caused by last case under law of 1850, 285; agitation in, for new slave law in 1860, memorials to, praying for repeal of law of 1850, attacks on slavery in, 286; repeal of fugitive slave legislation by, 288, 289, 358; Continental, incorporation of fugitive slave clause in Northwest Ordinance by, 293; attempts at amendment of law of 1793 in lower House, 295, in both Houses, 296; agitation for new slave law (1817), 296, 297, 301, 309–311; Kentucky resolutions against admission of fugitives to Canada, presented to, 299; Slave Law of 1850 adopted by, 311, 312, 314, 315; message of President Fillmore to, December, 1850, 318; Senate supports the President in enforcing Fugitive Slave Law, 319; Gerrit Smith, member of, 320; Sumner in Senate, on execution of, 325; Racine mass-meeting declares null and void the law of, 327, 328; charged with improper assumption of powers by convention in Cleveland, 336; complaints of Southern members of, on account of loss of slaves, 340–342; Southern members of, on existence of Underground Railroads, 351, 352; argument in, to prevent secession of border states, 355; caution of, in dealing with fugitive slave question in crisis of the War, 355; inexpediency of return of fugitives by the army, recognized by, 356; acts of, leading up to repeal of Fugitive Slave Law, 356; agitation in and out of, for rigorous Fugitive Slave Law, 357.

Congressmen, operators among, 92, 105–108; anti-slavery champions among, 173; pro-slavery champions among, 173.

Conlisk, James, 92.

Connecticut, colony of, 19; underground work of Samuel J. May in, 36, 109; anti-slavery men from, organize Scioto Company, 38; reward offered Indians by, for apprehending fugitives, 92; personal liberty law of, 245, 246, 309; law of colony of, against aiding fugitives, 292; emancipation by, 293.

Conservative party, affiliation of negro voters in Canada with, 233.

Constitution of United States, fugitive slave clause in, quoted, 20; effect of incorporation of fugitive slave clause in, 30; burned at meeting of abolitionists, 101; Giddings on relation of the law of 1850 to, 105; quoted in support of immediatism, 206; ineffectiveness of the fugitive slave clause in, 255; trial by jury provided for in amendments of, 257; amendment of, quoted against Fugitive Slave Law, 258; slaves not parties to, 259; slave-owner's rights under, 259, 261; paramount to Ordinance of 1787, 263; legislative warrant of Congress under, 264; effect on execution of, due to Prigg decision, 265; Prigg decision on language of, 267; amendments to, proposed by Buchanan in 1860, 286, 353, 354; adoption of Thirteenth Amendment to, 289, 356; fugitive slave clause embodied in, 293; disavowal of fugitive recovery clause of, by Liberty party, 310; Webster on disregard of the slave clause in, 314; limitations of state courts under, 330; Ohio urges repeal of laws injuring efficiency of, 354.

Contemporaneous documents, rarity of, 7; Still's collection of, 7, 8; Parker's memoranda, 8; notes left by John Brown, 8, 9, 165; records of Jirch Platt, 9; leaf from diary of Daniel Osborn, 9, 10; extant letters, 10; letter of William Steel, 51, 52; memorandum of David Putnam, Jr., 55; facsimile of message of John Stone, other messages, 57, 58; letter of Thomas Lee, 58, 59; letters of E. F. Pennypacker, 79 n., 143 n.; letter of Francis Jackson, 99; item from Theodore Parker's Journal, 109; letter of Parker, 110; letter of Rev. N. R. Johnston, 161; letter of McKiernon, 161, 162; letters relating to Harriet Tubman, 185, 186, 188, 189; certificate of clerk of court in Sloane's case, 277 n.; advertisement of runaway slave, 287; facsimile of Osborn's record, 344, 345; letter of Col. J. Bowles, 347–350.

Continental Congress, incorporation of slave clause in Northwest Ordinance by, 293.

Contributing members, significance of name, 67.

Conveyance of fugitive slaves, schedule of "trains," 55; variety of methods of, 59; by vehicle, 60, 61; as freight, 60, 155; by rail, 78–80, 142–145; by water, 81–84, 144, 145; methods employed by abductor Fairbank, 158, 160; in Brown's raid, 164, 165; in Drayton's expeditions, 172, 173.

Conway, Judge, 347.

Cook, Hon. B. C., counsel in fugitive slave cases, 283, 284.

Cornell, Cornelius, 124.

Corwin, R. C., 39.

Cotton-gin, effect of invention of, 26.

Counsel for fugitive slaves, 281–285, 308, 309, 353.

Court, decisions terminate slavery in Canada, 191–193; provision in state Fugitive Slave laws for action by, 237, 238; Wright vs. Deacon in, 256, 257; Peter *alias* Lewis Martin in, 257; Commonwealth vs. Griffith in, 258; Prigg vs. Pennsylvania in, 259–261, 264; State vs. Hoppess in, 262; Vaughan vs. Williams in, 262; Jones vs. Van Zandt in, 262; various courts on irreconcilability between law of 1793 and Ordinance of 1787, 262, 264; authority of United States commissioners, 265, 271; case of Sims in, 269, 270; Scott's case in, 269, 270; Miller vs. McQuerry, 269, 270; Booth's case in, 270, 279, 329, 330; case of *ex parte* Robinson in, 270; case of *ex parte* Simeon Bushnell in, 270; speech of Justice Nelson to grand jury in, 272; action for penalty under law of 1798 in, 273; prosecution in, 274; prosecution of John Van Zandt in, 274; Norris vs. Newton in, 276; Oliver vs. Weakley in, 276; case of Sloane in, 276, 277; case of F. D. Parish in, 277; Oberlin-Wellington rescue case in, 279, 336; arguments of Chase and Seward in, 282; hearing of fugitive Jim Gray in, 283, 284; provision for appeal to United States Circuit in proposed Fugitive Slave Law of 1860, 286; provision in House fugitive slave bill of 1817 in regard to proof of title before, 296, 297; constitutionality of law of 1850 contested in, 327; constitutional limitation of state, 330; clash between federal and state, 334, 335; effect of jurisdiction of United States, on abolitionists, 335; trial of the fugitive Anderson before the Canadian, 353.

Covenanters, friends of fugitives, 13–15, 32, 90, 115, 235. *See* Presbyterian Church.

Cowgill, Dr. Thomas, 38.

Craft, Ellen and William, 82, 252; rescue of, 317.

Crittenden, Gov. John J., pardons abductor Fairbank, 159.

Crocker, Mrs. Mary E., operator, 132.

Cross, Rev. John, prosecution of, 50, 51.

Crosswhite family, seizure of, 102.

Crothers, Rev. Samuel, 32.

450　INDEX

Cruse, David, victim of Brown's raid, 163.
Cummings, Jacob, 154.
Curtis, George T., on the power of a commissioner, 271.
Cushing, Deacon, arrest of, 283.

DALBY, Mr., fugitive slave of, 33.
Dana, Richard H., visit of, to Brown's farm at North Elba, 127; counsel for runaways, 283; counsel for Burns, 331.
Dane, Nathan, on rendition of slaves in Northwest Territory, 293.
Daniels, Jim, appeal of, to John Brown, 162.
Danvers Historical Society, report of, on route of U. G. R. R., 133.
Davis, Charles G., counsel for fugitives, 283.
Davis, Jefferson, on escape of slaves from Mississippi, 82, 312, 313; on prospects of non-execution of law of 1850, 315.
Davis, Joel P., map by, 140.
Dawes, Gen. R. R., on communication in underground service, 56 n.
Day, Dr., capture and incarceration of, 349.
Deacon, case of Wright vs., 256, 257.
Dean, John, counsel for fugitive slave, 285.
De Baptiste, George, agent, 70.
Declaration of Independence, quoted by abolitionists, 24; principles of, 30; as an "abolition tract," 31; preamble of, 89; quoted in support of immediatism, 306.
Defensive League of Freedom, proposed, 103, 104.
Delaware, reminiscences relating to, 11; anti-slavery Quakers in, 31; Joseph G. Walker of Wilmington, 67; Thomas Garrett, of Wilmington, 110, 111, 117, 322; route in, 117, 118; refugee from, 195; loss of slaves by, 312.
Democratic party, legislative action against Oberlin College proposed by, 97; character of, 100; congressional vote of, on Slave Law of 1850, 315; Compromise of 1850 regarded as a finality by, 320; governors belonging to, on personal liberty laws, 354.
Dennett, Mrs. Oliver, operator, 133.

Deportation, places of, for fugitive slaves, 36, 66, 82, 83, 145-148.
Destitution, among fugitives, 76-78, 109, 222, 223.
Detroit, crossing-place for runaways, 66, 147; agents in, 70; J. M. Howard, operator at, 106; secret paths leading to, 135, 138; arrival of John Brown and his abducted slaves in, 165; supplies for Canadian refugees shipped to, 203; fugitive settlers near, 236; loss of colored members from church of, 250.
Detroit River, escape of thousands across, 147.
Devices for secrecy, 14; need of, 47; midnight service one of the, 54-56; guarded communications one of the, 56-59; hidden methods of conveyance one of the, 59-61; zigzag routes one of the, 61, 62, 302; concealment of fugitives one of the, 62-64; use of disguises one of the, 64-67; multiple routes and switch connections one of the, 70, 137, 141; employed by abductor Rial Cheadle, 179; employed by Dr. A. M. Ross, 181, 182, 187; employed by Harriet Tubman, 187, 188; often neglected during period 1840-1860, 337.
Dewey, Rev. Dr., loyalty to Slave Law of, 238.
Dickey, Rev. William, 32.
Dickey family, 87.
Dillingham, Richard, charged with belonging to organized band of abductors, 30; attempted abduction by, 174, 175.
Disguises, used in helping fugitives, 64-67; employed by Fairbank, 160; kept by Joseph Sider for use in abductions, 157.
Dismal Swamp, place of refuge, 25.
District of Columbia, abduction from, 155; disappearance of slavery from, attributed to U. G. R. R., 341, 342.
Dixon, Richard, 38.
Dobbins, Rev. Robert B., 32.
Dodge, Hon. Simeon, on U. G. R. R. from 1840 to 1860, 36, 37; on route in New Hampshire, 132; an operator, 133.
Dodge, of Indiana, vote on Fugitive Slave Law of 1850, 314.
Doherty, Fisher, 65, 66.
Dolarson, George, agent, 70.
Donnell and Hamilton, Ray vs., case of, 278.

Dorsey, Basil, rescue of, 84, 85.
Douglas Bill, U. G. R. R. work before and after, 194.
Douglass, Frederick, aided in New York City, 35; collections made for fugitives by, 78; refugees shipped over New York Central by, 80; as agent in the South before his escape, 91, 118; on excitement involved in his secret work, 104; on Albany route, 125, 126; on Brown's plan of liberation, 166; on Harriet Tubman, 185; many runaways assisted by, 251, 253; a noted passenger of the U. G. R. R., 340.
Doyle, Dr., host of John Brown, 164.
Drayton, Capt. Daniel, abduction of slave family by, 172; expedition of, with steamer *Pearl*, 172-174.
Drayton, Hon. William, fugitive slave of, 33.
Dred Scott decision, denounced in eastern Ohio, 336.
Drew, Benjamin, on employments of Canadian refugees, 204; on Dresden and Dawn Colonies in Canada, 207; on effect of Slave Bill of 1850 on fugitive settlers in Northern states, 213; on morality in Dawn Settlement, 216; on early arrival of refugees in Canada, 218; list of refugee communities mentioned by, 219; on thrift of colored settlers in Canada, 227; on schools for refugees, 229.
Duncan, Rev. James, on immediate abolition, 304-306; political action against slavery early advocated by, 305 n.
Durkee, Chauncey, 278.
Dutch, agreement of New Haven with the, for surrender of fugitive slaves, 19.
Dutton, A. P., runaways sent by boat to Canada by, 82, 83.
Dyer, Dr. C. V., conductor, 144.

"EARLY SETTLEMENT and Growth of Western Iowa," chapters of, valuable for history of U. G. R. R., 7.
Eastern states, hidden routes leading to, 120.
Edgerton, Hon. Sidney, operator, 106.
Edwards, William, cause of flight of, 27.
Eells, Dr. Richard, case of, 278, 282.
Elgin Association, formation and purpose of, 202, 207; growth of, 208; improvement of, 209; Dr. Howe on, 212; regulations of, 215-217; new settlers, of, 218; special schools for negroes of, 229.
Elgin, Lord, participation of, in securing lands for Canadian refugees, 202, 207; on extradition of fugitive Anderson, 353.
Eliza, escape of, in *Uncle Tom's Cabin*, 322.
Emancipation, celebration of West Indian, by Canadian refugees, 226, 227; gradual, criticised by Rev. James Duncan, 305.
Emancipation Proclamation, Philadelphia Vigilance Committee terminated by, 75; restricted operation of, 287, 356.
Emerson, R. W., friend of Harriet Tubman, 186.
England, Rev. W. M. Mitchell in, his book entitled *Underground Railroad* published in, 3; fugitive slaves shipped to, 82, 133, 145; Cowper's stanza on hospitality of, to slaves, quoted, 149; act abolishing slavery in colonies of, 190; refuses extradition, 192; Clay on England's admission of fugitives to Canada, 201; money collected in, for benefit of refugees, 206; escape of fugitives to, after passage of law of 1850, 249; negotiations with, regarding extradition, 299, 300, 302; escape of William and Ellen Craft to, 317.
English Colonial Church and School Society, schools for refugees maintained by, 215.
English settlers, underground work of, 92.
Episcopal Church, appeal to societies of, 99.
Estimate of fugitives escaping into Ohio, same for Philadelphia, 346.
Eustace, Hon. J. V., counsel in fugitive slave case, 284.
Evans, John, 197.
Evans, Philip, 70.
Everett, John, conductor, 124.
Experiment, the, on number of lines of escape in Ohio, 135.

FAIRBANK, CALVIN, abductor, 28, 61, 150, 157-159, 251; devices of, 65, 160; on refugee settlers near Detroit, 236.

INDEX

Fairchild, James H., pamphlet on *The Underground Railroad* by, 5; on Oberlin as an anti-slavery centre, 89, 97.

Fairfield, John, the abductor, devices of, 65–67, 153, 178.

Falley, Lewis, map of underground routes in Indiana by, 137–139.

Federal Convention, a concession of, to slavery, 20; fugitive slave clause embodied in United States Constitution by, 293; work of, ratified by state conventions, 294.

Fessenden, Gen. Samuel, operator, 106, 133; address of, at funeral of Charles T. Torrey, 170.

Fifteenth Amendment, adoption of, celebrated in Cincinnati, 111.

Fillmore, Millard, pardon of Capt. Drayton by, 173; signed Fugitive Slave Law of 1850, 314; on the Fugitive Slave Law, 318; attempt of, to enforce the law, 319; connection of, with the Shadrach rescue and Christiana tragedy, 319.

Firelands Pioneer, on Underground Railroad, 5.

Fisher, Hon. M. M., on New Bedford route, 130.

Florida, a refuge for runaways, 25; escape of slave from Jacksonville, 81, 145; Capt. Walker's attempted abduction of slaves from, 170.

Foote, Mr., 173.

Forsyth, J. M., reminiscence of, 13.

Fort Malden, C.W. *See* Amherstburg.

Foster, Stephen and Abby Kelley, operators, 132.

Fountain, Capt., abduction by, from Virginia, 81.

Fountain City, Ind., work of Levi Coffin in, 111; multiple routes of, 141.

Fox, George, anti-slavery principles of, 93.

Frances, Dr., 109, 110.

Frazee, John H., operator, 88.

Frazier, Wm. A., reward for abduction of, 53.

Free Presbyterian Church, formation of, 96.

Freedman's Bureau, establishment of, 111.

Freedom, slaves' love of, 14, 25, 178, 195–197.

Free Soil party, 100, 306; principles of, 321; abolitionists' share in organization of, 326; state convention of, at time of attempted rescue of Burns, 332.

From Dixie to Canada, by H. U. Johnson, 4.

Fry, Gen. Speed S., 159, 160.

Fugitive slaves, memoranda of, in transit, 9, 10; hiding-places of, 13, 63, 64; routes of, in southern Illinois, 14, 15, 135, 139, 141; in eastern Indiana, 16, 137, 138, 141, 142; rendition of, in the colonies, 19, 20; refuges of, in the Southern states and adjoining regions, 25; United States census reports on, 26, 342, 343; by whom encouraged along the way, 32; rescue of, 38, 39, 83–86, 240, 273, 275, 276, 284, 336; earliest arrivals of, in Canada, 43; pursuit of, 51, 52; methods of conveying, 59–62; transportation of, over steam railroads, 59, 78–81, 122–124, 128, 130, 132, 133, 142–145, 164, 165; disguises furnished, 64–67; destitution among, 76–78, 109; transportation of, by boat, 82, 83, 146–148; escapes of, to England, 82, 133, 145, 249, 317; friends of, in Iowa, 95, 98, 194, 195; Oberlin, a well-known refuge for, 97; prosecutions for aiding, 102, 103, 254, 273–281, 283–285, 317; notable friends of, 104–112; main routes of, 118, 119, 134; routes of, through Pennsylvania, 120–123, through New Jersey and New York, 123–128, through Massachusetts, 128–133, through Vermont, 130, 131; James Freeman Clarke on protection given, in Boston, 132 n.; routes of, through New Hampshire and Maine, 133, 134, Ohio, 134–137, 140, Western states, 134–141; Ontario the goal of the great majority of, 140, 147; escapes of, by sea, 144, 145; journey of John Brown and party of, through Iowa, 164; use of, in Brown's plan of liberation, 167; delight of, on reaching Canada, 178, 196, 197; escape of, from Canada to United States, 190; rumors of Canada among, 192; numbers of, early forwarded to Canada, 192; resolution in Congress regarding friends of, 193; number of, arriving daily in Canada, 194; character of Canadian refugees, states whence they came, 195; general condition of, in Canada, 198; treatment of, in Canada, 199–201; attitude of Canadian government to-

INDEX 453

ward, 201-203; befriended by Indians in Canada, 203; colonies of, in Canada, 205; Dawn Settlement of, 205-207; Elgin Settlement of, 207, 209; occupation of, in the colonies, 207, 223, 224, 226; progress of, in Canada, 208, 209, 224-228; Refugees' Home Settlement of, 209, 210; purpose of the colonies, 210, 211; Howe's criticism of the colonies, 211, 212; defence of the colonies, 212-217; fugitive settlers in the towns of Canada, 217, 218, 225, 226; spread of, in Ontario, 218, 219; in the Eastern provinces, 219; number of abiding places for, in Canada, 219, 220; population of, in Canada, 220-222; destitute condition of, on arrival, 222, 223; domestic relations of, 227, 228; schools for, in Canada, 228-230; associations for self-improvement among, 230, 231; taxable property of, 232; political rights of, in Canada, 233; their value as citizens, 233, 234; numbers of, and risks of, settling in Northern states, 236-238; pursuit of, 240, 241, 317; seizure of, under law of 1850, 241, 242; increased difficulty of reclamation of, in Northern states, 242, 243; mass-meetings in favor of, 244; enactment of personal liberty laws in defence of, 245, 246; consternation among, in the North, due to law of 1850, 246-248, 316; Boston a favorite resort for, 246; exodus of, from the States, 249, 250; continued residence of, in the States after passage of law of 1850, 250, 251; underground men among, 251-253; question of state's power to legislate concerning, 260, 261; first congressional enactment concerning, questioned, 263, 264; effect of Prigg decision in Northern states, 265; penalties under law of 1850 for aiding, 271; fervor in aiding, after 1850, 273, 357; penalties for aiding, 273-281; counsel for, 281-285, 308, 309; arrest of friends of, 283-285; army officers forbidden to restore, 287; colonial laws against, 290-293; question of extradition of, in 1787, 293; Kentucky's protest against admission of, to Canada, 299; significance of diplomatic negotiations regarding, 300; effect of appeal of, 301; from the border and cotton states, 312; non-delivery of, as a Southern grievance, 314; as missionaries in the cause of freedom, 323, 348, 357; Garrison on, as public speakers, 325 n.; Sumner on the import of the appeal of, to Northern communities, 325; increasing number after 1850, 338; computation of number aided in Ohio and Philadelphia, 346; letter regarding aid given to, at Lawrence, Kan., 347-350; significance of controversy in regard to, 356.

Fugitive slave cases, 102, 103, 254, 273-281, 283-285, 317; during period 1840-1860, 337.

Fugitive Slave Law of 1793, substance of, 21, 22; inefficiency of, 22, 31, 47; support of state laws given to, 22, 237, 238; origin of demand for, 254; analysis and characterization of, 254, 255; appeal to Ordinance of 1787 for overthrow of, 262; court decisions on irreconcilability between Ordinance of 1787 and, 263; constitutionality of, 264, 265; prosecutions and penalties under, 272-281; Josiah Quincy counsel in one of the earliest cases under, 283; early resistance to, 294, 295; attempts at amendment of, 295-298; effect of Prigg decision on effectiveness of, 309.

Fugitive Slave Law of 1850, reason for enactment of, 2; destruction of records of fugitives aided, due to, 7, 10, 11; Parker's memoranda of resistance to, in Boston, 8; causes which led to enactment of, 22, 44, 173, 174, 265, 290, 309-311, 357; substance of, 23; effect of, 24, 25, 40, 44, 48, 71-76, 187, 193, 194, 213, 214, 240, 241, 249, 250, 316, 317, 321, 323, 337, 338; insistance of lower Southern states on enactment of, 30; penalties provided by, 48, 102; vigilance committees a product of, 71-76; denunciation of, by Theodore Parker, 90; appeal to churches evoked by, 98, 99; Defensive League of Freedom for persons violating, 103, 104; Congressman J. R. Giddings defies, 105; members of Congress violating, 106-108; other notable persons among violators of, 109-112; abductions following the passage of, 153-155, 159-166, 175, 181-183, 187-189; the U. G. R. R. and the, 193, 290; Dr. Howe on effect of, 194 n.;

454 INDEX

effect of, on the arrival of slaves in Canada, 194, 213, 214; Benj. Drew on effect of, 213; Josiah Henson on effect of, 214; homage paid to, 238, 239; resistance to, condemned by newspapers, 239; slave-hunting after enactment of, 240, 241; active resistance to, in the North, 243-246; object of, 243; consternation among fugitives in the North over, 246-248, exodus of fugitives from, and continued residence in Northern states after passage of, 249-251; grounds of attack upon legality of, 255; Prof. Eugene Wambaugh on the dilemma involved in, 256 n.; question of trial by jury under, 256, 257; Prigg decision leads to, 265; supplementary to law of 1793, 265; objectionable features of, 266-273; old and new arguments brought against, 268; remuneration of commissioners under, 271; prosecutions and penalties under, 272-281; public denunciation of, 272, 318, 327-329, 333, 336; failure of penalties under, to deter resistance to, 272, 273; arguments against, by Chase and Seward, 282; last case under, 285; amendment proposed in 1860 recognizing validity of, 286; after 1861, 287; repeal of, 288; efforts which led up to, 297, 298, 301; Webster's, Clay's, and Calhoun's support of, 314; enactment of, 314; by whom passed, 315; enforcement of, 316-318; open resistance to, 318-320; the law of 1850 and *Uncle Tom's Cabin*, 321; Sumner's efforts in Senate to secure repeal of, 324-326; open defiance of, during decade 1850-1860, 326 *et seq.*; penetrating criticism of, by able counsel, 327; pronounced unconstitutional by Wisconsin convention, 329; hostility to, in Illinois, 333; open violation of, in Oberlin-Wellington rescue case, 335; repeal of, demanded by Republican party, 337; Claiborne on the failure of, to make compensation to the South for abducted slaves, 341; violation of, charged against the North by Southern congressmen during sessions of 1860-1861, 351, 352; Buchanan on enforcement of, during his administration, 353; purpose of Lincoln to execute, 355; question of obligation to restore fugitives, 356.

Fuller, James C., 206.
Fullerton, Rev. Hugh S., 32.
Furber, James, operator, 133.
Fyffe, W. B., reminiscences of, entitled "History of Anti-Slavery Days," 6; map of route in Illinois, by, 139.

GALESBURG, ILL., old First Church of, as U. G. R. R. station, 64; anti-slavery Presbyterians in, 96; importance of, as a centre, 97.
Gallatin, on negotiations with England regarding extradition of fugitives, 299, 300.
Gannett, Dr. E. S., loyalty of, to Slave Law, 238.
Gardner, Ozem, 89.
Garland, B. W., claimant of Joshua Glover, 327.
Garner, Margaret, case of, 302; effect upon public opinion of case of, 302, 303.
Garretson, Joseph, 57.
Garrett, Thomas, reward for abduction of, 53; disguises provided by, 64; ships fugitives by boat, 82; a devotee of U. G. R. R., 110, 111; on Harriet Tubman, 188; aid given to Harriet Tubman by, 189; Mrs. H. B. Stowe on, 322.
Garrison, William Lloyd, abstinence from voting of, 100, 101; predecessors of, in advocacy of immediate abolition, 303-308; acquaintance of, with Rankin's *Letters on Slavery*, 308; address to Southern bondmen by, 310; on fugitives as public speakers, 325 n.; preparation of the way for, 357.
Garrisonian abolitionists, principles of, 100, 101.
Gay, Sydney Howard, an efficient agent, 108.
Geneva College, influence of, 115.
Geography of U. G. R. R., feasibility of representing the, 113; extent of, 113, 114; number and distribution of stations, 114, 115; Southern routes, 116-118; main channels of flight of slaves, 118, 119; lines of Pennsylvania, New Jersey, and New York, 119, 120; routes of eastern Pennsylvania, 120-122; routes of western Pennsylvania, 122, 123; outlets through New Jersey, 123-125; routes of New York, 125-128; routes of New England states, 128,

129; lines of Massachusetts, 129, 130, 132; routes of Vermont, 130, 131; branches of Rhode Island and Connecticut, 131; routes of New Hampshire, 132, 133; routes of Maine, 133, 134; secret paths in the Western states, 134; lines in Ohio, 135; routes of Illinois, Michigan, and Iowa, 135, 136; examination of map of Morgan County, O., 136, 137; study of Falley's map of Indiana and Michigan routes, 137-139; map of simple route in Illinois, noteworthy features of general map, 139; trend of lines, 139-141; multiple and intricate trails, 141; broken lines and isolated place names, 141, 142; river routes, 142; routes by rail, 142-144; routes by sea, 144, 145; terminal stations, 145-147; lines of lake travel, 147, 148; Canadian ports, 148, 149.

Georgia, route from northern, 119; in Brown's plan of liberation, 167; Canadian refugees from, 195; William and Ellen Craft from, 317; convention on execution of Fugitive Slave Law of 1850, 318, 319; charges of bad faith preferred against the North by Jones of, 351.

Germans, attitude of, toward fugitive slaves, 92, 93, 355, 356.

Gibbons, Daniel, number of fugitives aided by, 10, 87, 88.

Gibbs, Mr., agent, 126.

Gibbs, Jacob, assistant of Rev. Charles T. Torrey, 169.

Giddings, Joshua R., friend of bondmen, 7; source of abolition ideas of, 31; hiding-place in house of, 63; on attitude of North toward enforcement of law of 1850, 105, 106, 315, 316; champion of anti-slavery party in Congress, 173.

Gilliland, Rev. James, 32, 41, 95.

Giltner vs. Gorham, case of, 275.

Glover, Joshua, arrest of, as fugitive, 327; rescue of, 328, 329.

Glover, J. O., counsel for runaways, 284.

Goens, Reuben, visit to Canada by, 199.

Goodnow, Lyman, 92.

Gorham, Giltner vs., case of, 275.

Gorsuch, in Christiana case, 280, 319.

Grand Trunk Railroad, 80, 81, 133.

Grant, of firm of Baxter and, owners of Lewis Hayden, 158.

"Grape-vine telegraph," used by abolitionists, 56.

Gray, Jim, fugitive from Missouri, 283.

Gray, Jonathan H., 88.

Gray, O. C., counsel for runaways, 284.

Gray, Thomas L., reminiscences of, 6; number of slaves aided by, 89; on abductor Rial Cheadle, 178, 179.

Grier, Justice, charge of, to jury in the Mitchell case, 279; charge of, to jury in the Christiana case, 281.

Griffith, Commonwealth vs., case of, 258.

Grimes, Rev. Leonard B., organizer of Church of the Fugitive Slaves, 246, 250, 251.

Grinnell, Hon. J. B., receiver of fugitives, 58; "liberty room" in house of, 108; host of John Brown, 164.

Guilford College, N.C., organization of U. G. R. R. near, 40, 117.

Gunn, Erastus F., on route in Massachusetts.

HALE, JOHN P., a champion of anti-slavery party in Congress, 173.

Halliday, Simeon, counterpart of, in real life known by Mrs. Stowe, 322.

Hamilton, Ray vs. Donnell and, case of, 278.

Hamlet, James, case of, first under Slave Law of 1850, 269.

Hanway, Castner, part of, in Christiana case, 280, 281.

Harper, Jean, one of party abducted by John Brown, 163.

Harper's Ferry, prelude to, 162; plan of attack upon, reported by Hinton, 167; effect of attack upon, on value of slave property, 339.

Harrod, Leonard, on slave's desire for freedom, 195.

Harvard University, scholarship in, founded by escaped slave, Harriet Hayden, 158; action of overseers of, against Loring, 333.

Harwood, Edward, 64.

Haviland, Mrs. Laura S., on labors of abductor Fairfield, 153, 154; attempted abduction by, 171, 172; work of, in Refugees' Home, 210; Sunday-school of, for fugitives, 230; intercession of, for the runaway Anderson, 353.

Hayden, Harriet, bequest of, to Harvard University, 158.

INDEX

Hayden, Lewis, abduction of, 158; operator, 251, 252.
Hayes family, 15.
Hayes, Rutherford B., counsel in fugitive slave cases, 282; on effect of Margaret Garner case, 303.
Haywood, William, on underground route in Indiana, 16.
Henson, Josiah, knowledge of Canada carried among slaves by, 28; as abductor, 176–178; on condition of Canadian refugees, 198; founder of school in Canada, 205; on work of British and American Institute, 214; on morality of Dawn Settlement, 216; on refugee population, 220, 221; lumber industry established by, 223; lectures on farming by, 224; list of towns where refugees settled according to, 225; on number of fugitive settlers in Northern states, 237; on effects of Slave Law of 1850, 249; a notable passenger of U. G. R. R., 340.
Hiding-places, for fugitive slaves, 12, 13, 14, 25, 40, 62–65, 131, 248, 251, 252, 276, 280, 302.
Higginson, Col. T. W., indictment of, 103; connection with U. G. R. R., 105, 132; on continued residence of fugitives in Massachusetts after passage of law of 1850, 250; part of, in attempted rescue of Burns, 331, 332.
Hill *vs.* Low, case of, 273.
Hill, Leverett B., 88.
Hill, Milton, 88.
Hinton, Richard J., on escapes through Kansas, 114; on John Brown's plan of liberation, 166, 167; on Dr. A. M. Ross, 183 *n.*; on refugee population in Canada West, 221, 222.
History of Anti-Slavery Days, reminiscences by W. B. Fyffe entitled, 6.
History of Springfield, Mass., account of Connecticut River route in, 127.
Hodge, D. B., on abduction by Canadian refugee, 152.
Holmes, of Massachusetts, objections of, to bill of 1817 as basis of new Slave Law, 297.
Holt, Horace, special conveyance of, for fugitives, 60.
Hood family, 15.
Hood, John, 14.
Hooper, John H., agent, 253.

Hope, A. R., author of *Heroes in Homespun*, 2, 5.
Hopkins family, 87.
Hopkins, Capt. Amos, stowaway on brig of, 81.
Hopper, Isaac T., methods of secret emancipation early practised by, 34, 35, 346, 347; fugitives sent by sea by, 145.
Hoppess, State *vs.*, case of, 256, 257, 259, 262, 263.
Hossack, John, indicted for helping fugitives, 284.
Howard, Col. D. W. H., 37.
Howard, Edward, early operator, 37.
Howard, Senator Jacob M., 106.
Howe, Senator, of Wisconsin, bill for repeal of Fugitive Slave Law introduced by, 286.
Howe, Dr. S. G., on escape of slaves, 43, 44; on abductions by Canadian refugees, 152; on origin of U. G. R. R., 192; on effect of Slave Law of 1850, 194; on reception of fugitives in Canada, 201; on Elgin Settlement, 208, 209; criticism of refugee colonies by, 212–214; on organizations for relief of fugitives, 217; on number of colonies in Canada, 219; on refugee population of Canada, 220–222; on condition of farmers among Canadian refugees, 224, 225; on their thrift, 226 *n.*, 227; on their morality, 228; on their ability to read and write, 230; on their taxable property, 232; on their value as citizens, 234.
Hubbard, of Connecticut, on enlistment of colored soldiers, 288.
Hubbard and Company, fugitives shipped from warehouse of, 148.
Hudson, David, early operator, 37.
Hughes, Thomas, 49.
Hunn, Ezekiel, operator in Delaware, 117.
Hunn, John, operator in Delaware, 117.
Hunt, N. A., on abducting methods of Mission Institute, 155, 156.
Hurlburt, Chauncey, 16.
Hyde, Udney, agent of U. G. R. R., 69; defender of fugitive Addison White, 334.

ILLINOIS, U. G. R. R. in southern, 14, 15; prospect of organization of, as a slave-holding state, 18; anti-slavery sentiment in, 31; anti-slavery Southerners in, 32, 41, 91; rise of U. G. R. R. in, 41, 42; secret operations at Dwight, 61; reputed president of U. G. R. R. in, 69; underground helpers in, 70, 88, 92; transportation for fugitives by rail in, 79; emancipated slaves in, 93; Owen Lovejoy of, declares in Congress his right to aid slaves, 107; Rev. Asa Turner on hidden thoroughfares in, 114; population of various parts of, 115; favorable situation of, 134; distribution of lines in, 135; chart of route in, 139; trend of lines in, broken lines and isolated place-names in, 141; deportation of fugitives from Chicago, 147; abductors at southern extremity of, 151; abducting enterprises at Quincy, 155; vigorous work by abolitionists of, 194, 195; failure of, to pass full personal liberty law, 246; arrest of Owen Lovejoy and others, for aiding fugitives, 283; spirit of nullification in, 333.

Illinois Central Railroad, 79, 144.

Illinois River, a thoroughfare for fugitives, 82.

Immediate abolition, early advocates of, 303–306; Garrisonian movement, 307; early formulation of principle of, in underground neighborhoods, 357.

Independent, the, on escape of slaves from Missouri after 1850, 194; on "Ohio Underground Line," 195.

Indiana, Levi Coffin in, 4, 40, 41; newspaper contributions on routes of southern, 7; Grant County route in, 15, 16; prospect of organization of, as a slaveholding state, 18; anti-slavery Quakers in, 31; beginnings of the U. G. R. R. in, 40, 41, 117; Clay on enforcement of law of 1850 in, 48; slave-hunters in, 53, 54, 65; aid rendered by Female Anti-Slavery Association in, 77; transportation by rail in, 79, 144; emancipated slaves in, important underground centres in, 93; secret work of Quakers in eastern, 94; favorable situation of, 134; distribution of routes in, 135; Falley's map of lines in, 137–139; direction of routes in, 140; Fountain City route in, broken lines and isolated place-names in, 141; abductors along southern boundary of, 151; capture of abductor Concklin in, 161, 162; personal liberty law of, 245, 246; rescue in, 275, 276; principles of Rev. James Duncan, of southeastern, 304–306; vote of United States senators from, on law of 1850, 314.

Indians, effect of removal from Gulf states, 26, 308; aid given fugitives by, 37, 38, 91, 92; hospitality of, in Canada, 203; Dawn Institute attended by, 207.

Indian Territory, fugitives from, 284.

Insurrection of slaves, Brown's plan to arouse, 166–168; danger of, lessened by the U. G. R. R., 340.

Intelligencer, the, on "evil" of running off slaves, 194.

Iowa, reminiscences of the "Early Settlement and Growth of Western," 7; John Brown's journey through, 8, 9, 164; organized as free state, 18; anti-slavery Quakers in, 31, 33; rise of U. G. R. R. in, 42, 43; escape of Nuckolls' slaves through, 52; transportation by rail in, 79; Methodist operators in, 95; underground lines in, 98, 114, 135, 136; direction of routes in, broken lines and isolated place-names in, 141; abductors along frontier of, 151; underground activity of abolitionists of, 194, 195; failure of, to pass full personal liberty law, 246; capture of operators in, 284.

Irdell, on fugitive slave clause in Constitution, 294.

Irish settlers, underground work among, 92.

JACK *vs.* MARTIN, case of, 256, 257, 260.

Jackson, Andrew, supported by Illinois on nullification question, 333.

Jackson, Francis, letter of, regarding church contributions for fugitives, 99.

Jackson, William, 132; on settlement of Queen's Bush, Canada, 204, 205.

Jacksonville, escape from, 81, 145.

Jacob, Gov. Richard T., pardons abductor Fairbank, 159, 160.

Jefferson, Thomas, "abolition tract" by, 31.

Jerry rescue. *See* Rescue of Jerry McHenry.

Johnson, attorney-general of Pennsylvania, on unconstitutionality of Fugitive Slave Law, 264.

Johnson family, fugitive settlers near Detroit, 236.

Johnson, Gabe N., operator, 64.
Johnson, H. U., author of *From Dixie to Canada*, 2; characterization of his book, 4.
Johnson vs. Tompkins, case of, 273, 274.
Johnson, William, incident given by, showing misinformation about Canada among slaves, 197.
Johnston, Rev. N. R., letter of, on capture of abductor Concklin, 161.
Johnston, William, cause of flight of, 27.
Johnston, William A., on beginnings of U. G. R. R. in Ohio, 39.
Jolliffe, Amos A., on routes in western Pennsylvania, 123.
Jolliffe, John, counsel for fugitives, 282.
Jones, John W., colored agent, 128, 143, 252, 253.
Jones, of Georgia, brings charges against the North on account of U. G. R. R., 351.
Jones, of Indiana, vote of, on the Fugitive Slave Law, 314.
Jones, Thomas, on dissatisfaction in Refugees' Home Settlement, 216.
Jones vs. Van Zandt, case of, 262, 274, 275.
Jones, William Box P., transportation of, as freight, 60.
Jury trial, denial of, to fugitives, 256, 257.

KAGI and Stephens, responsible for shooting of David Cruse on Brown's raid, 163; arranges for eastern trip of Brown, 164, 165; Brown's plan of liberation related by, 166, 167.
Kanawha River, a thoroughfare for fugitives, 82.
Kansas, Brown's journey through, 8, 9, 136, 162-164; R. J. Hinton on escape of slaves through, 114, 119; personal liberty law of, 246; Bowles' letter on work of underground station of Lawrence, 347-350.
Kansas-Nebraska Act, appeal to the churches evoked by, 99; mass-meetings in opposition to, 328; relation of Glover and Burns cases to, 331.
Kauffman, Daniel, prosecution of, 102.
Kelly, Abby, disowned by Uxbridge monthly meeting, 49.
Kelsey, Capt., master of an "abolitionist" boat, 82.
Kenderdine, John, 274.

Kentucky, news of Canada early brought into, 27; abducting trip of Dr. A. M. Ross into, 28; knowledge of Canada among slaves in, 28, 29, 37; negotiations of, with adjoining free states for extradition of fugitives, 47; slave-hunters from, 53, 54; abduction of slaves from Covington, 61; fugitives from, 85, 109; Rev. John Rankin in, 109, 306; underground routes from, 119; incident of rescue from plantation of, 153; abduction of the Hayden family from Lexington, 158; visit of Mrs. Haviland to, for purpose of abducting slaves, 171, 172; Henson's abduction of slaves from, 177, 178; Elijah Anderson, abductor, imprisoned in, 183; abductions from, by John Mason, 184; Canadian refugees from, 195; effect of slave-breeding in, 228; John Van Zandt, anti-slavery man from, 274, 275; rescue of fugitives escaped from, 275, 276; Mallory of, on repeal of law of 1850, 288; resolution of, against admission of slaves to Canada, desirous of extradition of fugitives from, 299; Margaret Garner, a fugitive from, 302; petitions Congress for protection for slave-holder, 311; complaint of, against the free states, 312; residence of Harriet Beecher Stowe on borders of, 321; Senator Atchison of, on loss sustained by slave-owners of border states, 341; fugitives from, recorded by Osborn, 344, 345; Senator Polk on losses of, through underground channels, 352; reasons of, for remaining in the Union, 354, 356; insistence of, on retention of Fugitive Slave Law by the government, 356.
Kidnapping, of free persons in the North between 1850 and 1856, 240; along southern border of free states, 295; petition of Baltimore Quakers for protection of free negroes against, 296, 318; case of, 318.
Kightlinger, Jacob, informer, 50, 51.
Kilbourne, Col. James, aids in rescue of a fugitive, 38, 84.
King, on the proposition to prohibit slavery in the Northwest Territory, 293.
King, Rev. William, 207-209, 212; projector of Elgin Settlement, 202, 207; testimony of, concerning the settle-

ment, 208, 209; on morality of Elgin Settlement, 216; on the civil offices held by Canadian refugee settlers, 233.
Kinjeino, Chief, friend of fugitives, 37, 38, 92.
Kirkpatrick family, operators, 87.
Kirtland, Dr. Jared P., station-keeper, 104.
Knox College. *See* Galesburg, Ill.
Knox, Hon. Joseph, counsel in fugitive slave case, 284.
Knoxville, Ill., multiple routes of, 141.

Lake Shore Home Magazine, chapters of "Romances and Realities of the Underground Railroad" in, 4.
Lane Seminary, secession of students from, 97.
Langdon, Jervis, agent, 128, 252; forwards fugitives by rail, 143.
Langston, fined for aiding fugitives, 279.
Larnard, Hon. E. C., counsel in fugitive slave case, 284.
Latimer case, 337.
Lawrence, James, 162.
Lee, Judge Thomas, letter of, concerning family of fugitives, 58, 59.
Leeper, H. B., on beginnings of U. G. R. R. in Illinois, 41, 42; on number of negroes aided, 88.
Leeper, John, early operator, 41.
Leland, Judge E. S., counsel in fugitive slave cases, 283, 284.
Leonard, Mr., slave aided by, 154.
Letters of underground men, 10, 11. *See* Correspondence.
Letters on Slavery, by Rev. John Rankin, 308.
Lewis, Elijah, part in Christiana case, 280, 281.
Liberator, the, hiding-place over office of, 63; on flight of slaves after enactment of law of 1850, 249, 250.
Liberty party, in national politics, 100; Gen. Samuel Fessenden, nominee of, for governorship of Maine and for Congress, 106; part of Gerrit Smith in organization of, in New York, 107; motives of abolitionists for joining, 306; disavowal of fugitive recovery clause in Constitution by, 310; convention of, in Syracuse during Jerry rescue, 318, 320; abolitionists' share in organization of, 326.

Lightfoot, James, befriended by Josiah Henson, 177, 178.
Lincoln, Abraham, intervention of, in behalf of the abductor C. Fairbank, 159, 160; Proclamation of Emancipation by, 287; signs bill repealing Fugitive Slave Law, 288; mentioned, 330; election of, signal for secession, 352; efforts of, to preserve the Union, 355.
Linton, Seth, on an abduction by Canadian refugee, 152.
Livingston and La Salle counties, Ill., chart of simple line through, 139.
Lockhart, Rev. Jesse, 32.
Loguen, Rev. J. W., agent, 126, 251; first experience in Canada, 198; passenger on U. G. R. R., 340.
Loring, Edward G., on the power of a commissioner, 271; Burns remanded to slavery by, 332; removed from the office of judge of probate, 333.
Loring, Ellis Gray, 133; counsel for fugitive slaves, 283.
Louis, escape of, from court-room in Cincinnati, 85.
Louisiana, effect of purchase of, 26; abducting trip of A. M. Ross into, 28; fugitives from, 109; escape of abductor John Mason from New Orleans, 185; Canadian refugees from, 195; Elgin Settlement projected by Wm. King, former slaveholder of, 202, 207.
Louisville, Ky., agent in, 151.
Louisville, New Albany and Chicago Railroad, 79, 144.
Lovejoy, Elijah P., 107, 171.
Lovejoy, Hon. Owen, defies Fugitive Slave Law in Congress, 107; arrested for aiding fugitives, 283.
Low, case of Hill *vs.*, 273.
Lowell, poem of, read at the funeral of Charles T. Torrey, 170.
Lower Canada, underground route *via* Portland, Me., to, 133.
Lucas, Geo. W. S., colored agent of U. G. R. R., 70.
Lundy, Benjamin, 308.

McCLURKIN, Jas. B. and Thomas, 14, 15.
McCoy, William, reward for abduction of, 53.
McCrory, Robert, 38.
McHenry, Jerry, rescue of, 72, 86, 239, 318, 320, 326; place of embarkation of, for Canada, 127.

McIntire, Gen., a Virginian operator, 88.
McKiernon, on fate of abductor Miller, 161, 162.
McKim, J. Miller, on organization of Philadelphia Vigilance Committee, 75.
McLean, Judge, on the power of a commissioner, 270–272.
McQuerry, case of Miller *vs.*, 269, 271.
McQuerry, George Washington, seizure of, 241.
Madison, on the fugitive slave clause in the Constitution, 294.
Mad River Railroad, 78, 143.
Magazine of Western History, on U. G. R. R., 5.
Magill, Dr. Edward H., on lines of travel in eastern Pennsylvania, 122.
Mahan, Rev. John B., reward for abduction of, 53; on abduction of slaves from the South, 150.
Maine, rise of U. G. R. R. in, 37; steam railroad transportation for fugitives in, 80, 81; stowaways on vessels from Southern ports arrive in, 81; Gen. Samuel Fessenden, an operator in, 106; routes of, 133, 134; personal liberty law of, 246.
Mallory, of Kentucky, on repeal of Fugitive Slave Law, 288.
Mann, Mrs. Horace, friend of Harriet Tubman, 186.
Maps of U. G. R. R., method of preparation of, 113; general map, facing 113; map of lines of Chester and neighboring counties of Pennsylvania, facing 113; lines in Morgan County, O., 136; map of lines of Indiana and Michigan in 1848, 138; map of simple route through Livingston and La Salle counties, Ill., 139; map of network of routes through Greene, Warren and Clinton counties, O., 140.
Marsh, Gravner and Hannah, subjected to espionage, 50; conveyance of fugitives in market wagon by the latter, 60, 61.
Martin, case of Jack *vs.*, 256, 257, 260.
Martin, Lewis, case of, 256, 257, 259, 260, 263.
Maryland, abducting trip of A. M. Ross into, 28; knowledge of Canada among slaves in, 28, 29; fugitive shipped in a box from Baltimore, 60; number of slaves abducted from, by Charles T. Torrey, 88; reward offered to Indians for apprehending fugitives by, 91, 92; underground routes in, 117; steady loss from counties of, 119; movement of fugitives to Wilmington, 121; agents of U. G. R. R. in Baltimore, 151; escape of, and abductions by Harriet Tubman from, 186–189; Canadian refugees from, 195; fugitives from, in western Pennsylvania, 276; law against hospitality to fugitive slaves in, 291; resolution of legislature of, against harboring fugitives, 298; Rev. Geo. Bourne, a resident of, 303; Pratt of, on loss sustained by slave-owners of his state, 341.
Mason, John, abductor, 178, 183–185.
Mason, Lewis, counsel in fugitive slave case, 284.
Mason, of Massachusetts, on trial by jury for fugitives, 297.
Mason, of Virginia, on difficulty of recapturing fugitives, 243; on the Fugitive Slave Law, 311, 312; on loss sustained by slave-owners of his state, 341.
Massachusetts, extinction of slavery in, 17; anti-slavery Quakers in, 31; rise of U. G. R. R. in, 36, 37; steam railroad transportation for fugitives in, 80; refusal of German companies from, to aid in restoration of runaways, 92; underground centres in, 94; Constitution burned at Framingham, 101; Defensive League of Freedom proposed in, 103, 104; Theodore Parker, spiritual counsellor for fugitives in, 110; routes through, 128–130, 132; escape of slaves from Virginia to, 144; estimates of fugitive settlers in Boston and New Bedford, 235; indignation meetings in, against Slave Law of 1850, 244; personal liberty law of, 245, 246, 309; consternation among fugitive settlers in Boston caused by law of 1850, 246–248; continued residence of fugitives in, after enactment of law of 1850, 250; removal of fugitives from Pennsylvania to, after passage of law of 1850, 250; underground men among fugitives in, 251, 252; case of Commonwealth *vs.* Griffith tried in, 258, 259; emancipation by, 293; Holmes of, on House Fugitive Slave Bill of 1817, 297; **Mason** of, on House bill, 297; early pursuit in

INDEX

Boston and New Bedford, 302; anti-slavery societies of, 327; spirit of resistance to law of 1850 in, 327; public opinion in, after rendition of Burns, 333; amendment of personal liberty law of, 354.
Massachusetts Anti-Slavery Society, report of, on evasion of slaves, 193.
Massachusetts Bay, law of, against aiding fugitives, 292.
Matchett, Dr., 16.
May, Rev. S. J., connection with U. G. R. R., 105, 109, 131, 132; on Southern helpers of U. G. R. R., 116; friend of Harriet Tubman, 186; visits of, to Canadian refugees, 199; on number of fugitive settlers in Northern states, 237; on instances of regard paid to Fugitive Slave Law, 238; on Rev. J. W. Loguen, 251; one of leaders in the Jerry rescue case, 326.
Mechanicsburg, O., importance of stations at, 69, 70; attempted seizure of Addison White in, 241.
Merritt, Wm. H., colored operator, 92.
Messages, underground, 56-58.
Methodist Church, schism in, 40, 49; action against slavery taken by, 94; secession of the Church South, 95.
Methodists, Wesleyan, friends of fugitives, 32, 235; separation of, from M. E. Church, 50.
Methods, employed by some abductors, 151, 171, 179, 181, 182, 187.
Mexico, a refuge for fugitive slaves, 25; fugitive clause in treaty with United States of, 299.
Michigan, station in, 16; organized as free state, 18; anti-slavery Quakers in, 31; steam railroad transportation in, 79; number of fugitives forwarded through Schoolcraft, 88; Senator J. M. Howard an operator at Detroit, 106; stations in, 116; number of routes in, 135; Falley's map of lines in Indiana and, 137, 138, 139; direction of routes in, 141; steam railway branches of U. G. R. R. in, 144; supplies for fugitives sent to Detroit, 203; settlement of fugitives at Detroit, 236; personal liberty law of, 246; flight of slaves from Detroit, after enactment of law of 1850, 250.
Michigan Central Railroad, 79, 144.
Midland Monthly, the, on U. G. R. R., 5.

Miller, 318.
Miller, a depot agent for "fugitive goods," near Detroit, 203.
Miller, alias Seth Concklin, 161.
Miller, Col. Jonathan P., operator, 107.
Miller, Mrs. Elizabeth Smith, on use of a station on the St. Lawrence, 127 *n*.
Milligan, Rev. J. S. T., letter of, 13, 14.
Milligans, the, in southern Illinois, 15.
Miller *vs.* McQuerry, case of, 269.
Minnesota, failure to pass full liberty law in, 246.
Minnis, Wm., 65.
Mission for refugees in Canada, 194.
Mission Institute at Quincy, Ill., 155; anti-slavery spirit of, 155, 156.
Mississippi, abducting trip of A. M. Ross into, 29, 30; escape of slaves by boat from, 82; involved in Brown's scheme of liberation, 167; Jefferson Davis of, on escape of fugitives from cotton states, 312, 313; fugitive from Vicksburg, recorded by Osborn, 344.
Mississippi River, a thoroughfare for fugitives, 82, 312, 313; routes traced from, 134; terminals along, 136.
Missouri, Brown's raid into, 8, 108, 162-166; knowledge of Canada among slaves in, 29; Galesburg, Ill., a refuge for runaways from, 97; Grinnell, Ia., a refuge for runaways from, 98; egress of slaves from, 136; Chicago, the deportation point for fugitives from, 147; abductions from, 152; abduction from, by Burr, Work and Thompson, 156; effects of John Brown's raid in, 165; number of slaves escaping from, 194; escape of Wm. Wells Brown from, 252; grievance of, on account of loss of slaves, 312; Lawrence, Kan., as known in, 347; Senator Polk of, on the U. G. R. R., 351, 352.
Missouri Compromise (1820), 100; fugitive slave clause in, 298; set aside by Kansas-Nebraska Act, 331; together with law of 1850 produces crop of personal liberty bills, 245, 246, 338.
Mitchell, fined for aiding fugitives, 279.
Mitchell, Daniel, operator, 131.
Mitchell, Gethro and Anne, operators, 131.
Mitchell, Hon. Thomas, message sent by, 58.

Mitchell, Rev. W. M., author of *The Underground Railroad*, 2, 3; account of naming of the U. G. R. R. given by, 45, 46; on abductor John Mason, 183, 184; on number of Canadian refugees, 222; opinion of Canadian government on fugitives as settlers reported by, 233; on slave-hunting in Northern states, 239.
Monroe, Prof. James, on effect on public sentiment of Margaret Garner case, 303.
Montreal, objective point of fugitives, 140.
Moore, Dr. J. Wilson, on progress made by refugee settlers in Canada, 226, 227; on civil offices held by refugees, 233.
Moore, Eliakim H., on early assistance of fugitives, 38.
Moore, of Virginia, on loss sustained by slave-owners of his district, 341.
Moores, the, station-keepers, 15.
Morgan County, lines through portion of, 136, 137.
"Moses," name given to Harriet Tubman, 186.
Mott, Richard, M.C., operator, 92, 106.
Mullin, Job, on early operations, 38.
Multiple and intricate trails, 61, 62, 70, 121, 130, 141-146.
Myers, Stephen, colored agent of U. G. R. R., 70, 126.

NALLE, CHARLES, forcible rescue of, 85.
Nashville Daily Gazette, on trial of Richard Dillingham, 174, 175.
Nationality of underground helpers, 91, 92.
Neall, Daniel, 68.
Nebraska, escape of Nuckolls' slaves from, 52; egress of slaves from, 136.
Negroes, proposition to enslave free, 26; settlements of, resorted to by fugitives, 32; settlements of, in southern Ohio, 115; in New Jersey, 125; relative progress of colored people of Canada and free, of United States, 227; affiliations of voters among Canadian, 233; rights of, violated by Fugitive Slave Law, 261; participation of, in rescue of fugitives, 276, 332; petition against kidnapping of, 296; increase in number of fleeing, after passage of law of 1850, 316; arrest of free, 317, 318.
Nelson, Dr. David, 96; abducting enterprises of, 155.
Nelson, Judge, in decision in case of Jack vs. Martin, 257; on the Fugitive Slave Law, 272.
New Bedford, Mass., estimate of fugitive settlers in, 235, 236; Frederick Douglass in, 251.
Newberne, N.C., agent in, 68, 81, 117; escape of slaves from, 144.
New Brunswick, Canada, routes to, 133, 219.
New England, information secured concerning underground lines in, 11; slavery extinguished in, 17; anti-slavery settlement in, 31, 93, 171; rise of U. G. R. R. in, 36, 37; fugitives from the South landed on coast of, 81, 144; extent of underground system in, 113; settlers in Ohio from, 115; fugitives sent to, 121, 125; routes of, 128-134, 219; direction of routes in, 140, 195, 219; terminal stations in, 145; career of Lewis Hayden in, 158; stipulation for return of fugitives in agreement of Confederation of 1643, 292; memorial asking repeal of Fugitive Slave Law, from Quakers in, 324; sentiment in, adverse to the South's treatment of the compromises, 331.
New England Anti-Slavery Society, annual meeting of, at time of attempted rescue of Burns, 382.
New England Magazine, on Underground Railroad, 5, 6.
New Garden, Ind. *See* Fountain City, Ind.
New Hampshire, rise of Underground Railroad in, 36, 37; routes of, 132, 133; failure to pass full personal liberty law in, 246; early opposition to Fugitive Slave Law of 1793, 295.
New Haven, agreement of colony of, with New Netherlands for surrender of fugitives, 19.
New Jersey, slavery extinguished in, 17; anti-slavery Quakers in, 31; rise of Underground Railroad in, 34; routes of, 120, 121, 123-125; abductors along southern boundaries of, 151; settlement of fugitive slaves among Quakers at Greenwich, 236; sanction to Fugitive Slave Law, 246; slave-

INDEX 463

owner from, prosecuted, 274; penalties in, for transporting fugitives, 291, 292.
New Netherlands, agreement of colony of, with New Haven for surrender of fugitives, 19; aid prohibited to fugitives in, 290, 291.
New Orleans, escape of abductor John Mason from, to Canada, 185.
Newspapers, accounts of Underground Railroad in, 6, 7; anti-slavery, 168.
Newton, case of Norris vs., 275, 276.
New York, E. M. Pettit, conductor in southwestern, 4; slavery extinguished in, 31; rise of U. G. R. R. in, 34, 35; special agent in Albany, 70; effect of rescue of Jerry McHenry in central, 72; supplies for fugitives provided by Women's Anti-Slavery Society of Ellington, 77; steam railroad transportation in, 80; anti-slavery sentiment among Friends in, 93; favorable conditions for U. G. R. R. in western, 115; character of population in, 115; routes of, 120-128; direction of lines in, 140; broken lines and isolated place-names in, 141; terminal stations in, 145, 146; in the Patriot War, 193; settlement of fugitives in, 236; condemnation of Jerry rescue by many newspapers, 239; seizure of alleged fugitive in Poughkeepsie, 241; indignation meetings at Syracuse against law of 1850, 244, 320; personal liberty law of, 245, 246; flight of slaves from, 250; agents in, 251-253; abduction of free negroes from, 269; colonial law of, to prevent escape of fugitives to Canada, 292; address to slaves by Liberty party convention in, 310; address of Seward of, in behalf of fugitives, 313; Jerry rescue in Syracuse, 318; convention at Syracuse, sends congratulatory message to Wisconsin, 328, 329.
New York City, U. G. R. R. in, 35; Vigilance Committee of, 71; indignation meeting at Syracuse against Fugitive Slave Law, 244.
New York Central Railroad, 80.
New York Tribune, letter from John Brown to, 8, 9, 165, 166.
Niagara River, important crossing-places to Canada along, 146.
Nicholson, Valentine, method of disguise of fugitive employed by, 64, 65.

Nomenclature of stations in New Jersey, 124.
Norfolk, Va., escape by boat from, 81, 144, 145; natural route for escape of slave from, 118.
Norris vs. Newton, case of, 275, 276.
North American Review, on reclamation of fugitives in the North, 243.
North Carolina, Levi Coffin in, 4, 111; reminiscences relating to, 11; organization of U. G. R. R. in, (1819,) by Vestal and Levi Coffin, 40; escape of slaves from, 81, 144, 145; anti-slavery sentiment among Quakers in, 93; involved in Brown's plan of liberation, 167; Canadian refugees from, 195; law against aiding fugitives in colonial times, 292; Iredell on slave clause in Constitution before state convention of, 294; Clingman of, on value of fugitive settlers in Northern states, 341.
Northern Central Railroad, 80, 122, 128, 143, 252, 253.
Northern states, lack of formal organization in underground centres of, 69; steam railroad transportation for fugitive slaves in, 78-81; denunciation of law of 1850 in, 90, 243, 244, 318; list of, through which the underground system extended, 113, 114; most used underground routes in, 119; congested district in, 120, 121; favorable situation of Ohio, Indiana and Illinois for underground work, 134; sea routes to, 144; reception of abductor Capt. Walker in, 170, 171; effect of recital of Capt. Walker's experience upon, 171; appeal of fugitives to anti-slavery people in, 191; formation of lines of Underground Road in, during decade 1828-1838, 193; Canadian refugees visited by abolitionists from, 199-201; effect of apprenticeship of colored refugees in, 204, 212, 213; settlement of fugitives in, 235; number of and risks of fugitive settlers in, 237-240; slave-hunting in, 240, 241; effect of Fugitive Slave Law on fugitive slaves in, 241, 242, 246-248; increased difficulty of reclamation in, 242, 243; personal liberty laws enacted by, 245, 246; exodus of fugitives from, 249, 250; continued residence of fugitive slaves in, after law of 1850, 250, 251; underground men among fugitives in,

251-253; first Fugitive Slave Law stirs popular sense of justice in, 255; antagonism between state and federal Fugitive Slave laws, 259-260; non-interference of law of 1793 with laws of, 263; laws of, dealing with subject of fugitive slaves, 264; disinclination of, to restore fugitives after Prigg decision, 265; possibility of abduction of free negroes from, under law of 1850, 268, 269; counsel for fugitives in, 281-285; attitude of people toward proposed Fugitive Slave Bill of 1860, 286; object lessons in horrors of slavery in, 290; abduction of free negroes from, under law of 1793, 295; vote of members of Congress of, on proposed amendment to slave law of 1793, 296; proof of early anti-slavery sentiment in, 300; effect of fugitive slaves' appeal in, 300-303; effect of Garrisonian movement on resistance to Fugitive Slave Law in, 308, 309; attitude of population toward fugitives, 313; significance of vote on law of 1850, 314; era of slave-hunting in, 316; Webster's advocacy of obedience to law of 1850 throughout, 320; brought face to face with slavery by law of 1850, 321; effect of *Uncle Tom's Cabin* on people of, 323, 324; Mrs. H. B. Stowe, champion of victims of slavery in, 323; acceptance of Compromise of 1850 as a substantial political settlement in, 324; Sumner on import of the appeal of fugitive slaves to communities in, 325; open defiance to Fugitive Slave Law in, (1850-1860,) 326 *et seq.*; confederacy among cities of, proposed to defend fugitives from rendition, 328, 329; effect of Kansas-Nebraska Act on public feeling in, 331; double effect of law of 1850 in, 337, 338; charge of bad faith on part of, unsustained by statistics on fugitive slaves, 342, 343; underground operations the basis of important charges against, in crisis of 1850, 351, 352; efforts of Congress to appease spirit of secession, 354; protest against employment of troops from, as slave catchers, 355; effect of Underground Road in creating anti-slavery sentiment in, 357.

Northwest Ordinance, slavery excluded by, 17, 18; organization of states under, 18; fugitive slave clause in, quoted, 20, 293; alleged repugnancy of law of 1793 to, 255, 262, 263; alleged hostility between law of 1850 and, 268; protection afforded slave-owners by, 298.

Northwest Territory, slavery excluded from, 17; study of map of underground lines in, 120; multitude of lines within, 134, 135; appeal to Ordinance of, in effort to overthrow law of 1793, 262, 263; obligations of a state carved from, 263.

Norton, Mr., 258.

Notable persons among underground helpers, 104-112, 163-189.

Nova Scotia, disappearance of slavery from, 191; sea routes to, 219; fugitives sent from Boston to Halifax in, 248.

Nuckolls, escape of slaves of, 52.

Nullification, spirit of, in the North, 326-338.

Number, of underground helpers discovered, 87; of fugitives befriended by various operators, 87-89, 111; of fugitives using the valley of the Alleghanies, 118 *n.*; of fugitives sent over lines of southeastern Pennsylvania, 121; of fugitives aided by E. F. Pennypacker in two months, 143 *n.*; of terminal stations along northeastern boundary of Northern states, 145; impossibility of estimating, of fugitives emigrating from any one port, 146; of fugitives crossing Detroit River, 147; of fugitives helped by one man to Canada-bound vessels, 147; of deportation places along southwestern shore of Lake Michigan, 147; of resorts for refugees in Canada, 148, 149; of refugee abductors visiting the South annually, 152; abducted by Fairfield on one trip, 154; of slaves abducted by Fairbank, 160; of slaves abducted by Charles T. Torrey, 169; abducted by Drayton on the *Pearl* expedition, 172; of a party rescued by Josiah Henson, 177; total, abducted by Josiah Henson, 178; freed by Elijah Anderson, 183; freed by John Mason, 184; freed by Harriet Tubman, 186; forwarded by abolitionists in southern Ohio before the year 1817, 192; of slaves arriving

INDEX 465

daily at Amherstburg, Ontario, both before and after enactment of Fugitive Slave Law of 1850, 194; flocking into Canada, 200; of negro communities in Canada, 219, 220; of refugee population in Canada, 220–222, 313; estimated, of refugee settlers in Boston and New Bedford, 235, 236; of fugitive settlers in Northern states, 235–237; of arrests of fugitives between 1850 and 1856 recorded, 240, 241; of fugitives taking flight from Northern states after law of 1850, 249, 250; in companies transported by boat across Lake Erie by W. W. Brown, 252; increase in, of fugitives after passage of the law of 1850, 316; of slaves lost by the South through flight and abduction estimated, 341, 342; of fugitives given in census reports for 1850 and 1860, 342; aided by Osborn, as seen in record kept during five months, 344–346; of fugitives aided in Lawrence, Kan., during 1855–1859, 348; of negroes transported by American Colonization Society, 350; of underground operators in Ohio and other states, 351.

OBERLIN, a station, 89, 97, 98, 150; multiple routes of, 141; sentiment against abductions in, 150.

Oberlin College, 5; anti-slavery influence of, 33, 115; denomination and work of, 97, 98; C. Fairbank, abductor, student of, 157; interest of, in Oberlin-Wellington rescue, 336, 337; celebration at, over victory of abolitionists in Oberlin-Wellington case, 337.

Oberlin-Wellington rescue case, before United States District Court, 279; penalties levied in, 279; eminent attorneys in, 282; account of, 335–337.

Officers of the U. G. R. R., 67; title of "President" borne by Peter Stewart, 69; title of "President" bestowed upon Levi Coffin, 111, 112; Jacob Bigelow called "general manager" of a route, 117; a "general superintendent" mentioned, 125; Elijah Anderson designated "general superintendent" of U. G. R. R. in northwestern Ohio, 183.

Ohio, computation of number of slaves escaping into, 10, 346; special agents or conductors in, 13, 69, 70, 88, 89; organized as free state, 18; Fugitive Slave Law of, 22, 47, 48, 237, 238; underground stations on Western Reserve in, 1815, 28; anti-slavery sentiment in, 31, 32, 95, 96; rise of the U. G. R. R. in, 37–40; Clay declares law of 1850 is enforced in, 48; night service at stations in, 55, 56; steam railroad transportation in, 78, 79; underground operations in southern, 87, 184, 301; underground helpers of Scotch and Scotch-Irish descent in, 92; underground centres in, 93; denominational relations of operators in, 93, 95–98; Van Zandt case in, 102; prosecution of Rush R. Sloane of Sandusky, 102; notable operators in, 104–112; U. G. R. R. routes through, 113, 119; distribution of stations in, 114, 115; favorable situation of, 134; number of underground paths in, 135; lines through Morgan County, 136, 137; direction of routes in, 140, 141; terminal stations in, 146, 252; Detroit a receiving station for western routes of, 147; abductors along the southern boundaries of, 151; *Independent*, the, on increase in number of passengers of, 195; seizure of McQuerry in, 241; danger of slave-hunting in, 242; Slave Law denounced by meeting of Ashtabula County, 244; personal liberty law of, 246; dismissal of fugitives from custody at Sandusky, 276; Blake of, introduces bill praying for repeal of law of 1850, 286; Seward's address in, advising hospitality to fugitives, 313; Giddings on impossibility of enforcement of law of 1850 in, 315; contests between state and federal authorities in, 334; illustrated in Ad. White rescue case, 334, 335, and in Oberlin-Wellington case, 335–337; Oberlin-Wellington rescue commended by mass-meetings in eastern, 336; number of underground operators in, 351; states urged to repeal personal liberty laws by, 354.

Ohio River, a thoroughfare for fugitives, 82; routes traced northward from, 134; crossing-place on, 137; initial stations along the, 139; escape of Eliza across, at Ripley, 322.

Oliver, Rev. Thos. Clement, on routes of

466
INDEX

New Jersey, 123-125; on fugitive settlers in New Jersey, 236.
Oliver vs. Weakley, case of, 276.
Ontario, surviving fugitives in, 11; testimony of fugitives in, 27, 29, 76; fugitives conveyed by boat to Collingwood, 83; fugitives received by people of Chief Brant in, 92; goal of the great majority of runaways, 140; Clay on the admission of the refugee class by, 201; unsettled condition of, at time of beginning of immigration of fugitives into, 203; separate schools for negroes in, 229; action of Parliament of, in encouragement of fugitives, 233.
Ordinance of 1787. *See* Northwest Ordinance.
Organization, of the U. G. R. R., 67-70; U. G. R. R. work by an alleged regular, 279; league for self-protection among negroes in southeastern Pennsylvania, 280; formal organization of U. G. R. R. in Philadelphia, 309.
Orton, Prof. Edward, 35.
Osborn, Daniel, record kept by, as operator at Alum Creek Settlement, O., 345, 346.
Ottawa, Ill., multiple routes of, 141.

PAINE, BYRON, political reward of, for defence of Booth, 330.
Parish, F. D., fined for assisting runaways, 277, 278.
Parker, Asbury, fugitive, 76.
Parker, Chief Justice, on searching a citizen's house without warrant for a slave, 258.
Parker, Prof. L. F., on underground work in Iowa, 33, 42, 43, 98.
Parker, Theodore, scrap-book of, relating to renditions of Burns and Sims, 8; explanation of origin of vigilance committees given by, 71; public denunciation of Fugitive Slave Law of 1850 by, 90; indictment of, for attempted rescue of Burns, 103; journal and letter of, quoted, 109, 110; supporter of Dr. A. M. Ross, 180; on number of fugitives in Boston, 235; aid given by, to William and Ellen Craft, 317; part in the Burns rendition case, Boston, 331, 332.
Parker, William, leader in Christiana rescue case, 10; leader in league among fugitives for self-protection, 280.

Parliament, action by Ontario, in encouragement of fugitives, 233.
Patriot, the, Charles T. Torrey, editor of, 169.
Patriot War, part taken by fugitive slaves in, 193.
Patterson, Isaac, operator, 13.
Payne, George J., operator, 89.
Pearl, the schooner, capture of, 172, 173.
Peirce, I. Newton, message sent by, 57; connection with the U. G. R. R., 105, 143.
Penalties, levied for breaking the Fugitive Slave laws, 102, 103, 110; suffered by Burr, Work and Thompson, 156; paid by Calvin Fairbank and Miss Delia Webster for abducting Hayden family, 158, 159; suffered by Charles T. Torrey for abducting slaves, 169; suffered by Capt. Jonathan Walker for abduction of slaves, 170; fine and imprisonment of Capt. Drayton, 173; suffered by Richard Dillingham, 174, 175; imposed upon W. L. Chaplin for abduction of slaves, 176; suffered by Elijah Anderson, 183; created by Slave Law of 1850, 265, 266; failure of, under law of 1850 to deter resistance to the law, 272, 273; double penalty under law of 1793, 274, 275; for hindering arrest of fugitive slaves, 279; imposed on Booth for aiding in the Glover rescue, 329, 330.
Pennsylvania, slavery extinguished in, 17; anti-slavery sentiment in, 31, 33; rise of U. G. R. R. in, 37; steam railroad transportation in, 79, 80; operations in Lancaster County, 87; in Chester County, 88; protest of German Friends in, against slave-dealing, 93; numerous underground centres among Quakers of southeastern, 94; Presbytery of Mahoning, helps form a new church, 96; Presbyterian operators in western, 97; Unitarian centre at Meadville, 98; prosecution of Daniel Kauffman of Cumberland County, 102; Thomas Garrett, native of, 110; extent of U. G. R. R. system through, 113; favorable condition for U. G. R. R. in western, 115; study of map of U. G. R. R. lines in New Jersey, New York and, 120; routes of eastern, 121, 122; routes of western, 123; direction of lines in, 140; multiple and intricate

routes in southeastern, 141; broken lines and isolated place-names in, 141; terminal stations in, 144, 145; abductors along southern boundaries of, 151; fugitive settlers in northwestern, 236; Fugitive Slave Law of, 237, 238, 260; seizure of family of negroes at Uniontown in, 241; liberty law of, 246, 309; exodus of fugitives from, after enactment of law of 1850, 250; Prigg case in, 260, 261; law of, against aiding fugitives in colonial times, 292; emancipation by, 293; petition of Abolition Society of, for milder slave law, 296; Sergeant of, on House Fugitive Slave Bill of 1817, 297; complaints against people of, for harboring fugitives, 298; early pursuit in eastern, 302; Christiana case in, 317–319; kidnapping of free negro in, 318.

Pennsylvania Anti-Slavery Society, Wm. Still, clerk of, 3, 75; Harriet Tubman, a visitor at office of, 187.

Pennsylvania Railroad, 30.

Pennypacker, Elijah F., letter of, relating to fugitives, 79 n., 143 n.; stationkeeper, 121.

Personal liberty laws, object of, 245, 357; Buchanan's recommendations regarding, 286, 353, 354; of Massachusetts and other states, 309; enacted by Wisconsin, 330; slave-catchers indicted under, 336; characteristic of period 1840–1860, 337; induced by Missouri Compromise and law of 1850, 338; referred to as a grievance by Jones of Georgia, 351.

Peterboro, N.Y., station of Gerrit Smith in, 127, 128; visited by abductor A. M. Ross, 180; address to slaves issued from, 310.

Petersburg, Va., agent in, 118.

Pettijohn, Amos, reward for abduction of, 53.

Pettit, Eber M., author of *Sketches in the History of the Underground Railroad*, 2; characterization of his book, 4; on number of main routes in New York, 125.

Philadelphia, Vigilance Committee of, 3, 71, 75, 76, 80–82, 121, 145, 232; fugitives aided in, 10; continuous record of, as an underground centre, 34; anti-slavery sentiment among Friends in, 93; outlet from, 122; receives absconding chattels from Newberne, 144, from Baltimore, 151; trial of Christiana case in, 281, 319; counsel for fugitives in, 317; computation of fugitives aided in, 346, 347.

Philadelphia and Reading Railroad, 79, 143.

Phillips, Wendell, indictment of, 103; address in Faneuil Hall on the occasion of the Burns case, 332.

Piatt, slaves lost by family of, 283.

Pickard, S. T., on U. G. R. R. work in Portland, Me., 133.

Pickrell, Mahlon, on period of operations in Ohio, 39.

Pierce, Franklin, meaning of election of, 321.

Pierce, William S., counsel for fugitive slaves, 284.

Pinckney, on fugitive slave clause in the Constitution, 21, 294.

Pindall, of Virginia, on a bill for increased security of slave property, 296.

Pinkerton, Allen, friend of John Brown, 165.

Place, Maurice, 15, 16.

Platt, Jirch, diary of, 9; hiding-place on farm of, 63.

Poindexter, James, 253.

Poindexter, a colored abductor of Jackson, O., 151.

Poland, Hon. Joseph, operator, 107, 130.

Politics, of underground workers, 99–101; Canadian refugees in, 232, 233.

Polk, of Missouri, accusations against the North on account of U. G. R. R., 351, 352.

Porter, Rev. J., hiding-place in church of, 63.

Portsmouth, Va., escape of slaves from, 81, 144; agent in, 118.

Pratt, of Maryland, on Seward's speech advising hospitality to fugitives, 313; on loss sustained by slave-owners of his state, 341.

Prentiss, Henry J., 103.

Presbyterian Church, anti-slavery sentiment in, 31, 32, 95–97; J. J. Rice, missionary among Canadian refugees, minister of, 200; Rev. William King, minister of, 207; support of Elgin Settlement in Canada by, 208; Rev. John Rankin, pastor of a, 306.

Prigg *vs.* Pennsylvania, case of, 259, 260, 264–267, 289, 297, 309; new class of personal liberty laws following, 245, 246; effect of decision of, 309.

Prosecutions, for aiding fugitives, 102, 103, 254; cases of, under laws of 1793 and 1850, 273-281; for aiding fugitive slaves, 283-285; effect of prosecutions, 317; Prof. Edward Channing on importance of, 317 n.; of Booth for aiding in Glover rescue, 329, 330.

Pro-slavery sentiment in Congress, 173.

Providence and Worcester Railroad, 80, 130, 143.

Pursuit of fugitive slaves, 51, 52, 59, 65, 164, 302; increase in frequency of, 308; effect of Prigg decision on, 309; after passage of law of 1850, 316; instances of, 317.

Purvis, Robert, record of number of fugitives helped by, 10, 346; president of organized society of the U. G. R. R., 68, 309; account of the organization by, 68; chairman of the General Vigilance Committee of Philadelphia, 75; in rescue of Basil Dorsey, 85; New Jersey route described by, 125; on abduction by son of a planter, 153.

Putnam, David, underground letters of, 10 ; record of night service at station of, 55, 56; secret signal used by, 56; facsimile of message received by, 57.

Putnam, George W., on route in New Hampshire, 133.

QUAKERS, Levi Coffin one of the, 4; underground centres in communities of, 6, 90, 115-120, 125 ; Alum Creek Settlement of, 10; agents and operators among the, 31, 38, 39, 53, 92, 94, 98, 124, 131; pro-slavery sentiment among, 49 ; costume of, used as a disguise, 67; Washington's comment on a society of Philadelphia, 68; as conservators of abolition ideas, 93; result of appeal to societies of, in Massachusetts, 99; political affiliations of, 100; devotees of U. G. R. R. work among, 110-112; John Brown's party entertained by, in Iowa, 164; words of the Quaker poet, Whittier, quoted, 171; Quaker abductor Richard Dillingham, 174; at Richmond, Ind., befriend Josiah Henson, 177; at Fountain City, Ind., 199; visits of several, to Canadian refugees, 199; safety sought by fugitive settlers among, 235, 236; protection afforded fugitives by Quakers of New Bedford, Mass., 258; defendants in case of rescue, 274; in Christiana case, 280, 281; petition of Baltimore, against kidnapping, 296 ; memorial of, for repeal of Fugitive Slave Law, 324; record of fugitives in Alum Creek Settlement of, 344-346.

Quebec, early emigration of fugitive slaves to, 218.

Queen's Bush, early settlement of, by refugees, 204, 218.

Quincy, Ill., multiple routes of, 141.

Quincy, Josiah, his account of first known rescue of fugitive under arrest quoted, 83, 84; opponent of fugitive slave legislation, 283.

Quitman, Gen. John A., 341.

Quixot, Stephen, fugitive from Virginia, 51.

RACINE, WIS., Glover rescue in, 327.

Railroads, steam, use of, for transportation of fugitives, 35, 59, 78-81, 122-124, 128, 130, 132, 133, 142-145, 164, 165, 183; terminology of U. G. R. R. borrowed from vocabulary of, 67.

Railroad, Underground. See Underground Railroad.

Ramsey, Rev. R. G., on route in southern Illinois, 14.

Randolph, the slave, in case of Commonwealth vs. Griffith, 258.

Rankin, Rev. John, reward for abduction of, 53; secret cellar in barn of, 63; anti-slavery preaching and practice of, 96; station of, at Ripley, O., 109; on immediate abolition, 306, 307; Letters on Slavery by, 308.

Rantoul, Robert, Jr., counsel for fugitive slaves, 283.

Rathbun, Levi, station-keeper, 69, 70.

Ratliff, Hon. John, 15, 16.

Ray, Rev. Chas. B., on New York routes, 126.

Ray vs. Donnell and Hamilton, case of, 278.

Reading Railroad, 122.

Rebellion, Lincoln's proclamation regarding states continuing in, 287.

Recollections of an Abolitionist, by Dr. A. M. Ross, 179-183.

Redpath, James, on effects of John Brown's raid, 165.

Reed, Fitch, on arrival of abductor Fairfield and company of slaves in Canada, 154 n.
Reed, Gen., fugitives carried by boats of, 82.
Reed, John, on misinformation about Canada among slaves, 198.
Reform party, political affiliations of negro voters in Canada with, 233.
Refugees' Home Settlement, of Canadian refugees, 205, 209, 210; regulations of, 215-217; dissatisfaction in, 216, 217.
Reminiscences, collection of, 11; value of, 12-16.
Rendition of escaped slaves, early Northern sentiment on, Southern sentiment regarding, 21; question of, in crisis of 1851, 285; of Sims in Boston, 317; of Burns, 331-333.
Republican Leader, the, articles on the U. G. R. R. in, 6.
Republican party, effect of *Uncle Tom's Cabin* on young voters in, 324; forerunner of, in Wisconsin, 329; chief reliance of freedom declared to be in, repeal of Fugitive Slave Law demanded by, 337; organized U. G. R. R. said to be maintained by, 351; four governors belonging to, advise repeal of personal liberty bills, 354.
Rescue, of fugitives, 38, 39, 83-86, 240, 275, 276, 284, 336; attempts at, after 1850, 240, 273; provisions of law of 1850 to prevent, 266; of slaves, an expensive undertaking, 277; increase in frequency of, 308; during era of slave-hunting in the North, 316; of Shadrach, 317, 319; of Jerry McHenry, 318, 320; of Glover, 327-330; of Burns, attempted, 331-333.
Reynolds, Hon. John, on spirit of nullification in Illinois, 333, 334.
Rhode Island, anti-slavery Quakers in, 31; rise of U. G. R. R. in, 36; steam railroad transportation for fugitives in, 80; underground centres in, 94; routes of, 131; station at Valley Falls, 144; reception to Capt. Walker at Providence, 171; personal liberty law of, 245, 246, 309; colonial law against aiding fugitives in, 292; emancipation by, 293; repeal of personal liberty law by, 354.
Rhodes, James Ford, on the U. G. R. R., 1; on remote political effect of *Uncle Tom's Cabin*, 324; on spirit of the personal liberty laws, 338 n.
Rice, Rev. Isaac J., mission in Canada kept by, 194, 200; supplies kept for refugees by, 214.
Richardson, Lewis, cause of flight of, 27.
Richmond, Va., fugitive shipped from, in a box, 60; fugitives escape by boat from, 145.
Riddle, Albert G., counsel in Oberlin-Wellington case, 282.
Ripley, O., John Rankin in, 109, 306; abductor at, 153; escape of Eliza across Ohio River at, 322.
River routes of U. G. R. R., 81, 82, 118, 123, 129, 134, 138, 142; crossings on Detroit River, 147; Jefferson Davis on escape of slaves by Mississippi River, 312, 313.
Robin case, slavery terminated in Lower Canada by decision in, 191.
Robinson, case of *ex parte*, 270, 282.
Robinson, Rowland E., on routes in Vermont, 130.
Ross, Dr. A. M., abductor, 28-30, 178-182; as a naturalist, 183.
Ruggles, David, agent in New York City, 35, 126; Frederick Douglass befriended by, 71 n.
Russell, Hon. A. J., operator, 107.
Rycraft, colleague of Booth in the Glover rescue case, 329.

SABIN, HON. ALVAH, operator, 107.
Salsburg family, 87.
Sanborn, F. B., on Harriet Tubman, 186; on number of fugitive settlers in Northern states, 237; letter to, on the U. G. R. R. depot at Lawrence, Kan., 347-350.
San Domingo, servile insurrection in, 340.
Sandusky, Dayton and Cincinnati Railroad, 78.
Sandusky, Mansfield and Newark Railroad, 78.
Sandusky, O., first fugitive at, (1820,) 39; arrival of company of fugitives at, 76; boat service from, 83; prosecution of Rush R. Sloane of, 210, 276; as a terminal, 183, 185; trial of F. D. Parish of, 277.
Saxton, Gen. Rufus, on work of Harriet Tubman, 189.

Sayres, indictment of, for attempted abduction, 173.
Schooley, W. D., operator, 88.
Schools, for refugees in Canada, 199, 200, 205-208, 210, 214, 215, 228, 229; Sunday-schools, 330.
Scioto Company, organized by anti-slavery men, 38.
Scotch-Irish, the, in underground service, 92.
Scotch, the, in underground service, 92.
Scott, Gen. Winfield, presidential candidate of Whigs, 321.
Scott, James, tried for aiding in rescue of Shadrach, 269, 270.
Scripture, quoted by the abolitionists, 150, 306, 307.
Sea routes of the U. G. R. R., 81, 82, 118, 129, 133, 144, 145, 148, 219.
Seceders, friends of runaways, 13.
Secession, begun, 352, 353; efforts of the legislatures of the Northern states to appease the spirit of, 354; North's refusal to surrender fugitives one of the chief reasons for, 357.
Sentinel, the, articles in, on the Underground Railroad, 6.
Sentinel, the, chapters of "A History of Anti-Slavery Days" in, 6.
Sergeant, of Pennsylvania, on new Fugitive Slave Bill, 297.
Seward, F. W., on places of deportation of fugitive slaves, 145 *n*.
Seward, Wm. H., gives bail for Gen. Chaplin, 176; on Harriet Tubman, 185; aid given to Harriet Tubman by, 189; in the Van Zandt case, 282; speech advising hospitality to fugitive slaves, 313; signs the bond of rescuers of Jerry McHenry, 320.
Sewell, Samuel E., counsel for fugitive slaves, 283.
Shadrach, route taken by, after his rescue in Boston, 132; counsel in case of, 283; seizure of, 247; rescue of, 317, 319.
Shaw, Chief Justice, on Slave Law of 1793, 270.
Sheldon, Edward, indicted for helping fugitives, 284.
Shotwell, A. L., claimant of slave Tamar, 159.
Sider, Joseph, abductor, 60, 157.
Sidney, Allen, on misinformation about Canada among slaves, 197.

Signals, employed in the U. G. R. R. service, 125, 156.
Sims, Theodore Parker's memoranda on rendition of, 8; case of, in court, 269-271, 283; returned to slavery, 317.
Sketches in the History of the Underground Railroad, by E. M. Pettit, 2, 4.
Skillgess, Joseph, on fugitives passing through Ross County, O., 39.
Slave-hunters, authors of Levi Coffin's title "President of the U. G. R. R.," 111; at Detroit, 147; difficulties met by, 242, 243; imprisonment of, 273, 274; number of, increased after passage of the Fugitive Slave Law, 316; in the Oberlin-Wellington case, 335, 336; protest against the employment of Northern troops as, 355.
Slave-hunting, engagement of shiftless class in, 239; by Southern planters and their aids, 240; uncertainty of, in anti-slavery communities, 242, 243; Mr. Mason, of Virginia, on, 243; agents of slave-owners employed in, 316.
Slavery, character of, at beginning of nineteenth century, 25; changed character of later, 26; John Brown's plan of abolition of, 168; in Canada, 190, 191; attacks on, in Congress, 286; abolished in District of Columbia, 287; King's proposition to prohibit, in Northwest Territory, 293; conviction of sin of, in Northern states, 300, 301; pursuit of fugitives creates opposition to, in the North, 302; early advocacy of political action against, by Bourne and Duncan, Rev. John Rankin's hatred of, 306; address of Liberty party convention touching on, 310; effect of prosecution of U. G. R. R. workers on question of, 317; nationalized by law of 1850, 321; effects of, studied by Harriet Beecher Stowe, 321; renewal of consideration of question of, caused by *Uncle Tom's Cabin*, 324; U. G. R. R., the safety-valve of, 340; disappearance of, in District of Columbia attributed to the U. G. R. R. by Claiborne, 341, 342; extinction of, in the United States, 356, 358.
Slaves, desire for freedom among, 25, 195-197; purchase of, by Alabama, 26; incentives to flight of, 26, 27, 296; knowledge of Canada among, 28-

INDEX

30, 197; arrive as stowaways on the Maine coast, 133; steady increase in the number of, fleeing into Ohio, 135; from Virginia, 144; movement of, to inter-lake portion of Ontario, 147; abduction of, opposed by majority of abolitionists, 150; abduction of, by negroes, 151; abductions of, by Canadian refugees, 152; abductions of, by Southern whites, 153; abduction of, by Northern whites, 154, 155; abduction of, in District of Columbia, 155, abduction of, by Burr, Work and Thompson, 155, 156; abduction of, by Joseph Sider and Calvin Fairbank, 157–160; abduction of, by Seth Concklin, 160–162; abduction of, by John Brown, 162–165; effect of John Brown's raid upon Missouri, 165; Brown's plan for liberation of, 166–168; abductions of, in answer to appeal, 168, by Charles T. Torrey, 168–170, by Capt. Jonathan Walker, 170, 171, by Mrs. Laura S. Haviland, 171, 172; capture and incarceration of the, escaping on the steamer *Pearl*, 172, 173; abductions of, by Capt. Daniel Drayton, 172–174, by Richard Dillingham, 174, 175, by Wm. L. Chaplin, 175, 176, by Josiah Henson, 176–178, by Rial Cheadle, 178, 179, by Dr. A. M. Ross, 179–183, by the fugitive Elijah Anderson, 183, by the fugitive John Mason, 183–185, by the fugitive Harriet Tubman, 185–189; importation of, into Canada, 190, 191; Elgin Settlement in Canada started by a band of manumitted, 202, 207; Wilberforce Colony originally settled by group of emancipated, 218; domestic relations of, in Southern states, 227, 228; agents of U. G. R. R. appealed to for abduction of, 231, 232; Northern states an unsafe refuge for, 238, 239; purchase of, from their claimants, 241, 242; causes of flight of, 308; conditions favorable to escape of, 1840-1850, 309; effect of flight of, on Northern sentiment, 310; addresses to Southern, 310; address of Cazenovia convention to, 313; information about abolitionists among, 316; danger of uprising of, lessened by the U. G. R. R., 340; prospect of stampede of, from the border slave states, in case of secession, 355; chances for escape of, multiplied during War, 355.

Slave trade, effect of prohibition of, (1807,) 301.

Sloane, Hon. Rush R., on the U. G. R. R. in northwestern Ohio, 39; account given by, of the naming of the Road, 45; prosecution of, 102; incident of embarkation of company of refugees given by, 148 n.; on Elijah Anderson, abductor, 183; fined for assisting runaways, 276, 277.

Sloane, John, early operator, 37.

Sloane, J. R. W., 13.

Sloane, Prof. Wm. M., 13 n.

Sloane, Rev. William, 14, 15.

Smedley, R. C., author of *The Underground Railroad in Chester and Neighboring Counties of Pennsylvania*, 2, 4; account of naming of the U. G. R. R. by, 44, 45; on loss of bondmen by Maryland counties, 119; on numbers of fugitives sent to New England, 128, 129; on transportation of fugitives by rail, 143.

Smith, Gerrit, operator, 22, 27, 107; generosity of, 176; on Harriet Tubman, 185; defiant speech of, after Jerry rescue, 320; one of the leaders in the Jerry rescue, 326; counsel for the fugitive Wm. Anderson in Canada, 353.

Smith, James, 154.

Smith, William R., work of, in behalf of Gen. Chaplin, 176.

Snediger family, operators, 87.

Society of Friends. *See* Quakers.

Sorrick, Rev. R. S. W., on the condition of refugees in Oro, Ontario, 218; on the teachableness of the Canadian refugees, 224.

South Carolina, abducting trip of A. M. Ross into, 29; agent of U. G. R. R. in Newberne, 68; involved in Brown's plan of liberation, 167; Canadian refugees from, 195; Pinckney on slave clause in United States Constitution before state convention of, 294; doctrine of state sovereignty of, resisted by Wisconsin, 330; servile insurrections in, 340; Butler of, on loss sustained by slave-owners of Southern section, 341; withdrawal from the Union, 352.

Southern branches of the U. G. R. R., 116–119.

472   INDEX

Southern states, satisfaction with the fugitive slave clause in the Constitution in the, 21; complaints of, on account of losses of slave property, 22; refuges of runaways in the, 25; spread of the U. G. R. R. in, 28; knowledge about Canada among slaves in, 28, 29, 180–182, 192; self-interest of, manifest in the Fugitive Slave Law of 1850, 33; escapes by vessel from, 81, 133, 144; anti-slavery sentiment among white emigrants from, 90, 91; emigration of Quakers from, on account of slavery, 93 ; anti-slavery advocates among Presbyterian clergy in, 95; settlement of anti-slavery people from, in Ohio, 115; friends of fugitives in, 116; main channels of escape from, 119; abductions by whites from, 153, 154 ; Northern men in, encourage flight of slaves, 154, 155 ; expected effect of news of Brown's Missouri raid in, 165; Brown's plan for organizing insurrection in, 167, 168; Calhoun on expedition of the *Pearl* speaks for, 173, 174; expeditions for abduction of slaves to, 177, 178; operations of the abductor A. M. Ross in, 180–183; early emigration of negroes from, to Quebec, 219; domestic relations of slaves in, 227, 228; abductions of friends from, planned by the Canadian exiles, 231, 232; abducting trips of Canadian refugees to, 232; rights of recovery in the North claimed by people of, 237 ; slave-hunting by people from, before and after law of 1850, 240, 241; effect of law of 1850 upon, 243; Lincoln's proclamation of warning to, 287; the Underground Railroad as a grievance of, 290; sentiment in, concerning slave clause in Constitution, 294; complaints of members of Congress from, on score of treatment accorded runaways in the North, 295, 296; negotiations for return of fugitives to, 302; people of, aroused by addresses to slaves, 310; Calhoun on discontent in, 313; Webster on complaint of, in regard to non-rendition of fugitives, 314; Pres. Fillmore gives assurances to, regarding Fugitive Slave Law, 318; doctrine of state sovereignty of, resisted by Wisconsin, 330; work of the U. G. R. R. a real relief to, 340; estimates of loss sustained by slave-owners in various, 341, 342; decline of slave population in border states, shown in United States census reports, 343; comparison of numbers of negroes transported from, by U. G. R. R. and American Colonization Society, 350, 351; members of Congress from, on work of U. G. R. R., 351, 352; attempted conciliation of, 354; chances for escape of slaves multiplied throughout, 355; agitation by people of, for vigorous Fugitive Slave Law, 357.

Sowles, Hon. William, operator, 107.
Spalding, Rufus P., counsel in the Oberlin-Wellington case, 282.
Speed, John, 65.
Speed, Sidney, incident of unsuccessful pursuit narrated by, 65, 66.
Spradley, Wash, a colored abductor of Louisville, Ky., 151.
Sprague, Judge, on legal force of a commissioner's certificate, 270.
Springfield, Mass., "League of Gileadites" in, 71–75.
Stanton, Henry B., 169, 170.
State sovereignty, doctrine of, in the Northern states, 326–330.
Stations, in New Hampshire, 132; in Maine, 134; initial, in Ohio, 135; initial, in Iowa, 136; number and distribution of, in portion of Morgan County, O., 137; stations in Michigan, 138; corresponding stations in Falley's and the author's maps, 138, 139; initial, along the Ohio River, 139, 346; limited activity of, in eastern and western extremities of the free region, 141; isolated, in New York, Pennsylvania, Indiana and Illinois, 142; terminal, 145–148; cause of formation of initial, 295; Harriet B. Stowe's house one of the, 321.
Station-keepers of the U. G. R. R., significance of the name, 67; character of work of, 69; explanation of division of labor between special agents and, 70, 71; expense to, 76–78. *See* also Agents and Conductors.
Steele, Capt., master of a lake boat carrying fugitives, 82.
Steele, William, letter of, on escape of slave family, 51, 52.

Stephens, Alexander H., abduction of slave of, 176.
Stephens, Charles, in Brown's raid, 163–165; arranges for trip east of Brown and party, 164, 165.
Stevens, Thaddeus, operator, 106; in the Christiana case, 282.
Stevenson, Henry, on slaves' desire for freedom, 196.
Stewart, family of, fugitive settlers near Detroit, 236.
Stewart, John H., colored operator, 89.
Stewart, Peter, reputed President of the U. G. R. R., 69.
Still, Peter, a fugitive from Alabama, 160.
Still, William, author of *Underground Railroad Records*, 2, 3, 5, 8, 75; chairman of Vigilance Committee of Philadelphia, 8, 232; on instances of fugitives shipped as freight, 60; on stowaways from the South, 145; on value of Canadian refugees as citizens, 234 n.; coöperation of, with station at Elmira, 253.
Stone, Col. John, secret signal used by, 56; facsimile of message sent by, 57.
Story, Justice, on the Fugitive Slave Law, 245; on power of Congress to legislate on subject of fugitive slaves, 261.
Stout, Dr. Joseph, indicted for helping fugitive, 284.
Stow, L. S., on transportation of fugitives across Lake Erie, 146.
Stowe, Harriet Beecher, correctness of her representation in *Uncle Tom's Cabin*, 25, 322; material for *Uncle Tom's Cabin* gathered by, while living at Cincinnati, O., 105, 321; connection of, with the U. G. R. R., 105; influence of the slave controversy upon, 290; champion of fugitive slaves, 323.
Stowe, Prof. Calvin, model for a character in *Uncle Tom's Cabin*, 322.
Stowell, Martin, one of leaders in attempted rescue of Burns, 332.
Sturgeon, of Pennsylvania, supports the Fugitive Slave Law, 314.
Subterranean Pass Way of John Brown, 339, 357.
Sumner, Charles, efforts of, in behalf of Capt. Drayton, 173; on number of fugitives fleeing from Northern states after enactment of law of 1850, 249; efforts of, in Senate to secure repeal of Fugitive Slave Law, 324; champion in Senate of the fugitive slave and his friends, 325; reads a letter in the Senate on employment of Northern troops as slave-catchers, 355.
Supplies, for U. G. R. R. passengers, 76–78; furnished by Fred. Douglass, 78 n.; for Canadian refugees, 202, 214; gathered for fugitives in Lawrence, Kan., 348, 349.
Syracuse, Vigilance Committee of, 71, 72; rescue of Jerry McHenry in, 72, 86, 318, 326; passes distributed to runaways in, 80; underground work of Rev. S. J. May in, 109; fugitives sent by train to, 124; indignation meeting at, held after passage of law of 1850, 244; public action against Fugitive Slave Law in, 320; congratulatory message on Glover rescue from convention in, 328, 329.

TABOR COLLEGE, U. G. R. R. work of, 98.
Tamar, slave recovered by Fairbank, 159.
Taney, Judge, prosecution of Thomas Garrett before, 110.
Tappan, Lewis, supporter of Dr. A. M. Ross, 180.
Tennessee, abducting trip of Dr. A. M. Ross into, 28; John Rankin, a native of, 109; fugitives from, 109; underground route through eastern, 119; involved in Brown's plan of liberation, 167; Dillingham's attempted abduction of slaves from, 174, 175; Canadian refugees from, 195; fables about Canada circulated in, 198.
Terminal stations of U. G. R. R., 70, 76, 82, 83, 123, 126–128, 131, 133, 136, 138, 139, 145–149; in Canada, 148, 149.
Terminology of U. G. R. R., 67, 124.
Territories, slavery prohibited in the, 287.
Texas, question of annexation before Congress, 310; escape of slaves from western, 348.
Thirteenth Amendment to the Constitution, 356.
Thomas, Dr. Nathan M., operator, 88.
Thompson, George, a party in the case of Burr, Work and, 155, 156.
Thurston, Brown, operator, 37, 133.

Ticknor, George, on political effect of *Uncle Tom's Cabin*, 323.
Todd, Rev. John, author of reminiscences of "The Early Settlement and Growth of Western Iowa," 7; quoted, 43.
Todds, the, station-keepers, 15.
Toledo, O., boat service for runaways from, 83; U. G. R. R. helpers in, 92.
Tompkins, case of Johnson vs., 259, 273, 274.
Toombs, Robert, 173; abduction of slaves of, 176.
Toronto, Canada, mission work of Rev. W. M. Mitchell in, 3; goods received for Canadian refugees at, 202, 203; number of refugee settlers in, 220, 221; condition of fugitive settlers in, 226; Drew on condition of colored people in, 227; equal school privileges for whites and blacks in, 229; evening school for adult negroes in, 230.
Torrence, James W., method of, in conveying fugitives, 61.
Torrey, Rev. Charles T., abductor, 28, 168, 169; number of slaves abducted from Maryland by, 88; succeeded by Mr. Chaplin as editor of the Albany *Patriot*, 175.
Townsend, Martin I., on routes in New York, 126.
Townshend, Prof. Norton S., operator in Cincinnati, 104.
Treason, charged in Christiana case, 319; charged by Webster against transgressors of the law of 1850, 320.
Treatise on Slavery, in which is shown forth the evil of Slaveholding, both from the Light of Nature and Divine Revelation, immediate abolition advocated in, (1824,) 304-306.
Tribune, of New Lexington, O., on U. G. R. R., 6.
Troy, N.Y., rescue of fugitive Chas. Nalle in, 85.
"True Bands," societies for self-improvement among Canadian refugees, 230, 231.
Trueblood, E. Hicks, author of articles on U. G. R. R. in *Republican Leader*, 6.
Tubman, Harriet, mentioned, 6, 28, 178, 183; line of travel of, in Delaware, 118; character of, 185; work as an abductor, 186, 187; faith of, 188; most venturesome journey of, 188, 189; service of, as scout in the Civil War, 189; passenger on U. G. R. R., 340.
Turner, Rev. Asa, on U. G. R. R. lines in Iowa and Illinois, 114.

Uncle Tom's Cabin, correctness of representations in, 25, 322; sources of the knowledge of underground methods displayed in, 105, 321; political significance of, 321-324; Sumner on reception given to, 325; object of, 357.
Underground Railroad, as a subject for research, 1, 2; works on, 2, 3; articles on, 5-7; lack of contemporaneous documents relating to, 7; conditions of development of, 17, 18; numerous lines of, in Northern states, 22; early stations of, on Western Reserve, extended into Southern states, 28; effect of local conditions on growth of, 30; church connections of operators of, 32, 93-99; origin of, 33, 34, 191, 192; development of, 35-43, in New Jersey, 34, in New York, 34, 35, in New England, 36, in Ohio, 37-40, in North Carolina, 40, in Indiana, 40, 41, in Illinois, 41, 42, in Iowa, 42, 98, in Kansas, 43; activity of (1830-1840), 44, 308; activity of (1850-1860), 44, 71, 316, 317, 357; naming of, 44-46; midnight service on, 54-56; communications in work of, 56-59; methods of conveyance on, 59-61; nature of routes of, 61, 62, 70, 130, 141-146; variety of stations on, 62-64; use of disguises in work of, 64-67; lack of formal organization in, terminology of, 67; spontaneous character of, 69; places of deportation, 70, 145-147; terminal stations of, 70, 145-148; routes by rail, 78-81, 142-145; connection of Fred. Douglass with, 80, 91, 118, 251, 340; river routes, 81, 82, 142; traffic by water, 81-83, 142, 144-148, 219; routes by sea, 81, 129, 144, 145, 219; church connections of operators of, 94-97; notable operators of, 104-112, 155-189, 251-253; rise of, in Connecticut, 109; study of general map of, 113 *et seq.*; extent of system, 114; broken lines and isolated place-names, 115, 116, 123, 141, 142; lines of New York and New England states, of

INDEX

Wisconsin and Michigan, 116; organized in North Carolina, 117; Southern branches, 117-119; signals used on Delaware River, 125; relative number of routes in Western states, 134; local map of Morgan Co., O., 136, 137; map of Indiana and Michigan routes of, 137-139; map of line of, in Livingston and La Salle counties, Ill., 139; trend of routes of, 139-141; lines of lake travel, 147, 148; Canadian termini of, 148, 149, 200, 219, 220, 225; operations of, through Clinton, O., in year 1842, 153; route followed by Brown from Missouri to Canada, 163-166; Brown's proposed use of, 166; route through Morgan Co., O., 178, 179; through Pennsylvania to Erie, 181; made use of by abductor A. M. Ross, 181; "general superintendent" of, in northwestern Ohio, 183; Canada, the refuge of passengers of, 190; Dr. S. G. Howe, on the origin of, 192; development of, during decade 1828-1838, 193; increased efficiency of, due to law of 1850, 193, 338; ease of escape over, in later years of, 213; lines through New England to Quebec, 219; capacity of, for transportation of fugitives, 222; agents of, appealed to, for abduction of friends, 231; agents of, among fugitive settlers in Northern states, 251-253; explanation of secrecy of, 255; escapes from Indian Territory over, 284; political aspect of, 290; explanation of development of initial stations of, 295; early branches in Pennsylvania, 298; influence in spreading anti-slavery sentiment, 302; organization of, in Philadelphia, 309; grievance of border states due to, 312, 341, 342; most flourishing period of, 316; Harriet Beecher Stowe's house a station on, 321; rapid expansion of, during period 1840-1860, 337; the work of, a real relief to masters, 340; Osborn's record of fugitives aided during five months, 344, 345; computation of fugitives aided in Ohio and Philadelphia during 1830-1860, 346, 347; work of Lawrence station, in Kansas, described, 347-350; work of, compared with that of Colonization Society, 350, 351; organized societies of, said to be maintained by the Republican party, 351; relation of, to the Civil War, 357, 358.
Underground Railroad, the Rev. W. M. Mitchell, author of, 2, 3.
Underground Railroad in Chester and the Neighboring Counties of Pennsylvania, the, R. C. Smedley, author of, 2, 4.
Underground Railroad Records, by Wm. Still, 2, 3, 4; work of the Philadelphia Vigilance Committee revealed in, 75, 76; story of the abducting trip of Seth Concklin as given by, 160-162.
Unitarian Church, Rev. Theodore Parker a minister of, 8; underground work of Meadville Seminary of, 98; Rev. Samuel J. May, a clergyman of, 109.
United States, census reports of, on fugitive slaves, 26, 342; escape of fugitives from Canada to, 190; schoolteachers for Canadian refugees supported by religious societies of, 215; relative progress of Canadian negroes and free negroes in, 227; ministers of Canadian refugees canvass for money in, 231; fugitive slave cases before courts of, 257, 259-264, 269, 270, 272-282, 286; necessity of a uniform system of regulation regarding fugitive slaves throughout, 261; treason against, charged in Christiana case, 280; participation by President of, in Christiana case, 280, 281; fugitive slave clause embodied in Constitution of, 293; negotiations of, with England for extradition of fugitives, 299, 300; Senator Yulee on danger to the perpetuity of, 314; effect of Gerrit Smith's speech in the Anderson case in, 353; extinction of slavery in, 356.
United States Freedman's Inquiry Commission, Dr. S. G. Howe's report for, on Canadian refugees, 211.
Universalist Church, result of appeal to societies of, in Massachusetts, 99.

VAN DORN, Mr., operator, 88.
Van Zandt, case of Jones vs., 262, 278, 282; S. P. Chase and W. H. Seward in case of, 282; original of Van Tromp in *Uncle Tom's Cabin*, 322.
Vaughan vs. Williams, case of, 262.

Vermont, emancipation in, 17; rise of U. G. R. R. in, 36; steam railroad transportation for fugitives through, 81; public men, operators in, 106, 107; routes of, 126, 130; terminal stations in, 145; personal liberty law of, 245, 246, 309; emancipation by, 293; amendment of personal liberty law by, 354.

Vermont Central Railroad, 80, 130, 143, 145.

Vigilance Committee, of Philadelphia, 3, 4, 8; of Boston, 8; explanation of the origin of such bodies given by Theodore Parker, 71; organization and work of Syracuse, 71, 72; account of Boston, 72, 73; account of the formation and rules of the Springfield (Mass.) "League of Gileadites," 73-75; of Philadelphia, 75, 76; Female Anti-Slavery Association organizes a, 77; fugitives forwarded to New York City, by Philadelphia, 80; agents of, in Baltimore, 91, 117; appeal to churches of Massachusetts, by Boston, 98, 99; Theodore Parker appointed counsellor of fugitives in Massachusetts by, 110; fugitives sent by sea to Philadelphia, 145; of Cincinnati, consulted by Mrs. Haviland, 171; entreaties for aid to chairman of Philadelphia, 232; Philadelphia committee in Christiana case, 280; rescue of Jerry McHenry by Syracuse, 320; work of, in Milwaukee in Glover case, 328; work of Boston, in Burns case, 331; Purvis' record of fugitives aided by Philadelphia, 346, 347.

Vincent, James, counsel in fugitive slave case, 284.

Virginia, proposition to enslave free negroes in, 26; knowledge of Canada among slaves in, 26, 28, 29, 37; abducting trip of Dr. A. M. Ross into, 28; fugitives shipped in a box from, 61; fugitives escaping by vessel from, 81; runaways from, 85, 109, 252, 253, 258; reward offered to Indians in, for apprehending fugitives, 92; anti-slavery sentiment in Quaker meetings of, 93; agent in Petersburg, 118; natural route from Norfolk, 118; slaves escaping from, 144, 145; visitation of, by abductor, 151; abductor John Fairfield, of, 153; involved in Brown's plan of liberation, 167; Torrey's abduction of slaves from, 169; abductions by Rial Cheadle from, 179; knowledge of Canada spread by slaves from, 182; Rev. George Bourne, a resident of, 203; effect of slave-breeding in, 228; Mason of, on difficulty of recapturing fugitives, 243; prohibition of aid to fugitives in colonial, 291; Madison, on slave clause in the Constitution before state convention of, 294; desirous for extradition of fugitives from Canada, 299; Mason of, author of Slave Law of 1850, 311; Burns carried back to, 333; Richmond *Enquirer* on rendition of Burns, 333; Brown's method to weaken slavery in, 339; servile insurrection in, 340; Moore on loss borne by slaveowners of his district in, 341; Mason on loss sustained by slave-owners of, 341; decline in slave population of panhandle counties of, 343; fugitives from, recorded by Osborn, 345; reasons for loyalty of western, 354, 355.

Virginia and Kentucky resolutions, quoted by Wisconsin convention, 328, 329; quoted by mass convention at Cleveland, O., 336.

Von Holst, on the U. G. R. R., 1.

WABASH AND ERIE CANAL, thoroughfare for fugitives, 142.

Walker, Capt. Jonathan, work of, as an abductor, 168, 170, 171.

Walker, Edward, on the slave's desire for freedom, 196.

Walker, James, rescue of Piatt slaves by, 282, 283.

Walker, Joseph G., disguise provided for fugitive by, 67.

Wambaugh, Prof. Eugene, on the dilemma involved in the Fugitive Slave laws, 256 *n*.

War of 1812, knowledge of Canada spread by, 27, 28, 301.

War of Rebellion, Still's U. G. R. R. records concealed during, 8; underground work terminated by, 11; services of Harriet Tubman during, 186, 189; assaults on slavery justified by exigencies of, 286, 287; underground operations as a cause of, 290, 351, 352, 358; chances for escape of slaves multiplied during, 355; resort of slaves to Union forces at the outbreak of, 357.

Ware, J. R., station-keeper, 69, 70.

INDEX 477

Washington, D.C., route from, 117, 125; abduction of slaves from, by Capt. Drayton, 172, 173; abduction of slaves from, by Wm. L. Chaplin, 175, 176; occurrence of last fugitive slave case under law of 1850 in, 285.

Washington, George, letters of, (1786,) relating to fugitives, 33, 68; Fugitive Slave Law of 1793 signed by, 254; escaped slave of, 295, 324, 325.

Washington, Horace, 27.

Washington, Judge, in the case of Hill vs. Low, 273.

Washington, Lewis, agent, 253.

Weakley, case of Oliver vs., 276.

Webster, Daniel, supports Fugitive Slave Bill, 314, 315; on the necessity of the enforcement of Fugitive Slave Law of 1850, 320.

Webster, Miss Delia A., assistant of Fairbank in abduction of Hayden and family, 158, 159.

Weed, Thurlow, underground work of, 108.

Weeks, Dr. Stephen B., on underground work of the Coffins in North Carolina, 117.

Weiblen, John G., conveys fugitives by boat to Canada, 83.

Weimer, L. F., suit of, against Sloane, 276, 277.

Weldon, John, method of, in transporting fugitives, 61.

Wesley, John and Charles, views of, on slavery question, 94.

Wesleyan Methodists, friends of fugitives, 32; secession of, from M. E. Church, 94; operators among, 95, 168.

West, David, on the slave's desire for freedom, 196.

West, Hon. John, operator, 107.

West, Wm. H., counsel for Piatt slaves, 282, 283.

Western Reserve, early escapes across, 28, 301; anti-slavery sentiment in, 31, fugitive passengers from, 35; routes across, 123.

Western Reserve College, anti-slavery influence of, 115.

Western Reserve Historical Society publishes pamphlet on "U. G. R. R.," by Prof. J. H. Fairchild, 5.

Western states, routes of, 134–144.

West Indian Emancipation, celebration of, by Canadian refugees, 226, 227.

Weston, G. W., message of, 58.

Westwater, James M., hiding-place provided by, 63.

Wheaton, Chas. A., a leader in the Jerry rescue, 326.

Whig party, character of, 100; vote of, on the Fugitive Slave Law, 315; considers Compromise of 1850 a finality, 320; disinclination to vote for Gen. Winfield Scott, 321.

Whipper, Alfred, school-teacher among the refugees, 215.

Whipple. See Chas. Stephens.

White, Addison, attempted seizure of, 241; escape of, to Canada, 234.

White, Hon. Andrew D., letter of, on underground work of his father, 80.

White, Horace, railroad passes supplied to fugitives by, 80.

White, Isaac, 29.

White, John, slave befriended by Mrs. Haviland, 171, 172.

White, Joseph, operator, 97.

Whitfield, views on the slavery question, 94.

Whitman, of Massachusetts, on the bill securing to claimant of runaway right to prove title in courts of his own state, etc., 297.

Whitneys, of Concord, Mass., friends of Harriet Tubman, 186.

Whittier, John G., supporter of Liberty party, 100; on work of Rev. Charles T. Torrey, 170; stanza of "The Branded Hand," by, quoted, 171.

Wilberforce Colony in Canada, visited by Levi Coffin, 200, 220; origin of, 218; Dr. J. W. Moore on progress of fugitives in, 226, 227.

Willes, Rev. Dr., on refugee population in Canada, 222.

Willey, Rev. Austin, on escape of fugitives to New Brunswick, 219.

Williams, George W., the negro historian on U. G. R. R., 340.

Williams, case of Vaughan vs., 262.

Williams, John F., agent, 41.

Williams, Thomas, map of lines in Morgan County, O., by, 136.

Williams, W. B., on route from Washington, D.C., 117.

Wilmington, Del., underground work of Thomas Garrett in, 110, 111; station for Harriet Tubman, 118; movement of fugitives to, 121.

INDEX

Wilmington, N.C., escape of slaves from, 81, 144, 145.
Wilson, Henry, on U. G. R. R., 1, 37, 114; on abductions by Rev. Charles T. Torrey, 169; on number of fugitive settlers in Northern states, 237.
Wilson, John W., counsel in fugitive slave cases, 283.
Wilson, Rev. Hiram, receiving agent in Canada, 126; mission kept by, 194; schools supervised by, 199, 200; arranges with Canadian government for admission of supplies, 202; founder of school for refugees, 205; service of, in British and American Institute for refugees, 206, 207, 220; on number of Canadian refugees, 221.
Windsor, Ontario, visited by Fairfield, the abductor. 153, 154; arrival of Brown and his abducted slaves in, 165; private schools for negroes in, 229.
Winslow, Nathan, operator, 133.
Wisconsin, organized as free state, 17, 18; places of deportation in, 82, 116, 147; personal liberty law of, 246; Howe of, on law of 1850, 286; Glover rescue in, 327–330; determination of people of, shown in Booth case, 330.
Women's Anti-Slavery societies, supplies for passengers provided by, 77.
Woodford, Newton, indicted for helping fugitives, 284.
Woolman, John, precepts of, 49.
Work, Alanson, a party in the case of Burr, Work and Thompson, 155, 156.
Worthington, O., early rescue of a fugitive in, 38, 84.
Wright vs. Deacon, case of, 256, 257.
Wright, Judge Jabez, early operator, 39.
Wright, Peter, on the work of Canadian refugees, 205.
Wright, William and Phœbe, stationkeepers, 118 n.

YOKUM, WILLIAM, watchwords used by, 57.
Young, Rev. Joshua, operator. 130.
Yulee, of Florida, informs Senate of convention of runaway slaves in New York, 313.

ZIGZAG routes, 62, 131, 141.

A CATALOG OF SELECTED
DOVER BOOKS
IN ALL FIELDS OF INTEREST

A CATALOG OF SELECTED DOVER BOOKS IN ALL FIELDS OF INTEREST

100 BEST-LOVED POEMS, Edited by Philip Smith. "The Passionate Shepherd to His Love," "Shall I compare thee to a summer's day?" "Death, be not proud," "The Raven," "The Road Not Taken," plus works by Blake, Wordsworth, Byron, Shelley, Keats, many others. 96pp. 5 3/16 x 8 1/4. 0-486-28553-7

100 SMALL HOUSES OF THE THIRTIES, Brown-Blodgett Company. Exterior photographs and floor plans for 100 charming structures. Illustrations of models accompanied by descriptions of interiors, color schemes, closet space, and other amenities. 200 illustrations. 112pp. 8 3/8 x 11. 0-486-44131-8

1000 TURN-OF-THE-CENTURY HOUSES: With Illustrations and Floor Plans, Herbert C. Chivers. Reproduced from a rare edition, this showcase of homes ranges from cottages and bungalows to sprawling mansions. Each house is meticulously illustrated and accompanied by complete floor plans. 256pp. 9 3/8 x 12 1/4.
0-486-45596-3

101 GREAT AMERICAN POEMS, Edited by The American Poetry & Literacy Project. Rich treasury of verse from the 19th and 20th centuries includes works by Edgar Allan Poe, Robert Frost, Walt Whitman, Langston Hughes, Emily Dickinson, T. S. Eliot, other notables. 96pp. 5 3/16 x 8 1/4. 0-486-40158-8

101 GREAT SAMURAI PRINTS, Utagawa Kuniyoshi. Kuniyoshi was a master of the warrior woodblock print — and these 18th-century illustrations represent the pinnacle of his craft. Full-color portraits of renowned Japanese samurais pulse with movement, passion, and remarkably fine detail. 112pp. 8 3/8 x 11. 0-486-46523-3

ABC OF BALLET, Janet Grosser. Clearly worded, abundantly illustrated little guide defines basic ballet-related terms: arabesque, battement, pas de chat, relevé, sissonne, many others. Pronunciation guide included. Excellent primer. 48pp. 4 3/16 x 5 3/4.
0-486-40871-X

ACCESSORIES OF DRESS: An Illustrated Encyclopedia, Katherine Lester and Bess Viola Oerke. Illustrations of hats, veils, wigs, cravats, shawls, shoes, gloves, and other accessories enhance an engaging commentary that reveals the humor and charm of the many-sided story of accessorized apparel. 644 figures and 59 plates. 608pp. 6 1/8 x 9 1/4.
0-486-43378-1

ADVENTURES OF HUCKLEBERRY FINN, Mark Twain. Join Huck and Jim as their boyhood adventures along the Mississippi River lead them into a world of excitement, danger, and self-discovery. Humorous narrative, lyrical descriptions of the Mississippi valley, and memorable characters. 224pp. 5 3/16 x 8 1/4. 0-486-28061-6

ALICE STARMORE'S BOOK OF FAIR ISLE KNITTING, Alice Starmore. A noted designer from the region of Scotland's Fair Isle explores the history and techniques of this distinctive, stranded-color knitting style and provides copious illustrated instructions for 14 original knitwear designs. 208pp. 8 3/8 x 10 7/8. 0-486-47218-3

Browse over 9,000 books at www.doverpublications.com

CATALOG OF DOVER BOOKS

ALICE'S ADVENTURES IN WONDERLAND, Lewis Carroll. Beloved classic about a little girl lost in a topsy-turvy land and her encounters with the White Rabbit, March Hare, Mad Hatter, Cheshire Cat, and other delightfully improbable characters. 42 illustrations by Sir John Tenniel. 96pp. 5 3/16 x 8 1/4. 0-486-27543-4

AMERICA'S LIGHTHOUSES: An Illustrated History, Francis Ross Holland. Profusely illustrated fact-filled survey of American lighthouses since 1716. Over 200 stations — East, Gulf, and West coasts, Great Lakes, Hawaii, Alaska, Puerto Rico, the Virgin Islands, and the Mississippi and St. Lawrence Rivers. 240pp. 8 x 10 3/4. 0-486-25576-X

AN ENCYCLOPEDIA OF THE VIOLIN, Alberto Bachmann. Translated by Frederick H. Martens. Introduction by Eugene Ysaye. First published in 1925, this renowned reference remains unsurpassed as a source of essential information, from construction and evolution to repertoire and technique. Includes a glossary and 73 illustrations. 496pp. 6 1/8 x 9 1/4. 0-486-46618-3

ANIMALS: 1,419 Copyright-Free Illustrations of Mammals, Birds, Fish, Insects, etc., Selected by Jim Harter. Selected for its visual impact and ease of use, this outstanding collection of wood engravings presents over 1,000 species of animals in extremely lifelike poses. Includes mammals, birds, reptiles, amphibians, fish, insects, and other invertebrates. 284pp. 9 x 12. 0-486-23766-4

THE ANNALS, Tacitus. Translated by Alfred John Church and William Jackson Brodribb. This vital chronicle of Imperial Rome, written by the era's great historian, spans A.D. 14-68 and paints incisive psychological portraits of major figures, from Tiberius to Nero. 416pp. 5 3/16 x 8 1/4. 0-486-45236-0

ANTIGONE, Sophocles. Filled with passionate speeches and sensitive probing of moral and philosophical issues, this powerful and often-performed Greek drama reveals the grim fate that befalls the children of Oedipus. Footnotes. 64pp. 5 3/16 x 8 1/4. 0-486-27804-2

ART DECO DECORATIVE PATTERNS IN FULL COLOR, Christian Stoll. Reprinted from a rare 1910 portfolio, 160 sensuous and exotic images depict a breathtaking array of florals, geometrics, and abstracts — all elegant in their stark simplicity. 64pp. 8 3/8 x 11. 0-486-44862-2

THE ARTHUR RACKHAM TREASURY: 86 Full-Color Illustrations, Arthur Rackham. Selected and Edited by Jeff A. Menges. A stunning treasury of 86 full-page plates span the famed English artist's career, from *Rip Van Winkle* (1905) to masterworks such as *Undine, A Midsummer Night's Dream,* and *Wind in the Willows* (1939). 96pp. 8 3/8 x 11.
0-486-44685-9

THE AUTHENTIC GILBERT & SULLIVAN SONGBOOK, W. S. Gilbert and A. S. Sullivan. The most comprehensive collection available, this songbook includes selections from every one of Gilbert and Sullivan's light operas. Ninety-two numbers are presented uncut and unedited, and in their original keys. 410pp. 9 x 12.
0-486-23482-7

THE AWAKENING, Kate Chopin. First published in 1899, this controversial novel of a New Orleans wife's search for love outside a stifling marriage shocked readers. Today, it remains a first-rate narrative with superb characterization. New introductory Note. 128pp. 5 3/16 x 8 1/4. 0-486-27786-0

BASIC DRAWING, Louis Priscilla. Beginning with perspective, this commonsense manual progresses to the figure in movement, light and shade, anatomy, drapery, composition, trees and landscape, and outdoor sketching. Black-and-white illustrations throughout. 128pp. 8 3/8 x 11. 0-486-45815-6

Browse over 9,000 books at www.doverpublications.com

CATALOG OF DOVER BOOKS

THE BATTLES THAT CHANGED HISTORY, Fletcher Pratt. Historian profiles 16 crucial conflicts, ancient to modern, that changed the course of Western civilization. Gripping accounts of battles led by Alexander the Great, Joan of Arc, Ulysses S. Grant, other commanders. 27 maps. 352pp. 5⅜ x 8½. 0-486-41129-X

BEETHOVEN'S LETTERS, Ludwig van Beethoven. Edited by Dr. A. C. Kalischer. Features 457 letters to fellow musicians, friends, greats, patrons, and literary men. Reveals musical thoughts, quirks of personality, insights, and daily events. Includes 15 plates. 410pp. 5⅜ x 8½. 0-486-22769-3

BERNICE BOBS HER HAIR AND OTHER STORIES, F. Scott Fitzgerald. This brilliant anthology includes 6 of Fitzgerald's most popular stories: "The Diamond as Big as the Ritz," the title tale, "The Offshore Pirate," "The Ice Palace," "The Jelly Bean," and "May Day." 176pp. 5⅜ x 8½. 0-486-47049-0

BESLER'S BOOK OF FLOWERS AND PLANTS: 73 Full-Color Plates from Hortus Eystettensis, 1613, Basilius Besler. Here is a selection of magnificent plates from the *Hortus Eystettensis*, which vividly illustrated and identified the plants, flowers, and trees that thrived in the legendary German garden at Eichstätt. 80pp. 8⅜ x 11. 0-486-46005-3

THE BOOK OF KELLS, Edited by Blanche Cirker. Painstakingly reproduced from a rare facsimile edition, this volume contains full-page decorations, portraits, illustrations, plus a sampling of textual leaves with exquisite calligraphy and ornamentation. 32 full-color illustrations. 32pp. 9⅜ x 12¼. 0-486-24345-1

THE BOOK OF THE CROSSBOW: With an Additional Section on Catapults and Other Siege Engines, Ralph Payne-Gallwey. Fascinating study traces history and use of crossbow as military and sporting weapon, from Middle Ages to modern times. Also covers related weapons: balistas, catapults, Turkish bows, more. Over 240 illustrations. 400pp. 7¼ x 10⅛. 0-486-28720-3

THE BUNGALOW BOOK: Floor Plans and Photos of 112 Houses, 1910, Henry L. Wilson. Here are 112 of the most popular and economic blueprints of the early 20th century — plus an illustration or photograph of each completed house. A wonderful time capsule that still offers a wealth of valuable insights. 160pp. 8⅜ x 11. 0-486-45104-6

THE CALL OF THE WILD, Jack London. A classic novel of adventure, drawn from London's own experiences as a Klondike adventurer, relating the story of a heroic dog caught in the brutal life of the Alaska Gold Rush. Note. 64pp. 5³⁄₁₆ x 8¼. 0-486-26472-6

CANDIDE, Voltaire. Edited by Francois-Marie Arouet. One of the world's great satires since its first publication in 1759. Witty, caustic skewering of romance, science, philosophy, religion, government — nearly all human ideals and institutions. 112pp. 5³⁄₁₆ x 8¼. 0-486-26689-3

CELEBRATED IN THEIR TIME: Photographic Portraits from the George Grantham Bain Collection, Edited by Amy Pastan. With an Introduction by Michael Carlebach. Remarkable portrait gallery features 112 rare images of Albert Einstein, Charlie Chaplin, the Wright Brothers, Henry Ford, and other luminaries from the worlds of politics, art, entertainment, and industry. 128pp. 8⅜ x 11. 0-486-46754-6

CHARIOTS FOR APOLLO: The NASA History of Manned Lunar Spacecraft to 1969, Courtney G. Brooks, James M. Grimwood, and Loyd S. Swenson, Jr. This illustrated history by a trio of experts is the definitive reference on the Apollo spacecraft and lunar modules. It traces the vehicles' design, development, and operation in space. More than 100 photographs and illustrations. 576pp. 6¾ x 9¼. 0-486-46756-2

Browse over 9,000 books at www.doverpublications.com

CATALOG OF DOVER BOOKS

A CHRISTMAS CAROL, Charles Dickens. This engrossing tale relates Ebenezer Scrooge's ghostly journeys through Christmases past, present, and future and his ultimate transformation from a harsh and grasping old miser to a charitable and compassionate human being. 80pp. 5 3/16 x 8 1/4. 0-486-26865-9

COMMON SENSE, Thomas Paine. First published in January of 1776, this highly influential landmark document clearly and persuasively argued for American separation from Great Britain and paved the way for the Declaration of Independence. 64pp. 5 3/16 x 8 1/4. 0-486-29602-4

THE COMPLETE SHORT STORIES OF OSCAR WILDE, Oscar Wilde. Complete texts of "The Happy Prince and Other Tales," "A House of Pomegranates," "Lord Arthur Savile's Crime and Other Stories," "Poems in Prose," and "The Portrait of Mr. W. H." 208pp. 5 3/16 x 8 1/4. 0-486-45216-6

COMPLETE SONNETS, William Shakespeare. Over 150 exquisite poems deal with love, friendship, the tyranny of time, beauty's evanescence, death, and other themes in language of remarkable power, precision, and beauty. Glossary of archaic terms. 80pp. 5 3/16 x 8 1/4. 0-486-26686-9

THE COUNT OF MONTE CRISTO: Abridged Edition, Alexandre Dumas. Falsely accused of treason, Edmond Dantès is imprisoned in the bleak Chateau d'If. After a hair-raising escape, he launches an elaborate plot to extract a bitter revenge against those who betrayed him. 448pp. 5 3/16 x 8 1/4. 0-486-45643-9

CRAFTSMAN BUNGALOWS: Designs from the Pacific Northwest, Yoho & Merritt. This reprint of a rare catalog, showcasing the charming simplicity and cozy style of Craftsman bungalows, is filled with photos of completed homes, plus floor plans and estimated costs. An indispensable resource for architects, historians, and illustrators. 112pp. 10 x 7. 0-486-46875-5

CRAFTSMAN BUNGALOWS: 59 Homes from "The Craftsman," Edited by Gustav Stickley. Best and most attractive designs from Arts and Crafts Movement publication — 1903-1916 — includes sketches, photographs of homes, floor plans, descriptive text. 128pp. 8 1/4 x 11. 0-486-25829-7

CRIME AND PUNISHMENT, Fyodor Dostoyevsky. Translated by Constance Garnett. Supreme masterpiece tells the story of Raskolnikov, a student tormented by his own thoughts after he murders an old woman. Overwhelmed by guilt and terror, he confesses and goes to prison. 480pp. 5 3/16 x 8 1/4. 0-486-41587-2

THE DECLARATION OF INDEPENDENCE AND OTHER GREAT DOCUMENTS OF AMERICAN HISTORY: 1775-1865, Edited by John Grafton. Thirteen compelling and influential documents: Henry's "Give Me Liberty or Give Me Death," Declaration of Independence, The Constitution, Washington's First Inaugural Address, The Monroe Doctrine, The Emancipation Proclamation, Gettysburg Address, more. 64pp. 5 3/16 x 8 1/4. 0-486-41124-9

THE DESERT AND THE SOWN: Travels in Palestine and Syria, Gertrude Bell. "The female Lawrence of Arabia," Gertrude Bell wrote captivating, perceptive accounts of her travels in the Middle East. This intriguing narrative, accompanied by 160 photos, traces her 1905 sojourn in Lebanon, Syria, and Palestine. 368pp. 5 3/8 x 8 1/2. 0-486-46876-3

A DOLL'S HOUSE, Henrik Ibsen. Ibsen's best-known play displays his genius for realistic prose drama. An expression of women's rights, the play climaxes when the central character, Nora, rejects a smothering marriage and life in "a doll's house." 80pp. 5 3/16 x 8 1/4. 0-486-27062-9

Browse over 9,000 books at www.doverpublications.com

CATALOG OF DOVER BOOKS

DOOMED SHIPS: Great Ocean Liner Disasters, William H. Miller, Jr. Nearly 200 photographs, many from private collections, highlight tales of some of the vessels whose pleasure cruises ended in catastrophe: the *Morro Castle, Normandie, Andrea Doria, Europa,* and many others. 128pp. 8⅞ x 11¾. 0-486-45366-9

THE DORÉ BIBLE ILLUSTRATIONS, Gustave Doré. Detailed plates from the Bible: the Creation scenes, Adam and Eve, horrifying visions of the Flood, the battle sequences with their monumental crowds, depictions of the life of Jesus, 241 plates in all. 241pp. 9 x 12. 0-486-23004-X

DRAWING DRAPERY FROM HEAD TO TOE, Cliff Young. Expert guidance on how to draw shirts, pants, skirts, gloves, hats, and coats on the human figure, including folds in relation to the body, pull and crush, action folds, creases, more. Over 200 drawings. 48pp. 8¼ x 11. 0-486-45591-2

DUBLINERS, James Joyce. A fine and accessible introduction to the work of one of the 20th century's most influential writers, this collection features 15 tales, including a masterpiece of the short-story genre, "The Dead." 160pp. 5³⁄₁₆ x 8¼. 0-486-26870-5

EASY-TO-MAKE POP-UPS, Joan Irvine. Illustrated by Barbara Reid. Dozens of wonderful ideas for three-dimensional paper fun — from holiday greeting cards with moving parts to a pop-up menagerie. Easy-to-follow, illustrated instructions for more than 30 projects. 299 black-and-white illustrations. 96pp. 8⅜ x 11. 0-486-44622-0

EASY-TO-MAKE STORYBOOK DOLLS: A "Novel" Approach to Cloth Dollmaking, Sherralyn St. Clair. Favorite fictional characters come alive in this unique beginner's dollmaking guide. Includes patterns for Pollyanna, Dorothy from *The Wonderful Wizard of Oz,* Mary of *The Secret Garden,* plus easy-to-follow instructions, 263 black-and-white illustrations, and an 8-page color insert. 112pp. 8¼ x 11. 0-486-47360-0

EINSTEIN'S ESSAYS IN SCIENCE, Albert Einstein. Speeches and essays in accessible, everyday language profile influential physicists such as Niels Bohr and Isaac Newton. They also explore areas of physics to which the author made major contributions. 128pp. 5 x 8. 0-486-47011-3

EL DORADO: Further Adventures of the Scarlet Pimpernel, Baroness Orczy. A popular sequel to *The Scarlet Pimpernel,* this suspenseful story recounts the Pimpernel's attempts to rescue the Dauphin from imprisonment during the French Revolution. An irresistible blend of intrigue, period detail, and vibrant characterizations. 352pp. 5³⁄₁₆ x 8¼. 0-486-44026-5

ELEGANT SMALL HOMES OF THE TWENTIES: 99 Designs from a Competition, Chicago Tribune. Nearly 100 designs for five- and six-room houses feature New England and Southern colonials, Normandy cottages, stately Italianate dwellings, and other fascinating snapshots of American domestic architecture of the 1920s. 112pp. 9 x 12. 0-486-46910-7

THE ELEMENTS OF STYLE: The Original Edition, William Strunk, Jr. This is the book that generations of writers have relied upon for timeless advice on grammar, diction, syntax, and other essentials. In concise terms, it identifies the principal requirements of proper style and common errors. 64pp. 5⅜ x 8½. 0-486-44798-7

THE ELUSIVE PIMPERNEL, Baroness Orczy. Robespierre's revolutionaries find their wicked schemes thwarted by the heroic Pimpernel — Sir Percival Blakeney. In this thrilling sequel, Chauvelin devises a plot to eliminate the Pimpernel and his wife. 272pp. 5³⁄₁₆ x 8¼. 0-486-45464-9

Browse over 9,000 books at www.doverpublications.com

CATALOG OF DOVER BOOKS

AN ENCYCLOPEDIA OF BATTLES: Accounts of Over 1,560 Battles from 1479 B.C. to the Present, David Eggenberger. Essential details of every major battle in recorded history from the first battle of Megiddo in 1479 B.C. to Grenada in 1984. List of battle maps. 99 illustrations. 544pp. 6½ x 9¼. 0-486-24913-1

ENCYCLOPEDIA OF EMBROIDERY STITCHES, INCLUDING CREWEL, Marion Nichols. Precise explanations and instructions, clearly illustrated, on how to work chain, back, cross, knotted, woven stitches, and many more — 178 in all, including Cable Outline, Whipped Satin, and Eyelet Buttonhole. Over 1400 illustrations. 219pp. 8⅜ x 11¼. 0-486-22929-7

ENTER JEEVES: 15 Early Stories, P. G. Wodehouse. Splendid collection contains first 8 stories featuring Bertie Wooster, the deliciously dim aristocrat and Jeeves, his brainy, imperturbable manservant. Also, the complete Reggie Pepper (Bertie's prototype) series. 288pp. 5⅜ x 8½. 0-486-29717-9

ERIC SLOANE'S AMERICA: Paintings in Oil, Michael Wigley. With a Foreword by Mimi Sloane. Eric Sloane's evocative oils of America's landscape and material culture shimmer with immense historical and nostalgic appeal. This original hardcover collection gathers nearly a hundred of his finest paintings, with subjects ranging from New England to the American Southwest. 128pp. 10⅝ x 9.
0-486-46525-X

ETHAN FROME, Edith Wharton. Classic story of wasted lives, set against a bleak New England background. Superbly delineated characters in a hauntingly grim tale of thwarted love. Considered by many to be Wharton's masterpiece. 96pp. 5 3/16 x 8 ¼. 0-486-26690-7

THE EVERLASTING MAN, G. K. Chesterton. Chesterton's view of Christianity — as a blend of philosophy and mythology, satisfying intellect and spirit — applies to his brilliant book, which appeals to readers' heads as well as their hearts. 288pp. 5⅜ x 8½. 0-486-46036-3

THE FIELD AND FOREST HANDY BOOK, Daniel Beard. Written by a co-founder of the Boy Scouts, this appealing guide offers illustrated instructions for building kites, birdhouses, boats, igloos, and other fun projects, plus numerous helpful tips for campers. 448pp. 5 3/16 x 8¼. 0-486-46191-2

FINDING YOUR WAY WITHOUT MAP OR COMPASS, Harold Gatty. Useful, instructive manual shows would-be explorers, hikers, bikers, scouts, sailors, and survivalists how to find their way outdoors by observing animals, weather patterns, shifting sands, and other elements of nature. 288pp. 5⅜ x 8½. 0-486-40613-X

FIRST FRENCH READER: A Beginner's Dual-Language Book, Edited and Translated by Stanley Appelbaum. This anthology introduces 50 legendary writers — Voltaire, Balzac, Baudelaire, Proust, more — through passages from *The Red and the Black, Les Misérables, Madame Bovary*, and other classics. Original French text plus English translation on facing pages. 240pp. 5⅜ x 8½. 0-486-46178-5

FIRST GERMAN READER: A Beginner's Dual-Language Book, Edited by Harry Steinhauer. Specially chosen for their power to evoke German life and culture, these short, simple readings include poems, stories, essays, and anecdotes by Goethe, Hesse, Heine, Schiller, and others. 224pp. 5⅜ x 8½. 0-486-46179-3

FIRST SPANISH READER: A Beginner's Dual-Language Book, Angel Flores. Delightful stories, other material based on works of Don Juan Manuel, Luis Taboada, Ricardo Palma, other noted writers. Complete faithful English translations on facing pages. Exercises. 176pp. 5⅜ x 8½. 0-486-25810-6

Browse over 9,000 books at www.doverpublications.com